The American Counties

Origins of County Names, Dates of Creation, and Population Data, 1950–2000,
5th Edition

Joseph Nathan Kane
Charles Curry Aiken

The Scarecrow Press, Inc.
Lanham, Maryland • Toronto • Oxford
2005

SCARECROW PRESS, INC.

Published in the United States of America
by Scarecrow Press, Inc.
A wholly owned subsidary of The Rowman & Littlefield Publishing Group, Inc.
4501 Forbes Boulevard, Suite 200, Lanham, Maryland 20706
www.scarecrowpress.com

PO Box 317
Oxford
OX2 9RU, UK

British Library Cataloguing in Publication Information Available

Library of Congress Cataloging-in-Publication Data

Kane, Joseph Nathan, 1899–
   The American counties : origins of county names, dates of
creation and population data, 1950–2000 / Joseph Nathan Kane,
Charles Curry Aiken.— 5th ed.
   p. cm.
   Includes bibliographical references.
   ISBN 0-8108-5036-2 (alk. paper)
   1. United States—History, Local. I. Aiken, Charles Curry, 1940– II. Title.
E180.K3 2005
917.3'001'4—dc22

                                                           2004010154

⊗™ The paper used in this publication meets the minimum requirements of
American National Standard for Information Sciences—Permanence of Paper
for Printed Library Materials, ANSI/NISO Z39.48-1992.
Manufactured in the United States of America.

Contents

Preface   v

Introduction to the 4th Edition   vii

Introduction to the 5th Edition   xix

THE AMERICAN COUNTIES   1

Appendix A: Dates of County Creation   335

Appendix B: Counties by State   397

Appendix C: County Seats   469

Bibliography   527

About the Authors   529

Preface

I have always had an interest in counties. It grew out of an interest in geography. As a child I would make lists of the states and their capitals; I ranked them by area, population, and order of admission. I did about all I could with the (then) forty-eight states. I did the same, except for order of admission, for the countries of the world, which at the time amounted to not much more than fifty or sixty countries.

One day I came across *The World Almanac and Book of Facts*. It contained an alphabetical listing of the counties for each state. My mind raced with the possibilities. First I combined them all into one national, alphabetical list. Next came national rankings based on area and population and alphabetical listings of county seats. Then I did it all for each state. All of this was done without computers. I never did much with these lists except on trips with my family, when I could fascinate my parents and bore my brothers with national and state rankings as we entered a new county.

My interest in counties waned with college, career, and family responsibilities. My interest rekindled when I moved to Bloomington, Indiana. I was intrigued by the way county courthouses in southern Indiana were usually massive structures plopped down on a square in the middle of town. I took pictures of some nearby courthouses on family drives around Bloomington.

My employer in Bloomington was the U.S. Navy Safety School. My work as a safety instructor involved travel to naval bases on both coasts. These trips were usually for two weeks, giving me a weekend to kill. I hit on the idea of taking pictures of courthouses around the areas in which I was working as a good way to explore the surrounding territory. After getting pictures of most of the reachable courthouses around Norfolk, Charleston, Jacksonville, San Diego, San Francisco, etc., I realized that if I drove to these places from Bloomington, I could get courthouse pictures along the way. As often happens, a pastime became an obsession. Over the last twenty years, I have taken pictures of over 2,700 of the county courthouses in the United States. I was hooked on counties again.

I forget the nature of the research project that led me to Joseph Kane's *The American Counties*. I remember the sensation of discovering Kane being similar to my first encounter with *The World Almanac*. Here was a wealth of information on counties; not just the information I had manipulated before but the date a county was created and the origin of the county name. I was struck by the fact that here was an entire book devoted to counties—this meant that I was not alone in my interest in counties.

I bought a copy of the fourth edition of *The American Counties* (1983). I awaited the next edition that would include the 1990 census. When it was not forthcoming, I did not think much about it until the 2000 census was in progress. I thought it would be good to have *The American Counties* include the censuses from 1950 to 2000. Also, I had noted that some updating was required as some new counties had been created and others abolished and some county seats had been relocated since the publication of the first edition in 1953.

I contacted Scarecrow Press with a proposal to update *The American Counties*. The person I corresponded with said she would check with Mr. Kane for his concurrence to update his book. I was surprised to find that he was still alive (at 102!). I received Kane's approval through Scarecrow Press. I also received a letter from Kane's family saying he was very pleased that his book was going to be updated.

Joseph Kane has since died. I regret I did not conceive of this project earlier so I could have met him. I have no idea where he lived but I was probably close to him at one time or another in my travels. Mr. Kane did all the hard work: the concept, researching the name origins, and tracking down the dates that counties were created and the enumeration of the legislative acts creating counties. All I had to do was to verify some of them. This book is dedicated to Joseph Kane.

There are many people who helped make this edition what it is. The bibliography lists books and websites that provided information. I should also thank the numerous persons (usually library or county employees) who responded to my e-mails and letters as I tried to track down the proper spelling of a county or county seat or the date the county was created. The Government Documents Department of the Indiana University Library in Bloomington was also very helpful. I am, of course, responsible for any errors or omissions in this book. I would be remiss if I did not thank my wife for her patience during my many hours of monopolizing our computer during this project.

Charles C. Aiken

Introduction to the 4th Edition

The following is a reprint of Joseph Kane's introduction to the fourth edition of *The American Counties*. References to portions of the book that have been eliminated or heavily revised in this edition have been removed. Additions and corrections that can be incorporated into the text are enclosed in brackets; those that cannot are addressed in notes.

Much confusion exists about the derivation of the names of counties. There are [24] counties named Lincoln. The supposition is that they were named for President Lincoln. But as some of these counties were named before Abraham Lincoln was born, even the most patriotic, when confronted with the evidence, are obliged to admit that perhaps another Lincoln was intended. The Lincoln for whom [five] of these counties were named was Benjamin Lincoln, a major general in the Continental Army who was distinguished for his bravery. [Lincoln County, South Dakota, was named for Lincoln County, Maine, which was named for the town of Lincoln, England.] Twenty-three counties were named Franklin to honor Benjamin Franklin, but Franklin County in Idaho is named for Franklin B. Richards while Franklin County in Texas is named for Benjamin Cromwell Franklin.

So, it is fallacious to assume that a county was named for the most famous bearer of a name. Logan County, Arkansas, for example, was named for James Logan; Logan counties in Colorado, Kansas, Nebraska, North Dakota, and Oklahoma were named for John Alexander Logan. Logan, Illinois, was named for Dr. John Logan, while Logan, West Virginia, was named for John Logan, an Indian. [Logan counties in Kentucky and Ohio were named for Benjamin Logan.]

Of the [3,087] counties, 2,136 have been named for individuals. This figure includes the [204] counties named for [24] presidents. The president for whom the greatest number of counties was named was George Washington, who leads the list with 31, followed by Thomas Jefferson with 26. Jackson has [23] counties named for him, [including] Hickory County, Missouri, which perpetuates his nickname "Old Hickory." There are 20 counties named for Madison, 17 for Monroe, 17 for Lincoln, 12 for Grant, and 11 for Polk. Other presidents for whom counties have been named are John Adams, eight; Garfield, six; Van Buren, William Henry Harrison, Taylor and Pierce, four each; Fillmore and Buchanan, three each; John Quincy Adams, Cleveland, and Theodore Roosevelt, two each; and Tyler, Hayes, Arthur, McKinley, and Harding, one each.

Only one president had both his first and last name used as the name of a county. Millard Fillmore had Millard County named for him in Utah as well as Fillmore County in Minnesota and Nebraska. [Every president from Washington to Theodore Roosevelt, except Andrew Johnson and Benjamin Harrison, had at least one county named for him. Since Roosevelt, only one president, Harding, has had a county named for him.]

Nebraska with an even dozen leads with the greatest number of counties named for Presidents. Other high-ranking states are Iowa 11, Arkansas ten, and Mississippi[, Missouri,] and Wisconsin, . . . eight. [Six] states, Florida, Georgia, Indiana, . . . Ohio, Oklahoma, and Tennessee contain seven such counties. [Seven] states, Illinois, [Kentucky,] Louisiana, [Minnesota,] Oregon, Texas, and Washington, contain six presidential counties; seven states, Alabama, Colorado, Idaho, Kansas, [Montana,] . . . New Mexico and West Virginia, contain five such counties; [two] states, . . . New York and Pennsylvania, contain four; four states, Michigan, North Carolina, Utah, and Virginia, contain three; . . . and [eight] states, Maine, Maryland, Nevada, North Dakota, Rhode Island, [South Dakota,] Vermont, and Wyoming, contain one such county each. . . . [Ten] of the [50] states . . .—[Alaska,] Arizona, California, Connecticut, Delaware, Hawaii, Massachusetts, New Hampshire, New Jersey and South Carolina—have not named any counties for presidents.

There were [244] governors of colonies, territories, and states for whom [432] counties were named. The state with the greatest number of counties named for governors is Georgia with 40, followed by Kentucky, 24; Tennessee, 22; Missouri, 21; Texas, 20; Illinois and Iowa, 18; Indiana and West Virginia, 17; Arkansas, Mississippi, and Nebraska, 16; Ohio 13; and Alabama, Kansas, and Virginia, 12. Other states had fewer. The states with the greatest number of counties named for their own governors are Georgia, 29; Kentucky, 14; Virginia, ten; Mississippi, Nebraska, and Texas, nine; and Arkansas, North Carolina, and Tennessee, eight.

The state that honored the greatest number of governors of other states is West Virginia, with 17 such counties. West Virginia was once a part of Virginia and so honored governors of Virginia. Iowa follows with 16; Illinois, Missouri, and Tennessee, 14; Indiana, 13; Georgia and Texas, 11; Kentucky and Ohio, ten; and Alabama and Kansas, nine.

Greater in popularity than a governor was Benjamin Franklin of Pennsylvania for whom 23 counties were named. Of the colonial and state governors, the most honored governor was Patrick Henry of Virginia for whom ten counties were named, nine named Henry and one named Patrick. Excluding those Presidents of the United States who served also as governors, the governors for whom the greatest number of counties were named were Isaac Shelby of Kentucky, nine; Lewis Cass of Michigan and De Witt Clinton[1] of New York, both eight; Meriwether Lewis of Louisiana, six; and John Floyd[2] of Virginia and John Sullivan of New Hampshire, both four.

All of the states except Arizona, California, Connecticut, Delaware, Hawaii, Nevada, and Rhode Island have honored governors. Maryland, New Hampshire, and South Carolina honored their own governors but did not honor governors of other states. [Alaska,] Maine, Massachusetts, and West Virginia did not honor their own governors but named counties for governors of other states. Oklahoma honored its governor William Henry "Alfalfa" Murray by naming two counties for him, Murray and Alfalfa.

A breakdown of the [244] governors so honored shows that 30 who had 59 counties named for them had served also in the capacity of both U.S. Senator and Representative. In this list are included four counties named for William Henry Harrison, 21 named for Andrew Jackson, and one named for John Tyler, all of whom were also Presidents of the United States. There were 37 governors, for whom 80 counties are named, who served also in the U.S. Senate but not in the House of Representatives. Included in this group are 17 counties named for James Monroe and four counties named for Martin Van Buren, both of whom also served as presidents. There were 141 other governors for whom 243 counties were named. In this figure are included the 30 counties named for Thomas Jefferson, Grover Cleveland, and Theodore Roosevelt.

There are 574 counties named for the 288 men who served in the U.S. Congress. Of these, there were 175 counties named for 66 men who served as both senator and representative including the 30 listed in the governor group who served as senator, governor, and representative for whom 59 counties are named. There are 218 counties named for the 128 men who served as representatives (including the 35 listed in the governor group who served as governor and representative for whom 49 counties are named). There are 181 counties named for the 93 men who served as senators including the 37 senators listed in the governor group who served as governor and senator, for whom 80 counties are named.

Excluding presidents and governors, the persons for whom the greatest number of counties was named are Benjamin Franklin 23, and Francis Marion, Nathanael Greene, and the Marquis de Lafayette, 17 each. Fourteen counties are named Greene County, two are named Green County without the final "e" and one is named Greensville; 11 counties are named Fayette County and six counties are named Lafayette County.

Others for whom more than a dozen counties have been named are Richard Montgomery, 16; Henry Clay,[3] and Anthony Wayne, 15; Joseph Warren, 14; and Charles Carroll and Stephen Arnold Douglas, 12 each. Eleven counties are named for John Caldwell Calhoun, and ten counties each have been named for John Hancock, James Lawrence, Oliver Hazard Perry, and Zebulon Pike. Nine have each been named for Henry Knox, Daniel Morgan, and Israel Putnam. Eight each bear the names of Thomas Hart Benton,[4] Alexander Hamilton, William Jasper, Robert [Edward] Lee,[5] John Marshall, and Daniel Webster. Those for whom seven counties have been named are Daniel Boone, Robert Fulton, and Casimir Pulaski. Six counties have been named for each of the following: George Rogers Clark, George A. Custer, Johann De Kalb, Benjamin Lincoln,[6] Meriwether Lewis, [Nathaniel] Macon, and Hugh Mercer.[7]

Many counties have been named for an individual and immediate members of his family. For example, some of the counties named for King George II and is family are: Amelia, Augusta, Caroline, Frederick, Louisa, Lunenburg, Orange, Prince Edward, and Prince William. Some of the many counties named for the Calvert family are: Anne Arundel, Baltimore, Calvert, Caroline, Cecil, Charles, Harford, and Talbot.

Many fathers and sons have been honored by having counties named for them, the most prominent being the Adams family. Adams County in Idaho, Iowa, Mississippi, Nebraska, Ohio, Pennsylvania, Washington, and Wisconsin have been named for John Adams, the second President of the United States, while the counties in Illinois [and] Indiana . . . were named for his son, John Quincy Adams, the sixth President of the United States.

Dodge County in . . . Wisconsin is named for Henry Dodge while Dodge County, Nebraska, is named for his son, Augustus Caesar Dodge [Dodge County, Minnesota, is named for both Henry and Augustus]. Robertson County, Tennessee, is named for James Robertson, while Robertson County, Kentucky, is named for his son, George Robertson. Tazewell County, Virginia, is named for Henry Tazewell while Tazewell County, Illinois, is named for his son, Littleton Waller Tazewell. Several counties have been named for brothers, and in several instances individual brothers have had individual counties named for them.

Some counties with different names may trace the origin of their names to the same person. For example, King James II . . . was honored when New York and Wyoming used Albany, one of his titles, as the name of a county. He was similarly honored by Maine, Nebraska, Pennsylvania, South Carolina, and Virginia when York, another of his titles, was used. New York, N.Y. was also named for him, and Massachusetts named Dukes County to honor him. [Ulster, New York, is named for James II's title, Earl of Ulster.]

In some instances, counties have been named for both a person's first and last names, such as Charles Mix County, South Dakota; Kit Carson County, Colorado; Roger Mills County, Oklahoma; Ben Hill County, Georgia; and Jo Daviess County, Illinois. This practice is most prevalent in Texas where counties have been named for Jim Wells, Jim Hogg, Tom Green, Deaf Smith, and Jeff Davis. There is [also] a Jeff Davis County in Georgia . . . and Jefferson Davis County in both Louisiana and Mississippi.

American history is indelibly written in the names of counties. [Eighty-one] counties have been named for [15] signers of the Declaration of Independence, six of whom came from Virginia. They were Carter Braxton, Benjamin Harrison, Thomas Jefferson, Richard Henry Lee, Thomas Nelson, Jr., and George Wythe. The three signers so honored from Georgia were Button Gwinnett, Lyman Hall, and George Walton. The two signers from Pennsylvania, Benjamin Franklin and Benjamin Rush, also had counties named for them. Other signers and the colonies they represented were Samuel Huntington of Connecticut, Thomas McKean of Delaware, Charles Carroll of Maryland, . . . and John Adams of Massachusetts Bay.

[In addition to the 45 counties named for presidents who had served as vice presidents], nine Vice Presidents of the United States have had 28 counties named for them, the most favored one being John Caldwell Calhoun for whom 11 counties were named. Counties are named for Calhoun in Alabama, Arkansas, Florida, Georgia, Illinois, Iowa, Michigan, Mississippi, South Carolina, Texas, and West Virginia. Richard Mentor Johnson had five counties named for him: in Illinois, [Iowa,] Kentucky, Missouri, and Nebraska. Counties in Arkansas, Iowa, Missouri, and Texas have been named for George Mifflin Dallas. Counties have been named for George Clinton in New York and Ohio; for Schuyler Colfax in Nebraska and New Mexico. States having one county named for a vice president are New York (Daniel D. Tompkins); South Dakota (Hannibal Hamlin), and Washington (William R. King[8]).

County names have honored also many distinguished foreigners: Lafayette, Simon Bolivar, Edmund Burke, Thaddeus Kosciusko, Lajos Kossuth, Friederich von Humboldt, Baron von Steuben, Joseph Addison, Isaac Newton, Giacomo Beltrami, Robert Emmet, Arthur Onslow, etc. Texas remembered the slogan "Remember the Alamo" when it named its counties. Twelve heroic defenders who lost their lives on March 6, 1836, were honored by having counties named for them. The counties named for them were Bailey, Bowie, Cochran, Cottle, Crockett, Dickens, Floyd, Kent, Kimble, King, Lynn, and Travis. Crockett, Tennessee, was also named for one of these Alamo defenders.

Many counties have derived their names from descriptive words; 228 counties have been named for 141 descriptive words. The most commonly used word is "union," which is used 18 times by Arkansas, Florida, Georgia, Illinois, Indiana, Iowa, Kentucky, Louisiana, Mississippi, New Jersey, New Mexico, North Carolina, Ohio, Oregon, Pennsylvania, South Carolina, South Dakota, and Tennessee. The next most popular word is "lake," used 12 times for counties in California, Colorado, Florida, Illinois, Indiana, Michigan, Minnesota, Montana, Ohio, Oregon, South Dakota, and Tennessee.

Richland has been used five times (Louisiana, Montana, Ohio, South Carolina, and Wisconsin) and so has Saline (Arkansas, Illinois, Kansas, Missouri, and Nebraska) The words carbon, iron, liberty, and mineral have each been used four times. Counties named "Carbon" are in Montana, Pennsylvania, Utah, and Wyoming; "Iron" in Michigan, Missouri, Utah, and Wisconsin; "Liberty" in Florida, Georgia, Montana, and Texas, and "Mineral," in Colorado, Montana, Nevada, and West Virginia.

Each of the following descriptive words has been used three times as county names: Beaver, Buffalo, Cedar, Delta, Fairfield, Orange, Park, Rock, Summit, and Valley. Two counties have been named for each of the following words: Bath, Bay, Big Horn, Butte, Clearwater, Elk, Forest, Golden Valley, Grand, Highland, Limestone, Midland, Portage, Prairie, Red River, Trinity, and Vermilion.

Montana leads with descriptive county names having 27 counties, followed by Minnesota with 13; Florida, 12; Idaho and Texas, with 11 each; Nebraska, ten; Colorado, nine; [Alaska,] Ohio, Pennsylvania, and Wisconsin, eight each; Arkansas, Louisiana, Michigan, South Carolina, and Utah, seven each; and Wyoming, six. States having five counties named for descriptive words are California, Illinois, Kentucky, and South Dakota; Georgia and North Dakota have four each; Hawaii, Indiana, Mississippi, Missouri, Oklahoma, and Virginia, three each; Connecticut, Iowa, Kansas, Nevada, New Jersey, Oregon, Rhode Island, Tennessee, and West Virginia, two each; and Alabama, New Mexico, New York, North Carolina, Vermont, and Washington, one each.

French words account for the names of 43 counties located in 22 states. The only French word used more than once as the name of a county is Platte, used by Missouri, Nebraska, and Wyoming.[9] The state having the largest number of counties named for French words is Louisiana, which has seven parishes with the following names: East Baton Rouge, West Baton Rouge, Lafourc[h]e, Pointe Coupee, Rapides, Sabine, and Terrebonne. Wisconsin has the next-largest number of counties with French names. Its five French-named counties are Eau Clair, Fond du Lac, La Crosse, Racine, and Trempealeau.

There are four counties with French names in Minnesota: Lac qui Parle, Mille Lacs, Roseau, and Traverse; and four counties in Missouri; Moniteau, Maries, Ozark, and Platte. The three French-named counties in Nebraska are Box Butte, Loup, and

Platte. Ohio has two counties with French names, Belmont and Champaign; California has Butte and Siskiyou; and Oregon has Deschutes and Malheur. Other French words used as the names of counties are: Amite, Boise, Bon Homme, Cache, Chicot, Clarion, Des Moines, La Porte, Lamoille, Labette, Pend Oreille, Platte, Presque Isle, and Washita.

Spanish has a prominent place in county names. There are 69 counties whose names have been derived form 65 Spanish words. Most of these counties are located in California and Texas. Spanish words used by more that one county are Sierra (California and New Mexico), El Paso (Colorado and Texas), Escambia (Alabama and Florida), and Santa Cruz (California and Arizona).[10] In California, we find 18 counties with the following Spanish names: Alameda, Calaveras, Contra Costa, Del Norte, El Dorado, Fresno, Los Angeles, Madera, Mariposa, Merced, Nevada, Placer, Plumas, Sacramento, Santa Cruz, Sierra, Ventura, and Yuba.

Texas has 23 counties named for Spanish words as follows: Angelina, Atascosa, Bandera, Blanco, Bosque, Brazoria, Brazos, Colorado, Comal, Concho, El Paso, Frio, Lampasas, Lavaca, Llano, Matagorda, Nueces, Palo Pinto, Presidio, Refugio, Sabine, San Saba, and Val Verde. In Colorado, counties with Spanish names are: Alamosa, Conejos, Costilla, Dolores, El Paso, Huerfano, La Plata, Las Anim[a]s, Mesa, Pueblo, Rio Blanco, and Rio Grande. There are 16 other counties in seven states named for Spanish words.

There are 161 counties whose names have been derived from Indian words such as Alachua, Alamance, Allegan, Autauga, etc. Three Hawaiian counties are named for Polynesian descriptive words and one for a Polynesian demi-god. Michigan with 20 counties named for Indian words leads the states, followed by New York with 12, and Mississippi and Ohio with 11. Minnesota and Wisconsin have ten counties each named for Indian words. [Alaska has ten boroughs and census areas named from Aleut and Eskimo words.]

The other states with Indian-named counties follow: Washington, eight; Alabama, Florida, and Pennsylvania, six each; Maine and Oklahoma, five each; Georgia and Virginia, four each; and Arizona, North Carolina, South Carolina, Tennessee, Utah, and West Virginia, two each. The states with only one county with an Indian name are: Arkansas, Colorado, Kansas, Kentucky, Louisiana, Maryland, Massachusetts, Montana, Nebraska, Nevada, New Hampshire, New Jersey, North Dakota, Oregon, South Dakota, and Texas.

Sixty-one Indians have had their names immortalized by counties. There may also be other counties named for persons with Anglicized names who have Indian ancestry. The spelling of their names occasionally differs from that often found in histories and biographies. Among the Indian names are the names of seven Indian women whose names designate counties in eight states. They are Attala (Mississippi), Leelanau (Michigan), Marinette (Wisconsin), Sonoma (California), Tippah (Mississippi), Winona (Minnesota), and Pocahontas, whose name has been used by Iowa and West Virginia. The only Indian besides Pocahontas whose name is used more than once is Osceola for whom counties are named in Florida, Iowa, and Michigan.

The greatest use of Indian names is made by Oklahoma and Iowa. The 14 Indian-named Oklahoma counties are Adair, Atoka, Carter, Craig, Garvin, Johnston, Le Flore Love, McCurtain, McIntosh, Mayes, Pontotoc, Pushmataha, and Sequoyah; the ten counties in Iowa are Appanoose, Black Hawk, Keokuk, Mahaska, Osceola, Pocahontas, Poweshiek, Tama, Wapello, and Winneshiek. Six counties in Michigan bear Indian names: Leelanau, Mecosta, Missaukee, Newaygo, Osceola, and Sanilac. There are also six counties in Mississippi with Indian names: Attala, Itawamba, Leflore, Pontotoc, Tippah, and Tishomingo. California has four Indian-named counties: Marin, Solano, Sonoma, and Stanislaus. Six states have two Indian-named counties and 11 others have one county each.

In addition to naming counties for Indians and Indian words, 41 states have named 181 counties for Indian tribes. All states have honored an Indian tribe by naming a county for them except Delaware, Kentucky, Massachusetts, New Jersey, Rhode Island, Tennessee, and Vermont. Both Kansas and Oklahoma have 13 counties named for Indian tribes; North Carolina and Oregon have nine; Iowa, New York, Ohio, and Wisconsin have eight; and Arizona, California, Louisiana, and Washington have seven counties each. The most favored Indian tribe is the Cherokee for whom eight counties have been named. The Delaware and Ottawa tribes have each had four counties named for them. Sixteen tribes have had three counties named for them; 15 tribes have had two counties named for them.

Another source for the name of counties is words especially coined. In this group there are 28 counties in 18 states. The state that leads in creating names for counties is Michigan, which named counties: Alcona, Alpena, Arenac, Benzie, Hillsdale, Oceana, Oscoda, and Tuscola.

Eight states have named counties Columbia. They are Arkansas, Florida, Georgia, New York, Oregon, Pennsylvania, Washington, and Wisconsin. Arkansas adapted the word from Columbia, the goddess of Liberty; Washington from the *Columbia*, the first ship to carry the flag of the United States around the world, while the others named their counties Columbia in honor of Columbus. Other created names for counties are Columbiana, Ohio; Glades, Florida; Itasca, Minnesota; Kay, Oklahoma; Lonoke, Arkansas; Owyhee, Idaho; Pittsylvania, Virginia; Pondera, Montana; and Transylvania [North Carolina]. Eureka, Nevada, is derived from the Greek; Salem, New Jersey, from the Hebrew; and Schuylkill, Pennsylvania, from the Dutch.

Other sources of names for counties are those persons who have been designated saints. There are 41 counties named for 33 saints. Their names are preceded by the proper forms such as St., Ste., San, and Santa. The most popular name is San Juan for whom four counties have been named, and St. Charles, St. Francis, St. Joseph, St. Louis, and San Miguel for whom two counties have been named. The states having the most number of counties named for saints are California, nine; Louisiana, nine; Missouri, four; Florida, three; Texas, three; Colorado, two; New Mexico, two; and one each for Arkansas, Indiana, Maryland, Michigan, Minnesota, . . . Utah, Washington, and Wisconsin.

There are 45 counties named for women in 24 states. Among the women so honored are seven Indian women and four women who have been sainted. The only woman whose name has been used for more than one county is Pocahontas for whom counties have been named in Iowa and West Virginia. Two counties were named Mecklenburg (in North Carolina and Virginia) for Charlotte Sophia, Princess of Mecklenburg; and two counties named Guadalupe for Our Lady of Guadalupe. Two counties were named Caroline, each for a different person, and two counties were similarly named Florence.

The state most partial to the names of women for counties is Virginia, which has nine counties named for women as follows: Amelia, Augusta, Carolin[e], Charlotte, Elizabeth City [now part of the independent city of Hampton], Fluvanna, Louisa, Mecklenburg, and Princess Anne [now the independent city of Virginia Beach]. Five counties in Maryland have also been named for women: Anne Arundel, Caroline, Queen Anne's, Somerset, and Talbot. Pennsylvania named three counties for women: Huntingdon, Luzerne, and Montour. North Carolina also had named three counties for women: Dare, Mecklenburg, and Wake, as did Iowa: Bremer, Louisa, and Monona. Idaho, New Mexico, New York, and Texas named two counties for women, while 14 other states named one county.

Another source of county names is geography. There are 219 counties named for geographical locations. Since many mountains, valleys, rivers, and creeks bear the same name, it is not always possible to determine whether the county was named for the river, the mountain, the valley, or all of them.

It is not always possible to determine whether the counties have been named for certain areas or for the people who ruled them or those for whom the areas were named. For example, eight counties bear the name Cumberland. Disregarding whether these counties were named for the river, town, city, village, or other feature, one may claim that the counties named Cumberland were named for Cumberland, England. At the same time, it may be claimed that the counties were named for William Augustus, the Duke of Cumberland, while others may insist they were named for subsequent dukes.

In a similar vein, there is an Essex County in Massachusetts, New Jersey, New York, Vermont, and Virginia. One may contend that these counties were named for Robert Devereux, the Earl of Essex, but some may maintain that the counties were named for Essex, England, which area was ruled by Robert Devereux while he was Earl. Only rarely is the distinction made between the site and the ruler as in the case of Norborne Berkeley, the Baron of Botetourt. The county of Berkeley, West Virginia, is named for him, and the county of Botetourt, Virginia, is named for the site. [In this fifth edition the immediate source of a county's name, usually a geographic feature, is given with the origin of the feature's name also given.]

Quite frequently counties have used different names to honor the same person. The most conspicuous example of this is Fayette County (11 counties) and Lafayette County (six counties) both of whom are named for Lafayette. Nine counties are named Henry for Patrick Henry and one county is named Patrick for him. Two counties are named Dodge for Henry Dodge, and one county is named Henry in his honor. Three counties are named [DeSoto] for Hernando de Soto and one county is named Hernando. Eight of the counties are named Clinton for De Witt Clinton and one county is named De Witt. Two counties are named Fillmore and one county is named Millard to honor President Millard Fillmore.

Joseph Hamilton [Daveiss] is honored by three counties named Daviess, and one named Jo Daviess; Jefferson Davis was honored by two counties named Jefferson Davis and two named Jeff Davis. John Middleton Clayton was honored by Clayton, Iowa, and Clay, Arkansas. George Rogers Clark is honored by five counties named Clark and one named Clarke (with an "e"). Three counties are named for William Clark and five for Meriwether Lewis, and one county is named for both of them, Lewis and Clark County. William Pitt leads with the greatest number of deviations. There is a Pitt County in North Carolina, a Chatham County in both Georgia and North Carolina, and a Pittsylvania County in Virginia. [Actually, James II leads this category with five names, Albany, Dukes, New York, Ulster, and York, given to ten counties.]

States also have provided names for counties: they are Delaware County, Iowa; Nevada, Arkansas; Oregon, Missouri; Texas, Missouri; and Texas, Oklahoma. Indiana, Pennsylvania, was named for Indiana Territory; Republic, Kansas, for the Pawnee Republic, and Jersey, Illinois, for New Jersey.

Cities in the United States also have provided names for counties such as Dorchester, South Carolina; Lexington, South Carolina; Pittsburgh, Oklahoma [the county dropped the "h"]; Plymouth, Iowa, and Rutland, Vermont. And famous estates and residences also have been commemorated such as Ashland, Ohio, and Ashland, Wisconsin, both named for Henry Clay's estate; Vernon, Louisiana, and Vernon, Wisconsin, for George Washington's home at Mount Vernon; La Grange, Indiana, for Lafayette's home near Paris, and Arlington, Virginia, for John Custis's home.

Forts and military posts have lent their names to counties such as Duchesne, Utah, for Fort Duchesne, Pennsylvania; Fort Bend, Texas for Fort Bend (Texas); Defiance, Ohio for Fort Defiance (Ohio); and Massac, Illinois, for Fort Massac (Illinois).

Many counties have derived their names from other counties. Illinois named five of its counties for counties in Kentucky:

Christian, Hardin, Mason, Scott, and Woodford. Illinois named Champaign and Richland counties for counties of the same name in Ohio. Williamson, Illinois, was named for Williamson, Tennessee. Jones County and Walworth County in South Dakota were named for counties in Iowa and Wisconsin. Albany County and Chatauqua County, New York, have given their names to counties in Wyoming and Kansas, respectively. Orange County, Indiana, received its name from Orange County, North Carolina.

Although the preponderance of counties named for cities have derived their names from locations in England, [others] have resorted to [other] Old World cities. Some of the counties thus named are Geneva, Grenada (for Granada), Lorain, Medina, Athens, Goshen, and Marathon.

The New World was not neglected in naming counties. For example, Iowa named three of its counties Buena Vista, Cerro Gordo, and Palo Alto for battlegrounds in Mexico. Other names are Acadia, Louisiana; Hidalgo, New Mexico; Nassau, Florida; and Val Verde, Texas.

Although several counties have the same name, there are variations in spelling. There is an Allegany County in Maryland and New York, but North Carolina and Virginia have an Alleghany County, and Pennsylvania has an Allegheny County. There is a Pottawatomie County in Kansas and Oklahoma, but the county in Iowa is Pottawattamie County. Ohio has its Wyandot County whereas Kansas has Wyandotte County. Cheboygan County is in Michigan and Sheboygan County is in Wisconsin. [Vermilion County is in Illinois and Louisiana, and Vermillion County is in Indiana.]

This dissimilarity is true not only of Indian [and foreign] names but of English names. Loudon County in Tennessee and Loudoun County in Virginia are both named for the same man, John Campbell, the fourth Earl of Loudoun. In Ohio, there is a Clark County named for George Rogers Clark, but the county named for him in Virginia is Clarke County.

Some counties have the same sound but are spelled differently because they are named for different people, such as Kearney County Nebraska, and Kearny County, Kansas. Linn County, Iowa, and Lynn County, Texas, are similarly named for different people. There is a great diversity in the orthography of common names such as Smith and Smyth, Stanley, and Stanly, Stark and Starke, Stephens and Stevens, Storey and Story, etc.

More than one-third of the counties are located in seven states. Texas has the greatest number of counties, with 254. The six other states having 100 or more are Georgia, 159; Kentucky, 120; Missouri, 114; Kansas, 105; Illinois, 102; and North Carolina, 100. The state with the smallest number of counties is Delaware with only three counties. Texas has more counties than the total number of counties in 15 states. Louisiana is subdivided into 64 parishes, the equivalent of counties. [Alaska has 16 boroughs and 11 census areas that are the equivalent of counties.]

NOTES

1. Clinton has nine counting De Witt, Illinois.
2. Only one Floyd County, in Virginia, is named for Governor John Floyd. The other three are named for two other John Floyds.
3. Clay has 16 counties named for him.
4. Tennessee changed its honoree to David Benton.
5. Lee has nine counties named for him.
6. Benjamin Lincoln has five counties named for him.
7. Mercer has seven counties named for him.
8. The King County Council voted in 1968 to make Martin Luther King the county's honoree.
9. Butte is used by California, Idaho, and South Dakota; Box Butte is used by Nebraska. Champaign is used by Illinois and Ohio.
10. Nevada is used by Arkansas and California.

Table I.1. List of States with Number of Counties		**Table I.2. List of States by Number of Counties**	
Alabama	67	3	Delaware
Alaska*	27	4	Hawaii***
Arizona	15	5	Rhode Island**
Arkansas	75	8	Connecticut**
California	58	10	New Hampshire
Colorado	64	14	Massachusetts
Connecticut**	8	14	Vermont
Delaware	3	15	Arizona
Florida	67	16	Maine
Georgia	159	16	Nevada
Hawaii***	4	21	New Jersey
Idaho	44	23	Maryland
Illinois	102	23	Wyoming
Indiana	92	27	Alaska*
Iowa	99	29	Utah
Kansas	105	33	New Mexico
Kentucky	120	36	Oregon
Louisiana****	64	39	Washington
Maine	16	44	Idaho
Maryland	23	46	South Carolina
Massachusetts	14	53	North Dakota
Michigan	83	55	West Virginia
Minnesota	87	56	Montana
Mississippi	82	58	California
Missouri	114	62	New York
Montana	56	64	Colorado
Nebraska	93	64	Louisiana****
Nevada	16	66	South Dakota
New Hampshire	10	67	Alabama
New Jersey	21	67	Florida
New Mexico	33	67	Pennsylvania
New York	62	72	Wisconsin
North Carolina	100	75	Arkansas
North Dakota	53	77	Oklahoma
Ohio	88	82	Mississippi
Oklahoma	77	83	Michigan
Oregon	36	87	Minnesota
Pennsylvania	67	88	Ohio
Rhode Island**	5	92	Indiana
South Carolina	46	93	Nebraska
South Dakota	66	95	Tennessee
Tennessee	95	95	Virginia
Texas	254	99	Iowa
Utah	29	100	North Carolina
Vermont	14	102	Illinois
Virginia	95	105	Kansas
Washington	39	114	Missouri
West Virginia	55	120	Kentucky
Wisconsin	72	159	Georgia
Wyoming	23	254	Texas

*Alaska has 16 boroughs and 11 census areas.
**Connecticut and Rhode Island do not have county governments.
***Kalawao County is sometimes counted separate from Maui County giving Hawaii 5 counties.
****Louisiana parishes are the equivalents of counties.

Table I.3. Largest and Smallest Counties in Area (square miles)

Alabama	Baldwin	1,596
	Etowah	535
Alaska	Yukon-Koukuk	145,900
	Bristol Bay	505
Arizona	Coconino	18,617
	Santa Cruz	1,238
Arkansas	Union	1,039
	Lafayette	527
California	San Bernardino	20,053
	San Francisco	47
Colorado	Las Animas	4,773
	Broomfield	27
Connecticut	Litchfield	920
	Middlesex	369
Delaware	Sussex	938
	New Castle	426
Florida	Collier	2,025
	Union	240
Georgia	Ware	902
	Clarke	121
Hawaii	Hawaii	4,028
	Honolulu	600
Idaho	Idaho	8,485
	Payette	408
Illinois	McLean	1,184
	Putnam	160
Indiana	Allen	657
	Ohio	87
Iowa	Kossuth	973
	Dickinson	381
Kansas	Butler	1,428
	Wyandotte	151
Kentucky	Pike	788
	Gallatin	99
Louisiana	Vernon	1,328
	Orleans	181
Maine	Aroostook	6,672
	Sagadahoc	254
Maryland	Frederick	663
	Calvert	215
Massachusetts	Worcester	1,513
	Nantucket	48
Michigan	Marquette	1,821
	Benzie	321
Minnesota	Saint Louis	6,225
	Ramsey	156
Mississippi	Yazoo	919
	Alcorn	400
Missouri	Texas	1,179
	Worth	267
Montana	Beaverhead	5,542
	Silver Bow	718
Nebraska	Cherry	5,961
	Sarpy	241
Nevada	Nye	18,147
	Storey	263
New Hampshire	Grafton	1,800
	Strafford	369
New Jersey	Burlington	805
	Hudson	47

New Mexico	Catron	6,928
	Los Alamos	109
New York	Saint Lawrence	2,686
	New York	23
North Carolina	Robeson	949
	Chowan	173
North Dakota	McKenzie	2,742
	Eddy	630
Ohio	Ashtabula	702
	Lake	228
Oklahoma	Osage	2,251
	Marshall	371
Oregon	Harney	10,134
	Multnomah	435
Pennsylvania	Lycoming	1,235
	Montour	131
Rhode Island	Providence	413
	Bristol	25
South Carolina	Horry	1,134
	McCormick	360
South Dakota	Meade	3,471
	Clay	412
Tennessee	Shelby	755
	Trousdale	114
Texas	Brewster	6,193
	Rockwall	129
Utah	San Juan	7,820
	Davis	304
Vermont	Windsor	971
	Grand Isle	83
Virginia	Pittsylvania	971
	Arlington	26
Washington	Okanogan	5,268
	San Juan	175
West Virginia	Randolph	1,040
	Hancock	83
Wisconsin	Marathon	1,545
	Ozaukee & Pepin	232
Wyoming	Sweetwater	10,425
	Hot Springs	2,004

Table I.4.   Largest and Smallest Counties by Population (2000)

Alabama	Jefferson	662,047
	Greene	9,974
Alaska	Anchorage	260,283
	Yakutat	808
Arizona	Maricopa	3,072,149
	Greenlee	8,547
Arkansas	Pulaski	361,474
	Calhoun	5,744
California	Los Angeles	9,519,338
	Alpine	1,208
Colorado	Denver	554,636
	San Juan	558
Connecticut	Fairfield	882,567
	Windham	109,091
Delaware	New Castle	500,265
	Kent	126,697
Florida	Miami-Dade	2,253,362
	Liberty	7,021
Georgia	Fulton	816,006
	Taliaferro	2,077
Hawaii	Honolulu	876,156
	Kauai	58,463
Idaho	Ada	300,904
	Camas	991
Illinois	Cook	5,376,741
	Pope	4,413
Indiana	Marion	860,454
	Ohio	5,623
Iowa	Polk	374,601
	Adams	4,482
Kansas	Sedgwick	452,869
	Greeley	1,534
Kentucky	Jefferson	693,604
	Robertson	2,266
Louisiana	Orleans	484,674
	Tensas	6,618
Maine	Cumberland	265,612
	Piscataquis	17,235
Maryland	Montgomery	873,341
	Kent	19,197
Massachusetts	Middlesex	1,465,396
	Nantucket	9,520
Michigan	Wayne	2,061,162
	Keweenaw	2,301
Minnesota	Hennepin	1,116,200
	Traverse	4,134
Mississippi	Hinds	250,800
	Issaquena	2,274
Missouri	Saint Louis	1,016,315
	Worth	2,382
Montana	Yellowstone	129,352
	Petroleum	493
Nebraska	Douglas	463,585
	Arthur	444
Nevada	Clark	1,375,765
	Esmeralda	971
New Hampshire	Hillsborough	380,841
	Coos	33,111
New Jersey	Bergen	884,118
	Salem	64,285

New Mexico	Bernalillo	556,678
	Harding	810
New York	Kings	2,465,326
	Hamilton	5,379
North Carolina	Mecklenburg	695,454
	Tyrrell	4,149
North Dakota	Cass	123,138
	Slope	767
Ohio	Cuyahoga	1,393,978
	Vinton	12,806
Oklahoma	Oklahoma	660,448
	Cimarron	3,148
Oregon	Multnomah	660,486
	Wheeler	1,547
Pennsylvania	Philadelphia	1,517,550
	Forest	4,946
Rhode Island	Providence	621,602
	Bristol	50,648
South Carolina	Greenville	379,616
	McCormick	9,958
South Dakota	Minnehaha	148,281
	Jones	1,193
Tennessee	Shelby	897,472
	Pickett	4,945
Texas	Harris	3,400,578
	Loving	67
Utah	Salt Lake	898,387
	Daggett	921
Vermont	Chittenden	146,571
	Essex	6,459
Virginia	Fairfax	969,749
	Highland	2,536
Washington	King	1,737,034
	Garfield	2,397
West Virginia	Kanawha	200,073
	Wirt	5,873
Wisconsin	Milwaukee	940,164
	Menominee	4,562
Wyoming	Laramie	81,607
	Niobrara	2,407

Introduction to the 5th Edition

What is a county? To many people their county is just another layer of government collecting taxes and otherwise not very visible. Many people think of their county only during the county fair. Travelers may notice highway signs announcing their passing from one county to another. In many rural areas, the high school carries the county name and is a focal point of local pride.

If anybody thinks about his or her county it is usually as something that has just always been there and has always had a name that, unless named for a local geographic feature, has little, if any, current significance. This book offers a few facts about every county in the United States in hopes that it will spark the reader's interest to find out more about his/her county or other counties of interest. When was the county created? Who or what is it named for? Why? How does my county stack up against adjacent counties in area or population? Is my county older than the one next door?

A county can be defined politically, geographically, historically, statistically, or by any number of adverbial categories. This book follows the definition of the U.S. Department of Commerce that counties are the "first-order subdivisions" of each state. This simple definition expands beyond the word "county" to encompass the parishes of Louisiana, the boroughs and census areas of Alaska (the five boroughs of New York City are counties), and the independent cities in Maryland, Missouri, Nevada, and Virginia. Because the District of Columbia has no first-order subdivisions, it is in itself a first-order subdivision. Using this expanded definition, there are 3,142 first-order subdivisions in the United States: 3,007 counties; sixty-four parishes; forty-three independent cities; sixteen boroughs; eleven census areas; and one federal district.

The bibliography lists sources, most of which are very good, that are dedicated solely to population data, or name origins, or areas, or dates of creation. But no book, except this one, has all this county data in one place. Because of the multifaceted nature of this book, its information in any one area is less than that of books that are singularly devoted to such data.

Previous editions of *The American Counties* were limited to counties and Louisiana's parishes. Alaska's subdivisions were relegated to a separate section at the back of the book, as was a list of independent cities. Although this fifth edition retains the name of the previous editions, its coverage has expanded to include all first-order subdivisions. While more correct, the title *The American First-Order Subdivisions*, would be rather unwieldy. Unless otherwise noted, the term "county" as used in this book, including its title, refers to all first-order subdivisions.

This book is divided into five main sections. After the introductory material is the heart of the book: "The American Counties," an alphabetical listing of every county in the fifty states of the United States. The arrangement and contents of each entry in this section are discussed below. Appendix A "Dates of County Creation," is a list of counties in the order of creation from 1634 to 2001. Next is appendix B, "Counties by State," a listing of counties in each state. The list includes the county name, county seat, date of creation, and the number of the statute or other political action that created the county. Also included in this section are any county name changes. This is followed by appendix C, which is an alphabetical listing of county seats. Last is a bibliography of the main sources used in verifying or compiling the information in this book.

To make space for expanded discussions of county name origins, some information included in previous editions has been omitted from this edition. A list of counties whose names have changed from the original was deleted because this information is included in the main section and Appendix B. Another part omitted from Kane's earlier editions is the listing of the names of persons for whom counties were named. In many instances it is not certain for whom a county was named, and listing all possibilities would be cumbersome as well as misleading. Also, this information is included in "The American Counties" section. Two other omitted parts separately listed independent cities and Alaska's boroughs. These subdivisions are now included with all other counties in the main section.

It was decided to omit two features that were included in Kane's earlier editions: county nicknames and county bibliographies. It was easy to jettison the nicknames, most of which are no more than chamber of commerce contrivances—"The Swing Is to Palm Beach County for Fun," "The Playground of the Adirondacks," etc. It was more difficult to omit Kane's bibliographic entries in order to make more space for expanded discussions of county name origins. Kane's stated purpose in including bibliographic information was to assist researchers. Many of Kane's references, however, are by now over eighty years old, having been published during the heyday of county histories, roughly from 1880 to 1920. Like the county nicknames, many of the county histories of that and subsequent eras were prone to boosterism. The decision to omit the bibliographies was made easier by two considerations: (1) any researcher of a county will eventually be led to the county's local or state library or historical society; and (2) most U.S. counties have their own websites with links to myriad sources of information.

This book was prepared with the realization that each reader will turn first to his/her county. Some readers will be finding new information about their counties. Others will be checking this book to verify what they already know. Still other readers will be well versed in their county's history and will be evaluating the veracity of the information included. Every effort has been made to verify the accuracy of the information in this book knowing that if readers find errors regarding their counties, everything else in the book will be suspect. Readers are encouraged to inform the author of any errors or omissions so future editions can be as correct as possible.

Kalawao County, Hawaii, is included despite its dubious status as a county. Any reader wishing to exclude Kalawao County can place its area and population in Maui County with simple arithmetic. That portion of Yellowstone National Park located in Montana was recognized as a first-order subdivision until July 19, 1999, when it became part of Gallatin and Park Counties. The counties of Connecticut and Rhode Island do not have governmental structures. They are, however, geographical entities that are maintained for statistical, record-keeping, and some judicial functions.

In preparing this fifth edition, the organization of the previous editions has essentially been followed. The first line of each entry includes the name of the county and its state. The county seat and the area in square miles are given on the second line. The third line gives the county's decennial census totals from 2000 to 1950. The fourth line begins with the date the county was created. Also included, as applicable, are the dates the county was renamed, abolished, recreated, organized, deorganized, and/or reorganized. Following the date(s) is a brief description of the origin of the county's name and, if named for a person or persons, a brief sketch of biographical highlights of the person(s) so honored.

COUNTY NAME

The book's entries are arranged alphabetically by county and, if there is more than one of the same name, by state. There are no known disputed spellings of a county name, although some names are misspellings of their namesakes. For example, there are four counties named for Joseph Daveiss (including Jo Daviess, Illinois) and every one misspells the county name as "Daviess." Three of the four counties honoring John Stark spell his name correctly, but Indiana added an "e" when creating Starke County. Once a misspelling is enacted into law by a legislature, it is rarely corrected.

There is some confusion in the proper spacing in some county names. Are De Soto, La Salle, El Dorado, etc., one word or two? If one, is the third letter capitalized? An example is De Witt (two words) County, Illinois, and DeWitt (one word) County, Texas. Lagrange (lower case "g") is the county seat of LaGrange (upper case "G") County in Indiana. The first step in attempting to resolve these issues was to contact a county official or office listed on the National Association of Counties' website (http://www.naco.org). The final arbiter was the Geographic Names Information System (GNIS) of the U.S. Geological Survey, Department of the Interior (http://geonames.usgs.gov).

One hundred and seventy-six counties have changed their names. Some have changed names more than once, while others changed and then later reverted back to the original name. Some names are changed because the original was an Indian name that was too difficult to pronounce or spell, such as Warrosquyoake or Kautawubet. Often a change was made to honor a newly emerged hero or because the original honoree had fallen out of favor.

COUNTY SEAT

During the nineteenth century many towns vied to be their county's center of government. Such status would usually make the town a center of growth and commerce in addition to being a source of local pride. Theft of county records, gunfights, and even burning down the courthouse were sometimes resorted to in order to encourage the relocation of a county seat. By the early twentieth century, most counties had settled on their county seat, but county seats continue to be relocated—although by more peaceful processes. The cities or towns listed herein as county seats are consistent with the National Association of Counties and/or *The Handybook for Genealogists*.

The cities or towns identified with Alaska's boroughs are not county seats, but they serve the same function as administrative and judicial centers for their boroughs. Alaska's eleven census areas are administered by the state. Although there may be a locale within the census area from which a state official administrates, none are listed as such. Shannon and Todd Counties in South Dakota are not organized. They are administered by Fall River and Tripp Counties, respectively.

Connecticut abolished county government in 1960. Rhode Island's counties emerged from judicial districts and never have had complete county governmental functions or structures. The cities named as county seats for these two states are judicial or record-keeping centers that are listed by the National Association of Counties as functioning as county seats.

In previous editions of *The American Counties* some listings show two county seats for some counties, mostly in Arkansas and Mississippi. It may be that the courthouse and county seat are in separate cities or that governmental offices are divided between the two cities. In this edition, only one county seat is listed for each county, as named by the National Association of Counties and confirmed by *The Handybook for Genealogists*.

AREA

The second item on the second line of each county's entry is its area in square miles. The figure given is for land area exclusive of any water areas in the county. The county areas given in this edition are the ones used by the U.S. Census Bureau to compute population densities for the 2000 Census.

The area of a county changes more often than one would suspect. The area of coastal or riverine counties can fluctuate as land is lost to or reclaimed from the water. The creation of reservoirs can also reduce a county's land area. Boundary adjustments affect county areas. In Virginia, the establishment and growth of independent cities is done at the expense of surrounding counties.

POPULATION

On the third line of each county's entry is the county's population from the last six decennial censuses. The populations are listed from 2000 to 1950, reading left to right (2000, 1990, 1980, 1970, 1960, and 1950).

The population figures from 1990 and 2000 are from the Census Bureau's 2000 Census. The figures from 1950 to 1980 are from Kane's previous editions, verified against Richard L. Forstall, *Population of States and Counties of the United States: 1790–1990*, which is also available on the Internet at http://census.gov/population/cencounts/all190090.txt.

DATE OF CREATION

The fourth line of each county entry starts with the date the county was created. The six earliest counties were formed in Virginia in 1634; the last one, Broomfield, Colorado, was created November 15, 2001. The various factors considered in determining the date a county was created are discussed at the beginning of appendix A, "Dates of County Creation."

For some counties the date the county was created is followed by the date the county was organized. Many counties on the frontier were created when there were few, if any, settlers within the county. This was sometimes done by the legislature just to dispense with the business of establishing counties. Other times it was done at the behest of railroads to make the empty territory look settled. Some counties were later abolished or deorganized. This is noted in the date entry in the section "The American Counties" along with the date of any subsequent reorganization or recreation.

Some of these formally unorganized counties can easily be found by referring to a map showing county boundaries. The neat rectangular, if not actually square, counties in the Great Plains and Lower Michigan are indicative of boundaries established before anybody was there to complicate the process of creating county boundaries.

The date given for the creation of a county is the date it was established in its present location. If the county was abolished and subsequently recreated in its former location, the date given is the date the county was originally created. No dates of creation are given for Alaska's census areas. They evolved from former political subdivisions. Through 1960, Alaska's census was reported by divisions or districts that had some other governmental function, i.e., judicial divisions or election districts. During the 1960s, eight boroughs were incorporated as self-governing political jurisdictions; the remainder of the state was divided into twenty-one census divisions. By 1980, there were eleven boroughs and, through various boundary manipulations, twelve census divisions that by then were referred to as census areas. In 2000, there were sixteen boroughs and eleven census areas.

Some counties were abolished and the name was given to another county elsewhere. Seward County, Kansas, is a good example of a shifting county name, although there were many others in the Great Plains. The first Seward County was created in 1855 in southeastern Kansas as Godfroy County, one of Kansas's original counties. Its name was changed to Seward in 1861. In 1867, Seward County, which was never organized, was abolished when it was merged with Butler County to create Howard County. In 1873, a new Seward County was created in the southwestern corner of the state about 250 miles west of the first Seward County. In 1883, Seward absorbed two counties to its west: Kansas and Sumner. In 1886, Seward was organized and Morton and Stevens counties were created from where Kansas and Sumner had been. In the meantime, Howard County was divided into Chautauqua and Elk counties in 1875. The result of all this is that Seward County, Kansas, is listed as having been created in 1873 and organized in 1886.

In some states, the legislature specified the date the county would become effective. This is usually within a year of the creation date. The date listed is the date the legislation was passed creating the county. The effective date is included as applicable.

For some counties created during the colonial period, the only date that can be attributed with certainty is the convening date of the legislative session during which the county was created. The notation "session" is included after the date of creation for these counties. The date of creation for some counties in Kentucky and Tennessee have the "session" notation because they were created by the colonies of Virginia and North Carolina respectively. As a former part of Virginia, West Virginia also has some counties with the "session" notation.

In general, the date given for independent cities is the date the city became independent, not the date of its founding. Exceptions are Chesapeake, Hampton, Newport News, Suffolk, and Virginia Beach in Virginia, and Carson City, Nevada. These six cities merged with counties, and the date given is the date the original county was created.

NAME ORIGIN

The last part of each entry is the origin of the county's name. The "Introduction to the 4th Edition" in this book addresses the various categories into which county names can be grouped, such as presidents, military heroes, royalty, descriptive names, etc. Also explained in the "Introduction to the 4th Edition" is why Southern states that had been in the Confederacy have counties honoring Lincoln.

Each name origin begins with the name of the person, river, mountain, battle, or whatever else the county is named for. Sometimes the origin of the county's name is unknown or there are a number of possibilities. There may be two or more persons with the same name with valid claims to be the source of the county name. In some instances it is known that the county was named for a local mountain or river that has a foreign or Native American name, but the origin of that name is unknown. Because most Native Americans had no written language at the time a name was given to a local geographic feature, the meaning of such names is lost. Some consensus guesses are all that can be offered. These are listed as "Uncertain." Unless otherwise noted, the possibilities are offered in the order of decreasing plausibility.

If a county is named for a person, a brief biographical sketch is included. The brief biographical sketches given herein are not intended to portray the life of Washington or Jefferson. They, and others of their stature, do not need much explanation as to why they were honored by namesake counties. The biographical entries attempt to list the military, business, or political highlights of the person's life that connect the person, if not of national stature, with the county or state. In some instances, such as a private killed during the Civil War, little is known of the honoree's life other than his death.

The naming of a county was usually done by a gathering of settlers who petitioned for or otherwise sought the creation of the county. Sometimes the honoree has no discernable connection with the county or its state. This is usually the result of a prominent settler naming the county for a friend or relative who had nothing personally to do with the new county. Often the name of the town or county the settlers had come from was chosen or the name was the former home of one of the more prominent persons among the settlers.

Legislatures usually went along with the wishes of the local citizens in naming counties. However, many counties, especially in Michigan and the Great Plains, were created before anybody lived there, so the legislators selected the names of new counties. A practice prevalent in North Dakota, Oklahoma, and South Dakota—although it occurred in other states—was the naming of counties after persons who happened to be members of the legislature at the time counties were being named. Often such a person's life is unremarkable except for the happenstance of having been in the right place at the right time. Being on the committee that named counties was a virtual guarantee of eponymous immortality.

The meanings of Indian names are often unknown. The names we know today are often the result of being corrupted into whatever language was spoken by the Europeans who first encountered the Indians. Because the Europeans and Indians often had no idea what the other was saying, what was thought to be the name of the tribe could be almost anything the Indians thought the Europeans wanted to hear.

When more than one county is named for the same person, the first or most prominent county in that series contains the biographical sketch and the name is printed in italics. Other counties named for the same person have an asterisk (*) after the name. The same system of italics and asterisks is used when counties are named for the same Indian group or geographical feature.

Most of Virginia's independent cities are within a county; in fact, some are the county seat of the county of which they are independent. At the end of the entries for Virginia's independent cities, the counties they are associated with are given. This is so that readers who wish to can include the independent cities with the associated counties for statistical purposes.

There are many instances of spelling differences between a county's name and the name of the person or place for which the county is named. English spelling was fairly casual until the early nineteenth century even among literate people. The adoption of county names from French, Spanish, and other European languages further complicated spelling differences. The rendering of Indian names by Europeans offered many opportunities for variable spellings. Most of these spelling differences are fairly obvious and are usually not explained in this book. Where known, names that were misspelled by legislative actions are noted.

The American Counties

The information in this section is formatted as follows:

County Name   **State**
County Seat   Area (sq. mi.)
Population

2000	1990	1980	1970	1960	1950

Date of creation, organization, name changes, etc. Name origin.

A

Abbeville   **South Carolina**
Abbeville   508 sq. mi.

26,167	23,862	22,627	21,112	21,417	22,456

March 12, 1785. Town of Abbeville. Named for Abbeville, France.

Acadia   **Louisiana**
Crowley   655 sq. mi.

58,861	55,882	56,427	52,109	49,931	47,050

April 10, 1805. Acadian settlers from Nova Scotia, Canada; moved to Bourbon, Louisiana, 1755 after refusing to take oath of loyalty to England.

Accomack   **Virginia**
Accomac   455 sq. mi.

38,305	31,703	31,268	29,004	30,635	33,832

1661. Accomac Indians. Name of tribe, meaning "on the other side"; applied to all Indians on Virginia's eastern shore.

Ada   **Idaho**
Boise   1,055 sq. mi.

300,904	205,775	173,036	112,230	93,460	70,649

December 22, 1864. Ada Riggs (1856–1909). First American child born in Boise; daughter of H. C. Riggs, one of original incorporators of Boise, who erected first building in Boise and was a member of territorial legislature 1864.

Adair   **Iowa**
Greenfield   569 sq. mi.

8,243	8,409	9,509	9,487	10,893	12,292

January 15, 1851; organized May 6, 1854. *John Adair* (1757–1840). Served in Revolutionary War; major of Volunteers in expedition against Indians 1791–92; Kentucky House of Representatives 1793–95, 1800–03, and 1817; U.S. senator 1805–06;

aide to Governor Shelby at Battle of Thames 1813; commanded Kentucky rifle brigade under Andrew Jackson 1814–15; governor of Kentucky 1820–24; U.S. representative 1831–33.

Adair   **Kentucky**
Columbia   407 sq. mi.
17,244   15,360   15,233   13,037   14,699   17,603
December 11, 1801; effective April 1, 1802. John Adair.*

Adair   **Missouri**
Kirksville   567 sq. mi.
24,977   24,577   24,870   22,472   20,105   19,689
January 29, 1841. John Adair.*

Adair   **Oklahoma**
Stilwell   576 sq. mi.
21,038   18,421   18,575   15,141   13,112   14,918
July 16, 1907. Adair family. Cherokee family whose most prominent member was William P. Adair (?–1881); represented Cherokee Nation in Washington 1866–81; opposed influx of "boomers" into Oklahoma from Kansas 1879.

Adams   **Colorado**
Brighton   1,192 sq. mi.
363,857   265,038   245,944   185,789   120,296   40,234
April 15, 1901. Alva Adams (1850–1922). Colorado legislature 1876; governor of Colorado 1887–89, 1897–99, and 1905.

Adams   **Idaho**
Council   1,365 sq. mi.
3,476   3,254   3,347   2,877   2,978   3,347
March 3, 1911. *John Adams* (1735–1826). Continental Congress 1774–78; signer of Declaration of Independence 1776; commissioner to France 1777–78; negotiated peace treaty with England 1785–88; U.S. vice president 1789–97; 2nd U.S. president 1797–1801.

Adams   **Illinois**
Quincy   857 sq. mi.
68,277   66,090   71,622   70,861   68,467   64,690
January 13, 1825. John Quincy Adams (1767–1848). Son of John Adams; Massachusetts Senate 1802; U.S. senator 1803–08; U.S. minister to Russia 1809–14; negotiated Treaty of Ghent 1815; U.S. minister to Great Britain 1815–17; U.S. secretary of state 1817–25; 6th president of the U.S. 1825–29; U.S. representative 1831–48.

Adams   **Indiana**
Decatur   339 sq. mi.
33,625   31,095   29,619   26,871   24,643   22,393
February 7, 1835; organized January 23, 1836; effective March 1, 1836. John Quincy Adams.*

Adams   **Iowa**
Corning   424 sq. mi.
4,482   4,866   5,731   6,322   7,468   8,753
January 15, 1851; organized January 12, 1853; effective March 7, 1853. John Adams.*

Adams   **Mississippi**
Natchez   460 sq. mi.
34,340   35,356   38,035   37,293   37,730   32,256
April 2, 1799. John Adams.*

Adams   **Nebraska**
Hastings   563 sq. mi.

31,151   29,625   30,656   30,553   28,944   28,855
February 16, 1867; organized January 2, 1872. John Adams.*

Adams   **North Dakota**
Hettinger   988 sq. mi.
2,593   3,174   3,584   3,832   4,449   4,910
April 17, 1907. John Quincy Adams (1848–1919). General land and town-site agent for the Chicago, Milwaukee, St. Paul &
Pacific Railway when the county was created in 1907.

Adams   **Ohio**
West Union   584 sq. mi.
27,330   25,371   24,328   18,957   19,982   20,499
July 10, 1797. John Adams.*

Adams   **Pennsylvania**
Gettysburg   520 sq. mi.
91,292   78,274   68,292   56,937   51,906   44,197
January 22, 1800. John Adams.*

Adams   **Washington**
Ritzville   1,925 sq. mi.
16,428   13,603   13,267   12,014   9,929   6,584
November 28, 1883. John Adams.*

Adams   **Wisconsin**
Friendship   648 sq. mi.
18,643   15,682   13,457   9,234   7,566   7,906
March 11, 1848. John Adams.*

Addison   **Vermont**
Middlebury   770 sq. mi.
35,974   32,953   29,406   24,266   20,076   19,442
October 18, 1785. Joseph Addison (1672–1719). British undersecretary of state 1706; member of Parliament 1708–19; editor
of the *Spectator* 1711–12 and 1714; wrote tragedy "Cato" 1713; political newspaper, *The Freeholder* 1715–16; buried in Westminster Abbey.

Aiken   **South Carolina**
Aiken   1,073 sq. mi.
142,552   120,940   105,625   91,023   81,038   53,137
March 10, 1871. William Aiken (1806–87). South Carolina legislature 1838; governor of South Carolina 1844–46; president
of South Carolina Railway Company.

Aitkin   **Minnesota**
Aitkin   1,819 sq. mi.
15,301   12,425   13,404   11,403   12,162   14,327
May 23, 1857, as Aiken; name changed 1872; organized February 6, 1885. William Alexander Aitkin (1787–1851). Fur trader,
worked for the Fond du Lac department of the American Fur Company under John Jacob Astor.

Alachua   **Florida**
Gainesville   874 sq. mi.
217,955   181,596   151,348   104,764   74,074   57,026
December 29, 1824. Town of Alachua. Creek word of uncertain meaning; most possibilities refer to the marshes and sink holes
in the area.

Alamance   **North Carolina**
Graham   430 sq. mi.

130,800   108,213   99,136   96,362   85,674   71,220

January 29, 1849. Battle of Alamance. May 16, 1771, between Royal Governor William Tryon and the "Regulators," a group of settlers with various grievances against the Crown. Named for Alamance Creek, from an Indian word for "blue clay."

Alameda   **California**
Oakland   738 sq. mi.
1,443,741   1,279,182   1,105,379   1,073,184   908,209   740,315
March 25, 1853. Spanish word for "tree-lined road."

Alamosa   **Colorado**
Alamosa   723 sq. mi.
14,966   13,617   11,799   11,422   10,000   10,531
March 8, 1913. Alamosa Creek. Spanish for "cottonwood grove."

Albany   **New York**
Albany   523 sq. mi.
294,565   292,594   285,909   286,742   272,926   239,386
November 1, 1683. *King James II, Duke of York and Albany* (1633–1701). Second son of Charles I and Queen Henrietta Maria; named Duke of York and Albany 1643; succeeded to throne on death of brother Charles II 1685; King of England, Scotland, and Ireland 1685–88; escaped to France during "Glorious Revolution" 1688; defeated at the Battle of the Boyne by William of Orange 1690.

Albany   **Wyoming**
Laramie   4,273 sq. mi.
32,014   30,797   29,062   26,431   21,290   19,055
December 16, 1868. City of Albany, New York.

Albemarle   **Virginia**
Charlottesville   723 sq. mi.
79,236   68,040   55,783   37,780   30,969   26,662
May 6, 1744 (session). William Anne Keppel, Earl of Albemarle (1702–54). Aide-de-camp to George I 1727; absentee governor of Virginia 1737–54; brigadier general 1739; lieutenant general 1742; privy councilor 1751.

Alcona   **Michigan**
Harrisville   674 sq. mi.
11,719   10,145   9,740   7,113   6,352   5,856
April 1, 1840, as Negwegon; name changed March 8, 1843; organized March 12, 1869. Word for "beautiful plains" coined from Arabic, Ojibwa, and Latin.

Alcorn   **Mississippi**
Corinth   400 sq. mi.
34,558   31,722   33,036   27,179   25,282   27,158
April 15, 1870. James Lusk Alcorn (1816–94). Deputy sheriff Livingston County, Kentucky 1839–44; Kentucky House of Representatives 1843; Mississippi House of Representatives 1846 and 1856–57; Mississippi Senate 1848–54; opposed secession but served in Confederate army 1864–65; U.S. senator-elect but not seated 1865; governor of Mississippi 1870–71; U.S. senator 1871–77.

Aleutians East   **Alaska**
Sand Point   6,988 sq. mi.
2,697   2,464   [a]   [a]   [a]   [b]
October 23, 1987. *Aleut Eskimos. Aleut* means "the people." [(a) Part of Aleutians Census Area; (b) part of 3rd Judicial District.]

Aleutians West   **Alaska**
(Census Area)   4,397 sq. mi.

5,465   9,478   7,768[a]   8,057[a]   6,011[a]   [b]
Aleut Eskimos.* [(a) Aleutian Islands Census Area; (b) part of 3rd Judicial District.]

Alexander   **Illinois**
Cairo   236 sq. mi.
9,590   10,626   12,264   12,015   16,061   20,316
March 4, 1819. Dr. William M. Alexander (?–?). Physician; early Illinois settler; member, Illinois legislature 1820–24; Speaker, Illinois House of Representatives 1822.

Alexander   **North Carolina**
Taylorsville   260 sq. mi.
33,603   27,544   24,999   19,466   15,625   14,554
January 15, 1847. Uncertain. (1) Most probably William Julius Alexander (1797–1857); member of North Carolina legislature. (2) Abraham Alexander (1717–86), member of North Carolina Assembly. (3) Nathaniel Alexander (1756–1808), U.S. representative 1803–05; governor of North Carolina 1805–07.

Alexandria   **Virginia**
(Independent City)   15 sq. mi.
128,283   111,183   103,217   110,938   91,023   61,787
1852. John Alexander (1612–77). Acquired various grants in Virginia including Howson Patent on site of Alexandria 1669. (Associated counties: Arlington and Fairfax.)

Alfalfa   **Oklahoma**
Cherokee   867 sq. mi.
6,105   6,416   7,077   7,224   8,445   10,699
July 16, 1907. William Henry "Alfalfa Bill" Murray (see Murray, Oklahoma).

Alger   **Michigan**
Munising   918 sq. mi.
9,862   8,972   9,225   8,568   9,250   10,007
March 17, 1885. Russell Alexander Alger (1836–1907). Rose from private to captain, Michigan Volunteers, 1861; major and lieutenant colonel 1862; colonel and brevet brigadier general 1863; brevet major general, U.S. Volunteers, 1864; governor of Michigan, 1885–87; U.S. secretary of war 1897–99; U.S. senator 1902–07.

Allamakee   **Iowa**
Waukon   640 sq. mi.
14,675   13,855   15,108   14,968   15,982   16,351
February 20, 1847; organized March 6, 1849. Uncertain. (1) Allan Makee, Indian trader. (2) *Anameekee*, Sauk–Fox word for "thunder."

Allegan   **Michigan**
Allegan   827 sq. mi.
105,665   90,509   81,555   66,575   57,729   47,493
March 2, 1831; organized September 7, 1835. Corruption of "Allegany" (see Allegany, Maryland).

Allegany   **Maryland**
Cumberland   425 sq. mi.
74,930   74,946   80,548   84,044   84,169   89,556
December 25, 1789. Allegewi Indians. Name of prehistoric tribe, from *oolikhanna*, meaning "beautiful stream"; name applied to a river, mountain range, and a general name for Indians in the upper Ohio Valley. The "beautiful river" in this case is the Potomac River.

Allegany   **New York**
Belmont   1,030 sq. mi.
49,927   50,470   51,742   46,458   43,978   43,784
April 7, 1806. Allegheny Trail. Follows Allegheny River; named for Allegewi Indians (see Allegany, Maryland).

Alleghany **North Carolina**
Sparta 235 sq. mi.
10,677 9,590 9,587 8,134 7,734 8,155
1859. Uncertain. (1) Alleghany Indians. (2) Allegheny River. Both names stem from Allegewi Indians (see Allegany, Maryland).

Alleghany **Virginia**
Covington 445 sq. mi.
12,926 13,176 14,333 12,461 12,128 23,139
January 5, 1822. Allegheny Mountains. Named from Allegewi Indians (see Allegany, Maryland).

Allegheny **Pennsylvania**
Pittsburgh 730 sq. mi.
1,281,666 1,336,449 1,450,085 1,605,016 1,628,587 1,515,237
September 24, 1788. Allegheny River. Named from Allegewi Indians (see Allegany, Maryland).

Allen **Indiana**
Fort Wayne 657 sq. mi.
331,849 300,836 294,335 280,455 232,196 182,722
December 17, 1823; effective April 1, 1824. *John Allen* (1772–1813). Kentucky Senate; lieutenant colonel 1812; killed in River Raisin Massacre, 1813.

Allen **Kansas**
Iola 503 sq. mi.
14,385 14,638 15,654 15,043 16,369 18,187
August 30, 1855. William Allen (1803–79). U.S. representative from Ohio 1833–35; U.S. senator 1837–49; declined Democratic presidential nomination 1848; advocated free-soil policies popular in Kansas territorial legislature; governor of Ohio, 1874–76.

Allen **Kentucky**
Scottsville 346 sq. mi.
17,800 14,628 14,128 12,598 12,269 13,787
January 11, 1815. John Allen.*

Allen **Louisiana**
Oberlin 765 sq. mi.
25,440 21,226 21,390 20,794 19,867 18,835
June 12, 1912. Henry Watkins Allen (1820–66). Texas Volunteer 1842; Texas House of Representatives 1853; lieutenant colonel, 4th Louisiana Regiment; brigadier general in Confederate army 1863; wounded at Shiloh 1862; wounded in both cheeks at Baton Rouge 1862; Confederate governor of Louisiana 1864–65.

Allen **Ohio**
Lima 404 sq. mi.
108,473 109,755 112,241 111,144 103,691 88,183
February 12, 1820. Ethan Allen (1738–89). Served in French and Indian Wars; leader of Vermont's Green Mountain Boys; captured Fort Ticonderoga May 10, 1775; captured at Montreal 1775; exchanged 1778.

Allendale **South Carolina**
Allendale 408 sq. mi.
11,211 11,722 10,700 9,692 11,362 11,773
February 6, 1919. Town of Allendale. Named for Paul H. Allen (c1800–?), local landowner and first postmaster of Allendale, 1849.

Alpena **Michigan**
Alpena 574 sq. mi.
31,314 30,605 32,315 30,708 28,556 22,189

April 1, 1840, as Anamickee, name changed March 8, 1843; organized February 7, 1857. Contrived word combining Arab *al* with Ojibwa *pena*, meaning "partridge," to arrive at "partridge country."

Alpine   **California**
Markleeville   739 sq. mi.

1,208	1,113	1,097	484	397	241

March 16, 1864. Descriptive of location in Sierra Nevada Mountains.

Amador   **California**
Jackson   593 sq. mi.

35,100	30,039	19,314	11,821	9,990	9,151

May 11, 1854. Josef María Amador (1794–1883). Majordomo of Mission San Jose; early settler and miner.

Amelia   **Virginia**
Amelia Court House   357 sq. mi.

11,400	8,787	8,405	7,592	7,815	7,908

February 1, 1734 (session). Princess Amelia Sophie Eleanor (1711–86). Second daughter of King George II.

Amherst   **Virginia**
Amherst   475 sq. mi.

31,894	28,578	29,122	26,072	22,953	20,332

September 14, 1758 (session). Jeffrey Amherst (1717–97). Colonel 15th Regiment of Foot 1756–68; commissioned major general in America by William Pitt 1758; commander in chief of expedition to America; captain general and governor of Virginia 1759–68; made Baron Amherst 1776; commander in chief of British Army 1793–95; field marshal 1796.

Amite   **Mississippi**
Liberty   730 sq. mi.

13,599	13,328	13,369	13,763	15,573	19,261

February 24, 1809. Amite River. French *amité*, meaning "friendship."

Anchorage   **Alaska**
Anchorage   1,697 sq. mi.

260,283	226,338	174,431	124,542	82,833	[a]

September 13, 1963. Knik Anchorage. Ships' anchorage in Cook Inlet off shore from Alaskan Railroad construction camp at mouth of Ship Creek 1915. [(a) Part of 3rd Judicial District.]

Anderson   **Kansas**
Garnett   583 sq. mi.

8,110	7,803	8,749	8,501	9,035	10,267

August 30, 1855. Joseph C. Anderson (?–?). Elected to first Kansas territorial legislature by proslavery Missouri residents.

Anderson   **Kentucky**
Lawrenceburg   203 sq. mi.

19,111	14,571	12,567	9,358	8,618	8,984

January 16, 1827. Richard Clough Anderson (1788–1826). Kentucky House of Representatives 1815 and 1821–22, speaker 1822; U.S. House of Representatives 1817–21; U.S. minister to Colombia 1823; envoy extraordinary and minister plenipotentiary to the Panama Congress of Nations but died en route 1826.

Anderson   **South Carolina**
Anderson   718 sq. mi.

165,740	145,196	133,235	105,474	98,478	90,664

December 20, 1826. Robert Anderson (1741–1813). Captain, 3rd South Carolina Rangers 1775–79; rose from major to colonel 1781; adjutant general, South Carolina Militia; South Carolina legislature.

Anderson   **Tennessee**
Clinton   338 sq. mi.

71,330   68,250   67,346   60,300   60,032   59,407
November 6, 1801. Joseph Anderson (1757–1837). Brevet major; U.S. judge, Territory South of the Ohio River, 1791; U.S. senator from Tennessee 1791–1815; first comptroller of U.S. treasury, 1815–36.

Anderson   **Texas**
Palestine   1,071 sq. mi.
55,109   48,024   38,381   27,789   28 162   31,875
March 24, 1846; organized July 13, 1846. Kenneth Lewis Anderson (1805–45). Collector of customs, San Augustine, 1840; Texas House of Representatives 1841–42; district attorney for 5th District 1843; vice president of Texas Republic 1844–45.

Andrew   **Missouri**
Savannah   435 sq. mi.
16,492   14,632   13,980   11,913   11,062   11,727
January 29, 1841. Andrew Jackson Davis (?–?). Practiced law in St. Louis and Savannah, Missouri.

Andrews   **Texas**
Andrews   1,501 sq. mi.
13,004   14,338   13,323   10,372   13,450   5,002
August 21, 1876; organized 1910. Richard "Big Dick" Andrews (1814–35). Wounded at Battle of Gonzalez October 2, 1835; only Texan killed in Battle of Concepción, making him first Texas soldier killed in Texas Revolution October 28, 1835.

Androscoggin   **Maine**
Auburn   470 sq. mi.
103,793   105,259   99,657   91,279   86,312   83,594
March 18, 1854. Uncertain. (1) Arosaguntacook Indians; tribe whose name was applied by English to other tribes in area; name refers to curing and drying of fish. (2) Edmund Andros (1637–1714); British major; fought Dutch in West Indies; royal governor of New England 1686. (3) Androscoggin River; named for Arosaguntacook Indians.

Angelina   **Texas**
Lufkin   802 sq. mi.
80,130   69,884   64,172   49,349   39,814   36,032
April 22, 1846; organized July 13, 1846. Angelina River. Spanish for "little angel"; from name given to Indian girl at Mission San Francisco de los Tejas.

Anne Arundel   **Maryland**
Annapolis   416 sq. mi.
489,656   427,239   370,775   297,539   206,634   117,392
April 9, 1650, as Anne Arundel; name changed to Providence 1654; name restored 1658. Anne Arundell Calvert (1615–49). Daughter of Thomas, Lord Arundell of Wardour; wife of Cecilius Calvert, 2nd Lord Baltimore; mother of Charles Calvert.

Anoka   **Minnesota**
Anoka   424 sq. mi.
298,084   243,641   195,998   154,556   85,916   35,579
May 23, 1857. Town of Anoka. Dakota word for "on both sides of the river."

Anson   **North Carolina**
Wadesboro   532 sq. mi.
25,275   23,474   25,649   23,488   24,962   26,781
March 17, 1749 (session). George Lord Anson (1697–1762). British Navy captain 1723; admiral in command of naval forces along Carolina coast; voyage of circumnavigation 1740–44; 1st lord of the admiralty 1751–56 and 1757–62.

Antelope   **Nebraska**
Neligh   857 sq. mi.
7,452   7,965   8,675   9,047   10,176   11,624

March 1, 1871; organized October 1872. Descriptive of an individual antelope killed for food by Leander Gerrard who later proposed this name while a member of the Nebraska legislature.

Antrim   **Michigan**
Bellaire   477 sq. mi.
23,110   18,185   16,194   12,612   10,373   10,721
April 1, 1840, as Meegisee; name changed March 8, 1843; organized March 11, 1863. County Antrim, Ireland.

Apache   **Arizona**
Saint Johns   11,205 sq. mi.
69,423   61,591   52,108   32,298   30,438   27,767
February 14, 1879. Apache Indians. Name applied to several southwestern tribes. Uncertain. (1) *apa-ahwa-tche*, combining Yuman word for "men" with "fight" or "battle." (2) *apachu*, Zuni word meaning "enemy."

Appanoose   **Iowa**
Centerville   496 sq. mi.
13,721   13,743   15,511   15,007   16,015   19,683
February 17, 1843; organized January 3, 1846; effective August 3, 1846. Appanoose (?–1845). Chief of Sauk-Fox tribes; leader of peace faction during Black Hawk War 1832; name means "little child" or "chief when child."

Appling   **Georgia**
Baxley   509 sq. mi.
17,419   15,744   15,565   12,726   13,246   14,003
December 15, 1818. Daniel Appling (1787–1818). Lieutenant colonel, U.S. Army, 1805; fought in War of 1812; brevet lieutenant colonel at Battle of Sandy Creek 1814; awarded sword by Georgia legislature but died before presentation.

Appomattox   **Virginia**
Appomattox   334 sq. mi.
13,705   12,298   11,971   9,784   9,148   8,764
February 8, 1845. Appomatox River. Algonquin word describing "sinuous tidal estuary."

Aransas   **Texas**
Rockport   252 sq. mi.
22,497   17,892   14,260   8,902   7,006   4,252
September 18, 1871. Aransas River, Bay, and/or Pass. Named for a river in Spain: Rio Nuestra Señora de Aranzazu (Our Lady of Aranzazu), site of a palace in Spain.

Arapahoe   **Colorado**
Littleton   803 sq. mi.
487,967   391,511   293,621   162,142   113,426   52,125
November 1, 1861. Arapahoe Indians. From Pawnee *tirapihu* or *larapihu*, meaning "trader."

Archer   **Texas**
Archer City   910 sq. mi.
8,854   7,973   7,266   5,759   6,110   6,816
January 22, 1858; organized July 27, 1880. Dr. Branch Tanner Archer (1790–1856). One of three Texas commissioners sent to Washington to solicit U.S. aid 1835; speaker of Texas House of Representatives 1836; Texas secretary of war 1836–42.

Archuleta   **Colorado**
Pagosa Springs   1,350 sq. mi.
9,898   5,345   3,664   2,733   2,629   3,030
April 14, 1885. Uncertain. (1) Antonio D. Archuleta (1855–?); Colorado legislature 1876; Colorado Senate 1885. (2) José M. Archuleta (?–?); head of prominent family in Colorado. (3) Both Antonio and José Archuleta.

Arenac   **Michigan**
Standish   367 sq. mi.

| 17,269 | 14,931 | 14,706 | 11,149 | 9,860 | 9,644 |

March 2, 1831; abolished April 20, 1857; recreated April 1, 1883. Coined word from Latin *arena*, meaning "sand," and Algonquin *akee*, meaning "land."

Arkansas   **Arkansas**
De Witt   988 sq. mi.

| 20,749 | 21,653 | 24,175 | 23,347 | 23,355 | 23,665 |

December 31, 1813. Arkansas Indians. French corruption of Sioux word *quapaw* or *ugakhpa*, meaning "downstream people."

Arlington   **Virginia**
Arlington   26 sq. mi.

| 189,453 | 170,936 | 152,599 | 174,284 | 163,401 | 135,449 |

March 13, 1847, as Alexandria; name changed March 16, 1920. Arlington Estate. Home of George Washington Parke Custis, adopted grandson of George and Martha Custis Washington; Custis family estates in Virginia were named Arlington after their ancestral home in England.

Armstrong   **Pennsylvania**
Kittanning   654 sq. mi.

| 72,392 | 73,478 | 77,768 | 75,590 | 79,524 | 80,842 |

March 12, 1800. John Armstrong (1758–1843). On staffs of Generals Gates and Mercer in Revolutionary War; carried Mercer from Princeton battlefield 1776; Continental Congress 1778–80 and 1787–88; Pennsylvania secretary of state 1783–87; U.S. senator from New York 1800–02 and 1803–04; U.S. minister to France 1804–10; U.S. minister to Spain 1806; brigadier general 1812; U.S. secretary of war 1813–14.

Armstrong   **Texas**
Claude   914 sq. mi.

| 2,148 | 2,021 | 1,994 | 1,895 | 1,966 | 2,215 |

August 21, 1876; organized March 8, 1890. Armstrong family. Any one of up to six Texas pioneer families named Armstrong.

Aroostook   **Maine**
Caribou   6,672 sq. mi.

| 73,938 | 86,936 | 91,331 | 92,463 | 106,064 | 96,039 |

March 16, 1839. Aroostook River. Indian word of uncertain origin referring to a clear, smooth, or beautiful river.

Arthur   **Nebraska**
Arthur   715 sq. mi.

| 444 | 462 | 513 | 606 | 680 | 803 |

March 31, 1887; organized 1913. Chester Allen Arthur (1830–86). Brigadier general and quarter master general 1860–62; collector of Port of New York 1871–78; U.S. vice president 1881; 21st president of the United States 1881–85.

Ascension   **Louisiana**
Donaldsonville   292 sq. mi.

| 76,627 | 58,214 | 50,068 | 37,086 | 27,927 | 22,387 |

March 31, 1807. Ecclesiastical district of Ascension. Named for the ascension of Jesus into heaven.

Ashe   **North Carolina**
Jefferson   426 sq. mi.

| 24,384 | 22,209 | 22,325 | 19,571 | 19,768 | 21,878 |

November 18, 1799 (session). Samuel Ashe (1725–1813). Member of the North Carolina Council of Thirteen, served as president, 1776; Halifax Convention 1776; state Constitutional Convention 1776; chief justice of North Carolina 1777–95; governor of North Carolina 1795–98.

Ashland   **Ohio**
Ashland   424 sq. mi.

| 52,523 | 47,507 | 46,178 | 43,303 | 38,771 | 33,040 |

February 24, 1846. Ashland. Henry Clay's estate near Lexington, Kentucky.

Ashland   **Wisconsin**
Ashland   1,044 sq. mi.

| 16,866 | 16,307 | 16,783 | 16,743 | 17,375 | 19,461 |

March 27, 1860. Village of Ashland. From Ashland, Henry Clay's estate near Lexington, Kentucky.

Ashley   **Arkansas**
Hamburg   921 sq. mi.

| 24,209 | 24,319 | 26,538 | 24,976 | 24,220 | 25,660 |

November 30, 1848. Chester Ashley (1790–1848). U.S. senator from Arkansas 1844–48.

Ashtabula   **Ohio**
Jefferson   702 sq. mi.

| 102,728 | 99,821 | 104,215 | 98,237 | 93,067 | 78,695 |

February 10, 1807. Ashtabula River. European rendering of Delaware word meaning "fish river."

Asotin   **Washington**
Asotin   635 sq. mi.

| 20,551 | 17,605 | 16,823 | 13,799 | 12,909 | 10,878 |

October 27, 1883. Town of Asotin City. Named for Asotin Creek from Indian name meaning "eel creek."

Assumption   **Louisiana**
Napoleonville   339 sq. mi.

| 23,388 | 22,753 | 22,084 | 19,654 | 17,991 | 17,278 |

March 31, 1807. Church of the Assumption. First church built in Louisiana 1793; named for the festival of the assumption of the Virgin Mary following her death.

Atascosa   **Texas**
Jourdanton   1,232 sq. mi.

| 38,628 | 30,533 | 25,055 | 18,696 | 18,828 | 20,048 |

January 25, 1856; organized August 4, 1856. Atascosa River. Spanish word for "boggy."

Atchison   **Kansas**
Atchison   432 sq. mi.

| 16,774 | 16,932 | 18,397 | 19,165 | 20,898 | 21,496 |

August 30, 1855. *David Rice Atchison* (1807–86). Missouri House of Representatives 1834 and 1838; Platte County Circuit Court judge 1841; U.S. senator 1843–55, served several times as president pro tempore of the Senate.

Atchison   **Missouri**
Rock Port   545 sq. mi.

| 6,430 | 7,457 | 8,605 | 9,240 | 9,213 | 11,127 |

February 23, 1843, as Allen; name changed and organized February 14, 1845. David Rice Atchison.*

Athens   **Ohio**
Athens   507 sq. mi.

| 62,223 | 59,549 | 56,399 | 54,889 | 46,998 | 45,839 |

February 20, 1805. Athens, Greece.

Atkinson   **Georgia**
Pearson   338 sq. mi.

| 7,609 | 6,213 | 6,141 | 5,879 | 6,188 | 7,362 |

August 15, 1917. William Yates Atkinson (1854–99). Georgia Assembly 1886–94; governor of Georgia 1894–99.

Atlantic   **New Jersey**
Mays Landing   561 sq. mi.
252,552   224,327   194,119   175,043   160,880   132,399
February 7, 1837. Atlantic Ocean.

Atoka   **Oklahoma**
Atoka   978 sq. mi.
13,879   12,778   12,748   10,972   10,352   14,269
July 16, 1907. Charles Atoka (?–?). Choctaw chief; signed Treaty of Dancing Rabbit Creek, leading to removal of Choctaws to Oklahoma 1830; member of Choctaw Council; *atoka* resembles Choctaw word for "ball ground" and may have been given to Atoka in recognition of his prowess as a ballplayer.

Attala   **Mississippi**
Kosciusko   735 sq. mi.
19,661   18,481   19,865   19,570   21,335   26,652
December 23, 1833. Fictitious Indian heroine in *The Interesting History of Atala, the Beautiful Indian of the Mississippi* by Francois Rene, Vicomte de Chateaubriand, 1801.

Audrain   **Missouri**
Mexico   693 sq. mi.
25,853   23,599   26,458   25,362   26,079   23,829
January 12, 1831; organized 1836. Uncertain. (1) Samuel Audrain (?–?); first settler in the area. (2) James H. Audrain (1782–1831); Missouri legislature 1830–31.

Audubon   **Iowa**
Audubon   443 sq. mi.
6,830   7,334   8,559   9,595   10,919   11,579
January 15, 1851; organized July 9, 1855. John James Audubon (1785–1851). Naturalist and ornithologist; *Birds of America*, 1839.

Auglaize   **Ohio**
Wapakoneta   401 sq. mi.
46,611   44,585   42,554   38,602   36,147   30,637
February 14, 1848. Auglaize River. European rendering of Indian word meaning "fallen timbers."

Augusta   **Virginia**
Staunton   970 sq. mi.
65,615   54,677   53,732   44,220   37,363   34,154
August 1, 1738 (session). Augusta of Saxe-Gotha (1719–72). Wife of Frederick, Prince of Wales; mother of King George III.

Aurora   **South Dakota**
Plankinton   708 sq. mi.
3,058   3,135   3,638   4,183   4,749   5,020
February 22, 1879; organized August 29, 1881. Aurora. Roman goddess of the dawn.

Austin   **Texas**
Bellville   653 sq. mi.
23,590   19,832   17,726   13,831   13,777   14,663
March 17, 1836. Stephen Fuller Austin (1793–1836). Missouri territorial legislature 1814–20; judge for 1st Judicial District of Arkansas 1820; surveyed and explored Texas for colonization 1822; defeated by Sam Houston for president of the Republic of Texas 1836; appointed Texas secretary of state by Houston 1836.

Autauga   **Alabama**
Prattville   596 sq. mi.
43,671   34,222   32,259   24,460   18,739   18,186
November 21, 1818. Autauga Creek. Indian word *atagi*, meaning "land of plenty."

Avery   **North Carolina**
Newland   247 sq. mi.
17,167   14,867   14,409   12,655   12,009   13,352
February 23, 1911. Waightstill Avery (1741–1821). Mecklenburg Convention 1775; North Carolina legislature 1776; attorney general of North Carolina 1777–79; colonel of Jones County Militia in Revolutionary War 1779; North Carolina House of Commons 1782–83 and 1793; North Carolina Senate 1796; fought duel with Andrew Jackson 1788.

Avoyelles   **Louisiana**
Marksville   832 sq. mi.
41,481   39,159   41,393   37,751   37,606   38,031
March 31, 1807. Avoyel Indians. Uncertain meaning; possibilities include "flint people" and "nation [or people] of the rocks."

B

Baca   **Colorado**
Springfield   2,556 sq. mi.
4,517   4,556   5,419   5,674   6,310   7,964
April 16, 1889. Baca family. Early settlers in southeast Colorado; Felipe Baca donated land for town site of Trinidad, Colorado.

Bacon   **Georgia**
Alma   285 sq. mi.
10,103   9,566   9,379   8,233   8,359   8,940
July 27, 1914. Augustus Octavius Bacon (1839–1914). Adjutant, 9th Georgia Regiment, 1861–62; captain, Confederate army; Georgia House of Representatives 1871–86, served two years as speaker pro tempore and eight years as Speaker; U.S. senator 1895–1914.

Bailey   **Texas**
Muleshoe   827 sq. mi.
6,594   7,064   8,168   8,487   9,090   7,592
August 21, 1876; organized 1917. Peter James Bailey III (1812–36). Private from Springfield, Kentucky; killed in defense of the Alamo 1836.

Baker   **Florida**
Macclenny   585 sq. mi.
22,259   18,486   15,289   9,242   7,363   6,313
February 8, 1861. James McNair Baker (1821–92). Solicitor of Eastern Circuit 1859–62; Confederate Senate 1862–64; associate justice of Florida Supreme Court 1866; judge, 4th Judicial Circuit, 1881.

Baker   **Georgia**
Newton   343 sq. mi.
4,074   3,615   3,808   3,875   4,543   5,952
December 12, 1825. Col. John Baker (?–1792). Lieutenant in British army; member of Georgia Provisional Congress; served with patriots in Revolutionary War.

Baker   **Oregon**
Baker City   3,068 sq. mi.
16,741   15,317   16,134   14,919   17,295   16,175
September 22, 1862. Edward Dickinson Baker (1811–61). Private in Black Hawk War 1832; Illinois House of Representatives 1837; Illinois Senate 1840–44; colonel, 4th Illinois Volunteer Infantry, 1846; U.S. representative 1845–47 and 1849–51; U.S. senator from Oregon 1860–61; colonel, 71st Regiment of Pennsylvania Volunteer Infantry, 1861; major general of Volunteers, 1861; killed at Battle of Balls Bluff, October 21, 1861.

Baldwin   **Alabama**
Bay Minette   1,596 sq. mi.

| 140,415 | 98,280 | 78,556 | 59,382 | 49,088 | 40,997 |

December 21, 1809. *Abraham Baldwin* (1754–1807). Tutor at Yale 1775–79; Chaplain, 2nd Continental Brigade, 1777–83; Georgia House of Representatives 1785; Continental Congress 1785–88; president, University of Georgia, 1786–1801; federal Constitutional Convention 1787; U.S. representative 1789–99; U.S. senator 1799–1807.

Baldwin   **Georgia**
Milledgeville   258 sq. mi.

| 44,700 | 39,530 | 34,686 | 34,240 | 34,064 | 29,706 |

May 11, 1803; organized, 1807. Abraham Baldwin.*

Ballard   **Kentucky**
Wickliffe   251 sq. mi.

| 8,286 | 7,902 | 8,798 | 8,276 | 8,291 | 8,545 |

February 15, 1842. Bland Williams Ballard (1761–1853). Accompanied George Rogers Clark on Piqua expedition; guided Generals Scott and Wilkinson; captain and major in War of 1812; wounded and captured at Battle of the River Raisin 1813.

Baltimore   **Maryland**
Towson   599 sq. mi.

| 754,292 | 692,134 | 655,615 | 621,077 | 492,428 | 270,273 |

June 30, 1695. *Baltimore, Ireland.* Irish barony of the Calvert family; George Calvert made 1st Lord Baltimore by James I; Cecilius Calvert, 2nd Baron of Baltimore, granted colony in Maryland by Charles I.

Baltimore   **Maryland**
(Independent City)   81 sq. mi.

| 651,154 | 736,014 | 786,775 | 905,759 | 939,024 | 949,708 |

July 4, 1851. Baltimore, Ireland.*

Bamberg   **South Carolina**
Bamberg   393 sq. mi.

| 16,658 | 16,902 | 18,118 | 15,950 | 16,274 | 17,533 |

February 25, 1897. Town of Bamberg. Grew from station owned by Bamberg family on stage line between Charleston and Augusta.

Bandera   **Texas**
Bandera   792 sq. mi.

| 17,645 | 10,562 | 7,084 | 4,747 | 3,892 | 4,410 |

January 26, 1856; organized March 10, 1856. Bandera Mountains and/or Pass. Spanish for "flag"; also may be named for a Spanish general named Bandera.

Banks   **Georgia**
Homer   234 sq. mi.

| 14,422 | 10,308 | 8,702 | 6,833 | 6,497 | 6,935 |

December 11, 1858. Richard E. Banks (1784–1850). Popular physician who traveled in the area.

Banner   **Nebraska**
Harrisburg   746 sq. mi.

| 819 | 852 | 918 | 1,034 | 1,269 | 1,325 |

November 6, 1888. Hyperbole describing county's future. County's founders wanted to give the impression that their county would be the best in Nebraska.

Bannock   **Idaho**
Pocatello   1,113 sq. mi.

| 75,565 | 66,026 | 65,421 | 52,200 | 49,342 | 41,745 |

March 6, 1893. Bannack Indians. From Shoshone words *bamp,* meaning "hair," and *nack,* meaning "backward"; describes Bannack practice of wearing hair pulled back in tufts.

Baraga   **Michigan**
L'Anse   904 sq. mi.

| 8,746 | 7,954 | 8,484 | 7,789 | 7,151 | 8,037 |

February 19, 1875. Irenaeus Frederich Baraga (1791–1868). Austrian missionary; ordained priest 1823; arrived in U.S. 1830; wrote Chippewa grammar 1850 and Chippewa dictionary 1853; consecrated bishop 1853; established schools in Ohio and Michigan for Chippewa and Ottawa Indians 1830–68.

Barber   **Kansas**
Medicine Lodge   1,134 sq. mi.

| 5,307 | 5,874 | 6,548 | 7,016 | 8,713 | 8,521 |

February 26, 1867, as Barbour; spelling corrected March 1, 1883. Thomas W. Barber (?–1855). Free-state martyr; murdered near Lawrence, Kansas, December 6, 1855.

Barbour   **Alabama**
Clayton   885 sq. mi.

| 29,038 | 25,417 | 24,756 | 22,543 | 24,700 | 28,892 |

December 18, 1832. James Barbour (1775–1842). Virginia House of Delegates 1796–1812, Speaker, 1809–12; governor of Virginia 1812–14; U.S. senator 1815–25; U.S. secretary of war in cabinet of John Quincy Adams 1825–28; U.S. minister to England 1828–29.

Barbour   **West Virginia**
Philippi   341 sq. mi.

| 15,557 | 15,699 | 16,639 | 14,030 | 15,474 | 19,745 |

March 3, 1843. Philip Pendleton Barbour (1783–1841); Virginia House of Delegates 1812–14; U.S. representative 1814–25 and 1827–30, Speaker, 1821–22; Virginia general court judge 1826–27; judge U.S. Circuit Court for the Eastern District of Virginia 1830–36; U.S. Supreme Court justice 1836–41.

Barnes   **North Dakota**
Valley City   1,492 sq. mi.

| 11,775 | 12,545 | 13,960 | 14,669 | 16,719 | 16,884 |

January 4, 1873, as Burbank; name changed January 14, 1875. Alanson H. Barnes (1818–90). Justice of Dakota Territory Supreme Court 1873–81.

Barnstable   **Massachusetts**
Barnstable   396 sq. mi.

| 222,230 | 186,605 | 147,925 | 96,656 | 70,286 | 46,805 |

June 2, 1685. Town of Barnstable. Named for Barnstaple, Devonshire, England.

Barnwell   **South Carolina**
Barnwell   548 sq. mi.

| 23,478 | 20,293 | 19,868 | 17,176 | 17,659 | 17,266 |

1798. Uncertain. (1) John Barnwell (?–?); Provisional Congress 1775–76; general in South Carolina militia; South Carolina legislature; elected to U.S. Congress but did not serve. (2) Robert Barnwell (1761–1814); lieutenant in Revolutionary War; captured by British 1780, released 1781; delegate to 3rd Continental Congress; U.S. representative 1791–93; South Carolina legislature. (3) Village of Barnwell; named for John Barnwell (c1671–1724); immigrated to Carolina from Ireland 1701; active in colonial government of South Carolina.

Barren   **Kentucky**
Glasgow   491 sq. mi.

| 38,033 | 34,001 | 34,009 | 28,677 | 28,303 | 28,461 |

December 20, 1798. "Kentucky barrens," descriptive of treeless prairie.

Barron   **Wisconsin**
Barron   863 sq. mi.

| 44,963 | 40,750 | 38,730 | 33,955 | 34,270 | 34,703 |

March 19, 1859, as Dallas; name changed March 4, 1869. Henry D. Barron (1833–82). Waukesha postmaster 1853–57; Wisconsin legislature, Speaker 1866 and 1873; declined appointment as chief justice of Dakota Territory Supreme Court 1869; Wisconsin Senate; judge of circuit court 1876–82.

Barrow   **Georgia**
Winder   162 sq. mi.
46,144   29,721   21,354   16,859   14,485   13,115
July 7, 1914. Dr. David Crenshaw Barrow (1852–1929). Adjunct professor of mathematics, University of Georgia, 1878 and 1899; professor of engineering 1883; chancellor of the University of Georgia 1907–25.

Barry   **Michigan**
Hastings   556 sq. mi.
58,755   50,057   45,781   38,166   31,738   26,183
October 29, 1829; organized March 5, 1839. *William Taylor Barry* (1784–1835). Kentucky House of Representatives 1807; U.S. representative 1810–11; War of 1812 aide-de-camp to General Shelby; Battle of the Thames October 5, 1813; Speaker, Kentucky House of Representatives 1814; U.S. senator 1814–16; judge of the Circuit Court for the 11th District of Kentucky 1816–17; Kentucky Senate 1817–21; lieutenant governor 1820; Kentucky secretary of state 1824; chief justice, Kentucky Court of Appeals, 1825; U.S. postmaster general 1829–35; appointed envoy extraordinary and minister plenipotentiary to Spain, died en route 1835.

Barry   **Missouri**
Cassville   779 sq. mi.
34,010   27,547   24,408   19,597   18,921   21,755
January 5, 1835. Uncertain. (1) William Taylor Barry.* (2) John Barry (?–1803); merchant seaman; captain, Continental navy; captured British tender *Essex* 1776, first British ship captured by commissioned American ship.

Bartholomew   **Indiana**
Columbus   407 sq. mi.
71,435   63,657   65,088   57,022   48,198   36,108
January 8, 1821; effective February 12, 1821. Joseph Bartholomew (1766–1840). Served in Revolutionary War; served with General Wayne in Northwest Territory 1792; lieutenant colonel, Indiana Militia; wounded at battle of Tippecanoe, November 7, 1811; major general, War of 1812; Indiana legislature 1819.

Barton   **Kansas**
Great Bend   894 sq. mi.
28,205   29,382   31,343   30,663   32,368   29,909
February 26, 1867. Clara H. Barton (1821–1912). Volunteer nurse in Civil War; called "Angel of the Battlefield"; superintendent of nurses for the Army of the James 1864; organizer and first president of American Red Cross, 1881; urged U.S. ratification of Geneva Convention 1882.

Barton   **Missouri**
Lamar   594 sq. mi.
12,541   11,312   11,292   10,431   11,113   12,678
December 12, 1855. David Barton (1783–1837). Attorney general of Missouri 1813; first circuit judge of Howard County 1815, presiding judge, 1816; territorial House of Representatives 1818; president of Missouri Constitutional Convention 1820; U.S. senator 1821–31; Missouri Senate 1834; circuit judge at Boonville 1835.

Bartow   **Georgia**
Cartersville   459 sq. mi.
76,019   55,911   40,760   32,663   28,267   27,370
December 3, 1832, as Cass; name changed, December 6, 1861. Francis S. Bartow (1816–61). Georgia legislature; Confederate Congress; brigadier general Confederate army; killed at Manassas Plains July 21, 1861.

Bastrop   **Texas**
Bastrop   888 sq. mi.
57,733   38,263   24,726   17,297   16,925   19,622

March 17, 1836, as Mina; name changed December 18, 1837. Felipe Enrique Neri, Baron of Bastrop (c1766–1827). Established unsuccessful German colony in Louisiana 1795; assisted Moses and Stephen Austin in establishing Anglo-American colony in Mexican Texas.

Bates   **Missouri**
Butler   848 sq. mi.

16,653	15,025	15,873	15,468	15,905	17,534

January 29, 1841. Uncertain; one of two brothers. (1) Edward Bates (1793–1869); War of 1812; Missouri Constitutional Convention 1820; Missouri legislature 1822; U.S. representative 1827–29; U.S. attorney general 1861–64. (2) Frederick Bates (1777–1825); judge of Michigan Territory 1805; secretary of Louisiana Territory 1806; governor of Missouri Territory 1809–10; governor of Missouri 1824–25.

Bath   **Kentucky**
Owingsville   279 sq. mi.

11,085	9,692	10,025	9,235	9,114	10,410

January 15, 1811. Descriptive of local medicinal bathing springs.

Bath   **Virginia**
Warm Springs   532 sq. mi.

5,048	4,799	5,860	5,192	5,335	6,296

December 14, 1790. Descriptive of local sulfur bathing springs.

Baxter   **Arkansas**
Mountain Home   554 sq. mi.

38,386	31,186	27,409	15,319	9,943	11,683

March 24, 1873. Elisha Baxter (1827–99). Arkansas legislature 1854 and 1858; raised 4th Arkansas Mounted Infantry for Union army 1861; chief justice of Arkansas 1864; circuit judge 1868–72; governor of Arkansas 1872–74.

Bay   **Florida**
Panama City   764 sq. mi.

148,217	126,994	97,740	75,283	67,131	42,689

April 24, 1913. St. Andrew's Bay.

Bay   **Michigan**
Bay City   444 sq. mi.

110,157	111,723	119,881	117,339	107,042	88,461

April 20, 1857. Saginaw Bay.

Bayfield   **Wisconsin**
Washburn   1,476 sq. mi.

15,013	14,008	13,822	11,683	11,910	13,760

February 19, 1845, as La Pointe; name changed April 12, 1866. Town of Bayfield. Named for Henry W. Bayfield (1795–1885); admiral, British Royal Navy; surveyed Lakes Superior, Erie, and Huron, 1822–23.

Baylor   **Texas**
Seymour   871 sq. mi.

4,093	4,385	4,919	5,221	5,893	6,875

February 1, 1858; organized April 12, 1879. Henry Weidner Baylor (1818–54). Comanche campaign 1840; surgeon 1st Regiment, Texas Mounted Riflemen, during Mexican War.

Beadle   **South Dakota**
Huron   1,259 sq. mi.

17,023	18,253	19,195	20,877	21,682	21,082

February 22, 1879; organized July 9, 1880. William Henry Harrison Beadle (1838–1915). Private, lieutenant, and captain with Company A, 31st Indiana Volunteer Infantry during Civil War; lieutenant colonel, Michigan Sharpshooters; brevet colonel of

Volunteers; brevet brigadier general; provost marshal at Utica 1865; mustered out 1866; surveyor general of Dakota Territory 1869–73; government surveyor 1873–79; Dakota territorial House of Representatives 1877; private secretary to territorial governor 1878; superintendent of public instruction 1879–86; director of Indian School, Salem, Oregon, 1888–89; president of South Dakota State Normal School 1899–1905; professor emeritus of history 1905–11.

Bear Lake   **Idaho**
Paris   971 sq. mi.
6,411   6,084   6,931   5,801   7,148   6,834
January 5, 1875. Bear Lake. Named Black Bear Lake by Donald McKenzie for numerous bears in the area 1818.

Beaufort   **North Carolina**
Washington   828 sq. mi.
44,958   42,283   40,355   35,980   36,014   37,134
December 3, 1705, as Pamptecough; name changed 1712. *Henry Somerset, 2nd Duke of Beaufort* (1684–1714). One of several lords proprietor of Carolina; inherited proprietorship from his mother 1709.

Beaufort   **South Carolina**
Beaufort   587 sq. mi.
120,937   86,425   65,364   51,136   44,187   26,993
March 12, 1785. Town of Beaufort. Named for Henry Somerset, 2nd Duke of Beaufort.*

Beauregard   **Louisiana**
DeRidder   1,160 sq. mi.
32,986   30,083   29,692   22,888   19,191   17,766
June 12, 1912. Pierre Gustave Toutant Beauregard (1818–93). Graduated West Point 1838; served in Army engineering department 1840–45; wounded twice in Mexican War 1846; brevet major, captain of engineers, 1853; superintendent of West Point 1861, resigned; joined Confederate army; defended Charleston and directed bombardment of Fort Sumter April 12, 1861; Battle of Bull Run July 21, 1861; promoted to general 1862; president of New Orleans, Jackson, and Mississippi Railroad Co.; adjutant general of Louisiana; manager of Louisiana State Lottery.

Beaver   **Oklahoma**
Beaver   1,814 sq. mi.
5,857   6,023   6,806   6,282   6,965   7,411
1890, as County 7; name changed July 16, 1907. Beaver River. Descriptive of numerous beaver dams.

Beaver   **Pennsylvania**
Beaver   434 sq. mi.
181,412   186,093   204,441   208,418   206,948   175,192
March 12, 1800. Beaver River. Descriptive of numerous beaver dams.

Beaver   **Utah**
Beaver   2,590 sq. mi.
6,005   4,765   4,378   3,800   4,331   4,856
January 5, 1856. Beaver River. Descriptive of numerous beaver dams.

Beaverhead   **Montana**
Dillon   5,542 sq. mi.
9,202   8,424   8,186   8,187   7,194   6,671
February 2, 1865. Beaverhead River. Descriptive of a rock in the river that resembles the head of a beaver.

Becker   **Minnesota**
Detroit Lakes   1,310 sq. mi.
30,000   27,881   29,336   24,372   23,959   24,836
March 18, 1858; organized March 1, 1871. George Loomis Becker (1829–1904). Brigadier general 1858; mayor of St. Paul 1856; land commissioner of St. Paul and Pacific RR Co. 1862; Minnesota legislature 1868–71; Minnesota Railroad and Warehouse Commission 1855–1901.

Beckham **Oklahoma**
Sayre 902 sq. mi.
19,799 18,812 19,243 15,754 17,782 21,627
July 16, 1907. John Crepps Wickliffe Beckham (1869–1940). Kentucky House of Representatives 1899; governor of Kentucky 1900–07; U.S. senator 1915–21.

Bedford **Pennsylvania**
Bedford 1,015 sq. mi.
49,984 47,919 46,784 42,353 42,451 40,775
March 9, 1771. Uncertain. (1) Town of Bedford. (2) Fort Bedford. Both town and fort are named for *John Russell II, Duke of Bedford* (1710–71); 1st lord of the admiralty 1744; Privy councilor 1744; major general 1755; lord lieutenant of Ireland 1755–61; chancellor of University of Dublin 1765.

Bedford **Tennessee**
Shelbyville 474 sq. mi.
37,586 30,411 27,916 25,039 23,150 23,627
December 3, 1807. Thomas Bedford (1758–1804). Captain, Continental army; Virginia House of Delegates 1788; immigrated to Tennessee 1795.

Bedford **Virginia**
Bedford 755 sq. mi.
60,371 45,656 34,927 26,728 31,028 29,627
February 27, 1752 (session). John Russell II, Duke of Bedford.*

Bedford **Virginia**
(Independent City) 7 sq. mi.
6,299 6,073 5,991 6,011 (a) (a)
August 30, 1968. John Russell II, Duke of Bedford.* (Associated county: Bedford.) [(a) Part of Bedford County.]

Bee **Texas**
Beeville 880 sq. mi.
32,359 25,135 26,030 22,737 23,755 18,174
December 8, 1857; organized January 25, 1858. Bernard E. Bee (1787–1853). Joined Texas Army under Thomas J. Rusk; secretary of treasury in Texas ad interim government; secretary of war under Sam Houston; secretary of state under Mirabeau; Texas minister to the U.S. 1838–41; opposed U.S. annexation of Texas; returned to South Carolina 1846.

Belknap **New Hampshire**
Laconia 401 sq. mi.
56,325 49,216 42,884 32,267 28,912 26,632
December 22, 1840. Jeremy Belknap (1744–98). Congregational pastor, Dover, New Hampshire, 1767–86; pastor, Federal Street Church, Boston, Massachusetts, 1787–98; founded Massachusetts Historical Society 1792; wrote *History of New Hampshire* and other books.

Bell **Kentucky**
Pineville 361 sq. mi.
30,060 31,506 34,330 31,087 35,336 47,602
February 28, 1867, as Josh Bell; name changed 1873. Joshua Fry Bell (1811–70). U.S. representative 1845–47; Kentucky secretary of state 1849; Kentucky House of Representatives 1862–67; declined Union Democrat nomination for governor 1863.

Bell **Texas**
Belton 1,060 sq. mi.
237,974 191,088 157,889 124,483 94,097 73,824
January 22, 1850; organized August 1, 1850. Peter Hansborough Bell (1812–98). Battle of San Jacinto 1836; Texas assistant adjutant general 1837; Texas inspector general 1839; captain, Texas Volunteer Rangers, 1845–46; lieutenant colonel, Mounted Volunteers, 1846; colonel 1848–49; governor of Texas 1849–53; U.S. representative 1853–57; colonel, North Carolina Regiment 1861.

Belmont   **Ohio**
Saint Clairsville   537 sq. mi
70,226   71,074   82,569   80,917   83,864   87,740
September 7, 1801. French for "beautiful mountain."

Beltrami   **Minnesota**
Bemidji   2,505 sq. mi.
39,650   34,384   30,982   26,373   23,425   24,962
February 28, 1866; organized April 6, 1897. Giacomo Constantino Beltrami (1779–1855). Exiled from Italy and migrated to U.S. 1821; explored upper Mississippi River and incorrectly believed he found its source.

Benewah   **Idaho**
Saint Maries   776 sq. mi.
9,171   7,937   8,292   6,230   6,036   6,173
January 23, 1915. Benewah (?–?). Chief of Coeur d'Alene Indians.

Ben Hill   **Georgia**
Fitzgerald   252 sq. mi.
17,484   16,245   16,000   13,171   13,633   14,879
July 31, 1906. Benjamin Harvey Hill (1823–82). Georgia House of Representatives 1851; Georgia Senate 1859–60; delegate, Confederate Provisional Congress, 1861; senator, Confederate Congress, 1861–65; U.S. representative 1875–77; U.S. senator 1877–82.

Bennett   **South Dakota**
Martin   1,185 sq. mi.
3,574   3,206   3,044   3,088   3,053   3,396
March 9, 1909; organized April 27, 1912. Granville G. Bennett (1833–1910). Civil War 1861–65; Iowa legislature 1865–71; associate judge, Dakota Territory Supreme Court, 1875–78; Dakota Territory delegate to Congress 1879–81; practiced law in Yankton and Deadwood.

Bennington   **Vermont**
Bennington   676 sq. mi.
36,994   35,845   33,345   29,282   25,088   24,115
February 11, 1779 (session). Town of Bennington. Named for Benning Wentworth (1696–1770). Royal governor of New Hampshire 1741–66; granted land for town of Bennington 1749; donated 500 acres to Dartmouth College 1768.

Benson   **North Dakota**
Minnewaukan   1,381 sq. mi.
6,964   7,198   7,944   8,245   9,435   10,675
March 9, 1883. Bertil W. Benson (?–c1907). Land agent for Northern Pacific Railroad; Dakota territorial legislature 1883–84.

Bent   **Colorado**
Las Animas   1,514 sq. mi.
5,998   5,048   5,945   6,493   7,419   8,775
February 11, 1870. Bent's Fort. The Bent brothers built three forts in Colorado; the last and biggest was on the Arkansas River 1853. The four Bent brothers were all involved in trapping and trading with the Indians: Charles (1799–1847), William (1809–69), George (1814–47), and Robert (1816–41). William was most responsible for the forts.

Benton   **Arkansas**
Bentonville   846 sq. mi.
153,406   97,499   78,115   50,476   36,272   38,076
September 30, 1836. *Thomas Hart Benton* (1782–1858). Tennessee Senate 1809–11; colonel, Tennessee Volunteers, 1812–13; colonel, U.S. infantry, 1813–15; U.S. senator 1821–51; U.S. representative 1853–55; advocate of westward expansion.

Benton   **Indiana**
Fowler   406 sq. mi.

| 9,421 | 9,441 | 10,218 | 11,262 | 11,912 | 11,462 |

February 18, 1840. Thomas Hart Benton.*

Benton **Iowa**
Vinton 716 sq. mi.

| 25,308 | 22,429 | 23,649 | 22,885 | 23,422 | 22,656 |

December 21, 1837; organized January 17, 1845; effective March 1, 1845. Thomas Hart Benton.*

Benton **Minnesota**
Foley 408 sq. mi.

| 34,226 | 30,185 | 25,187 | 20,841 | 17,287 | 15,911 |

October 27, 1849; effective March 31, 1851. Thomas Hart Benton.*

Benton **Mississippi**
Ashland 407 sq. mi.

| 8,026 | 8,046 | 8,153 | 7,505 | 7,723 | 8,793 |

July 21, 1870. Samuel Benton (1820–64). Mississippi legislature; Mississippi Secession Convention 1861; rose from captain to colonel Confederate army 1861–64; died from wounds received at Battle of Atlanta July 22, 1864.

Benton **Missouri**
Warsaw 706 sq. mi.

| 17,180 | 13,859 | 12,183 | 9,695 | 8,737 | 9,080 |

January 3, 1835. Thomas Hart Benton.*

Benton **Oregon**
Corvallis 676 sq. mi.

| 78,153 | 70,811 | 68,211 | 53,776 | 39,165 | 31,570 |

December 23, 1847. Thomas Hart Benton.*

Benton **Tennessee**
Camden 395 sq. mi.

| 16,537 | 14,524 | 14,901 | 12,126 | 10,662 | 11,495 |

December 19, 1835; effective January 1, 1836. Originally named for Thomas Hart Benton* who became unpopular in Tennessee for moderate position on slavery and abolition. Tennessee legislature declared January 26, 1852 "That the county of Benton retain its original name in honor of David Benton an old and respectable citizen of said county." David Benton (1779–1860); War of 1812; active in creation of Benton County.

Benton **Washington**
Prosser 1,703 sq. mi.

| 142,475 | 112,560 | 109,444 | 67,540 | 62,070 | 51,370 |

March 8, 1905. Thomas Hart Benton.*

Benzie **Michigan**
Beulah 321 sq. mi.

| 15,998 | 12,200 | 11,205 | 8,593 | 7,834 | 8,306 |

February 27, 1863; organized March 30,1869. Uncertain. (1) Betsie River from French *bec scies,* referring to saw-bill ducks in the area. (2) Village of Benzonia; disputed origin; either Hebrew or Greek–Latin, meaning "sons of light," or "life," or "toil," or "Zion." (3) Coined word from "Benzonia" and "Betsie."

Bergen **New Jersey**
Hackensack 234 sq. mi.

| 884,118 | 825,380 | 845,385 | 898,012 | 780,255 | 539,139 |

March 1, 1683. Village of Bergen. Named for city of Bergen-op-zoom, Holland.

Berkeley **South Carolina**
Moncks Corner 1,098 sq. mi.

142,651   128,776   94,727   56,199   38,196   30,251
January 31, 1882. Original proprietary county of Berkeley (1682–1798); named for one of two brothers or both; both were among eight original lords proprietor of Carolina. (1) John Berkeley (1607–78); special ambassador to Sweden; English army officer against Scots; member of Parliament; lord lieutenant of Ireland; proprietor of New Jersey. (2) William Berkeley (1606–77); royal governor of Virginia.

Berkeley   **West Virginia**
Martinsburg   321 sq. mi.
75,905   59,253   46,775   36,356   33,791   30,359
February 10, 1772 (session). *Norborne Berkeley, Lord Botetourt* (1718–70). Member of Parliament 1741–63; created peer 1764; colonial governor of Virginia 1768–70; favored colonists but dissolved the legislature 1769.

Berks   **Pennsylvania**
Reading   859 sq. mi.
373,638   336,523   312,509   296,382   275,414   255,740
October 14, 1751 (session). Berkshire County, England.

Berkshire   **Massachusetts**
Pittsfield   931 sq. mi.
134,953   139,352   145,110   149,402   142,135   132,966
May 28, 1760 (session); effective June 30, 1761. Berkshire County, England.

Bernalillo   **New Mexico**
Albuquerque   1,166 sq. mi.
556,678   480,577   419,700   315,774   262,199   145,673
January 9, 1852. Town of Bernalillo. Named for any one of six members of the Gonzales–Bernal family, which settled in New Mexico in the 17th century; *illo* is Spanish diminutive suffix that may have been applied to a "junior" member of the Bernal family.

Berrien   **Georgia**
Nashville   452 sq. mi.
16,235   14,153   13,525   11,556   12,038   13,966
February 25, 1856. *John Macpherson Berrien* (1781–1856). Solicitor general for Eastern Circuit of Georgia 1809; judge, Eastern Judicial Circuit, 1810–21; colonel of cavalry 1810; Georgia Senate 1822–23; U.S. senator 1825–29 and 1841–52; U.S. attorney general 1829–31.

Berrien   **Michigan**
Saint Joseph   571 sq. mi.
162,453   161,378   171,276   163,875   149,865   115,702
October 29, 1829; organized September 1, 1831. John Macpherson Berrien.*

Bertie   **North Carolina**
Windsor   699 sq. mi.
19,773   20,388   21,024   20,528   24,350   26,439
October 2, 1722 (session). Uncertain; either James Bertie (1673–1735) or both brothers, James and Henry Bertie (1675–1735); both were lords proprietor of Carolina.

Bethel   **Alaska**
(Census Area)   40,633 sq. mi.
16,006   13,656   10,999   9,885[a]   7,838[a]   [b]
Bethel Mission. Hebrew "house of God" (Genesis 35:1); name given to Moravian church mission, 1884. [(a) Includes Kuskokwim Census Division; (b) part of 4th Judicial District.]

Bexar   **Texas**
San Antonio   1,247 sq. mi.

1,392,931   1,185,394   988,800   830,460   687,151   500,460

March 17, 1836. Uncertain. (1) Presidio, village, or municipality of San Antonio de Bexar. (2) Balthasar Manuel de Zuñiga y Guzmán Sotomayor y Sarmiento, second son of the Duke of Bexar, was viceroy of New Spain (Mexico) at time presidio was founded 1718.

Bibb   **Alabama**
Centreville   623 sq. mi.
20,826   16,576   15,723   13,812   14,357   17,987
February 7, 1818, as Cahawba; name changed December 2, 1820. *William Wyatt Bibb* (1781–1820). Physician; Georgia House of Representatives 1803–05; U.S. representative 1807–13; U.S. senator 1813–16; governor of Alabama Territory 1817–19; first governor of Alabama 1819–20.

Bibb   **Georgia**
Macon   250 sq. mi.
153,887   149,967   150,256   143,418   141,249   114,079
December 9, 1822. William Wyatt Bibb.*

Bienville   **Louisiana**
Arcadia   811 sq. mi.
15,752   15,979   16,387   16,024   16,726   19,105
March 14, 1848. Jean Baptiste Le Moyne, Sieur de Bienville (1680–1765). Explored Mississippi with his brother Pierre, Sieur de Iberville 1699; founded Mobile 1702, and New Orleans 1718; French governor of Louisiana intermittingly 1706–40; returned to France 1743.

Big Horn   **Montana**
Hardin   4,995 sq. mi.
12,671   11,337   11,096   10,057   10,007   9,824
January 13, 1913. Big horn sheep.

Big Horn   **Wyoming**
Basin   3,137 sq. mi.
11,461   10,525   11,896   10,202   11,898   13,176
March 12, 1890. Uncertain. (1) Big horn sheep. (2) Big Horn Mountains; named for the sheep.

Big Stone   **Minnesota**
Ortonville   497 sq. mi.
5,820   6,285   7,716   7,941   8,954   9,607
February 20, 1862; organized February 8, 1881. Big Stone Lake. Translation of Dakota name referring to granite outcrops near the lake.

Billings   **North Dakota**
Medora   1,151 sq. mi.
888   1,108   1,138   1,198   1,513   1,777
February 10, 1879; organized April 30, 1886. Frederick Billings (1823–90). Original partner, Northern Pacific Railroad 1870; proposed reorganization plan 1875; elected president 1879, resigned 1881.

Bingham   **Idaho**
Blackfoot   2,095 sq. mi.
41,735   37,583   36,489   29,167   28,218   23,271
January 13, 1885. Henry Harrison Bingham (1841–1912). Rose from 1st lieutenant to captain, Pennsylvania Volunteer Infantry, 1862; brevet major 1864; Congressional Medal of Honor 1864; brevet lieutenant colonel, colonel, and brigadier general, 1865; Philadelphia postmaster 1867–72; U.S. representative from Pennsylvania 1879–1912; friend of Idaho territorial governor William Bunn.

Blackford   **Indiana**
Hartford City   165 sq. mi.

14,048   14,067   15,570   15,888   14,792   14,026
February 15, 1838; effective April 2, 1838; organized January 29, 1839. Isaac Newton Blackford (1786–1859). Clerk and recorder of Washington County 1813; clerk of Indiana territorial legislature 1814; judge of district court 1814; Speaker, Indiana legislature, 1816; judge of Indiana Supreme Court 1817–52; judge of U.S. Court of Claims 1855–59.

Black Hawk   **Iowa**
Waterloo   567 sq. mi.
128,012   123,798   137,961   132,916   122,482   100,448
February 17, 1843; organized August 17, 1853. Black Hawk (1767–1838). Chief of Sauk–Fox alliance; warrior at age of 17; sided with British in War of 1812; leader in Black Hawk War 1832; captured at Battle of Bad Axe River, August 2, 1832.

Bladen   **North Carolina**
Elizabethtown   875 sq. mi.
32,278   28,663   30,491   26,477   28,881   29,703
1734 (session). Martin Bladen (1680–1746). Colonel of English foot soldiers in Europe; comptroller of the mint 1714; member of Parliament 1715–46; supervised colonial affairs as commissioner of trade and plantations 1717–46.

Blaine   **Idaho**
Hailey   2,645 sq. mi.
18,991   13,552   9,841   5,749   4,598   5,384
March 5, 1895. *James Gillespie Blaine* (1830–93). Maine House of Representatives 1859–62, Speaker, 1861–62; U.S. representative 1863–76, Speaker of the House 1869–75; U.S. senator 1876–81; U.S. secretary of state 1881 and 1889–92; republican candidate for presidency 1884.

Blaine   **Montana**
Chinook   4,226 sq. mi.
7,009   6,728   6,999   6,727   8,091   8,516
February 29, 1912. James Gillespie Blaine.*

Blaine   **Nebraska**
Brewster   711 sq. mi.
583   675   867   847   1,016   1,203
March 5, 1885; organized June 24, 1886. James Gillespie Blaine.*

Blaine   **Oklahoma**
Watonga   928 sq. mi.
11,976   11,470   13,443   11,794   12,077   15,049
1892, as County C; name changed July 16, 1907. James Gillespie Blaine.*

Blair   **Pennsylvania**
Hollidaysburg   526 sq. mi.
129,144   130,542   136,621   135,356   137,270   139,154
February 26, 1846. John Blair (?–1832). Pennsylvania legislature; supported construction of canals and railroads.

Blanco   **Texas**
Johnson City   711 sq. mi.
8,418   5,972   4,681   3,567   3,657   3,780
February 12, 1858; organized April 12, 1858. Blanco River. Spanish for "white"; named for white, chalky limestone in region.

Bland   **Virginia**
Bland   359 sq. mi.
6,871   6,514   6,349   5,423   5,982   6,436
March 30, 1861. Richard Bland (1710–76). Virginia House of Burgesses 1742–75; Continental Congress 1774–75; Virginia House of Delegates 1776.

Bleckley   **Georgia**
Cochran   217 sq. mi.

11,666	10,430	10,767	10,291	9,642	9,218

July 30, 1912. Logan Edwin Bleckley (1827–1907). Solicitor general of Atlanta 1852–56; private in Civil War 1861; Georgia Supreme Court reporter 1864–67; associate justice, Georgia Supreme Court, 1875–87; chief justice of Georgia Supreme Court 1887–94.

Bledsoe   **Tennessee**
Pikeville   406 sq. mi.

12,367	9,669	9,478	7,643	7,811	8,561

November 30, 1807. Uncertain; one or more members of pioneer Bledsoe family. (1) Abraham Bledsoe (?–?); major, Continental army. (2) Anthony Bledsoe (1733–88); father of Abraham. (3) Isaac Bledsoe (1735–93); brother of Anthony. (4) Thomas, Anthony Jr., and/or Henry Bledsoe; sons of Anthony, nephews of Isaac.

Blount   **Alabama**
Oneonta   646 sq. mi.

51,024	39,248	36,459	26,853	25,449	28,975

February 6, 1818. Willie G. Blount (1768–1835). Tennessee legislature; governor of Tennessee 1809–15; sent aid to eastern Mississippi Territory (Alabama) during Creek wars.

Blount   **Tennessee**
Maryville   559 sq. mi.

105,823	85,969	77,770	63,744	57,525	54,691

July 11, 1795. William Blount (1749–1800). Paymaster, 3rd North Carolina Regiment 1778; North Carolina House of Commons 1780–89; Continental Congress 1782–83, 1786, and 1787; federal Constitutional Convention 1787; North Carolina Senate 1788–90; governor of Territory South of the Ohio River (Tennessee) 1790–96; superintendent of Indian affairs 1790–96; North Carolina Constitutional Convention 1796; U.S. senator from Tennessee 1796–97; president, Tennessee Senate, 1797.

Blue Earth   **Minnesota**
Mankato   752 sq. mi.

55,941	54,044	52,314	52,322	44,385	38,327

March 5, 1853. Blue Earth River. English translation of Sisseton *mahkahto,* describing color of river from deposits of blue-green clay.

Boise   **Idaho**
Idaho City   1,902 sq. mi.

6,670	3,509	2,999	1,763	1,646	1,776

February 4, 1864. Boise River. French *bois* meaning "woods."

Bolivar   **Mississippi**
Cleveland   876 sq. mi.

40,633	41,875	45,965	49,409	54,464	63,004

February 9, 1836. Simón Bolívar y Ponte (1783–1830). Defeated Spanish in South America, leading to independence for Bolivia, Colombia, Ecuador, Peru, and Venezuela; "the George Washington of South America."

Bollinger   **Missouri**
Marble Hill   621 sq. mi.

12,029	10,619	10,301	8,820	9,167	11,019

March 1, 1851. George F. Bollinger (1770–1842). Early settler; emigrated from North Carolina to Cape Girardeau 1796; led twenty North Carolina families to Missouri 1799; Missouri Senate, president pro tempore 1828.

Bond   **Illinois**
Greenville   380 sq. mi.

17,633	14,991	16,224	14,012	14,060	14,157

January 4, 1817. Shadrach Bond (1773–1832). Legislative council of Indiana Territory 1805–08; congressional delegate from Illinois Territory 1812–14; land office receiver of public moneys 1814–18; first governor of Illinois 1818–22; registrar of land office for Kaskaskia, 1823–32.

Bon Homme   **South Dakota**
Tyndall   563 sq. mi.
7,260   7,089   8,059   8,577   9,229   9,440
April 5, 1862. Town of Bonhomme. Named from an island in the Missouri River; from French phrase *bon homme Jacques*, meaning "good man Jack" or "good fellow," the French equivalent of Uncle Sam.

Bonner   **Idaho**
Sandpoint   1,738 sq. mi.
36,835   26,622   24,163   15,560   15,587   14,853
February 21, 1907; effective March 18, 1907. Edwin L. Bonner (?–?). Built ferry across Kootenai River, site of town of Bonners Ferry 1864.

Bonneville   **Idaho**
Idaho Falls   1,868 sq. mi.
82,522   72,207   65,980   51,250   46,906   30,210
February 7, 1911. Benjamin Louis Eulalie de Bonneville (1796–1878). Graduated West Point 1815; captain of infantry 1825; explored California and Rocky Mountain regions on military leave of absence 1831–36; major 1845; lieutenant colonel 1849; colonel 1855; retired brevet brigadier general 1865.

Boone   **Arkansas**
Harrison   591 sq. mi.
33,948   28,297   26,067   19,073   16,116   16,260
April 9, 1869. Uncertain. (1) *Daniel Boone* (1734–1820). Explorer; American militia under British General Braddock during French and Indian Wars 1755; developed Wilderness Road to Kentucky 1775; emigrated to Missouri 1798. (2) Intended to be named "Boon" because new county was seen as a boon to local residents.

Boone   **Illinois**
Belvidere   281 sq. mi.
41,786   30,806   28,630   25,440   20,326   17,070
March 4, 1837. Daniel Boone.*

Boone   **Indiana**
Lebanon   423 sq. mi.
46,107   38,147   36,446   30,870   27,543   23,993
January 29, 1830; effective April 1, 1830. Daniel Boone.*

Boone   **Iowa**
Boone   571 sq. mi.
26,224   25,186   26,184   26,470   28,037   28,139
January 13, 1846; organized October 1, 1849. Nathan Boone (1780–?). Youngest son of Daniel Boone*; accompanied father to Missouri 1798; captain, Missouri Militia 1808; major 1815; Missouri Constitutional Convention 1820; surveyed parts of Louisiana Purchase; captain, Black Hawk War 1832; lieutenant colonel 1835.

Boone   **Kentucky**
Burlington   246 sq. mi.
85,991   57,589   45,842   32,812   21,940   13,015
December 13, 1798; effective June 1, 1799. Daniel Boone.*

Boone   **Missouri**
Columbia   685 sq. mi.
135,454   112,379   100,376   80,911   55,202   48,432
November 16, 1820; effective January 1, 1821. Daniel Boone.*

Boone   **Nebraska**
Albion   687 sq. mi.
6,259   6,667   7,391   8,190   9,134   10,721
March 1, 1871; organized March 28, 1871. Daniel Boone.*

Boone   **West Virginia**
Madison   503 sq. mi.
25,535   25,870   30,447   25,118   28,764   33,173
March 11, 1847. Daniel Boone.*

Borden   **Texas**
Gail   899 sq. mi.
729   799   859   888   1,076   1,106
August 21, 1876; organized March 17, 1891. Gail Borden, Jr. (1801–74). Surveyor of Stephen Austin's colony 1830; publisher of *Telegraph* and *Texas Register* 1835; collector for port of Galveston 1837–38 and 1841–43; inventor of condensed milk.

Bosque   **Texas**
Meridian   989 sq. mi.
17,204   15,125   13,401   10,966   10,809   11,836
February 4, 1854; organized August 7, 1854. Bosque River. Spanish word meaning "forest" or "woodland"; descriptive of the thick vegetation along the river.

Bossier   **Louisiana**
Benton   839 sq. mi.
98,310   86,088   80,721   64,519   57,622   40,139
February 24, 1843. Pierre Evariste John Baptiste Bossier (1797–1844). Louisiana Senate 1833–43; U.S. representative 1843–44.

Botetourt   **Virginia**
Fincastle   543 sq. mi.
30,496   24,992   23,270   18,193   16,715   15,766
November 7, 1769 (session). Norborne Berkeley, Lord Botetourt* (see Berkeley, West Virginia).

Bottineau   **North Dakota**
Bottineau   1,669 sq. mi.
7,149   8,011   9,239   9,496   11,315   12,140
January 4, 1873; organized July 22, 1884. Pierre Bottineau (?–1895). French–Canadian scout, guide, translator, and fur trader; assisted U.S. Army against Sioux 1863; guided railroad survey party 1869.

Boulder   **Colorado**
Boulder   742 sq. mi.
291,288   225,339   189,625   131,889   74,254   48,296
November 1, 1861. City of Boulder. Named from Boulder Creek; descriptive of large rocks in the area.

Boundary   **Idaho**
Bonners Ferry   1,269 sq. mi.
9,871   8,332   7,289   6,371   5,809   5,908
January 23, 1915. International boundary. Descriptive of only county in Idaho bordering on Canada.

Bourbon   **Kansas**
Fort Scott   637 sq. mi.
15,379   14,966   15,969   15,215   16,090   19,153
August 30, 1855. Bourbon County, Kentucky.

Bourbon   **Kentucky**
Paris   291 sq. mi.

19,360   19,236   19,405   18,476   18,178   17,752
October 17, 1785 (session); effective May 1, 1786. French royal family from 1589 (Henry IV) to 1792 (Louis XVI). France was most important ally of American colonists against England.

Bowie   **Texas**
New Boston   888 sq. mi.
89,306   81,665   75,301   67,813   59,971   61,966
December 17,1840; organized 1846. James Bowie (1795–1836). Resident of San Antonio; colonel of Texas Volunteers; battle of Concepción 1835; killed at the Alamo March 6, 1836; inventor of Bowie knife.

Bowman   **North Dakota**
Bowman   1,162 sq. mi.
3,242   3,596   4,229   3,901   4,154   4,001
March 8, 1883; abolished November 30, 1896; recreated May 24, 1901; organized April 17, 1907. Edward M. Bowman (?–?). Member of Dakota Territorial Assembly 1883–84.

Box Butte   **Nebraska**
Alliance   1,075 sq. mi.
12,158   13,130   13,696   10,094   11,688   12,279
November 2, 1886; organized April 23, 1887. Box Butte, natural landmark shaped like a box; French *butte,* meaning "mound" or "isolated elevation."

Box Elder   **Utah**
Brigham City   5,723 sq. mi.
42,745   36,485   33,222   28,129   25,061   19,734
January 5, 1856. Box elder trees.

Boyd   **Kentucky**
Catlettsburg   160 sq. mi.
49,752   51,150   55,513   52,376   52,163   49,949
February 16, 1860. Linn Boyd (1800–59). Kentucky legislature 1827–30 and 1831–32; U.S. representative 1835–37 and 1839–55; Speaker of the House 1852–55; elected lieutenant governor of Kentucky but was too ill to serve 1859.

Boyd   **Nebraska**
Butte   540 sq. mi.
2,438   2,835   3,331   3,752   4,513   4,911
March 20, 1891; organized August 29, 1891. James E. Boyd (1834–1906). Manager of City Gas Works of Omaha 1868–69; president of Omaha Board of Trade 1868–69; clerk of Douglas County 1857; clerk of Buffalo County; Nebraska legislature 1866; Nebraska Constitutional Convention 1871 and 1875; mayor of Omaha 1881–82 and 1885–87; governor of Nebraska 1891, removed because citizenship contested; declared citizen, 1892; resumed governorship 1892–93.

Boyle   **Kentucky**
Danville   182 sq. mi.
27,697   25,641   25,066   21,090   21,257   20,532
February 15, 1842. John Boyle (1774–1834). Kentucky House of Representatives 1800; U.S. representative 1803–09; declined appointment to be governor of Illinois Territory 1809; judge, Kentucky Court of Appeals, 1809–10; chief justice, Kentucky Court of Appeals, 1810–26; U.S. judge for District of Kentucky 1826–34.

Bracken   **Kentucky**
Brooksville   203 sq. mi.
8,279   7,766   7,738   7,227   7,422   8,424
December 14, 1796. Uncertain. (1) William Bracken (?–?); member of survey parties of Kentucky River and Falls of the Ohio (Louisville); early settler of Kentucky; killed by Indians. (2) Big and Little Bracken Creeks; named for William Bracken.

Bradford   **Florida**
Starke   293 sq. mi.

26,088   22,515   20,023   14,625   12,446   11,457

December 21, 1858, as New River; name changed December 6, 1861. Richard Bradford (c1839–61). First Florida officer killed in Civil War, at battle of Santa Rosa Island, October 9, 1861.

Bradford   **Pennsylvania**
Towanda   1,151 sq. mi.
62,761   60,967   62,919   57,962   54,925   51,722

February 21, 1810, as Ontario; name changed March 24, 1812. William Bradford (1755–95). Private 1776; captain and colonel 1777; resigned 1779; attorney general of Pennsylvania 1780–91; associate justice of Pennsylvania Supreme Court 1791; U.S. attorney general 1794–95.

Bradley   **Arkansas**
Warren   651 sq. mi.
12,600   11,793   13,803   12,778   14,029   15,987

December 18, 1840. Hugh Bradley (?–?). Captain under General Jackson at New Orleans; Arkansas territorial legislature.

Bradley   **Tennessee**
Cleveland   329 sq. mi.
87,965   73,712   67,547   50,686   38,324   32,338

February 10, 1836. Edward Bradley (?–1829). Lieutenant colonel, 1st Regiment, Tennessee Volunteers, 1812–15; wounded during Creek War 1813; Tennessee legislature 1813–15.

Branch   **Michigan**
Coldwater   507 sq. mi.
45,787   41,502   40,188   37,906   34,903   30,202

October 29, 1829; organized March 1, 1833. John Branch (1782–1863). North Carolina Senate 1811–17 and 1822, Speaker 1815–17; governor of North Carolina 1817–20; U.S. senator 1823–29; secretary of the navy 1829–31; U.S. representative 1831–33; governor of Florida Territory 1844–45.

Brantley   **Georgia**
Nahunta   444 sq. mi.
14,629   11,077   8,701   5,940   5,891   6,387

August 14, 1920. Uncertain. (1) Benjamin D. Brantley (1832–91); private, Confederate army; Georgia House of Representatives; Pierce County treasurer. (2) William G. Brantley (1860–1934); son of Benjamin; Georgia House of Representatives 1884–85; Georgia Senate 1886–87; U.S. representative 1897–1913.

Braxton   **West Virginia**
Sutton   513 sq. mi.
14,702   12,998   13,894   12,666   15,152   18,082

January 15, 1836. Carter Braxton (1736–97). Virginia House of Burgesses 1761–71 and 1775; Continental Congress 1775–76, 1777–83, and 1785; signer of Declaration of Independence 1776; Virginia Council of State 1786–91 and 1794–97.

Brazoria   **Texas**
Angleton   1,386 sq. mi.
241,767   191,707   169,587   108,312   76,204   46,549

March 17, 1836. *Brazos River*. Spanish *Rio de los Brazos de Dios* (Arms of God River); longest river in Texas.

Brazos   **Texas**
Bryan   586 sq. mi.
152,415   121,862   93,588   57,978   44,895   38,390

January 30, 1841, as Navasota; name changed January 28, 1842; organized February 6, 1843. Brazos River.*

Breathitt   **Kentucky**
Jackson   495 sq. mi.
16,100   15,703   17,004   14,221   15,490   19,964

February 8, 1839. John Breathitt (1786–1834). Kentucky legislature 1811; lieutenant governor 1828–32; governor of Kentucky 1832–34; died in office 1834.

Breckinridge	**Kentucky**				
Hardinsburg	572 sq. mi.				
18,648	16,312	16,861	14,789	14,734	15,528

December 9, 1799. John Breckinridge (1760–1806). Elected to Virginia House of Burgesses 1780, but denied seat because of age (20); Virginia Militia; Kentucky attorney general 1795–97; Kentucky House of Representatives 1798–1800, Speaker, 1799–1800; U.S. senator 1801–05; U.S. attorney general 1805–06.

Bremer	**Iowa**				
Waverly	438 sq. mi.				
23,325	22,813	24,820	22,737	21,108	18,884

January 15, 1851; organized August 15, 1853. Frederika Bremer (1801–65). Swedish traveler and feminist author; first book published 1828; books had wide popularity.

Brevard	**Florida**				
Titusville	1,018 sq. mi.				
476,230	398,978	272,959	230,006	111,435	23,653

March 14, 1844, as St. Lucie; name changed January 6, 1855. Theodore Washington Brevard (1804–77). Lawyer; judge, Macon County, Alabama, 1847; Florida comptroller 1855–61.

Brewster	**Texas**				
Alpine	6,193 sq. mi.				
8,866	8,681	7,573	7,780	6,434	7,309

February 2, 1887; organized February 26, 1887. Henry Percy Brewster (1816–84). Private in Texas Army 1836; private secretary to General Houston 1836; Texas secretary of war 1836; district attorney, 2nd Judicial District, 1840–43; Texas attorney general 1847–49; adjutant general and chief of staff under Confederate general Albert Johnston; Texas commissioner of insurance, statistics, and history 1883.

Briscoe	**Texas**				
Silverton	900 sq. mi.				
1,790	1,971	2,579	2,794	3,577	3,528

August 21, 1876; organized January 11, 1892. Andrew Briscoe (1810–49). Captain of Liberty Volunteers at battle of Concepción 1835; signer, Texas Declaration of Independence 1836; captain of infantry regulars at battle of San Jacinto 1836; chief justice of Harrisburg, Texas, 1836–39; railroad builder and promoter 1840–41.

Bristol	**Massachusetts**				
Taunton	556 sq. mi.				
534,678	506,325	474,641	444,301	398,488	381,569

June 2, 1685. Town of Bristol, Rhode Island. Boundary change moved Bristol from Massachusetts to Rhode Island 1746.

Bristol	**Rhode Island**				
Bristol	25 sq. mi.				
50,648	48,859	46,942	45,937	37,146	29,079

February 17, 1747. Town of Bristol. Named for Bristol, England.

Bristol	**Virginia**				
(Independent City)	13 sq. mi.				
17,367	18,426	19,042	14,857	17,144	15,954

February 12, 1890. Bristol, England. (Associated county: Washington.)

Bristol Bay	**Alaska**				
Naknek	505 sq. mi.				
1,258	1,410	1,094	1,147	(a)	(b)

October, 1962. Bristol Bay. Named by Captain James Cook (1778) for Admiral Augustus John Hervey, 3rd Earl of Bristol; lord of the British admiralty 1771–75. [(a) Part of Bristol Bay (Dillingham) Census Area; (b) part of 4th Judicial District.]

Broadwater **Montana**
Townsend 1,191 sq. mi.

4,385	3,318	3,267	2,526	2,804	2,922

February 9, 1897. Colonel Charles A. Broadwater (1840–92). Miner; constructed Fort Maginnis; railroad baron James Hill's manager in Montana; president, Mountain Central Railroad; urged expansion of Great Northern Railroad in Montana.

Bronx **New York**
Bronx 42 sq. mi.

1,332,650	1,203,789	1,168,972	1,471,701	1,424,815	1,451,277

April 19, 1912. Bronx Borough. From Bronx River; corruption of "Bronck's River," a small stream named for Jonas Bronck (?–1643), first settler north of Harlem River 1641.

Brooke **West Virginia**
Wellsburg 89 sq. mi.

25,447	26,992	31,117	29,685	28,940	26,904

November 30, 1796. Robert Brooke (1751–99); captured twice during Revolutionary War; Virginia House of Delegates 1791–94; governor of Virginia 1794–96; Virginia attorney general 1798.

Brookings **South Dakota**
Brookings 794 sq. mi.

28,220	25,207	24,332	22,158	20,046	17,851

April 5, 1862; organized January 13, 1871. Wilmot Wood Brookings (1833–1905). Pioneer settler 1857; lost both feet to frostbite 1858; Dakota Council 1862–63; Speaker of the House 1864–65; superintendent in charge of building road from Minnesota boundary to Crow Creek Agency 1865–68; associate justice of Dakota Territory Supreme Court 1869–73; Constitutional Convention 1883 and 1885.

Brooks **Georgia**
Quitman 494 sq. mi.

16,450	15,398	15,255	13,739	15,292	18,169

December 11, 1858. Preston Smith Brooks (1819–57). South Carolina legislature; captain in Mexican War; U.S. representative 1853–57; severely caned Senator Charles Sumner of Massachusetts because of anti-Southern speech 1856.

Brooks **Texas**
Falfurrias 943 sq. mi.

7,976	8,204	8,428	8,005	8,609	9,195

March 11, 1911; organized 1912. James Abijah Brooks (1855–1944). Cattle business 1876–80; Texas Ranger 1882, captain 1889, resigned 1906; Texas House of Representatives 1909–11; Brooks County judge 1911–39.

Broome **New York**
Binghamton 707 sq. mi.

200,536	212,160	213,648	221,815	212,661	184,698

March 28, 1806. John Broome (1738–1810). Committee of Safety; New York Constitutional Convention 1777; president of New York City Chamber of Commerce 1794; New York Senate; lieutenant governor 1804–10.

Broomfield **Colorado**
Broomfield 27 sq. mi.

38,272[a]	24,638[a]	[a]	[a]	[a]	[a]

November 15, 2001. City of Broomfield. [(a) City of Broomfield included in parts of Adams, Boulder, Jefferson, and Weld counties. 2000 and 1990 populations listed for these counties also include Broomfield's population.]

Broward **Florida**
Fort Lauderdale 1,205 sq. mi.

1,623,018   1,255,488   1,018,200   620,100   333,946   83,933

April 30, 1915. Napoleon Bonaparte Broward (1857–1910). Smuggled arms to Cuban revolutionaries fighting Spain; sheriff of Duval County, Florida, 1887–1900; Florida legislature 1900; Florida Board of Health 1900–04; governor of Florida 1905–09.

Brown   **Illinois**
Mount Sterling   306 sq. mi.
6,950   5,836   5,411   5,586   6,210   7,132
February 1, 1839. *Jacob J. Brown* (1775–1828). Brigadier general, New York Volunteers 1813; brigadier general, U.S. Army 1813; major general 1814; army commander in chief 1821–28; received Thanks of Congress and gold medal for actions at Chippewa, Niagara, and Erie.

Brown   **Indiana**
Nashville   312 sq. mi.
14,957   14,080   12,377   9,057   7,024   6,209
February 4, 1836; effective April 1, 1836. Jacob Brown.*

Brown   **Kansas**
Hiawatha   571 sq. mi.
10,724   11,128   11,955   11,685   13,229   14,651
August 30, 1855. Uncertain. (1) Albert Gallatin Brown (1813–80); Mississippi House of Representatives 1835–39; U.S. representative 1839–41 and 1847–53; judge of the Circuit Superior Court 1842–43; governor of Mississippi 1844–48; U.S. senator 1854–61; captain, Mississippi Infantry; Confederate Senate 1862; brigadier general, Mississippi Militia; proslavery record popular in Kansas legislature. (2) Orville H. Browne (?–?); Kansas territorial legislature. County was created as "Browne" but the "e" was omitted from the county seal and never replaced.

Brown   **Minnesota**
New Ulm   611 sq. mi.
26,911   26,984   28,645   28,887   27,676   25,895
February 20, 1855; organized February 11, 1856. Joseph Renshaw Brown (1805–70). Fourteen-year-old drummer boy at Fort St. Anthony (Snelling); trader with Sioux; negotiated treaties with Dakotas and Chippewas; secretary, Minnesota Territorial Council 1849–51; Minnesota territorial printer 1853–54; chief clerk, Minnesota House of Representatives 1853; Minnesota Council, 1854–55; Minnesota territorial House of Representatives 1857.

Brown   **Nebraska**
Ainsworth   1,221 sq. mi.
3,525   3,657   4,377   4,021   4,436   5,164
February 19, 1883. Five members of Nebraska legislature named Brown at time of county's creation.

Brown   **Ohio**
Georgetown   492 sq. mi.
42,285   34,966   31,920   26,635   25,178   22,221
December 27, 1817; effective March 1, 1818. Jacob Brown.*

Brown   **South Dakota**
Aberdeen   1,713 sq. mi.
35,460   35,580   36,962   36,920   34,106   32,617
February 22, 1879; organized September 14, 1880. Alfred Brown (1836–1919). Canadian; arrived Dakota Territory 1874; Dakota territorial legislature 1879.

Brown   **Texas**
Brownwood   944 sq. mi.
37,674   34,371   33,057   25,877   24,728   28,607
August 27, 1856; organized March 2, 1857. Henry Stevenson Brown (1793–1834). War of 1812; operated keel boats to New Orleans 1814–24; moved to Texas 1824; trader with Indians and Mexicans 1824–32; fought Waco Indians 1825; captured Mexican fort at Velasco 1832; delegate to Texas convention 1832–33.

Brown   **Wisconsin**
Green Bay   529 sq. mi.

226,778	194,594	175,280	158,244	125,082	98,314

October 26, 1818. Jacob Brown.*

Brule   **South Dakota**
Chamberlain   819 sq. mi.

5,364	5,485	5,245	5,870	6,319	6,076

January 14, 1875. Brule tribe of Sioux Indians. Derisively called *sicangu* by Pawnees, meaning "burned thighs," possibly the result of a prairie fire set by Pawnees; translated by French to *brulé* (burned).

Brunswick   **North Carolina**
Bolivia   855 sq. mi.

73,143	50,985	35,777	24,223	20,278	19,238

January 30, 1764 (session). Former town of Brunswick. Named for George I*, Duke of Brunswick-Lunenburg (see King George, Virginia).

Brunswick   **Virginia**
Lawrenceville   566 sq. mi.

18,419	15,987	15,632	16,172	17,779	20,136

November 2, 1720 (session). House of Brunswick. Named for George I*, Duke of Brunswick-Lunenburg (see King George, Virginia)

Bryan   **Georgia**
Pembroke   442 sq. mi.

23,417	15,438	10,175	6,539	6,226	5,965

December 19, 1793. Jonathan Bryan (1708–88). Established colony of Georgia with James Oglethorpe 1732; King's Council for Georgia; became active opponent of England; suspended from council by George III 1769; Georgia Provincial Congress 1775; prisoner for two years following capture by British on Long Island.

Bryan   **Oklahoma**
Durant   909 sq. mi.

36,534	32,089	30,535	25,552	24,252	28,999

July 16, 1907. William Jennings Bryan (1860–1925). U.S. representative from Nebraska 1891–95; advocate for the poor; defeated as presidential candidate 1896, 1900, and 1908; assisted in developing Oklahoma Constitution 1907; U. S. secretary of state 1913–15.

Buchanan   **Iowa**
Independence   571 sq. mi.

21,093	20,844	22,900	21,746	22,293	21,927

December 21, 1837; organized October 4, 1847. *James Buchanan* (1791–1868). War of 1812; Pennsylvania House of Representatives 1814–15; U.S. representative 1821–31; U.S. minister to Russia 1832–34; U.S. senator 1845–49; U.S. secretary of state 1845–49; U.S. minister to Great Britain 1853–56; 15th president of the United States 1857–61.

Buchanan   **Missouri**
Saint Joseph   410 sq. mi.

85,998	83,083	87,888	86,915	90,581	96,826

December 31, 1838. James Buchanan.*

Buchanan   **Virginia**
Grundy   504 sq. mi.

26,978	31,333	37,989	32,071	36,724	35,748

February 13, 1858. James Buchanan.*

Buckingham   **Virginia**
Buckingham   581 sq. mi.

15,623   12,873   11,751   10,597   10,877   12,288
September 14, 1758 (session). Uncertain. (1) Buckinghamshire, England. (2) One of many Dukes of Buckingham; most likely John Sheffield, 1st Duke of Buckingham and Normandy (?–1721); court favorite of Charles II, James II, William and Mary, and Queen Anne; suitor to Anne; made duke on first day of Anne's reign 1702.

Bucks   **Pennsylvania**
Doylestown   607 sq. mi.
597,635   541,174   479,211   415,056   308,567   144,620
March 10, 1682. Buckinghamshire, England. Home of William Penn.

Buena Vista   **Iowa**
Storm Lake   575 sq. mi.
20,411   19,965   20,774   20,693   21,189   21,113
January 15, 1851; organized November 20, 1858. *Battle of Buena Vista*, February 22–23, 1847. U.S. victory, under Zachary Taylor, against much larger Mexican force led by General Santa Anna.

Buena Vista   **Virginia**
(Independent City)   7 sq. mi.
6,349   6,406   6,717   6,425   6,300   5,214
1892. Buena Vista Furnace which provided cannon balls used at Battle of Buena Vista.* (Associated county: Rockbridge.)

Buffalo   **Nebraska**
Kearney   968 sq. mi.
42,259   37,447   34,797   31,222   26,236   25,134
March 14, 1855. Descriptive of bison herds in area.

Buffalo   **South Dakota**
Gann Valley   471 sq. mi.
2,032   1,759   1,795   1,739   1,547   1,615
January 6, 1864; organized January 13, 1873. Descriptive of bison herds in area.

Buffalo   **Wisconsin**
Alma   684 sq. mi.
13,804   13,584   14,309   13,743   14,202   14,719
July 6, 1853. Buffalo River. Named for bison herds in the area.

Bullitt   **Kentucky**
Shepherdsville   299 sq. mi.
61,236   47,567   43,346   26,090   15,726   11,349
December 13, 1796. Alexander Scott Bullitt (c1761–1816). Virginia legislature 1782; Kentucky Statehood Convention 1788; Kentucky Constitutional Conventions 1792 and 1799; Kentucky senate 1792–1800 and 1804–08; lieutenant governor of Kentucky 1800–04.

Bulloch   **Georgia**
Statesboro   682 sq. mi.
55,983   43,125   35,785   31,585   24,263   24,740
February 8, 1796. Archibald Bulloch (1730–77). Lieutenant in South Carolina Regiment 1757; Speaker, Georgia Royal Assembly, 1775–76; president, Georgia Provisional Congress, 1775–76; Continental Congress 1775–76; commander in chief of Georgia forces 1776–77; Governor of Georgia 1776–77.

Bullock   **Alabama**
Union Springs   625 sq. mi.
11,714   11,042   10,596   11,824   13,462   16,054
December 5, 1866. Edward C. Bullock (1825–61). Alabama Senate; colonel, Confederate army; died at Mobile of typhoid fever.

Buncombe **North Carolina**
Asheville 656 sq. mi.
206,330 174,821 160,934 145,056 130,074 124,403
December 5, 1791 (session). Edward Buncombe (1742–78). Colonel of North Carolina Militia 1771; clerk of county court 1774–77; colonel, North Carolina Minutemen 1775; battle of Brandywine 1777; wounded at Germantown, October 4, 1777; prisoner of British 1778.

Bureau **Illinois**
Princeton 869 sq. mi.
35,503 35,688 39,114 38,541 37,594 37,711
February 28, 1837. Bureau Creek. Named for Pierre de Buero (?–?); French trader; established trading post on Illinois River 1818.

Burke **Georgia**
Waynesboro 830 sq. mi.
22,243 20,579 19,349 18,255 20,596 23,458
February 5, 1777. *Edmund Burke* (1729–97). Elected to Parliament 1765; urged repeal of Stamp Act and advocated conciliation with American colonies.

Burke **North Carolina**
Morganton 507 sq. mi.
89,148 75,744 72,504 60,364 52,701 45,518
April 8, 1777. Uncertain. (1) Edmund Burke.* (2) Thomas Burke (c1747–83); North Carolina Provisional Congress 1774–76; Continental Congress 1776–81; Volunteer at battle of Brandywine 1777; governor of North Carolina 1781–82; British prisoner for four months, escaped January 16, 1782.

Burke **North Dakota**
Bowbells 1,104 sq. mi.
2,242 3,002 3,822 4,739 5,886 6,621
February 8, 1910. John Burke (1859–1937). North Dakota House of Representatives 1891–92; North Dakota Senate 1893–95; governor of North Dakota 1907–13; treasurer of the U.S., 1913; North Dakota Supreme Court.

Burleigh **North Dakota**
Bismarck 1,633 sq. mi.
69,416 60,131 54,811 40,714 34,016 25,673
January 4, 1873; organized September 25, 1873. Walter A. Burleigh (1820–96). Physician in Maine and Pennsylvania; Indian agent at Yankton Sioux 1863; Dakota Territory congressional delegate 1865–69; Dakota territorial legislature 1877–78; South Dakota Senate 1893.

Burleson **Texas**
Caldwell 666 sq. mi.
16,470 13,625 12,313 9,999 11,177 13,000
March 24, 1846; organized July 13, 1846. Edward Burleson (1798–1852). War of 1812, battle of Horseshoe Bend, Alabama, and battle of New Orleans; Mexican War, commander of Texas forces, major 1835; battle of San Jacinto 1836; senator in first Texas Congress 1836; vice president of Texas Republic 1841; brigadier general in command of Texas troops 1838–41; Texas state Senate 1848–52, president, 1852.

Burlington **New Jersey**
Mount Holly 805 sq. mi.
423,394 395,066 362,542 323,132 224,499 135,910
May 17, 1694. Town of Burlington. Corruption of Bridlington, England.

Burnet **Texas**
Burnet 996 sq. mi.
34,147 22,677 17,803 11,420 9,265 10,356

February 5, 1852; organized August 7, 1854. David Gouverneur Burnet (1788–1870). Lieutenant of forces seeking liberation of Venezuela from Spain 1806; one of three Texas district judges 1834–36; president ad interim, Texas colonial government 1836; Texas vice president 1838–41; elected to U.S. Senate but was denied seat 1866.

Burnett   **Wisconsin**
Siren   822 sq. mi.
15,674   13,084   12,340   9,276   9,214   10,236
March 31, 1856. Thomas Pendleton Burnett (1800–46). Sub-Indian agent, Prairie du Chien 1830; district attorney for western Michigan Territory 1835; reporter, Wisconsin territorial Supreme Court, 1835; Wisconsin territorial legislature; Wisconsin Constitutional Convention 1846.

Burt   **Nebraska**
Tekamah   493 sq. mi.
7,791   7,868   8,813   9,247   10,192   11,536
November 23, 1854. Francis Burt (1807–54). Member, South Carolina Nullification Convention 1832; South Carolina legislature 1832–44; South Carolina treasurer 1844; editor, Pendleton *Messenger* 1847–51; South Carolina Constitutional Convention 1852; auditor of U.S. treasury 1853; territorial governor of Nebraska, served two days before his death, 1854.

Butler   **Alabama**
Greenville   777 sq. mi.
21,399   21,892   21,680   22,007   24,560   29,228
December 13, 1819. William Butler (?–1818). Georgia legislature; Georgia Militia; early settler in county area; killed by Indians at Butler Springs, March 20, 1818.

Butler   **Iowa**
Allison   580 sq. mi.
15,305   15,731   17,668   16,953   17,467   17,394
January 15, 1851; organized October 2, 1854. *William Orlando Butler* (1791–1880). Private, Kentucky Volunteers; wounded at battle of the Thames, October 6, 1813; imprisoned in Canada; returned as captain; brevet major at battle of New Orleans 1815; aide to General Jackson 1816–17; Kentucky House of Representatives 1817–18; U.S. representative 1839–43; major general, Kentucky Volunteers, 1846; received Thanks of Congress and a sword for gallantry at Monterrey, Mexico; unsuccessful Democratic candidate for vice president 1848; declined appointment as governor of Nebraska Territory 1855; delegate to Peace Conference 1861.

Butler   **Kansas**
El Dorado   1,428 sq. mi.
59,482   50,580   44,782   38,658   38,395   31,001
August 30, 1855; organized February 11, 1859. Andrew Pickens Butler (1796–1857). South Carolina legislature 1824; South Carolina Senate 1824–33; judge of South Carolina Session Court 1833; judge of South Carolina Court of Common Pleas 1835–46; U.S. senator 1846–57; proslavery views popular in Kansas territorial legislature.

Butler   **Kentucky**
Morgantown   428 sq. mi.
13,010   11,245   11,064   9,723   9,586   11,309
January 18, 1810. *Richard Butler* (1743–91). Major 1776; lieutenant colonel 1777; colonel, 9th Pennsylvania Regiment, fought at Saratoga and Stony Point 1779; commissioner to negotiate treaty with Iroquois 1783; superintendent of Indian affairs, northern district; justice of common pleas, Allegheny County 1788; Pennsylvania Senate 1790; major general under General Arthur St. Clair against Indian tribes in the Northwest Territory; killed November 3, 1791.

Butler   **Missouri**
Poplar Bluff   698 sq. mi.
40,867   38,765   37,693   33,529   34,656   37,707
February 27, 1849. William Orlando Butler.*

Butler   **Nebraska**
David City   584 sq. mi.

8,767   8,601   9,330   9,461   10,312   11,432
January 26, 1856; organized October 21, 1868. William Orlando Butler.*

Butler   **Ohio**
Hamilton   467 sq. mi.
332,807   291,479   258,787   226,207   199,076   147,203
March 24, 1803. Richard Butler.*

Butler   **Pennsylvania**
Butler   789 sq. mi.
174,083   152,013   142,912   127,941   114,639   97,320
March 12, 1800. Richard Butler.*

Butte   **California**
Oroville   1,639 sq. mi.
203,171   182,120   143,851   101,969   82,030   64,930
February 18, 1850, Sutter Buttes. Sutter Buttes is a landmark in Sacramento Valley. From French word for "isolated hill" or "mound."

Butte   **Idaho**
Arco   2,233 sq. mi.
2,899   2,918   3,342   2,925   3,498   2,722
February 6, 1917. Uncertain. (1) Buttes in general in the area. (2) Three Buttes, a local landmark; from French *trios buttes*. (3) Big Butte; largest of the Three Buttes. (See Butte, California.)

Butte   **South Dakota**
Belle Fourche   2,249 sq. mi.
9,094   7,914   8,372   7,825   8,592   8,161
March 2, 1883. Numerous buttes in the area. (See Butte, California.)

Butts   **Georgia**
Jackson   187 sq. mi.
19,522   15,326   13,665   10,560   8,976   9,079
December 24, 1825. Samuel Butts (1777–1814). Private in Georgia Regiment 1812, elected captain; killed at battle of Chillabee, January 27, 1814.

C

Cabarrus   **North Carolina**
Concord   364 sq. mi.
131,063   98,935   85,895   74,629   68,137   63,783
November 15, 1792 (session). Stephen Cabarrus (1754–1808). North Carolina House of Commons 1784–1805; first board of trustees, University of North Carolina 1789.

Cabell   **West Virginia**
Huntington   282 sq. mi.
96,784   96,827   106,835   106,918   108,202   108,035
January 2, 1809. William H. Cabell (1772–1853). Virginia Assembly 1795 and 1798; governor of Virginia 1805–08; judge of General Court 1808; judge of Circuit Court of Appeals 1811; judge of Court of Appeals 1830.

Cache   **Utah**
Logan   1,165 sq. mi.
91,391   70,183   57,176   42,331   35,788   33,536
January 5, 1856. Cache Valley. From French *cacher,* meaning "to hide"; refers to trappers' practice of hiding pelts for later retrieval.

Caddo   **Louisiana**
Shreveport   882 sq. mi.
252,161   248,253   252,358   230,184   223,859   176,547
January 18, 1838. *Caddo Indians*. Contraction of "Kadohadacho," meaning "real chiefs."

Caddo   **Oklahoma**
Anadarko   1,278 sq. mi.
30,150   29,550   30,905   28,931   28,621   34,913
1901, as County I; organized and name changed November 8, 1902. Caddo Indians.*

Calaveras   **California**
San Andreas   1,020 sq. mi.
40,554   31,998   20,710   13,585   10,289   9,902
February 18, 1850. Calaveras River. Spanish word meaning "skulls"; possibly from skeletal remains found at site of Indian battle.

Calcasieu   **Louisiana**
Lake Charles   1,071 sq. mi.
183,577   168,134   167,223   145,415   145,475   89,635
March 24, 1840. Uncertain. (1) Calcasieu River. (2) French corruption of name of Atakapa chief Crying Eagle, whose battle cry sounded like an eagle's cry. (3) Colloquial French *quelques chaux,* meaning "some cabbages"; refers to cabbage grown by settlers.

Caldwell   **Kentucky**
Princeton   347 sq. mi.
13,060   13,232   13,473   13,179   13,073   13,199
January 13, 1809. *John W. Caldwell* (1757–1804). Major general; served with George Rogers Clark 1786; Kentucky Conventions 1787–89; Kentucky Senate, 1792–93; lieutenant governor of Kentucky 1804; died while presiding over Senate at Frankfort.

Caldwell   **Louisiana**
Columbia   529 sq. mi.
10,560   9,810   10,761   9,354   9,004   10,293
March 6, 1838. *Mathew Caldwell* (1798–1842). Battle of San Jacinto 1836; signer of Texas Declaration of Independence 1836; commanded Texas Rangers 1838–39; one of the commanders against Comanches at Plum Creek 1840; captured by Mexico while scouting for Santa Fe expedition 1841; released 1842.

Caldwell   **Missouri**
Kingston   429 sq. mi.
8,969   8,380   8,660   8,351   8,830   9,929
December 29, 1836. Uncertain. (1) John Caldwell.* (2) Mathew Caldwell.*

Caldwell   **North Carolina**
Lenoir   472 sq. mi.
77,415   70,709   67,746   56,689   49,552   43,352
January 11, 1841. Joseph Caldwell (1773–1835). Professor of mathematics; first president of the University of North Carolina 1804–12 and 1817–35.

Caldwell   **Texas**
Lockhart   546 sq. mi.
32,194   26,392   23,637   21,178   17,222   19,350
March 6, 1848; organized August 7, 1848. Mathew Caldwell.*

Caledonia   **Vermont**
Saint Johnsbury   651 sq. mi.

29,702   27,846   25,808   22,789   22,786   24,049
November 5, 1792; organized 1796. Latin name for Scotland.

Calhoun   **Alabama**
Anniston   608 sq. mi.
112,249   116,034   119,761   103,092   95,878   79,539
December 18, 1832, as Benton; name changed January 29, 1856. *John Caldwell Calhoun* (1782–1850). South Carolina House of Representatives 1808–09; U.S. representative 1811–17; secretary of war 1817–25; vice president of U.S. 1825–32; U.S. senator 1832–43 and 1845–50; secretary of state 1844–45.

Calhoun   **Arkansas**
Hampton   628 sq. mi.
5,744   5,826   6,079   5,573   5,991   7,132
December 6, 1850. John Caldwell Calhoun.*

Calhoun   **Florida**
Blountstown   567 sq. mi.
13,107   11,011   9,294   7,624   7,422   7,922
January 26, 1838. John Caldwell Calhoun.*

Calhoun   **Georgia**
Morgan   280 sq. mi
6,320   5,013   5,717   6,606   7,341   8,578
February 20, 1854. John Caldwell Calhoun.*

Calhoun   **Illinois**
Hardin   254 sq. mi.
5,084   5,322   5,867   5,675   5,933   6,898
January 10, 1825. John Caldwell Calhoun.*

Calhoun   **Iowa**
Rockwell City   570 sq. mi.
11,115   11,508   13,542   14,287   15,923   16,925
January 15, 1851, as Fox; name changed January 22, 1853; organized November 7, 1855. John Caldwell Calhoun.*

Calhoun   **Michigan**
Marshall   709 sq. mi.
137,985   135,982   141,557   141,963   138,858   120,813
October 29, 1829; organized April 1, 1833. John Caldwell Calhoun.*

Calhoun   **Mississippi**
Pittsboro   587 sq. mi.
15,069   14,908   15,664   14,623   15,941   18,369
March 8, 1852. John Caldwell Calhoun.*

Calhoun   **South Carolina**
Saint Matthews   380 sq. mi.
15,185   12,753   12,206   10,780   12,256   14,753
February 14, 1908. John Caldwell Calhoun.*

Calhoun   **Texas**
Port Lavaca   512 sq. mi.
20,647   19,053   19,574   17,831   16,592   9,222
April 4, 1846; organized July 13, 1846. John Caldwell Calhoun.*

Calhoun   **West Virginia**
Grantsville   281 sq. mi.
7,582   7,885   8,250   7,046   7,948   10,259
March 5, 1856. John Caldwell Calhoun.*

Callahan   **Texas**
Baird   899 sq. mi.
12,905   11,859   10,992   8,205   7,929   9,087
February 1, 1858; organized July 3, 1877. James Hughes Callahan (1814–56). Texas Volunteer; captured at Goliad 1836; escaped massacre; captain, Texas Rangers; led three companies against Indians 1855; killed 1856.

Callaway   **Missouri**
Fulton   839 sq. mi.
40,766   32,809   32,252   25,850   23,858   23,316
November 25, 1820. James Callaway (1783–1815). Grandson of Daniel Boone; 2nd lieutenant in company of Rangers 1813; captain, July 1814; killed in battle with Indians March 7, 1815.

Calloway   **Kentucky**
Murray   386 sq. mi.
34,177   30,735   30,031   27,692   20,972   20,147
December 19, 1821; organized 1823. Richard Callaway (c1722–80). Major, French and Indian Wars; constructed fort at Boonesborough; traced Wilderness Road from Clinch River to Boonesborough; represented Kentucky County in Virginia House of Burgesses; killed by Indians while constructing ferry across Kentucky River. (Variation in spelling due to uncorrected clerical error.)

Calumet   **Wisconsin**
Chilton   320 sq. mi.
40,631   34,291   30,867   27,604   22,268   18,840
December 7, 1836; organized 1850. Menominee village. From French word for shepherd's pipe, applied to Indian pipes.

Calvert   **Maryland**
Prince Frederick   215 sq. mi.
74,563   51,372   34,638   20,682   15,826   12,100
July 3, 1654; name changed to Patuxent October 31, 1654; renamed Calvert December 31, 1658. Uncertain; one of three, or all three, members of Calvert family. (1) George Calvert, 1st Baron of Baltimore (c1580–1632); knighted 1617; secretary of state for James I 1619; resigned 1624; raised to Irish peerage as Baron of Baltimore 1625; petitioned James I for a land grant in North America as a haven for Catholics; died before charter was signed for Maryland tract. (2) Cecilius Calvert* (see Cecil, Maryland). (3) Leonard Calvert (1606–47); second son of George Calvert; appointed lieutenant-general (governor) of Maryland by his brother Cecilius 1633–43 and 1644–47.

Camas   **Idaho**
Fairfield   1,075 sq. mi.
991   727   818   728   917   1,079
February 6, 1917. Big Camas Prairie. From Chinook word *kamass,* meaning "sweet"; name of root prized by Indians for food.

Cambria   **Pennsylvania**
Ebensburg   688 sq. mi.
152,598   163,029   183,263   186,785   203,283   209,541
March 26, 1804; organized 1807. Cambria Township. Medieval name for Wales.

Camden   **Georgia**
Woodbine   630 sq. mi.
43,664   30,167   13,371   11,334   9,975   7,322
February 5, 1777. *Charles Pratt, Earl of Camden* (1714–94). British attorney general 1757; chief justice, Court of Common Pleas, 1761–66; House of Lords 1766; opposed Stamp Act and tax on American colonies as unconstitutional; lord chancellor 1766–60; lord president of council 1782 and 1784–94.

Camden   **Missouri**
Camdenton   655 sq. mi.

| 37,051 | 27,495 | 20,017 | 13,315 | 9,116 | 7,861 |

January 29, 1841, as Kinderhook; name changed February 23, 1843. Camden County, North Carolina.

Camden   **New Jersey**
Camden   222 sq. mi.

| 508,932 | 502,824 | 471,650 | 456,291 | 392,035 | 300,743 |

March 13, 1844. Village of Camden. Named for Charles Pratt, Earl of Camden.*

Camden   **North Carolina**
Camden   241 sq. mi.

| 6,885 | 5,904 | 5,829 | 5,453 | 5,598 | 5,223 |

April 8, 1777. Charles Pratt, Earl of Camden.*

Cameron   **Louisiana**
Cameron   1,313 sq. mi.

| 9,991 | 9,260 | 9,336 | 8,194 | 6,909 | 6,244 |

March 15, 1870. *Simon Cameron* (1799–1889). U.S. senator from Pennsylvania 1845–49, 1857–61, and 1867–77; U.S. secretary of war 1861–62; organized Union forces 1862; U.S. minister to Russia 1862.

Cameron   **Pennsylvania**
Emporium   397 sq. mi.

| 5,974 | 5,913 | 6,674 | 7,096 | 7,586 | 7,023 |

March 29, 1860. Simon Cameron.*

Cameron   **Texas**
Brownsville   906 sq. mi.

| 335,227 | 260,120 | 209,727 | 140,368 | 151,098 | 125,170 |

February 12, 1848; organized August 7, 1858. Ewen Cameron (1811–43). Kentucky Volunteer in Texas Revolution; leader in Mier expedition to Mexico 1842; captured 1842; led prison escape but recaptured 1843; shot by order of Santa Anna April 25, 1843.

Camp   **Texas**
Pittsburg   198 sq. mi.

| 11,549 | 9,904 | 9,275 | 8,005 | 7,849 | 8,740 |

April 6, 1874; organized June 20, 1874. John Lafayette Camp (1828–91). Captain, Upshur County Militia 1861; colonel, 14th Texas Regulars, Confederate army 1861; twice wounded and captured; elected U.S. representative but was refused a seat 1866; Texas Senate, 1874; district judge, 1878.

Campbell   **Kentucky**
Newport   152 sq. mi.

| 88,616 | 83,866 | 83,317 | 88,501 | 86,803 | 76,196 |

December 17, 1794. John Campbell (c1735–1799). Served under General Braddock in French and Indian Wars; fur trader; taken prisoner by British and held at Montreal during Revolutionary War; represented Jefferson County (Kentucky) in Virginia legislature; Kentucky Constitutional Convention 1792; Kentucky legislature; died on floor of Kentucky Senate.

Campbell   **South Dakota**
Mound City   736 sq. mi.

| 1,782 | 1,965 | 2,243 | 2,866 | 3,531 | 4,046 |

January 8, 1873; organized April 17, 1884. Norman B. Campbell (?–?). Dakota territorial legislature 1872–73.

Campbell   **Tennessee**
Jacksboro   480 sq. mi.

| 39,854 | 35,079 | 34,923 | 26,045 | 27,936 | 34,369 |

September 11, 1806. Uncertain. (1) Arthur Campbell (c1742–1811); volunteered for militia at age 15; captured by Indians and taken to Great Lakes area; commander of frontier militia units during Revolutionary War; leader of State of Franklin movement. (2) George Washington Campbell (1769–1848); U.S. representative from Tennessee 1803–09; judge, Tennessee Supreme Court of Errors and Appeals, 1809–11; U.S. senator 1811–14 and 1815–18; U.S. secretary of treasury 1814; U.S. minister to Russia 1818–21.

Campbell   **Virginia**
Rustberg   504 sq. mi.
51,078   47,572   45,424   43,319   32,958   28,877
November 5, 1781 (session). William Campbell (1745–81). Captain, 1st Virginia Regiment, 1775; resigned 1776; colonel, Virginia Militia, 1777–80; battle of Kings Mountain October 7, 1780; battle of Guilford Courthouse March 15, 1781; died of illness during early stages of siege of Yorktown.

Campbell   **Wyoming**
Gillette   4,797 sq. mi.
33,698   29,370   24,367   12,957   5,861   4,839
February 13, 1911. Uncertain; either John Campbell alone or both John and Robert Campbell. (1) John Allen Campbell (1835–80); 2nd lieutenant, Volunteers 1861; major 1862; assistant adjutant general 1862; brevet colonel, Volunteers 1865; brevet brigadier general 1865; mustered out 1866; 2nd lieutenant, Regular Army; 1867; brevet 1st lieutenant 1867; assistant secretary of war, resigned, 1869; first territorial governor of Wyoming 1896–75. (2) Robert Campbell (1804–79); trapper in northern Rockies; established trading post which became Fort Laramie.

Canadian   **Oklahoma**
El Reno   900 sq. mi.
87,697   74,409   56,452   32,245   24,727   25,644
1889. North and South Canadian Rivers. Uncertain. (1) From French Canadian trappers. (2) From Spanish *cañada*, meaning "canyon." (3) From Caddoan name meaning "red river."

Candler   **Georgia**
Metter   247 sq. mi.
9,577   7,744   7,518   6,412   6,672   8,063
July 17, 1914. Allen Daniel Candler (1834–1910). Private, Company H, 34th Georgia Regiment, 1861; captain 1863; lieutenant colonel, 4th Georgia Reserves 1864; colonel 1864; wounded at Kennesaw Mountain; lost eye at Jonesboro; vice president, Monroe Female College 1865–66; principal, Clayton High School 1867–69; president of Bailey Institute 1870–71; mayor of Jonesboro, Tennessee, 1866; mayor of Gainesville, Georgia, 1872; Georgia House of Representatives 1873–77; Georgia Senate 1878–79; U.S. representative 1883–91; Georgia secretary of state 1894–98; governor of Georgia 1899–1902.

Cannon   **Tennessee**
Woodbury   266 sq. mi.
12,826   10,467   10,234   8,467   8,537   9,174
January 31, 1836. Newton Cannon (1781–1842). Tennessee legislature 1811; private in Creek War, advanced to captain and colonel of Tennessee mounted rifles, 1813; U.S. representative 1814–17 and 1819–23; negotiated treaty with Chickasaws 1819; governor of Tennessee 1836–39.

Canyon   **Idaho**
Caldwell   590 sq. mi.
131,441   90,076   83,756   61,288   57,662   53,597
March 7, 1891. Uncertain. (1) Canyon of the Boise River. (2) Snake River Canyon.

Cape Girardeau   **Missouri**
Jackson   579 sq. mi.
68,693   61,633   58,837   49,350   42,020   38,397
October 1, 1812. Spanish district of Cape Girardeau. Name of promontory on Mississippi River north of town of Cape Girardeau. Named for Jean B. Girardot (?–?); French soldier stationed at Kaskaskia, Illinois, 1704–20; established trading post at Cape Girardeau 1733; resigned French military 1735.

Cape May   **New Jersey**
Cape May Court House   255 sq. mi.
102,326   95,089   82,266   59,554   48,555   37,131
November 12, 1692. Cape May. Named by Cornelius Jacobsen Mey (?–?); navigator on exploration of North America 1614; led Dutch West India Company expedition, explored Delaware River, 1623; first director general of Dutch West India Company's New Netherlands (New York) 1624–25.

Carbon   **Montana**
Red Lodge   2,048 sq. mi.
9,552   8,080   8,099   7,080   8,317   10,241
March 4, 1895. Local coal deposits.

Carbon   **Pennsylvania**
Jim Thorpe   381 sq. mi.
58,802   56,846   53,285   50,573   52,889   57,558
March 13, 1843. Local coal deposits.

Carbon   **Utah**
Price   1,478 sq. mi.
20,422   20,228   22,179   15,647   21,135   24,901
March 8, 1894. Local coal deposits.

Carbon   **Wyoming**
Rawlins   7,896 sq. mi.
15,639   16,659   21,896   13,354   14,937   15,742
December 16, 1868. Local coal deposits.

Caribou   **Idaho**
Soda Springs   1,766 sq. mi.
7,304   6,963   8,695   6,534   5,976   5,576
February 11, 1919. Caribou Mountains. Named for Caribou City, which flourished near site of gold discovery by prospector Cariboo Fairchild (or Fairbanks) who arrived in Idaho from Caribou, British Columbia, 1860.

Carlisle   **Kentucky**
Bardwell   192 sq. mi.
5,351   5,238   5,487   5,354   5,608   6,206
April 3, 1886. John Griffin Carlisle (1835–1910). Kentucky House of Representatives 1859–61; Kentucky Senate 1866–71; lieutenant governor of Kentucky 1871–75; U.S. representative 1877–93; Speaker of the House 1883–89; U.S. senator 1890–93; secretary of the treasury 1893–97.

Carlton   **Minnesota**
Carlton   860 sq. mi.
31,671   29,259   29,936   28,072   27,932   24,584
May 23, 1857; organized February 18, 1870. Reuben B. Carlton (1812–63). Indian agent at Fond du Lac; Minnesota Senate 1858; promoted transportation improvements to attract settlers.

Caroline   **Maryland**
Denton   320 sq. mi.
29,772   27,035   23,143   19,781   19,462   18,234
December 5, 1773; organized 1774. Caroline Calvert Eden (c1734–84). Second sister of Frederick Calvert, the last Lord Baltimore; wife of Robert Eden, colonial governor of Maryland; Eden family left for England 1776.

Caroline   **Virginia**
Bowling Green   533 sq. mi.
22,121   19,217   17,904   13,925   12,725   12,471

February 1, 1727 (session). Princess Wilhelmina Caroline of Anspach (1683–1737). Daughter of John Frederick, Margrave of Brandenburg-Anspach; married George Augustus, Prince of Hanover; became Princess of Wales when father-in-law became George I of England 1714; Queen of England when husband became George II 1727.

Carroll   **Arkansas**
Berryville   630 sq. mi.

| 25,357 | 18,654 | 16,203 | 12,301 | 11,284 | 13,244 |

November 1, 1833. *Charles Carroll* (1737–1832). Continental commissioner to Canada 1776; Continental Congress 1776–78; signer of Declaration of Independence 1776; Maryland Senate 1777–1800; U.S. senator 1789–92; last surviving signer of Declaration of Independence.

Carroll   **Georgia**
Carrollton   499 sq. mi.

| 87,268 | 71,422 | 56,346 | 45,404 | 36,451 | 34,112 |

December 11, 1826. Charles Carroll.*

Carroll   **Illinois**
Mount Carroll   444 sq. mi.

| 16,674 | 16,805 | 18,779 | 19,276 | 19,507 | 18,976 |

February 22, 1839. Charles Carroll.*

Carroll   **Indiana**
Delphi   372 sq. mi.

| 20,165 | 18,809 | 19,722 | 17,734 | 16,934 | 16,010 |

January 7, 1828; effective May 1, 1828. Charles Carroll.*

Carroll   **Iowa**
Carroll   569 sq. mi.

| 21,421 | 21,423 | 22,951 | 22,912 | 23,431 | 23,065 |

January 15, 1851; organized August 17, 1855. Charles Carroll.*

Carroll   **Kentucky**
Carrollton   130 sq. mi.

| 10,155 | 9,292 | 9,270 | 8,523 | 7,978 | 8,517 |

February 9, 1838. Charles Carroll.*

Carroll   **Maryland**
Westminster   449 sq. mi.

| 150,897 | 123,372 | 96,356 | 69,006 | 52,785 | 44,907 |

January 19, 1837. Charles Carroll.*

Carroll   **Mississippi**
Carrollton   628 sq. mi.

| 10,769 | 9,237 | 9,776 | 9,397 | 11,177 | 15, 499 |

December 23, 1833. Charles Carroll.*

Carroll   **Missouri**
Carrollton   695 sq. mi.

| 10,285 | 10,748 | 12,131 | 12,565 | 13,847 | 15,589 |

January 2, 1833. Charles Carroll.*

Carroll   **New Hampshire**
Ossipee   934 sq. mi.

| 43,666 | 35,410 | 27,931 | 18,548 | 15,829 | 15,868 |

December 22, 1840. Charles Carroll.*

Carroll	**Ohio**				
Carrollton	395 sq. mi.				
28,836	26,521	25,598	21,579	20,857	19,039

December 25, 1832. Charles Carroll.*

Carroll	**Tennessee**				
Huntingdon	599 sq. mi.				
29,475	27,514	28,285	25,741	23,476	26,553

November 7, 1821. William Carroll (1788–1844). General under Andrew Jackson at Battle of New Orleans 1815; governor of Tennessee 1821–27 and 1829–35.

Carroll	**Virginia**				
Hillsville	476 sq. mi.				
29,245	26,594	27,270	23,092	23,178	26,695

January 17, 1842. Charles Carroll.*

Carson	**Texas**				
Panhandle	923 sq. mi.				
6,516	6,576	6,672	6,358	7,781	6,852

August 21, 1876; organized June 26, 1888. Samuel Price Carson (1798–1838). North Carolina Senate 1822–24; U.S. representative 1825–33; North Carolina Senate 1834; North Carolina Constitutional Convention 1835; signer, Texas Declaration of Independence 1836; Texas Constitutional Convention 1836; Texas secretary of state 1836–38; commissioner to Washington to intercede for Texas.

Carson City	**Nevada**				
(Independent City)	143 sq. mi.				
52,457	40,443	32,022	15,468	8,063[a]	4,172[a]

November 25, 1861, as Ormsby County; consolidated with Carson City 1969. *Christopher "Kit" Carson (1809–68).* Guide on Fremont's expeditions 1842–43 and 1845; Indian agent 1853–61; served in southwest against Indians during Civil War; brevet brigadier general 1865. [(a) Ormsby County]

Carter	**Kentucky**				
Grayson	411 sq. mi.				
26,889	24,340	25,060	19,850	20,817	22,559

February 9, 1838. William G. Carter (?–1850). Kentucky Senate 1834–38; large landowner; moved to Arkansas; died of cholera on visit to Lexington, Kentucky.

Carter	**Missouri**				
Van Buren	508 sq. mi.				
5,941	5,515	5,428	3,878	3,973	4,777

March 10, 1859. Zimri A. Carter (1794–1870). Pioneer; first settler in county; judge of county court.

Carter	**Montana**				
Ekalaka	3,340 sq. mi.				
1,360	1,503	1,799	1,956	2,493	2,798

February 22, 1917. Thomas Henry Carter (1854–1911). Congressional delegate from Montana Territory 1889; U.S. representative 1889–91; commissioner of General Land Office 1891–93; U.S. senator 1895–1901 and 1905–11.

Carter	**Oklahoma**				
Ardmore	824 sq. mi.				
45,621	42,919	43,610	37,349	39,040	36,455

July 16, 1907. Uncertain. (1) Benjamin Wisner Carter (1837–94); Cherokee Indian; superintendent of Chickasaw Male Academy; captain in Confederate army; Oklahoma territorial judge. (2) Charles David Carter (1868–1929); son of Benjamin Carter; mineral trustee for Choctaw and Chickasaw nations; U.S. representative 1907–27. (3) Carter family, including Benjamin and Charles as well as Nathaniel G. Carter (c1770–?) and David Carter (1812–67), grandfather and father of Benjamin, respectively.

Carter   **Tennessee**
Elizabethton   341 sq. mi.
56,742   51,505   50,205   42,575   41,578   42,432
April 9, 1796. Landon Carter (1760–1800). Active in Watauga Settlement and Revolutionary War; North Carolina legislature; advocate of the State of Franklin.

Carteret   **North Carolina**
Beaufort   520 sq. mi.
59,383   52,556   41,092   31,603   30,940   23,059
1722. *John Carteret, Earl of Granville* (1690–1763). House of Lords 1711; English ambassador to Sweden 1719; lord lieutenant of Ireland 1724–30; opposed Sir Robert Walpole in House of Commons; one of the lords proprietors of Carolina; refused to sell his share to the king, 1728; became Earl of Granville 1744; lord president of Council 1751–63.

Carver   **Minnesota**
Chaska   357 sq. mi.
70,205   47,915   37,046   28,310   21,358   18,155
February 20, 1855. Jonathon Carver (1732–80). Military leader; captain in French and Indian War 1755; wintered in Minnesota 1766–67; signed Indian treaty 1767; moved to England and wrote descriptions of his explorations of upper Mississippi River.

Cascade   **Montana**
Great Falls   2,698 sq. mi.
80,357   77,691   80,696   81,804   73,418   53,027
September 12, 1887. Great Falls of the Missouri River.

Casey   **Kentucky**
Liberty   446 sq. mi.
15,447   14,211   14,818   12,930   14,327   17,446
November 14, 1806. William Casey (1754–1816). Veteran of Revolutionary War; moved to Kentucky from Virginia 1780; lieutenant colonel of militia 1792; Kentucky legislature; 2nd Kentucky Constitutional Convention 1799.

Cass   **Illinois**
Virginia   376 sq. mi.
13,695   13,437   15,084   14,219   14,539   15,097
March 3, 1837. *Lewis Cass* (1782–1866). Ohio House of Representatives 1806; U.S. marshal, Ohio District 1807–12; colonel, 27th Regiment, U.S. Infantry 1813; brigadier general 1813; military and civil governor of Michigan Territory 1813–30; U.S. secretary of war 1831–36; U.S. minister to France 1836–42; U.S. senator 1845–48 and 1849–57; unsuccessful Democratic candidate for president, lost to Zachary Taylor, 1848; U.S. secretary of state 1857–60.

Cass   **Indiana**
Logansport   413 sq. mi.
40,930   38,413   40,936   40,456   40,931   38,793
December 18, 1828; effective April 14, 1829. Lewis Cass.*

Cass   **Iowa**
Atlantic   564 sq. mi.
14,684   15,128   16,932   17,007   17,919   18,532
January 15, 1851; organized March 7, 1853. Lewis Cass.*

Cass   **Michigan**
Cassopolis   492 sq. mi.
51,104   49,477   49,499   43,312   36,932   28,185
October 29, 1829. Lewis Cass.*

Cass   **Minnesota**
Walker   2,018 sq. mi.

27,150 21,791 21,050 17,323 16,720 19,468
March 31, 1851; organized May 4, 1872; deorganized 1876; reorganized 1897. Lewis Cass.*

Cass   **Missouri**
Harrisonville   699 sq. mi.
82,092 63,808 51,029 39,448 29,702 19,325
March 3, 1835, as Van Buren; name changed February 19, 1849. Lewis Cass.*

Cass   **Nebraska**
Plattsmouth   559 sq. mi.
24,334 21,318 20,297 18,076 17,281 16,361
November 3, 1854; organized 1857. Lewis Cass.*

Cass   **North Dakota**
Fargo   1,765 sq. mi.
123,138 102,874 88,247 73,653 66,947 58,877
January 4, 1873; organized October 27, 1873. George W. Cass (1810–88). West Point 1832; assisted building of Cumberland Road 1832–36; president of Northern Pacific Railroad when railroad reached Dakota Territory 1873.

Cass   **Texas**
Linden   937 sq. mi.
30,438 29,982 29,430 24,133 23,496 26,732
April 25, 1846, as Cass; organized July 13, 1846; name changed to Davis, December 17, 1861; renamed Cass, May 16, 1871. Lewis Cass.*

Cassia   **Idaho**
Burley   2,566 sq. mi.
21,416 19,532 19,427 17,017 16,121 14,629
February 20, 1879. Cassia Creek. Named for cassia plant (wild senna), a variety of cinnamon.

Castro   **Texas**
Dimmitt   898 sq. mi.
8,285 9,070 10,556 10,394 8,923 5,417
August 21, 1876; organized 1891. Henri Castro (1786–1865). Republic of Texas counsel general in Paris; established Castro's Colony, a settlement of French immigrants, 1842; founded other French colonies in Texas 1844–47.

Caswell   **North Carolina**
Yanceyville   425 sq. mi.
23,501 20,693 20,705 19,055 19,912 20,870
April 8, 1777. Richard Caswell (1729–89). North Carolina Assembly 1769–71; delegate, Continental Congress 1774–76; brigadier general 1776; Halifax Convention 1776; governor of North Carolina 1775–79 and 1784–87; battle of Camden 1780; North Carolina Senate 1788.

Catahoula   **Louisiana**
Harrisonburg   704 sq. mi.
10,920 11,065 12,287 11,769 11,421 11,834
March 23, 1808. Catahoula Lake. Named for Catahoula Indians. Meaning of name is uncertain; most suggestions refer to lake or water.

Catawba   **North Carolina**
Newton   400 sq. mi.
141,685 118,412 105,208 90,873 73,191 61,794
December 12, 1842. Uncertain. (1) Catawba Indians; first encountered by Europeans in western South Carolina; sided with colonists in Revolutionary War; moved to North Carolina 1840; uncertain origin of name. (2) Catawba River; named for Catawba Indians.

Catoosa   **Georgia**
Ringgold   162 sq. mi.
53,282   42,464   36,991   28,271   21,101   15,146
December 5, 1853. Catoosa Springs. Cherokee *gatusi,* meaning "hill" or "small mountain."

Catron   **New Mexico**
Reserve   6,928 sq. mi.
3,543   2,563   2,720   2,198   2,773   3,533
February 25, 1921. Thomas Benton Catron (1840–1921). Confederate army 1860–64; district attorney, 3rd District, New Mexico, 1866–68; attorney general of New Mexico 1869; U.S. attorney 1870; Territorial Council 1884, 1888, 1890, 1905, and 1909; congressional delegate from New Mexico Territory 1895–97; U.S. senator 1912–17.

Cattaraugus   **New York**
Little Valley   1,310 sq. mi.
83,955   84,234   85,697   81,666   80,187   77,901
March 11, 1808; organized 1817. Cattaraugus Creek. Seneca Indian word meaning "bad smelling banks"; refers to gas deposits in area.

Cavalier   **North Dakota**
Langdon   1,488 sq. mi.
4,831   6,064   7,636   8,213   10,064   11,840
January 4, 1873; organized July 8, 1884. Charles Turner Cavaleer (1818–1902). Minnesota territorial librarian 1849; collector of customs for Minnesota Territory at Pembina 1851; fur trader; postmaster, Pembina, Dakota Territory, 1864–84; mayor of Pembina; believed to be first settler in what is now North Dakota. (Surname spelled both ways, usually with double "e.")

Cayuga   **New York**
Auburn   693 sq. mi.
81,963   82,313   79,894   77,439   73,942   70,136
March 8, 1799. Cayuga Indians. Members of Iroquois League. Name may mean "where they haul boats out" or "from the water to the shore."

Cecil   **Maryland**
Elkton   348 sq. mi.
85,951   71,347   60,430   53,291   48,408   33,356
December 31, 1674. *Cecilius Calvert* (1605–75). 2nd Lord Baltimore; son of George Calvert; received grant originally requested by his father from James I, following George's death 1632; never visited Maryland tract but managed it from England; father of Charles Calvert* (see Charles, Maryland).

Cedar   **Iowa**
Tipton   580 sq. mi.
18,187   17,381   18,635   17,655   17,791   16,910
December 21, 1837. Cedar River. Also called Red Cedar River for trees in area.

Cedar   **Missouri**
Stockton   476 sq. mi.
13,733   12,093   11,894   9,424   9,185   10,663
February 14, 1845. Cedar Creek. Descriptive of trees in area.

Cedar   **Nebraska**
Hartington   740 sq. mi.
9,615   10,131   11,375   12,192   13,368   13,843
February 12, 1857. Descriptive of trees in area.

Centre   **Pennsylvania**
Bellefonte   1,108 sq. mi.

135,758   123,786   112,760   99,267   78,580   65,922

February 13, 1800. Descriptive of county's location at geographical center of Pennsylvania.

Cerro Gordo   Iowa
Mason City   568 sq. mi.
46,447   46,733   48,458   49,335   49,894   46,053

January 15, 1851; organized December 29, 1855. Battle of Cerro Gordo. U.S. victory in Mexican War, April 17–18, 1847.

Chaffee   Colorado
Salida   1,013 sq. mi.
16,242   12,684   13,227   10,162   8,298   7,168

November 1, 1861, as Lake; name changed February 10, 1879. Jerome Bunty Chaffee (1825–86). One of the founders of Denver; Colorado Territory House of Representatives 1861–63, Speaker, 1863; president, First National Bank of Denver 1865–80; congressional delegate from Colorado 1871–75; U.S. senator 1876–79.

Chambers   Alabama
Lafayette   597 sq. mi.
36,583   36,876   39,191   36,356   37,828   39,528

December 18, 1832. Henry H. Chambers (1790–1826). Physician; surgeon on staff of General Andrew Jackson; Alabama Constitutional Convention 1819; Alabama House of Representatives 1820; U.S. senator 1825–26.

Chambers   Texas
Anahuac   599 sq. mi.
26,031   20,088   18,538   12,187   10,379   7,871

February 12, 1858; organized August 2, 1858. Thomas Jefferson Chambers (1802–65). Surveyor general of Texas 1829; state attorney of Coahuila and Texas 1834; major general of reserves 1836; Secession Convention 1861; unsuccessful attempt to raise a company for Confederate army 1862; volunteer in Hood's Texas Brigade 1862–63; assassinated March 15, 1865.

Champaign   Illinois
Urbana   997 sq. mi.
179,669   173,025   166,392   163,281   132,436   106,100

February 20, 1833. Champaign County, Ohio.

Champaign   Ohio
Urbana   429 sq. mi.
38,890   36,019   33,649   30,491   29,714   26,793

February 20, 1805; effective March 1, 1805. From French *champagne,* meaning "open, level country."

Chariton   Missouri
Keytesville   756 sq. mi.
8,438   9,202   10,489   11,084   12,720   14,944

November 16, 1820. Uncertain. (1) Chariton River; named for one of two fur trappers: John Chariton (?–?) or John Chorette (?–1795). (2) Town of Chariton; named for Chariton River; flooded 1824; abandoned by last resident 1832.

Charles   Maryland
La Plata   461 sq. mi.
120,546   101,154   72,751   47,678   32,572   23,415

July 10, 1658. *Charles Calvert* (1637–1715), 3rd Lord Baltimore. Son of Cecilius Calvert (see Cecil, Maryland) and Anne Arundell Calvert (see Anne Arundel, Maryland); governor of Maryland 1660–84; retained proprietary rights after Maryland became royal colony 1691.

Charles City   Virginia
Charles City   183 sq. mi.
6,926   6,282   6,692   6,158   5,492   4,676

1634. Charles City. Named for King Charles I (1600–1649); Duke of Albany 1600; Duke of York 1605; Prince of Wales on death of older brother, Henry Frederick, 1612; King of England 1625–49; married Henrietta Maria, daughter of Henri IV of France, May 11, 1625; crowned February 2, 1626; beheaded January 30, 1649.

Charles Mix   **South Dakota**
Lake Andes   1,098 sq. mi.
9,350   9,131   9,680   9,994   11,785   15,558
May 8, 1862; deorganized 1864; reorganized 1879. Charles H. Mix (1833–1909). Moved to Dakota Territory 1852; Indian agent 1858; 1st lieutenant, 1st Minnesota Cavalry; commandant of Fort Abercrombie in northeast Dakota Territory 1864.

Charleston   **South Carolina**
Charleston   919 sq. mi.
309,969   295,039   276,974   247,650   216,382   164,856
1769. City of Charleston. Named for *King Charles II* (1630–85); Prince of Wales from birth; King of England 1660–85; crowned April 23, 1661, following death of Cromwell; married Katherine Braganza, Infanta of Portugal, May 21, 1662; known as the "Merry Monarch."

Charlevoix   **Michigan**
Charlevoix   417 sq. mi.
26,090   21,468   19,907   16,541   13,421   13,475
April 1, 1840, as Reshkauko; name changed March 8, 1843; abolished January 29, 1853; recreated April 1, 1869. Pierre Francois Xavier de Charlevoix (1682–1761). Jesuit historian and explorer; traveled through the Great Lakes and Illinois and Mississippi Rivers to New Orleans 1720–22.

Charlotte   **Florida**
Port Charlotte   694 sq. mi.
141,627   110,975   58,460   27,559   12,594   4,286
April 23, 1921. Charlotte Harbor. Named for *Charlotte Sophia of Mecklenburg-Strelitz* (1744–1818); married King George III 1761; mother of Kings George IV and William IV.

Charlotte   **Virginia**
Charlotte Court House   475 sq. mi.
12,472   11,688   12,266   11,551   13,368   14,057
May 26, 1764 (session). Charlotte Sophia of Mecklenburg-Strelitz.*

Charlottesville   **Virginia**
(Independent City)   10 sq. mi.
45,049   40,341   39,916   38,880   29,427   25,969
1888. Charlotte Sophia of Mecklenburg-Strelitz.* (Associated county: Albemarle.)

Charlton   **Georgia**
Folkston   781 sq. mi.
10,282   8,496   7,343   5,680   5,313   4,821
February 18, 1854. Uncertain. (1) Robert Milledge Charlton (1807–54); Georgia legislature 1829; U.S. district attorney 1830; judge of the Superior Court for the Eastern District of Georgia 1832; U.S. senator 1851–52; mayor of Savannah. (2) Thomas U. P. Charlton (1779–1835); Georgia legislature 1800; attorney general of Georgia; mayor of Savannah.

Chase   **Kansas**
Cottonwood Falls   776 sq. mi.
3,030   3,021   3,309   3,408   3,921   4,831
February 11, 1859. Salmon Portland Chase (1808–73). Cincinnati City Council 1840; U.S. senator 1849–53 and two days in 1861; governor of Ohio 1855–59; U.S. secretary of the treasury 1861–64; Chief Justice of U.S. 1864–73; presided over President Johnson's impeachment trial 1868.

Chase   **Nebraska**
Imperial   895 sq. mi.

4,068   4,381   4,758   4,129   4,317   5,176
February 27, 1873; organized April 24, 1886. Champion S. Chase (1820–98). Paymaster in Union army; Nebraska attorney general 1867–69; mayor of Omaha 1874–75, 1879–80, and 1883–84; member, first board of regents, University of Nebraska.

Chatham   **Georgia**
Savannah   438 sq. mi.
232,048   216,935   202,226   187,767   188,299   151,481
February 5, 1777. *William Pitt, Earl of Chatham* (1708–78). English statesman; entered Parliament 1735; secretary of state 1756; strengthened British fleet during Seven Years' War 1756–63; opposed British policies in American colonies; prime minister 1766–68.

Chatham   **North Carolina**
Pittsboro   683 sq. mi.
49,329   38,759   33,415   29,554   26,785   25,392
December 5, 1770 (session). William Pitt, Earl of Chatham.*

Chattahoochee   **Georgia**
Cusseta   249 sq. mi.
14,882   16,934   21,732   25,813   13,011   12,149
February 13, 1854. Chattahoochee River. From Indian *chatto hoche,* meaning "painted stone"; after red and pink stones along river.

Chattooga   **Georgia**
Summerville   313 sq. mi.
25,470   22,242   21,856   20,541   19,954   21,197
December 28, 1838. Chattooga River. Possible Cherokee borrowing of Creek *tsatu gi*, *chato-algi*, or *chato-agi,* meaning "full of rocks."

Chautauqua   **Kansas**
Sedan   642 sq. mi.
4,359   4,407   5,016   4,642   5,956   7,376
March 3, 1875; effective June 1, 1875. Chautauqua County, New York.

Chautauqua   **New York**
Mayville   1,062 sq. mi.
139,750   141,895   146,925   147,305   145,377   135,189
March 11, 1808; organized 1811. Chautauqua Lake. Contraction of Seneca phrase of unknown origin; most suggestions pertain to lakes or fish.

Chaves   **New Mexico**
Roswell   6,071 sq. mi.
61,382   57,849   51,103   43,335   57,649   40,605
February 25, 1889. José F. Chaves (1833–1904). New Mexico territorial legislature; lieutenant colonel in Union army; New Mexico Territory congressional delegate; murdered 1904.

Cheatham   **Tennessee**
Ashland City   303 sq. mi.
35,912   27,140   21,616   13,199   9,428   9,167
February 28, 1856. Edwin Saunders Cheatham (1818–78). President of Louisville & Nashville Railroad; Tennessee legislature under Union and Confederacy; Speaker of Tennessee Senate during Confederacy.

Cheboygan   **Michigan**
Cheboygan   716 sq. mi.
26,448   21,398   20,649   16,573   14,550   13,731
April 1, 1840; organized January 29, 1853. Uncertain. *He* is Ojibwa for "big" and *boygan* means "pipe"; may refer to a geographic feature or a specific body of water.

Chelan   **Washington**
Wenatchee   2,921 sq. mi.
66,616   52,250   45,061   41,355   40,744   39,301
March 13, 1899. Lake Chelan. Indian word for "deep water."

Chemung   **New York**
Elmira   408 sq. mi.
91,070   95,195   97,656   101,537   98,706   86,827
March 29, 1836. Chemung River. Delaware village and word meaning "big horn."

Chenango   **New York**
Norwich   894 sq. mi.
51,401   51,768   49,344   46,368   43,243   39,138
March 15, 1798. Uncertain. (1) Chenango River. (2) Chenango Lake. (3) Onondaga village on Chenango River. Onondaga word meaning "large bull-thistle."

Cherokee   **Alabama**
Centre   553 sq. mi.
23,988   19,543   18,760   15,606   16,303   17,634
January 9, 1836. *Cherokee Indians*. Cherokee word *chera,* meaning "fire" or Chickasaw word, *chiluk-ki,* for "cave people."

Cherokee   **Georgia**
Canton   424 sq. mi.
141,903   90,204   51,699   31,059   23,001   20,750
December 26, 1831. Cherokee Indians.*

Cherokee   **Iowa**
Cherokee   577 sq. mi.
13,035   14,098   16,238   17,269   18,598   19,052
January 15, 1851; organized October 2, 1858. Cherokee Indians.*

Cherokee   **Kansas**
Columbus   587 sq. mi.
22,605   21,374   22,304   21,549   22,279   25,144
August 30, 1855, as McGee; name changed and county organized February 18, 1860. Cherokee Indians.*

Cherokee   **North Carolina**
Murphy   455 sq. mi.
24,298   20,170   18,933   16,330   16,335   18,294
January 4, 1839. Cherokee Indians.*

Cherokee   **Oklahoma**
Tahlequah   751 sq. mi.
42,521   34,049   30,684   23,174   17,762   18,989
July 16, 1907. Cherokee Indians.*

Cherokee   **South Carolina**
Gaffney   393 sq. mi.
52,537   44,506   40,983   36,791   35,205   34,992
February 25, 1897. Cherokee Indians.*

Cherokee   **Texas**
Rusk   1,052 sq. mi.
46,659   41,049   38,127   32,008   33,120   38,694
April 11, 1846; organized July 13, 1846. Cherokee Indians.*

Cherry   **Nebraska**
Valentine   5,961 sq. mi.

| 6,148 | 6,307 | 6,758 | 6,846 | 8,218 | 8,397 |

February 23, 1883; organized April 4, 1883. Samuel A. Cherry (1850–81). Graduate of West Point; lieutenant, 5th Cavalry; killed near Rock Creek, Dakota Territory.

Chesapeake   **Virginia**
(Independent City)   341 sq. mi.

| 199,184 | 151,976 | 114,486 | 89,580 | 73,647[a] | 110,371[b] |

1691 as Norfolk; consolidation of city of South Norfolk and Norfolk County into independent city of Chesapeake January 1, 1963. Chesapeake Bay. Indian name meaning "mother of waters" or "great salt bay"; corrupted from *tschiswapeki* or *k'tschis-chwapeki,* compounded from *kitschi,* meaning "highly salted" and *peek,* meaning "body of water." [(a) Norfolk County (51,612) and city of South Norfolk (22,035). (b) Norfolk County (99,937) and city of South Norfolk (10,434).]

Cheshire   **New Hampshire**
Keene   707 sq. mi.

| 73,825 | 70,121 | 62,116 | 52,364 | 43,342 | 38,811 |

April 29, 1769. Cheshire County, England.

Chester   **Pennsylvania**
West Chester   756 sq. mi.

| 433,501 | 379,396 | 316,660 | 278,311 | 210,608 | 159,141 |

March 10, 1682. City of Chester, England.

Chester   **South Carolina**
Chester   581 sq. mi.

| 34,068 | 32,170 | 30,148 | 29,811 | 30,888 | 32,597 |

March 12, 1785. Chester County, Pennsylvania.

Chester   **Tennessee**
Henderson   289 sq. mi.

| 15,540 | 12,819 | 12,727 | 9,927 | 9,569 | 11,149 |

March 4, 1879. Robert I. Chester (1793–1892). Postmaster of Jackson, Tennessee; quartermaster, 4th Tennessee Regiment, War of 1812; Tennessee legislature; U.S. marshal.

Chesterfield   **South Carolina**
Chesterfield   799 sq. mi.

| 42,768 | 38,577 | 38,161 | 33,667 | 33,717 | 36,236 |

March 12, 1785. *Philip Dormer Stanhope, 4th Earl of Chesterfield* (1694–1773). Member of Parliament 1716–26; ambassador to The Hague 1728–32 and 1744; lord lieutenant of Ireland 1745–46; wrote letters to his son, published after his death.

Chesterfield   **Virginia**
Chesterfield   426 sq. mi.

| 259,903 | 209,274 | 141,372 | 76,855 | 71,197 | 40,400 |

May 1, 1749; effective May 25, 1749. Earl of Chesterfield.*

Cheyenne   **Colorado**
Cheyenne Wells   1,781 sq. mi.

| 2,231 | 2,397 | 2,153 | 2,396 | 2,789 | 3,453 |

March 25, 1889. *Cheyenne Indians.* Dakota (Sioux) word for "aliens" or "scarred arms"; from Cheyenne warrior practice of scarring left arms.

Cheyenne   **Kansas**
Saint Francis   1,020 sq. mi.

| 3,165 | 3,243 | 3,678 | 4,256 | 4,708 | 5,668 |

March 6, 1873; organized April 1, 1886. Cheyenne Indians.*

Cheyenne   **Nebraska**
Sidney   1,196 sq. mi.
9,830   9,494   10,057   10,778   14,848   12,081
June 22, 1867; organized December 17, 1870. Cheyenne Indians.*

Chickasaw   **Iowa**
New Hampton   505 sq. mi.
13,095   13,295   15,437   14,969   15,034   15,228
January 15, 1851; organized September 12, 1853. *Chickasaw Indians.* Lived in northern Mississippi and western Tennessee; relocated to Indian Territory (Oklahoma) in 1830s.

Chickasaw   **Mississippi**
Houston   502 sq. mi.
19,440   18,085   17,853   16,805   16,891   18,951
February 9, 1836. Chickasaw Indians.*

Chicot   **Arkansas**
Lake Village   644 sq. mi.
14,117   15,713   17,793   18,164   18,990   22,306
October 25, 1823. Point Chicot. Uncertain. (1) French word for "stub." (2) Indian village named Chiska.

Childress   **Texas**
Childress   710 sq. mi.
7,688   5,953   6,950   6,605   8,421   12,123
August 21, 1876; organized April 11, 1877. George Campbell Childress (1804–41). One of five commissioners who drafted Texas Declaration of Independence 1836; Constitutional Convention 1836; committed suicide at Galveston.

Chilton   **Alabama**
Clanton   694 sq. mi.
39,593   32,458   30,612   25,180   25,693   26,922
December 30, 1868, as Baker; name changed December 17, 1874. William Parish Chilton (1810–71). Alabama legislature 1839; Alabama Supreme Court 1847–56, chief justice 1852–56; Alabama Senate 1859; Provisional Congress of the Confederacy 1860; Confederate Congress 1861–65.

Chippewa   **Michigan**
Sault Sainte Marie   1,561 sq. mi.
38,543   34,604   29,029   32,412   32,655   29,206
December 22, 1826; effective February 1, 1827. *Chippewa Indians*. Algonquin linguistic family; controlled much of western Great Lakes area. Name is corruption of *Ojibwa*, another name for the tribe; meaning may refer to roasting meat.

Chippewa   **Minnesota**
Montevideo   583 sq. mi.
13,088   13,228   14,941   15,109   16,320   16,739
February 20, 1862; organized January 9, 1869. Chippewa River. Named for Chippewa Indians.*

Chippewa   **Wisconsin**
Chippewa Falls   1,010 sq. mi.
55,195   52,360   52,127   47,717   45,096   42,839
February 3, 1845; organized 1852. Chippewa River. Named for Chippewa Indians.*

Chisago   **Minnesota**
Center City   418 sq. mi.
41,101   30,521   25,717   17,492   13,419   12,669
March 31, 1851; organized January 1, 1852. Chisago Lake. American coinage from Indian words *kichi*, for "large" and *saga*, for "beautiful."

Chittenden   **Vermont**
Burlington   539 sq. mi.

146,571	131,761	115,534	99,131	74,425	62,570

October 22, 1787. Thomas Chittenden (1730–97). 14th Connecticut Regiment 1767–73; colonel 1773; moved to New Hampshire grants (Vermont) 1774; active in fight for New Hampshire independence from England; unofficial governor of Vermont while seeking independence from New Hampshire; first governor of Vermont 1791–97.

Choctaw   **Alabama**
Butler   914 sq. mi.

15,922	16,018	16,839	16,589	17,870	19,152

December 29, 1847. *Choctaw Indians*. Large tribe in southern Mississippi and Alabama; ceded lands in 1830's and removed to Indian Territory (Oklahoma).

Choctaw   **Mississippi**
Ackerman   419 sq. mi.

9,758	9,071	8,996	8,440	8,423	11,009

December 23, 1833. Choctaw Indians.*

Choctaw   **Oklahoma**
Hugo   774 sq. mi.

15,342	15,302	17,203	15,141	16,637	20,405

July 16, 1907. Choctaw Indians.*

Chouteau   **Montana**
Fort Benton   3,973 sq. mi.

5,970	5,452	6,092	6,473	7,348	6,974

February 2, 1865. Chouteau family of fur traders. Most likely Pierre Chouteau (1789–1865); Missouri Constitutional Convention 1820; headed western department of American Fur Company for John Jacob Astor; bought out Astor; first fur company to take steamboat up the Missouri River to Montana.

Chowan   **North Carolina**
Edenton   173 sq. mi.

14,526	13,506	12,558	10,764	11,729	12,540

1670. Uncertain. (1) Chowan River. (2) Chowanoc Indians; name may mean "people of the south."

Christian   **Illinois**
Taylorville   709 sq. mi.

35,372	34,418	36,446	35,948	37,207	38,816

February 15, 1839, as Dane; name changed February 1, 1840. Christian County, Kentucky.

Christian   **Kentucky**
Hopkinsville   721 sq. mi.

72,265	68,941	66,878	56,224	56,904	42,359

December 13, 1796; effective March 1, 1797. William Christian (?–1786). Officer in French and Indian Wars; colonel of militia 1774; Virginia legislature; moved to Kentucky 1785; killed by Indians.

Christian   **Missouri**
Ozark   563 sq. mi.

54,285	32,644	22,402	15,124	12,359	12,412

March 8, 1859. Christian County, Kentucky.

Churchill   **Nevada**
Fallon   4,929 sq. mi.

23,982	17,938	13,917	10,513	8,452	6,161

November 25, 1861; organized 1864. Fort Churchill. Named for General Sylvester Churchill (1783–1862); commissioned 1812; inspector general of the army 1841; cited for valor at battle of Buena Vista 1847, promoted to brigadier general.

Cibola   **New Mexico**
Grants   4,539 sq. mi.
25,595   23,794   (a)   (a)   (a)   (a)
January 19, 1981. Seven Cities of Cíbola. Fabled cities of great wealth believed to be in southwestern U.S.; sought by Francisco Coronado 1540–42. [(a) Part of Valencia County.]

Cimarron   **Oklahoma**
Boise City   1,835 sq. mi.
3,148   3,301   3,648   4,145   4,496   4,589
July 16, 1907. Cimarron River. Spanish for "unruly."

Citrus   **Florida**
Inverness   584 sq. mi.
118,085   93,515   54,703   19,196   9,268   6,111
June 2, 1887. Descriptive of citrus fruit grown in area.

Clackamas   **Oregon**
Oregon City   1,868 sq. mi.
338,391   278,850   241,919   166,088   113,038   86,716
July 5, 1843. Clackama Indians. Chinookan tribe living at lower end of Clackamas River; encountered by Lewis and Clark 1806.

Claiborne   **Louisiana**
Homer   755 sq. mi.
16,851   17,405   17,095   17,024   19,407   25,063
March 13, 1828. *William Charles Coles Claiborne* (1775–1817). Tennessee Constitutional Convention 1796; judge of Superior Court 1796; U.S. representative 1791–1801; governor of Mississippi Territory 1801–05; commissioner to accept transfer of Louisiana from France 1803; governor of Orleans Territory 1804–12; first governor of Louisiana 1812–16; U.S. senator 1817.

Claiborne   **Mississippi**
Port Gibson   487 sq. mi.
11,831   11,370   12,279   10,086   10,845   11,944
January 27, 1802. William Charles Coles Claiborne.*

Claiborne   **Tennessee**
Tazewell   434 sq. mi.
29,862   26,137   24,595   19,420   19,067   24,788
October 29, 1801. William Charles Coles Claiborne.*

Clallam   **Washington**
Port Angeles   1,739 sq. mi.
64,525   56,464   51,648   34,770   30,022   26,396
April 26, 1854. Clallam Indians. Lived on Strait of Juan de Fuca; name means "brave people."

Clare   **Michigan**
Harrison   567 sq. mi.
31,252   24,952   23,822   16,695   11,647   10,253
April 1, 1840, as Kaykakee; name changed March 8, 1843; organized March 13, 1871. County Clare, Ireland.

Clarendon   **South Carolina**
Manning   607 sq. mi.
32,502   28,450   27,464   25,604   29,490   32,215
March 12, 1785; abolished 1800; recreated 1855. Edward Hyde, 3rd Earl of Clarendon (1661–1724). Colonel, Royal Regiment of Dragoons, 1685–88; captain general and governor in chief of New York and New Jersey 1701–08; commander in chief of the militia and forces of Connecticut and East and West Jersey 1701; vice admiral of New York and East and West Jersey 1701–08; privy councilor 1711; envoy extraordinary to Hanover 1714.

Clarion   **Pennsylvania**
Clarion   602 sq. mi.
41,765   41,699   43,362   38,414   37,408   38,344
March 11, 1839. Clarion River. French for "clear sounding."

Clark   **Arkansas**
Arkadelphia   865 sq. mi.
23,546   21,437   23,326   21,537   20,950   22,998
December 15, 1818; effective March 1, 1819. *William Clark* (1770–1838). Frontier service against Indians 1791–96; led Lewis and Clark Expedition with Meriwether Lewis 1804–07; resigned from army 1807; brigadier general of militia for Louisiana Territory and superintendent of Indian affairs at St. Louis 1807; governor of Missouri Territory 1813–20; surveyor general for Illinois, Missouri, and Arkansas.

Clark   **Idaho**
Dubois   1,765 sq. mi.
1,022   762   798   741   915   918
February 1, 1919. Sam K. Clark (?–?). Pioneer cattleman; Idaho legislature; first state senator from county.

Clark   **Illinois**
Marshall   502 sq. mi.
17,008   15,921   16,913   16,216   16,546   17,362
March 22, 1819. *George Rogers Clark* (1752–1818). Frontier leader; surveyor; volunteer under governor Dunmore of Virginia against Shawnee Indians; major of militia 1776; lieutenant colonel 1777; captured British garrison at Vincennes 1779; brigadier general of Continental army 1781.

Clark   **Indiana**
Jeffersonville   375 sq. mi.
96,472   87,777   88,838   75,876   62,795   48,330
February 3, 1801. George Rogers Clark.*

Clark   **Kansas**
Ashland   975 sq. mi.
2,390   2,418   2,599   2,896   3,396   3,946
February 26, 1867; abolished 1883; recreated March 7, 1885; organized May 5, 1885. Charles F. Clarke (?–1862). Captain, 6th Kansas Cavalry; died at Memphis December 10, 1862. Final "e" dropped in legislation.

Clark   **Kentucky**
Winchester   254 sq. mi.
33,144   29,496   28,322   24,090   21,075   18,898
December 6, 1792; effective February 1, 1793. George Rogers Clark.*

Clark   **Missouri**
Kahoka   507 sq. mi.
7,416   7,547   8,493   8,260   8,725   9,003
December 16, 1836. William Clark.*

Clark   **Nevada**
Las Vegas   7,910 sq. mi.
1,375,765   741,459   463,087   273,288   127,016   48,289
February 5, 1909; effective July 1, 1909. William Andrews Clark (1839–1925). Placer miner in Montana 1863–65; major of battalion that pursued Chief Joseph 1877; president of Montana Constitutional Convention 1884 and 1889; U.S. senator 1899–1900 and 1901–07; supported railroad through southern Nevada.

Clark   **Ohio**
Springfield   400 sq. mi.

144,742   147,548   150,236   157,115   131,440   111,661
December 26, 1817; effective March 1, 1818. George Rogers Clark.*

Clark   **South Dakota**
Clark   958 sq. mi.
4,143   4,403   4,894   5,515   7,134   8,369
January 8, 1873; organized May 23, 1881. Newton Clark (?–?). First schoolteacher in Sioux Falls; Dakota territorial legislature 1872–73.

Clark   **Washington**
Vancouver   628 sq. mi.
345,238   238,053   192,227   128,454   93,809   85,307
June 27, 1844, as Vancouver; name changed September 3, 1849. William Clark.*

Clark   **Wisconsin**
Neillsville   1,216 sq. mi.
33,557   31,647   32,910   30,361   31,527   32,459
July 6, 1853; organized 1857. George Rogers Clark.*

Clarke   **Alabama**
Grove Hill   1,238 sq. mi.
27,867   27,240   27,702   26,724   25,738   26,548
December 10, 1812. Uncertain. (1) *Elijah Clarke* (1733–99); general, Continental army; served with Pickens; siege of Augusta 1781. (2) John Clark (1766–1832); son of Elijah; Revolutionary War; general in War of 1812; Georgia legislature; governor of Georgia 1819–23; dropped "e" from family name.

Clarke   **Georgia**
Athens   121 sq. mi.
101,489   87,594   74,498   65,177   45,363   36,550
December 5, 1801. Elijah Clarke.*

Clarke   **Iowa**
Osceola   431 sq. mi.
9,133   8,287   8,612   7,581   8,222   9,369
January 13, 1846; organized August 21, 1851. James Clarke (1812–50). Printer, first Wisconsin territorial legislature, 1836; established Burlington, Iowa, *Gazette* 1837; secretary of Iowa Territory; territorial governor of Iowa, 1845–46.

Clarke   **Mississippi**
Quitman   691 sq. mi.
17,955   17,313   16,945   15,049   16,493   19,362
December 23, 1833. Joshua G. Clarke (?–1828). Mississippi territorial legislature; Mississippi Constitutional Convention 1817; Mississippi Supreme Court 1818; chancellor of Mississippi Supreme Court of Chancery 1821–28.

Clarke   **Virginia**
Berryville   177 sq. mi.
12,652   12,101   9,965   8,102   7,942   7,074
March 8, 1836. George Rogers Clark.* (Spelling error in legislation never corrected.)

Clatsop   **Oregon**
Astoria   827 sq. mi.
35,630   33,301   32,489   28,473   27,380   30,776
June 22, 1844. Clatsop Indians. Chinook group, northwestern Oregon; Lewis and Clark wintered with Clatsops 1805–06.

Clay   **Alabama**
Ashland   605 sq. mi.

14,254 13,252 13,703 12,636 12,400 13,929

December 7, 1866. *Henry Clay* (1777–1852). Kentucky House of Representatives 1803 and 1808–09; U.S. senator 1806–07, 1810–11, 1831–42, and 1849–1852; U.S. representative 1811–14, 1815–21, and 1823–25; U.S. secretary of state 1825–29; unsuccessful presidential candidate on Whig ticket 1824, 1832, and 1844.

Clay　　　　　　　　**Arkansas**
Piggott　　　　　　　　639 sq. mi.
17,609 18,107 20,616 18,771 21,258 26,674

March 24, 1873, as Clayton; name changed December 6, 1875. Uncertain. (1) Continued to be named for John Middleton Clayton* (see Clayton, Iowa) after name change. (2) Henry Clay.*

Clay　　　　　　　　**Florida**
Green Cove Springs　　601 sq. mi.
140,814 105,986 67,052 32,059 19,535 14,323

December 31, 1858. Henry Clay.*

Clay　　　　　　　　**Georgia**
Fort Gaines　　　　　　195 sq. mi.
3,357 3,364 3,553 3,636 4,551 5,844

February 16, 1854. Henry Clay.*

Clay　　　　　　　　**Illinois**
Louisville　　　　　　　469 sq. mi.
14,560 14,460 15,283 14,735 15,815 17,445

December 23, 1824. Henry Clay.*

Clay　　　　　　　　**Indiana**
Brazil　　　　　　　　　358 sq. mi.
26,556 24,705 24,862 23,933 24,207 23,918

February 12, 1825; effective April 1, 1825. Henry Clay.*

Clay　　　　　　　　**Iowa**
Spencer　　　　　　　　569 sq. mi.
17,372 17,585 19,576 18,464 18,504 18,103

January 15, 1851; organized October 15, 1858. Henry Clay, Jr. (1807–47). Graduated West Point 1831; brevet 2nd lieutenant 1831; resigned 1831; lieutenant colonel, 2nd Kentucky Volunteers, 1846; killed at the battle of Buena Vista February 23, 1847.

Clay　　　　　　　　**Kansas**
Clay Center　　　　　　644 sq. mi.
8,822 9,158 9,802 9,890 10,675 11,697

February 20, 1857; organized 1866. Henry Clay.*

Clay　　　　　　　　**Kentucky**
Manchester　　　　　　471 sq. mi.
24,556 21,746 22,752 18,481 20,748 23,116

December 2, 1806; effective April 1, 1807. Green Clay (1757–1826). Surveyor in Kentucky 1777; Virginia legislature 1788–89; Kentucky legislature 1793–94; Kentucky Constitutional Convention 1799; Kentucky Senate 1795–98 and 1807; led 3,000 volunteers to aid Fort Meigs 1813; commanded Fort Meigs 1813; major general, Kentucky militia.

Clay　　　　　　　　**Minnesota**
Moorhead　　　　　　　1,045 sq. mi.
51,229 50,422 49,327 46,585 39,080 30,363

March 18, 1858, as Breckinridge; name changed March 6, 1862; organized February 27, 1872. Henry Clay.*

Clay　　　　　　　　**Mississippi**
West Point　　　　　　409 sq. mi.

21.979   21,120   21,082   18,840   18,933   17,757
May 12, 1871, as Colfax; name changed April 10, 1876. Henry Clay.*

Clay   **Missouri**
Liberty   396 sq. mi.
184,006   153,411   136,488   123,322   87,474   45,221
January 2, 1822. Henry Clay.*

Clay   **Nebraska**
Clay Center   573 sq. mi.
7,039   7,123   8,106   8,266   8,717   8,700
February 16, 1867. Henry Clay.*

Clay   **North Carolina**
Hayesville   215 sq. mi.
8,775   7,155   6,619   5,180   5,526   6,006
February 20, 1861. Henry Clay.*

Clay   **South Dakota**
Vermillion   412 sq. mi.
13,537   13,186   13,689   12,923   10,810   10,993
April 10, 1862. Henry Clay.*

Clay   **Tennessee**
Celina   236 sq. mi.
7,976   7,238   7,676   6,624   7,289   8,701
June 24, 1870. Henry Clay.*

Clay   **Texas**
Henrietta   1,098 sq. mi.
11,006   10,024   9,582   8,079   8,351   9,896
December 24, 1857; organized 1861; deorganized 1862; reorganized May 27, 1873. Henry Clay.*

Clay   **West Virginia**
Clay   342 sq. mi.
10,330   9,983   11,265   9,330   11,942   14,961
March 29, 1858. Henry Clay.*

Clayton   **Georgia**
Jonesboro   143 sq. mi.
236,517   182,052   150,357   98,043   46,365   22,872
November 30, 1858. Augustin Smith Clayton (1783–1839). Georgia legislature 1810–12; clerk, Georgia House of Representatives 1813–15; Georgia Senate 1826–27; judge of Georgia Superior Court 1819–31; U.S. representative 1832–35.

Clayton   **Iowa**
Elkader   779 sq. mi.
18,678   19,054   21,098   20,606   21,962   22,522
December 21, 1837. *John Middleton Clayton* (1796–1856). Delaware House of Representatives 1824; Delaware secretary of state 1826–28; U.S. senator 1845–49; U.S. secretary of state 1849–50.

Clear Creek   **Colorado**
Georgetown   395 sq. mi.
9,322   7,619   7,308   4,819   2,793   3,289
November 1, 1861. Clear Creek. Descriptive.

Clearfield   **Pennsylvania**
Clearfield   1,147 sq. mi.
83,382   78,097   83,578   74,619   81,534   85,957
March 26, 1804. Descriptive of land cleared by Indians.

Clearwater   **Idaho**
Orofino   2,461 sq. mi.
8,930   8,505   10,390   10,871   8,548   8,217
February 27, 1911. Clearwater River. Translation of "Koos-koos-kia," Indian name for the river.

Clearwater   **Minnesota**
Bagley   995 sq. mi.
8,423   8,309   8,761   8,013   8,864   10,204
December 20, 1902. Clearwater River and Lake. Translation of Chippewa names for the river and lake.

Cleburne   **Alabama**
Heflin   560 sq. mi.
14,123   12,730   12,595   10,996   10,911   11,904
December 6, 1866. *Patrick Ronayne Cleburne* (1828–64). Immigrated to New Orleans from Ireland 1849; druggist; captain and colonel, 15th Arkansas Infantry; brigadier general and major general 1862; battle of Shiloh April 6–7, 1962; battles of Missionary Ridge, Ringgold Gap, Resaca, and New Hope Church; killed at battle of Franklin, Tennessee, November 30, 1864.

Cleburne   **Arkansas**
Heber Springs   553 sq. mi.
24,046   19,411   16,909   10,349   9,059   11,487
February 20, 1883. Patrick Ronayne Cleburne.*

Clermont   **Ohio**
Batavia   452 sq. mi.
177,977   150,187   128,483   95,725   80,530   42,182
December 6, 1800. Uncertain. (1) City of Clermont-Ferrand, France. (2) Anglicized combination of French *cler*, approximating "clear," and *mont*, meaning "mount."

Cleveland   **Arkansas**
Rison   598 sq. mi.
8,571   7,781   7,868   6,605   6,944   8,956
April 17, 1873, as Dorsey; name changed March 5, 1885. *Stephen Grover Cleveland* (1837–1908). Sheriff, Erie County, New York, 1870–73; mayor of Buffalo 1881–82; governor of New York 1883–85; 22nd and 24th president of the U.S. 1885–89 and 1893–97.

Cleveland   **North Carolina**
Shelby   465 sq. mi.
96,287   84,714   83,435   72,556   66,048   64,357
January 11, 1841, as Cleaveland; spelling changed to more familiar spelling of President Cleveland's name 1885. Benjamin Cleaveland (1738–1806). Ensign, 2nd North Carolina Regiment 1775; lieutenant and captain 1776; retired 1778; colonel, North Carolina militia 1778; hero, battle of Kings Mountain 1780

Cleveland   **Oklahoma**
Norman   536 sq. mi.
208,016   174,253   133,173   81,839   47,600   41,443
1890. Stephen Grover Cleveland.*

Clifton Forge   **Virginia**
(Independent City)   3 sq. mi.
4,289   4,679   5,046   5,501   5,268   5,795

1906; reverted to incorporated town status in Alleghany County July 1, 2001. James Clifton's iron furnace in Iron Gate Gorge 1828. (Associated county: Alleghany.)

Clinch   **Georgia**
Homerville   809 sq. mi.
6,878   6,160   6,660   6,405   6,545   6,007
February 14, 1850. Duncan Lamont Clinch (1787–1849). 1st lieutenant, 3rd Infantry, U.S. Army 1808; captain 1810; lieutenant colonel 1813; colonel 1819; brevet brigadier general for ten years' service 1829; 1st and 2nd Seminole Wars 1835; resigned 1836; U.S. Representative from Georgia 1844–45.

Clinton   **Illinois**
Carlyle   474 sq. mi.
35,535   33,944   32,617   28,315   24,029   22,594
December 27, 1824. *De Witt Clinton* (1769–1828). Secretary to Governor George Clinton; New York Assembly 1798; New York Senate 1798–1802 and 1806–11; U.S. senator 1802–03; mayor of New York City 1803–07, 1810–11, and 1813–15; governor of New York 1817–21 and 1825–28; led development of Erie Canal.

Clinton   **Indiana**
Frankfort   405 sq. mi.
33,866   30,974   31,545   30,547   30,765   29,734
January 29, 1830; effective March 1, 1830. De Witt Clinton.*

Clinton   **Iowa**
Clinton   695 sq. mi.
50,149   51,040   57,122   56,749   55,060   49,664
December 21, 1837; organized January 5, 1841. De Witt Clinton.*

Clinton   **Kentucky**
Albany   197 sq. mi.
9,634   9,135   9,321   8,174   8,886   10,605
February 20, 1836. De Witt Clinton.*

Clinton   **Michigan**
Saint Johns   571 sq. mi.
64,753   57,883   55,893   48,492   37,969   31,195
March 2, 1831; organized March 12,1839. De Witt Clinton.*

Clinton   **Missouri**
Plattsburg   419 sq. mi.
18,979   16,595   15,916   12,462   11,588   11,726
January 2, 1833. De Witt Clinton.*

Clinton   **New York**
Plattsburgh   1,039 sq. mi.
79,894   85,969   80,750   72,934   72,722   53,622
March 17, 1788. *George Clinton* (1739–1812). Clerk of the Court of Common Pleas of New York 1759; district attorney 1765; New York Assembly 1768; Continental Congress 1775–76; brigadier general 1777; governor of New York 1777–95 and 1801–04; vice president of U.S. 1805–12; uncle of De Witt Clinton.

Clinton   **Ohio**
Wilmington   411 sq. mi.
40,543   35,415   34,603   31,464   30,004   25,572
February 19, 1810. George Clinton.*

Clinton   **Pennsylvania**
Lock Haven   891 sq. mi.

| 37,914 | 37,182 | 38,971 | 37,721 | 37,619 | 36,532 |

June 21, 1839. De Witt Clinton.*

Cloud   **Kansas**
Concordia   716 sq. mi.

| 10,268 | 11,023 | 12,494 | 13,466 | 14,407 | 16,104 |

February 27, 1860, as Shirley; abolished 1865; recreated as Shirley 1866; name changed February 26, 1867. William F. Cloud (1825–1905). Mexican War; captain, Ohio Volunteer Militia 1848; enlisted Union army 1861; battles of Wilson's Creek and Cane Hill; colonel, 2nd Kansas Cavalry.

Coahoma   **Mississippi**
Clarksdale   554 sq. mi.

| 30,622 | 31,665 | 36,918 | 40,447 | 46,212 | 49,361 |

February 9, 1836. Choctaw word for "red panther." Uncertain source of name. (1) Chickasaw chief Coahoma, also known as William McGillivray (c1750–c1840), captain under Washington. (2) "Sweet Coahoma," an Indian princess, daughter of a chief from a family named Sheriff.

Coal   **Oklahoma**
Coalgate   518 sq. mi.

| 6,031 | 5,780 | 6,041 | 5,525 | 5,546 | 8,056 |

July 16, 1907. Descriptive of coal deposits in the area.

Cobb   **Georgia**
Marietta   340 sq. mi.

| 607,751 | 447,745 | 297,718 | 196,793 | 114,174 | 61,830 |

December 3, 1832. Thomas Willis Cobb (1784–1830). U.S. representative from Georgia 1817–21 and 1823–24; U.S. senator 1824–28; judge of Superior Court of Georgia 1828.

Cochise   **Arizona**
Bisbee   6,169 sq. mi.

| 117,755 | 97,624 | 85,686 | 61,910 | 55,039 | 31,488 |

February 1, 1881. Cochise (?–1874). Chief of Chiracahua Apaches; fought against U.S. 1861–71; moved tribe to reservation 1871.

Cochran   **Texas**
Morton   775 sq. mi.

| 3,730 | 4,377 | 4,825 | 5,326 | 6,417 | 5,928 |

August 21, 1876; organized 1924. Robert Cochran (1810–36). Settled in Texas 1835; private; killed at the Alamo March 6, 1836.

Cocke   **Tennessee**
Newport   434 sq. mi.

| 33,565 | 29,141 | 28,792 | 25,283 | 23,390 | 22,991 |

October 9, 1797; name changed to Union January 28, 1846; renamed Cocke January 3, 1850. William Cocke (1748–1828). Explored Tennessee with Daniel Boone; led Virginians against Indians 1776; Virginia House of Burgesses; moved to Tennessee 1776; Tennessee Constitutional Convention 1796; U.S. senator 1796–97 and 1799–1805; judge of 1st Circuit 1809; Mississippi legislature 1813; served under General Jackson, War of 1812; Chickasaw Nation Indian agent 1814.

Coconino   **Arizona**
Flagstaff   18,617 sq. mi.

| 116,320 | 96,591 | 75,008 | 48,326 | 41,857 | 23,910 |

February 19, 1891. Corruption of Hopi name for its neighboring tribes, the Havasupai and Yavapai. Most suggested translations are derogatory or refer to water.

Codington   **South Dakota**
Watertown   688 sq. mi.

25,897   22,698   20,885   19,140   20,220   18,944
February 15, 1877; organized August 7, 1878. G. S. Codington (?–?). Circuit-riding Protestant clergyman; Dakota territorial legislature 1877–78.

Coffee   **Alabama**
New Brockton   679 sq. mi.
43,615   40,240   38,533   34,872   30,583   30,720
December 29, 1841. *John Coffee* (1772–1833). Business partner of Andrew Jackson; surveyor; colonel, Tennessee Volunteers 1812–13; brigadier general, Tennessee Mounted Riflemen, 1813; wounded in battle of New Orleans 1815; U.S. surveyor of public lands 1817.

Coffee   **Georgia**
Douglas   599 sq. mi.
37,413   29,592   26,894   22,828   21,953   23,961
February 9, 1854. John Coffee (1782–1836). General of Georgia militia, Creek War, 1814; Georgia senate 1819–27; U.S. representative 1833–36; cousin of John Coffee listed above.

Coffee   **Tennessee**
Manchester   429 sq. mi.
48,014   40,339   38,311   32,572   28,603   23,049
January 8, 1836. John Coffee (1772–1833).*

Coffey   **Kansas**
Burlington   630 sq. mi.
8,865   8,404   9,370   7,397   8,403   10,408
August 30, 1855; organized 1859. Asbury M. Coffey (1804–79). Osage River Indian Agency; Kansas territorial legislature; favored slavery but supported preservation of Union; colonel, Confederate army in Indian Territory (Oklahoma).

Coke   **Texas**
Robert Lee   899 sq. mi.
3,864   3,424   3,196   3,087   3,589   4,045
March 13, 1889; organized April 23, 1889. Richard Coke (1829–97). Private, Confederate army; advanced to captain 1861–65; district court judge at Waco 1865; judge of Texas Supreme Court 1866, removed 1867; governor of Texas 1874–76; U.S. senator 1877–85.

Colbert   **Alabama**
Tuscumbia   595 sq. mi.
54,984   51,666   54,519   49,632   46,506   39,561
February 6, 1867; abolished 1867; recreated 1869. George Colbert (1744–1839) and Levi Colbert (1759–1834). Brothers; Chickasaw Indian chiefs Tootemastubbie (George) and Itawamba Mingo (Levi; see Itawamba, Mississippi); George owned ferry on Natchez Trace.

Cole   **Missouri**
Jefferson City   391 sq. mi.
71,397   63,579   56,663   46,228   40,761   35,464
November 16, 1820. Stephen Cole (c1792–1822). Early pioneer of central Missouri; traded on Santa Fe Trail; killed by Indians on Rio Grande.

Coleman   **Texas**
Coleman   1,260 sq. mi.
9,235   9,710   10,439   10,288   12,458   15,503
February 1, 1858; organized October 6, 1864. Robert M. Coleman (1797–1837). Aide-de-camp of General Houston at battle of San Jacinto 1836; signer, Texas Declaration of Independence 1836; Texas Ranger 1836–37; drowned in Brazos River.

Coles   **Illinois**
Charleston   508 sq. mi.

| 53,196 | 51,644 | 52,260 | 47,815 | 42,860 | 40,328 |

December 25, 1830. Edward Coles (1786–1868). Private secretary to President Madison 1809–15; mission to Moscow 1816; settled in Illinois 1818; governor of Illinois 1822–26; freed his slaves and gave each 160 acres of land.

Colfax   **Nebraska**
Schuyler   413 sq. mi.

| 10,441 | 9,139 | 9,890 | 9,498 | 9,595 | 10,010 |

February 15, 1869. *Schuyler Colfax* (1823–85). Editor and proprietor, *Valley Register*, St. Joseph, Indiana, 1845; Indiana Constitutional Convention 1850; U.S. representative 1855–69; U.S. vice president 1869–73.

Colfax   **New Mexico**
Raton   3,757 sq. mi.

| 14,189 | 12,925 | 13,667 | 12,170 | 13,806 | 16,761 |

January 25, 1869. Schuyler Colfax.*

Colleton   **South Carolina**
Walterboro   1,056 sq. mi.

| 38,264 | 34,377 | 31,676 | 27,622 | 27,816 | 28,242 |

1682; abolished 1769; recreated 1798. John Colleton (1608–66). Loyalist in English Civil War; lived in Barbados during Interregnum; one of eight original lords proprietors of Carolina 1663.

Collier   **Florida**
Naples   2,025 sq. mi.

| 251,377 | 152,099 | 85,971 | 38,040 | 15,753 | 6,488 |

May 8, 1923. Barron Gift Collier (1873–1939). Industrialist; owned Florida real estate and hotels; reclaimed sections of the Everglades.

Collin   **Texas**
McKinney   848 sq. mi.

| 491,675 | 264,036 | 144,576 | 66,920 | 41,247 | 41,692 |

April 3, 1846; organized July 13, 1846. Collin McKinney (1766–1861). Texas Constitutional Convention 1836; signer, Texas Declaration of Independence 1836; Texas Republic legislature; insisted that new counties in north Texas have straight boundaries.

Collingsworth   **Texas**
Wellington   919 sq. mi.

| 3,206 | 3,573 | 4,648 | 4,755 | 6,276 | 9,139 |

August 21, 1876; organized September 30, 1890. James T. Collinsworth (1806–38). Texas Constitutional Convention 1836; major and aide-de-camp to General Houston 1836; Texas Senate 1836; first chief justice, Texas Republic 1837; accidental death by drowning. (Uncorrected spelling error added "g" to county's name.)

Colonial Heights   **Virginia**
(Independent City)   7 sq. mi.

| 16,897 | 16,064 | 16,509 | 15,097 | 9,587 | 6,077 |

1948. Elevated position where Lafayette placed his field pieces, known as "colonials," to bombard British at Petersburg 1781. (Associated county: Chesterfield.)

Colorado   **Texas**
Columbus   963 sq. mi.

| 20,390 | 18,383 | 18,823 | 17,638 | 18,463 | 17,576 |

March 17, 1836; organized 1837. Colorado River. Spanish for "colored"; refers to reddish silt in river.

Colquitt   **Georgia**
Moultrie   552 sq. mi.

| 42,053 | 36,645 | 35,376 | 32,200 | 34,048 | 33,999 |

February 25, 1856. Walter Terry Colquitt (1799–1855). Judge of the Chattahochee Circuit 1826; Methodist preacher 1827; Georgia Senate 1834 and 1837; U.S. representative 1839–42; U.S. senator 1843–48.

Columbia   **Arkansas**
Magnolia   766 sq. mi.
25,603   25,691   26,644   25,952   26,400   28,770
December 17, 1852. Columbia, goddess of liberty.

Columbia   **Florida**
Lake City   797 sq. mi.
56,513   42,613   35,399   25,250   20,077   18,216
February 4, 1832. *Christopher Columbus* (1451–1506). Latinized name; Italian navigator; sailed from Palos, Spain, August 3, 1492; discovered San Salvador October 12, 1492, effective European discovery of America.

Columbia   **Georgia**
Evans   290 sq. mi.
89,288   66,031   40,118   22,327   13,423   9,525
December 10, 1790. Christopher Columbus.*

Columbia   **New York**
Hudson   636 q. mi.
63,094   62,982   59,487   51,519   47,322   43,182
April 4, 1786. Christopher Columbus.*

Columbia   **Oregon**
Saint Helens   657 sq. mi.
43,560   37,557   35,646   28,790   22,379   22,967
January 16, 1854. *Columbia River*; named for the ship *Columbia,* in which Captain Gray sailed up the river 1792.

Columbia   **Pennsylvania**
Bloomsburg   486 sq. mi.
64,151   63,202   61,967   55,114   53,489   53,460
March 22, 1813. Christopher Columbus.*

Columbia   **Washington**
Dayton   869 sq. mi.
4,064   4,024   4,057   4,439   4,569   4,860
November 11, 1875. Columbia River.*

Columbia   **Wisconsin**
Portage   774 sq. mi.
52,468   45,088   43,222   40,150   36,708   34,023
February 3, 1846. Christopher Columbus.*

Columbiana   **Ohio**
Lisbon   532 sq. mi.
112,075   108,276   113,572   108,310   107,004   98,920
March 25, 1803. Christopher Columbus.*

Columbus   **North Carolina**
Whiteville   937 sq. mi.
54,749   49,587   51,037   46,937   48,973   50,621
December 15, 1808. Christopher Columbus.*

Colusa   **California**
Colusa   1,151 sq. mi.

18,804   16,275   12,791   12,430   12,075   11,651
February 18, 1850 as Colusi; organized 1851; name changed 1854. Colus Indian tribe. Name may mean "scratch" or "scratcher."

Comal   **Texas**
New Braunfels   561 sq. mi.
78,021   51,832   36,446   24,165   19,844   16,357
March 24, 1846. Spanish word for "basin" or "griddle"; from the surrounding landscape.

Comanche   **Kansas**
Coldwater   788 sq. mi.
1,967   2,313   2,554   2,702   3,271   3,888
February 26, 1867; organized February 27, 1885. *Comanche Indians*. From Ute word meaning "enemy."

Comanche   **Oklahoma**
Lawton   1,069 sq. mi.
114,996   111,486   112,456   108,144   90,803   55,165
1901. Comanche Indians.*

Comanche   **Texas**
Comanche   938 sq. mi.
14,026   13,381   12,617   11,898   11,865   15,516
January 25, 1856; organized March 17, 1856. Comanche Indians.*

Concho   **Texas**
Paint Rock   991 sq. mi.
3,966   3,044   2,915   2,937   3,672   5,078
February 1, 1858; organized March 11, 1879. Concho River. Spanish word for "shell."

Concordia   **Louisiana**
Vidalia   696 sq. mi.
20,247   20,828   22,981   22,578   20,467   14,398
April 10, 1805. New Concordia. Spanish military post named for good relations (concord) between the Spanish and American settlers.

Conecuh   **Alabama**
Evergreen   851 sq. mi.
14,089   14,054   15,884   15,645   17,762   21,776
February 13, 1818. Conecuh River. Uncertain origin. (1) Muskogee word for "crooked." (2) Corruption of Creek word *econneka,* meaning "land of cane."

Conejos   **Colorado**
Conejos   1,287 sq. mi.
8,400   7,453   7,794   7,846   8,428   10,171
November 1, 1861, as Guadalupe; name changed November 7, 1861. Conejos River and town of Conejos. Spanish for "rabbits."

Contra Costa   **California**
Martinez   720 sq. mi.
948,816   803,732   656,380   558,389   409,030   298,984
February 18, 1850. Spanish for "opposite coast" (across San Francisco Bay from San Francisco).

Converse   **Wyoming**
Douglas   4,255 sq. mi.
12,052   11,128   14,069   5,938   6,366   5,933
March 9, 1888. Amasa R. Converse (1842–85). Merchant, stockman, and banker; treasurer, Wyoming Territory 1875–76 and 1877–79.

Conway   **Arkansas**
Morrilton   556 sq. mi.
20,336   19,151   19,505   16,805   15,430   18,137
October 20, 1825; effective January 1, 1826. Henry Wharton Conway (1793–1827). Navy ensign and lieutenant 1813; clerk, U.S. Treasury 1817; moved to Arkansas Territory 1820; congressional delegate from Arkansas Territory 1823–27; killed in duel by Robert Crittenden (see Crittenden, Arkansas).

Cook   **Georgia**
Adel   229 sq. mi.
15,771   13,456   13,490   12,129   11,822   12,201
July 30, 1918. Philip Cook (1817–94). Georgia Senate 1859–60 and 1863–1864; private, Confederate army 1861; brigadier general 1863; U.S. representative 1873–83; Georgia secretary of state 1890–94.

Cook   **Illinois**
Chicago   946 sq. mi.
5,376,741   5,105,067   5,253,655   5,492,369   5,129,725   4,508,792
January 15, 1831. Daniel Pope Cook (1794–1827). First attorney general of Illinois, March 5 to 15, 1819; U.S. representative 1819–27.

Cook   **Minnesota**
Grand Marais   1,451 sq. mi.
5,168   3,868   4,092   3,423   3,377   2,900
March 9, 1874; organized April 6, 1897. Michael Cook (1828–64). Minnesota territorial and state senator 1857–62; major, 10th Minnesota Regiment, 1864; died from wounds received at battle of Nashville December 16, 1864.

Cooke   **Texas**
Gainesville   874 sq. mi.
36,363   30,777   27,656   23,471   22,560   22,146
March 20, 1848; organized March 10, 1849. William G. Cooke (1808–47). Captain of the New Orleans Greys in Texas Revolution at Bexar December 5, 1835; battle of San Jacinto 1836; quartermaster general of Texas Army 1839.

Cooper   **Missouri**
Boonville   565 sq. mi.
16,670   14,835   14,643   14,732   15,448   16,608
December 17, 1818. Uncertain. (1) Benjamin Cooper (1784–1867); early settler; Missouri Senate 1820. (2) Sarshall (or Sarshel) Cooper (1762–1815); built Cooper's Fort on Missouri River; War of 1812; killed by Indians.

Coos   **New Hampshire**
Lancaster   1,800 sq. mi.
33,111   34,828   35,147   34,291   37,140   35,932
December 24, 1803; effective March 1, 1805. Uncertain. (1) Indian word meaning "crooked"; refers to the Connecticut River. (2) Corruption of Indian word *cohos,* meaning "pines."

Coos   **Oregon**
Coquille   1,600 sq. mi.
62,779   60,273   64,047   56,515   54,955   42,265
December 22, 1853. Kusan Indians; meaning of name unknown. Inhabited area around Coos Bay.

Coosa   **Alabama**
Rockford   652 sq. mi.
12,202   11,063   11,377   10,662   10,726   11,766
December 18, 1832. Coosa River. Cherokee word for "rippling."

Copiah   **Mississippi**
Hazlehurst   777 sq. mi.

| 28,757 | 27,592 | 26,503 | 24,749 | 27,051 | 30,493 |

January 21, 1823. Combination of Indian words *koi* (panther) and *panya* (screaming).

Corson **South Dakota**
McIntosh 2,473 sq. mi.

| 4,181 | 4,195 | 5,196 | 4,994 | 5,798 | 6,168 |

March 2, 1909. Dighton Corson (c1827–1915). Wisconsin legislature 1857–58; Nevada district attorney and state attorney; Nevada Constitutional Convention 1885 and 1889; first judge, Supreme Court of South Dakota 1889–1913.

Cortland **New York**
Cortland 500 sq. mi.

| 48,599 | 48,963 | 48,820 | 45,894 | 41,113 | 37,158 |

April 8, 1808. Pierre van Cortlandt (1721–1814). French and Indian Wars; provincial legislature of New York; New York Constitutional Convention; lieutenant governor of New York 1777–95.

Coryell **Texas**
Gatesville 1,052 sq. mi.

| 74,978 | 64,213 | 56,767 | 35,311 | 23,961 | 16,284 |

February 4, 1854; organized March 11, 1854. James Coryell (c1801–37). Settled in Texas 1829; Texas Ranger 1836; killed by Indians while exploring silver mine, May 27, 1837.

Coshocton **Ohio**
Coshocton 564 sq. mi.

| 36,655 | 35,427 | 36,024 | 33,486 | 32,224 | 31,141 |

January 31, 1810; organized 1811. Delaware Indian village. From Delaware word *koshachkink* (one of many variations), meaning "union of waters" or "ferry."

Costilla **Colorado**
San Luis 1,227 sq. mi.

| 3,663 | 3,190 | 3,071 | 3,091 | 4,219 | 6,067 |

November 1, 1861. Costilla River and town of Costilla, New Mexico. Spanish for "rib"; possibly for a long, sweeping curve in the river.

Cottle **Texas**
Paducah 901 sq. mi.

| 1,904 | 2,247 | 2,947 | 3,204 | 4,207 | 6,099 |

August 21, 1876; organized January, 1892. George Washington Cottle (1798–1836). Private, resident of Gonzales, Texas; killed at Alamo March 6, 1836.

Cotton **Oklahoma**
Walters 637 sq. mi.

| 6,614 | 6,651 | 7,338 | 6,832 | 8,031 | 10,180 |

August 27, 1912. Descriptive. Name drawn from a hat by citizens of the area.

Cottonwood **Minnesota**
Windom 640 sq. mi.

| 12,167 | 12,694 | 14,854 | 14,887 | 16,166 | 15,763 |

May 23, 1857; organized July 4, 1873. Cottonwood River. English translation of Dakota name *waraju* for trees along the river.

Covington **Alabama**
Andalusia 1,034 sq. mi.

| 37,631 | 36,478 | 36,850 | 34,079 | 35,631 | 40,373 |

December 7, 1821. *Leonard Wailes Covington* (1768–1813). U.S. Army 1792; lieutenant of dragoons 1793; served with General Wayne 1794; resigned 1795; Maryland House of Delegates; U.S. representative 1805–07; lieutenant colonel and colonel of Light Dragoons 1809; brigadier general 1813; mortally wounded at battle of Chrysler's Field November 11, 1813.

Covington   **Mississippi**
Collins   414 sq. mi.
19,407   16,527   15,927   14,002   13,637   16,036
February 5, 1819. Leonard Wailes Covington.*

Covington   **Virginia**
(Independent City)   6 sq. mi.
6,303   6,991   9,063   10,060   11,062   (a)
1952. Uncertain. (1) Peter Covington (?–?); early settler. (2) Leonard Wailes Covington.* [(a) Part of Alleghany County.] (Associated county: Alleghany.)

Coweta   **Georgia**
Newman   443 sq. mi.
89,215   53,853   39,268   32,310   28,893   27,786
December 11, 1826. Coweta Indians. Named from Creek word *kawita*, perhaps for "falls" on the Chattahoochee River; also name for Lower Creeks.

Cowley   **Kansas**
Winfield   1,126 sq. mi.
36,291   36,915   36,824   35,012   37,861   36,905
February 26, 1867; organized 1870. Matthew Cowley (?–1864). 1st lieutenant, Company I, 9th Kansas; died at Little Rock, Arkansas, October 7, 1864.

Cowlitz   **Washington**
Kelso   1,139 sq. mi.
92,948   82,119   79,548   68,616   57,801   53,369
April 21, 1854. Uncertain. (1) Cowlitz Indians; from Cowlitz word meaning "capturing the medicine spirit"; refers to practice of Cowlitz youths to commune with spirits. (2) Cowlitz River; named from Cowlitz Indians.

Craig   **Oklahoma**
Vinita   761 sq. mi.
14,950   14,104   15,014   14,722   16,303   18,263
July 16, 1907. Granville C. Craig (1849–?). Cherokee merchant and stockman; arrived in Oklahoma 1873.

Craig   **Virginia**
New Castle   331 sq. mi.
5,091   4,372   3,948   3,524   3,356   3,452
March 21, 1851. Robert Craig (1792–1852). Virginia House of Delegates 1817–18, 1825–29, and 1850–52; Virginia Board of Public Works 1820–23; U.S. representative 1829–33 and 1835–41.

Craighead   **Arkansas**
Jonesboro   711 sq. mi.
82,148   68,956   63,239   52,068   47,303   50,613
February 19, 1859. Thomas B. Craighead (1800–?). Arkansas Senate; opposed creation of county, which was named for him during his absence from Senate.

Crane   **Texas**
Crane   786 sq. mi.
3,996   4,652   4,600   4,172   4,699   3,965
February 26, 1887; organized 1927. William Carey Crane (1816–85). Ordained Baptist minister 1838; president of Mississippi Female College 1851–57; president of Baylor University 1863–85.

Craven   **North Carolina**
New Bern   708 sq. mi.
91,436   81,613   71,043   62,554   58,773   48,823

December 3, 1705, as Archdale; name changed 1712. Uncertain. (1) William Craven, Earl of Craven (1606–97); English military officer; knighted 1627; supporter of Charles I; one of original eight lords proprietor of Carolina 1663; made Earl of Craven 1664. (2) William, Lord Craven (1668–1711); inherited Carolina proprietorship on death of William Craven 1697; 2nd Lord Craven; lord lieutenant of Berkshire 1702. (3) William, Lord Craven (1700–39); inherited Carolina proprietorship on death of 2nd Lord Craven 1711; sold proprietorship to crown 1729.

Crawford   **Arkansas**
Van Buren   595 sq. mi.
53,247   42,493   36,892   25,677   21,318   22,727
October 18, 1820. *William Harris Crawford* (1772–1834). Georgia House of Representatives 1803–07; U.S. senator 1807–13; president pro tempore of the Senate 1812; U.S. minister to France 1813–15; U.S. secretary of war 1815–16; U.S. secretary of the treasury 1816–25; Georgia circuit judge 1827–34.

Crawford   **Georgia**
Roberta   325 sq. mi.
12,495   8,991   7,684   5,748   5,816   6,080
December 9, 1822. William Harris Crawford.*

Crawford   **Illinois**
Robinson   444 sq. mi.
20,452   19,464   20,818   19,824   20,751   21,137
December 31, 1816. William Harris Crawford.*

Crawford   **Indiana**
English   306 sq. mi.
10,743   9,914   9,820   8,033   8,379   9,289
January 29, 1818; effective February 15, 1818. Uncertain. (1) *William Crawford* (1732–82). Surveyor; served under General Braddock; captain 1761; Pontiac's War 1763–64; in Revolutionary War fought in battles of Long Island, Trenton, Princeton; resigned as colonel 1781; fought Wyandot and Delaware Indians on Sandusky River; captured, tortured and burned at the stake June 1782. (2) William Harris Crawford.*

Crawford   **Iowa**
Denison   714 sq. mi.
16,942   16,775   18,935   18,780   18,569   19,741
January 15, 1851; organized September 3, 1855. William Harris Crawford.*

Crawford   **Kansas**
Girard   593 sq. mi.
38,242   35,568   37,916   37,850   37,032   40,231
February 13, 1867; organized March 3, 1868. Samuel J. Crawford (1835–1913). Kansas legislature 1861; resigned and organized company of volunteers, chosen captain, promoted to colonel, brevet brigadier general 1864; governor of Kansas 1865–68; resigned to command 19th Kansas Cavalry against Indians 1868.

Crawford   **Michigan**
Grayling   558 sq. mi.
14,273   12,260   9,465   6,482   4,971   4,151
April 1, 1840, as Shawano; name changed March 8, 1843; organized March 22, 1879. William Crawford.*

Crawford   **Missouri**
Steelville   743 sq. mi.
22,804   19,173   18,300   14,828   12,647   11,615
January 23, 1829. William Harris Crawford.*

Crawford   **Ohio**
Bucyrus   402 sq. mi.

46,966   47,870   50,075   50,364   46,775   38,738
February 12, 1820; organized 1826. William Crawford.*

Crawford   **Pennsylvania**
Meadville   1,013 sq. mi.
90,366   86,169   88,869   81,342   77,956   78,948
March 12, 1800. William Crawford.*

Crawford   **Wisconsin**
Prairie du Chien   573 sq. mi.
17,243   15,940   16,556   15,252   16,351   17,652
October 26, 1818. Fort Crawford. Named for William Harris Crawford.*

Creek   **Oklahoma**
Sapulpa   956 sq. mi.
67,367   60,915   59,016   45,532   40,495   43,143
July 16, 1907. Creek Indians. Occupied most of Alabama and Georgia; defeated by U.S. in Creek War 1813–14; removed to Indian Territory (Oklahoma) by 1841.

Crenshaw   **Alabama**
Luverne   610 sq. mi.
13,665   13,635   14,110   13,188   14,909   18,981
November 24, 1866. Anderson Crenshaw (1786–1847). First graduate from College of Columbia 1806; Alabama Circuit Court judge 1821–38; judge, Alabama Supreme Court 1838; Court of Chancery 1838–47.

Crisp   **Georgia**
Cordele   274 sq. mi.
21,996   20,011   19,489   18,087   17,768   17,663
August 17, 1905. Charles Frederick Crisp (1845–96). Confederate army 1861–64; lieutenant, prisoner of war 1864; released 1865; solicitor general of Southwestern Judicial Circuit 1872–77; judge of Superior Court 1877–82; U.S. representative from Georgia 1883–96.

Crittenden   **Arkansas**
Marion   610 sq. mi.
50,866   49,939   49,499   48,106   47,564   47,184
October 22, 1825; effective January 1, 1826. Robert Crittenden (1797–1834). War of 1812; secretary of Arkansas Territory; mortally wounded Congressman Henry Wharton Conway in a duel 1827 (see Conway, Arkansas).

Crittenden   **Kentucky**
Marion   362 sq. mi.
9,384   9,196   9,207   8,493   8,648   10,818
January 26, 1842. John Jordan Crittenden (c1787–1863). Attorney general of Illinois Territory 1809–10; in War of 1812 on staff of General Shelby at battle of the Thames 1813; Kentucky legislature 1811–17, Speaker 1817; Kentucky Senate 1817–19; Kentucky House of Representatives 1825 and 1829–32; U.S. district attorney 1827–29; nominated to U.S. Supreme Court but not confirmed 1828; U.S. senator 1835–41, 1842–48 and 1855–61; U.S. attorney general 1841 and 1850–53; governor of Kentucky 1848–50; U.S. representative 1861–63.

Crockett   **Tennessee**
Alamo   265 sq. mi.
14,532   13,378   14,941   14,402   14,594   16,624
December 20, 1845; abolished 1846; recreated 1871; organized 1872. *David "Davy" Crockett* (1786–1836). Creek Indian campaign 1813–14; Tennessee House of Representatives 1821–25; U.S. representative 1827–31 and 1833–35; aided Texas independence; killed at the Alamo March 6, 1836.

Crockett   **Texas**
Ozona   2,807 sq. mi.

4,099   4,078   4,608   3,885   4,209   3,981
January 22, 1875; organized July 14, 1891. David Crockett.*

Crook   **Oregon**
Prineville   2,979 sq. mi.
19,182   14,111   13,091   9,985   9,430   8,991
October 24, 1882. *George Crook* (1829–90). Graduated U.S. Military Academy 1852; lieutenant in Oregon Territory 1852–60; major general 1860; commander of districts of Idaho and Arizona 1866–72.

Crook   **Wyoming**
Sundance   2,859 sq. mi.
5,887   5,294   5,308   4,535   4,691   4,738
December 8, 1875. George Crook.*

Crosby   **Texas**
Crosbyton   900 sq. mi.
7,072   7,304   8,859   9,085   10,347   9,582
August 21, 1876; organized September 11, 1886. Stephen Crosby (1808–69). Steamboat captain; chief clerk in Texas Land Office 1853–57 and 1859–67.

Cross   **Arkansas**
Wynne   616 sq. mi.
19,526   19,225   20,434   19,783   19,551   24,757
November 15,1862. Uncertain. (1) David Cross (?–1874); colonel, Confederate army 1861; resigned for poor health 1862. (2) Edward Cross (1798–1887). U.S. judge for Arkansas Territory 1830; U.S. surveyor general for Arkansas 1836–38; U.S. representative 1839–45; Arkansas Supreme Court judge 1845–55; attorney general of Arkansas 1874.

Crow Wing   **Minnesota**
Brainerd   997 sq. mi.
55,099   44,249   41,722   34,826   32,134   30,875
May 23, 1857; deorganized 1858; reorganized 1866; deorganized 1867; reorganized March 3, 1870. Crow Wing River. Translation of Chippewa name *kayaugeweguan,* meaning "crow's wing" or "crow's feather."

Crowley   **Colorado**
Ordway   789 sq. mi.
5,518   3,946   2,928   3,086   3,978   5,222
May 29, 1911. John H. Crowley (1849–?). Colorado House of Representatives 1893–94 and 1897–98; Colorado Board of Horticulture 1899–1905; Colorado Senate 1911.

Culberson   **Texas**
Van Horn   3,812 sq. mi.
2,975   3,407   3,315   3,429   2,794   1,825
March 10, 1911; organized 1912. David Browning Culberson (1830–1900). Texas legislature 1859; entered Confederate army as private; colonel, 18th Texas Infantry, adjutant general of Texas with rank of colonel; Texas House of Representatives 1864; Texas Senate 1873–75; U.S. representative 1875–97; commissioner to codify U.S. laws 1897–1900.

Cullman   **Alabama**
Cullman   738 sq. mi.
77,483   67,613   61,642   52,445   45,572   49,046
January 24, 1877. John Gottfried Cullman (c1825–95). Emigrated from Germany to U.S. 1866; founded town of Cullman as German colony 1873.

Culpeper   **Virginia**
Culpeper   381 sq. mi.
34,262   27,791   22,620   18,218   15,088   13,242

March 23, 1748. Thomas Culpeper, Lord Culpeper (1635–89). Received 31-year grant from King Charles II for entire Virginia colony 1673; purchased rights of Earl of Arlington 1675; proclaimed governor of Virginia for life 1675; commission declared forfeited 1683.

Cumberland   **Illinois**
Toledo   346 sq. mi.
11,253   10,670   11,062   9,772   9,936   10,496
March 2, 1843. Cumberland Road. First national thoroughfare, opened 1818 from Cumberland, Maryland, to Wheeling, Virginia (West Virginia). (See Cumberland, Kentucky.)

Cumberland   **Kentucky**
Burkesville   306 sq. mi.
7,147   6,784   7,289   6,850   7,835   9,309
December 14, 1798. Cumberland River. Named for *William Augustus, Duke of Cumberland* (1721–65). Second son of King George II and Queen Caroline; privy councillor 1742; major general 1742; lieutenant general 1743; captain general of the army 1745–57; commanded English troops at the battle of Culloden, Scotland, 1745; defeated Scottish Highlanders. Cumberland Road, Cumberland River, and Cumberland Mountains were named for him.

Cumberland   **Maine**
Portland   836 sq. mi.
265,612   243,135   215,789   192,528   182,751   169,201
May 28, 1760 (session); effective November 1, 1760. William Augustus, Duke of Cumberland.*

Cumberland   **New Jersey**
Bridgeton   489 sq. mi.
146,438   138,053   132,866   121,374   106,850   88,597
January 19, 1748. William Augustus, Duke of Cumberland.*

Cumberland   **North Carolina**
Fayetteville   653 sq. mi.
302,963   274,566   247,160   212,042   148,418   96,006
February 19, 1754 (session). William Augustus, Duke of Cumberland.*

Cumberland   **Pennsylvania**
Carlisle   550 sq. mi.
213,674   195,257   178,541   158,177   124,816   94,457
January 27, 1750. Cumberlandshire, England. "Land of the Cumbri" (Welsh).

Cumberland   **Tennessee**
Crossville   682 sq. mi.
46,802   34,736   28,676   20,733   19,135   18,877
November 16, 1855. Cumberland Mountains. Named for Duke of Cumberland.*

Cumberland   **Virginia**
Cumberland   298 sq. mi.
9,017   7,825   7,881   6,179   6,360   7,252
March 23, 1749. Duke of Cumberland.*

Cuming   **Nebraska**
West Point   572 sq. mi.
10,203   10,117   11,664   12,034   12,435   12,994
March 16, 1855. Thomas B. Cuming (1828–58). Acting governor of Nebraska Territory 1854–55 and 1857–58; secretary of Nebraska Territory 1854–58.

Currituck   **North Carolina**
Currituck   262 sq. mi.

18,190   13,736   11,089   6,976   6,601   6,201
1670. Currituck Indians. Members of Algonquin tribes; traditional translation of name is "wild geese."

Curry   **New Mexico**
Clovis   1,406 sq. mi.
45,044   42,207   42,019   39,517   32,691   23,251
February 25, 1909. George Curry (c1862–1947). Deputy treasurer, Lincoln County, New Mexico, 1886–87; county clerk 1888; lieutenant and captain in Roosevelt's Rough Riders in Spanish–American War 1898; sheriff, Otero County 1899; provost marshal and provost judge of provinces in Philippine Islands 1899–1907; governor of New Mexico Territory 1907–11; U.S. representative 1912–13; state historian of New Mexico 1945–47.

Curry   **Oregon**
Gold Beach   1,627 sq. mi.
21,137   19,327   16,992   13,006   13,983   6,048
December 18, 1855. George Law Curry (1820–78). Emigrated to Oregon 1846; Oregon legislature 1848–49 and 1851; acting secretary of Oregon legislature 1849; third editor of *Oregon Spectator*, first newspaper west of the Rockies 1846; territorial governor of Oregon 1853 and 1854–59.

Custer   **Colorado**
Westcliffe   739 sq. mi.
3,503   1,926   1,528   1,120   1,305   1,573
March 9, 1877. *George Armstrong Custer* (1839–76). Graduated West Point 1851; 2nd lieutenant at battle of Bull Run; brevet colonel for Yellow Tavern 1864; brevet colonel for Winchester 1864; brevet brigadier general 1865; led campaign against Cheyennes 1868; sent to Dakota Territory 1873; killed with his entire command at Little Big Horn, June 25, 1876.

Custer   **Idaho**
Challis   4,925 sq. mi.
4,342   4,133   3,385   2,967   2,996   3,318
January 8, 1881; effective April 1, 1882. General Custer Mine. Named for George Armstrong Custer.*

Custer   **Montana**
Miles City   3,783 sq. mi.
11,696   11,697   13,109   12,174   13,227   12,661
February 2, 1865, as Big Horn; name changed February 16, 1877. George Armstrong Custer.*

Custer   **Nebraska**
Broken Bow   2,576 sq. mi.
11,793   12,270   13,877   14,092   16,517   19,170
February 17, 1877; organized June 27, 1877. George Armstrong Custer.*

Custer   **Oklahoma**
Arapaho   987 sq. mi.
26,142   26,897   25,995   22,665   21,040   21,097
1892, as County G; name changed November 8, 1892; organized 1898. George Armstrong Custer.*

Custer   **South Dakota**
Custer   1,558 sq. mi.
7,275   6,179   6,000   4,698   4,906   5,517
January 11, 1875; organized April 26, 1877. George Armstrong Custer.*

Cuyahoga   **Ohio**
Cleveland   458 sq. mi.
1,393,978   1,412,140   1,498,400   1,721,300   1,647,895   1,389,532
February 10, 1807; organized February 10, 1808. Cuyahoga River. Indian word meaning "crooked."

D

Dade   **Georgia**
Trenton   174 sq. mi.
15,154   13,147   12,318   9,910   8,666   7,364
December 25, 1837. *Francis Langhorne Dade* (1793–1835). 3rd lieutenant in U.S. Infantry 1813; 1st lieutenant 1816; captain 1818; brevet major 1828; killed in ambush by Seminole chiefs Micanope and Jumper, December 28, 1835.

Dade   **Missouri**
Greenfield   490 sq. mi.
7,923   7,449   7,383   6,850   7,577   9,324
January 29, 1841. Francis Langhorne Dade.*

Daggett   **Utah**
Manila   698 sq. mi.
921   690   769   666   1,164   364
March 4, 1917; organized March 4, 1919. Ellsworth Daggett (1845–1923). Surveyor-general of Utah Territory 1888; surveyor of canal system for Daggett section of Utah.

Dakota   **Minnesota**
Hastings   570 sq. mi.
355,904   275,227   194,279   139,808   78,303   49,019
October 27, 1849; organized March 5, 1853. *Dakota Indians*. Commonly known as "Sioux," which is a Chippewa–French derogatory name (see Sioux, Iowa). The Sioux called themselves "Lakota" or "Dakota," meaning "friends" or "allies."

Dakota   **Nebraska**
Dakota City   264 sq. mi.
20,253   16,742   16,573   13,137   12,168   10,401
March 7, 1855; organized January 5, 1857. Dakota Indians.*

Dale   **Alabama**
Ozark   561 sq. mi.
49,129   49,633   47,821   52,938   31,066   20,828
December 22, 1824; effective October 1825. Samuel Dale (1772–1841). Indian scout 1793; major against Creeks 1794; colonel of militia; brigadier general; Alabama legislature 1819–20 and 1824–28; Mississippi legislature 1836.

Dallam   **Texas**
Dalhart   1,505 sq. mi.
6,222   5,461   6,531   6,012   6,302   7,640
August 21, 1876; organized September 8, 1891. James Wilmer Dallam (1818–47). Compiler of *A Digest of the Laws of Texas: Opinions of the Supreme Court of Texas from 1840–41*; died at New Orleans while on a trip to establish a newspaper at Indianola, Texas.

Dallas   **Alabama**
Selma   981 sq. mi.
46,365   48,130   53,981   55,296   56,667   56,270
February 9, 1818. *Alexander James Dallas* (1759–1817). U.S. district attorney in Pennsylvania 1810–14; U.S. secretary of the treasury 1814–15; acting U.S. secretary of war 1815.

Dallas   **Arkansas**
Fordyce   667 sq. mi.
9,210   9,614   10,515   10,022   10,522   12,416
January 1, 1845. *George Mifflin Dallas* (1792–1864). Solicitor of the U.S. Bank 1815–17; deputy attorney general 1817; mayor of Philadelphia 1829; U.S. district attorney for Eastern District of Pennsylvania 1829–31; U.S. senator 1831–33; attorney general of Pennsylvania 1833–35; U.S. minister to Russia 1837–39; vice president of U.S. 1845–49; U.S. minister to Great Britain 1856–61.

Dallas   **Iowa**
Adel   586 sq. mi.

40,750	29,755	29,513	26,085	24,123	23,661

January 13, 1846; organized March 1, 1847. George Mifflin Dallas.*

Dallas   **Missouri**
Buffalo   542 sq. mi.

15,661	12,646	12,096	10,054	9,314	10,392

January 29, 1841, as Niangua; name changed December 16, 1844. George Mifflin Dallas.*

Dallas   **Texas**
Dallas   880 sq. mi.

2,218,899	1,852,810	1,556,390	1,327,321	951,527	614,799

March 30, 1846; organized July 10, 1846. Uncertain. Probably named for George Mifflin Dallas.* Other suggestions include (1) either Walter R. or James L. Dallas, soldiers in Texas Army; (2) U.S. Navy commodore A. J. Dallas; (3) Alexander James Dallas*; (4) Joseph Dallas (?–?), an early settler in area.

Dane   **Wisconsin**
Madison   1,202 sq. mi.

426,526	367,085	323,545	290,272	222,095	169,357

December 7, 1836; organized 1839. Nathan Dane (1752–1835). Massachusetts House of Representatives 1782–85; Continental Congress 1785–88; Massachusetts Senate 1790–91 and 1794–97; Essex County judge of Court of Common Pleas 1794; commissioner to codify laws of Massachusetts 1795; author of 8-volume *Abridgement and Digest of American Law* 1829.

Daniels   **Montana**
Scobey   1,426 sq. mi.

2,017	2,266	2,835	3,083	3,755	3,946

August 30, 1920. Mansfield A. Daniels (1858–1919). Pioneer rancher; one of first settlers in area 1901.

Danville   **Virginia**
(Independent City)   43 sq. mi.

48,411	53,056	45,642	46,391	46,577	35,066

1890. Dan River. Origin of name uncertain; possibly for Dan River, Israel, source of Jordan River. (Associated county: Pittsylvania.)

Dare   **North Carolina**
Manteo   384 sq. mi.

29,967	22,746	13,377	6,995	5,935	5,405

February 2, 1870. Virginia Dare (1587–?). First child of English settlers born in America, August 18, 1587; granddaughter of John White, governor of Virginia Colony on Roanoke Island; vanished with Roanoke Colony.

Darke   **Ohio**
Greenville   600 sq. mi.

53,309	53,619	55,096	49,141	45,612	41,799

January 3, 1809; organized 1817. William Darke (1736–1801). Served under General Braddock at Fort Duquesne 1755; Indian fighter 1755–70; Continental army 1775; captain, 8th Virginia 1776; major 1777; wounded and captured at Germantown 1777; exchanged 1780; lieutenant colonel 4th Virginia 1781; lieutenant colonel, militia 1781; retired 1783; brigadier general; federal Constitutional Convention 1788; lieutenant colonel, Kentucky Militia at St. Clair's defeat 1791.

Darlington   **South Carolina**
Darlington   561 sq. mi.

67,394	61,851	62,717	53,442	52,928	50,016

March 12, 1785. Darlington, England.

Dauphin   **Pennsylvania**
Harrisburg   525 sq. mi.

251,798   237,813   232,317   223,834   220,255   197,784
March 4, 1785. Louis Joseph Xavier, Dauphin of France (1781–89). Eldest son of King Louis XVI and Marie Antoinette; a sickly child; died at age seven. "Dauphin" has been the hereditary title of the eldest son of the King of France since 1349. County was named to honor alliance with France during Revolutionary War.

Davidson   **North Carolina**
Lexington   552 sq. mi.
147,246   126,677   113,162   95,627   79,493   62,244
December 9, 1822. *William Lee Davidson* (1746–81). Major, 4th North Carolina 1776; lieutenant colonel 1777; brigadier general, North Carolina Militia; battle of Camden 1780; killed at battle of Cowan's Pass, January 17, 1781.

Davidson   **Tennessee**
Nashville   502 sq. mi.
569,891   510,784   477,811   448,003   399,743   321,758
April 18, 1783 (session). William Lee Davidson.*

Davie   **North Carolina**
Mocksville   265 sq. mi.
34,835   27,859   24,599   18,855   16,728   15,420
December 20, 1836. William Richardson Davie (1756–1820). Captain in Pulaski's Legion 1779; colonel, North Carolina Cavalry 1780; federal Constitutional Convention 1787; brigadier general, U.S. Army 1798; governor of North Carolina 1798–99; peace commissioner to France 1799.

Daviess   **Indiana**
Washington   431 sq. mi.
29,820   27,533   27,836   26,602   26,636   26,762
December 24, 1816; effective February 15, 1817. *Joseph Hamilton Daveiss* (1774–1811). U.S. district attorney for Kentucky; prosecuted Aaron Burr for treason 1807; killed at battle of Tippecanoe 1811. Daveiss's name is misspelled by all the states that named a county for him.

Daviess   **Kentucky**
Owensboro   462 sq. mi.
91,545   87,189   85,949   79,486   70,588   57,241
January 14, 1815. Joseph Hamilton Daveiss.*

Daviess   **Missouri**
Gallatin   567 sq. mi.
8,016   7,865   8,905   8,420   9,502   11,180
December 29, 1836. Joseph Hamilton Daveiss.*

Davis   **Iowa**
Bloomfield   503 sq. mi.
8,541   8,312   9,104   8,207   9,199   9,959
February 17, 1843; organized March 1, 1844. Garrett Davis (1801–72). Kentucky House of Representatives 1833–35; U.S. representative 1839–47; U.S. senator 1861–72.

Davis   **Utah**
Farmington   304 sq. mi.
238,994   187,941   146,540   99,028   64,760   30,867
March 3, 1852. Daniel C. Davis (1804–50). Captain of Company E, Mormon Battalion 1846; mustered out of army 1847; opened wagon road from Utah to California 1848.

Davison   **South Dakota**
Mitchell   435 sq. mi.
18,741   17,503   17,820   17,319   16,681   16,522

January 8, 1873; organized July 31, 1874. Henry C. Davison (?–1874). Merchant; one of first homesteaders in the area 1869; filed claim at Riverside, Dakota Territory, 1872.

Dawes   **Nebraska**
Chadron   1,396 sq. mi.
9,060   9,021   9,609   9,693   9,536   9,708
February 19, 1885. James William Dawes (1845–87). Nebraska Constitutional Convention 1875; Nebraska Senate 1876; governor of Nebraska 1883–87.

Dawson   **Georgia**
Dawsonville   211 sq. mi.
15,999   9,429   4,774   3,639   3,590   3,712
December 3, 1857. William Crosby Dawson (1798–1856). Clerk, Georgia House of Representatives; compiler of laws of Georgia 1820–30; captain, Volunteer company, Creek War 1836; U.S. representative 1836–41; judge of Superior Court of Ocmulgee Circuit Court 1845; U.S. senator 1849–55.

Dawson   **Montana**
Glendive   2,373 sq. mi.
9,059   9,505   11,805   11,269   12,314   9,092
January 15, 1869. Andrew Dawson (1817–71). Trapper and trader, American Fur Company.

Dawson   **Nebraska**
Lexington   1,013 sq. mi.
24,365   19,940   22,304   19,467   19,405   19,393
January 11, 1860; organized 1871. Jacob Dawson (?–?). Newspaper publisher; postmaster of Lancaster (now Lincoln) 1864–68.

Dawson   **Texas**
Lamesa   902 sq. mi.
14,985   14,349   16,184   16,604   19,185   19,113
August 21, 1876; organized February 13, 1905. Nicholas Mosby Dawson (1808–42). 2nd lieutenant at battle of San Jacinto 1836; lieutenant in Company C 1837; captain of Volunteer company 1842; killed by Mexican cavalry at Dawson Massacre, September 8, 1842.

Day   **South Dakota**
Webster   1,029 sq. mi.
6,267   6,978   8,133   8,713   10,516   12,294
October 1, 1879; organized January 2, 1882. Merritt H. Day (1844–1900). Pioneer; Civil War; Dakota territorial legislature 1879–89; commander, South Dakota State Militia in Messiah War against Sioux 1890.

Deaf Smith   **Texas**
Hereford   1,497 sq. mi.
18,561   19,153   21,165   18,999   13,187   9,111
August 21, 1876; organized December 1, 1890. Erastus "Deaf Smith" Smith (1787–1837). Settled in Texas 1821; scout for Sam Houston, battle of Concepción 1835; destroyed Vince's Bridge before battle of San Jacinto 1836; captain of Ranger company 1837; lost hearing from childhood disease.

Dearborn   **Indiana**
Lawrenceburg   305 sq. mi.
46,109   38,835   34,291   29,430   28,674   25,141
March 7, 1803. Henry Dearborn (1751–1829). Captain in Stark's Regiment 1775; fought at battle of Bunker Hill 1775; storming of Quebec 1775; taken prisoner, released on parole 1776; fought at battles of Stillwater (1777), Saratoga (1777), Monmouth (1778), and Newton (1779); deputy quartermaster with rank of colonel on General Washington's staff 1781; brigadier general of militia 1787; major general 1789; U.S. marshal for district of Maine 1789; U.S. representative from Massachusetts 1793–97; U.S. secretary of war 1801–09; collector of the Port of Boston 1809–12; senior major general, U.S. Army 1812; U.S. minister to Portugal 1822–24.

DeBaca   **New Mexico**
Fort Sumner   2,325 sq. mi.
2,240   2,252   2,454   2,547   2,991   3,464
February 28, 1917. Ezequiel Cabeza de Baca (1864–1917). Publisher and business manager of Spanish-language newspaper; lieutenant governor of New Mexico 1911–16; governor of New Mexico 1917; died six weeks after taking office.

Decatur   **Georgia**
Bainbridge   597 sq. mi.
28,240   25,511   25,495   22,310   25,203   23,620
December 8, 1823. *Stephen Decatur* (1779–1820). Commanded schooner *Enterprise* in Tripolitan War 1804; War of 1812; forced Barbary pirates to submit to terms; commissioner of the navy 1815; killed in a duel by Commodore James Barron, March 22, 1820.

Decatur   **Indiana**
Greensburg   373 sq. mi.
24,555   23,645   23,841   22,738   20,019   18,218
December 31, 1821; effective March 4, 1822. Stephen Decatur.*

Decatur   **Iowa**
Leon   532 sq. mi.
8,689   8,338   9,794   9,737   10,539   12,601
January 13, 1846; organized May 6, 1850. Stephen Decatur.*

Decatur   **Kansas**
Oberlin   894 sq. mi.
3,472   4,021   4,509   4,988   5,778   6,185
March 6, 1873; organized 1879. Stephen Decatur.*

Decatur   **Tennessee**
Decaturville   334 sq. mi.
11,731   10,472   10,857   9,457   8,324   9,442
November 1845. Stephen Decatur.*

Deer Lodge   **Montana**
Anaconda   737 sq. mi.
9,417   10,278   12,518   15,652   18,640   16,553
February 2, 1865. Town of Deer Lodge. Descriptive of a site where deer were frequently seen, near a landmark resembling an Indian lodge.

Defiance   **Ohio**
Defiance   411 sq. mi.
39,500   39,350   39,987   36,949   31,508   25,925
March 4, 1845. Fort Defiance Established by General Anthony Wayne 1794.

DeKalb   **Alabama**
Fort Payne   778 sq. mi.
64,452   54,651   53,658   41,981   41,417   45,048
January 9, 1836. *Johann Kalb, Baron de Kalb* (1721–80). Brigadier in French army 1764; aided American colonists, commissioned major general in Continental army 1777; mortally wounded at battle of Camden August 16, 1780.

DeKalb   **Georgia**
Decatur   268 sq. mi.
665,865   545,837   483,024   415,387   256,782   136,395
December 9, 1822. Johann Kalb, Baron de Kalb.*

DeKalb　　　　　　**Illinois**
Sycamore　　　　　　634 sq. mi.
88,969　　　77,932　　　74,624　　　71,654　　　51,714　　　40,781
March 4, 1837. Johann Kalb, Baron de Kalb.*

DeKalb　　　　　　**Indiana**
Auburn　　　　　　　363 sq. mi.
40,285　　　35,324　　　33,606　　　30,837　　　28,271　　　26,023
February 7, 1835; organized January 14, 1837; effective May 1, 1837. Johann Kalb, Baron de Kalb.*

DeKalb　　　　　　**Missouri**
Maysville　　　　　　424 sq. mi.
11,597　　　9,967　　　8,222　　　7,305　　　7,226　　　8,047
February 25, 1845. Johann Kalb, Baron de Kalb.*

DeKalb　　　　　　**Tennessee**
Smithville　　　　　　305 sq. mi.
17,423　　　14,360　　　13,589　　　11,151　　　10,774　　　11,680
December 11, 1837; organized 1838. Johann Kalb, Baron de Kalb.*

Delaware　　　　　**Indiana**
Muncie　　　　　　　393 sq. mi.
118,769　　　119,659　　　128,587　　　129,219　　　110,938　　　90,252
January 26, 1827; effective April 1, 1827. *Delaware Indians*. Named for Delaware River (see Delaware, New York). Originally lived in New Jersey and Pennsylvania; migrated west 1720–70.

Delaware　　　　　**Iowa**
Manchester　　　　　578 sq. mi.
18,404　　　18,035　　　18,933　　　18,770　　　18,483　　　17,734
December 21, 1837; organized November 19, 1841. Uncertain. (1) State of Delaware in appreciation of the services of Senator John Middleton Clayton of Delaware in creation of Wisconsin Territory, which included Iowa. (2) Delaware County, New York.

Delaware　　　　　**New York**
Delhi　　　　　　　　1,446 sq. mi.
48,055　　　47,225　　　46,824　　　44,718　　　43,540　　　44,420
March 10, 1797. *Delaware River*. Named for Thomas West, 3rd Baron De La Warr (1577–1618); first colonial governor of Virginia 1609; resided in Virginia 1610–11; returned to England 1611; died en route on second voyage to Virginia 1618.

Delaware　　　　　**Ohio**
Delaware　　　　　　442 sq. mi.
109,989　　　66,929　　　53,840　　　42,908　　　36,107　　　30,278
February 10, 1808. Delaware Indians.*

Delaware　　　　　**Oklahoma**
Jay　　　　　　　　　741 sq. mi.
37,077　　　28,070　　　23,946　　　17,767　　　13,198　　　14,734
July 16, 1907. Delaware Indians.*

Delaware　　　　　**Pennsylvania**
Media　　　　　　　　184 sq. mi.
550,864　　　547,651　　　555,007　　　600,035　　　553,154　　　414,234
September 26, 1789. Delaware River.*

Del Norte　　　　　**California**
Crescent City　　　　1,008 sq. mi.

27,507   23,460   18,217   14,580   17,771   8,078
March 2, 1857. Spanish for "of the north"; descriptive of county's location in northwest corner of the state.

Delta   **Colorado**
Delta   1,142 sq. mi.
27,834   20,980   21,225   15,286   15,602   17,365
February 11, 1883. City of Delta. Descriptive of the city's location at the Uncompahgre River delta.

Delta   **Michigan**
Escanaba   1,170 sq. mi.
38,520   37,780   38,947   35,924   34,298   32,913
March 9, 1843; organized March 12, 1861. Descriptive of the county's shape, similar to the Greek letter *delta*.

Delta   **Texas**
Cooper   277 sq. mi.
5,327   4,857   4,839   4,927   5,860   8,964
July 29, 1870; organized October 6, 1870. Greek letter *delta*. Descriptive of the triangular shape of the county.

Denali   **Alaska**
Healy   12,750 sq. mi.
1,893   (a)   (a)   (a)   (a)   (b)
December, 1990. Denali Mountain. Tanana name for Mount McKinley, meaning "the big one" or "the high one." [(a) Part of Yukon-Koyukuk Census Area; (b) part of 4th Judicial District.]

Dent   **Missouri**
Salem   754 sq. mi.
14,927   13,702   14,517   11,457   10,445   10,936
February 10, 1851. Lewis Dent (1808–80). Settler 1835; Missouri legislature 1851.

Denton   **Texas**
Denton   889 sq. mi.
432,976   273,525   143,126   75,633   47,432   41,365
April 11, 1846; organized July 13, 1846. John B. Denton (1806–41). Itinerant minister; lawyer; missionary; captain and aide to Colonel Edward H. Tarrant; killed near Fort Worth in attack against Indians, May 22, 1841.

Denver   **Colorado**
Denver   153 sq. mi.
554,636   467,610   492,365   514,678   493,887   415,786
March 18, 1901. City of Denver. Named for James William Denver (1817–92); captain under General Scott 1847–48; California Senate 1851; California secretary of state 1852; U.S. representative 1855–57; commissioner of Indian affairs 1857 and 1858–59; governor of Kansas Territory 1857–58; brigadier general, Union army 1861; resigned 1863.

Deschutes   **Oregon**
Bend   3,018 sq. mi.
115,367   74,958   62,142   30,442   23,100   21,812
December 13, 1916. Deschutes River. From French *Riviére des Chutes*, meaning "river of the falls."

Desha   **Arkansas**
Arkansas City   765 sq. mi.
15,341   16,798   19,760   18,761   20,770   25,155
December 12, 1838. Benjamin Desha (?–1835). Captain, War of 1812.

Des Moines   **Iowa**
Burlington   416 sq. mi.
42,351   42,614   46,203   46,982   44,605   42,056

September 6, 1834; effective October 1, 1834. Des Moines River. From Moingwena Indians, possibly referring to the loon that is one of their totems; rendered by French as *riviére des moines*.

DeSoto **Florida**
Arcadia 637 sq. mi.

32,209	23,865	19,039	13,060	11,683	9,242

May 19, 1887. *Hernando de Soto* (1496–1542). Spanish conqueror and explorer; served under Pizarro in Panama and Peru; received title governor of Florida and Cuba from Charles I; explored southeast U.S.; sighted Mississippi River 1541; contracted fever and died 1542; buried in Mississippi River.

De Soto **Louisiana**
Mansfield 877 sq. mi.

25,494	25,346	25,727	22,764	24,248	24,398

April 1, 1843. Hernando de Soto.*

DeSoto **Mississippi**
Hernando 478 sq. mi.

107,199	67,910	53,930	35,885	23,891	24,599

February 9, 1836. Hernando de Soto.*

Deuel **Nebraska**
Chappell 440 sq. mi.

2,098	2,237	2,462	2,717	3,125	3,330

November 6, 1888; organized January 21, 1889. Henry Porter Deuell (1836–1914). Agent Kansas City & St. Joseph Railroad 1888; Omaha passenger agent 1888–96; Chicago, Burlington & Quincy station agent in Omaha 1896; auditor, Douglas County 1899–1901.

Deuel **South Dakota**
Clear Lake 624 sq. mi.

4,498	4,522	5,289	5,686	6,782	7,689

April 5, 1862; organized May 20, 1878. Jacob Smith Deuel (1830–98). Dakota territorial legislature 1862–63; owned small store and sawmill; moved to Nebraska 1863.

Dewey **Oklahoma**
Taloga 1,000 sq. mi.

4,743	5,551	5,922	5,656	6,051	8,789

1892, as County D; name changed November 8, 1898. George Dewey (1837–1917). Graduated U.S. Naval Academy 1858; served under Admiral Farragut in Civil War 1861; commanded Asiatic squadron in Spanish–American War 1897; won battle of Manila Bay, May 1, 1898; appointed first admiral of the navy 1899.

Dewey **South Dakota**
Timber Lake 2,303 sq. mi.

5,972	5,523	5,366	5,170	5,257	4,968[a]

January 8, 1873, as Rusk; name changed March 9, 1883; organized December 3, 1910. William Pitt Dewey (1833–1900). Pioneer; Dakota territorial surveyor general 1873–77; Dakota territorial legislature 1883. [(a) Includes Armstrong (52)]

De Witt **Illinois**
Clinton 398 sq. mi.

16,798	16,516	18,108	16,975	17,253	16,894

March 1, 1839. De Witt Clinton* (see Clinton, Illinois).

DeWitt **Texas**
Cuero 909 sq. mi.

20,013	18,840	18,903	18,660	20,693	22,973

March 24, 1846; organized July 13, 1846. Green C. De Witt (1787–1835). Captain, War of 1812; established small colony in Mexico 1825; represented Gonzalez in Convention of 1833.

Dickens   **Texas**
Dickens   904 sq. mi.
2,762   2,571   3,539   3,737   4,963   7,177
August 21, 1876; organized March 14, 1891. James R. Dimpkins (?–1836). Englishman; captain, New Orleans Greys; siege of Bexar; killed at the Alamo; listed on the Alamo monument as "J. Dickens."

Dickenson   **Virginia**
Clintwood   332 sq. mi.
16,395   17,620   19,806   16,077   20,211   23,393
March 3, 1880. William J. Dickenson (1828–1907). Virginia legislature; one of founders of Readjuster political party, popular in Virginia in late 19th century.

Dickey   **North Dakota**
Ellendale   1,131 sq. mi.
5,757   6,107   7,207   6,976   8,147   9,121
March 5, 1881; August 31, 1882. George H. Dickey (1858–1923). Attorney; Dakota territorial legislature 1881.

Dickinson   **Iowa**
Spirit Lake   381 sq. mi.
16,424   14,909   15,629   12,565   12,574   12,756
January 15, 1851; organized August 3, 1857. *Daniel Stevens Dickinson* (1800–66). New York Assembly 1837–40; lieutenant governor of New York 1842–44; U.S. senator 1844–51; attorney general of New York 1861; U.S. attorney for the Southern District of New York 1865–66.

Dickinson   **Kansas**
Abeline   848 sq. mi.
19,344   18,958   20,175   19,993   21,572   21,190
February 20, 1857. Daniel Stevens Dickinson.*

Dickinson   **Michigan**
Iron Mountain   766 sq. mi.
27,472   26,831   25,341   23,753   23,917   24,844
May 21, 1891. Donald McDonald Dickinson (1846–1917). Chairman, Michigan Democratic state committee; postmaster general of the U.S. 1887–89.

Dickson   **Tennessee**
Charlotte   490 sq. mi.
43,156   35,061   30,037   21,977   18,839   18,805
October 25, 1803. William Dickson (1770–1816). Physician; Tennessee House of Representatives 1799–1803; U.S. representative 1801–07; trustee of University of Nashville 1806–16.

Dillingham   **Alaska**
(Census Area)   18,675 sq. mi.
4,922   4,012   4,616   3,485[a]   4,024[a]   [b]
William Paul Dillingham (1843–1923). Governor of Vermont 1888–90; U.S. senator 1903–23; led Senate subcommittee tour of Alaska 1903; became Senate's "authority" on Alaska. [(a) Bristol Bay Census Area; (b) part of 3rd Judicial District.]

Dillon   **South Carolina**
Dillon   405 sq. mi.
30,722   29,114   31,083   28,838   30,584   30,930
February 15, 1910. Town of Dillon. Named for James W. Dillon (1826–1913); merchant; persuaded Florence Railroad Company to build station on site that became town of Dillon 1881.

Dimmit   **Texas**
Carrizo Springs   1,331 sq. mi.

10,248   10,433   11,367   9,039   10,095   10,654

February 1, 1858; organized November 2, 1880. Philip Dimmit (1801–41). Captain of troops at Goliad after its capture; took poison rather than go to Mexican prison at siege of Bexar July 1841.

Dinwiddie   **Virginia**
Dinwiddie   504 sq. mi.

24,533   20,960   22,602   25,046   22,183   18,839

February 27, 1752 (session). Robert Dinwiddie (c1693–1770). Lieutenant governor of Royal Province of Virginia 1751–56 and 1756–58; fought French; returned to England 1758.

District of Columbia   (Federal District)
Washington   61 sq. mi.

572,059   606,900   638,333   756,510   763,956   802,178

July 16, 1790. Christopher Columbus.* (See Columbia, Florida.)

Divide   **North Dakota**
Crosby   1,260 sq. mi.

2,283   2,899   3,494   4,564   5,566   5,967

December 9, 1910. Uncertain. (1) Descriptive of divide between Missouri and Red Rivers, which runs across county. (2) In honor of vote to divide county from Williams County.

Dixie   **Florida**
Cross City   704 sq. mi.

13,827   10,585   7,751   5,480   4,479   3,928

April 25, 1921. Nickname for the South. Derived from French *dix*, meaning "ten"; refers to $10.00 bank notes printed by Citizens Bank of New Orleans.

Dixon   **Nebraska**
Ponca   476 sq. mi.

6,339   6,143   7,137   7,453   8,106   9,129

January 26, 1856; organized November 1, 1858. Unknown early settler named Dixon.

Doddridge   **West Virginia**
West Union   320 sq. mi.

7,403   6,994   7,433   6,389   6,970   9,026

February 4, 1845. Philip Doddridge (1773–1832). Virginia House of Delegates 1815–16, 1822–23, and 1828–29; Virginia Constitutional Convention 1829; U.S. representative 1829–32.

Dodge   **Georgia**
Eastman   500 sq. mi.

19,171   17,607   16,955   15,658   16,483   17,865

October 26, 1870. William Earle Dodge (1805–83). Merchant; delegate to peace convention to prevent Civil War 1861; U.S. representative from New York 1866–67; urged moderation in Reconstruction; owned vast tracts of pine lands in Georgia; president, National Temperance Society 1865–83.

Dodge   **Minnesota**
Mantorville   440 sq. mi.

17,731   15,731   14,773   13,037   13,259   12,624

February 20, 1855. *Henry Dodge* (1782–1867) and *Augustus Caesar Dodge* (1812–83). (1) Henry served in War of 1812; in Black Hawk War and other Indian wars; major, U.S. Rangers 1832; resigned from army with rank of colonel 1836; governor of Wisconsin Territory 1836–41 and 1845–48; congressional delegate from Wisconsin Territory 1841–45; U.S. senator 1848–57; declined appointment as governor of Washington Territory. (2) Augustus was son of Henry; congressional delegate from Iowa Territory 1840–48; U.S. senator 1848–55; U.S. minister to Spain 1855.

Dodge   **Nebraska**
Fremont   534 sq. mi.

36,160   34,500   35,847   34,782   32,471   26,265
November 23, 1854; organized January 6, 1857. Augustus Caesar Dodge.*

Dodge   **Wisconsin**
Juneau   882 sq. mi.
85,897   76,559   75,064   69,004   63,170   57,611
December 7, 1836; organized 1844. Henry Dodge.*

Dolores   **Colorado**
Dove Creek   1,067 sq. mi.
1,844   1,504   1,658   1,641   2,196   1,966
February 19, 1881. Dolores River. From Spanish *Rio de Nuestra Señora de los Dolores* (River of Our Lady of Sorrows); named when a member of a Spanish exploration party drowned in the river.

Dona Ana   **New Mexico**
Las Cruces   3,807 sq. mi.
174,682   135,510   96,340   69,773   59,948   39,557
January 9, 1852. Village of Dona Ana. Origin of name is unknown; possibilities include (1) Doña Ana Robledo (?–?), a local widow known for her charity; (2) Señorita Ana; legendary maiden captured by Indians; (3) Doña Ana María, Niña de Córdoba (?–?), sheep rancher in 17th century.

Doniphan   **Kansas**
Troy   392 sq. mi.
8,249   8,134   9,268   9,107   9,574   10,499
August 30, 1855. Alexander William Doniphan (1808–87). Missouri legislature 1836, 1840, and 1854; brigadier general in Missouri Militia to drive Mormons out of Missouri 1838; colonel of 1st Regiment of Missouri Mounted Volunteers in Mexican War 1846; battles of Chihuahua and Saltillo 1847.

Donley   **Texas**
Clarendon   930 sq. mi.
3,828   3,696   4,075   3,641   4,449   6,216
August 21, 1876; organized March 22, 1882. Stockton P. Donley (1821–71). District attorney, 6th Texas Judicial District 1852; Confederate army 1861; Texas Supreme Court 1866, removed 1867.

Dooly   **Georgia**
Vienna   393 sq. mi.
11,525   9,901   10,826   10,404   11,474   14,159
May 15, 1821. John Dooly (1740–80). Captain, 1st Georgia Regiment 1775; resigned 1776; colonel, Georgia Militia; murdered in home by Tories August 1780.

Door   **Wisconsin**
Sturgeon Bay   483 sq. mi.
27,961   25,690   25,029   20,106   20,685   20,870
February 11, 1851; organized 1861. Porte de Morte (Death's Door). French name given to strait with hazardous currents flowing between islands at entrance to Green Bay.

Dorchester   **Maryland**
Cambridge   558 sq. mi.
30,674   30,236   30,623   29,405   29,666   27,815
February 16, 1669. Uncertain. (1) Edward Sackville, 4th Earl of Dorset (1591–1652); member of Parliament; English ambassador to France; governor of Bermuda Islands Company; privy councilor; lord chamberlain to Queen Henrietta Maria, wife of Charles I. (2) Richard Sackville, 5th Earl of Dorset (1622–77); friend of the Calverts; member of Parliament 1640–43; court favorite of Charles II; succeeded as 5th Earl of Dorset, July 17, 1652.

Dorchester   **South Carolina**
Saint George   575 sq. mi.

96,413   83,060   58,761   32,276   24,383   22,601
February 25, 1897. Town of Dorchester. Named for town of Dorchester, Massachusetts.

Dougherty   **Georgia**
Albany   330 sq. mi.
96,065   96,311   100,718   89,639   75,680   43,617
December 15, 1853. Charles Dougherty (1801–53). Judge of the Western Circuit; leader of Georgia's Whig Party.

Douglas   **Colorado**
Castle Rock   840 sq. mi.
175,766   60,391   25,153   8,407   4,816   3,507
November 1, 1861. *Stephen Arnold Douglas* (1813–61). Illinois House of Representatives 1836–37; Illinois secretary of state 1840–41; U.S. representative 1843–47; U.S. senator 1847–61; Lincoln–Douglas debates 1858; Democratic nominee for president, defeated by Lincoln 1861.

Douglas   **Georgia**
Douglasville   199 sq. mi.
92,174   71,120   54,573   28,659   16,741   12,173
October 17, 1870. Stephen Arnold Douglas.*

Douglas   **Illinois**
Tuscola   417 sq. mi.
19,922   19,464   19,774   18,997   19,243   16,706
February 8, 1859. Stephen Arnold Douglas.*

Douglas   **Kansas**
Lawrence   457 sq. mi.
99,962   81,798   67,640   57,932   43,720   34,086
August 30, 1855. Stephen Arnold Douglas.*

Douglas   **Minnesota**
Alexandria   634 sq. mi.
32,821   28,674   27,839   22,892   21,313   21,304
March 8, 1858. Stephen Arnold Douglas.*

Douglas   **Missouri**
Ava   815 sq. mi.
13,084   11,876   11,594   9,268   9,653   12,638
October 29, 1857. Stephen Arnold Douglas.*

Douglas   **Nebraska**
Omaha   331 sq. mi.
463,585   416,444   397,038   389,455   343,490   281,020
November 23, 1854. Stephen Arnold Douglas.*

Douglas   **Nevada**
Minden   710 sq. mi.
41,259   27,637   19,421   6,882   3,481   2,029
November 25, 1861. Stephen Arnold Douglas.*

Douglas   **Oregon**
Roseburg   5,037 sq. mi.
100,399   94,649   93,748   71,743   68,458   54,549
January 7, 1852. Stephen Arnold Douglas.*

Douglas   **South Dakota**
Armour   434 sq. mi.
3,458   3,746   4,181   4,569   5,113   5,636
January 8, 1873; organized June 7, 1882. Stephen Arnold Douglas.*

Douglas   **Washington**
Waterville   1,821 sq. mi.
32,603   26,205   22,144   16,787   14,890   10,817
November 28, 1883. Stephen Arnold Douglas.*

Douglas   **Wisconsin**
Superior   1,309 sq. mi.
43,287   41,758   44,421   44,657   45,008   46,715
February 9, 1854. Stephen Arnold Douglas.*

Drew   **Arkansas**
Monticello   828 sq. mi.
18,723   17,369   17,910   15,157   15,213   17,959
November 26, 1846. Thomas Stevenson Drew (1802–79). Merchant; schoolteacher; county clerk 1823–25; Arkansas constitutional Convention 1836; governor of Arkansas 1844–49.

Dubois   **Indiana**
Jasper   430 sq. mi.
39,674   36,616   34,238   30,934   27,463   23,785
December 20, 1817; effective February 1, 1818. Toussaint Dubois (1764–1816). French soldier; Indian trader; served under William Henry Harrison against Indians; battle of Tippecanoe 1811; drowned in Little Wabash River.

Dubuque   **Iowa**
Dubuque   608 sq. mi.
89,143   86,403   93,745   90,609   80,048   71,337
September 6, 1834; effective October 1, 1834. Julien Dubuque (1762–1810). First settler in Iowa; received option from Indians to operate lead mines.

Duchesne   **Utah**
Duchesne   3,238 sq. mi.
14,371   12,645   12,565   7,299   7,179   8,134
March 3, 1913. Duchesne River. Origin of name is unknown; possibilities include (1) French trapper named Du Chasne or Du Chesne; (2) Mother Rose Philippine Duchesne (1769–1852), founder of U.S. branch of Society of the Sacred Heart; (3) André Duchesne (1584–1640), French geographer and historian; and (4) Ute word meaning "dark canyon."

Dukes   **Massachusetts**
Edgartown   104 sq. mi.
14,987   11,639   8,942   6,117   5,829   5,633
June 22, 1695. King James II, Duke of York and Albany* (see Albany, New York.)

Dundy   **Nebraska**
Benkelman   920 sq. mi.
2,292   2,582   2,861   2,926   3,570   4,354
February 27, 1873; organized June 12, 1884. Elmer S. Dundy (1830–96). Nebraska territorial legislature 1858–61; Nebraska Territory Supreme Court 1863–67; U.S. Circuit Court 1867–96.

Dunklin   **Missouri**
Kennett   546 sq. mi.
33,155   33,112   36,324   33,742   39,139   45,329
February 14, 1845. Daniel Dunklin (1790–1844). Sheriff, Washington County, Missouri; Constitutional Convention 1820; lieutenant governor 1828; governor of Missouri 1833–36; surveyor general of Missouri, Illinois, and Arkansas, 1836.

Dunn **North Dakota**
Manning 2,010 sq. mi.
3,600 4,005 4,627 4,895 6,350 7,212
March 9, 1883; abolished 1896; recreated May 24, 1901; organized January 17, 1908. John P. Dunn (1839–1917). Homesteaded 1873; mayor of Bismarck, North Dakota 1884–85.

Dunn **Wisconsin**
Menomonie 852 sq. mi.
39,858 35,909 34,314 29,154 26,156 27,341
February 3, 1854; organized 1857. Charles Dunn (1799–1872). Illinois legislature; first chief justice of Wisconsin Territory 1836; Wisconsin Senate 1853–56.

DuPage **Illinois**
Wheaton 334 sq. mi.
904,161 781,666 658,835 491,882 313,459 154,599
February 9, 1839. Du Page River. Named for an early French Indian trader who had a trading post on the banks of the river about 1800.

Duplin **North Carolina**
Kenansville 818 sq. mi.
49,063 39,995 40,952 38,015 40,270 41,074
March 17, 1749 (session). George Henry Hay, Viscount Dupplin and Earl of Kinnoull (1710–87). English nobleman, made Viscount Dupplin 1627; British Parliament 1741–58; commissioner of Irish revenue; ambassador-extraordinary to Portugal.

Durham **North Carolina**
Durham 290 sq. mi.
223,314 181,835 152,785 132,681 111,995 101,639
February 28, 1881. City of Durham. Named for Dr. Bartlett Durham (1822–58); donated land for railroad station which became Durhamville.

Dutchess **New York**
Poughkeepsie 802 sq. mi.
280,150 259,462 245,055 222,295 176,008 136,781
November 1, 1683; organized 1713. Mary Beatrice of Modena, Duchess of York and Albany (1658–1718). Daughter of Alfonso IV, Duke of Modena; second wife of James II, Duke of York and Albany; Queen Consort of England 1685–88; fled to France during English Civil War.

Duval **Florida**
Jacksonville 774 sq. mi.
778,879 672,971 571,003 528,865 455,411 304,029
August 12, 1822. *William Pope DuVal* (1784–1854). Captain of Kentucky Mounted Rangers 1812; U.S. representative 1813–15; U.S. judge East Florida District 1821; governor of Florida Territory 1822–34; law agent in Florida 1841.

Duval **Texas**
San Diego 1,793 sq. mi.
13,120 12,918 12,517 11,722 13,398 15,643
February 1, 1858; organized November 7, 1876. Uncertain. (1) All three Duval brothers, sons of William Pope DuVal*: Burr H. Duval (1809–36), captain of Kentucky Mustangs, massacred at Goliad, Texas, March 27, 1836; John C. Duval (1816–96), followed brother Burr to Texas, escaped massacre at Goliad; Thomas H. Duval (1813–80), federal judge 1865. (2) Burr Duval only.

Dyer **Tennessee**
Dyersburg 511 sq. mi.
37,279 34,854 34,663 30,427 29,537 33,473
October 16, 1823. Robert Henry Dyer (c1774–1826). War of 1812; Natchez expedition; Creek War; battle of New Orleans 1815; Seminole campaign 1818.

E

Eagle **Colorado**
Eagle 1,688 sq. mi.
41,659 21,928 13,320 7,498 4,677 4,488
February 11, 1883. Eagle River. Uncertain. (1) Name of Ute chief. (2) Descriptive of the numerous eagles in the area.

Early **Georgia**
Blakely 511 sq. mi.
12,354 11,854 13,158 12,682 13,151 17,413
December 15, 1818; organized December 24, 1825. Peter Early (1773–1817). U.S. representative from Georgia 1803–07; first judge of the Superior Court of the Ocmulgee Circuit 1807–13; governor of Georgia 1813–15; Georgia Senate 1815–17.

East Baton Rouge **Louisiana**
Baton Rouge 455 sq. mi.
412,852 380,105 366,191 285,167 230,058 158,236
December 22, 1810. French for "red stick." French Canadian explorer Pierre le Moyne, Sieur d'Iberville noted a "reddened maypole" marking the boundary between Indian hunting areas 1699; the pole may also have had religious significance.

East Carroll **Louisiana**
Lake Providence 421 sq. mi.
9,421 9,709 11,772 12,884 14,433 16,302
March 28, 1877. Carroll Parish. Named for Charles Carroll (see Carroll, Arkansas); Carroll Parish (est. March 14, 1832) divided into east and west parishes 1877.

East Feliciana **Louisiana**
Clinton 453 sq. mi.
21,360 19,211 19,015 17,657 20,198 19,133
February 17, 1824. Feliciana Parish. Named for Spanish Distrito de Feliciana in West Florida; claimed by U.S. 1810; Feliciana Parish (est. December 7, 1810) divided into east and west parishes 1824. Origin of name is uncertain; possibilities include (1) Spanish for "land of happiness" or "happy land"; (2) Maria Feliciana (Felicite) de Saint-Maxent (?–?), French wife of Bernardo de Galvez, Spanish governor of Louisiana.

Eastland **Texas**
Eastland 926 sq. mi.
18,297 18,488 19,480 18,092 19,526 23,942
February 1, 1858; organized December 2, 1873. William Mosby Eastland (1806–43). 1st lieutenant; fought Waco Indians 1835; battle of San Jacinto 1836; captain 1836–38; executed on orders of Santa Anna, March 25, 1843.

Eaton **Michigan**
Charlotte 576 sq. mi.
103,655 92,879 88,337 68,892 49,684 40,023
October 29, 1829; organized December 29, 1837. John Henry Eaton (1790–1856). Tennessee House of Representatives 1815–16; U.S. senator 1818–29; U.S. secretary of war 1829–31; governor of Florida Territory 1834–36; envoy extraordinary and minister plenipotentiary to Spain 1836–40.

Eau Claire **Wisconsin**
Eau Claire 638 sq. mi.
93,142 85,183 78,805 67,219 58,300 54,187
October 6, 1856. Eau Claire River. French for "clear water."

Echols **Georgia**
Statenville 404 sq. mi.
3,754 2,334 2,297 1,924 1,876 2,494
December 13, 1858. Robert M. Echols (c1800–47). Georgia Assembly; colonel, 13th U.S. Infantry Regiment 1847; brevet brigadier general 1847; thrown from his horse during a dress parade and died at Natural Bridge, Mexico, December 3, 1847.

Ector　　　　　　　　**Texas**
Odessa　　　　　　　　901 sq. mi.
121,123　　　118,934　　　115,374　　　91,805　　　90,995　　　42,102
February 26, 1887; organized January 6, 1891. Matthew Duncan Ector (1822–79). Texas legislature; 3rd Texas Cavalry; brigadier general in the Army of Cumberland; district judge 1866; judge of the 6th District Court of Texas 1874; judge of the Court of Appeals 1876–79.

Eddy　　　　　　　　**New Mexico**
Carlsbad　　　　　　　4,182 sq. mi.
51,658　　　48,605　　　47,855　　　41,119　　　50,783　　　40,640
February 25, 1889. Charles B. Eddy (1857–?). Cattleman; manager of Carlsbad irrigation project in Pecos Valley 1889–94.

Eddy　　　　　　　　**North Dakota**
New Rockford　　　　　630 sq. mi.
2,757　　　2,951　　　3,554　　　4,103　　　4,936　　　5,732
March 31, 1885; organized April 27, 1885. Ezra B. Eddy (1829–85). 1st lieutenant, Minnesota Volunteer Infantry, 1861; merchant; founder of First National Bank, Fargo, 1878

Edgar　　　　　　　　**Illinois**
Paris　　　　　　　　624 sq. mi.
19,704　　　19,595　　　21,725　　　21,591　　　22,550　　　23,407
January 3, 1823. John Edgar (?–1832). Officer in British navy during American Revolution; deserted to American side; judge of Common Pleas Court; Northwest territorial legislature; major general of militia.

Edgecombe　　　　　**North Carolina**
Tarboro　　　　　　　505 sq. mi.
55,606　　　56,558　　　55,988　　　52,341　　　54,226　　　51,634
April 4, 1741. Richard Edgcumbe, Baron Edgcumbe (1680–1758). British Parliament 1701; lord of English treasury 1716; vice treasurer, treasurer of war, and paymaster general of His Majesty's services in Ireland; major general 1755.

Edgefield　　　　　**South Carolina**
Edgefield　　　　　　502 sq. mi.
24,595　　　18,375　　　17,528　　　15,692　　　15,735　　　16,591
March 12, 1785. Uncertain. (1) Descriptive of early settlement located on the edge of an Indian battlefield. (2) Describes county's location on the western edge of the state.

Edmonson　　　　　　**Kentucky**
Brownsville　　　　　303 sq. mi.
11,644　　　10,357　　　9,962　　　8,751　　　8,085　　　9,376
January 12, 1825. John Edmonson (?–1813). Virginia militia; battle of King's Mountain 1780; raised company of volunteer riflemen, commissioned colonel 1812; killed at Frenchtown battle on the Raisin River, Michigan, January 18, 1813.

Edmunds　　　　　　**South Dakota**
Ipswich　　　　　　　1,146 sq. mi.
4,367　　　4,356　　　5,159　　　5,548　　　6,079　　　7,275
January 8, 1873; organized July 27, 1883. Newton Edmunds (1819–1908). Chief clerk in surveyor's office 1861; sought peace with Indians; governor of Dakota Territory 1863–66; banker.

Edwards　　　　　　**Illinois**
Albion　　　　　　　222 sq. mi.
6,971　　　7,440　　　7,961　　　7,090　　　7,940　　　9,056
November 28, 1814. Ninian Edwards (1775–1833). Kentucky House of Representatives 1796–97; judge of Kentucky General Court 1803; judge of Kentucky Circuit Court; judge of Court of Appeals 1806; Kentucky chief justice 1808; governor of Illinois Territory 1809–18; U.S. senator from Illinois 1818–24; governor of Illinois 1826–30.

Edwards   **Kansas**
Kinsley   622 sq. mi.
3,449   3,787   4,271   4,581   5,118   5,936
March 7, 1874. William Corydon Edwards (1846–1922). Lumber merchant; Kansas secretary of state 1895–97.

Edwards   **Texas**
Rocksprings   2,120 sq. mi.
2,162   2,266   2,033   2,107   2,317   2,908
February 1, 1858; organized April 10, 1883. Hayden Edwards (1771–1849). Founded colony at Nacagdoches 1825; expelled by Mexican governor 1826; leader of Fredonian Rebellion 1826.

Effingham   **Georgia**
Springfield   479 sq. mi.
37,535   25,687   18,327   13,632   10,144   9,133
February 5, 1777. *Thomas Howard, 3rd Earl of Effingham* (1746–91). 1st Regiment of Foot Guards 1766; captain, 22nd Regiment 1772; deputy earl marshal of England 1777–82; lieutenant colonel, British army 1782; resigned commission rather than fight Americans.

Effingham   **Illinois**
Effingham   479 sq. mi.
34,264   31,704   30,944   24,608   23,107   21,675
February 15, 1831; organized 1833. Uncertain. (1) Edward Effingham (?–?); general, Black Hawk War 1832; U.S. surveyor; surveyed county. (2) Thomas Howard, 3rd Earl of Effingham.*

Elbert   **Colorado**
Kiowa   1,851 sq. mi.
19,872   9,646   6,850   3,903   3,708   4,477
February 2, 1874. Samuel Hitt Elbert (1833–1907). Secretary of Colorado Territory 1862; Colorado territorial legislature 1869; governor of Colorado Territory 1873–74; Colorado Supreme Court justice 1876–80; chief justice, Colorado Supreme Court 1880–83.

Elbert   **Georgia**
Elberton   369 sq. mi.
20,511   18,949   18,758   17,262   17,835   18,585
December 10, 1790. Samuel Elbert (1743–82). Captain, Grenadier Company 1774; member of Georgia Council of Safety 1775; lieutenant colonel and colonel 1776; expedition against English in East Florida 1777; defended Savannah; wounded and taken prisoner at Briar Creek 1779; brevet brigadier general 1782; governor of Georgia 1785–86; major general of militia.

El Dorado   **California**
Placerville   1,711 sq. mi.
156,299   125,995   85,812   43,833   29,390   16,207
February 18, 1850. Spanish for "the gilded one," from myth of a king covered in gold dust each day. Descriptive of local gold deposits.

Elk   **Kansas**
Howard   647 sq. mi.
3,261   3,327   3,918   3,858   5,048   6,679
March 3, 1875; effective June 1, 1875. Elk River. Descriptive of the numerous elk ranging in the area.

Elk   **Pennsylvania**
Ridgway   829 sq. mi.
35,112   34,878   38,338   37,770   37,328   34,503
April 18, 1843. Descriptive of elk herds in the area.

Elkhart   **Indiana**
Goshen   464 sq. mi.

| 182,791 | 156,198 | 137,330 | 126,529 | 106,790 | 84,512 |

January 29, 1830; effective April 1, 1830. Uncertain. (1) Elkhart River, named by Miamis from a heart-shaped island in the river. (2) Elkhart Indians.

Elko   **Nevada**
Elko   17,179 sq. mi.

| 45,291 | 33,530 | 17,269 | 13,958 | 12,011 | 11,654 |

March 5, 1869. Town of Elko. Name of uncertain origin and meaning; at least seven different new towns were named "Elko" by railroads.

Elliott   **Kentucky**
Sandy Hook   234 sq. mi.

| 6,748 | 6,455 | 6,908 | 5,933 | 6,330 | 7,085 |

January 26, 1869. Uncertain. (1) John L. Elliott (1794–1855); ran away to Virginia as a youth and assumed the name Isaac Lowe; War of 1812; returned to Kentucky and resumed true name 1825; Kentucky House of Representatives 1836–37; Kentucky Senate 1851–53. (2) John Milton Elliott (1820–79); son of John L.; Kentucky House of Representatives 1847 and 1861; U.S. representative 1853–59; 1st and 2nd Confederate Congresses; circuit judge 1868–74; judge of Court of Appeals 1876–79; assassinated at Frankfort 1879.

Ellis   **Kansas**
Hays   900 sq. mi.

| 27,507 | 26,004 | 26,098 | 24,730 | 21,270 | 19,043 |

February 26, 1867. George Ellis (?–1864). 1st lieutenant, Company I, 12th Kansas Infantry; killed at Jenkins Ferry, April 30, 1864.

Ellis   **Oklahoma**
Arnett   1,229 sq. mi.

| 4,075 | 4,497 | 5,596 | 5,129 | 5,457 | 7,326 |

July 16, 1907. Albert H. Ellis (c1867–?). Delegate and 2nd vice president, Oklahoma Constitutional Convention 1907.

Ellis   **Texas**
Waxahachie   940 sq. mi.

| 111,360 | 85,167 | 59,743 | 46,638 | 43,395 | 45,645 |

December 20, 1849; organized August 5, 1850. Richard Ellis (1781–1846). Alabama Constitutional Convention 1819; Alabama Supreme Court 1819–25; president of Texas Convention of 1836; signer, Texas Declaration of Independence; Texas Republic Senate 1836–40.

Ellsworth   **Kansas**
Ellsworth   716 sq. mi.

| 6,525 | 6,586 | 6,640 | 6,146 | 7,677 | 8,465 |

February 26, 1867. Fort Ellsworth. Named for Allen Ellsworth (c1831–?); 2nd lieutenant, Company H, 7th Iowa Cavalry 1863; supervised construction of fort later named for him 1864.

Elmore   **Alabama**
Wetumpka   621 sq. mi.

| 65,874 | 49,210 | 43,390 | 33,535 | 30,524 | 31,649 |

February 15, 1866. John Archer Elmore (1762–1834). Revolutionary War; South Carolina legislature; moved to Alabama 1819; Alabama legislature 1821.

Elmore   **Idaho**
Mountain Home   3,078 sq. mi.

| 29,130 | 21,205 | 21,565 | 17,479 | 16,719 | 6,687 |

February 7, 1889. Ida Elmore Mine; region's most productive gold and silver mine during 1860's. Name origin unknown.

El Paso   **Colorado**
Colorado Springs   2,126 sq. mi.

516,929   397,014   309,424   235,972   143,742   74,523
November 1, 1861. Spanish for "the pass"; refers to Ute Pass near Pike's Peak.

El Paso   **Texas**
El Paso   1,013 sq. mi.
679,622   591,610   479,899   359,291   314,070   194,968
January 3, 1850; organized March 7, 1871. City of El Paso. From Spanish "El Paso del Norte" (The Pass of the North), or "El Paso del Rio del Norte" (The Pass of the River of the North). Both names refer to the Rio Grande's passage through local mountains.

Emanuel   **Georgia**
Swainsboro   686 sq. mi.
21,837   20,546   20,795   18,189   17,815   19,789
December 10, 1812. David Emanuel (1742–1808). Revolutionary War; Georgia legislature; president of Georgia Senate; governor of Georgia 1801.

Emery   **Utah**
Castle Dale   4,452 sq. mi.
10,860   10,332   11,451   5,137   5,546   6,304
February 12, 1880. George W. Emery (1830–1909). Governor of Utah Territory 1875–80; balanced handling of Mormon–U.S. issues.

Emmet   **Iowa**
Estherville   396 sq. mi.
11,027   11,569   13,336   14,009   14,871   14,102
January 15, 1851; organized February 7, 1859. *Robert Emmet* (1778–1803). Irish patriot and fighter; captured and executed September 20, 1803, for his activity in the Irish Rebellion.

Emmet   **Michigan**
Petoskey   468 sq. mi.
31,437   25,040   22,992   18,331   15,904   16,534
April 1, 1840, as Tonedagana; name changed March 8, 1843; organized January 29, 1853. Robert Emmet.*

Emmons   **North Dakota**
Linton   1,510 sq. mi.
4,331   4,830   5,877   7,200   8,462   9,715
February 10, 1879; organized November 9, 1883. James A. Emmons (1845–1919). Steamboat operator; Bismarck merchant.

Emporia   **Virginia**
(Independent City)   7 sq. mi.
5,665   5,306   4,840   5,300   (a)   (a)
July 31, 1967. Latin for "center of trade." [(a) Part of Greensville County.] (Associated county: Greensville.)

Erath   **Texas**
Stephenville   1,086 sq. mi.
33,001   27,991   22,560   18,141   16,236   18,434
January 25, 1856; organized August 4, 1856. George Bernard Erath (1813–91). Austrian; moved to Texas 1833; Moore's expedition against Indians 1835; battle of San Jacinto 1836; captain, Texas Rangers 1839; Indian fighter 1839–41; Somervell expedition 1842; Texas Republic legislature 1843–45; first Texas state legislature 1846; Texas Senate 1857–61 and 1874; Texas regiment 1861–64.

Erie   **New York**
Buffalo   1,044 sq. mi.
950,265   968,532   1,015,472   1,113,491   1,064,688   899,238
April 2, 1821. *Erie Indians*. Lived between Lake Erie and Ohio River; eradicated by Iroquois 1655; unknown origin of name; may be Iroquois for "long tail" or "cat people."

Erie   **Ohio**
Sandusky   255 sq. mi.
79,551   76,779   79,655   75,909   68,000   52,565
March 15, 1838. Erie Indians.*

Erie   **Pennsylvania**
Erie   802 sq. mi.
280,843   275,572   279,780   263,654   250,682   219,388
March 12, 1800; organized 1803. Lake Erie. Named for Erie Indians.*

Escambia   **Alabama**
Brewton   947 sq. mi.
38,440   35,518   38,440   34,906   33,511   31,443
December 10, 1868. *Escambia River*. Name of unknown origin; possibly from Spanish *cambiar*, meaning "to exchange."

Escambia   **Florida**
Pensacola   662 sq. mi.
294,410   262,798   233,794   205,334   173,829   112,706
July 21, 1821. Escambia River.*

Esmeralda   **Nevada**
Goldfield   3,589 sq. mi.
971   1,344   777   629   619   614
November 25, 1861. Esmeralda Mining District. From Spanish for "emerald."

Essex   **Massachusetts**
Salem   501 sq. mi.
723,419   670,080   633,632   637,887   568,831   522,384
May 10, 1643. *Essex County, England*.

Essex   **New Jersey**
Newark   126 sq. mi.
793,633   778,206   851,116   929,986   923,545   905,949
March 1, 1683. Essex County, England.*

Essex   **New York**
Elizabethtown   1,797 sq. mi.
38,851   37,152   36,176   34,631   35,300   35,036
March 1, 1799. Uncertain. (1) Town of Essex. (2) Essex County, Massachusetts.

Essex   **Vermont**
Guildhall   665 sq. mi.
6,459   6,405   6,313   5,416   6,083   6,257
November 5, 1792; organized 1800. Uncertain. (1) Essex County, England.* (2) *Robert Devereux, 2nd Earl of Essex* (1567–1601); court favorite of Elizabeth I; lord lieutenant of Ireland 1599; fell out of favor and executed for treason 1601.

Essex   **Virginia**
Tappahannock   258 sq. mi.
9,989   8,689   8,864   7,099   6,690   6,530
April 16, 1692 (session). Uncertain. (1) Essex County, England.* (2) Robert Devereux, 2nd Earl of Essex.*

Estill   **Kentucky**
Irvine   254 sq. mi.
15,307   14,614   14,495   12,752   12,466   14,677

January 27, 1808; effective April 1, 1808. James Estill (1750–82). Captain; killed leading pursuit of Indians in retaliation for a raid.

Etowah   **Alabama**
Gadsden   535 sq. mi.
103,459   99,840   103,057   94,144   96,980   93,892
December 7, 1866, as Baine; abolished December 3, 1867; reestablished as Etowah December 3, 1868. Cherokee word of unknown meaning; may mean "pine tree."

Eureka   **Nevada**
Eureka   4,176 sq. mi.
1,651   1,547   1,198   948   767   896
March 1, 1873. Town of Eureka. Greek for "I have found it!"; from exclamation associated with discoveries of gold.

Evangeline   **Louisiana**
Ville Platte   664 sq. mi.
35,434   33,274   33,343   31,932   31,639   31,629
June 15, 1910. Evangeline, legendary heroine of Longfellow's poem *Evangeline*.

Evans   **Georgia**
Claxton   185 sq. mi.
10,495   8,724   8,428   7,290   6,952   6,653
August 11, 1914. Clement Anselm Evans (1833–1911). Judge of Stewart County Court 1854; Georgia Senate 1859; private, 31st Georgia; major 1861; colonel 1862; brigadier general 1863; wounded at Gettysburg 1863; battle of the Wilderness 1864; Methodist minister 1866.

F

Fairbanks North Star   **Alaska**
Fairbanks   7,366 sq. mi.
82,840   77,720   53,983   45,864   43,412   [a]
January 1, 1964. "North Star" was selected by school children in a contest to name the borough; "Fairbanks," for the city of Fairbanks, was added to avoid confusion with North Slope Borough. Charles Warren Fairbanks (1852–1918); U.S. senator from Indiana 1897–1905; headed U.S. delegation to joint high commission with Canada; U.S. vice president 1905–09. [(a) Part of 4th Judicial District.]

Fairfax   **Virginia**
Fairfax   395 sq. mi.
969,749   818,584   596,901   455,021   275,002   98,557
May 6, 1742 (session). Thomas Fairfax, 6th Baron Fairfax of Cameron (1692–1782). Inherited title from his father and extensive land holdings in America from his mother.

Fairfax   **Virginia**
(Independent City)   6 sq. mi.
21,498   19,622   19,390   21,970   [a]   [a]
June 30, 1961. Fairfax County, Virginia. [(a) Part of Fairfax County.] (Associated county: Fairfax.)

Fairfield   **Connecticut**
Bridgeport   626 sq. mi.
882,567   827,645   807,143   792,814   653,589   504,342
May 10, 1666 (session). City of Fairfield. Descriptive of area's topography.

Fairfield   **Ohio**
Lancaster   505 sq. mi.

| 122,759 | 103,461 | 93,678 | 73,301 | 63,912 | 52,130 |

December 9, 1800. Descriptive of rolling farm land.

Fairfield   **South Carolina**
Winnsboro   687 sq. mi.

| 23,454 | 22,295 | 20,700 | 19,999 | 20,713 | 21,780 |

March 12, 1785. Uncertain. Most suggestions concern the nature of the landscape.

Fallon   **Montana**
Baker   1,620 sq. mi.

| 2,837 | 3,103 | 3,763 | 4,050 | 3,997 | 3,660 |

December 9, 1913. Benjamin O'Fallon (1793–1842). Indian agent for Missouri River tribes; expedition to Yellowstone River 1825.

Fall River   **South Dakota**
Hot Springs   1,740 sq. mi.

| 7,453 | 7,353 | 8,439 | 7,505 | 10,688 | 10,439 |

April 3, 1883. Fall River. Descriptive of falls and rapids; translation of Indian name.

Falls   **Texas**
Marlin   769 sq. mi.

| 18,576 | 17,712 | 17,946 | 17,300 | 21,263 | 26,724 |

January 28, 1850; organized August 5, 1850. Falls of Brazos River.

Falls Church   **Virginia**
(Independent City)   2 sq. mi.

| 10,377 | 9,578 | 9,515 | 10,772 | 10,192 | 7,535 |

1948. Anglican church built near falls of Potomac 1734. (Associated county: Fairfax.)

Fannin   **Georgia**
Blue Ridge   386 sq. mi.

| 19,798 | 15,992 | 14,748 | 13,357 | 13,620 | 15,192 |

January 21, 1854. *James Walker Fannin* (1805–36). Native of Georgia; hero of battle of Concepción, Texas, 1835; defeated at Goliad, killed by order of Santa Anna March 27, 1836.

Fannin   **Texas**
Bonham   891 sq. mi.

| 31,242 | 24,804 | 24,285 | 22,705 | 23,880 | 31,253 |

December 14, 1837; organized 1840. James Walker Fannin.*

Faribault   **Minnesota**
Blue Earth   714 sq. mi.

| 16,181 | 16,937 | 19,714 | 20,896 | 23,685 | 23,879 |

February 20, 1855; organized May 1, 1857. Jean Baptiste Faribault (1774–1860). French Canadian fur trader; agent in the northwest for the American Fur Company 1796–1806; taught agriculture to Indians.

Faulk   **South Dakota**
Faulkton   1,000 sq. mi.

| 2,640 | 2,744 | 3,327 | 3,893 | 4,397 | 4,752 |

January 8, 1873; organized November 5, 1883. Andrew Jackson Faulk (1814–98). Post trader to Yankton Indians 1861; oil business at Oil City, Pennsylvania 1864–66; governor of Dakota Territory and superintendent of Indian affairs 1866–69; mayor of Yankton; clerk of federal and territorial courts.

Faulkner   **Arkansas**
Conway   647 sq. mi.

86,014   60,006   46,192   31,572   24,303   25,289
April 12, 1873. Sanford C. Faulkner (1803–74). Confederate officer; composer of *The Arkansas Traveler*.

Fauquier   **Virginia**
Warrenton   650 sq. mi.
55,139   48,741   35,889   26,375   24,066   21,248
September 14, 1758 (session). Francis Fauquier (1704–68). Royal Society 1754; lieutenant governor of Virginia 1758–68; opposed colonial attempts of government and self-expression; defended western frontier during French and Indian Wars.

Fayette   **Alabama**
Fayette   628 sq. mi.
18,495   17,962   18,809   16,252   16,148   19,388
December 20, 1824. Marie Jean Paul Roch Yves Gilbert Motier, *Marquis de Lafayette* (1757–1834). Resigned from French military service to aid American cause of independence; commissioned as major general in Continental army 1777; returned to Paris 1781; commander in chief of French National Guard 1789; captured by Austrians 1792; revisited U.S. 1784 and 1824–25.

Fayette   **Georgia**
Fayetteville   197 sq. mi.
91,263   62,415   29,043   11,364   8,199   7,978
May 15, 1821. Marquis de Lafayette.*

Fayette   **Illinois**
Vandalia   716 sq. mi.
21,802   20,893   22,167   20,752   21,946   24,582
February 14, 1821. Marquis de Lafayette.*

Fayette   **Indiana**
Connersville   215 sq. mi.
25,588   26,015   28,272   26,216   24,454   23,391
December 28, 1818; effective January 1, 1819. Marquis de Lafayette.*

Fayette   **Iowa**
West Union   731 sq. mi.
22,008   21,843   25,488   26,898   28,581   28,294
December 21, 1837; organized August 26, 1850. Marquis de Lafayette.*

Fayette   **Kentucky**
Lexington   285 sq. mi.
260,512   225,366   204,165   174,323   131,906   100,746
May 1, 1780 (session); effective November 1, 1780. Marquis de Lafayette.*

Fayette   **Ohio**
Washington Court House   407 sq. mi.
28,433   27,466   27,467   25,461   24,775   22,554
February 19, 1810. Marquis de Lafayette.*

Fayette   **Pennsylvania**
Uniontown   790 sq. mi.
148,644   145,351   159,417   154,667   169,340   189,899
September 26, 1783. Marquis de Lafayette.*

Fayette   **Tennessee**
Somerville   705 sq. mi.
28,806   25,559   25,305   22,692   24,577   27,535
September 29, 1824. Marquis de Lafayette.*

Fayette   **Texas**
La Grange   950 sq. mi.

| 21,804 | 20,095 | 18,832 | 17,650 | 20,384 | 24,176 |

December 14, 1837; organized January, 1838. Marquis de Lafayette.*

Fayette   **West Virginia**
Fayetteville   664 sq. mi.

| 47,579 | 47,952 | 57,863 | 49,332 | 61,731 | 82,443 |

February 28, 1831. Marquis de Lafayette.*

Fentress   **Tennessee**
Jamestown   499 sq. mi.

| 16,625 | 14,669 | 14,826 | 12,593 | 13,288 | 14,917 |

November 28, 1823. James Fentress (1763–1843). Tennessee House of Representatives 1809–23, Speaker 1820–23.

Fergus   **Montana**
Lewistown   4,339 sq. mi.

| 11,893 | 12,083 | 13,076 | 12,611 | 14,018 | 14,015 |

March 12, 1885. John Fergus (1813–1902). Montana territorial legislature; initiated idea for Yellowstone National Park; Montana Constitutional Convention.

Ferry   **Washington**
Republic   2,204 sq. mi.

| 7,260 | 6,295 | 5,811 | 3,655 | 3,889 | 4,096 |

February 18, 1899. Elisha Peyre Ferry (1825–95). Illinois Constitutional Convention 1861; bank commissioner 1861–63; surveyor general of Washington Territory 1869; governor of Washington Territory 1872–80; governor of Washington 1889–93.

Fillmore   **Minnesota**
Preston   861 sq. mi.

| 21,122 | 20,777 | 21,930 | 21,916 | 23,768 | 24,465 |

March 5, 1853. *Millard Fillmore* (1800–74). New York Assembly 1829–31; U.S. representative 1833–35 and 1837–43; New York comptroller 1847–49; vice president of U.S. 1849–50; 13th president of U.S. 1850–53; unsuccessful Whig candidate for president 1852.

Fillmore   **Nebraska**
Geneva   576 sq. mi.

| 6,634 | 7,103 | 7,920 | 8,137 | 9,425 | 9,610 |

January 26, 1856; organized April 21, 1871. Millard Fillmore.*

Finney   **Kansas**
Garden City   1,302 sq. mi.

| 40,523 | 33,070 | 23,825 | 18,947 | 16,093 | 15,092 |

March 6, 1873, as Sequoyah; name changed February 21, 1883. David W. Finney (1839–1916). Private to sergeant, Union army 1861–65; Kansas legislature; lieutenant governor of Kansas 1881–85.

Fisher   **Texas**
Roby   901 sq. mi.

| 4,344 | 4,842 | 5,891 | 6,344 | 7,865 | 11,023 |

August 21, 1876; organized April 27, 1886. Samuel Rhoads Fisher (1794–1839). Texas Constitutional Convention 1836; signer, Texas Declaration of Independence 1836; secretary of Texas Navy.

Flagler   **Florida**
Bunnell   485 sq. mi.

| 49,832 | 28,701 | 10,913 | 4,454 | 4,566 | 3,367 |

April 28, 1917. Henry Morrison Flagler (1830–1913). Capitalist and industrialist; made fortune in oil industry; developed railroads and hotels in Florida.

Flathead   **Montana**
Kalispell   5,098 sq. mi.
74,471   59,218   51,966   39,460   32,965   31,495
February 6, 1893. Salish Indians. Named Flatheads by Lewis and Clark, but did not flatten heads as did tribes farther West; Lewis and Clark may have noted flat-headed Indians, perhaps captives, among the Salish.

Fleming   **Kentucky**
Flemingsburg   351 sq. mi.
13,792   12,292   12,323   11,366   10,890   11,962
February 10, 1798; effective March 1, 1798. John Fleming (1735–?). Surveyor; explored Ohio River 1776.

Florence   **South Carolina**
Florence   800 sq. mi.
125,761   114,344   110,163   89,636   84,438   79,710
December 22, 1888. City of Florence. Named for Florence Harllee (1848–?); daughter of General W. W. Harllee, railroad president.

Florence   **Wisconsin**
Florence   488 sq. mi.
5,088   4,590   4,172   3,298   3,437   3,756
March 18, 1882. Mine and town of Florence. Named for Florence Hulst (?–?); wife of Nelson P. Hulst; first American woman to settle in region. Mine and town were originally named Eagle, then renamed because there already was a town of Eagle in Wisconsin.

Floyd   **Georgia**
Rome   513 sq. mi.
90,565   81,251   79,800   73,742   69,130   62,899
December 3, 1832. John Floyd (1769–1839). Brigadier general, Georgia Militia 1813–15; fought Creek and Choctaw Indians; Georgia House of Representatives 1820–27; U.S. representative 1827–29.

Floyd   **Indiana**
New Albany   148 sq. mi.
70,823   64,404   61,169   55,622   51,397   43,955
January 2, 1819; effective February 1, 1819. Uncertain. (1) Davis Floyd (1772–?); Indiana territorial legislature 1805–06; indicted for associating with Aaron Burr in his conspiracy with Spain, sentenced to half-hour in jail; U.S. land claims commissioner in Florida. (2) John Floyd* (see Floyd, Kentucky).

Floyd   **Iowa**
Charles City   501 sq. mi.
16,900   17,058   19,597   19,860   21,102   21,505
January 15, 1851; organized September 4, 1854. Uncertain. (1) Charles Floyd (?–1804); sergeant in Lewis and Clark expedition; only fatality on expedition; buried in Iowa. (2) William Floyd (1734–1821); New York Colonial Senate; Continental Congress 1774–77 and 1778–83; signer of Declaration of Independence; major general, New York Militia; U.S. representative 1789–91.

Floyd   **Kentucky**
Prestonburg   394 sq. mi.
42,441   43,586   48,764   35,889   41,642   53,500
December 13, 1799. *John Floyd* (1751–83). Virginia surveyor in Kentucky; Continental navy; captured by British but escaped; killed by Indians.

Floyd   **Texas**
Floydada   992 sq. mi.
7,771   8,497   9,834   11,044   12,369   10,535
August 21, 1876; organized May 28, 1890. Dolphin Ward Floyd (1804–36). Resident of Gonzales, Texas; killed at the Alamo, March 6, 1836.

Floyd   **Virginia**
Floyd   381 sq. mi.
13,874   12,005   11,563   9,775   10,462   11,351
January 15, 1831. John Floyd (1783–1837). Justice of the peace for Montgomery County, Virginia, 1807; major, Virginia Militia 1807–12; brigadier general of militia 1813; Virginia House of Delegates 1814–15; U.S. representative 1817–29; governor of Virginia 1830–34.

Fluvanna   **Virginia**
Palmyra   287 sq. mi.
20,047   12,429   10,244   7,621   7,227   7,121
May 5, 1777 (session). Fluvanna River. Combined from Latin *fluvius,* meaning "river," and "anna," for Queen Anne (see Queen Anne's, Maryland).

Foard   **Texas**
Crowell   707 sq. mi.
1,622   1,794   2,158   2,211   3,125   4,216
March 3, 1891; organized April 27, 1891. Robert Levi Foard (1831–98). Maryland attorney; moved to Texas 1852; 1st lieutenant, Colorado County Militia 1861; major, 13th Texas Infantry 1863; served in Texas and Louisiana.

Fond du Lac   **Wisconsin**
Fond du Lac   723 sq. mi.
97,296   90,083   88,964   84,567   75,085   67,829
December 7, 1836; organized 1844. City of Fond du Lac. French for "end of the lake"; describes city's location at southern end of Lake Winnebago.

Ford   **Illinois**
Paxton   486 sq. mi.
14,241   14,275   15,265   16,382   16,606   15,901
February 17, 1859. Thomas Ford (1800–50). Newspaperman, St. Louis 1824; Illinois state attorney 1829–33; judge of 6th Circuit 1836; judge, Chicago Municipal Court 1837; Illinois Supreme Court 1840; governor of Illinois 1842–46.

Ford   **Kansas**
Dodge City   1,099 sq. mi.
32,458   27,463   24,315   22,587   20,938   19,670
March 6, 1873; organized 1873. James Hobart Ford (?–1867). Captain, Colorado Infantry 1861; major 1862; colonel 1863; brevet brigadier general of Volunteers 1864; honorable discharge 1865.

Forest   **Pennsylvania**
Tionesta   428 sq. mi.
4,946   4,802   5,072   4,926   4,485   4,944
April 11, 1848; organized 1857. Descriptive of forests in the region.

Forest   **Wisconsin**
Crandon   1,014 sq. mi.
10,024   8,776   9,044   7,691   7,542   9,437
April 11, 1885. Descriptive of forests in the region.

Forrest   **Mississippi**
Hattiesburg   467 sq. mi.
72,604   68,314   66,018   57,849   52,722   45,055
April 19, 1906; organized January 6, 1908. Nathan Bedford Forrest (1821–77). Enlisted in mounted rifle company 1861; lieutenant colonel with volunteer company 1861; battle of Sacramento December 26, 1861; battle of Fort Donelson February 11, 1862; captured Murfreesboro 1862; brigadier general 1862; twenty-nine horses were shot from under him in his numerous engagements.

Forsyth   **Georgia**
Cumming   226 sq. mi.

98,407   44,083   27,958   16,928   12,170   11,005

December 3, 1832. John Forsyth (1780–1841). Georgia attorney general 1808; U.S. representative 1813–18 and 1823–27; U.S. senator 1818–19 and 1829–34; U.S. minister to Spain 1819–23; governor of Georgia 1827–29; U.S. secretary of state 1834–41.

Forsyth   **North Carolina**
Winston-Salem   410 sq. mi.
306,067   265,878   243,683   214,348   189,428   146,135

January 16, 1849. Benjamin Forsyth (c1775–1814). 2nd lieutenant, North Carolina Infantry 1800; captain of riflemen 1808; North Carolina legislature 1807–08; commanded assault at Gananoque, Upper Canada, 1812; brevet lieutenant colonel at Elizabethtown; killed near Odelltown, New York, June 28, 1814.

Fort Bend   **Texas**
Richmond   875 sq. mi.
354,452   225,421   130,846   52,314   40,527   31,056

December 29, 1837; organized January 1838. Fort Bend; located at a bend of the Brazos River 1821.

Foster   **North Dakota**
Carrington   635 sq. mi.
3,759   3,983   4,611   4,832   5,361   5,337

January 4, 1873; organized October 11, 1883. James S. Foster (1828–90). Established colony in Dakota Territory 1864; Dakota Territory commissioner of immigration.

Fountain   **Indiana**
Covington   396 sq. mi.
17,954   17,808   19,033   18,257   18,706   17,836

December 20, 1825; effective April 1, 1826. James Fountain (also Fontaine) (?–1790). Militia major; killed in battle on Maumee River.

Franklin   **Alabama**
Russellville   636 sq. mi.
31,223   27,814   28,350   23,933   21,988   25,705

February 6, 1818; effective June 1, 1818. *Benjamin Franklin* (1706–90). Printer and editor; founded *Pennsylvania Gazette* 1728; clerk, Pennsylvania General Assembly 1736–50; postmaster of Philadelphia 1737; Provincial Assembly 1744–45; deputy postmaster general of the British North American colonies 1753–74; Continental Congress 1775–76; signed Declaration of Independence 1776; Pennsylvania Constitutional Convention 1776; commissioner and minister to France 1776–85; governor of Pennsylvania 1785–88; federal Constitutional Convention 1787.

Franklin   **Arkansas**
Ozark   610 sq. mi.
17,771   14,897   14,705   11,301   10,213   12,358

December 19, 1837. Benjamin Franklin.*

Franklin   **Florida**
Apalachicola   544 sq. mi.
11,057   8,967   7,661   7,065   6,576   5,814

February 8, 1832. Benjamin Franklin.*

Franklin   **Georgia**
Carnesville   263 sq. mi.
20,285   16,650   15,185   12,784   13,274   14,446

February 25, 1784. Benjamin Franklin.*

Franklin   **Idaho**
Preston   665 sq. mi.

11,329   9,232   8,895   7,373   8,457   9,867

January 20, 1913. Town of Franklin. Named for Franklin Dewey Richards (1821–99). High priest, Church of Latter-Day Saints 1844; led group of settlers to Salt Lake Valley 1848; ordained one of twelve apostles February 12, 1849; Utah legislature 1849; president, Utah legislature 1856; regent, University of Deseret; brigadier general, Nauvoo Legion 1859; judge of Weber County Probate and County Court 1869–83; historian, Mormon Church 1889–99.

Franklin   **Illinois**
Benton   412 sq. mi.
39,018   40,319   43,201   38,329   39,281   48,685
January 2, 1818. Benjamin Franklin.*

Franklin   **Indiana**
Brookville   386 sq. mi.
22,151   19,580   19,612   16,943   17,015   16,034
November 27, 1810; effective January 1, 1811. Benjamin Franklin.*

Franklin   **Iowa**
Hampton   582 sq. mi.
10,704   11,364   13,036   13,255   15,472   16,268
January 15, 1851; organized March 3, 1856. Benjamin Franklin.*

Franklin   **Kansas**
Ottawa   574 sq. mi.
24,784   21,994   22,062   20,007   19,548   19,928
August 20, 1855. Benjamin Franklin.*

Franklin   **Kentucky**
Frankfort   210 sq. mi.
47,687   43,781   41,830   34,481   29,421   25,933
December 7, 1794; effective May 10, 1795. Benjamin Franklin.*

Franklin   **Louisiana**
Winnsboro   624 sq. mi.
21,263   22,387   24,141   23,946   26,088   29,376
March 1, 1843. Benjamin Franklin.*

Franklin   **Maine**
Farmington   1,698 sq. mi.
29,467   29,008   27,098   22,444   20,069   20,682
March 20, 1838; effective May 9, 1838. Benjamin Franklin.*

Franklin   **Massachusetts**
Greenfield   702 sq. mi.
71,535   70,092   64,317   59,210   54,864   52,747
June 24, 1811; effective December 2, 1811. Benjamin Franklin.*

Franklin   **Mississippi**
Meadville   565 sq. mi.
8,448   8,377   8,208   8,011   9,286   10,929
December 21, 1809. Benjamin Franklin.*

Franklin   **Missouri**
Union   923 sq. mi.
93,807   80,603   71,233   55,116   44,566   36,046
December 11, 1818. Benjamin Franklin.*

Franklin   **Nebraska**
Franklin   576 sq. mi.
3,574   3,938   4,377   4,566   5,449   7,096
February 16, 1867; organized June 21, 1871. Benjamin Franklin.*

Franklin   **New York**
Malone   1,631 sq. mi.
51,134   46,540   44,929   43,931   44,742   44,830
March 11, 1808. Benjamin Franklin.*

Franklin   **North Carolina**
Louisburg   492 sq. mi.
47,260   36,414   30,055   26,820   28,755   31,341
April 14, 1778 (session). Benjamin Franklin.*

Franklin   **Ohio**
Columbus   540 sq. mi.
1,068,978   961,437   869,132   833,249   682,962   503,410
March 30, 1803. Benjamin Franklin.*

Franklin   **Pennsylvania**
Chambersburg   772 sq. mi.
129,313   121,082   113,629   100,833   88,172   75,927
September 9, 1784. Benjamin Franklin.*

Franklin   **Tennessee**
Winchester   555 sq. mi.
39,270   34,725   31,983   27,244   25,528   25,431
December 3, 1807. Benjamin Franklin.*

Franklin   **Texas**
Mount Vernon   286 sq. mi.
9,458   7,802   6,893   5,291   5,101   6,257
March 6, 1875; organized April 30, 1975. Benjamin Cromwell Franklin (1805–73). District judge, Republic of Texas 1836; expedition against Indians 1837; captain, Texas Army 1836; battle of San Jacinto 1836; judge, Brazoria Judicial District 1837–39; Texas legislature 1845.

Franklin   **Vermont**
Saint Albans   637 sq. mi.
45,417   39,980   34,788   31,282   29,474   29,894
November 5, 1792; organized 1796. Benjamin Franklin.*

Franklin   **Virginia**
Rocky Mount   692 sq. mi.
47,286   39,549   35,740   26,858   25,925   24,560
October 17, 1785 (session). Benjamin Franklin.*

Franklin   **Virginia**
(Independent City)   8 sq. mi.
8,346   7,864   7,308   6,880   (a)   (a)
December 21, 1961. Uncertain. (1) Benjamin Franklin.* (2) Early storekeeper named Franklin in Franklin Depot, city's original name. [(a) Part of Southampton County.] (Associated county: Southampton.)

Franklin   **Washington**
Pasco   1,242 sq. mi.

49,347   37,473   35,025   25,816   23,342   13,563
November 28, 1883. Benjamin Franklin.*

Frederick   Maryland
Frederick   663 sq. mi.
195,277   150,208   114,792   84,927   71,930   62,287
June 10, 1748. Uncertain. (1) Frederick Calvert, 6th and last Baron of Baltimore (1731–71); 5th Palatine of Maryland; son of Lord Charles Calvert; made Baron of Baltimore 1751; tried to give title to Henry Harford, his illegitimate son (see Harford, Maryland). (2) *Frederick Louis*, Duke of Gloucester (1707–51); eldest son of George II; made Duke of Gloucester 1717; Duke of Edinburgh 1727; Prince of Wales 1729; father of George III.

Frederick   Virginia
Winchester   415 sq. mi.
59,209   45,723   34,150   28,893   21,941   17,537
August 1, 1738 (session). Frederick Louis.*

Fredericksburg   Virginia
(Independent City)   11 sq. mi.
19,279   19,027   15,322   14,450   13,639   12,158
1879. Frederick Louis.* (Associated county: Spotsylvania.)

Freeborn   Minnesota
Albert Lea   708 sq. mi.
32,584   33,060   36,329   38,064   37,891   34,517
February 20, 1855; organized March 6, 1857. William Freeborn (1816–?). Minnesota territorial legislature 1854–57; emigrated to Montana 1864, to California 1868.

Freestone   Texas
Fairfield   877 sq. mi.
17,867   15,818   14,830   11,116   12,525   15,696
September 6, 1850; organized July 6, 1851. Descriptive term to distinguish local stone deposits and county name from adjacent Limestone County.

Fremont   Colorado
Canon City   1,533 sq. mi.
46,145   32,273   28,676   21,942   20,196   18,366
November 1, 1861. *John Charles Fremont* (1813–90). Led five explorations of far West; called "the Pathfinder"; major, California Volunteers 1846; lieutenant colonel, U.S. Mounted Rifles 1846; ordered to act as governor of California; tried by court martial, found guilty, pardoned by President Polk, resigned from army 1848; U.S. senator 1850–51; unsuccessful Republican candidate for president 1856; major general, U.S. Army, commanded Western District 1861; governor of Arizona Territory 1878–81.

Fremont   Idaho
Saint Anthony   1,867 sq. mi.
11,819   10,937   10,813   8,710   8,679   9,351
March 4, 1893. John Charles Fremont.*

Fremont   Iowa
Sidney   511 sq. mi.
8,010   8,226   9,401   9,282   10,282   12,323
February 24, 1847; organized September 10, 1849. John Charles Fremont.*

Fremont   Wyoming
Lander   9,182 sq. mi.
35,804   33,662   38,992   28,352   26,168   19,580
March 5, 1884. John Charles Fremont.*

Fresno   **California**
Fresno   5,963 sq. mi.
799,407   667,490   514,621   413,053   365,945   276,515
April 19, 1856. Spanish for "ash tree."

Frio   **Texas**
Pearsall   1,133 sq. mi.
16,252   13,472   13,785   11,159   10,112   10,357
February 1, 1858; organized July 20, 1871. Frio River. Spanish for "cold."

Frontier   **Nebraska**
Stockville   975 sq. mi.
3,099   3,101   3,647   3,982   4,311   5,282
January 17, 1872; organized February 5, 1872. Descriptive of county's location at time of creation.

Fulton   **Arkansas**
Salem   618 sq. mi.
11,642   10,037   9,975   7,699   6,657   9,187
December 21, 1842; effective January 1, 1843. William Savin Fulton (1795–1844). Staff of Colonel Armistead in defense of Fort McHenry 1813; private secretary to General Andrew Jackson in the Seminole War 1818; editor of Florence, Alabama, *Gazette* 1821; judge of county court 1822; secretary of Arkansas Territory 1829–35; governor of Arkansas Territory 1835–36; U.S. senator 1836–44.

Fulton   **Georgia**
Atlanta   529 sq. mi.
816,006   648,951   589,904   607,592   556,326   473,572
December 20, 1853. Uncertain. (1) Hamilton Fulton (?–1834); chief engineer of Georgia 1819–29; proposed and surveyed railroad through region. (2) *Robert Fulton* (1765–1815). Inventor, experimented with a submarine boat in France 1801; invented naval mines; built the steamboat *Clermont,* which sailed up Hudson River 1807.

Fulton   **Illinois**
Lewistown   866 sq. mi.
38,250   38,080   43,687   41,890   41,954   43,716
January 28, 1823. Robert Fulton.*

Fulton   **Indiana**
Rochester   369 sq. mi.
20,511   18,840   19,335   16,984   16,957   16,565
February 7, 1835; organized January 23, 1836; effective April 1, 1836. Robert Fulton.*

Fulton   **Kentucky**
Hickman   209 sq. mi.
7,752   8,271   8,971   10,183   11,256   13,668
January 15, 1845. Robert Fulton.*

Fulton   **New York**
Johnstown   496 sq. mi.
55,073   54,191   55,153   52,637   51,304   51,021
April 18, 1838. Robert Fulton.*

Fulton   **Ohio**
Wauseon   407 sq. mi.
42,084   38,498   37,751   33,071   29,301   25,580
February 28, 1850. Robert Fulton.*

Fulton   **Pennsylvania**
McConnellsburg   438 sq. mi
14,261   13,837   12,842   10,776   10,597   10,387
April 19, 1850. Robert Fulton.*

Furnas   **Nebraska**
Beaver City   718 sq. mi.
5,324   5,553   6,486   6,897   7,711   9,385
February 27, 1873. Robert Wilkinson Furnas (1824–1905). Editor, Troy, Ohio, *Times* 1826–31; editor, *Nebraska Advertiser* 1855–61; Nebraska Legislative Assembly 1856–60; organized and commanded three regiments of Indians 1861; colonel, 2nd Nebraska Cavalry 1861; colonel, U.S. Army 1862; governor of Nebraska 1873–75; regent, University of Nebraska 1875–81; author of numerous agricultural and horticultural reports.

G

Gadsden   **Florida**
Quincy   516 sq. mi.
45,087   41,105   41,565   39,184   41,989   36,457
June 24, 1823. James Gadsden (1788–1858). War of 1812; aide-de-camp to General Jackson 1818; led removal of Seminoles to Florida 1820; U.S. minister to Mexico 1853; negotiated Gadsden Purchase with Mexico 1854.

Gage   **Nebraska**
Beatrice   855 sq. mi.
22,993   22,794   24,456   25,719   26,818   28,052
March 16, 1855; organized March 13, 1858. William D. Gage (1803–85). Methodist clergyman; chaplain of Nebraska territorial legislature; treasurer of Otoe County 1855–56; Cass County commissioner 1857.

Gaines   **Texas**
Seminole   1,502 sq. mi.
14,467   14,123   13,150   11,593   12,267   8,909
August 21, 1876; organized October 24, 1905. James Gaines (1776–1856). Mexican army 1813; first judge of Sabine, Texas; signer of Texas Declaration of Independence 1836; Texas Senate 1838–42; California gold rush 1849.

Galax   **Virginia**
(Independent City)   8 sq. mi.
6,837   6,670   6,524   6,278   5,254   (a)
November 30, 1953. Native decorative evergreen tree. [(a) Part of Carroll and Grayson counties.] (Associated counties: Carroll and Grayson.)

Gallatin   **Illinois**
Shawneetown   324 sq. mi.
6,445   6,909   7,590   7,418   7,638   9,818
September 14, 1812. *Abraham Alfonse Albert Gallatin* (1761–1849). Pennsylvania Constitutional Convention 1789; Pennsylvania House of Representatives 1790–92; election as U.S. senator declared void 1794; U.S. representative 1795–1801; U.S. secretary of the treasury 1802–14; U.S. minister to France 1815–23; U.S. minister to Great Britain 1826–27.

Gallatin   **Kentucky**
Warsaw   99 sq. mi.
7,870   5,393   4,842   4,134   3,867   3,969
December 14, 1798; effective May 13, 1799. Abraham Alfonse Albert Gallatin.*

Gallatin   **Montana**
Bozeman   2,606 sq. mi.
67,831   50,463   42,865   32,505   26,045   21,902
February 2, 1865. Gallatin River. Named for Abraham Alfonse Albert Gallatin* by Lewis and Clark 1805.

Gallia   **Ohio**
Gallipolis   469 sq. mi.
31,069   30,954   30,098   25,239   26,120   24,910
March 25, 1803. France. From "Gaul," the Latin name for France.

Galveston   **Texas**
Galveston   398 sq. mi.
250,158   217,399   195,940   169,812   140,364   113,066
May 15, 1838; organized 1839. Bernardo de Galvez (1746–86). Served in Spanish army in Portugal 1762, in New Spain (Mexico) against the Apaches, and in Algiers; governor of Spanish Province of Louisiana 1777; fought British 1783; captain at Baton Rouge and Mobile 1780, at Pensacola 1781; viceroy of New Spain 1785.

Garden   **Nebraska**
Oshkosh   1,704 sq. mi.
2,292   2,460   2,802   2,929   3,472   4,114
November 2, 1909. Descriptive of hoped-for future as the "garden spot of the West."

Garfield   **Colorado**
Glenwood Springs   2,947 sq. mi.
43,791   29,974   22,514   14,821   12,017   11,625
February 10, 1883. *James Abram Garfield* (1831–81). President, Hiram College 1857–61; Ohio Senate 1859; lieutenant colonel and colonel, 42nd Regiment Ohio Volunteer Infantry 1861; brigadier general of Volunteers 1862; major general 1863; U.S. representative 1863–80; 20th president of the U.S. 1881; assassinated July 2, 1881, died September 19, 1881.

Garfield   **Montana**
Jordan   4,668 sq. mi.
1,279   1,589   1,656   1,796   1,981   2,172
February 7, 1919. James Abram Garfield.*

Garfield   **Nebraska**
Burwell   570 sq. mi.
1,902   2,141   2,363   2,411   2,699   2,912
November 8, 1884. James Abram Garfield.*

Garfield   **Oklahoma**
Enid   1,058 sq. mi.
57,813   56,735   62,820   55,365   52,975   52,820
1893, as County O; name changed November 6, 1894. James Abram Garfield.*

Garfield   **Utah**
Panguitch   5,174 sq. mi.
4,735   3,980   3,673   3,157   3,577   4,151
March 9, 1882. James Abram Garfield.*

Garfield   **Washington**
Pomeroy   711 sq. mi.
2,397   2,248   2,468   2,911   2,976   3,204
November 29, 1881. James Abram Garfield.*

Garland   **Arkansas**
Hot Springs   677 sq. mi.
88,068   73,397   70,531   54,131   46,697   47,102
April 5, 1873. Augustus Hill Garland (1832–99). Confederate Provisional Congress 1861; Confederate House of Representatives and Senate; U.S. senator from Arkansas, denied seat 1867; governor of Arkansas 1874–76; U.S. senator 1877–85; U.S. attorney general 1885–89.

Garrard **Kentucky**
Lancaster 231 sq. mi.
14,792 11,579 10,853 9,457 9,747 11,029
December 17, 1796; effective June 1, 1797. James Garrard (1749–1822). Captain of militia 1776–77; Virginia legislature 1779; Kentucky Constitutional Convention 1792; governor of Kentucky 1796–1804.

Garrett **Maryland**
Oakland 648 sq. mi.
29,846 28,138 26,498 21,476 20,420 21,259
April 1, 1872. John Work Garrett (1820–84). Industrialist and financier; director of Baltimore & Ohio Railroad 1858–84; interested in mercantile endeavors, steamship lines, telegraph cables, etc.

Garvin **Oklahoma**
Pauls Valley 807 sq. mi.
27,210 26,605 27,856 24,874 28,290 29,500
July 16, 1907. Samuel Garvin (1844–1908). Merchant; member of Chickasaw tribal organization.

Garza **Texas**
Post 896 sq. mi.
4,872 5,143 5,336 5,289 6,611 6,281
August 21, 1876; organized June 15, 1907. Uncertain. (1) Gerónimo Garza (?–?); head of one of first thirteen families to arrive in Texas from Canary Islands 1731; settled in San Antonio. (2) The Garza family.

Gasconade **Missouri**
Hermann 521 sq. mi.
15,342 14,006 13,181 11,478 12,195 12,342
November 25, 1820; effective January 1, 1821. Gasconade River. Name of uncertain origin. (1) French *gascon,* meaning "braggart" or "boaster"; applied to settlers or Indians along the river. (2) Gascony, France.

Gaston **North Carolina**
Gastonia 356 sq. mi.
190,365 175,093 162,568 148,415 127,074 110,836
December 21, 1846. William Gaston (1778–1844). North Carolina Senate 1800, 1812, and 1818–19; North Carolina House of Representatives 1824, 1827–29, and 1831; North Carolina Supreme Court 1833–44; wrote state song, "The Old North State."

Gates **North Carolina**
Gatesville 341 sq. mi.
10,516 9,305 8,875 8,524 9,254 9,555
April 14, 1778 (session). Horatio Gates (1728–1806). Under General Cornwallis in Nova Scotia 1749–50; under General Braddock, wounded at Fort Duquesne 1755; conquest of Martinique 1761; lived in England 1762–72; adjutant general and brigadier general, Continental army 1775; major general 1776; defeated Burgoyne at battle of Saratoga 1777; awarded congressional medal for surrender of British army 1777; battle of Camden 1780; New York legislature 1800–01.

Geary **Kansas**
Junction City 385 sq. mi.
27,947 30,453 29,852 28,111 28,779 21,671
August 30, 1855, as Davis; organized 1857; name changed February 28, 1889. John White Geary (1819–73). Pennsylvania infantry in Mexican War, wounded at Chapultepec 1846; postmaster of San Francisco and general mail agent 1849; first mayor of San Francisco 1850; governor of Kansas Territory 1856–57; brigadier general of Volunteers 1862; military governor of Savannah 1864; governor of Pennsylvania 1867–73.

Geauga **Ohio**
Chardon 404 sq. mi.
90,895 81,129 74,474 62,977 47,573 26,646
December 31, 1805; effective March 1, 1806. Grand River. From Indian name for the river, Sheauga sepe (Raccoon River).

Gem   **Idaho**
Emmett   563 sq. mi.
15,181   11,844   11,972   9,387   9,127   8,730
March 19, 1915. Uncertain. Best guess is from Idaho's motto, "Gem of the Mountains."

Genesee   **Michigan**
Flint   640 sq. mi.
436,141   430,459   450,449   444,341   374,313   270,963
March 28, 1835; organized April 4, 1836. Genesee County, New York.

Genesee   **New York**
Batavia   494 sq. mi.
60,370   60,060   59,400   58,722   53,994   47,584
March 30, 1802; organized 1803. Genesee River Valley. Seneca word for "beautiful valley."

Geneva   **Alabama**
Geneva   576 sq. mi.
25,764   23,647   24,253   21,924   22,310   25,899
December 26, 1868. Town of Geneva. Named for Geneva, Switzerland.

Gentry   **Missouri**
Albany   492 sq. mi.
6,861   6,848   7,887   8,060   8,793   11,036
February 12, 1841; organized 1843. Richard Gentry (1788–1837). Captain in militia; Missouri Senate 1826 and 1828; major general 1832; commander of Missouri troops in Black Hawk War; postmaster Columbia, Missouri; killed fighting Seminoles at Okeechobee, Florida, December 25, 1837.

George   **Mississippi**
Lucedale   478 sq. mi.
19,144   16,673   15,297   12,459   11,098   10,012
March 16, 1910. James Zachariah George (1826–97). Mexican War 1846; reporter, Mississippi Supreme Court 1854; captain, colonel, and brigadier general, Confederate army; Mississippi Supreme Court 1879; U.S. senator 1881–97.

Georgetown   **South Carolina**
Georgetown   815 sq. mi.
55,797   46,302   42,461   33,500   34,798   31,762
1769. City of Georgetown. Named for *George II* (1683–1760); George Augustus; married Caroline of Anspach 1705; elected Prince of Hanover; fought under Marlborough; made Prince of Wales 1714; succeeded to throne 1727; last British monarch to lead troops, in battle of Dettingen 1743.

Gibson   **Indiana**
Princeton   489 sq. mi.
32,500   31,913   33,156   30,444   29,949   30,720
March 9, 1813; effective April 1, 1813. John Gibson (1740–1822). Soldier in French and Indian Wars 1756; Revolutionary War colonel, general 1777; judge, Court of Common Pleas; secretary of Indiana Territory 1800–16.

Gibson   **Tennessee**
Trenton   603 sq. mi.
48,152   46,315   49,467   47,871   44,699   48,132
October 21, 1823; organized January 5, 1824. John H. Gibson (?–1823). Lieutenant, Tennessee Militia 1811; major in General Jackson's Natchez expedition 1812–13.

Gila   **Arizona**
Globe   4,768 sq. mi.
51,335   40,216   37,080   29,255   25,745   24,158

February 8, 1881. Gila River. Uncertain origin; may be (1) Moorish word via Spain; (2) Yuman name for the river; (3) Indian word meaning "spider"; (4) tribal name; or (5) a corruption of any of the above.

Gilchrist	**Florida**				
Trenton	349 sq. mi.				
14,437	9,667	5,767	3,551	2,868	3,499

December 4, 1925. Albert Waller Gilchrist (1858–1926). Florida Southern Railroad 1885–87; brigadier general, Florida Militia 1898; enlisted as private in Company C, 3rd U.S. Volunteer Infantry 1898; served at Santiago, Cuba 1899; Florida House of Representatives 1893–1903; governor of Florida 1909–13.

Giles	**Tennessee**				
Pulaski	611 sq. mi.				
29,447	25,741	24,625	22,138	22,410	26,961

November 14, 1809. *William Branch Giles* (1762–1830). U.S. representative from Virginia 1790, supported Tennessee statehood; U.S. senator 1804–15; governor of Virginia 1827–30.

Giles	**Virginia**				
Pearisburg	357 sq. mi.				
16,657	16,366	17,810	16,741	17,219	18,956

January 16, 1806; effective May 1, 1806. William Branch Giles.*

Gillespie	**Texas**				
Fredericksburg	1,061 sq. mi.				
20,814	17,204	13,532	10,553	10,048	10,520

February 23, 1848; organized June 3, 1848. Robert Addison Gillespie (1815–46). Somervell expedition 1842; Texas Ranger, wounded 1844; killed in charge of Bishop's Palace, Monterrey, Mexico, September 21, 1846.

Gilliam	**Oregon**				
Condon	1,204 sq. mi.				
1,915	1,717	2,057	2,342	3,069	2,817

February 25, 1885. Cornelius Gilliam (1798–1848). Sheriff, Clay County, Missouri; Black Hawk War; captain, Seminole War 1837; commander of forces of provisional government; Cayuse War, accidentally shot March 24, 1848.

Gilmer	**Georgia**				
Ellijay	427 sq. mi.				
23,456	13,368	11,110	8,956	8,922	9,963

December 3, 1832. George Rockingham Gilmer (1790–1859). 1st lieutenant in campaign against Creeks 1813–15; Georgia House of Representatives 1821–23; trustee, University of Georgia 1826–27; U.S. representative 1827–29 and 1833–35; governor of Georgia 1829–31 and 1837–39.

Gilmer	**West Virginia**				
Glenville	340 sq. mi.				
7,160	7,669	8,334	7,782	8,050	9,746

February 3, 1845. Thomas Walker Gilmer (1802–44). Virginia House of Delegates 1829–36 and 1839–40, Speaker 1834–36; governor of Virginia 1840–41; U.S. representative 1841–44; secretary of the navy 1844; killed in explosion aboard USS *Princeton* during demonstration of new guns.

Gilpin	**Colorado**				
Central City	150 sq. mi.				
4,757	3,070	2,441	1,272	685	850

November 1, 1861. William Gilpin (1815–94). Withdrew from West Point 1836; 2nd lieutenant, 2nd Dragoons 1836; 1st lieutenant 1836; Seminole War 1838; resigned 1838; 1st Missouri Volunteers in Mexican War 1846; governor of Colorado Territory, dismissed by President Lincoln 1861.

Glacier	**Montana**
Cut Bank	2,995 sq. mi.

13,247   12,121   10,628   10,783   11,565   9,645
February 17, 1919. Glacier National Park. Descriptive of numerous glaciers within the park.

Glades   **Florida**
Moore Haven   774 sq. mi.
10,576   7,591   5,992   3,669   2,950   2,199
April 23, 1921. Florida Everglades.

Gladwin   **Michigan**
Gladwin   507 sq. mi.
26,023   21,896   19,957   13,471   10,769   9,451
March 2, 1831; organized April 18, 1875. Henry Gladwin (1729–91). British officer during French and Indian Wars; defended Fort Detroit during Pontiac's Rebellion 1763; returned to England before American Revolution.

Glascock   **Georgia**
Gibson   144 sq. mi.
2,556   2,357   2,382   2,280   2,672   3,579
December 19, 1857. Thomas Glascock (1790–1841). Georgia Constitutional Convention 1798; captain of Volunteers, War of 1812; brigadier general, Seminole War 1817; Georgia House of Representatives intermittently between 1821 and 1839; U.S. representative 1835–39.

Glasscock   **Texas**
Garden City   901 sq. mi.
1,406   1,447   1,304   1,155   1,118   1,089
April 4, 1887; organized March 28, 1893. George Washington Glasscock (1810–68). Flatboating partner of Abraham Lincoln in Illinois; built flour mill at Austin, Texas; Texas legislature.

Glenn   **California**
Willows   1,315 sq. mi.
26,453   24,798   21,350   17,521   17,245   15,448
March 11, 1891. Hugh J. Glenn (1824–82). Mexican War; successful wheat grower known as "the Wheat King"; California Board of Agriculture.

Gloucester   **New Jersey**
Woodbury   325 sq. mi.
254,673   230,082   199,917   172,681   134,840   91,727
May 28, 1686. Gloucester and/or Gloucestershire, England.

Gloucester   **Virginia**
Gloucester   217 sq. mi.
34,780   30,131   20,107   14,059   11,919   10,343
1651. Uncertain. (1) Gloucester and/or Gloucestershire, England. (2) Henry, Duke of Gloucester (1640–60); son of King Charles I and Queen Henrietta Maria; younger brother of Charles I and James I; died of smallpox.

Glynn   **Georgia**
Brunswick   422 sq. mi.
67,568   62,496   54,981   50,528   41,954   29,046
February 5, 1777. John Glynn (1722–79). Member of English parliament; ally of American colonists.

Gogebic   **Michigan**
Bessemer   1,102 sq. mi.
17,370   18,052   19,686   20,676   24,370   27,053
February 7, 1887. Lake Gogebic and *Gogebic Iron Mining District*. From European rendering of Indian name for the lake.

Golden Valley   **Montana**
Ryegate   1,175 sq. mi.

1,042	912	1,026	931	1,203	1,337

October 4, 1920. Promotional name.

Golden Valley   **North Dakota**
Beach   1,002 sq. mi.

1,924	2,108	2,391	2,611	3,100	3,499

November 19, 1912. Golden Valley Land and Cattle Company. Extensive land-holding company located in St. Paul, Minnesota.

Goliad   **Texas**
Goliad   854 sq. mi.

6,928	5,980	5,193	4,869	5,429	6,219

March 17, 1836; organized 1837. Mexican municipality of Goliad. Derived from an anagram of [H]idalgo (see Hidalgo, New Mexico).

Gonzalez   **Texas**
Gonzalez   1,068 sq. mi.

18,628	17,205	16,883	16,375	17,845	21,164

March 17, 1836; organized 1837. Mexican municipality and battle of Gonzales. Named for Rafael Gonzalez (1789–1857); 2nd lieutenant 1814; 1st lieutenant 1815; captain 1818; lieutenant colonel 1821; governor of Coahuila, Mexico, and Texas 1824–26.

Goochland   **Virginia**
Goochland   284 sq. mi.

16,863	14,163	11,761	10,069	9,206	8,934

February 1, 1727 (session). Sir William Gooch (1681–1751). Lieutenant colonel; governor of Virginia 1727–37 and 1737–40; assumed command of British forces to attack Carthagena, New Granada (Colombia), upon death of General Spotwood; wounded and contracted fever, returned to Virginia and governed colony 1741–49; major general 1747; baronet 1748.

Goodhue   **Minnesota**
Red Wing   758 sq. mi.

44,127	40,690	38,749	34,763	33,035	32,118

March 5, 1853; organized June 15, 1854. James Madison Goodhue (1810–52). Owned *Wisconsin Herald* 1845–49; published *Minnesota Pioneer*, first newspaper in Minnesota 1849.

Gooding   **Idaho**
Gooding   731 sq. mi.

14,155	11,633	11,874	8,645	9,544	11,101

January 28, 1913. Frank Robert Gooding (1859–1929). Idaho Senate 1898–1902; governor of Idaho 1905–09; U.S. senator 1921–28.

Gordon   **Georgia**
Calhoun   356 sq. mi.

44,104	35,072	30,070	23,570	19,228	18,922

February 13, 1850. William Washington Gordon (1796–1842). Graduated West Point 1814; 3rd lieutenant 1815; aide to General Gaines, resigned 1815; president of Georgia Central Railroad 1836–42.

Goshen   **Wyoming**
Torrington   2,225 sq. mi.

12,538	12,373	12,040	10,885	11,941	12,634

February 9, 1911. Uncertain. (1) Biblical land of Goshen. (2) Goshen Hole, livestock and oil region in the county, named for any one of an Assiniboine trapper, one of two French trappers, or a local cowboy.

Gosper   **Nebraska**
Elwood   458 sq. mi.

2,143	1,928	2,140	2,178	2,489	2,734

November 26, 1873. John J. Gosper (?–1913). Lieutenant, Company I, 8th Illinois Cavalry and 29th Regiment Colored Troops; Nebraska secretary of state 1873–75; secretary of Arizona Territory 1877.

Gove   **Kansas**
Gove City   1,071 sq. mi.
3,068   3,231   3,726   3,940   4,107   4,447
March 2, 1868; organized September 2, 1886. Grenville L. Gove (c1841–64). Private, Company F, 6th Kansas Cavalry; raised Company G, 11th Kansas Cavalry, commissioned 1st lieutenant 1862; captain 1864; died of illness November 7, 1864.

Grady   **Georgia**
Cairo   458 sq. mi.
23,659   20,279   19,845   17,826   18,015   18,928
August 17, 1905; effective January 1, 1906. *Henry Woodfin Grady* (1850–89). Georgia representative of *New York Herald* 1871; editor and part owner of *Atlanta Constitution* 1880; nationally recognized advocate of South during Reconstruction.

Grady   **Oklahoma**
Chickasha   1,101 sq. mi.
45,516   41,747   39,490   29,354   29,590   34,872
July 16, 1907. Henry Woodfin Grady.*

Grafton   **New Hampshire**
North Haverhill   1,713 sq. mi.
81,743   74,929   65,806   54,914   48,857   47,923
April 29, 1769; organized 1773. Augustus Henry Fitzroy, 3rd Duke of Grafton (1735–1811). English secretary of state for Northern Department 1765–66; first minister 1768–70; Lord Privy Seal 1771–75 and 1782–83.

Graham   **Arizona**
Safford   4,629 sq. mi.
33,489   26,554   22,862   16,578   14,045   12,985
March 10, 1881. Graham Mountain. Named for James D. Graham (1799–1865); graduate of West Point; lieutenant colonel; surveyed West and Southwest.

Graham   **Kansas**
Hill City   898 sq. mi.
2,946   3,543   3,995   4,751   5,586   5,020
February 26, 1867; organized 1880. John L. Graham (1832–63). Captain, Company D, 8th Kansas Regiment; killed at Chicka-mauga, September 19 1863.

Graham   **North Carolina**
Robbinsville   292 sq. mi.
7,993   7,196   7,217   6,562   6,432   6,886
January 30, 1872. William Alexander Graham (1804–75). North Carolina House of Commons 1836, Speaker 1838 and 1840; U.S. senator 1840–43; governor of North Carolina 1845–49; U.S. secretary of the navy 1850–52; unsuccessful candidate for U.S. vice president 1852; North Carolina Senate 1854, 1862, and 1865; Confederate Senate 1863; elected to U.S. Senate but credentials not presented 1866; arbiter in Virginia–Maryland boundary dispute 1873–75.

Grainger   **Tennessee**
Rutledge   280 sq. mi.
20,659   17,095   16,751   13,948   12,506   13,086
April 22, 1796. Mary Grainger Blount (?–1802). Daughter of Caleb Grainger, Wilmington, North Carolina; married William Blount (see Blount, Tennessee), only governor of the Territory South of the Ohio (Tennessee), February 12, 1778; popular first lady.

Grand   **Colorado**
Hot Sulphur Springs   1,847 sq. mi.

12,442   7,966   7,475   4,107   3,557   3,963
February 2, 1874. *Grand River*. Alternative name for Colorado River until officially changed to "Colorado" by Congress 1921.

Grand   **Utah**
Moab   3,682 sq. mi.
8,485   6,620   8,241   6,688   6,345   1,903
March 13, 1890. Grand River.*

Grand Forks   **North Dakota**
Grand Forks   1,438 sq. mi.
66,109   70,683   66,100   61,102   48,677   39,443
January 4, 1873; organized March 2, 1875. Town of Grand Forks. Named for location at junction of Red River and Red Lake River.

Grand Isle   **Vermont**
North Hero   83 sq. mi.
6,901   5,318   4,613   3,574   2,927   3,406
November 9, 1802; organized November 2, 1805; effective December 1, 1805. Grand Isle. Largest island in Lake Champlain.

Grand Traverse   **Michigan**
Traverse City   465 sq. mi.
77,654   64,273   54,899   39,175   33,490   28,598
April 7, 1851. Grand Traverse Bay. From French phrase meaning "long crossing"; describes the larger of two openings crossed in navigating northeastern Lake Michigan.

Granite   **Montana**
Philipsburg   1,727 sq. mi.
2,830   2,548   2,700   2,737   3,014   2,773
March 2, 1893. Granite Mountain Silver Mine. Mountain was named for its granite content.

Grant   **Arkansas**
Sheridan   632 sq. mi.
16,464   13,948   13,008   9,711   8,294   9,024
February 4, 1869. *Ulysses Simpson Grant* (1822–85). Graduated West Point 1843; Mexican War; resigned 1854; re-enlisted as colonel June 17, 1861; brigadier general and major general; received Lee's surrender, Appomattox Court House April 9, 1865; first General of the U.S. 1866; 18th president of the U.S. 1869–77.

Grant   **Indiana**
Marion   414 sq. mi.
73,403   74,169   80,934   83,955   74,741   62,156
February 10, 1831; effective April 1, 1831. *Samuel Grant* (1762–89) and Moses Grant (1768–89). Brothers from Kentucky killed in skirmish with Indians in Switzerland County, Indiana, August 1789.

Grant   **Kansas**
Ulysses   575 sq. mi.
7,909   7,159   6,977   5,961   5,269   4,638
March 6, 1873; organized 1889. Ulysses Simpson Grant.*

Grant   **Kentucky**
Williamstown   260 sq. mi.
22,384   15,737   13,308   9,999   9,489   9,809
February 12, 1820. Uncertain. (1) John Grant (1754–1826); pioneer salt producer. (2) Samuel Grant.* (3) Squire Grant (1764–1833); surveyor; Kentucky Senate 1801–06.

Grant   **Louisiana**
Colfax   645 sq. mi.

18,698   17,526   16,703   13,671   13,330   14,263
March 4, 1869. Ulysses Simpson Grant.*

Grant   **Minnesota**
Elbow Lake   546 sq. mi.
6,289   6,246   7,171   7,462   8,870   9,542
March 6, 1868; organized March 1, 1883. Ulysses Simpson Grant.*

Grant   **Nebraska**
Hyannis   776 sq. mi.
747   769   877   1,019   1,009   1,057
March 31, 1887; organized May 13, 1888. Ulysses Simpson Grant.*

Grant   **New Mexico**
Silver City   3,966 sq. mi.
31,002   27,676   26,204   22,030   18,700   21,649
January 30, 1868. Ulysses Simpson Grant.*

Grant   **North Dakota**
Carson   1,659 sq. mi.
2,841   3,549   4,274   5,009   6,248   7,114
November 25, 1916. Ulysses Simpson Grant.*

Grant   **Oklahoma**
Medford   1,001 sq. mi.
5,144   5,689   6,518   7,117   8,140   10,461
1893, as County L; name changed November 6, 1894. Ulysses Simpson Grant.*

Grant   **Oregon**
Canyon City   4,529 sq. mi.
7,935   7,853   8,210   6,996   7,726   8,329
October 14, 1864. Ulysses Simpson Grant.*

Grant   **South Dakota**
Milbank   683 sq. mi.
7,847   8,372   9,013   9,005   9,913   10,233
January 8, 1873; organized June 17, 1878. Ulysses Simpson Grant.*

Grant   **Washington**
Ephrata   2,681 sq. mi.
74,698   54,758   48,522   41,881   46,477   24,346
February 24, 1909. Ulysses Simpson Grant.*

Grant   **West Virginia**
Petersburg   477 sq. mi.
11,299   10,428   10,210   8,607   8,304   8,756
February 14, 1866. Ulysses Simpson Grant.*

Grant   **Wisconsin**
Lancaster   1,148 sq. mi.
49,597   49,264   51,736   48,398   44,419   41,460
December 8, 1836; effective March 4, 1837. Uncertain. (1) Cuthbert Grant (c1791–1854); fur trapper. (2) Grant River; named for Cuthbert Grant or his father, James Grant (?–?).

Granville   **North Carolina**
Oxford   531 sq. mi.

48,498   38,345   34,043   32,762   33,110   31,793
June 28, 1746 (session). John Carteret, Earl of Granville.* (See Carteret, North Carolina).

Gratiot   **Michigan**
Ithaca   570 sq. mi.
42,285   38,982   40,448   39,246   37,012   33,429
March 2, 1831; organized February 3, 1855. Uncertain. (1) Charles Gratiot (1786–1855); graduated West Point 1806; chief engineer in army 1812 and 1828–38; attack on Fort Meigs 1813; brevet colonel 1814; Fort Mackinac 1814; directed construction of Fort Gratiot 1814; brevet brigadier general 1828. (2) Fort Gratiot; named for Charles Gratiot; located at head of St. Clair River.

Graves   **Kentucky**
Mayfield   556 sq. mi.
37,028   33,550   34,049   30,939   30,021   31,364
December 19, 1821; organized 1824. Benjamin Graves (1771–1813). Major in regiment of Colonel Lewis 1812; colonel 1812; killed at battle of River Raisin 1813.

Gray   **Kansas**
Cimarron   869 sq. mi.
5,904   5,396   5,138   4,516   4,380   4,894
March 5, 1887; organized July 20, 1887. Alfred Gray (1830–80). Kansas legislature 1861; Union army quartermaster 1862–64; secretary of Kansas Board of Agriculture 1873–80.

Gray   **Texas**
Pampa   928 sq. mi.
22,744   23,967   26,386   26,949   31,535   24,728
August 21, 1876; organized May 27, 1902. Peter W. Gray (1819–74). Captain, 2nd Brigade, Texas Army 1840; district attorney 1841; alderman, Houston 1841; Texas Congress; Texas Senate; district judge 1861–64; Confederate Congress 1861–63; justice, Texas Supreme Court 1874.

Grays Harbor   **Washington**
Montesano   1,917 sq. mi.
67,194   64,175   66,314   59,553   54,465   53,644
April 14, 1854, as Chehalis; name changed March 15, 1915. Grays Harbor. Named for Robert Gray (1755–1806); Boston trader; commanded first circumnavigation of the world under the American flag 1787–90; entered Columbia River and named it for his ship *Columbia* 1792.

Grayson   **Kentucky**
Leitchfield   504 sq. mi.
24,053   21,050   20,854   16,445   15,834   17,063
January 25, 1810; effective April 1, 1810. *William Grayson* (c1736–90). Captain of independent company of cadets, Prince William County, Virginia 1774; aide-de-camp to General Washington 1776; organized Grayson's additional Continental Regiment 1777; colonel 1777; battle of Monmouth 1778; Continental Congress 1784–87; Virginia Constitutional Convention 1788; U.S. senator 1789–90.

Grayson   **Texas**
Sherman   934 sq. mi.
110,595   95,021   89,796   83,225   73,043   70,467
March 17, 1846; organized July 13, 1846. Peter William Grayson (1788–1838). Aide-de-camp to Stephen Austin 1835; attorney general of Republic of Texas 1836–37; mediator at Washington, D.C., between Texas and Mexico 1836; committed suicide.

Grayson   **Virginia**
Independence   443 sq. mi.
17,917   16,278   16,579   15,439   17,390   21,379
November 7, 1792. William Grayson.*

Greeley   **Kansas**
Tribune   778 sq. mi.
1,534   1,774   1,845   1,819   2,087   2,010
March 6, 1873; organized July 9, 1888. *Horace Greeley* (1811–72). Founded *New York Tribune* 1841; U.S. representative 1848–49; commissioner to the Paris Exposition 1855; defeated for presidency 1872; popularized phrase "Go West, young man."

Greeley   **Nebraska**
Greeley   570 sq. mi.
2,714   3,006   3,462   4,000   4,595   5,575
March 1, 1871; organized January 20, 1873. Horace Greeley.*

Green   **Kentucky**
Greensburg   289 sq. mi.
11,518   10,371   11,043   10,350   11,249   11,261
December 20, 1792; effective January 1, 1793. Nathanael Greene.* (See Greene, Alabama.)

Green   **Wisconsin**
Monroe   584 sq. mi.
33,647   30,339   30,012   26,714   25,851   24,172
December 8, 1836; organized 1838. Uncertain. (1) Nathanael Greene* (see Greene, Alabama). (2) Descriptive of local forests.

Greenbrier   **West Virginia**
Lewisburg   1,021 sq. mi.
34,435   34,693   37,665   32,090   34,446   39,295
October 20, 1777 (session); effective March 1, 1778. Greenbrier River. Translation of French name Ronceverte, from *ronce,* meaning "brier" or "bramble," and *verte,* meaning "green."

Greene   **Alabama**
Eutaw   646 sq. mi.
9,974   10,153   11,021   10,650   13,600   16,482
December 13, 1819. *Nathanael Greene* (1742–86). Brigadier general, Rhode Island troops 1775; brigadier general Continental army 1775; major general 1776; quartermaster general 1778–80; commanded Army of the South 1780; president of the court of inquiry for Major André; resigned from army 1783.

Greene   **Arkansas**
Paragould   578 sq. mi.
37,331   31,804   30,744   24,765   25,198   29,149
November 5, 1833; effective November 1, 1834. Nathanael Greene.*

Greene   **Georgia**
Greensboro   388 sq. mi.
14,406   11,793   11,391   10,212   11,193   12,843
February 3, 1786. Nathanael Greene.*

Greene   **Illinois**
Carrollton   543 sq. mi.
14,761   15,317   16,661   17,014   17,460   18,852
January 20, 1821. Nathanael Greene.*

Greene   **Indiana**
Bloomfield   542 sq. mi.
33,157   30,410   30,416   26,894   26,327   27,886
January 5, 1821; effective February 5, 1821. Nathanael Greene.*

Greene   **Iowa**
Jefferson   568 sq. mi.
10,366   10,045   12,119   12,716   14,379   15,544
January 15, 1851; organized August 25, 1853. Nathanael Greene.*

Greene   **Mississippi**
Leakesville   713 sq. mi.
13,299   10,220   9,827   8,545   8,366   8,215
December 9, 1811. Nathanael Greene.*

Greene   **Missouri**
Springfield   675 sq. mi.
240,391   207,949   185,302   152,929   126,276   104,823
January 2, 1833. Nathanael Greene.*

Greene   **New York**
Catskill   648 sq. mi.
48,195   44,739   40,861   33,136   31,372   28,745
March 25, 1800. Nathanael Greene.*

Greene   **North Carolina**
Snow Hill   265 sq. mi.
18,974   15,384   16,117   14,967   16,741   18,024
November 18, 1799 (session). Nathanael Greene.*

Greene   **Ohio**
Xenia   415 sq. mi.
147,886   136,731   129,769   125,057   94,642   58,892
March 24, 1803; effective May 1, 1803. Nathanael Greene.*

Greene   **Pennsylvania**
Waynesburg   576 sq. mi.
40,672   39,550   40,476   36,090   39,424   45,394
February 9, 1796. Nathanael Greene.*

Greene   **Tennessee**
Greenville   622 sq. mi.
62,909   55,853   54,422   47,630   42,163   41,048
April 18, 1783 (session). Nathanael Greene.*

Greene   **Virginia**
Stanardsville   157 sq. mi.
15,244   10,297   7,625   5,248   4,715   4,745
January 24, 1838. Nathanael Greene.*

Green Lake   **Wisconsin**
Green Lake   354 sq. mi.
19,105   18,651   18,370   16,878   15,418   14,749
March 5, 1858. Green Lake. Translation of Indian name describing lake's color.

Greenlee   **Arizona**
Clifton   1,847 sq. mi.
8,547   8,008   11,406   10,330   11,509   12,805
March 10, 1909. Mason Greenlee (1835–1903). Early prospector and mineral surveyor in area.

Greensville   **Virginia**
Emporia   295 sq. mi.
11,560   8,853   10,903   9,604   16,155   16,319
October 16, 1780 (session). Uncertain. (1) Nathanael Greene* (see Greene, Alabama). (2) Sir Richard Grenville (?–1591); member of Parliament; established colony at Roanoke 1585; died in naval combat against Spain.

Greenup   **Kentucky**
Greenup   346 sq. mi.
36,891   36,742   39,132   33,192   29,238   24,887
December 12, 1803. Christopher Greenup (1750–1818). Colonel, Revolutionary War; Indian wars; admitted to bar 1783; clerk of district court at Harrodsburg, Kentucky, 1785–92; Virginia House of Delegates 1785; U.S. representative from Kentucky 1792–97; Kentucky House of Representatives 1798 and 1809; clerk of Kentucky Senate 1799–1802; judge of circuit court 1802; Franklin County justice of the peace 1812.

Greenville   **South Carolina**
Greenville   790 sq. mi.
379,616   320,167   287,913   240,546   209,776   168,152
March 22, 1786. Uncertain. (1) Nathanael Greene* (see Greene, Alabama). (2) Isaac Green (1762–?); early settler 1785, established grist mill on Reedy River. (3) Descriptive of local foliage.

Greenwood   **Kansas**
Eureka   1,140 sq. mi.
7,673   7,847   8,764   9,141   11,253   13,574
August 30, 1855; organized February 27, 1860. Alfred Burton Greenwood (1811–89). Arkansas House of Representatives 1842–45; Arkansas prosecuting attorney 1845–51; Arkansas circuit judge 1851–53; U.S. representative 1853–59; U.S. commissioner of Indian affairs 1859–61; Confederate House of Representatives 1862–65.

Greenwood   **South Carolina**
Greenwood   456 sq. mi.
66,271   59,567   57,847   49,686   44,346   41,628
March 2, 1897. City of Greenwood. Descriptive of local foliage.

Greer   **Oklahoma**
Mangum   639 sq. mi.
6,061   6,559   7,028   7,979   8,877   11,749
1886 by Texas; declared part of Oklahoma by Congress May 4, 1896. John A. Greer (1802–55). Texas Republic legislature 1837–45; Texas secretary of treasury; lieutenant governor of Texas; died while campaigning for governor.

Gregg   **Texas**
Longview   274 sq. mi.
111,379   104,948   99,487   75,929   69,436   61,258
April 12, 1873; organized June 28, 1873. John Gregg (1828–64). Judge of the 13th District 1856–60; delegate to Provisional Congress of the Confederacy 1860; organized 7th Regiment, Texas Volunteers 1861; captured at Fort Donelson; brigadier general 1862; killed near Fort Harrison October 7, 1864.

Gregory   **South Dakota**
Burke   1,016 sq. mi.
4,792   5,359   6,015   6,710   7,399   8,556
May 8, 1862; organized September 5, 1898. John Shaw Gregory (1831–?). Graduate, U.S. Naval Academy; Dakota territorial legislature 1862–66; U.S. Indian agent for Poncas.

Grenada   **Mississippi**
Grenada   422 sq. mi.
23,263   21,555   21,043   19,854   18,409   18,830
May 9, 1870. City of Grenada. Named for city and province of Granada, Spain.

Griggs   **North Dakota**
Cooperstown   709 sq. mi.
2,754   3,303   3,714   4,184   5,023   5,460
February 18, 1881; organized June 16, 1882. Alexander Griggs (1838–1903). Mississippi River steamboat pilot; moved to Red River; one of founders of Grand Forks; North Dakota Constitutional Convention 1889.

Grimes   **Texas**
Anderson   794 sq. mi.
23,552   18,828   13,580   11,855   12,709   15,135
April 6, 1846; organized July 15, 1846. Jesse Grimes (1788–1866). Elected 1st lieutenant of 1st Company 1829; general council 1835; signer, Texas Declaration of Independence 1836; company of volunteers 1836; Texas Senate 1836–37; Texas legislature 1841–45.

Grundy   **Illinois**
Morris   420 sq. mi.
37,535   32,337   30,582   26,535   22,350   19,217
February 7, 1841; organized May 24, 1841. *Felix Grundy* (1777–1840). Kentucky House of Representatives 1800–05; judge, Kentucky Supreme Court 1806, Chief Justice 1807; U.S. representative from Tennessee 1829–38; U.S. attorney general 1838–39; U.S. senator 1839–40.

Grundy   **Iowa**
Grundy Center   503 sq. mi.
12,369   12,029   14,366   14,119   14,132   13,722
January 15, 1851; organized December 25, 1856. Felix Grundy.*

Grundy   **Missouri**
Trenton   436 sq. mi.
10,432   10,536   11,959   11,819   12,220   13,220
January 29, 1841. Felix Grundy.*

Grundy   **Tennessee**
Altamont   361 sq. mi.
14,332   13,362   13,787   10,631   11,512   12,558
January 29, 1844. Felix Grundy.*

Guadalupe   **New Mexico**
Santa Rosa   3,030 sq. mi.
4,680   4,156   4,496   4,969   5,610   6,772
February 26, 1891, as Guadalupe; name changed to Leonard Wood 1903; renamed Guadalupe 1905. *Our Lady of Guadalupe*, patron saint of Mexico. Spanish rendering of the name Virgin Mary called herself during her appearance to an Aztec peasant 1531.

Guadalupe   **Texas**
Seguin   711 sq. mi.
89,023   64,873   46,708   33,554   29,017   25,392
March 30, 1846. Guadalupe River. Named for Our Lady of Guadalupe.*

Guernsey   **Ohio**
Cambridge   522 sq. mi.
40,792   39,024   42,024   37,665   38,579   38,452
January 31, 1810. Isle of Guernsey, England.

Guilford   **North Carolina**
Greensboro   649 sq. mi.
421,048   347,420   317,154   288,590   246,520   191,057
December 5, 1770 (session). Francis North, Earl of Guilford (1704–90). British parliament 1727; governor of the royal princes Edward August and George William Frederick, future George III; personal favorite of George III and Queen Charlotte Sophia.

Gulf **Florida**
Port Saint Joe 555 sq. mi.

| 13,332 | 11,504 | 10,658 | 10,096 | 9,937 | 7,460 |

June 6, 1925. Gulf of Mexico. Descriptive of county's location on the gulf.

Gunnison **Colorado**
Gunnison 3,239 sq. mi.

| 13,956 | 10,273 | 10,689 | 7,578 | 5,477 | 5,716 |

March 9, 1877. The Gunnison Country. Area of western Colorado named for John William Gunnison (1812–53); graduated West Point 1837; 2nd lieutenant, 2nd Cavalry, 1837; Cherokee War 1837–38; Seminole campaign 1839; 1st lieutenant 1846; captain 1853; killed by Indians near Sevier Lake, Utah, October 26, 1853, while surveying Pacific railroad route.

Guthrie **Iowa**
Guthrie Center 591 sq. mi.

| 11,353 | 10,935 | 11,983 | 12,243 | 13,607 | 15,197 |

January 15, 1851. Edwin Guthrie (1806–47). Captain of Iowa Volunteers in Mexican War 1847; died of wounds received at La Hoya June 20, 1847.

Gwinnett **Georgia**
Lawrenceville 433 sq. mi.

| 588,448 | 352,910 | 166,903 | 72,349 | 43,541 | 32,320 |

December 15, 1818. Button Gwinnett (1732–77). President, Georgia Provisional Council; Continental Congress 1776–77; signer, Declaration of Independence 1776; Georgia Constitutional Convention 1777; acting president and commander in chief of Georgia 1777; killed in duel with General Lachlan McIntosh (see McIntosh (3), Georgia).

H

Haakon **South Dakota**
Phillip 1,813 sq. mi.

| 2,196 | 2,624 | 2,794 | 2,802 | 3,303 | 3,167 |

November 1914; organized February 8, 1915. King Haakon VII of Norway (1872–1957). Second son of Frederick VIII of Denmark; married Princess Maud, youngest daughter of Edward VII of England 1896; chosen as King of Norway after independence from Sweden 1905; crowned King of Norway June 22, 1906; headed government-in-exile during World War II 1940–45.

Habersham **Georgia**
Clarkesville 278 sq. mi.

| 35,902 | 27,621 | 25,020 | 20,691 | 18,116 | 16,553 |

December 15, 1818. Joseph Habersham (1751–1815). Major, lieutenant colonel, colonel, 1st Georgia Regiment 1776; resigned 1778; Continental Congress 1785–86; U.S. postmaster general 1795–1801.

Haines **Alaska**
Haines 2,344 sq. mi.

| 2,392 | 2,117 | 1,680 | 1,504 | (a) | (b) |

August 1968. Haines Mission. Named for Mrs. F. E. Haines, secretary of the Presbyterian mission board that had raised money for the mission; mission founded by Reverend Eugene S. Willard 1881. [(a) Part of Lynn Canal–Icy Straits Census District; (b) part of 1st Judicial District.]

Hale **Alabama**
Greensboro 644 sq. mi.

| 17,185 | 15,498 | 15,604 | 15,888 | 19,537 | 20,832 |

January 30, 1867. Stephen F. Hale (1816–62). Graduated from law school 1839; Mexican War 1846–48; lieutenant colonel, 11th Alabama Infantry Regiment 1861; died in combat near Richmond.

Hale **Texas**
Plainview 1,005 sq. mi.

36,602   34,671   37,592   34,137   36,798   28,211
August 21, 1876; organized August 4, 1888. John C. Hale (1806–36). Migrated to Texas 1831; lieutenant in Captain Bryant's company; killed at battle of San Jacinto April 21, 1836.

Halifax   **North Carolina**
Halifax   725 sq. mi.
57,370   55,516   55,286   53,884   58,956   58,377
December 12, 1754 (session). George Montagu Dunk, *2nd Earl of Halifax* (1716–71). President, board of trade 1748–61; lord lieutenant of Ireland 1761–63; 1st lord of the Admiralty 1762; secretary of state 1762; Lord Privy Seal 1770.

Halifax   **Virginia**
Halifax   819 sq. mi.
37,355   36,030[a]   37,692[a]   36,965[a]   39,611[a]   41,442
February 27, 1752 (session); effective May 10, 1752. Earl of Halifax.* [(a) Includes independent city of South Boston: 1990, 6,997; 1980, 7,093; 1970, 6,889; 1960, 5,974]

Hall   **Georgia**
Gainesville   394 sq. mi.
139,277   95,428   75,649   59,405   49,739   40,113
December 15, 1818. Lyman Hall (1731–90). Provisional Council of Georgia 1774–75; Continental Congress 1774–80; signer of Declaration of Independence 1776; physician; governor of Georgia 1783.

Hall   **Nebraska**
Grand Island   546 sq. mi.
53,534   48,925   47,690   42,851   35,757   32,186
November 4, 1858; organized January 7, 1867. Augustus Hall (1814–61). Assistant U.S. marshal in Ohio 1839; prosecuting attorney, Union County, Ohio, 1840–42; U.S. representative from Iowa 1855–57; chief justice, Nebraska Territory 1858–61.

Hall   **Texas**
Memphis   903 sq. mi.
3,782   3,905   5,594   6,015   7,322   10,930
August 21, 1876; organized June 23, 1890. Warren D. C. Hall (1788–1867). Mexican army 1812; resigned 1814; committee of safety 1835; adjutant general, Republic of Texas 1835; secretary of war, Republic of Texas.

Hamblen   **Tennessee**
Morristown   161 sq. mi.
58,128   50,480   49,300   38,696   33,092   23,976
June 8, 1870. Hezekiah Hamblen (1775–1855). Lawyer and landowner; Hawkins County Court.

Hamilton   **Florida**
Jasper   515 sq. mi.
13,327   10,930   8,761   7,787   7,705   8,981
December 26, 1827. *Alexander Hamilton* (1757–1804). Captain of artillery, Continental army 1776; aide-de-camp to General Washington 1777–81; Continental Congress 1782–83 and 1787–88; New York Assembly 1787; Constitutional Convention 1788; U.S. secretary of the treasury 1789–95; mortally wounded in duel with Aaron Burr July 11, 1804.

Hamilton   **Illinois**
McLeansboro   435 sq. mi.
8,621   8,499   9,172   8,665   10,010   12,356
February 8, 1821. Alexander Hamilton.*

Hamilton   **Indiana**
Noblesville   398 sq. mi.
182,740   108,936   82,027   54,532   40,132   28,491
January 8, 1823; effective April 7, 1823. Alexander Hamilton.*

Hamilton   **Iowa**
Webster City   577 sq. mi.
16,438   16,071   17,862   18,383   20,032   19,660
December 22, 1856. William H. Hamilton (c1816–?). Probate judge of Dubuque County; president of Iowa Senate 1856–57.

Hamilton   **Kansas**
Syracuse   996 sq. mi.
2,670   2,388   2,514   2,747   3,144   3,696
March 6, 1873; organized January 29, 1886. Alexander Hamilton.*

Hamilton   **Nebraska**
Aurora   544 sq. mi.
9,403   8,862   9,301   8,867   8,714   8,778
February 16, 1867; organized October 1870. Alexander Hamilton.*

Hamilton   **New York**
Lake Pleasant   1,720 sq. mi.
5,379   5,279   5,034   4,714   4,367   4,105
April 12, 1816; organized 1847. Alexander Hamilton.*

Hamilton   **Ohio**
Cincinnati   407 sq. mi.
845,303   866,228   873,224   924,018   864,121   723,952
January 2, 1790. Alexander Hamilton.*

Hamilton   **Tennessee**
Chattanooga   542 sq. mi.
307,896   285,536   287,740   254,236   237,905   208,255
October 25, 1819. Alexander Hamilton.*

Hamilton   **Texas**
Hamilton   836 sq. mi.
8,229   7,733   8,297   7,198   8,488   10,660
January 22, 1858. James Hamilton (1786–1857). Major, War of 1812; mayor of Charleston, South Carolina, 1822–24; U.S. representative 1822–29; governor of South Carolina 1830–32; brigadier general of South Carolina troops 1833; Texas Republic diplomatic agent in Europe; drowned in Gulf of Mexico.

Hamlin   **South Dakota**
Hayti   507 sq. mi.
5,540   4,974   5,261   5,172   6,303   7,058
January 8, 1873; organized September 10, 1878. Hannibal Hamlin (1809–91). U.S. representative from Maine 1843–47; U.S. senator 1848–57, 1857–61, and 1869–81; governor of Maine 1857; U.S. vice president 1861–65; enlisted in Maine State Guards as private for sixty days 1864; collector of the Port of Boston 1865–66; U.S. minister to Spain 1881–82.

Hampden   **Massachusetts**
Springfield   618 sq. mi.
456,228   456,310   443,018   459,050   429,353   367,971
February 25, 1812; effective August 1, 1812. John Hampden (1594–1643). English patriot; resisted attempt of King Charles I to force loans and raise taxes; Short Parliament 1640; arrested and involved in lawsuit against King; impeached by attorney general 1642; mortally wounded in English Civil War 1643.

Hampshire   **Massachusetts**
Northampton   529 sq. mi.
152,251   146,568   138,813   123,981   103,229   87,594
May 7, 1662. Hampshire County, England.

Hampshire   **West Virginia**
Romney   642 sq. mi.
20,203   16,498   14,867   11,710   11,705   12,577
February 27, 1752 (session); effective December 13, 1753. Hampshire County, England.

Hampton   **South Carolina**
Hampton   560 sq. mi.
21,386   18,191   18,159   15,878   17,425   18,027
February 18, 1878. Wade Hampton (1818–1902). South Carolina legislature; colonel, Confederate army; lieutenant general 1864; governor of South Carolina 1877–79; U.S. senator 1879–91.

Hampton   **Virginia**
(Independent City)   52 sq. mi.
146,437   133,793   122,617   120,779   89,258   60,994[a]
1634, as Elizabeth City County; independent city of Hampton created 1634; merged with Elizabeth City County July 1, 1952. Henry Wriothesley, 3rd Earl of Southampton (see Southampton, Virginia). [(a) Includes Elizabeth City County (55,028)]

Hancock   **Georgia**
Sparta   473 sq. mi.
10,076   8,908   9,466   9,019   9,979   11,052
December 17, 1793. *John Hancock* (1737–93). Massachusetts provisional legislature 1766–72; Continental Congress 1775–80 and 1785–86, president 1775–77; first signer of Declaration of Independence 1776; major general, Massachusetts Militia; Massachusetts Constitutional Convention 1780; governor of Massachusetts 1780–85 and 1787–93.

Hancock   **Illinois**
Carthage   795 sq. mi.
20,121   21,373   23,877   23,645   24,574   25,790
January 13, 1825; organized 1829. John Hancock.*

Hancock   **Indiana**
Greenfield   306 sq. mi.
55,391   45,527   43,939   35,096   26,665   20,332
January 26, 1827; organized March 1, 1828. John Hancock.*

Hancock   **Iowa**
Garner   571 sq. mi.
12,100   12,638   13,833   13,227   14,604   15,077
January 15, 1851; organized November 25, 1858. John Hancock.*

Hancock   **Kentucky**
Hawesville   189 sq. mi.
8,392   7,864   7,742   7,080   5,330   6,009
January 3, 1829. John Hancock.*

Hancock   **Maine**
Ellsworth   1,588 sq. mi.
51,791   46,948   41,781   34,590   32,293   32,105
June 25, 1789; effective May 1, 1790. John Hancock.*

Hancock   **Mississippi**
Bay Saint Louis   477 sq. mi.
42,967   31,760   24,537   17,387   14,039   11,891
December 18, 1812. John Hancock.*

Hancock   **Ohio**
Findlay   531 sq. mi.

71,295   65,536   64,581   61,217   53,686   44,280
February 12, 1820; organized 1828. John Hancock.*

Hancock   **Tennessee**
Sneedville   222 sq. mi.
6,786   6,739   6,887   6,719   7,757   9,116
January 7, 1844. John Hancock.*

Hancock   **West Virginia**
New Cumberland   83 sq. mi.
32,667   35,233   40,418   39,749   39,615   34,388
January 15, 1848. John Hancock.*

Hand   **South Dakota**
Miller   1,437 sq. mi.
3,741   4,272   4,948   5,883   6,712   7,149
January 8, 1873; organized September 1, 1882. George H. Hand (1837–91). Union aArmy 1864; U.S. attorney for Dakota Territory 1866–69; secretary of Dakota Territory 1874–83.

Hanover   **Virginia**
Hanover   473 sq. mi.
86,320   63,306   50,398   37,479   27,550   21,985
November 2, 1720 (session). George I,* Duke of Hanover (see King George, Virginia).

Hansford   **Texas**
Spearman   920 sq. mi.
5,369   5,848   6,209   6,351   6,208   4,202
August 21, 1876; organized March 11, 1889. John M. Hansford (?–1844). Immigrated to Texas 1837; judge of 7th Judicial District 1840–42; Texas attorney general; killed by Regulators 1844.

Hanson   **South Dakota**
Alexandria   435 sq. mi.
3,139   2,994   3,415   3,781   4,584   4,896
January 13, 1871; organized August 16, 1873. Joseph R. Hanson (1837–1917). Legislature of Dakota Territory 1864–65; territorial auditor; judge advocate; Sioux agent 1865–70.

Haralson   **Georgia**
Buchanan   282 sq. mi.
25,690   21,966   18,422   15,927   14,543   14,663
January 26, 1856. Hugh Anderson Haralson (1805–54). Georgia House of Representatives 1831–32; Georgia Senate 1837–38; major general, Georgia Militia 1838–50; U.S. representative 1843–51.

Hardee   **Florida**
Wauchula   637 sq. mi.
26,938   19,499   19,379   14,889   12,370   10,073
April 23, 1921. Cary Augustus Hardee (1876–1957). Florida attorney, 3rd Judicial Circuit 1905–13; Speaker, Florida House of Representatives 1915–17; governor of Florida 1921–25.

Hardeman   **Tennessee**
Bolivar   668 sq. mi.
28,105   23,377   23,873   22,435   21,517   23,311
October 16, 1823. Thomas Jones Hardeman (1788–1854). Colonel, Tennessee Militia, War of 1812; brigade quartermaster in the Natchez expedition 1812–13; member of Texas Republic Congress; associate justice, Bastrop County, Texas, 1843; chief justice, Bastrop County 1845; Most Worshipful Grand Master of Texas Free and Accepted Masons 1850. Brother of Bailey Hardeman (see below).

Hardeman   **Texas**
Quanah   695 sq. mi.
4,724   5,283   6,368   6,795   8,275   10,212
February 1, 1858; organized December 1, 1884. Bailey Hardeman (1795–1836). West Tennessee Volunteer, War of 1812; 1st lieutenant 1813; signer, Texas Declaration of Independence 1836; ad interim secretary of treasury, Texas Republic 1836. Brother of Thomas Hardeman (see above).

Hardin   **Illinois**
Elizabethtown   178 sq. mi.
4,800   5,189   5,383   4,914   5,879   7,530
March 2, 1839. Hardin County, Kentucky.

Hardin   **Iowa**
Eldora   569 sq. mi.
18,812   19,094   21,776   22,248   22,533   22,218
January 15, 1851; organized March 2, 1853. John J. Hardin (1810–47). Colonel, Mexican War, killed in battle of Buena Vista.

Hardin   **Kentucky**
Elizabethtown   628 sq. mi.
94,174   89,240   88,917   78,421   67,789   50,312
December 15, 1792; effective February 20, 1793. *John Hardin* (1753–92). Governor Dunmore's expedition 1774; 2nd lieutenant, 8th Pennsylvania, Continental army 1777; resigned as 1st lieutenant 1779; Indian fighter; brigadier general, Kentucky Militia 1792; killed by Indians while on peace mission.

Hardin   **Ohio**
Kenton   470 sq. mi.
31,945   31,111   32,719   30,813   29,633   28,673
February 12, 1820; organized 1833. John Hardin.*

Hardin   **Tennessee**
Savannah   578 sq. mi.
25,578   22,633   22,280   18,212   17,397   16,908
November 13, 1819. Joseph Hardin (1734–1801). North Carolina Minutemen; Continental army; legislature of Territory South of the Ohio (Tennessee) 1794–95, Speaker 1795.

Hardin   **Texas**
Kountze   894 sq. mi.
48,073   41,320   40,721   29,996   24,629   19,535
January 22, 1858; organized August 2, 1858. Five Hardin brothers: Benjamin (1796–1850), Augustine (1797–1871), William (1801–39), Franklin (1803–78), and Milton (1813–94). Migrated to Texas 1825; all were active in Texas independence movement.

Harding   **New Mexico**
Mosquero   2,125 sq. mi.
810   987   1,090   1,348   1,874   3,013
March 4, 1921. Warren Gamaliel Harding (1865–1923). Editor, Marion, Ohio, *Star* 1884; Ohio Senate 1899–1903; lieutenant governor of Ohio 1904–05; U.S. senator 1915–21; 29th president of the U.S. 1921–23.

Harding   **South Dakota**
Buffalo   2,671 sq. mi.
1,353   1,669   1,700   1,855   2,371   2,289
March 5, 1881; abolished November 8, 1898; recreated November 3, 1908; organized January 30, 1911. John A. Harding (?–?). Miner in Black Hills; Speaker, Dakota territorial legislature, 1881.

Hardy   **West Virginia**
Moorefield   583 sq. mi.

| 12,669 | 10,977 | 10,030 | 8,855 | 9,308 | 10,032 |

October 17, 1785 (session). Samuel Hardy (1758–85). Virginia House of Delegates 1780; executive council 1781; Continental Congress 1783–85.

Harford   **Maryland**
Bel Air   440 sq. mi.

| 218,590 | 182,132 | 145,930 | 115,378 | 76,722 | 51,782 |

March 2, 1774. Henry Harford (1758–1834). Last proprietor of Maryland; son of Frederick, 6th Lord Baltimore; did not inherit title, because of illegitimate birth (see Frederick (1), Maryland).

Harlan   **Kentucky**
Harlan   467 sq. mi.

| 33,202 | 36,574 | 41,889 | 37,370 | 51,107 | 71,751 |

January 28, 1819. Silas Harlan (1753–1782). Major; served with George Rogers Clark; killed at battle of Blue Licks, last battle of American Revolution August 19, 1782.

Harlan   **Nebraska**
Alma   553 sq. mi.

| 3,786 | 3,810 | 4,292 | 4,357 | 5,081 | 7,189 |

June 3, 1871; organized July 29, 1872. Uncertain. (1) James Harlan (1820–99); U.S. senator from Iowa 1855–65 and 1867–72; supported development of West by homesteads, college land grants, and railroads; secretary of interior 1865–66. (2) Thomas Harlan (?–?); founded colony on Republican River. (3) Unidentified nephew of James Harlan.

Harmon   **Oklahoma**
Hollis   538 sq. mi.

| 3,283 | 3,793 | 4,519 | 5,136 | 5,852 | 8,079 |

June 2, 1909. Judson Harmon (1846–1927). Judge of Common Pleas Court, Ohio 1876; judge of Superior Court of Cincinnati 1878–87; U.S. attorney general 1895–97; governor of Ohio 1909–13.

Harnett   **North Carolina**
Lillington   595 sq. mi.

| 91,025 | 67,822 | 59,570 | 49,667 | 48,236 | 47,605 |

February 7, 1855. Cornelius Harnett (1723–81). North Carolina legislature 1770–71; Wilmington Committee of Safety 1774; author of the Halifax Resolves 1776; Continental Congress 1777–80; died of disease contracted while paroled British prisoner.

Harney   **Oregon**
Burns   10,134 sq. mi.

| 7,609 | 7,060 | 8,314 | 7,215 | 6,744 | 6,113 |

February 25, 1889. William Selby Harney (1800–89). 2nd lieutenant 1818; 1st lieutenant 1819; captain 1825; Black Hawk War 1832; major and paymaster 1833; lieutenant colonel 1836; 2nd Seminole War 1835–42; Mexican War 1847; brigadier general 1858; assigned to command Department of Oregon; brevet brigadier general 1865.

Harper   **Kansas**
Anthony   801 sq. mi.

| 6,536 | 7,124 | 7,778 | 7,871 | 9,541 | 10,263 |

February 26, 1867; organized 1873. Marion Harper (?–1863). Enlisted in Union army 1861; 1st sergeant, Company E, 2nd Kansas; died from wounds at Waldron, Arkansas, December 30, 1863.

Harper   **Oklahoma**
Buffalo   1,039 sq. mi.

| 3,562 | 4,063 | 4,715 | 5,151 | 5,956 | 5,977 |

July 16, 1907. Oscar G. Harper (1874–?). Postmaster of Brule (later Buffalo) 1899; clerk, Oklahoma Constitutional Convention 1907.

Harris   **Georgia**
Hamilton   464 sq. mi.

| 23,695 | 17,788 | 15,464 | 11,520 | 11,167 | 11,265 |

December 14, 1827. Charles Harris (1772–1827). Lawyer, alderman or mayor (first alderman) of Savannah, Georgia, intermittently 1802–27; offered many judicial posts but declined them.

Harris **Texas**
Houston 1,729 sq. mi.

| 3,400,578 | 2,818,199 | 2,409,547 | 1,741,912 | 1,243,158 | 806,701 |

March 17, 1836, as Harrisburg; organized 1837; name changed December 28, 1839. Community of Harrisburg. Named for John Richardson Harris (1790–1829); established trading post 1824; operated boats between Texas and New Orleans; died of yellow fever at New Orleans.

Harrison **Indiana**
Corydon 485 sq. mi.

| 34,325 | 29,890 | 27,276 | 20,423 | 19,207 | 17,858 |

October 11, 1808; effective December 1, 1808. *William Henry Harrison* (1773–1841). Indian Wars; captain, commanding Fort Washington 1797; secretary of Northwest Territory 1798–99; congressional delegate from Northwest Territory 1799–1800; governor of Indiana Territory 1800–11; Indian commissioner 1801–13; defeated Indians at Tippecanoe 1811 and at Thames 1813; awarded Congressional medal; major general, U.S. Army 1813; U.S. representative from Ohio 1816–19; Ohio Senate 1819–21; U.S. senator 1825–28; U.S. minister to Colombia 1828–29; 9th president of the U.S. March 4 to April 4, 1841.

Harrison **Iowa**
Logan 697 sq. mi.

| 15,666 | 14,730 | 16,348 | 16,240 | 17,600 | 19,560 |

January 15, 1851; organized March 7, 1853. William Henry Harrison.*

Harrison **Kentucky**
Cynthiana 310 sq. mi.

| 17,983 | 16,248 | 15,166 | 14,158 | 13,704 | 13,736 |

December 21, 1793; effective February 1, 1794. Benjamin Harrison (c1745–1808). Colonel, Continental army; Kentucky Constitutional Convention 1792; general, Kentucky Militia; Kentucky legislature 1793.

Harrison **Mississippi**
Gulfport 581 sq. mi.

| 189,601 | 165,365 | 157,665 | 134,582 | 119,489 | 84,073 |

February 5, 1841. William Henry Harrison.*

Harrison **Missouri**
Bethany 725 sq. mi.

| 8,850 | 8,469 | 9,890 | 10,257 | 11,603 | 14,107 |

February 14, 1845. Albert Gallatin Harrison (1800–39). Board of Visitors, U.S. Military Academy 1828; commissioner to adjust land titles of Spanish grants 1829–35; U.S. representative from Missouri 1835–39.

Harrison **Ohio**
Cadiz 404 sq. mi.

| 15,856 | 16,085 | 18,152 | 17,013 | 17,995 | 19,054 |

January 12, 1813. William Henry Harrison.*

Harrison **Texas**
Marshall 899 sq. mi.

| 62,110 | 57,483 | 52,265 | 44,841 | 45,594 | 47,745 |

January 28, 1839; organized June 18, 1842. Jonas Harrison (1777–1837). Lawyer; collector of customs at Niagara Falls; master of chancery, New York; migrated to Texas 1820; active in Texas independence movement.

Harrison **West Virginia**
Clarksburg 416 sq. mi.

68,652   69,371   77,710   73,028   77,856   85,296

May 3, 1784 (session); effective July 20, 1784. Benjamin Harrison (1726–91). Virginia House of Burgesses 1749–75; Continental Congress 1774–77; signer, Declaration of Independence 1776; Speaker, Virginia House of Delegates 1778–81 and 1785; Virginia Constitutional Convention 1788; governor of Virginia 1781–84. Father of President William Henry Harrison and great-grandfather of President Benjamin Harrison.

Harrisonburg   **Virginia**
(Independent City)   18 sq. mi.
40,468   30,707   19,671   14,605   11,916   10,810

1916. Thomas Harrison (1704–85). Early settler; donated land for courthouse and county seat for Rockingham County. (Associated county: Rockingham.)

Hart   **Georgia**
Hartwell   232 sq. mi.
22,997   19,712   18,585   15,814   15,229   14,495

December 7, 1853. Nancy Morgan Hart (1735–1830). Married Benjamin Hart of Kentucky; moved to Elbert County, Georgia; a sharpshooter and patriot reported to have routed and captured many Tories; named *Wahatchee* (War Woman) by local Indians.

Hart   **Kentucky**
Munfordville   416 sq. mi.
17,445   14,890   15,402   13,980   14,119   15,321

January 28, 1819. Nathaniel G. S. Hart (?–1813). Captured at battle of River Raisin June 18, 1813; massacred by Indians.

Hartford   **Connecticut**
Hartford   735 sq. mi.
857,183   851,783   807,766   816,737   689,555   539,661

May 10, 1666 (session). City of Hartford. Named for Hertford, Hertfordshire, England.

Hartley   **Texas**
Channing   1,462 sq. mi.
5,537   3,634   3,987   2,782   2,171   1,913

August 21, 1876; organized February 9, 1891. Hartley brothers, Oliver and Rufus. (1) Oliver Cromwell Hartley (1823–59) private, Mexican War; compiled *A Digest of Laws of Texas* 1848–49; Texas legislature 1851–52; reporter of decisions of Texas supreme court 1859. (2) Rufus K. Hartley (?–?); reporter, Texas Supreme Court 1854.

Harvey   **Kansas**
Newton   539 sq. mi.
32,869   31,028   30,531   27,236   25,865   21,698

February 29, 1872. James Madison Harvey (1833–94). Government surveyor in Southwest; enlisted in Union army 1861; mustered out of Kansas Volunteer Infantry as captain 1864; Kansas House of Representatives 1865–66; Kansas Senate 1867–68; governor of Kansas 1869–73; U.S. senator 1874–77.

Haskell   **Kansas**
Sublette   577 sq. mi.
4,307   3,886   3,814   3,672   2,990   2,606

March 5, 1887. Dudley Chase Haskell (1842–83). Owned Colorado silver mine 1859; army quartermaster 1861–62; declined Prohibition Party nomination for U.S. presidency 1874; Kansas House of Representatives 1876; U.S. representative 1877–83.

Haskell   **Oklahoma**
Stigler   577 sq. mi.
11,792   10,940   11,010   9,578   9,121   13,313

July 16, 1907. Charles Nathaniel Haskell (1860–1933). Oklahoma Constitutional Convention 1906; governor of Oklahoma 1907–11.

Haskell   **Texas**
Haskell   903 sq. mi.

6,093   6,820   7,725   8,512   11,174   13,736

February 1, 1858; organized January 13, 1885. Charles Ready Haskell (1817–36). Enlisted under Fannin; Battle of Coleto; killed in Goliad Massacre March 27, 1836.

Hawaii   **Hawaii**
Hilo   4,028 sq. mi.
148,677   120,317   92,053   63,468   61,332   68,350

July 1905. Island of Hawaii. Possible origins of name include (1) Hawaiki, legendary home of Hawaiians near Tahiti; (2) Hawaii-Loa, legendary Polynesian fisherman who discovered Hawaii; (3) Polynesian word for "beyond the doors of death," referring to a mythical land.

Hawkins   **Tennessee**
Rogersville   487 sq. mi.
53,563   44,565   43,751   33,726   30,468   30,494

November 18, 1786 (session). Benjamin Hawkins (1754–1816). French interpreter for General Washington in Revolutionary War; North Carolina House of Commons 1778, 1779, and 1784; Continental Congress 1781–84 and 1786–87; U.S. senator 1789–95; Indian agent for all tribes south of the Ohio River 1796–1816.

Hayes   **Nebraska**
Hayes Center   713 sq. mi.
1,068   1,222   1,356   1,530   1,919   2,404

February 19, 1877. Rutherford Birchard Hayes (1822–93). Cincinnati city solicitor 1857–59; major and lieutenant colonel, Ohio Volunteer Infantry 1861; colonel 1862; brigadier general 1864; brevet major general 1865; resigned 1865; U.S. representative 1865–67; governor of Ohio 1868–72 and 1876–77; 19th president of the U.S. 1877–81.

Hays   **Texas**
San Marcos   678 sq. mi.
97,589   65,614   40,594   27,642   19,934   17,840

March 1, 1848; organized August 7, 1848. John Coffee Hays (1817–83). Surveyor; moved to Texas 1837; captain, Texas Rangers; colonel, 1st Regiment Mounted Troops, under General Taylor; battles of Monterrey and Mexico City 1846; resigned 1848; sheriff, San Francisco County, California, 1849–53; surveyor general of California 1859.

Haywood   **North Carolina**
Waynesville   554 sq. mi.
54,033   46,942   46,495   41,710   39,711   37,631

December 15, 1808. John Haywood (1755–1827). Clerk of North Carolina Senate 1781–86; treasurer of North Carolina 1787–1827; one of original trustees of University of North Carolina 1789–1827.

Haywood   **Tennessee**
Brownsville   533 sq. mi.
19,797   19,437   20,318   19,596   23,393   26,212

November 3, 1823. John Haywood (1753–1826). Attorney general of North Carolina 1791–94; judge of Superior Court of North Carolina 1794–1800; settled in Tennessee 1810; judge, Tennessee Supreme Court 1816–26.

Heard   **Georgia**
Franklin   296 sq. mi.
11,012   8,628   6,520   5,354   5,333   6,975

December 22, 1830. Stephen Heard (1740–1815). Governor of Georgia 1780; battle of Kettle Creek 1781; de facto president of Georgia Government Council 1781; president, Georgia Council 1794–95; chief justice, Georgia Inferior Court.

Hemphill   **Texas**
Canadian   910 sq. mi.
3,351   3,720   5,304   3,084   3,185   4,123

August 21, 1876; organized July 5, 1887. John Hemphill (1803–62). 2nd lieutenant, Seminole War 1836; moved to Texas 1838; judge, 4th Judicial District of Texas 1840–42; chief justice, Texas Supreme Court 1846–58; U.S. senator 1859–61, expelled; Provisional Congress of Confederate States 1861.

Hempstead   **Arkansas**
Hope   729 sq. mi.
23,587   21,621   23,635   19,308   19,661   25,080
December 15, 1818; effective March 1, 1819. Edward Hempstead (1780–1817). Attorney general, Territory of Upper Louisiana; Speaker, territorial legislature; congressional delegate from Missouri Territory.

Henderson   **Illinois**
Oquawka   379 sq. mi.
8,213   8,096   9,114   8,451   8,237   8,416
January 20, 1841. Uncertain. (1) Henderson River. (2) Henderson County, Kentucky. Both are named for Richard Henderson* (see Henderson, Kentucky).

Henderson   **Kentucky**
Henderson   440 sq. mi.
44,829   43,044   40,849   36,031   33,519   30,715
December 21, 1798; effective May 15, 1799. *Richard Henderson* (1735–85). Attorney; purchased land from Cherokee Nation to create Transylvania, covering about half of Kentucky 1775.

Henderson   **North Carolina**
Hendersonville   374 sq. mi.
89,173   69,285   58,580   42,804   36,163   30,921
December 15, 1838. Leonard Henderson (1772–1833). Judge, North Carolina Appellate Court 1808–18; North Carolina Supreme Court 1818–29, chief justice 1829.

Henderson   **Tennessee**
Lexington   520 sq. mi.
25,522   21,844   21,390   17,291   16,115   17,173
November 7, 1821. James Henderson (?–1815). Colonel, Tennessee Militia; quartermaster on staff of General Jackson on Natchez expedition 1812–13; killed at battle of New Orleans.

Henderson   **Texas**
Athens   874 sq. mi.
73,277   58,543   42,606   26,466   21,786   23,405
April 27, 1846; organized July 13, 1846. James Pinckney Henderson (1808–58). Brigadier general, Texas Army 1836; attorney general, Republic of Texas 1836; Texas secretary of state 1837; Texas representative in Europe 1838; Texas minister to the U.S. 1844; Texas Constitutional Convention 1845; governor of Texas 1846–47; major general, U.S. Army, voted a sword by Congress for bravery at Monterrey; U.S. senator 1857–58.

Hendricks   **Indiana**
Danville   408 sq. mi.
104,093   75,717   69,804   53,974   40,896   24,594
December 20, 1823; effective April 1, 1824. William Hendricks (1782–1850). Secretary, Indiana territorial General Assembly 1814–15; secretary, Indiana Constitutional Convention 1816; U.S. representative 1816–22; governor of Indiana 1822–25; U.S. senator 1825–37; trustee, Indiana University 1829–40.

Hendry   **Florida**
La Belle   1,153 sq. mi.
36,210   25,773   18,599   11,859   8,119   6,051
May 11, 1923. Francis Asbury Hendry (1833–1917). Cattleman; Florida legislature; voted against secession but served as captain in Confederate cavalry.

Hennepin   **Minnesota**
Minneapolis   557 sq. mi.
1,116,200   1,032,431   941,411   960,080   842,854   676,579
March 6, 1852. Louis Hennepin (1640–1701). Roman Catholic friar; explored Great Lakes with La Salle 1679; explored upper Mississippi River 1680.

Henrico   **Virginia**
Richmond   238 sq. mi.
262,300   217,881   180,735   154,364   117,339   57,340
1634. Settlement of Henrico. Named for Henry Frederick, Prince of Wales (1594–1612); eldest son of James I and Queen Anne; made Earl of Chester and Prince of Wales 1610; died before becoming king.

Henry   **Alabama**
Abbeville   562 sq. mi.
16,310   15,374   15,302   13,254   15,286   18,674
December 13, 1819. *Patrick Henry* (1736–99). Virginia House of Burgesses 1765; Continental Congress 1774–76; speech before Virginia Provisional Congress, "Give me liberty or give me death" 1775; governor of Virginia 1776–79 and 1784–86; Constitutional Convention 1788; elected to Virginia Senate but died before taking office 1799.

Henry   **Georgia**
McDonough   323 sq. mi.
119,341   58,741   36,309   23,724   17,619   15,857
May 15, 1821. Patrick Henry.*

Henry   **Illinois**
Cambridge   823 sq. mi.
51,020   51,159   57,968   53,217   49,317   46,492
January 13, 1825; organized 1837. Patrick Henry.*

Henry   **Indiana**
New Castle   393 sq. mi.
48,508   48,139   53,336   52,603   48,899   45,505
December 31, 1821; effective June 1, 1822. Patrick Henry.*

Henry   **Iowa**
Mount Pleasant   434 sq. mi.
20,336   19,226   18,890   18,114   18,187   18,708
December 7, 1836. Henry Dodge* (see Dodge, Minnesota).

Henry   **Kentucky**
New Castle   289 sq. mi.
15,060   12,823   12,740   10,910   10,987   11,394
December 14, 1798; effective June 1, 1799. Patrick Henry.*

Henry   **Missouri**
Clinton   702 sq. mi.
21,997   20,044   19,672   18,451   19,226   20,043
December 13, 1834, as Rives; name changed February 15, 1841. Patrick Henry.*

Henry   **Ohio**
Napoleon   417 sq. mi.
29,210   29,108   28,383   27,058   25,392   22,423
February 12, 1820; organized 1834. Patrick Henry.*

Henry   **Tennessee**
Paris   562 sq. mi.
31,115   27,888   28,656   23,749   22,275   23,828
November 7, 1821. Patrick Henry.*

Henry   **Virginia**
Martinsville   382 sq. mi.

57,930   56,942   57,654   50,901   40,335   31,219
October 7, 1776 (session). Patrick Henry.*

Herkimer   **New York**
Herkimer   1,411 sq. mi.
64,427   65,797   66,714   67,633   66,370   61,407
February 16, 1791. Nicholas Herkimer (1728–77). Brigadier general, New York Militia 1775; mortally wounded at battle of Oriskany.

Hernando   **Florida**
Brooksville   478 sq. mi.
130,802   101,115   44,469   17,004   11,205   6,693
February 24, 1843; name changed to Benton March 6, 1844; renamed Hernando December 24, 1850. Hernando de Soto* (see DeSoto, Florida).

Hertford   **North Carolina**
Winton   353 sq. mi.
22,601   22,523   23,368   23,529   22,718   21,453
December 12, 1754 (session). Francis Seymour Conway, Earl of Hertford (1719–94). Privy councillor of Ireland 1749; ambassador extraordinary and plenipotentiary to Paris 1763–65; lord lieutenant of Ireland 1765–66; lord chamberlain of the household 1766–82.

Hettinger   **North Dakota**
Mott   1,132 sq. mi.
2,715   3,445   4,275   5,075   6,317   7,100
March 9, 1883; organized April 17, 1907. Mathias Hettinger (1810–90). Banker and brewer in Illinois; father-in-law of Erastis A. Williams, who proposed county name in Dakota territorial legislature (see Williams, North Dakota).

Hickman   **Kentucky**
Clinton   244 sq. mi.
5,262   5,566   6,065   6,264   6,747   7,778
December 19, 1821. Paschal Hickman (?–1813). Battle of Fallen Timbers 1794; lieutenant, Kentucky Militia 1802; captured and killed at battle of Raisin River.

Hickman   **Tennessee**
Centerville   613 sq. mi.
22,295   16,754   15,151   12,096   11,862   13,353
December 3, 1807. Edwin (or Edmund) Hickman (?–1785). Explorer and surveyor; killed by Indians while exploring Duck River.

Hickory   **Missouri**
Hermitage   399 sq. mi.
8,940   7,335   6,367   4,481   4,516   5,387
February 14, 1845. Andrew Jackson. From Jackson's nickname "Old Hickory." (See Jackson, Alabama.)

Hidalgo   **New Mexico**
Lordsburg   3,446 sq. mi.
5,932   5,958   6,049   4,734   4,961   5,095
February 25, 1919. Uncertain. (1) Treaty of Guadalupe Hidalgo; ended Mexican War 1848. (2) *Miguel Hidalgo y Castilla* (1753–1811). Mexican priest; began movement of Mexican independence from Spain by leading parishioners to seize prison at Dolores 1810; defeated at Aculo 1810, and Calderon 1811; executed as rebel August 1, 1811.

Hidalgo   **Texas**
Edinburg   1,570 sq. mi.
569,463   383,545   283,229   181,535   180,904   160,446
January 24, 1852; organized August 7, 1852. Miguel Hidalgo y Castilla.*

Highland   **Ohio**
Hillsboro   553 sq. mi.

40,875	35,728	33,477	28,996	29,716	28,188

February 18, 1805; effective May 1, 1805. Descriptive of land between Scioto and Little Miami rivers.

Highland   **Virginia**
Monterey   416 sq. mi.

2,536	2,635	2,937	2,529	3,221	4,069

March 19, 1847. Descriptive of location in Allegheny Mountains.

Highlands   **Florida**
Sebring   1,028 sq. mi.

87,366	68,432	47,526	29,507	21,338	13,636

April 23, 1921. Descriptive of relatively hilly landscape.

Hill   **Montana**
Havre   2,896 sq. mi.

16,673	17,654	17,985	17,358	18,653	14,285

February 28, 1912. James Jerome Hill (1838–1916). Railroad builder and philanthropist; vice president of St. Paul and Manitoba Railway Company 1882, president 1883; founded Great Northern Railway 1893.

Hill   **Texas**
Hillsboro   962 sq. mi.

32,321	27,146	25,024	22,596	23,650	31,982

February 7, 1853; organized May 14, 1853. George Washington Hill (1814–60). Surgeon at Fort Houston 1836–37; Texas Congress; secretary of war and navy 1843–44, Republic of Texas; returned to medical practice 1847.

Hillsborough   **Florida**
Tampa   1,051 sq. mi.

998,948	834,054	646,960	490,265	397,788	249,894

January 25, 1834. Hillsborough Bay. Named for *Wills Hill, Earl of Hillsborough* (1718–93); privy councillor of Ireland 1746; English secretary of state for the colonies 1768–72; councilor of King George III.

Hillsborough   **New Hampshire**
Nashua   876 sq. mi.

380,841	336,073	276,608	223,941	178,161	156,987

April 29, 1769. Wills Hill, Earl of Hillsborough.*

Hillsdale   **Michigan**
Hillsdale   599 sq. mi.

46,527	43,431	42,071	37,171	34,742	31,916

October 29, 1829; organized February 11, 1835. Descriptive of hilly landscape.

Hinds   **Mississippi**
Jackson   869 sq. mi.

250,800	254,441	250,998	214,973	187,045	142,164

February 12, 1821. Thomas Hinds (1780–1840). War of 1812; brevetted for gallantry at New Orleans; representative from Mississippi in negotiations with Choctaws; U.S. representative from Mississippi 1828–31.

Hinsdale   **Colorado**
Lake City   1,118 sq. mi.

790	467	408	202	208	263

February 10, 1874. George A. Hinsdale (1826–74). Nebraska territorial legislature; lieutenant governor of Colorado 1865; territorial council 1868, president 1870.

Hitchcock   **Nebraska**
Trenton   710 sq. mi.
3,111   3,750   4,079   4,051   4,829   5,867
February 27, 1873; organized August 30, 1873. Phineas Warrener Hitchcock (1831–81). U.S. marshal 1861–64; congressional delegate from Nebraska Territory 1865–67; surveyor general of Nebraska and Iowa 1867–69; U.S. senator from Nebraska 1871–77.

Hocking   **Ohio**
Logan   423 sq. mi.
28,241   25,533   24,304   20,322   20,168   19,520
January 3, 1818. Hocking River. Named from Delaware Indian words *hockhock,* for "gourd" or "bottle," and *ing,* meaning "place," describes river's bottle-like appearance nearby.

Hockley   **Texas**
Levelland   908 sq. mi.
22,716   24,199   23,230   20,396   22,340   20,407
August 21, 1876; organized February 1921. George Washington Hockley (1802–54). Chief of staff under Sam Houston 1835; battle of San Jacinto 1836; colonel of ordnance 1836; Texas Republic secretary of war 1838 and 1841.

Hodgeman   **Kansas**
Jetmore   860 sq. mi.
2,085   2,177   2,269   2,662   3,115   3,310
February 26, 1867, as Hageman; name changed 1868; organized 1879. Amos Hodgman (?–1863). Captain, Company H, 7th Kansas; died of wounds at Wyatt, Mississippi, October 16, 1863. Added letter "e" is misspelling of county name.

Hoke   **North Carolina**
Raeford   391 sq. mi.
33,646   22,856   20,383   16,436   16,356   15,756
February 7, 1911. Robert Frederick Hoke (1837–1912). Private, 1st North Carolina Volunteers 1861; major and lieutenant colonel, 33rd North Carolina Infantry; colonel, 11th North Carolina Regiment; brigadier general 1863; major general 1864; surrendered at Durham Station 1865; president, Georgia, Carolina and Northern Railway Company.

Holmes   **Florida**
Bonifay   482 sq. mi.
18,564   15,778   14,723   10,720   10,844   13,988
January 8, 1848. Holmes Creek. Uncertain origin. (1) Thomas J. Holmes (?–?); moved from North Carolina to Florida c1830; (2) Anglo-Indian named Holmes; killed by Andrew Jackson's troops; (3) Holmes Creek, named for either of the above.

Holmes   **Mississippi**
Lexington   756 sq. mi.
21,609   21,604   22,970   23,120   27,096   33,301
February 19, 1833. David Holmes (1770–1832). U.S. representative from Virginia 1797–1809; governor, Mississippi Territory 1809–17; governor of Mississippi 1817–20 and 1826; U.S. senator 1820–25.

Holmes   **Ohio**
Millersburg   423 sq. mi.
38,943   32,849   29,416   23,024   21,591   18,760
January 20, 1824; organized 1825. Andrew Hunter Holmes (?–1814). Captain, 24th Mississippi Infantry 1812; major 1813; brevet major 1814; killed at Fort Mackinac, Michigan, August 4, 1814.

Holt   **Missouri**
Oregon   462 sq. mi.
5,351   6,034   6,882   6,654   7,885   9,833
January 29, 1841, as Nodaway; name changed February 15, 1841. David Rice Holt (1803–40). Minister and physician; Missouri legislature 1840.

Holt   **Nebraska**
O'Neill   2,413 sq. mi.

11,551	12,599	13,552	12,933	13,722	14,859

January 13, 1860, as West; name changed January 9, 1862; organized July 13, 1876. Joseph Holt (1807–94). U.S. commissioner of patents 1857; U.S. postmaster general 1859–61; U.S. secretary of war 1861; judge advocate general, U.S. Army 1862–75.

Honolulu   **Hawaii**
Honolulu   600 sq. mi.

876,156	836,231	762,565	629,176	500,409	353,020

July 1905. City of Honolulu. Most suggestions of name's origin refer to Hawaiian word meaning sheltered bay or harbor.

Hood   **Texas**
Granbury   422 sq. mi.

41,100	28,981	17,714	6,368	5,443	5,287

November 2, 1866; organized December 25, 1866. John Bell Hood (1831–79). Graduated U.S. Military Academy 1853; 3rd lieutenant 1855; 1st lieutenant 1858; resigned to join Confederate army 1861; commanded 4th Texas Infantry 1861; brigadier general and major general 1862; lieutenant general 1864; lost right leg at Chickamauga 1863; succeeded General Johnston in command of Army of Tennessee 1864; defeated at Nashville, relieved of command 1865; died of yellow fever at New Orleans 1879.

Hood River   **Oregon**
Hood River   522 sq. mi.

20,411	16,903	15,835	13,187	13,395	12,740

June 23, 1908. Hood River. Named for its source on Mount Hood, which was named in 1792 for Samuel Hood, Baron Hood of Catherington (1724–1816); British navy; commanded North American fleet 1767–70; member of Parliament; vice admiral 1787; lord of the admiralty 1788–93; admiral 1794; made Viscount Hood 1796.

Hooker   **Nebraska**
Mullen   721 sq. mi.

783	793	990	939	1,130	1,061

March 29, 1889; organized April 13, 1889. Joseph Hooker (1814–79). Graduated U.S. Military Academy 1837; 1st lieutenant 1838; brevet captain 1846; captain 1848; major 1847; lieutenant colonel 1847; resigned 1853; brigadier general of Volunteers 1861; major general of Volunteers 1862; brigadier general U.S. Army 1862; voted Thanks of Congress 1864; brevet major general 1865; retired 1868.

Hopewell   **Virginia**
(Independent City) 10 sq. mi.

22,354	23,101	23,397	23,471	17,895	10,219

1916. Hopewell Farm. Ñamed for ship *Hopewell*, which brought Francis Eppes (1627–c1678), early settler, to Virginia. (Associated county: Prince George.)

Hopkins   **Kentucky**
Madisonville   551 sq. mi.

46,519	46,126	46,174	38,167	38,458	38,815

December 9, 1806; effective May 1, 1807. Samuel Hopkins (1753–1819). Captain, 6th Virginia Regiment 1776; major 1777; wounded at Germantown 1777; lieutenant colonel 1778; taken prisoner at Charleston 1780; exchanged 1781; Kentucky legislature; major general, War of 1812; U.S. representative 1813–14.

Hopkins   **Texas**
Sulphur Springs   782 sq. mi.

31,960	28,833	25,247	20,710	18,594	23,490

March 25, 1846; organized July 13, 1846. David Hopkins (1825–?) and his family. Early settlers in area.

Horry   **South Carolina**
Conway   1,134 sq. mi.

196,629   144,053   101,419   69,992   68,247   59,820

December 19, 1801. Peter Horry (c1747–1815). Captain, 2nd South Carolina Regiment 1775; major 1776; colonel, South Carolina Militia 1779–81; brigadier general; wounded at Eutaw Springs 1781.

Hot Spring   **Arkansas**
Malvern   615 sq. mi.
30,353   26,115   26,819   21,963   21,893   22,181

November 2, 1829. Uncertain. (1) Hot springs that are now in Garland County. (2) Hot Springs National Park.

Hot Springs   **Wyoming**
Thermopolis   2,004 sq. mi.
4,882   4,809   5,710   4,952   6,365   5,250

February 9, 1911. Descriptive of mineral springs in the area.

Houghton   **Michigan**
Houghton   1,012 sq. mi.
36,016   35,446   37,872   34,652   35,654   39,771

March 19, 1845; organized May 18, 1846. Douglas Houghton (1809–45). Professor of chemistry and natural history, Rensselaer Polytechnic Institute 1828–30; Michigan state geologist 1838–41; drowned in Lake Superior.

Houston   **Alabama**
Dothan   580 sq. mi.
88,787   81,331   74,632   56,574   50,718   46,522

February 9, 1903. George Smith Houston (1808–79). Alabama House of Representatives 1832; Alabama state attorney 1836; U.S. representative 1841–49 and 1851–61, withdrew 1861, elected but not allowed to take seat 1866; governor of Alabama 1874–78; U.S. senator 1879.

Houston   **Georgia**
Perry   377 sq. mi.
110,765   89,208   77,605   62,924   39,154   20,964

May 15, 1821. John Houston (1744–96). Chairman, Georgia Sons of Liberty 1774; Continental Congress 1775–76; Georgia Executive Council 1777; governor of Georgia 1778–79 and 1784–85.

Houston   **Minnesota**
Caledonia   558 sq. mi.
19,718   18,497   18,382   17,556   16,588   14,435

February 23, 1854. *Samuel Houston* (1793–1863). Served under General Jackson as sergeant in Creek War, lieutenant 1814; Tennessee adjutant general 1820; major general 1821; U.S. representative 1823–27; governor of Tennessee 1827–29; member of Texas Constitutional Convention 1835; signed Texas Declaration of Independence 1836; commander in chief of Texas Army; defeated Santa Anna in battle of San Jacinto April 21, 1836; president, Republic of Texas 1836–38 and 1841–44; U.S. senator 1846–59; governor of Texas 1860–61; refused to take oath of allegiance to the Confederate States and was deposed March 18, 1861.

Houston   **Tennessee**
Erin   200 sq. mi.
8,088   7,018   6,871   5,845   4,794   5,318

January 23, 1871. Samuel Houston.*

Houston   **Texas**
Crockett   1,231 sq. mi.
23,185   21,375   22,299   17,855   19,376   22,825

June 12, 1837. Samuel Houston.*

Howard   **Arkansas**
Nashville   587 sq. mi.

| 14,300 | 13,569 | 13,459 | 11,412 | 10,878 | 13,342 |

April 17, 1873. James Howard (?–?). Arkansas Senate 1867.

Howard **Indiana**
Kokomo 293 sq. mi.

| 84,964 | 80,827 | 86,896 | 83,198 | 69,509 | 54,498 |

January 15, 1844 as Richardville; effective May 1, 1844; name changed December 28, 1846. *Tilghman Ashurst Howard* (1797–1844). Tennessee Senate 1824; Indiana district attorney 1833–37; U.S. representative 1839–40; U.S. charge d'affaires to Republic of Texas 1844.

Howard **Iowa**
Cresco 473 sq. mi.

| 9,932 | 9,809 | 11,114 | 11,442 | 12,734 | 13,105 |

January 15, 1851; organized September 15, 1855. Tilgham Ashurst Howard.*

Howard **Maryland**
Ellicott City 252 sq. mi.

| 247,842 | 187,328 | 118,572 | 61,911 | 36,152 | 23,119 |

July 4, 1851. John Edgar Howard (1752–1827). Commanded company at battle of White Plains 1776; captain 1776; major 1777; lieutenant colonel and colonel 1778; received thanks and medal from Congress for gallantry at Cowpens 1781; wounded at Eutaw Springs 1781; retired 1783; Continental Congress 1784–88; governor of Maryland 1788–91; Maryland Senate 1791–95; U.S. senator 1796–1803.

Howard **Missouri**
Fayette 466 sq. mi.

| 10,212 | 9,631 | 10,008 | 10,561 | 10,859 | 11,857 |

January 13, 1816. Benjamin Howard (1760–1814). Kentucky House of Representatives 1800; U.S. representative 1807–10; governor of Louisiana Territory 1810–12; brigadier general 1813; commanded military department west of the Mississippi River.

Howard **Nebraska**
Saint Paul 569 sq. mi.

| 6,567 | 6,055 | 6,773 | 6,807 | 6,541 | 7,226 |

March 1, 1871; organized March 9, 1871. Oliver Otis Howard (1830–1909). Graduated West Point 1854; served in Seminole War; colonel of Maine Volunteer Regiment in Civil War, made brigadier general of Volunteers; battle of Bull Run; lost right arm at battle of Fair Oaks; commanded Army of the Cumberland; brigadier general in Regular Army 1864; commissioner of Freedmen's Bureau 1865; president of Howard University 1869–73; superintendent of West Point 1881; major general 1886; retired 1894.

Howard **Texas**
Big Spring 903 sq. mi.

| 33,627 | 32,343 | 33,142 | 37,796 | 40,139 | 26,722 |

August 21, 1876; organized June 15, 1882. Volney Erskine Howard (1809–89). Mississippi House of Representatives 1836; injured in duel with Hiram G. Runnels (see Runnels (2), Texas) 1840; Texas state Constitutional Convention 1845; U.S. representative 1849–53; Los Angeles, California, district attorney 1861–70; judge of Los Angeles Superior Court 1878–79.

Howell **Missouri**
West Plains 928 sq. mi.

| 37,238 | 31,447 | 28,807 | 23,521 | 22,027 | 22,725 |

March 2, 1857. Uncertain. (1) James (or Josiah) Howell (?–?) first settler in area 1832. (2) Howell Valley; named for James Howell.

Hubbard **Minnesota**
Park Rapids 922 sq. mi.

| 18,376 | 14,939 | 14,098 | 10,583 | 9,962 | 11,085 |

February 26, 1883. Lucius Frederick Hubbard (1836–1913). Established Red Wing, Minnesota, *Republican* 1857; private, 5th Minnesota Infantry 1861; captain, lieutenant colonel, and colonel 1862; wounded at Corinth 1862; wounded at Nashville, brevet brigadier general 1864; railroad operations 1868; Minnesota Senate 1872–76; governor of Minnesota 1882–87; brigadier general in Spanish–American War.

Hudson   **New Jersey**
Jersey City   47 sq. mi.
608,975   553,099   556,972   609,266   610,734   647,437
February 22, 1840. Henry Hudson (c1569–c1611). English navigator, sought Northwest Passage; sailed from Amsterdam in *Half Moon* to New York Bay 1609; sailed up North (Hudson) River to site of Albany; set adrift by his mutinous crew on the *Discoverie* 1611.

Hudspeth   **Texas**
Sierra Blanca   4,571 sq. mi.
3,344   2,915   2,728   2,392   3,343   4,298
February 16, 1917. Claude Benton Hudspeth (1877–1941). Texas House of Representatives 1902–06; Texas Senate 1906–18; U.S. representative 1919–31.

Huerfano   **Colorado**
Walsenburg   1,591 sq. mi.
7,862   6,009   6,440   6,590   7,867   10,549
November 1, 1861. Huerfano River. Spanish word for "orphan"; refers to an isolated cone-shaped butte on the Huerfano River.

Hughes   **Oklahoma**
Holdenville   807 sq. mi.
14,154   13,023   14,338   13,228   15,144   20,664
July 16, 1907. William C. Hughes (1869–1938). Oklahoma Constitutional Convention 1907; chairman, State Board of Affairs 1931–35.

Hughes   **South Dakota**
Pierre   741 sq. mi.
16,481   14,817   14,220   11,632   12,725   8,111
January 8, 1873; organized November 26, 1880. Alexander Hughes (1846–1907). Union army at age fifteen; Dakota territorial legislature 1872–73; president of Dakota territorial legislature 1872–73; attorney general of Dakota Territory; attorney for Northern Pacific Railroad.

Humboldt   **California**
Eureka   3,572 sq. mi.
126,518   119,118   108,514   99,692   104,892   69,241
May 12, 1853. Humboldt Bay. Named in 1850 for *Friedrich Heinrich Alexander von Humboldt* (1769–1859); German naturalist, explorer, and statesman; mine assessor in Prussia 1792–97; explored Latin America 1799–1804.

Humboldt   **Iowa**
Dakota City   434 sq. mi.
10,381   10,756   12,246   12,519   13,156   13,117
January 15, 1851; abolished January 24, 1855; recreated August 31, 1857. Friedrich von Humboldt.*

Humboldt   **Nevada**
Winnemucca   9,648 sq. mi.
16,106   12,844   9,434   6,375   5,708   4,838
November 25, 1861. Humboldt River. Named for Friedrich von Humboldt.*

Humphreys   **Mississippi**
Belzoni   418 sq. mi.

11,206   12,134   13,931   14,601   19,093   23,115

March 28, 1918. Benjamin Grubb Humphreys (1808–82). Dismissed from West Point for discipline 1828; Mississippi legislature 1837; Mississippi Senate 1839; captain and colonel, 21st Mississippi Regiment; promoted to brigadier general for gallantry 1863; wounded 1864; governor of Mississippi 1865–66.

Humphreys   **Tennessee**
Waverly   532 sq. mi.
17,929   15,795   15,957   13,560   11,511   11,030

October 19, 1809. Parry Wayne Humphreys (c1778–1839). Judge, Tennessee Superior Court 1807–09; judge, Tennessee Judicial Circuit 1809–13 and 1818–36; U.S. representative 1813–15.

Hunt   **Texas**
Greenville   841 sq. mi.
76,596   64,343   55,248   47,948   39,399   42,731

April 11, 1846; organized July 12, 1846. Memucan Hunt (1807–56). Major general, Texas Army 1836; minister of Texas Republic to U.S. to secure recognition of Texas 1836; secretary of Texas Navy 1838–39; boundary commissioner 1839; adjutant general, Somervell expedition 1842; Texas legislature 1852.

Hunterdon   **New Jersey**
Flemington   430 sq. mi.
121,989   107,776   87,361   69,718   54,107   42,736

March 13, 1714. Robert Hunter (?–1734). Major general, English Army; appointed governor of Virginia 1707; captured at sea by French, never reached Virginia; appointed governor of New York and East and West Jersey 1710; resigned 1719; governor of Jamaica 1727–34.

Huntingdon   **Pennsylvania**
Huntingdon   874 sq. mi.
45,586   44,164   42,253   39,108   39,457   40,872

September 20, 1787. Town of Huntingdon. Named for Selina Shirley Hastings, Countess of Huntingdon (1707–91); daughter of Washington Shirley, 2nd Earl of Huntingdon; wife of Theophilus Hastings, 9th Earl of Huntingdon; interested in religion and missionary work.

Huntington   **Indiana**
Huntington   383 sq. mi.
38,075   35,427   35,596   34,970   33,814   31,400

February 2, 1832; effective April 1, 1832; organized February 1, 1834. Samuel Huntington (1731–96). Continental Congress 1776, president 1779–81; signer of Declaration of Independence; chief justice, Connecticut Superior Court 1784; lieutenant governor of Connecticut 1785; governor of Connecticut 1786–96.

Huron   **Michigan**
Bad Axe   837 sq. mi.
36,079   34,951   36,459   34,083   34,006   33,149

April 1, 1840; organized January 25, 1859. Uncertain. (1) *Huron Indians*; Iroquois linguistic family; lived near Georgian Bay, Canada; moved into Ohio and Michigan c1650; ceded lands in Ohio by treaty with U.S. 1805; moved to Kansas 1842; removed to Indian Territory (Oklahoma) 1867. From French *hures,* meaning "wild boar," or *huron,* meaning "knave" or "ruffian." (2) Lake Huron; named for Huron Indians.

Huron   **Ohio**
Norwalk   493 sq. mi.
59,487   56,420   54,608   49,587   47,326   39,353

February 7, 1809; organized 1815. Huron Indians.*

Hutchinson   **South Dakota**
Olivet   813 sq. mi.
8,075   8,262   9,350   10,379   11,085   11,423

May 8, 1862; organized January 13, 1871. John S. Hutchinson (1829–89). Secretary of Dakota Territory 1861–65; acting governor, Dakota Territory 1861–63

Hutchinson   **Texas**
Stinnett   887 sq. mi.
23,857   25,689   26,304   24,443   34,419   31,580
August 21, 1876; organized 1901. Anderson Hutchinson (1798–1853). District judge, Republic of Texas; taken prisoner while presiding at court when San Antonio was captured 1842; moved to Mississippi.

Hyde   **North Carolina**
Swanquarter   613 sq. mi.
5,826   5,411   5,873   5,571   5,765   6,479
December 3, 1705, as Wickham; name changed 1712. Edward Hyde, Earl of Clarendon (1661–1723). Deputy governor of North Carolina; appointed governor of New York and New Jersey 1701; dissolved colonial assemblies; replaced by Lord Lovelace 1708; returned to England; imprisoned for debts; paid and released.

Hyde   **South Dakota**
Highmore   861 sq. mi.
1,671   1,696   2,069   2,515   2,602   2,811
January 8, 1873; organized October 1, 1883. James Hyde (1842–1902). Company B, 2nd Battalion, 16th U.S. Infantry 1862; confined three months in Libby Prison and eleven months at Andersonville; honorable discharge 1865; Dakota territorial legislature 1872.

I

Iberia   **Louisiana**
New Iberia   575 sq. mi.
73,266   68,297   63,752   57,397   51,657   40,059
October 30, 1868. City of New Iberia. Named for the Iberian Peninsula.

Iberville   **Louisiana**
Plaquemine   619 sq. mi.
33,320   31,049   32,159   30,746   29,939   26,750
April 10, 1805. Pierre le Moyne, Sieur d'Iberville (1661–1706). French navy; assisted in capture of English forts at Hudson Bay 1686; captured Fort Severns and Albany 1689; built Fort Biloxi 1699; captured Nevis Island 1706.

Ida   **Iowa**
Ida Grove   432 sq. mi.
7,837   8,365   8,908   9,190   10,269   10,697
January 15, 1851; organized January 1, 1859. Mount Ida, Island of Crete, Greece.

Idaho   **Idaho**
Grangeville   8,485 sq. mi.
15,511   13,783   14,769   12,891   13,542   11,423
February 4, 1864. Shoshone phrase *ee-da-how,* roughly equivalent to greeting "good morning."

Imperial   **California**
El Centro   4,175 sq. mi.
142,361   109,303   92,110   74,492   72,105   62,975
August 6, 1907; organized August 26, 1907. Imperial Valley. Named for Imperial Land Company, which sold land in Colorado desert.

Independence   **Arkansas**
Batesville   764 sq. mi.

34,233   31,192   30,147   22,723   20,048   23,488
October 23, 1820. United States Declaration of Independence.

Indiana   **Pennsylvania**
Indiana   829 sq. mi.
89,605   89,994   92,281   79,451   75,366   77,106
March 30, 1803; organized 1806. Latin construction for "Land of Indians."

Indian River   **Florida**
Vero Beach   503 sq. mi.
112,947   90,208   59,896   35,992   25,309   11,872
May 30, 1925. Indian River. Named for the Ays Indians living in the area.

Ingham   **Michigan**
Mason   559 sq. mi.
279,320   281,912   275,520   261,039   211,296   172,941
October 29, 1829; organized June 14, 1838. Samuel Delucenna Ingham (1779–1860). Pennsylvania House of Representatives 1806–08; U.S. representative 1813–18 and 1822–29; secretary of Pennsylvania 1819–20; U.S. secretary of the treasury 1829–31; various commercial and industrial endeavors.

Inyo   **California**
Independence   10,203 sq. mi.
17,945   18,281   17,895   15,571   11,684   11,658
March 22, 1866. Inyo Mountains. From local Indian word for "dwelling place of a great spirit."

Ionia   **Michigan**
Ionia   573 sq. mi.
61,518   57,024   51,815   45,848   43,132   38,158
March 2, 1831; organized April 3, 1837. Ancient Greek district of Ionia, Asia Minor.

Iosco   **Michigan**
Tawas City   549 sq. mi.
27,339   30,209   28,349   24,905   16,505   10,906
April 1, 1840, as Kanotin; name changed March 8, 1843; organized February 16, 1857. Fictional Indian hero in *Algic Researches,* by Henry Rowe Schoolcraft 1839 (see Schoolcraft, Michigan).

Iowa   **Iowa**
Marengo   586 sq. mi.
15,671   14,630   15,429   15,419   16,396   15,835
February 17, 1843; organized July 1, 1845. Iowa River. Named for *Iowa Indians*; from French rendering of Dakota name "Ouaouiatonon" that eventually mutated into "Iowa." May have meant "sleepy ones" or "drowsy ones."

Iowa   **Wisconsin**
Dodgeville   763 sq. mi.
22,780   20,150   19,802   19,306   19,631   19,610
October 9, 1829. Iowa Indians.*

Iredell   **North Carolina**
Statesville   576 sq. mi.
122,660   92,931   82,538   72,197   62,526   56,303
November 3, 1788 (session). James Iredell (1751–99). Collector of customs, Edenton 1768–76; Superior Court judge; attorney general of North Carolina; influential in ratification of federal constitution; U.S. Supreme Court 1790–99.

Irion   **Texas**
Mertzon   1,051 sq. mi.

1,771   1,629   1,386   1,070   1,183   1,590
March 7, 1889; organized April 16, 1889. Robert Anderson Irion (1804–61). Physician; Texas Senate 1836–37; Texas secretary of state 1837–38.

Iron   **Michigan**
Crystal Falls   1,166 sq. mi.
13,138   13,175   13,635   13,813   17,184   17,692
April 3, 1885. Descriptive of iron ore deposits.

Iron   **Missouri**
Ironton   551 sq. mi.
10,697   10,726   11,084   9,529   8,041   9,458
February 17, 1857. Descriptive of iron ore deposits.

Iron   **Utah**
Parowan   3,298 sq. mi.
33,779   20,789   17,349   12,177   10,795   9,642
January 31, 1850, as Little Salt Lake; name changed December 3, 1850. Descriptive of iron ore deposits.

Iron   **Wisconsin**
Hurley   757 sq. mi.
6,861   6,153   6,730   6,533   7,830   8,714
March 1, 1893. Gogebic Iron District. (See Gogebic, Michigan.)

Iroquois   **Illinois**
Watseka   1,116 sq. mi.
31,334   30,787   32,976   33,532   33,562   32,348
February 26, 1833. Iroquois River. Named for Iroquois Indians; confederation of tribes in New York; origin of name uncertain; may refer to "snake" or "extended lodge."

Irwin   **Georgia**
Ocilla   357 sq. mi.
9,931   8,649   8,988   8,036   9,211   11,973
December 15, 1818. Jared Irwin (c1751–1818). Brigadier general, Georgia Militia; Georgia Constitutional Convention 1789; Georgia legislature 1790; governor of Georgia 1796–98 and 1806–09.

Isabella   **Michigan**
Mount Pleasant   574 sq. mi.
63,351   54,624   54,110   44,594   35,348   28,964
March 2, 1831; organized February 11, 1859. Queen Isabella of Castile and León (1451–1504). United Spain with husband ,King Ferdinand of Aragón and Catalonia; financed Columbus's voyage of discovery 1492.

Isanti   **Minnesota**
Cambridge   439 sq. mi.
31,287   25,921   23,600   16,560   13,530   12,123
February 13, 1857; deorganized 1858; reorganized 1871. Santee (or Izaty) Indians. Division of Dakota Indians; name may mean "knife Indians."

Island   **Washington**
Coupeville   208 sq. mi.
71,558   60,195   44,048   27,011   19,638   11,079
January 6, 1853. Islands of Puget Sound.

Isle of Wight   **Virginia**
Isle of Wight   316 sq. mi.

| 29,728 | 25,053 | 21,603 | 18,285 | 17,164 | 14,906 |

1634 as Warrosquyoake; name changed 1637. Isle of Wight, England.

Issaquena   **Mississippi**
Mayersville   413 sq. mi.

| 2,274 | 1,909 | 2,513 | 2,737 | 3,576 | 4,966 |

January 23, 1844. Deer Creek. Choctaw name from *isi,* meaning "deer," and *okhina,* meaning "stream."

Itasca   **Minnesota**
Grand Rapids   2,665 sq. mi.

| 43,992 | 40,863 | 43,069 | 35,530 | 38,006 | 33,321 |

October 27, 1849; organized March 6, 1857; deorganized 1858; reorganized 1891. Itasca Lake. Contrived word from last two syllables of Latin *veritas* (truth) and first syllable of *caput* (head), signifying the lake as the source of the Mississippi River.

Itawamba   **Mississippi**
Fulton   532 sq. mi.

| 22,770 | 20,017 | 20,518 | 16,847 | 15,080 | 17,216 |

February 9, 1836. Levi Colbert (1759–1834). Mixed French and Chickasaw ancestry; called Itawamba Mingo (Bench Chief) by Chickasaw for bravery in defending village from attack by another tribe.

Izard   **Arkansas**
Melbourne   581 sq. mi.

| 13,249 | 11,364 | 10,768 | 7,381 | 6,766 | 9,953 |

October 27, 1825; effective January 1, 1826. George Izard (1776–1828). Lieutenant of artillery 1794; in charge of Charleston Harbor fortifications 1798; on staff of General Alexander Hamilton 1799; resigned as captain of artillery 1803; colonel of U.S. Artillery in War of 1812; brigadier general 1813; major general 1814; governor of Arkansas Territory 1825–28.

J

Jack   **Texas**
Jacksboro   917 sq. mi.

| 8,763 | 6,981 | 7,408 | 6,711 | 7,418 | 7,755 |

August 27, 1856; organized July 1, 1857. Jack brothers. (1) William Houston Jack (1806–44); Georgia legislature 1829; battle of San Jacinto 1836; Texas secretary of state 1836; Texas House of Representatives; Texas Senate. (2) Patrick Churchill Jack (1808–44); delegate to conventions of 1822 and 1823; Texas House of Representatives 1837–38; district attorney, 1st Judicial District 1840, and 6th Judicial District 1841; died of yellow fever.

Jackson   **Alabama**
Scottsboro   1,079 sq. mi.

| 53,926 | 47,796 | 51,407 | 39,202 | 36,681 | 38,998 |

December 13, 1819. *Andrew Jackson* (1767–1845). Tennessee Constitutional Convention 1788; U.S. representative 1796–97; U.S. senator 1797–98 and 1823–25; judge, Tennessee Supreme Court 1798–1804; major general of Volunteers 1812–14; fought in Creek War 1813; brigadier general U.S. Army and major general 1814; defeated British at battle of New Orleans 1815; received gold medal and Thanks of Congress 1815; captured Florida 1817; military governor of Florida 1821–22; 7th president of the United States 1829–37.

Jackson   **Arkansas**
Newport   634 sq. mi.

| 18,418 | 18,944 | 21,646 | 20,452 | 22,843 | 25,912 |

November 5, 1829; effective December 25, 1829. Andrew Jackson.*

Jackson   **Colorado**
Walden   1,613 sq. mi.

| 1,577 | 1,605 | 1,863 | 1,811 | 1,758 | 1,976 |

May 5, 1909. Andrew Jackson.*

Jacskon   **Florida**
Marianna   916 sq. mi.
46,755   41,375   39,154   34,434   36,208   34,645
August 12, 1822. Andrew Jackson.*

Jackson   **Georgia**
Jefferson   342 sq. mi.
41,589   30,005   25,343   21,093   18,499   18,997
February 11, 1796. James Jackson (1757–1806). Lieutenant, wounded at Midway, Georgia; brigadier general 1778; U.S. representative from Georgia 1789–91; U.S. senator 1793–95 and 1801–06; governor of Georgia 1798–1801.

Jackson   **Illinois**
Murphysboro   588 sq. mi.
59,612   61,067   61,522   55,008   42,151   38,124
January 10, 1816. Andrew Jackson.*

Jackson   **Indiana**
Brownstown   509 sq. mi.
41,335   37,730   36,523   33,187   30,556   28,237
December 18, 1815; effective January 1, 1816. Andrew Jackson.*

Jackson   **Iowa**
Maquoketa   636 sq. mi.
20,296   19,950   22,503   20,839   20,754   18,622
December 21, 1837. Andrew Jackson.*

Jackson   **Kansas**
Holton   656 sq. mi.
12,657   11,525   11,644   10,342   10,309   11,098
August 30, 1855, as Calhoun; name changed February 11, 1859. Andrew Jackson.*

Jackson   **Kentucky**
McKee   346 sq. mi.
13,495   11,955   11,996   10,005   10,677   13,101
February 2, 1858. Andrew Jackson.*

Jackson   **Louisiana**
Jonesboro   570 sq. mi.
15,397   15,705   17,321   15,963   15,828   15,434
February 27, 1845. Andrew Jackson.*

Jackson   **Michigan**
Jackson   707 sq. mi.
158,422   149,756   151,495   143,274   131,994   107,925
October 29, 1829; organized August 1, 1832. Andrew Jackson.*

Jackson   **Minnesota**
Jackson   702 sq. mi.
11,268   11,677   13,690   14,352   15,501   16,306
May 23, 1857; deorganized 1862; reorganized 1866. Uncertain. (1) Andrew Jackson.* (2) Henry Jackson (1811–57); one of first merchants in St. Paul 1842; justice of the peace 1843; postmaster 1846–49; Wisconsin territorial legislature 1847–48; Minnesota territorial legislature.

Jackson   **Mississippi**
Pascagoula   727 sq. mi.

131,420   115,243   118,015   87,975   55,522   31,401
December 18, 1812. Andrew Jackson.*

Jackson   **Missouri**
Kansas City   605 sq. mi.
654,880   633,232   629,266   654,558   622,732   541,035
December 15, 1826. Andrew Jackson.*

Jackson   **North Carolina**
Sylva   491 sq. mi.
33,121   26,846   25,811   21,593   17,780   19,261
January 29, 1851. Andrew Jackson.*

Jackson   **Ohio**
Jackson   420 sq. mi.
32,641   30,230   30,592   27,174   29,372   27,767
January 12, 1816. Andrew Jackson.*

Jackson   **Oklahoma**
Altus   803 sq. mi.
28,439   28,764   30,356   30,902   29,736   20,082
July 16, 1907. Uncertain. (1) Andrew Jackson.* (2) Thomas Jonathon "Stonewall" Jackson* (see Stonewall, Texas).

Jackson   **Oregon**
Medford   2,785 sq. mi.
181,269   146,389   132,456   94,533   73,962   58,510
January 12, 1852. Andrew Jackson.*

Jackson   **South Dakota**
Kadoka   1,869 sq. mi.
2,930   2,811   3,437   2,920[a]   3,027[a]   3,319[a]
March 8, 1883; eliminated June 3, 1909; recreated November 3, 1914; organized February 9, 1915. John R. Jackson (?–?). Dakota territorial legislature 1879 and 1883. [(a) Includes Washabaugh: 1970, 1,389; 1960, 1,042; 1950, 1,551]

Jackson   **Tennessee**
Gainesboro   309 sq. mi.
10,984   9,297   9,398   8,141   9,233   12,348
November 6, 1801. Andrew Jackson.*

Jackson   **Texas**
Edna   829 sq. mi.
14,391   13,039   13,352   12,975   14,040   12,916
March 17, 1836; organized 1837. Municipality of Jackson. Named for Andrew Jackson.*

Jackson   **West Virginia**
Ripley   466 sq. mi.
28,000   25,938   25,794   20,903   18,541   15,299
March 1, 1831. Andrew Jackson.*

Jackson   **Wisconsin**
Black River Falls   987 sq. mi.
19,100   16,588   16,831   15,325   15,151   16,073
February 11, 1853. Andrew Jackson.*

James City   **Virginia**
Williamsburg   143 sq. mi.

48,102   34,859   22,763   17,853   11,539   6,317

1634. Town of Jamestown. Named for King James I of England (1566–1625); became James VI of Scotland as an infant on death of mother, Mary, Queen of Scots 1567; chosen as successor of cousin Elizabeth I 1603; sponsored King James Version of the Bible 1611.

Jasper   **Georgia**
Monticello   370 sq. mi.
11,426   8,453   7,553   5,760   6,135   7,473

December 10, 1807, as Randolph; name changed December 10, 1812. *William Jasper* (c1750–79). Private and sergeant, William Moultrie's 2nd South Carolina Infantry, 1775; made heroic rescue of a flag at Fort Moultrie; with friend, John Newton* (see Newton, Georgia), distinguished himself during siege of Savannah June 28, 1775, by rescuing American prisoners and capturing British troops; killed while planting South Carolina flag at battle of Savannah October 9, 1779.

Jasper   **Illinois**
Newton   494 sq. mi.
10,117   10,609   11,318   10,741   11,346   12,266

February 15, 1831; organized 1835. William Jasper.*

Jasper   **Indiana**
Rensselaer   560 sq. mi.
30,043   24,960   26,138   20,429   18,842   17,031

February 7, 1835; organized February 17, 1838; effective March 15, 1838. William Jasper.*

Jasper   **Iowa**
Newton   730 sq. mi.
37,213   34,795   36,425   35,425   35,282   32,305

January 13, 1846. William Jasper.*

Jasper   **Mississippi**
Bay Springs   676 sq. mi.
18,149   17,114   17,265   15,994   16,909   18,912

December 23, 1833. William Jasper.*

Jasper   **Missouri**
Carthage   640 sq. mi.
104,686   90,465   86,958   79,852   78,863   79,106

January 29, 1841. William Jasper.*

Jasper   **South Carolina**
Ridgeland   656 sq. mi.
20,678   15,487   14,504   11,885   12,237   10,995

January 30, 1912. William Jasper.*

Jasper   **Texas**
Jasper   937 sq. mi.
35,604   31,102   30,781   24,692   22,100   20,049

March 17, 1836. William Jasper.*

Jay   **Indiana**
Portland   384 sq. mi.
21,806   21,512   23,239   23,575   22,572   23,157

February 7, 1835; organized January 30, 1836; effective March 1, 1836. John Jay (1745–1829). Continental Congress 1774–77, 1778, and 1779, president 1778–79; chief justice, New York Supreme Court, 1777–78; U.S. minister to Spain 1779; minister to negotiate peace treaty with England 1781; secretary of foreign affairs 1784–89; first chief justice of the U.S. 1789–95; U.S. minister to Great Britain 1794–95; Jay Treaty 1794; governor of New York 1795–1801.

Jeff Davis   **Georgia**
Hazlehurst   333 sq. mi.
12,684   12,032   11,473   9,425   8,914   9,299
August 18, 1905; effective January 1, 1906. *Jefferson Davis* (1808–89). Graduated West Point 1828; Black Hawk War 1830–31; U.S. representative from Mississippi 1845–46; commanded Mississippi Riflemen under General Taylor in Mexico 1846; declined appointment as brigadier general 1847; U.S. senator 1847–51 and 1857–61, resigned 1861; U.S. secretary of war 1853–57; major general of Mississippi Militia 1861; president, Provisional Confederate Congress 1861; president of the Confederacy 1862–65; captured 1865; indicted for treason 1866; paroled 1867.

Jeff Davis   **Texas**
Fort Davis   2,264 sq. mi.
2,207   1,946   1,647   1,527   1,582   2,090
March 15, 1887; organized May 24, 1887. Jefferson Davis.*

Jefferson   **Alabama**
Birmingham   1,113 sq. mi.
662,047   651,525   671,324   644,991   634,864   558,928
December 13, 1819. *Thomas Jefferson* (1743–1826). Virginia House of Burgesses 1769–74; Continental Congress 1775–76 and 1783–85; author and signer of Declaration of Independence 1776; governor of Virginia 1779–81; Virginia House of Delegates 1782; U.S. minister to France 1784–87; U.S. secretary of state 1790–93; vice president of the U.S. 1797–1801; 3rd president of the U.S. 1801–09.

Jefferson   **Arkansas**
Pine Bluff   885 sq. mi.
84,278   85,487   90,718   85,329   81,373   76,075
November 2, 1829; effective January 1, 1830. Thomas Jefferson.*

Jefferson   **Colorado**
Golden   772 sq. mi.
527,056   438,430   371,753   233,031   127,520   55,687
November 1, 1861. Jefferson Territory. Name of provisional government until Congress chose "Colorado"; named for Thomas Jefferson.*

Jefferson   **Florida**
Monticello   598 sq. mi.
12,902   11,296   10,703   8,778   9,543   10,413
January 6, 1827. Thomas Jefferson.*

Jefferson   **Georgia**
Louisville   528 sq. mi.
17,266   17,408   18,403   17,174   17,468   18,855
February 20, 1796. Thomas Jefferson.*

Jefferson   **Idaho**
Rigby   1,095 sq. mi.
19,155   16,543   15,304   11,619   11,672   10,495
February 18, 1913. Thomas Jefferson.*

Jefferson   **Illinois**
Mount Vernon   571 sq. mi.
40,045   37,020   36,552   31,446   32,315   35,892
March 26, 1819. Thomas Jefferson.*

Jefferson   **Indiana**
Madison   361 sq. mi.

31,705   29,797   30,419   27,006   24,061   21,613
November 23, 1810; effective February 1, 1811. Thomas Jefferson.*

Jefferson   **Iowa**
Fairfield   435 sq. mi.
16,181   16,310   16,316   15,774   15,818   15,696
January 21, 1839. Thomas Jefferson.*

Jefferson   **Kansas**
Oskaloosa   536 sq. mi.
18,426   15,905   15,207   11,945   11,252   11,084
August 30, 1855. Thomas Jefferson.*

Jefferson   **Kentucky**
Louisville   385 sq. mi.
693,604   664,937   685,004   695,055   610,947   484,615
May 1, 1780 (session); effective November 1, 1780. Thomas Jefferson.*

Jefferson   **Louisiana**
Gretna   307 sq. mi.
455,466   448,306   454,592   337,568   208,769   103,873
February 11, 1825. Thomas Jefferson.*

Jefferson   **Mississippi**
Fayette   519 sq. mi.
9,740   8,653   9,181   9,295   10,142   11,306
April 2, 1799, as Pickering; name changed January 11, 1802. Thomas Jefferson.*

Jefferson   **Missouri**
Hillsboro   657 sq. mi.
198,099   171,380   146,183   105,248   66,377   38,007
December 8, 1818. Thomas Jefferson.*

Jefferson   **Montana**
Boulder   1,657 sq. mi.
10,049   7,939   7,019   5,238   4,297   4,014
February 2, 1865. Jefferson River. Named by Lewis and Clark for Thomas Jefferson* 1805.

Jefferson   **Nebraska**
Fairbury   573 sq. mi.
8,333   8,759   9,817   10,436   11,620   13,623
January 26, 1856, as Jones; organized October 23, 1865; name changed 1867. Thomas Jefferson.*

Jefferson   **New York**
Watertown   1,272 sq. mi.
111,738   110,943   88,151   88,508   87,835   85,521
March 28, 1805. Thomas Jefferson.*

Jefferson   **Ohio**
Steubenville   410 sq. mi.
73,894   80,298   91,564   96,193   99,201   96,495
July 27, 1797. Thomas Jefferson.*

Jefferson   **Oklahoma**
Waurika   759 sq. mi.

| 6,818 | 7,010 | 8,183 | 7,125 | 8,192 | 11,122 |

July 16, 1907. Thomas Jefferson.*

Jefferson   **Oregon**
Madras   1,781 sq. mi.

| 19,009 | 13,676 | 11,599 | 8,548 | 7,130 | 5,536 |

December 12, 1914. Mount Jefferson. Named by Lewis and Clark for Thomas Jefferson* 1806.

Jefferson   **Pennsylvania**
Brookville   655 sq. mi.

| 45,932 | 46,083 | 48,303 | 43,695 | 46,792 | 49,147 |

March 26, 1804; organized 1830. Thomas Jefferson.*

Jefferson   **Tennessee**
Dandridge   274 sq. mi.

| 44,294 | 33,016 | 31,284 | 24,940 | 21,493 | 19,667 |

June 11, 1792. Thomas Jefferson.*

Jefferson   **Texas**
Beaumont   904 sq. mi.

| 252,051 | 239,397 | 250,938 | 244,773 | 245,659 | 195,083 |

March 17, 1836; organized 1837. Municipality of Jefferson. Named for Thomas Jefferson.*

Jefferson   **Washington**
Port Townsend   1,814 sq. mi.

| 25,953 | 20,146 | 15,965 | 10,661 | 9,639 | 11,618 |

December 22, 1852. Thomas Jefferson.*

Jefferson   **West Virginia**
Charles Town   210 sq. mi.

| 42,190 | 35,926 | 30,302 | 21,280 | 18,665 | 17,184 |

January 8, 1801. Thomas Jefferson.*

Jefferson   **Wisconsin**
Jefferson   557 sq. mi.

| 74,021 | 67,783 | 66,152 | 60,060 | 50,094 | 43,069 |

December 7, 1836; organized 1839. Thomas Jefferson.*

Jefferson Davis   **Louisiana**
Jennings   652 sq. mi.

| 31,435 | 30,722 | 32,168 | 29,554 | 29,825 | 26,298 |

June 12, 1912. Jefferson Davis* (see Jeff Davis, Georgia).

Jefferson Davis   **Mississippi**
Prentiss   408 sq. mi.

| 13,962 | 14,051 | 13,846 | 12,936 | 13,540 | 15,500 |

March 31, 1906. Jefferson Davis *(see Jeff Davis, Georgia).

Jenkins   **Georgia**
Millen   350 sq. mi.

| 8,575 | 8,247 | 8,841 | 8,332 | 9,148 | 10,264 |

August 17, 1905. Charles Jones Jenkins (1805–83). Georgia legislature 1830 and 1836–49, Speaker 1840, 1843, and 1845; Georgia attorney general 1831; solicitor general of Georgia Middle Circuit 1831; Georgia Senate 1856; Georgia Supreme Court 1860; governor of Georgia 1865–67; president, Georgia Constitutional Convention, 1877.

Jennings   **Indiana**
Vernon   377 sq. mi.

27,554	23,661	22,854	19,454	17,267	15,250

December 27, 1816; effective February 1, 1817. Jonathon Jennings (1784–1834). Clerk, Indiana territorial legislature 1807; congressional delegate from Indiana 1809–16; Indiana Constitutional Convention 1816; first governor of Indiana 1816–22; U.S. representative 1822–31; one of three commissioners appointed by President Jackson to settle Indian claims 1833.

Jerauld   **South Dakota**
Wessington Springs   530 sq. mi.

2,295	2,425	2,929	3,310	4,048	4,476

March 9, 1883. H. A. Jerauld (?–?). Dakota territorial legislature 1883–84.

Jerome   **Idaho**
Jerome   600 sq. mi.

18,342	15,138	14,840	10,253	11,712	12,080

February 8, 1919. Uncertain. (1) Jerome Hill (?–?) one of developers of Twin Falls North Side Irrigation Project. (2) Jerome Kuhn (?–?); son-in-law of Jerome Hill. (3) Jerome Kuhn, Jr. (?–?); grandson of Jerome Hill and nephew of Jerome Kuhn. (4) Village of Jerome; named for Jerome Kuhn.

Jersey   **Illinois**
Jerseyville   369 sq. mi.

21,668	20,539	20,538	18,492	17,023	15,264

February 28, 1839. Town of Jerseyville. Named for state of New Jersey.

Jessamine   **Kentucky**
Nicholasville   173 sq. mi.

39,041	30,508	26,146	17,430	13,625	12,458

December 19, 1798; effective February 1, 1799. Uncertain. (1) Jessamine flower; a type of jasmine that grows in the area. (2) Jessamine River; named for the flower. (3) Both the flower and the creek.

Jewell   **Kansas**
Mankato   909 sq. mi.

3,791	4,251	5,241	6,099	7,217	9,698

February 26, 1867; organized 1870. Lewis R. Jewell (1822–1862). Lieutenant colonel, 6th Kansas Cavalry; died of wounds at Cone Hill, Arkansas, November 30, 1862.

Jim Hogg   **Texas**
Hebbronville   1,136 sq. mi.

5,281	5,109	5,168	4,654	5,022	5,389

March 31, 1913. James S. Hogg (1851–1906). Established *Longview News* 1871; attorney, Wood County 1878–80; district attorney, 7th Judicial District 1880–84; attorney general of Texas 1886–90; governor of Texas 1891–95.

Jim Wells   **Texas**
Alice   865 sq. mi.

39,326	37,679	36,498	33,032	34,548	27,991

March 25, 1911; organized 1912. James Babbidge Wells (1850–1923). Brownsville lawyer; improved relations with Mexico by defending Spanish and Mexican land titles in southern Texas.

Jo Daviess   **Illinois**
Galena   601 sq. mi.

22,289	21,821	23,520	21,766	21,821	21,459

February 17, 1827. Joseph Hamilton Daveiss* (see Daviess, Indiana).

Johnson   **Arkansas**
Clarksville   662 sq. mi.

22,781   18,221   17,423   13,630   12,421   16,138
November 16, 1833; effective December 25, 1833. Benjamin Johnson (1784–1849). Judge, Arkansas territorial Supreme Court; judge, District of Arkansas 1836–49.

Johnson   **Georgia**
Wrightsville   304 sq. mi.
8,560   8,329   8,660   7,727   8,048   9,893
December 11, 1858. Herschel Vespasian Johnson (1812–80). U.S. senator from Georgia 1848–49; judge, Superior Court of Okmulgee Circuit, 1849–53; governor of Georgia 1853–57; Confederate Senate 1862–65; president, Georgia Constitutional Convention, 1865; elected U.S. senator but failed to qualify 1866; judge, Middle Circuit of Georgia, 1873–80

Johnson   **Illinois**
Vienna   345 sq. mi.
12,878   11,347   9,624   7,550   6,928   8,729
September 14, 1812. *Richard Mentor Johnson* (1780–1850). Kentucky House of Representatives 1804–07, 1819, and 1841–42; U.S. representative 1807–19 and 1829–37; colonel, Kentucky Volunteers in Lower Canada 1813; battle of the Thames 1813; presented sword by Congress for heroism; U.S. senator 1819–29; vice president of U.S. 1837–41.

Johnson   **Indiana**
Franklin   320 sq. mi.
115,209   88,109   77,240   61,138   43,704   26,183
December 31, 1822; effective May 5, 1823. John Johnson (1776–1816). Indiana territorial legislature 1805–09; served on board to establish Vincennes University; Indiana Supreme Court 1816. .

Johnson   **Iowa**
Iowa City   614 sq. mi.
111,006   96,119   81,717   72,127   53,663   45,766
December 21, 1837; organized July 4, 1838. Richard Mentor Johnson.*

Johnson   **Kansas**
Olathe   477 sq. mi.
451,086   355,054   270,269   217,662   143,792   62,783
August 30, 1855. Thomas Johnson (1802–65). Shawnee Manual Training School 1838; missionary to Shawnees 1829–58; Kansas territorial legislature 1855; robbed and murdered for pro-Unionist sympathies.

Johnson   **Kentucky**
Paintsville   262 sq. mi.
23,445   23,248   24,432   17,539   19,748   23,846
February 24, 1843. Richard Mentor Johnson.*

Johnson   **Missouri**
Warrensburg   830 sq. mi.
48,258   42,514   39,059   34,172   28,981   20,716
December 13, 1834. Richard Mentor Johnson.*

Johnson   **Nebraska**
Tecumseh   376 sq. mi.
4,488   4,673   5,285   5,743   6,281   7,251
March 2, 1855. Richard Mentor Johnson.*

Johnson   **Tennessee**
Mountain City   298 sq. mi.
17,499   13,766   13,745   11,569   10,765   12,278
January 2, 1836. Uncertain. (1) Cave Johnson (1793–1866); prosecuting attorney, Montgomery County, Tennessee, 1817; U.S. representative 1829–37 and 1839–45; U.S. postmaster general 1845–49; judge, 7th Judicial Circuit, 1850–51; president, Bank of Tennessee, 1854–60. (2) Thomas Johnson (?–?); early settler; justice of the peace.

Johnson   **Texas**
Cleburne   729 sq. mi.
126,811   97,165   67,649   45,769   34,720   31,390
February 13, 1854; organized August 7, 1854. Middleton Tate Johnson (1810–66). Alabama legislature 1844; battle of Monterrey under General Taylor; commanded Texas Rangers 1848–50; surveyed Southern Pacific Railroad west of Fort Worth 1851; Texas Senate 1851; Texas legislature 1866.

Johnson   **Wyoming**
Buffalo   4,166 sq. mi.
7,075   6,145   6,700   5,587   5,475   4,707
December 8, 1875, as Pease; name changed December 13, 1879. Edward P. Johnson (1842–79). Union army; U.S. attorney for Wyoming Territory.

Johnston   **North Carolina**
Smithfield   792 sq. mi.
121,965   81,306   70,599   61,737   62,936   65,906
June 28, 1746 (session). Gabriel Johnston (c1698–1752). Colonial governor of North Carolina 1734–52.

Johnston   **Oklahoma**
Tishomingo   645 sq. mi.
10,513   10,032   10,356   7,870   8,517   10,608
July 16, 1907. Douglas Hancock Johnston (?–?). Superintendent of Bloomfield Academy, Indian Territory 1882–98; governor of Chickasaw Nation 1898–1939.

Jones   **Georgia**
Gray   394 sq. mi.
23,639   20,739   16,579   12,218   8,468   7,538
December 10, 1807. James Jones (?–1801). 1st lieutenant, Georgia Militia 1790; Georgia House of Representatives 1796–98; Georgia Constitutional Convention 1798; U.S. representative 1799–1801.

Jones   **Iowa**
Anamosa   575 sq. mi.
20,221   19,444   20,401   19,868   20,693   19,401
December 21, 1837; organized January 24, 1839; effective June 1, 1839. George Wallace Jones (1804–96). Clerk of U.S. courts in Missouri 1860; congressional delegate from Michigan and Wisconsin territories 1835–39; surveyor of public lands, Wisconsin and Iowa territories 1840; U.S. senator from Iowa 1848–59.

Jones   **Mississippi**
Laurel   694 sq. mi.
64,958   62,031   61,912   56,357   59,542   57,235
January 24, 1826; name changed to Davis 1865; renamed Jones 1869. John Paul Jones (1747–92). Born in Scotland as John Paul; 3rd mate of ship in slave trade; on a ship as a passenger, Jones brought ship to port after captain died, appointed as ship's master 1766; added "Jones" to his name and fled to America to avoid murder charge on British merchantman 1773; 1st lieutenant in Continental navy on *Alfred* 1775; captain of *Bonhomme Richard*; captured British ship *Serapis* September 23, 1779; admiral in Russian navy 1788.

Jones   **North Carolina**
Trenton   472 sq. mi.
10,381   9,414   9,705   9,779   11,005   11,004
April 14, 1778 (session). Willie Jones (1741–1801). Aide-de-camp of royal governor 1774; refused appointment to royal council 1774; delegate to Continental Congress 1780–81; opposed ratification of federal constitution 1788.

Jones   **South Dakota**
Murdo   971 sq. mi.
1,193   1,324   1,463   1,882   2,066   2,281
January 15, 1916; organized January 16, 1917. Jones County, Iowa.

Jones   **Texas**
Anson   931 sq. mi.
20,785   16,490   17,268   16,106   19,299   22,147
February 1, 1858; organized June 13, 1881. Anson Jones (1798–1858). Surgeon at battle of San Jacinto 1836; apothecary general of Texas Army; Texas Congress 1837–38; Texas secretary of state 1841–44; president of Texas Republic 1844–46.

Josephine   **Oregon**
Grants Pass   1,640 sq. mi.
75,726   62,649   58,855   35,746   29,917   26,542
January 22, 1856. Josephine Creek. Named for Virginia Josephine Rollins (also Rawlings) (1833–?); daughter of a local miner; settled in Oregon 1850.

Juab   **Utah**
Nephi   3,392 sq. mi.
8,238   5,817   5,530   4,574   4,597   5,981
March 3, 1852. Uncertain. (1) Indian word *yoab,* meaning "thirsty plain." (2) An Indian friendly to settlers in the area.

Judith Basin   **Montana**
Stanford   1,870 sq. mi.
2,329   2,282   2,646   2,667   3,085   3,200
December 10, 1920. Judith River Basin. Named for Julia "Judith" Hancock Clark (1791–1820), wife of Captain William Clark who named river after his wife 1805.

Juneau   **Alaska**
Juneau   2,717 sq. mi.
30,711   26,751   19,528   13,556   9,745   [a]
December 1971. Joseph Juneau (1826–99). Discovered gold on Gold Creek; laid out town site 1880. [(a) Part of 1st Judicial District.]

Juneau   **Wisconsin**
Mauston   768 sq. mi.
24,316   21,650   21,039   18,455   17,490   18,930
October 13, 1856. Solomon Juneau (1793–1856). Agent of Northwest Fur Company and of American Fur Company; mayor of Milwaukee 1846.

Juniata   **Pennsylvania**
Mifflintown   392 sq. mi.
22,821   20,625   19,188   16,712   15,874   15,243
March 2, 1831. Juniata River. Corruption of Indian word meaning "projecting rock"; for a prominent rock on the river.

K

Kalamazoo   **Michigan**
Kalamazoo   562 sq. mi.
238,603   223,411   212,378   201,550   169,712   126,707
October 29, 1829; organized October 1, 1830. Kalamazoo River. Indian word meaning "boiling pot"; for bubbling rapids in the river.

Kalawao   **Hawaii**
(Administered by State)   13 sq. mi.
147   130   144   172   279   340
July 1905. Hawaiian word for "mountain area." (Kalawao is usually included in Maui County.)

Kalkaska   **Michigan**
Kalkaska   561 sq. mi.

| 16,571 | 13,497 | 10,952 | 5,272 | 4,382 | 4,597 |

April 1, 1840, as Wabassee; name changed to Kalcasca March 8, 1843; organized and spelling changed January 27, 1871. Uncertain. (1) Chippewa word for "burned over." (2) A name contrived by Henry Schoolcraft* and Lewis Cass* from elements of both their names (see Schoolcraft, Michigan, and Cass, Illinois).

Kanabec **Minnesota**
Mora 525 sq. mi.

| 14,996 | 12,802 | 12,161 | 9,775 | 9,007 | 9,192 |

March 13, 1858; organized November 4, 1881. Snake River. From Ojibway name for the river, meaning "snake."

Kanawha **West Virginia**
Charleston 903 sq. mi.

| 200,073 | 207,619 | 231,414 | 229,515 | 252,925 | 239,629 |

November 14, 1788. Kanawha River. Named for Kanawha Indians, an Algonquin tribe.

Kandiyohi **Minnesota**
Willmar 796 sq. mi.

| 41,203 | 38,761 | 36,763 | 30,548 | 29,987 | 28,644 |

March 20, 1858; deorganized 1866; reorganized 1871. Kandiyohi lakes. Sioux name for a group of lakes, meaning "where the buffalo-fish come."

Kane **Illinois**
Geneva 520 sq. mi.

| 404,119 | 317,471 | 278,405 | 251,005 | 208,246 | 150,388 |

January 16, 1836. Elias Kent Kane (1794–1835). Judge of Illinois Territory 1816; Illinois Constitutional Convention 1818; Illinois secretary of state 1818–21; Illinois House of Representatives 1824; U.S. senator 1825–35.

Kane **Utah**
Kanab 3,992 sq. mi.

| 6,046 | 5,169 | 4,024 | 2,421 | 2,667 | 2,299 |

January 16, 1864. Thomas Leiper Kane (1822–83). Colonel, Mormon battalion during Mexican War; represented Brigham Young in his dispute with Governor Cummings during Mormon War 1858; lieutenant colonel, 13th Pennsylvania 1861; wounded at Dranesville 1861, and at Harrisburg 1862; brigadier general of Volunteers 1862; brevet major general for service at Gettysburg 1863.

Kankakee **Illinois**
Kankakee 677 sq. mi.

| 103,833 | 96,255 | 102,926 | 97,250 | 92,063 | 73,524 |

February 11, 1853. Kankakee River. Corruption of Indian word meaning "low land" or "swampy country."

Karnes **Texas**
Karnes City 750 sq. mi.

| 15,446 | 12,455 | 13,593 | 13,462 | 14,995 | 17,139 |

February 4, 1854; February 27, 1854. Henry Wax Karnes (1812–40). Emigrated from Tennessee to Texas 1831; Texas Scout and Ranger; commanded troops under General Houston; battle of San Antonio December 5–9, 1835; captain of cavalry at San Jacinto 1836; fought Indians 1836–40; died of yellow fever.

Kauai **Hawaii**
Lihue 622 sq. mi.

| 58,463 | 51,177 | 39,082 | 29,761 | 28,176 | 29,905 |

July 1905. Island of Kauai. Polynesian word of unknown origin; possibilities range from "drying place" to "source of water."

Kaufman **Texas**
Kaufman 786 sq. mi.

| 71,313 | 52,220 | 39,015 | 32,392 | 29,931 | 31,170 |

February 26, 1848; organized August 7, 1848. David Spangler Kaufman (1813–51). Texas House of Representatives 1839–43; Texas Senate 1843–45; Texas Republic charge d'affaires to U.S. 1845; U.S. representative 1846–51.

Kay   **Oklahoma**
Newkirk   919 sq. mi.

| 48,080 | 48,056 | 48,852 | 48,791 | 51,042 | 48,892 |

1893, as County K; name changed and organized 1895. The letter "K." Some early Oklahoma districts were identified by letters.

Kearney   **Nebraska**
Minden   516 sq. mi.

| 6,882 | 6,629 | 7,053 | 6,707 | 6,580 | 6,409 |

January 10, 1860; organized June 17, 1872. Fort Kearney. Named for Stephen Watts Kearny (1794–1848); 1st lieutenant 1812; battle of Queenstown Heights 1812; remained in army and advanced to lieutenant colonel of dragoons 1833; colonel 1836; brigadier general 1846; wounded twice at San Pascual 1846; brevet major general 1846; proclaimed himself governor of California March–June 1847; military and civil governor of Vera Cruz 1848. The misspelling reportedly originated in the War Department.

Kearny   **Kansas**
Lakin   871 sq. mi.

| 4,531 | 4,027 | 3,435 | 3,047 | 3,108 | 3,492 |

March 6, 1873, as Kearney; abolished 1883; recreated March 5, 1887, as Kearny; organized February 25, 1889. Philip Kearny (1815–62). Lieutenant, 1st Dragoons 1837 and 1841–46; 1st lieutenant 1839; resigned; reinstated as captain 1846; brevet major 1847 for gallantry at battles of Contreras and Churubusco, Mexico; resigned 1851; brigadier general commanding 1st New Jersey Brigade in Army of the Potomac 1861; major general of Volunteers 1862; killed at battle of Chantilly (Ox Hill) September 1, 1862.

Keith   **Nebraska**
Ogallala   1,061 sq. mi.

| 8,875 | 8,584 | 9,364 | 8,487 | 7,958 | 7,449 |

February 27, 1873; organized June 9, 1873. Morell C. Keith (1824–99). Cattleman; promoted railroads and irrigation.

Kemper   **Mississippi**
De Kalb   766 sq. mi.

| 10,453 | 10,356 | 10,148 | 10,233 | 12,277 | 15,893 |

December 23, 1833. Reuben Kemper (?–1827). Adventurer; with brothers Nathan and Samuel, made raids into Spanish West Florida 1804–10.

Kenai Peninsula   **Alaska**
Soldotna   16,013 sq. mi.

| 49,691 | 40,802 | 25,282 | 16,586[a] | 9,053[a] | [b] |

September 13, 1963. Kenai Indians. From "Kenayskaya," the Russian name for Cook Inlet. [Includes Seward: 1970, 2,336; 1960, 2,956. (b) Part of 3rd Judicial District.]

Kendall   **Illinois**
Yorkville   321 sq. mi.

| 54,544 | 39,413 | 37,202 | 26,374 | 17,540 | 12,115 |

February 19, 1841. Amos Kendall (1789–1869). Auditor of U.S. treasury; U.S. postmaster general 1835–40; president of Columbia Institution for the Deaf and Dumb; publisher of Washington, D.C., *Evening Star*.

Kendall   **Texas**
Boerne   662 sq. mi.

| 23,743 | 14,589 | 10,635 | 6,964 | 5,889 | 5,423 |

January 10, 1862; organized February 18, 1862. George Wilkins Kendall (1809–67). Journalist; one of the founders and correspondent, New Orleans *Picayune*; captain, Santa Fe expedition 1841; captured and imprisoned 1841–43; wrote *The War Between the United States and Mexico* 1851.

Kenedy   **Texas**
Sarita   1,457 sq. mi.
414   460   543   678   884   632
April 2, 1921. Mifflin Kenedy (1818–95). Sailed to the Orient 1834–36; steamship clerk and captain 1836–42; sailed on *Champion* 1842–46; on USS *Corvette* on Rio Grande; shipping business 1850–74; half interest in King Ranch 1860–68; acquired Laurelos Ranch 1868; sold both ranches 1882; owned part of Texas narrow-gauge railroad 1876–81.

Kennebec   **Maine**
Augusta   868 sq. mi.
117,114   115,904   109,889   95,247   89,150   83,881
February 20, 1799; effective April 1, 1799. Kennebec River. Abnaki name meaning "long reach."

Kenosha   **Wisconsin**
Kenosha   273 sq. mi.
149,577   128,181   123,137   117,917   100,615   75,238
January 30, 1850. City of Kenosha. From Indian name for the Pike River, meaning "fish."

Kent   **Delaware**
Dover   590 sq. mi.
126,697   110,993   98,219   81,892   65,651   37,870
1680 as Saint Jones; name changed December 31, 1683. Kent County, England.

Kent   **Maryland**
Chestertown   279 sq. mi.
19,197   17,842   16,695   16,146   15,481   13,677
August 2, 1642. Kent Island. Named for Kent County, England.

Kent   **Michigan**
Grand Rapids   856 sq. mi.
574,335   500,631   444,506   411,044   363,187   288,292
March 2, 1831; organized April 4, 1836. James Kent (1763–1847). New York legislature 1796; New York City recorder 1791; New York Supreme Court 1798–1804, chief justice, 1804–14; chancellor 1814–23.

Kent   **Rhode Island**
West Warwick   170 sq. mi.
167,090   161,135   154,163   142,382   112,619   77,763
June 11, 1750. Kent County, England.

Kent   **Texas**
Jayton   902 sq. mi.
859   1,010   1,145   1,434   1,727   2,249
August 21, 1876; organized November 8, 1892. Andrew Kent (1798–1836). Resident of Gonzales; private, killed at the Alamo March 6, 1836.

Kenton   **Kentucky**
Covington   162 sq. mi.
151,464   142,031   137,058   129,440   120,700   104,254
January 29, 1840. Simon Kenton (1755–1836). Pioneer scout, served with Daniel Boone and George Rogers Clark; Indian fighter, joined Kentucky troops at the battle of the Thames, 1813.

Keokuk   **Iowa**
Sigourney   579 sq. mi.
11,400   11,624   12,921   13,943   15,492   16,797
December 21, 1837; organized February 5, 1844; effective March 1, 1844. Keokuk (1780–1848). Ally of U.S. in War of 1812; leader in Black Hawk War 1832; appointed chief of Sauks by General Winfield Scott 1832; claimed Iowa by conquest at Washington Conference.

Kern **California**
Bakersfield 8,141 sq. mi.
661,645 543,477 403,089 329,162 291,984 228,309
April 2, 1866. Kern River. Named for Edward M. Kern (1823–63); topographer and artist; served with Fremont; Bear Flag Revolt 1846; participated in relief of Donner Party 1847.

Kerr **Texas**
Kerrville 1,106 sq. mi.
43,653 36,304 28,780 19,454 16,800 14,022
January 26, 1856; organized March 22, 1856. James Kerr (1790–1850). Texas Republic Constitutional Convention 1836; Texas Republic Congress.

Kershaw **South Carolina**
Camden 726 sq. mi.
52,647 43,599 39,015 34,727 33,585 32,287
February 19, 1791. Joseph Kershaw (1727–91). Colonel, South Carolina Militia 1777–80; taken prisoner at Charleston May 12, 1780.

Ketchikan Gateway **Alaska**
Ketchikan 1,233 sq. mi.
14,070 13,828 11,316 10,041 10,070[a] [b]
September 13, 1963. Ketchikan River. Tlinglit word believed to mean "eagle wing river"; for water spraying over a boulder in the Ketchikan River. "Gateway" refers to Ketchikan's position as the first stop in Alaska for ferries and ships arriving from the south on the Inward Passage. [(a) Includes Outer Ketchikan; (b) part of 1st Judicial District]

Kewaunee **Wisconsin**
Kewaunee 343 sq. mi.
20,187 18,878 19,539 18,961 18,282 17,366
April 16, 1852; organized 1859. Kewaunee River. From Chippewa word meaning "prairie hen" or "wild duck."

Keweenaw **Michigan**
Eagle River 541 sq. mi.
2,301 1,701 1,963 2,264 2,417 2,918
March 11, 1861; organized August 1, 1861. Keweenaw Peninsula. From Indian word for "portage" or "detour."

Keya Paha **Nebraska**
Springview 773 sq. mi.
983 1,029 1,301 1,340 1,672 2,160
November 4, 1884; organized February 9, 1885. Keya Paha River. Dakota phrase meaning "turtle hill"; for small round hills in area.

Kidder **North Dakota**
Steele 1,351 sq. mi.
2,753 3,332 3,833 4,362 5,386 6,168
January 4, 1873; organized March 22, 1881. Jefferson Parish Kidder (1815–83). Vermont Constitutional Convention 1843; Vermont state's attorney 1843–47; Vermont senate 1847–48; lieutenant governor of Vermont 1853–54; Minnesota House of Representatives 1863–64; associate justice, Dakota Territory Supreme Court 1865–75 and 1879–83; congressional delegate from Dakota Territory 1875–79.

Kimball **Nebraska**
Kimball 952 sq. mi.
4,089 4,108 4,882 6,009 7,975 4,283
November 6, 1888; organized January 22, 1889. Town of Kimball. Named for Thomas Lord Kimball (1831–99); jeweler in Maine; worked for Pennsylvania Railroad Company; general ticket and passenger agent for Union Pacific Railroad 1871.

Kimble   **Texas**
Junction   1,251 sq. mi.
4,468   4,122   4,063   3,904   3,943   4,619
January 22, 1858; organized January 3, 1876. George C. Kimble (1803–36). Resident of Gonzales; died at the Alamo March 6, 1836.

King   **Texas**
Guthrie   912 sq. mi.
356   354   425   464   640   870
August 21, 1876; organized 1891. William P. King (1820–36). Resident of Gonzales; private; youngest Texan killed at the Alamo March 6, 1836.

King   **Washington**
Seattle   2,126 sq. mi.
1,737,034   1,507,319   1,269,749   1,156,633   935,014   732,992
December 22, 1852. William King and Martin Luther King. (1) Originally named for William Rufus de Vane King (1786–1853); North Carolina House of Commons 1807–09; city solicitor, Wilmington, North Carolina, 1810; U.S. representative 1811–16; secretary of U.S. legations at Naples and St. Petersburg 1817–18; U.S. senator from Alabama 1819–44 and 1848–52; U.S. minister to France 1844–46; U.S. vice president March 4 to April 18, 1853. (2) King County Council voted, February 24, 1986, to make Martin Luther King (1929–68) the honoree of the county's name; leading civil rights activist; followed nonviolent tactics; assassinated April 4, 1968.

King and Queen   **Virginia**
King and Queen Court House   316 sq. mi.
6,630   6,289   5,968   5,491   5,889   6,299
April 16, 1691 (session). King William III (1650–1702) and Queen Mary II (1662–94). (1) William III* (see King William, Virginia). (2) Mary II was eldest surviving child of James II; sister of Queen Anne; married her Protestant cousin William of Orange 1677; jointly ruled England 1689–94.

Kingfisher   **Oklahoma**
Kingfisher   903 sq. mi.
13,926   13,212   14,187   12,857   10,635   12,860
1890. Town of Kingfisher. Named for Kingfisher Creek; origin of name is uncertain. (1) Belted kingfisher bird; common to area. (2) King Fisher (?–?), a settler who operated a stagecoach on the Chisholm Trail. (3) King Fisher (?–?), local cattleman and rancher.

King George   **Virginia**
King George   180 sq. mi.
16,803   13,527   10,543   8,039   7,243   6,710
November 2, 1720 (session). *George I* (1660–1727). German Duke of Brunswick-Lunenburg; Elector of Hanover 1698; great-grandson of James I of England; ascended English throne on death of heirless Queen Anne in favor of Catholic James Stuart 1714.

Kingman   **Kansas**
Kingman   863 sq. mi.
8,673   8,292   8,960   8,886   9,958   10,324
February 29, 1872; organized February 27, 1874. Samuel Austin Kingman (1818–1904). County clerk 1842; county attorney 1844; Kentucky legislature 1849–50 and 1851; Kansas Constitutional Convention 1857; associate justice, Kansas Supreme Court 1861–65, chief justice 1866–77.

Kings   **California**
Hanford   1,391 sq. mi.
129,461   101,469   73,738   64,610   49,954   46,768
March 22, 1893. Kings River. Named by Spanish explorers *Rio de los Santos Reyes* (River of the Holy Kings) for the three magi at the birth of Jesus.

Kings **New York**
Brooklyn 71 sq. mi.
2,465,326 2,300,664 2,230,936 2,602,012 2,627,319 2,738,175
November 1, 1683. King Charles II* (see Charleston, South Carolina).

Kingsbury **South Dakota**
De Smet 838 sq. mi.
5,815 5,925 6,679 7,657 9,227 9,962
January 8, 1873; organized February 18, 1880. Brothers George Washington and T. A. Kingsbury. (1) George Washington Kingsbury (1837–1925); Dakota territorial legislature 1872–73; one of the founders of Yankton *Press and Dakotan* 1861; South Dakota Board of Charities and Corrections 1897–1901; wrote *History of Dakota Territory*. (2) T. A. Kingsbury (?–?); Dakota territorial legislature.

King William **Virginia**
King William 275 sq. mi.
13,146 10,913 9,334 7,497 7,563 7,589
December 5, 1700 (session). *William Nassau, Prince of Orange, King William III* (1650–1702). Nephew of King Charles II; married his cousin Mary, daughter of King James II, presumptive heir of British throne 1677; invaded England during Glorious Revolution 1688; ruled England jointly with Mary until her death 1689–94; ruled alone 1694–1702.

Kinney **Texas**
Brackettville 1,363 sq. mi.
3,379 3,119 2,279 2,006 2,452 2,668
January 28, 1850; organized February 7, 1874. Henry Lawrence Kinney (1814–62). Founder of Corpus Christi; Republic of Texas legislature; Texas Senate 1845–53; filibuster in Central America; returned to Texas legislature, resigned over secession 1861.

Kiowa **Colorado**
Eads 1,771 sq. mi.
1,622 1,688 1,936 2,029 2,425 3,003
April 11, 1889. *Kiowa Indians*. From Kiowa phrase *ka-i-gwu,* meaning "principal people."

Kiowa **Kansas**
Greensburg 722 sq. mi.
3,278 3,660 4,046 4,088 4,626 4,743
February 26, 1867; abolished 1875; recreated February 10, 1886; organized March 23, 1886. Kiowa Indians.*

Kiowa **Oklahoma**
Hobart 1,015 sq. mi.
10,227 11,347 12,711 12,532 14,825 18,926
1901. Kiowa Indians.*

Kit Carson **Colorado**
Burlington 2,161 sq. mi.
8,011 7,140 7,599 7,530 6,957 8,600
April 11, 1889. Christopher "Kit" Carson* (see Carson City, Nevada).

Kitsap **Washington**
Port Orchard 396 sq. mi.
231,969 189,731 147,152 101,732 84,176 75,724
January 16, 1857, as Slaughter; name changed July 13, 1857. Kitsap (?–1860). Important chief in Puget Sound area; medicine man and ruthless warrior; name means "brave."

Kittitas **Washington**
Ellensburg 2,297 sq. mi.

33,362   26,725   24,877   25,039   20,467   22,235
November 24, 1883. Uncertain. (1) Indian word for "gray gravel bank." (2) K'tatas Indians; name means "shoal people," refering to living on Yakima River.

Kittson   **Minnesota**
Hallock   1,097 sq. mi.
5,285   5,767   6,672   6,853   8,343   9,649
October 27, 1849 as Pembina; organized March 4, 1852; deorganized March 5, 1853; name changed March 9, 1878; reorganized April 6, 1897. Norman Wolford Kittson (1814–88). Fur trader; manager, American Fur Company; Minnesota territorial legislature 1851–55; mayor of St. Paul, 1858; interested in steamboat, barge, and steamship lines.

Klamath   **Oregon**
Klamath Falls   5,944 sq. mi.
63,775   57,702   59,117   50,021   47,475   42,150
October 17, 1882. Uncertain. (1) Klamath Indians; derived from "Tlamatl," the Chinook name for a Modoc tribe. (2) Klamath Lakes; named for Klamath Indians.

Kleberg   **Texas**
Kingsville   871 sq. mi.
31,549   30,274   33,358   33,166   30,052   21,991
February 27, 1913; organized June 27, 1939. Robert Justus Kleberg (1803–88). German immigrant; fought at battle of San Jacinto 1836; chief justice of Austin and De Witt Counties.

Klickitat   **Washington**
Goldendale   1,872 sq. mi.
19,161   16,616   15,822   12,138   13,455   12,049
December 20, 1859. Klickitat Indians. Possibly from an Indian word meaning "robber."

Knott   **Kentucky**
Hindman   352 sq. mi.
17,649   17,906   17,940   14,698   17,362   20,320
May 5, 1884. James Proctor Knott (1830–1911). Missouri House of Representatives 1857–71; Missouri attorney general 1859–60; U.S. representative from Kentucky 1867–71 and 1875–83; governor of Kentucky 1883–87; Kentucky Constitutional Convention 1891; professor of civics and economics, Centre College 1892–94, dean of Law School 1894–1901.

Knox   **Illinois**
Galesburg   716 sq. mi.
55,836   56,393   61,607   61,280   61,280   54,366
January 13, 1825; organized 1830. *Henry Knox* (1750–1806). Continental army; battle of Bunker Hill 1775; colonel, Continental Regiment of Artillery 1775; brigadier general and chief of artillery 1776; major general 1782; commander in chief of the army 1783–84; West Point commandant 1782; first U.S. secretary of war 1789–95.

Knox   **Indiana**
Vincennes   516 sq. mi.
39,256   39,884   41,838   41,546   41,591   43,415
June 20, 1790. Henry Knox.*

Knox   **Kentucky**
Barbourville   388 sq. mi.
31,795   29,676   30,239   23,689   25,258   30,409
December 19, 1799; effective June 2, 1800. Henry Knox.*

Knox   **Maine**
Rockland   366 sq. mi.

| 39,618 | 36,310 | 32,941 | 29,013 | 28,575 | 28,121 |

March 9, 1860; effective April 1, 1860. Henry Knox.*

Knox   **Missouri**
Edina   506 sq. mi.

| 4,361 | 4,482 | 5,508 | 5,692 | 6,558 | 7,617 |

February 14, 1845. Henry Knox.*

Knox   **Nebraska**
Center   1,108 sq. mi.

| 9,374 | 9,534 | 11,457 | 11,723 | 13,300 | 14,820 |

February 10, 1857, as L'eau qui Court; name changed to Emmett February 18, 1867; organized and name changed to Knox February 21, 1873. Henry Knox.*

Knox   **Ohio**
Mount Vernon   527 sq. mi.

| 54,500 | 47,473 | 46,304 | 41,795 | 38,808 | 35,287 |

January 30, 1808. Henry Knox.*

Knox   **Tennessee**
Knoxville   508 sq. mi.

| 382,032 | 335,749 | 319,694 | 276,293 | 250,523 | 223,007 |

June 11, 1792. Henry Knox.*

Knox   **Texas**
Benjamin   849 sq. mi.

| 4,253 | 4,837 | 5,329 | 5,972 | 7,857 | 10,082 |

February 1, 1858; organized March 20, 1886. Henry Knox.*

Kodiak Island   **Alaska**
Kodiak   6,560 sq. mi.

| 13,913 | 13,309 | 9,939 | 9,409 | 7,174 | (a) |

September 1963. Innuit word *kaniag* or *kikhtak,* meaning "island." [(a) Part of 3rd Judicial District.]

Koochiching   **Minnesota**
International Falls   3,102 sq. mi.

| 14,355 | 16,299 | 17,571 | 17,131 | 18,190 | 16,910 |

December 19, 1906. Falls of the Rainy River. From Cree name of river, describing the mist over the falls.

Kootenai   **Idaho**
Coeur d'Alene   1,245 sq. mi.

| 108,685 | 69,795 | 59,770 | 35,332 | 29,556 | 24,947 |

December 22, 1864; organized 1881. Kutenai Indians. General agreement that name means "water people."

Kosciusko   **Indiana**
Warsaw   538 sq. mi.

| 74,057 | 65,294 | 59,555 | 48,127 | 40,373 | 33,002 |

February 7, 1835; organized February 4, 1836; effective June 1, 1836. Thaddeus Andrzej Bonawentura Kosciusko (1746–1817). Polish patriot, emigrated to America 1776; served in Revolutionary War; colonel of engineers 1776; brevet brigadier general 1783; returned to Poland 1786; appointed major general and later commander in chief of Polish insurgent army.

Kossuth   **Iowa**
Algona   973 sq. mi.

| 17,163 | 18,591 | 21,891 | 22,937 | 25,314 | 26,241 |

January 15, 1851; organized March 1, 1856. Lajos (or Louis) Kossuth (1802–94). Led Hungarian Revolution against Austria 1848–49; Hungarian minister of finance 1848; appointed governor of Hungary; sought refuge in Turkey 1849; toured U.S., hailed as "Hungarian George Washington."

L

Labette   **Kansas**
Oswego   649 sq. mi.
22,835   23,693   25,682   25,775   26,805   29,285
February 7, 1867. Labette River. Uncertain origin; possibilities include (1) Pierre Labette (?–?), local French trapper and guide; (2) corruption of French *la bete,* meaning "beast," or French Canadian "skunk."

Lackawanna   **Pennsylvania**
Scranton   459 sq. mi.
213,295   219,039   227,908   234,107   234,531   257,396
August 21, 1878. Lackawanna River. Uncertain origin; most likely the Delaware word *lechauhanne,* meaning "stream that forks."

Laclede   **Missouri**
Lebanon   766 sq. mi.
32,513   27,158   24,323   19,944   18,991   19,010
February 24, 1849. Pierre Lacléde Liguest (1724–78). French fur trader in Missouri River Valley; established trading post which became St. Louis 1763.

Lac qui Parle   **Minnesota**
Madison   765 sq. mi.
8,067   8,924   10,592   11,164   13,330   14,545
March 6, 1871; organized January 7, 1873. Lac qui Parle. French for "lake which talks"; possibly referrs to an echo.

La Crosse   **Wisconsin**
La Crosse   453 sq. mi.
107,120   97,904   91,056   80,468   72,465   67,587
March 1, 1851; organized May, 1851. City of La Crosse. French word meaning "crosier," given to an Indian game played with a long, hooked stick.

Lafayette   **Arkansas**
Lewisville   527 sq. mi.
8,559   9,643   10,213   10,018   11,030   13,203
October 15, 1827; effective February 1, 1828. Marquis de Lafayette.* (See Fayette, Alabama.)

Lafayette   **Florida**
Mayo   543 sq. mi.
7,022   5,578   4,035   2,892   2,889   3,440
December 23, 1856. Marquis de Lafayette.* (See Fayette, Alabama.)

Lafayette   **Louisiana**
Lafayette   270 sq. mi.
190,503   164,762   150,017   109,716   84,656   57,743
January 17, 1823. Marquis de Lafayette.* (See Fayette, Alabama.)

Lafayette   **Mississippi**
Oxford   631 sq. mi.
38,744   31,826   31,030   24,181   21,355   22,798
February 9, 1836. Marquis de Lafayette.* (See Fayette, Alabama.)

Lafayette   **Missouri**
Lexington   629 sq. mi.
32,960   31,107   29,925   26,626   25,274   25,272
November 16, 1820, as Lillard; name changed February 16, 1825. Marquis de Lafayette.* (See Fayette, Alabama.)

Lafayette   **Wisconsin**
Darlington   634 sq. mi.
16,137   16,076   17,412   17,456   18,142   18,137
January 31, 1846. Marquis de Lafayette.* (See Fayette, Alabama.)

Lafourche   **Louisiana**
Thibodaux   1,085 sq. mi.
89,974   85,860   82,483   68,941   55,381   42,209
County created April 10, 1805; abolished 1845. Parish created March 31, 1807, as Interior; name changed to Lafourche Interior 1812; name changed to Lafourche 1853. Bayou Lafourche. French for "the fork."

LaGrange   **Indiana**
Lagrange   380 sq. mi.
34,909   29,477   25,550   20,890   17,380   15,347
February 2, 1832; effective April 1, 1832. Home of Marquis de Lafayette* near Paris, France (see Fayette, Alabama).

Lake   **California**
Lakeport   1,258 sq. mi.
58,309   50,631   36,366   19,548   13,786   11,481
May 20, 1861. Clear Lake.

Lake   **Colorado**
Leadville   377 sq. mi.
7,812   6,007   8,830   8,282   7,101   6,150
November 1, 1861, as Carbonate; name changed February 10, 1879. Twin Lakes.

Lake   **Florida**
Tavares   953 sq. mi.
210,528   152,104   104,870   69,305   57,383   36,340
May 27, 1887. Descriptive of numerous lakes in area.

Lake   **Illinois**
Waukegan   448 sq. mi.
644,356   516,418   440,372   382,638   293,656   179,097
March 1, 1839. Uncertain. (1) Lake Michigan. (2) Descriptive of numerous lakes in area.

Lake   **Indiana**
Crown Point   497 sq. mi.
484,564   475,594   522,965   546,253   513,269   368,152
January 28, 1836; organized January 16, 1837; effective February 15, 1837. Lake Michigan.

Lake   **Michigan**
Baldwin   567 sq. mi.
11,333   8,583   7,711   5,661   5,338   5,257
April 1, 1840, as Aishcum; name changed March 8, 1843; organized May 1, 1871. Descriptive of numerous lakes in area.

Lake   **Minnesota**
Two Harbors   2,099 sq. mi.
11,058   10,415   13,043   13,351   13,702   7,781

February 20, 1855, as Superior; name changed to St. Louis March 3, 1855; name changed to Lake March 1, 1856; organized February 27, 1891. Lake Superior.

Lake   **Montana**
Polson   1,494 sq. mi.
26,507   21,041   19,056   14,445   13,104   13,835
May 11, 1923. Flathead Lake.

Lake   **Ohio**
Painesville   228 sq. mi.
227,511   215,499   212,801   197,200   148,700   75,979
March 6, 1840. Lake Erie.

Lake   **Oregon**
Lakeview   8,136 sq. mi.
7,422   7,186   7,532   6,343   7,158   6,649
October 24, 1874. Descriptive of numerous lakes in area.

Lake   **South Dakota**
Madison   563 sq. mi.
11,276   10,550   10,724   11,456   11,764   11,792
January 8, 1873. Descriptive of numerous lakes in area.

Lake   **Tennessee**
Tiptonville   163 sq. mi.
7,954   7,129   7,455   7,896   9,572   11,655
June 24, 1870. Reelfoot Lake.

Lake and Peninsula   **Alaska**
King Salmon   23,782 sq. mi.
1,823   1,668   (a)   (b)   (b)   (c)
April 1989. Lake Iliamna, largest lake in Alaska, and Alaskan Peninsula. [(a) Part of Dillingham Census Area; (b) part of Bristol Bay Census Area; (c) part of 3rd and 4th Judicial Districts.]

Lake of the Woods   **Minnesota**
Baudette   1,297 sq. mi.
4,522   4,076   3,764   3,987   4,304   4,955
November 28, 1922. Lake of the Woods. Translation of French *Lac de Bois*; describes a lake surrounded by trees in an otherwise prairie region.

Lamar   **Alabama**
Vernon   605 sq. mi.
15,904   15,715   16,453   14,335   14,271   16,441
February 4, 1867, as Jones; abolished November 13, 1867; recreated as Sanford October 8, 1868; name changed February 8, 1877. *Lucius Quintus Cincinnatus Lamar* (1825–93). Georgia House of Representatives 1853; U.S. representative from Mississippi 1857–60 and 1873–77; lieutenant colonel and colonel, 18th Mississippi Regiment; diplomatic mission to Russia, France, and England for the Confederacy 1863; professor of political economy, University of Mississippi 1866, professor of law 1867; U.S. senator 1877–85; U.S. secretary of interior 1885–88; U.S. Supreme Court justice 1888–93.

Lamar   **Georgia**
Barnesville   185 sq. mi.
15,912   13,038   12,215   10,688   10,240   10,242
August 17, 1920. Lucius Lamar.*

Lamar   **Mississippi**
Purvis   497 sq. mi.

39,070   30,424   22,821   15,209   13,675   13,225
February 19, 1904. Lucius Lamar.*

Lamar   **Texas**
Paris   917 sq. mi.
48,499   43,949   42,156   36,062   34,234   43,033
December 17, 1840; organized February 1841. Mirabeau Buonaparte Lamar (1798–1859). Editor, Columbus, Georgia, *Enquirer* 1826; commanded cavalry, battle of San Jacinto 1836; Republic of Texas attorney general, secretary of war, vice president 1836–38, and president 1838–41.

Lamb   **Texas**
Littlefield   1,016 sq. mi.
14,709   15,072   18,669   17,770   21,896   20,015
August 21, 1876; organized June 20, 1908. George A. Lamb (1814–36). 2nd lieutenant; killed at battle of San Jacinto April 21, 1836.

Lamoille   **Vermont**
Hyde Park   461 sq. mi.
23,233   19,735   16,767   13,309   11,027   11,388
October 26, 1835; organized 1836. Lamoille River. Named *La Mouette*, "the seagull," by French explorer Champlain 1609; name erroneously transcribed as *La Mouelle* and corrupted to Lamoille.

LaMoure   **North Dakota**
LaMoure   1,147 sq. mi.
4,701   5,383   6,473   7,117   8,705   9,498
January 4, 1873; organized October 22, 1881. Judson La Moure (1839–1918). Dakota territorial legislature 1872–88; North Dakota Senate 1889–1913.

Lampasas   **Texas**
Lampasas   712 sq. mi.
17,762   13,521   12,005   9,323   9,418   9,929
February 1, 1856; organized March 10, 1856. Lampasas River. Spanish for "water lilies."

Lancaster   **Nebraska**
Lincoln   839 sq. mi.
250,291   213,641   192,884   167,972   155,272   119,742
March 6, 1855. Lancaster city and county, Pennsylvania.

Lancaster   **Pennsylvania**
Lancaster   949 sq. mi.
470,658   422,822   362,346   319,693   278,359   234,717
October 14, 1728 (session). Lancashire, England.

Lancaster   **South Carolina**
Lancaster   549 sq. mi.
61,351   54,516   53,361   43,328   39,352   37,071
March 12, 1785. Lancaster city and county, Pennsylvania.

Lancaster   **Virginia**
Lancaster   133 sq. mi.
11,567   10,896   10,129   9,126   9,174   8,640
1652. Lancaster and Lancashire, England.

Lander   **Nevada**
Battle Mountain   5,494 sq. mi.

5,794   6,266   4,076   2,666   1,566   1,850

December 19, 1862. Frederick William Lander (1821–62). Rose from surveyor to chief engineer of Northern Pacific; negotiated brief peace with Northern Paiutes; commissioned Union brigadier general 1861; wounded at Edwards' Ferry, October 1861.

Lane   **Kansas**
Dighton   717 sq. mi.
2,155   2,375   2,472   2,707   3,060   2,808

March 6, 1873; organized June 3, 1886. James Henry Lane (1814–66). Colonel in Mexican War 1846–47; 3rd Indiana Volunteers 1846–47; 5th Indiana Infantry 1847–48; lieutenant governor of Indiana 1849; U.S. representative 1853–55; U.S. senator from Kansas 1861–66; brigadier general of Volunteers 1861–62.

Lane   **Oregon**
Eugene   4,554 sq. mi.
322,959   282,912   275,226   213,358   162,890   125,776

January 28, 1851. Joseph Lane (1801–81). Indiana House of Representatives 1822–23, 1831–33, and 1838–39; Indiana Senate 1844–46; colonel and brigadier general, Indiana Volunteer Regiment, 1846; brevet major general 1847; honorable discharge 1848; governor of Oregon Territory 1849–50 and 1853; congressional delegate from Oregon 1851–59; U.S. senator 1859–1861; Southern democratic vice presidential nominee with John Breckinridge 1860.

Langlade   **Wisconsin**
Antigo   873 sq. mi.
20,740   19,505   19,978   19,220   19,916   21,975

February 27, 1879, as New; name changed February 19, 1880. Charles Michel Mouet de Langlade (1729–1800). Allied with French in French and Indian Wars; at Quebec with General Montcalm 1759; warned British of Pontiac's Rebellion 1763; opposed American Revolution; led Loyalists against George Rogers Clark; operated trading post at Green Bay.

Lanier   **Georgia**
Lakeland   187 sq. mi.
7,241   5,531   5,654   5,031   5,097   5,151

August 11, 1919. Sidney C. Lanier (1842–81). Tutor, Oglethorpe College 1860–61; private in Macon Volunteers 1861; wrote many poems about Georgia and the South; practiced law at Macon 1868–72; lecturer in English literature at Johns Hopkins University.

La Paz   **Arizona**
Parker   4,500 sq. mi.
19,715   13,844   (a)   (a)   (a)   (a)

November 2, 1983. Spanish for "peace." [(a) Part of Yuma County.]

Lapeer   **Michigan**
Lapeer   654 sq. mi.
87,904   74,768   70,038   52,317   41,926   35,794

September 10, 1822; organized February 2, 1835. Flint River. From Indian name for river meaning "flint"; refers to deposits near the river; French translated Indian name as "La Pierre," which was corrupted by English into "lapeer."

La Plata   **Colorado**
Durango   1,692 sq. mi.
43,941   32,284   27,424   19,199   19,225   14,880

February 10, 1874. La Plata River and Mountains. Spanish for "silver"; describes rich deposits in the region.

LaPorte   **Indiana**
La Porte   598 sq. mi.
110,106   107,066   108,632   105,342   95,111   76,808

January 9, 1832; effective April 1, 1832. French for "door" or "port"; describes a natural opening in the forest connecting two prairies.

Laramie   **Wyoming**
Cheyenne   2,686 sq. mi.
81,607   73,142   68,649   56,360   60,149   47,662
January 9, 1867. Jacques La Ramee (c1784–1821). French Canadian trapper; killed by Indians near Laramie River.

Larimer   **Colorado**
Fort Collins   2,601 sq. mi.
251,494   186,136   149,184   89,900   53,343   43,554
November 1, 1861. William Larimer (1809–75). Pioneer; a founder of Denver; recruited Coloradans for Union army.

Larue   **Kentucky**
Hodgenville   263 sq. mi.
13,373   11,679   11,922   10,672   10,346   9,956
March 4, 1843. John P. LaRue (1746–92). Pioneer and landowner.

La Salle   **Illinois**
Ottawa   1,135 sq. mi.
111,509   106,913   112,033   111,409   110,800   100,610
January 15, 1831. *Rene Robert Cavalier, Sieur de la Salle* (1643–87). French explorer; traveled down Mississippi River to Gulf of Mexico, claiming the territory for France; named territory Louisiana for Louis XIV 1682; killed by his men.

La Salle   **Louisiana**
Jena   624 sq. mi.
14,282   13,662   17,004   13,295   13,011   12,717
July 3, 1908. Robert Cavalier de la Salle.*

La Salle   **Texas**
Cotulla   1,489 sq. mi.
5,866   5,254   5,514   5,014   5,972   7,485
February 1, 1858; organized November 2, 1880. Robert Cavalier de la Salle.*

Las Animas   **Colorado**
Trinidad   4,773 sq. mi.
15,207   13,765   14,897   15,744   19,983   25,902
February 9, 1866; effective November 1, 1866. Purgatoire River. Spanish for "the souls," from their name for the river, El Rio de las Animas Perdidas en Purgatoria (River of the Souls Lost in Purgatory).

Lassen   **California**
Susanville   4,557 sq. mi.
33,828   27,598   21,661   14,960   13,597   18,474
April 1, 1864. Mount Lassen. Named for Peter Lassen (1793–1859); Danish pioneer; led immigrant band to Sacramento Valley 1848; killed by Indians near Pyramid Lake, Nevada, April 26, 1859.

Latah   **Idaho**
Moscow   1,077 sq. mi.
34,935   30,617   28,749   24,891   21,170   20,971
December 22, 1864. Latah Creek. Coined word from first syllables of Nez Perce words *la-kah* (pine tree) and *taho* (pestle).

Latimer   **Oklahoma**
Wilburton   722 sq. mi.
10,692   10,333   9,840   8,601   7,738   9,690
July 16, 1907. James S. Latimer (1855–1941). Station agent for Choctaw, Oklahoma & Gulf Railroad; Oklahoma Constitutional Convention 1907.

Lauderdale   **Alabama**
Florence   669 sq. mi.

| 87,966 | 79,661 | 80,546 | 68,111 | 61,622 | 54,179 |

February 6, 1818; effective June 1, 1818. *James Lauderdale* (1780–1814). Lieutenant colonel; wounded at Talladega fighting against Creeks 1813; colonel; killed at New Orleans December 23, 1814.

Lauderdale **Mississippi**
Meridian 704 sq. mi.

| 78,161 | 75,555 | 77,285 | 67,087 | 67,119 | 64,171 |

December 23, 1833. James Lauderdale.*

Lauderdale **Tennessee**
Ripley 470 sq. mi.

| 27,101 | 23,491 | 24,555 | 20,271 | 21,844 | 25,047 |

November 24, 1835. James Lauderdale.*

Laurel **Kentucky**
London 436 sq. mi.

| 52,715 | 43,438 | 38,982 | 27,386 | 24,901 | 25,797 |

December 12, 1825. Uncertain. (1) Descriptive of mountain laurel flowers. (2) Laurel River; named for the flowers.

Laurens **Georgia**
Dublin 812 sq. mi.

| 44,874 | 39,988 | 36,990 | 32,738 | 32,313 | 33,123 |

December 10, 1807. John Laurens (1754–82). Lieutenant colonel under General Washington; wounded at battle of Germantown October 4, 1777; envoy extraordinary to France; captured British redoubt at Yorktown 1781; killed in skirmish at Combahee River, South Carolina, August 27, 1782.

Laurens **South Carolina**
Laurens 715 sq. mi.

| 69,567 | 58,092 | 52,214 | 49,713 | 47,609 | 46,974 |

March 12, 1785. Henry Laurens (1724–92). President of Continental Congress 1777–78; appointed minister to Holland in 1779 but his ship was captured by English and he was imprisoned; exchanged for Lord Cornwallis; one of signers of preliminary treaties of peace with England.

Lavaca **Texas**
Hallettsville 970 sq. mi.

| 19,210 | 18,690 | 19,004 | 17,903 | 20,174 | 22,159 |

April 6, 1846; organized 1852. Lavaca River. Spanish for "cow"; for the bison in the area.

Lawrence **Alabama**
Moulton 693 sq. mi.

| 34,803 | 31,513 | 30,170 | 27,281 | 24,501 | 27,128 |

February 6, 1818; effective June 1, 1818. *James Lawrence* (1781–1813). American naval commander; served in war against Tripolitan pirates 1804; promoted to captain 1812; commanded *Chesapeake*; mortally wounded in battle with British frigate *Shannon* June 1, 1813; gave order while dying "Don't give up the ship."

Lawrence **Arkansas**
Walnut Ridge 587 sq. mi.

| 17,774 | 17,457 | 18,447 | 16,320 | 17,267 | 21,303 |

January 15, 1815; effective March 1, 1815. James Lawrence.*

Lawrence **Illinois**
Lawrenceville 372 sq. mi.

| 15,452 | 15,972 | 17,807 | 17,522 | 18,540 | 20,539 |

January 16, 1821. James Lawrence.*

Lawrence   **Indiana**
Bedford   449 sq. mi.
45,922   42,836   42,472   38,038   36,564   34,346
January 7, 1818; effective March 16, 1818. James Lawrence.*

Lawrence   **Kentucky**
Louisa   419 sq. mi.
15,569   13,998   14,121   10,726   12,134   14,418
December 14, 1821. James Lawrence.*

Lawrence   **Mississippi**
Monticello   431 sq. mi.
13,258   12,458   12,518   11,137   10,215   12,639
December 22, 1814. James Lawrence.*

Lawrence   **Missouri**
Mount Vernon   613 sq. mi.
35,204   30,236   28,973   24,585   23,260   23,420
February 14, 1845. James Lawrence.*

Lawrence   **Ohio**
Ironton   455 sq. mi.
62,319   61,834   63,849   56,868   55,438   49,115
December 21, 1815; organized 1817. James Lawrence.*

Lawrence   **Pennsylvania**
New Castle   360 sq. mi.
94,643   96,246   107,150   107,374   112,965   105,120
March 20, 1849. USS *Lawrence*. Flagship of Oliver Perry at battle of Lake Erie; named for James Lawrence.*

Lawrence   **South Dakota**
Deadwood   800 sq. mi.
21,802   20,655   18,339   17,453   17,075   16,648
January 11, 1875; organized March 5, 1877. John Lawrence (?–1889). Early settler of Sioux Falls 1858; 2nd lieutenant, Dakota Militia; Dakota territorial legislature 1863–64 and 1874–75; superintendent of Sioux City–Fort Randall wagon road 1868; county treasurer 1877–78.

Lawrence   **Tennessee**
Lawrenceburg   617 sq. mi.
39,926   35,303   34,110   29,097   28,049   28,818
October 21, 1817. James Lawrence.*

Lea   **New Mexico**
Lovington   4,393 sq. mi.
55,511   55,765   55,993   49,554   53,429   30,717
March 7, 1917. Joseph C. Lea (1841–1904). Colonel, Confederate army; pioneer of Chaves County 1876; first mayor of Roswell.

Leake   **Mississippi**
Carthage   583 sq. mi.
20,940   18,436   18,790   17,085   18,660   21,610
December 23, 1833. Walter Leake (1762–1825). Virginia legislature 1805; judge of Mississippi Territory 1807; U.S. senator from Mississippi 1817–20; U.S. marshal for Mississippi District 1820; governor of Mississippi 1822–25.

Leavenworth   **Kansas**
Leavenworth   463 sq. mi.

68,691   64,371   54,809   53,340   48,524   42,361

August 30, 1855. Fort Leavenworth. Named for Henry Leavenworth (1783–1834); captain, 25th Infantry 1812; major 1813; brevet lieutenant colonel for distinguished service at Niagara Falls, Upper Canada, 1814; lieutenant colonel 1818; defeated Aricaras 1823; brevet brigadier general for ten years' service 1824; colonel 1825; built Fort Leavenworth 1827.

Lebanon   **Pennsylvania**
Lebanon   362 sq. mi.
120,327   113,744   108,582   99,665   90,853   81,683

February 16, 1813. Lebanon Township (or Borough). Named for Mount Lebanon, Lebanon; name suggested by cedar trees.

Lee   **Alabama**
Opelika   609 sq. mi.
115,092   87,146   76,283   61,268   49,754   45,073

December 5, 1866. *Robert Edward Lee* (1807–70). Graduated from West Point 1829; Mexican War, wounded at Chapultepec; superintendent of West Point 1852; resigned as colonel, U.S. Army 1861; commanded Confederate Army of Northern Virginia 1861–65; surrendered at Appomattox Court House 1865; president of Washington College (Washington and Lee).

Lee   **Arkansas**
Marianna   602 sq. mi.
12,580   13,053   15,539   18,884   21,001   24,322

April 17, 1873. Robert Edward Lee.*

Lee   **Florida**
Fort Myers   804 sq. mi.
440,888   335,113   205,266   105,216   54,539   23,404

May 13, 1887. Robert Edward Lee.*

Lee   **Georgia**
Leesburg   356 sq. mi.
24,757   16,250   11,684   7,044   6,204   6,674

December 11, 1826. Richard Henry Lee (1732–94). Justice of the peace, Westmoreland County, Virginia, 1757; Virginia House of Burgesses 1758–75; Continental Congress 1774–80 and 1784–87; introduced independence resolution 1776; signer of Declaration of Independence 1776; Virginia House of Delegates 1777, 1780, and 1785; U.S. senator 1789–92.

Lee   **Illinois**
Dixon   725 sq. mi.
36,062   34,392   36,328   37,947   38,749   36,451

February 27, 1839. Uncertain. (1) *Henry Lee* (1756–1818). Captain, Virginia Dragoons, 1776; nicknamed "Light Horse Harry"; voted Thanks of Congress and gold medal 1779; lieutenant colonel 1780; major general 1798–1800; Continental Congress 1785–88; governor of Virginia 1791–94; commanded troops in Whiskey Rebellion 1794; U.S. representative 1799–1801; wrote Washington funeral oration "first in war, first in peace, ..." (2) Robert Edward Lee.*

Lee   **Iowa**
Fort Madison   517 sq. mi.
38,052   38,687   43,106   42,996   44,207   43,102

December 7, 1836. Uncertain. (1) Albert M. Lea (1808–?); graduate of West Point 1831; explored Iowa for fort sites 1835; wrote *Notes on the Wisconsin Territory,* which applied name "Iowa" to the region 1836; acting secretary of war in cabinet of President Fillmore; served as engineer in Confederate army; transcription error misspelled name. (2) Robert Edward Lee.* (3) William E. Lee (?–?); member of New York land speculation enterprise with large holdings in Iowa.

Lee   **Kentucky**
Beattyville   210 sq. mi.
7,916   7,422   7,754   6,587   7,420   8,739

January 29, 1870. Uncertain. (1) Robert Edward Lee.* (2) Lee County, Virginia.

Lee   **Mississippi**
Tupelo   450 sq. mi.
75,755   65,581   57,061   46,148   40,589   38,237
October 26, 1866. Robert Edward Lee.*

Lee   **North Carolina**
Sanford   257 sq. mi.
49,040   41,374   36,718   30,467   26,561   23,522
March 6, 1907. Robert Edward Lee.*

Lee   **South Carolina**
Bishopville   410 sq. mi.
20,119   18,437   18,929   18,323   21,832   23,173
February 25, 1902. Robert Edward Lee.*

Lee   **Texas**
Giddings   629 sq. mi.
15,657   12,854   10,952   8,048   8,949   10,144
April 14, 1874; organized June 2, 1974. Robert Edward Lee.*

Lee   **Virginia**
Jonesville   437 sq. mi.
23,589   24,496   25,956   20,321   25,824   36,106
October 25, 1792 (session). Henry Lee.*

Leelanau   **Michigan**
Leland   348 sq. mi.
21,119   16,527   14,007   10,872   9,321   8,647
April 1, 1840; organized February 27, 1863. Leelinau, fictitious Chippewa maiden. Recorded as "Leelanau" in Henry Schoolcraft's *Algic Researches,* a collection of Indian tales.

Leflore   **Mississippi**
Greenwood   592 sq. mi.
37,947   37,341   41,525   42,111   47,142   51,813
March 15, 1871. *Greenwood Le Flore* (1800–65). Choctaw chieftan; owned large cotton plantation; oversaw removal of
Choctaws to Indian Territory (Oklahoma) 1830; Mississippi Senate 1841–44; opposed secession.

Le Flore   **Oklahoma**
Poteau   1,586 sq. mi.
48,109   43,270   40,698   32,137   29,106   35,276
July 16, 1907. *Greenwood Le Flore.**

Lehigh   **Pennsylvania**
Allentown   347 sq. mi.
312,090   291,130   272,349   255,304   227,536   198,207
March 6, 1812. Lehigh River. Delaware word *lechauwekenk,* meaning "at the forks"; shortened to *lecha* and further corrupted.

Lemhi   **Idaho**
Salmon   4,564 sq. mi.
7,806   6,899   7,460   5,566   5,816   6,278
January 9, 1869. Fort Lemhi. Established by Mormons 1855; abandoned 1858; named for King Limhi from the *Book of Mormon.*

Lenawee   **Michigan**
Adrian   751 sq. mi.

98,890   91,476   89,948   81,609   77,789   64,629
September 10, 1822; organized November 20, 1826. Indian word for "man" or "people."

Lenoir   **North Carolina**
Kinston   400 sq. mi.
59,648   57,274   59,819   55,204   55,276   45,953
December 5, 1791 (session). William Lenoir (1751–1839). Captain, battle of King's Mountain, wounded in arm and side, 1780; served in North Carolina Militia from sergeant to major general; North Carolina legislature; president of Board of University of North Carolina.

Leon   **Florida**
Tallahassee   667 sq. mi.
239,452   192,493   148,655   103,047   74,225   51,590
December 29, 1824. Juan Ponce de León (1460–1521). Spanish explorer; governor of Puerto Rico 1510; discoverer of Florida 1513; wounded on second expedition to Florida, returned to Cuba where he died.

Leon   **Texas**
Centerville   1,072 sq. mi.
15,335   12,665   9,594   8,738   9,951   12,024
March 17, 1846; organized July 13, 1846. Uncertain. (1) Alonso de León (1637–91); Spanish explorer of Texas; checked French advances into Texas. (2) Martín de León (1765–1833); pioneer rancher; established De Leon's colony with colonists from Mexico, Ireland, and U.S. (3) Leon Prairie; commemorating the killing of a lion (Spanish *león*), or more likely a yellow wolf.

Leslie   **Kentucky**
Hyden   404 sq. mi.
12,401   13,642   14,882   11,623   10,941   15,537
March 29, 1878; effective April 15, 1878. Preston Hopkins Leslie (1819–1907). Monroe County attorney 1842–44; Kentucky House of Representatives 1844 and 1850; Kentucky Senate 1851 and 1867; governor of Kentucky 1871–75; circuit judge 1881; governor of Montana Territory 1887–89; U.S. district attorney for Montana 1894–98.

Le Sueur   **Minnesota**
Le Center   449 sq. mi.
25,426   23,239   23,434   21,332   19,906   19,088
March 5, 1853. Pierre Charles le Sueur (1657–1704) Trader, miner, fur trader; built fort on Prairie Island near Red Wing 1695; ascended Mississippi to Mankato, built fort 1700; explored valley of Mississippi River.

Letcher   **Kentucky**
Whitesburg   339 sq. mi.
25,277   27,000   30,687   23,165   30,102   39,522
March 3, 1842. Robert Perkins Letcher (1788–1861). Kentucky House of Representatives 1813–15, 1817, and 1836–38; U.S. representative 1823–33 and 1834–35; governor of Kentucky 1840–44; U.S. minister to Mexico 1849–52.

Levy   **Florida**
Bronson   1,118 sq. mi.
34,450   25,923   19,870   12,756   10,364   10,637
March 10, 1845. David Levy (1810–86). Congressional delegate from Florida 1841–45; Florida Constitutional Convention 1845; U.S. senator 1845–51 and 1855–61; Confederate Congress 1861–65; changed name to David Levy Yulee 1846.

Lewis   **Idaho**
Nezperce   479 sq. mi.
3,747   3,516   4,118   3,867   4,423   4,208
March 3, 1911. *Meriwether Lewis* (1774–1809). Served in army against Whiskey Rebellion 1794; lieutenant 1795; captain 1797; private secretary to President Jefferson 1801–03; commanded expedition with Captain William Clark to Pacific 1803; returned to Washington 1807; governor of Louisiana Territory 1807–09.

Lewis **Kentucky**
Vanceburg 484 sq. mi.
14,092 13,029 14,545 12,355 13,115 13,520
December 2, 1806; effective April 1, 1807. Meriwether Lewis.*

Lewis **Missouri**
Monticello 505 sq. mi.
10,494 10,233 10,901 10,993 10,984 10,733
January 2, 1833. Meriwether Lewis.*

Lewis **New York**
Lowville 1,275 sq. mi.
26,944 26,796 25,035 23,644 23,249 22,521
March 28, 1805. Morgan Lewis (1754–1844). Continental army 1774; colonel and chief of staff to General Gates; quartermaster general of Northern Army; New York legislature; attorney general of New York; governor of New York 1804–07; major general in War of 1812.

Lewis **Tennessee**
Hohenwald 282 sq. mi.
11,367 9,247 9,700 6,761 6,269 6,078
December 21, 1843; abolished 1866; recreated 1867. Meriwether Lewis.*

Lewis **Washington**
Chehalis 2,408 sq. mi.
68,600 59,358 56,025 45,467 41,858 43,755
December 21, 1845. Meriwether Lewis.*

Lewis **West Virginia**
Weston 382 sq. mi.
16,919 17,223 18,813 17,847 19,711 21,074
December 18, 1816. Charles Lewis (?–1774). Virginia House of Burgesses; colonel in Revolutionary War; killed at battle of Point Pleasant October 10, 1774.

Lewis and Clark **Montana**
Helena 3,461 sq. mi.
55,716 47,495 43,039 33,281 28,006 24,540
February 2, 1865, as Edgerton; name changed December 20, 1867; effective March 1, 1868. Lewis and Clark expedition. Led by Meriwether Lewis* (see Lewis, Idaho) and William Clark* (see Clark, Arkansas).

Lexington **South Carolina**
Lexington 699 sq. mi.
216,014 167,611 140,353 89,012 60,726 44,279
March 12, 1785; abolished 1800; recreated 1804. *Battle of Lexington*, Massachusetts. First battle of Revolutionary War April 19, 1775.

Lexington **Virginia**
(Independent City) 2 sq. mi.
6,867 6,959 7,292 7,597 (a) (a)
December 31, 1965. Battle of Lexington.* [(a) Part of Rockbridge County.] (Associated county: Rockbridge.)

Liberty **Florida**
Bristol 836 sq. mi.
7,021 5,569 4,260 3,379 3,138 3,182
December 15, 1855. Descriptive of American ideal of freedom.

Liberty   **Georgia**
Hinesville   519 sq. mi.
61,610   52,745   37,583   17,569   14,487   8,444
February 5, 1777. Commemorates leading role played by local residents in American independence movement.

Liberty   **Montana**
Chester   1,430 sq. mi.
2,158   2,295   2,329   2,359   2,624   2,180
February 11, 1920. Commemoration of U.S. victory in World War I.

Liberty   **Texas**
Liberty   1,160 sq. mi.
70,154   52,726   47,088   33,014   31,595   26,729
March 17, 1836; organized 1837. Villa de la Santissima Trinidad de la Libertad. Mexican municipality 1831; name translates as "Town of the Most Holy Trinity of Liberty." Reference to holy trinity may have been to indicate Anglos' required conversion to Roman Catholicism.

Licking   **Ohio**
Newark   687 sq. mi.
145,491   128,300   120,981   107,799   90,242   70,645
January 30, 1808. Licking River. Named for salt licks in area.

Limestone   **Alabama**
Athens   568 sq. mi.
65,676   54,135   46,005   41,699   36,513   35,766
February 6, 1818. Limestone Creek. Descriptive of local limestone deposits.

Limestone   **Texas**
Groesbeck   909 sq. mi.
22,051   20,946   20,224   18,100   20,413   25,251
April 11, 1846; organized August 18, 1846. Descriptive of local limestone deposits.

Lincoln   **Arkansas**
Star City   561 sq. mi.
14,492   13,690   13,369   12,913   14,447   17,079
March 28, 1871. *Abraham Lincoln* (1809–65). Captain, Sangamon County Rifles in Black Hawk War, 1832; postmaster New Salem, Illinois, 1833–36; deputy county surveyor 1834–36; Illinois House of Representatives 1834–41; U.S. representative 1847–49; 16th president of the U.S. 1861–65; assassinated April 14, 1865.

Lincoln   **Colorado**
Hugo   2,586 sq. mi.
6,087   4,529   4,663   4,836   5,310   5,909
April 11, 1889. Abraham Lincoln.*

Lincoln   **Georgia**
Lincolnton   211 sq. mi.
8,348   7,442   6,716   5,895   5,906   6,462
February 20, 1796. *Benjamin Lincoln* (1733–1810). Major general in Continental army 1776; siege of Yorktown, received Cornwallis's sword in surrender, 1781; secretary of war 1781–83; put down Shay's Rebellion 1787; lieutenant governor of Massachusetts 1788; collector of the Port of Boston 1789–1808.

Lincoln   **Idaho**
Shoshone   1,206 sq. mi.
4,044   3,308   3,436   3,057   3,686   4,256
March 18, 1895. Abraham Lincoln.*

Lincoln   **Kansas**
Lincoln   719 sq. mi.
3,578   3,653   4,145   4,582   5,556   6,643
February 26, 1867. Abraham Lincoln.*

Lincoln   **Kentucky**
Stanford   336 sq. mi.
23,361   20,045   19,053   16,668   16,503   18,668
May 1, 1780 (session); effective November 1, 1780. Benjamin Lincoln.*

Lincoln   **Louisiana**
Ruston   471 sq. mi.
42,509   41,745   39,763   33,800   28,535   25,782
February 27, 1873. Abraham Lincoln.*

Lincoln   **Maine**
Wiscasset   456 sq. mi.
33,616   30,357   25,691   20,537   18,497   18,004
May 28, 1760 (session); effective November 1, 1760. Town of Lincoln, England.

Lincoln   **Minnesota**
Ivanhoe   537 sq. mi.
6,429   6,890   8,207   8,143   9,651   10,150
November 4, 1873; organized February 9, 1881. Abraham Lincoln.*

Lincoln   **Mississippi**
Brookhaven   586 sq. mi.
33,166   30,278   30,174   26,198   26,759   27,899
April 7, 1870. Abraham Lincoln.*

Lincoln   **Missouri**
Troy   630 sq. mi.
38,944   28,892   22,193   18,041   14,783   13,748
December 14, 1818. Lincoln counties, Kentucky and North Carolina.

Lincoln   **Montana**
Libby   3,613 sq. mi.
18,837   17,481   17,752   18,063   12,537   8,693
March 9, 1909; effective July 1, 1909. Abraham Lincoln.*

Lincoln   **Nebraska**
North Platte   2,564 sq. mi.
34,632   32,508   36,455   29,538   28,491   27,380
January 7, 1860, as Shorter; name changed December 11, 1861; organized October 1, 1866. Abraham Lincoln.*

Lincoln   **Nevada**
Pioche   10,634 sq. mi.
4,165   3,775   3,732   2,557   2,431   3,837
February 26, 1866. Abraham Lincoln.*

Lincoln   **New Mexico**
Carrizozo   4,831 sq. mi.
19,411   12,219   10,997   7,560   7,744   7,409
January 16, 1869. Abraham Lincoln.*

Lincoln   **North Carolina**
Lincolton   299 sq. mi.
63,780   50,319   42,372   32,682   28,814   27,459
April 14, 1778 (session). Benjamin Lincoln.*

Lincoln   **Oklahoma**
Chandler   958 sq. mi.
32,080   29,216   26,601   19,482   18,783   22,102
1891. Abraham Lincoln.*

Lincoln   **Oregon**
Newport   980 sq. mi.
44,479   38,889   35,264   25,755   24,635   21,308
February 20, 1893. Abraham Lincoln.*

Lincoln   **South Dakota**
Canton   578 sq. mi.
24,131   15,427   13,942   11,761   12,371   12,767
April 5, 1862; organized December 30, 1867. Lincoln County, Maine.

Lincoln   **Tennessee**
Fayetteville   570 sq. mi.
31,340   28,157   26,483   24,318   23,829   25,624
November 14, 1809. Benjamin Lincoln.*

Lincoln   **Washington**
Davenport   2,311 sq. mi.
10,184   8,864   9,604   9,572   10,919   10,970
November 24, 1883. Abraham Lincoln.*

Lincoln   **West Virginia**
Hamlin   437 sq. mi.
22,108   21,382   23,675   18,912   20,267   22,466
February 23, 1867. Abraham Lincoln.*

Lincoln   **Wisconsin**
Merrill   883 sq. mi.
29,641   26,993   26,555   23,499   22,338   22,235
March 4, 1874; organized 1875. Abraham Lincoln.*

Lincoln   **Wyoming**
Kemmerer   4,069 sq. mi.
14,573   12,625   12,177   8,640   9,018   9,023
February 20, 1911. Abraham Lincoln.*

Linn   **Iowa**
Cedar Rapids   717 sq. mi.
191,701   168,767   169,775   163,213   136,899   104,274
December 21, 1837; organized January 15, 1839; effective June 1, 1839. *Lewis Fields Linn* (1795–1843). Surgeon in Colonel Henry Dodge's mounted riflemen War of 1812; graduated as doctor 1815; authority on Asiatic cholera 1817; Missouri Senate 1820; French Land Claims Commission in Missouri 1832; U.S. senator 1833–43.

Linn   **Kansas**
Mound City   599 sq. mi.
9,570   8,254   8,234   7,770   8,274   10,053
August 30, 1855. Lewis Fields Linn.*

Linn　　　　　　　**Missouri**
Linneus　　　　　　　620 sq. mi.
13,754　　　13,885　　　15,495　　　15,125　　　16,815　　　18,865
January 6, 1837. Lewis Fields Linn.*

Linn　　　　　　　**Oregon**
Albany　　　　　　　2,292 sq. mi.
103,069　　　91,227　　　89,495　　　71,914　　　58,867　　　54,317
December 28, 1847. Lewis Fields Linn.*

Lipscomb　　　　　**Texas**
Lipscomb　　　　　　932 sq. mi.
3,057　　　3,143　　　3,766　　　3,486　　　3,406　　　3,658
August 21, 1876; organized June 6, 1887. Abner S. Lipscomb (1789–1856). Alabama territorial legislature 1818; Alabama Supreme Court 1820, chief justice, 1824; moved to Texas 1838; Texas secretary of state 1839–40; Texas Constitutional Convention 1845; Texas Supreme Court 1846–58.

Litchfield　　　　　**Connecticut**
Litchfield　　　　　　920 sq. mi.
182,193　　　174,092　　　156,769　　　144,091　　　119,856　　　98,872
October 14, 1751 (session). Town of Litchfield. Named for Litchfield, England 1719.

Little River　　　　**Arkansas**
Ashdown　　　　　　532 sq. mi.
13,628　　　13,966　　　13,952　　　11,194　　　9,211　　　11,690
March 5, 1867. Little River. Forms northern boundary of county.

Live Oak　　　　　**Texas**
George West　　　　　1,036 sq. mi.
12,309　　　9,556　　　9,606　　　6,697　　　7,846　　　9,054
February 2, 1856; organized August 4, 1856. Descriptive of trees in the area.

Livingston　　　　　**Illinois**
Pontiac　　　　　　　1,044 sq. mi.
39,678　　　39,301　　　41,381　　　40,690　　　40,341　　　37,809
February 27, 1837. *Edward Livingston* (1764–1836). U.S. representative from New York 1801; U.S. district attorney 1801–03; mayor of New York City 1801–03; on staff of General Jackson at battle of New Orleans 1815; Louisiana House of Representatives 1820; U.S. representative 1823–29; U.S. senator 1829–31; U.S. secretary of state 1829–31; U.S. minister to France 1833–35.

Livingston　　　　　**Kentucky**
Smithland　　　　　　316 sq. mi.
9,804　　　9,062　　　9,219　　　7,596　　　7,029　　　7,184
December 13, 1798; effective May 1799. *Robert R. Livingston* (1746–1813). New York City recorder 1773–75; Provincial Convention 1775; Continental Congress 1775–77 and 1779–81; New York Constitutional Convention 1777; secretary of foreign affairs 1781–83; chancellor of New York 1777–1801; administered oath of office to President Washington April 30, 1789; U.S. minister to France 1801–04; negotiated Louisiana Purchase 1803.

Livingston　　　　　**Louisiana**
Livingston　　　　　　648 sq. mi.
91,814　　　70,526　　　58,806　　　36,511　　　26,974　　　20,054
February 10, 1832. Uncertain. (1) Edward Livingston.* (2) Robert R. Livingston.*

Livingston　　　　　**Michigan**
Howell　　　　　　　568 sq. mi.

156,951   115,645   100,239   58,967   38,233   26,725
March 21, 1833; organized March 24, 1836. Edward Livingston.*

Livingston   **Missouri**
Chillicothe   535 sq. mi.
14,558   14,592   15,739   15,368   15,771   16,532
January 6, 1837. Edward Livingston.*

Livingston   **New York**
Geneseo   632 sq. mi.
64,328   62,372   57,006   54,041   44,053   40,257
February 23, 1821. Robert R. Livingston.*

Llano   **Texas**
Llano   935 sq. mi.
17,044   11,631   10,144   6,979   5,240   5,377
February 1, 1856; organized August 4, 1856. Llano River. Spanish for "plain."

Logan   **Arkansas**
Paris   710 sq. mi.
22,486   20,557   20,144   16,789   15,957   20,260
March 22, 1871, as Sarber; name changed December 14, 1875. James Logan (?–1859). Early settler in western Arkansas c1829; Arkansas legislature 1836.

Logan   **Colorado**
Sterling   1,839 sq. mi.
20,504   17,567   19,800   18,852   20,302   17,187
February 25, 1887. *John Alexander Logan* (1826–86). Mexican War, 2nd lieutenant, 1st Illinois Infantry 1847; clerk of Jackson County, Illinois, court 1849; Illinois House of Representatives 1852–53 and 1856–57; prosecuting attorney, 3rd Judicial District of Illinois, 1853–57; U.S. representative 1859–62 and 1867–71; colonel, 31st Illinois Infantry, 1861; brigadier general of Volunteers 1862; major general of Volunteers 1862–65; U.S. senator 1871–77 and 1879–86; Republican nominee for vice president with James G. Blaine 1884.

Logan   **Illinois**
Lincoln   618 sq. mi.
31,183   30,798   31,802   33,538   33,656   30,671
February 15, 1839. John Logan (1788–1852). Corporal, Black Hawk War; Illinois General Assembly; father of John Alexander Logan.*

Logan   **Kansas**
Oakley   1,073 sq. mi.
3,046   3,081   3,478   3,814   4,036   4,206
March 4, 1881, as Saint John; name changed February 24, 1887; organized September 17, 1887. John Alexander Logan.*

Logan   **Kentucky**
Russellville   556 sq. mi.
26,573   24,416   24,138   21,793   20,896   22,335
June 28, 1792; effective September 1, 1792. *Benjamin Logan* (c1743–1802). Indian fighter; built fort at Stanford, Kentucky, 1776; Virginia legislature; Kentucky Constitutional Convention 1792; Kentucky legislature.

Logan   **Nebraska**
Stapleton   571 sq. mi.
774   878   983   991   1,108   1,357
February 24, 1885. John Alexander Logan.*

Logan   **North Dakota**
Napoleon   993 sq. mi.
2,308   2,847   3,493   4,245   5,369   6,357
January 4, 1873; organized September 1, 1884. John Alexander Logan.*

Logan   **Ohio**
Bellefontaine   458 sq. mi.
46,005   42,310   39,155   35,072   34,803   31,329
December 30, 1817. Benjamin Logan.*

Logan   **Oklahoma**
Guthrie   744 sq. mi.
33,924   29,011   26,881   19,645   18,662   22,170
1890. John Alexander Logan.*

Logan   **West Virginia**
Logan   454 sq. mi.
37,710   43,032   50,679   46,269   61,570   77,391
January 12, 1824. John Logan (c1725–80). Mingo chief named Tah-gah-jute; took name of a friend, John Logan, private secretary to William Penn; friendly to settlers until family massacred by settlers 1774; led Indians in Lord Dunmore's War 1774; led raids against settlements during American Revolution.

Long   **Georgia**
Ludowici   401 sq. mi.
10,304   6,202   4,524   3,746   3,874   3,598
August 14, 1920. Crawford Williamson Long (1815–78). Physician; first physician to use ether as anesthetic during surgery, Jefferson, Georgia, 1842.

Lonoke   **Arkansas**
Lonoke   766 sq. mi.
52,828   39,268   34,518   26,249   24,551   27,278
April 16, 1873. Descriptive. Contraction of "lone oak," after a tree used in early surveys.

Lorain   **Ohio**
Elyria   493 sq. mi.
284,664   271,126   274,909   256,843   217,500   148,162
December 26, 1822; organized January 21, 1824. Lorraine, France.

Los Alamos   **New Mexico**
Los Alamos   109 sq. mi.
18,343   18,115   17,599   15,198   13,037   10,746
March 16, 1949. City of Los Alamos. Spanish for "cottonwood trees"; for trees in the area.

Los Angeles   **California**
Los Angeles   4,061 sq. mi.
9,519,338   8,863,164   7,477,503   7,032,075   6,038,771   4,151,687
February 18, 1850. Los Angeles River and City. From Spanish name, El Rio Nuestra Señora la Reína de los Ángeles de Portiúncula (The River of Our Lady, the Queen of the Angels of Portiuncula). Portiuncula is the site of a shrine to the Virgin Mary in Assisi, Italy.

Loudon   **Tennessee**
Loudon   229 sq. mi.
39,086   31,255   28,553   24,266   23,757   23,182
June 2, 1870, as Christiana; name changed July 7, 1870. Fort Loudon. Named for *John Campbell, Earl of Loudoun* (1705–82); British army 1726; lost Forts Oswego and William Henry in French and Indian Wars; governor general of Virginia 1756; failed at invasion of Canada; recalled 1757; acting commander of British troops in Portugal 1762–63; general 1770.

Loudoun   **Virginia**
Leesburg   520 sq. mi.
169,599   86,129   57,427   37,150   24,549   21,147
March 25, 1757 (session). John Campbell, Earl of Loudoun.*

Louisa   **Iowa**
Wapello   402 sq. mi.
12,183   11,592   12,055   10,682   10,290   11,101
December 7, 1836. Uncertain. (1) Louisa Massey (?–?). Pioneer heroine who shot and wounded her brother's murderer shortly before county was created. (2) Louisa County, Virginia.

Louisa   **Virginia**
Louisa   497 sq. mi.
25,627   20,325   17,825   14,004   12,959   12,826
May 6, 1742 (session). Princess Louise (1724–51). Eighth and youngest child of King George II of England and Queen Caroline; married Frederick V of Denmark 1744.

Loup   **Nebraska**
Taylor   570 sq. mi.
712   683   859   854   1,097   1,348
February 23, 1883. North Loup River. French for "wolf."

Love   **Oklahoma**
Marietta   515 sq. mi.,
8,831   8,157   7,469   5,637   5,862   7,721
July 16, 1907. Love family. Prominent Chickasaw family, most notably Overton Love (1820–1907); arrived in Indian Territory (Oklahoma) 1838; represented Chickasaw Nation in dealings with U.S.

Loving   **Texas**
Mentone   673 sq. mi.
67   107   91   164   226   227
February 26, 1887; organized 1931. Oliver Loving (c1812–1867). Cattleman and trail driver; supplied cattle and hogs to Confederate government; developed Goodnight-Loving Trail; killed by Indians.

Lowndes   **Alabama**
Hayneville   718 sq. mi.
13,473   12,658   13,253   12,897   15,417   18,018
January 20, 1830. *William Jones Lowndes* (1782–1822). South Carolina House of Representatives 1806–10; captain of Militia 1807; U.S. representative 1811–22; died and buried at sea en route to England.

Lowndes   **Georgia**
Valdosta   504 sq. mi.
92,115   75,981   67,972   55,112   49,270   35,211
December 23, 1825. William Jones Lowndes.*

Lowndes   **Mississippi**
Columbus   502 sq. mi.
61,586   59,308   57,304   49,700   46,639   37,852
January 30, 1830. William Jones Lowndes.*

Lubbock   **Texas**
Lubbock   899 sq. mi.
242,628   222,636   211,651   179,295   156,271   101,048
August 21, 1876; organized March 10, 1891. Thomas S. Lubbock (1817–62). Texas Revolution, siege of Bexar; captured 1841; escaped 1842; lieutenant colonel, Confederate army; helped form Terry's Texas Rangers 1861.

Lucas   **Iowa**
Chariton   431 sq. mi.
9,422   9,070   10,313   10,163   10,923   12,069
January 13, 1846; organized January 15, 1849; effective July 4, 1849. *Robert Lucas* (1781–1853). Scioto County, Ohio, surveyor, 1804; major general, Ohio Militia; captain in U.S. Army 1812; Ohio legislature 1816–32; governor of Ohio 1832–36; governor of Iowa Territory 1838–41.

Lucas   **Ohio**
Toledo   340 sq. mi.
455,054   462,361   471,741   484,370   456,931   395,551
June 20, 1835. Robert Lucas.*

Luce   **Michigan**
Newberry   903 sq. mi.
7,024   5,763   6,659   6,789   7,827   8,147
March 1, 1887. Cyrus Gray Luce (1824–1905). Supervisor of Gilead Township 1842–54; Michigan legislature 1854; Michigan Senate 1865 and 1876; Michigan Constitutional Convention 1867; governor of Michigan 1887–96.

Lumpkin   **Georgia**
Dahlonega   284 sq. mi.
21,016   14,573   10,762   8,728   7,241   6,574
December 3, 1832. Wilson Lumpkin (1783–1870). Georgia House of Representatives 1808–12; Georgia Senate 1812–15; U.S. representative 1815–17 and 1827–31; governor of Georgia 1831–35; U.S. senator 1837–41.

Luna   **New Mexico**
Deming   2,965 sq. mi.
25,016   18,110   15,585   11,706   9,839   8,753
March 16, 1901. Solomon Luna (1858–1912). Sheep rancher; New Mexico Constitutional Convention 1910.

Lunenburg   **Virginia**
Lunenburg   432 sq. mi.
13,146   11,419   12,124   11,687   12,523   14,116
May 6, 1745 (session). George II,* Duke of Brunswick-Lunenburg. (See Georgetown, South Carolina.)

Luzerne   **Pennsylvania**
Wilkes-Barre   891 sq. mi.
319,250   328,149   343,079   342,301   346,972   392,241
September 25, 1786. Anne Cesar, Chevalier de la Luzerne (1741–91). French army during Seven Years' War; French minister to the U.S. 1779; raised money for American cause.

Lycoming   **Pennsylvania**
Williamsport   1,235 sq. mi.
120,044   118,710   118,416   113,296   109,367   101,249
April 13, 1795. Lycoming Creek. Corruption of Delaware word for "sandy creek."

Lyman   **South Dakota**
Kennebec   1,640 sq. mi.
3,895   3,638   3,864   4,060   4,428   4,572
January 8, 1873; organized May 21, 1893. William P. Lyman (c1833–c1880). Served with General Harney in punitive expedition against Indians 1855; early settler in southeastern Dakota Territory; operated ferry and trading post on James River; Dakota territorial legislature 1873.

Lynchburg   **Virginia**
(Independent City)   49 sq. mi.
65,269   66,049   66,743   54,083   54,790   47,727

August 27, 1852. John Lynch (c1740–1820). Built ferry across James River 1757; ferry landing grew into town. (Associated counties: Bedford and Campbell.)

Lynn   **Texas**
Tahoka   892 sq. mi.
6,550   6,758   8,605   9,107   10,914   11,030
August 21, 1876; organized 1903. William Linn (?–1836). At Alamo from Boston via New Orleans; private under Captain Blazeby. (County name is misspelled.)

Lyon   **Iowa**
Rock Rapids   588 sq. mi.
11,763   11,952   12,896   13,340   14,468   14,697
January 15, 1851, as Buncombe; name changed September 11, 1862; organized January 1, 1872. *Nathaniel Lyon* (1818–61). Graduated West Point 1841; Seminole War 1841–42; Mexican War 1846–47; captain 1851; commanded U.S. arsenal at St. Louis; killed leading 1st Iowa Infantry at battle of Wilson Creek, Missouri, August 10, 1861.

Lyon   **Kansas**
Emporia   851 sq. mi.
35,935   34,732   35,108   32,071   26,928   26,576
August 30, 1855, as Breckenridge; organized February 17, 1857; name changed February 5, 1862. Nathaniel Lyon.*

Lyon   **Kentucky**
Eddyville   216 sq. mi.
8,080   6,624   6,490   5,562   5,924   6,853
January 14, 1854. Uncertain. (1) Chittenden Lyon (1787–1842); Kentucky House of Representatives 1822–24; Kentucky Senate 1824–27; U.S. representative 1827–35. (2) Matthew Lyon (1749–1822); father of Chittenden Lyon; Vermont legislature; U.S. representative from Vermont 1797–1800; U.S. representative from Kentucky 1803–11.

Lyon   **Minnesota**
Marshall   714 sq. mi.
25,425   24,789   25,207   24,273   22,655   22,253
March 6, 1868. Nathaniel Lyon.*

Lyon   **Nevada**
Yerington   1,994 sq. mi.
34,501   20,001   13,594   8,221   6,143   3,679
November 25, 1861. Uncertain. (1) Nathaniel Lyon.* (2) Robert Lyon (?–?); Indian scout; Pyramid Lake Indian War 1860.

M

Mackinac   **Michigan**
Saint Ignance   1,022 sq. mi.
11,943   10,674   10,178   9,660   10,853   9,287
October 26, 1818, as Michilimackinac; name changed January 26, 1837. Indian word meaning "turtle."

Macomb   **Michigan**
Mount Clemens   480 sq. mi.
788,149   717,400   694,600   625,309   405,804   184,961
January 15, 1818. Alexander Macomb (1782–1841). Enlisted U.S. Army 1799; appointed brigadier general 1814; commanded northern frontier on Lake Champlain, defeated British squadron; received Thanks of Congress and gold medal for victory at Plattsburgh 1814; commander in chief of the army 1835–41.

Macon   **Alabama**
Tuskegee   611 sq. mi.

24,105   24,928   26,829   24,841   26,717   30,561
December 18, 1832. *Nathaniel Macon* (1757–1837). Revolutionary War; North Carolina Senate 1780–82 and 1784–85; U.S. representative 1791–1815, Speaker 1801–07; U.S. senator 1815–28; president, North Carolina Constitutional Convention 1835.

Macon   **Georgia**
Oglethorpe   403 sq. mi.
14,074   13,114   14,003   12,933   13,170   14,213
December 14, 1837. Nathaniel Macon.*

Macon   **Illinois**
Decatur   581 sq. mi.
114,706   117,206   131,375   125,010   118,257   98,853
January 19, 1829. Nathaniel Macon.*

Macon   **Missouri**
Macon   804 sq. mi.
15,762   15,345   16,313   15,432   16,473   18,332
January 6, 1837. Nathaniel Macon.*

Macon   **North Carolina**
Franklin   516 sq. mi.
29,811   23,499   20,178   15,788   14,935   16,174
1828. Nathaniel Macon.*

Macon   **Tennessee**
Lafayette   307 sq. mi.
20,386   15,906   15,700   12,315   12,197   13,599
January 18, 1842. Nathaniel Macon.*

Macoupin   **Illinois**
Carlinville   864 sq. mi.
49,019   47,679   49,384   44,557   43,524   44,210
January 17, 1829. Macoupin Creek. Indian word for "white potato."

Madera   **California**
Madera   2,136 sq. mi.
123,109   88,090   63,116   41,519   40,468   36,964
March 11, 1893. Town of Madera. Spanish for "lumber" or "timber."

Madison   **Alabama**
Huntsville   805 sq. mi.
276,700   238,912   196,966   186,540   117,348   72,903
December 13, 1808. *James Madison* (1751–1836). General Assembly of Virginia 1776; Continental Congress 1780–83 and 1786–88; federal Constitutional Convention 1787; U.S. representative 1789–97; U.S. secretary of state 1801–09; 4th president of the U.S. 1809–17.

Madison   **Arkansas**
Huntsville   837 sq. mi.
14,243   11,618   11,373   9,453   9,068   11,734
September 30, 1836. Madison County, Alabama.

Madison   **Florida**
Madison   692 sq. mi.
18,733   16,569   14,894   13,481   14,154   14,197
December 26, 1827. James Madison.*

Madison   **Georgia**
Danielsville   284 sq. mi.
25,730   21,050   17,747   13,517   11,246   12,238
December 5, 1811. James Madison.*

Madison   **Idaho**
Rexburg   472 sq. mi.
27,467   23,674   19,480   13,452   9,417   9,156
February 18, 1913. James Madison.*

Madison   **Illinois**
Edwardsville   725 sq. mi.
258,941   249,238   247,691   250,934   224,689   182,307
September 14, 1812. James Madison.*

Madison   **Indiana**
Anderson   452 sq. mi.
133,358   130,669   139,336   138,451   125,819   103,911
January 4, 1823; effective July 1, 1823. James Madison.*

Madison   **Iowa**
Winterset   561 sq. mi.
14,019   12,483   12,597   11,558   12,295   13,131
January 13, 1846; organized February 19, 1849. James Madison.*

Madison   **Kentucky**
Richmond   441 sq. mi.
70,872   57,508   53,352   42,730   33,482   31,179
October 17, 1785 (session); effective August 1, 1788. James Madison.*

Madison   **Louisiana**
Tallulah   624 sq. mi.
13,728   12,463   15,975   15,065   16,444   17,451
January 19, 1838. James Madison.*

Madison   **Mississippi**
Canton   717 sq. mi.
74,674   53,794   41,613   29,737   32,904   33,860
January 29, 1828. James Madison.*

Madison   **Missouri**
Fredericktown   497 sq. mi.
11,800   11,127   10,725   8,641   9,366   10,380
December 14, 1818. James Madison.*

Madison   **Montana**
Virginia City   3,587 sq. mi.
6,851   5,989   5,448   5,014   5,211   5,998
February 2, 1865. Madison River. Named for James Madison* by Lewis and Clark 1805.

Madison   **Nebraska**
Madison   573 sq. mi.
35,226   32,655   31,382   27,402   25,145   24,338
January 26, 1856; organized April 6, 1868. City of Madison, Wisconsin. Named for James Madison.*

Madison   **New York**
Wampsville   656 sq. mi.

| 69,441 | 69,120 | 65,150 | 62,864 | 54,635 | 46,214 |

March 21, 1806. James Madison.*

Madison   **North Carolina**
Marshall   449 sq. mi.

| 19,635 | 16,953 | 16,827 | 16,003 | 17,217 | 20,522 |

January 27, 1851. James Madison.*

Madison   **Ohio**
London   465 sq. mi.

| 40,213 | 37,068 | 33,004 | 28,318 | 26,454 | 22,300 |

February 16, 1810. James Madison.*

Madison   **Tennessee**
Jackson   557 sq. mi.

| 91,837 | 77,982 | 74,546 | 65,727 | 60,655 | 60,128 |

November 7, 1821. James Madison.*

Madison   **Texas**
Madisonville   470 sq. mi.

| 12,940 | 10,931 | 10,649 | 7,693 | 6,749 | 7,996 |

January 27, 1853; organized August 7, 1854. James Madison.*

Madison   **Virginia**
Madison   321 sq. mi.

| 12,520 | 11,949 | 10,232 | 8,638 | 8,187 | 8,273 |

December 4, 1792 (session); effective May 1, 1793. James Madison.*

Magoffin   **Kentucky**
Salyersville   309 sq. mi.

| 13,332 | 13,077 | 13,515 | 10,443 | 11,156 | 13,839 |

February 22, 1860. Beriah Magoffin (1815–85). Kentucky Senate 1850; governor of Kentucky 1859–62, resigned; Kentucky House of Representatives 1867.

Mahaska   **Iowa**
Oskaloosa   571 sq. mi.

| 22,335 | 21,522 | 22,867 | 22,177 | 23,602 | 24,672 |

February 17, 1843; organized February 5, 1844; effective March 1, 1844. Mahaska (1784–1834). Iowa chief; signed treaties with U.S. 1824, 1825, and 1830; killed by disgruntled Indian Mahaska had turned over to U.S.; name means "white cloud."

Mahnomen   **Minnesota**
Mahnomen   556 sq. mi.

| 5,190 | 5,044 | 5,535 | 5,638 | 6,341 | 7,059 |

December 27, 1906. Chippewa word for "wild rice," a major part of their diet.

Mahoning   **Ohio**
Youngstown   415 sq. mi.

| 257,555 | 264,806 | 289,487 | 303,424 | 300,480 | 257,629 |

February 16, 1846. Mahoning River. Delaware word for salt licks.

Major   **Oklahoma**
Fairview   957 sq. mi.

| 7,545 | 8,055 | 8,772 | 7,529 | 7,808 | 10,279 |

July 16, 1907. John C. Major (1863–1937). Oklahoma territorial legislature; Oklahoma Constitutional Convention; Oklahoma legislature 1907–37.

Malheur   **Oregon**
Vale   9,887 sq. mi.
31,615   26,038   26,896   23,169   22,764   23,223
February 17, 1887. Malheur River. French for "misfortune" or "mishap"; name given to river by French trappers who lost a cache of furs.

Manassas   **Virginia**
(Independent City)   10 sq. mi.
35,135   27,957   15,438   (a)   (a)   (a)
May 1, 1975. Manassas Junction. Railroad hub named for Manassas Gap, which was named for Manahoac Indians. (Associated county: Prince William.)

Manassas Park   **Virginia**
(Independent City)   2 sq. mi.
10,290   6,734   6,524   (a)   (a)   (a)
June 1, 1975. Manassas, Virginia. (Associated county: Prince William.)

Manatee   **Florida**
Bradenton   741 sq. mi.
264,002   211,707   148,442   97,115   69,168   34,704
January 9, 1855. Descriptive of sea cows or manatees. From Spanish *mamati*, which is derived from Carib word for female breast, a distinguishing feature of manatees.

Manistee   **Michigan**
Manistee   544 sq. mi.
24,527   21,265   23,019   20,094   19,042   18,524
April 1, 1840; organized February 13, 1855. Manistee River. Indian word, possibly meaning "lost river" or "island in the river."

Manitowoc   **Wisconsin**
Manitowoc   592 sq. mi.
82,887   80,421   82,918   82,294   75,215   67,159
December 7, 1836; organized 1848. Manitowoc River. From *manitou*, Algonquin word referring to "spirit world."

Marathon   **Wisconsin**
Wausau   1,545 sq. mi.
125,834   115,400   111,270   97,457   88,874   80,337
February 9, 1850. Battle of Marathon, Greece.

Marengo   **Alabama**
Linden   977 sq. mi.
22,539   23,084   25,047   23,819   27,098   29,494
February 6, 1818. Marengo, Italy; site of Napoleon's victory over Austria June 14, 1800.

Maricopa   **Arizona**
Phoenix   9,203 sq. mi.
3,072,149   2,122,101 1,509,052   967,522   663,510   331,770
February 14, 1871. Maricopa Indians. From Spanish *mariposa* (butterfly); for their colorfully painted faces and hair.

Maries   **Missouri**
Vienna   528 sq. mi.
8,903   7,976   7,551   6,851   7,282   7,423
March 2, 1855. Maries and Little Maries rivers. From French *marais,* meaning "marsh" or "swamp."

Marin   **California**
San Rafael   520 sq. mi.

247,289	230,096	222,568	206,038	146,820	85,619

February 18, 1850. Marin Bay, Islands, and Peninsula; origin uncertain. (1) Bay in San Francisco Bay between San Quentin and San Pedro points (now San Rafael Bay) named "Bahía de Nuestra Señora del Rosario la Marinera" by Spanish explorer Juan de Ayala 1775; islands in the bay called "Islas de Marín" by 1834 and Marin Islands by 1850. (2) Chief of the Licatiuts; baptized "El Marinero" (the mariner). (3) Local Indian baptized "Marinero" because of his knowledge of San Francisco Bay.

Marinette   **Wisconsin**
Marinette   1,402 sq. mi.

43,384	40,548	39,314	35,810	34,660	35,748

February 27, 1879. City of Marinette. Named for Marguerite Chevalier (1793–1865); daughter of Menominee chief; nicknamed "Marinette" after Marie Antoinette; with husband, competed with American Fur Company.

Marion   **Alabama**
Hamilton   741 sq. mi.

31,214	29,830	30,041	23,788	21,837	27,264

February 13, 1818. *Francis Marion* (1732–95). Brigadier general; commander of Marion's brigade; known as "the Swamp Fox"; harassed English troops during Revolutionary War; won battle of Eutaw Springs; South Carolina Senate 1782–90.

Marion   **Arkansas**
Yellville   598 sq. mi.

16,140	12,001	11,334	7,000	6,041	8,609

November 3, 1835, as Searcy; effective December 25, 1835; name changed September 29, 1836. Francis Marion.*

Marion   **Florida**
Ocala   1,579 sq. mi.

258,916	194,833	122,488	69,030	51,616	38,187

March 14, 1844. Francis Marion.*

Marion   **Georgia**
Buena Vista   367 sq. mi.

7,144	5,590	5,297	5,099	5,477	6,521

December 24, 1827. Francis Marion.*

Marion   **Illinois**
Salem   572 sq. mi.

41,691	41,561	43,523	38,986	39,349	41,700

January 24, 1823. Francis Marion.*

Marion   **Indiana**
Indianapolis   396 sq. mi.

860,454	797,159	765,233	792,299	697,567	551,777

December 31, 1821; effective April 1, 1822. Francis Marion.*

Marion   **Iowa**
Knoxville   554 sq. mi.

32,052	30,001	29,669	26,352	25,886	25,930

June 10, 1845. Francis Marion.*

Marion   **Kansas**
Marion   943 sq. mi.

13,361	12,888	13,522	13,935	15,143	16,307

August 30, 1855; abolished 1857; recreated February 17, 1860; organized 1865. Marion County, Ohio.

Marion   **Kentucky**
Lebanon   346 sq. mi.
18,212   16,499   17,910   16,714   16,887   17,212
January 25, 1834. Francis Marion.*

Marion   **Mississippi**
Columbia   542 sq. mi.
25,595   25,544   25,708   22,871   23,293   23,967
December 9, 1811. Francis Marion.*

Marion   **Missouri**
Palmyra   438 sq. mi.
28,289   27,682   28,638   28,121   29,522   29,765
December 14, 1822; organized December 23, 1826. Francis Marion.*

Marion   **Ohio**
Marion   404 sq. mi.
66,217   64,274   67,974   64,724   60,221   49,959
February 12, 1820; organized 1824. Francis Marion.*

Marion   **Oregon**
Salem   1,184 sq. mi.
284,834   228,483   204,692   151,309   120,888   101,401
July 5, 1843, as Champoeg; name changed September 3, 1849. Francis Marion.*

Marion   **South Carolina**
Marion   489 sq. mi.
35,466   33,899   34,179   30,270   32,014   33,110
1798. Francis Marion.*

Marion   **Tennessee**
Jasper   498 sq. mi.
27,776   24,860   24,416   20,577   21,036   20,520
November 20, 1817. Francis Marion.*

Marion   **Texas**
Jefferson   381 sq. mi.
10,941   9,984   10,360   8,517   8,049   10,172
February 8, 1860; organized March 16, 1860. Francis Marion.*

Marion   **West Virginia**
Fairmont   310 sq. mi.
56,598   57,249   65,789   61,356   63,717   71,521
January 14, 1842. Francis Marion.*

Mariposa   **California**
Mariposa   1,451 sq. mi.
17,130   14,302   11,108   6,015   5,064   5,145
February 18, 1850. Mariposa Creek. Spanish for "butterfly."

Marlboro   **South Carolina**
Bennettsville   480 sq. mi.
28,818   29,361   31,634   27,151   28,529   31,766
March 12, 1785. John Churchill, Duke of Marlborough (1650–1722). Supported William III; made Earl of Marlborough 1689; commanded English forces in Ireland 1689; elevated by Queen Anne to Duke of Marlborough, a title rarely given to people outside of royalty 1702; War of Spanish Succession victories at Blenheim (1704), Ramillies (1706), and Malplaquet (1709).

Marquette   **Michigan**
Marquette   1,821 sq. mi.

64,634	70,887	74,101	64,686	56,154	47,654

March 9, 1843; organized December 1, 1851. *Jacques Marquette* (1637–75). French explorer and Jesuit missionary; accompanied Louis Joliet in exploring Mississippi River to the mouth of the Arkansas River, returned by way of Illinois River, opening best route between Great Lakes and Mississippi River 1673.

Marquette   **Wisconsin**
Montello   455 sq. mi.

15,832	12,321	11,672	8,865	8,516	8,839

December 7, 1836; organized 1848. Jacques Marquette.*

Marshall   **Alabama**
Guntersville   567 sq. mi.

82,231	70,832	65,622	54,211	48,018	45,090

January 9, 1836. *John Marshall* (1755–1835). Officer in Virginia Militia 1777–81; House of Burgesses 1780 and 1782–88; federal Constitutional Convention 1788; U.S. commissioner to France 1797–98; U.S. representative 1799–1800; U.S. secretary of state 1800; chief justice of the U.S. 1801–35.

Marshall   **Illinois**
Lacon   386 sq. mi.

13,180	12,846	14,479	13,302	13,334	13,025

January 19, 1839. John Marshall.*

Marshall   **Indiana**
Plymouth   444 sq. mi.

45,128	42,182	39,155	34,986	32,443	29,468

February 7, 1835; organized February 4, 1836; effective April 1, 1836. John Marshall.*

Marshall   **Iowa**
Marshalltown   572 sq. mi.

39,311	38,276	41,652	41,076	37,984	35,611

January 13, 1846; organized October 1, 1849. John Marshall.*

Marshall   **Kansas**
Marysville   903 sq. mi.

10,965	11,705	12,787	13,139	15,598	17,926

August 30, 1855. Francis J. Marshall (1816–95). Operated ferry across Big Blue River 1850; trading post for California immigrants 1851; Kansas territorial legislature 1855; defeated as pro-slavery candidate for governor 1857.

Marshall   **Kentucky**
Benton   305 sq. mi.

30,125	27,205	25,637	20,381	16,736	13,387

February 12, 1842. John Marshall.*

Marshall   **Minnesota**
Warren   1,772 sq. mi.

10,155	10,993	13,027	13,060	14,262	16,125

February 25, 1879; organized March 11, 1881. William Rainey Marshall (1825–96). Surveyor of Wisconsin lands 1847; Wisconsin legislature 1848; banker 1855–57; established newspaper in St. Paul 1861; lieutenant colonel, 7th Minnesota Infantry 1862; won battle of Wood Lake 1862; colonel 1863; fought Sioux 1863; brevet brigadier general 1865; governor of Minnesota 1866–70.

Marshall   **Mississippi**
Holly Springs   706 sq. mi.

34,993   30,361   29,296   24,027   24,503   25,106
February 9, 1836. John Marshall.*

Marshall   **Oklahoma**
Madill   371 sq. mi.
13,184   10,829   10,550   7,682   7,263   8,177
July 16, 1907. Elizabeth Ellen Marshall Henshaw (c1834–94). Mother of George Henshaw, delegate to Oklahoma Constitutional Convention; Henshaw had county named after his mother's side of the family, which had links to John Marshall.*

Marshall   **South Dakota**
Britton   838 sq. mi.
4,576   4,844   5,404   5,965   6,663   7,835
March 10, 1885. Marshall Vincent (?–?). Homesteaded in Day County, Dakota Territory, 1881; opened flour mill in Britton 1883; Day County commissioner when Marshall County created from northern Day County.

Marshall   **Tennessee**
Lewisburg   375 sq. mi.
26,767   21,539   19,968   17,319   16,859   17,768
February 20, 1836. John Marshall.*

Marshall   **West Virginia**
Moundsville   307 sq. mi.
35,519   37,356   41,608   37,598   38,041   36,893
March 12, 1835. John Marshall.*

Martin   **Florida**
Stuart   556 sq. mi.
126,731   100,900   64,014   28,035   16,932   7,807
May 30, 1925. John W. Martin (1884–1958). Mayor of Jacksonville 1917–24; governor of Florida 1925–29.

Martin   **Indiana**
Shoals   336 sq. mi.
10,369   10,369   11,001   10,969   10,608   10,678
January 17, 1820; effective February 1, 1820. Uncertain. (1) Thomas Martin (?–1819); resident of Newport, Kentucky; major in Continental army. (2) Jeremiah Martin (?–?); Kentucky Volunteer, War of 1812; battle of the Thames. (3) Thomas E. Martin (?–?); early settler and road supervisor.

Martin   **Kentucky**
Inez   231 sq. mi.
12,578   12,526   13,925   9,377   10,201   11,677
March 10, 1870. John Preston Martin (1811–62). Kentucky House of Representatives 1841–43; U.S. representative 1845–47; Kentucky Senate 1855–59.

Martin   **Minnesota**
Fairmont   709 sq. mi.
21,802   22,914   24,687   24,316   26,986   25,655
May 23, 1857; organized December 16, 1857. Uncertain. (1) Henry Martin (1829–1908); Connecticut bank commissioner 1854–56; resident of Minnesota Territory 1856–57. (2) Morgan L. Martin (1805–87); Wisconsin territorial delegate to Congress 1845–46; introduced legislation to create Minnesota Territory 1846. (3) Martin McLeod* (see McLeod, Minnesota).

Martin   **North Carolina**
Williamston   461 sq. mi.
25,593   25,078   25,948   24,730   27,139   27,938
March 2, 1774. Josiah Martin (1737–86). Officer in British army 1757–69; royal governor of North Carolina 1771–75; forced to flee and rejoined British army during American Revolution; served with Cornwallis in capture of Charleston 1780. Although

named for a British officer who fought against the American colonists, the county's name was not changed but was shifted to honor Alexander Martin (1740–1807); governor of North Carolina 1782–85 and 1789–92; U.S. senator 1793–98.

Martin   **Texas**
Stanton   915 sq. mi.

4,746	4,956	4,684	4,774	5,068	5,541

August 21, 1876; organized November 14, 1884. Wylie Martin (1776–1842). Scout for General Harrison 1813; captain, U.S. Army, resigned his commission (1823) after killing a man in a duel and moved to Texas 1825; member of conventions to establish separate government for American section of Texas; fought in Texas Army; Texas Republic legislature.

Martinsville   **Virginia**
(Independent City)   11 sq. mi.

15,416	16,162	18,149	19,653	18,798	17,251

1928. Joseph Martin (1740–1808). Early settler 1792. (Associated county: Henry.)

Mason   **Illinois**
Havana   539 sq. mi.

16,038	16,269	19,492	16,161	15,193	15,326

January 20, 1841. Mason County, Kentucky.

Mason   **Kentucky**
Maysville   241 sq. mi.

16,800	16,666	17,765	17,273	18,454	18,486

November 5, 1788; effective May 1, 1789. *George Mason* (1725–92). Virginia House of Burgesses 1759; Virginia Convention 1775; authored Virginia Declaration of Rights 1776; Virginia Assembly 1776–80 and 1786–88; federal Constitutional Convention 1787.

Mason   **Michigan**
Ludington   495 sq. mi.

28,274	25,537	26,365	22,612	21,929	20,474

April 1, 1840, as Notipekago; name changed March 8, 1843; organized February 13, 1855. Stevens Thomson Mason (1811–43). Secretary and acting governor of Michigan Territory 1831–35; governor of Michigan 1835–38.

Mason   **Texas**
Mason   932 sq. mi.

3,738	3,423	3,683	3,356	3,780	4,945

January 22, 1858; organized August 2, 1858. Fort Mason. Built on Comanche Creek 1851; abandoned 1859. Name of uncertain origin. (1) George T. Mason (?–1846), 2nd lieutenant in 2nd U.S. Dragoons, died in combat near Brownsville April 25, 1846, in action with Mexico that precipitated Mexican War; (2) Richard B. Mason (1797–1850), Black Hawk War, brevet brigadier general in Mexican War, military governor of California.

Mason   **Washington**
Shelton   961 sq. mi.

49,405	38,341	31,184	20,918	16,251	15,022

March 13, 1854, as Sawamish; name changed January 8, 1864. Charles H. Mason (1830–59). Secretary of Washington Territory; acting territorial governor during Yakima War 1855–58.

Mason   **West Virginia**
Point Pleasant   432 sq. mi.

25,957	25,178	27,045	24,306	24,459	23,537

January 2, 1804. George Mason.*

Massac   **Illinois**
Metropolis   239 sq. mi.

15,161	14,752	14,990	13,889	14,341	13,594

February 8, 1843. Fort Massac. Grew from French trading post on Ohio River 1702. Name is of uncertain origin. (1) Most likely for Claude Louis, Marquis de Massiac (1686–1770); French minister of marine and colonies 1758; ordered conversion of the trading post to a fort on Ohio River 1758. (2) Two Frenchmen associated with the early fort whose names are similar to "Massac." (3) Corruption of French *massacre*; for supposed slaughter of French soldiers by Indians.

Matagorda   **Texas**
Bay City   1,114 sq. mi.
37,957   36,928   37,828   27,913   25,744   21,559
March 17, 1836; organized 1837. Matagorda Bay and Mexican municipality. Spanish for "canebrake."

Matanuska-Susitna   **Alaska**
Palmer   24,682 sq. mi.
59,322   39,683   17,816   6,509   5,188   3,534
January 1964. "Matanuska" from Russian *matanooski* for "Copper River people"; "Susitna" from Russian rendering of Tanaina name for "sandy river."

Mathews   **Virginia**
Mathews   86 sq. mi.
9,207   8,348   7,995   7,168   7,121   7,148
December 16, 1790. Uncertain. (1) George Mathews (1739–1812); colonel in Virginia regiments during American Revolution; U.S. representative from Georgia; governor of Georgia 1787–88. (2) Thomas Mathews (?–?). Captain, possibly colonel, in Continental army; Speaker, Virginia House of Delegates 1788–94.

Maui   **Hawaii**
Wailuku   1,159 sq. mi.
128,094   100,374   70,847   45,984   42,576   48,179
July 1905. Island of Maui. Named for Polynesian demi-god who brought the land out of the sea and separated the sky from the earth.

Maury   **Tennessee**
Columbia   613 sq. mi.
69,498   54,812   51,095   43,376   41,699   40,368
November 16, 1807. Abram P. Maury (1766–1825). Tennessee Senate 1805 and 1819; commissioner to sell Cherokee Indian lands.

Maverick   **Texas**
Eagle Pass   1,280 sq. mi.
47,297   36,378   31,398   18,093   14,508   12,292
February 2, 1856; organized July 13, 1871. Samuel Augustus Maverick (1803–70). Signed Texas Declaration of Independence 1836; captured by Mexican army; elected to Texas Republic legislature while in Mexican prison 1845. Maverick did not brand his cattle, and "maverick" became a synonym for unbranded cattle and "nonconformist."

Mayes   **Oklahoma**
Pryor   656 sq. mi.
38,369   33,366   32,261   23,302   20,073   19,743
July 16, 1907. Uncertain. (1) Joel B. Mayes (1833–91); Cherokee; private in 1st Confederate Indian Brigade; Cherokee Supreme Court; principal chief of Cherokee Nation 1887–91. (2) Samuel Houston Mayes (1845–1927); principal chief of Cherokee Nation 1895–99.

McClain   **Oklahoma**
Purcell   570 sq. mi.
27,740   22,795   20,291   14,157   12,740   14,681
July 16, 1907. Charles M. McClain (1840–1915). Enlisted in Confederate army 1861; moved to Chickasaw Nation, Indian Territory (Oklahoma) 1885; Oklahoma Constitutional Convention 1906–07.

McCone   **Montana**
Circle   2,643 sq. mi.
1,977   2,276   2,702   2,875   3,321   3,258
February 20, 1919. George McCone (1854–1929). Cattle and sheep rancher; arrived in Montana Territory 1882; Montana legislature 1900; Montana Senate; lobbied for creation of county.

McCook   **South Dakota**
Salem   575 sq. mi.
5,832   5,688   6,444   7,246   8,268   8,828
January 8, 1873; organized June 15, 1878. Edwin S. McCook (1837–73). Graduated from U.S. Naval Academy; captain, Union army 1861; resigned as brevet brigadier general 1864; secretary of Dakota Territory 1872–73; killed in saloon fight, September, 1873.

McCormick   **South Carolina**
McCormick   360 sq. mi.
9,958   8,868   7,797   7,955   8,629   9,577
February 19, 1916. Cyrus Hall McCormick (1809–84). Perfected reaping machine 1834; large land holdings in county.

McCracken   **Kentucky**
Paducah   251 sq. mi.
65,514   62,879   61,310   58,281   57,306   49,137
December 17, 1824; organized 1825. Virgil McCracken (?–1813). Kentucky legislature 1810–11; raised company of soldiers in War of 1812; wounded and captured at battle of River Raisin; massacred by Indian captors, who were allies of British.

McCreary   **Kentucky**
Whitley City   428 sq. mi.
17,080   15,603   15,634   12,548   12,463   16,660
March 12, 1912. James B. McCreary (1838–1918). Enlisted in Confederate army 1861; lieutenant colonel 1863; Kentucky House of Representatives 1869–73, Speaker 1871 and 1873; governor of Kentucky 1875–79 and 1911–15; U.S. representative 1885–97; U.S. senator 1903–09.

McCulloch   **Texas**
Brady   1,069 sq. mi.
8,205   8,778   8,735   8,571   8,815   11,701
August 27, 1856; organized 1876. Benjamin McCulloch (1811–62). Battle of San Jacinto 1836; Texas Congress 1839; Mexican War, battles of Monterrey, Buena Vista, and Mexico City; U.S. marshal in Texas 1853; brigadier general, Confederate army; killed at Pea Ridge.

McCurtain   **Oklahoma**
Idabel   1,852 sq. mi.
34,402   33,433   36,151   28,642   25,851   31,588
July 16, 1907. Green McCurtain (1848–1910). Choctaw National Council 1874–80; treasurer, Choctaw Nation 1888–92; Choctaw National Senate 1892–94; chief, Choctaw Nation 1896–1900 and 1902–04.

McDonald   **Missouri**
Pineville   540 sq. mi.
21,681   16,938   14,917   12,357   11,798   14,144
March 3, 1849. Alexander McDonald (?–?). American Revolution; sergeant under General Francis Marion.

McDonough   **Illinois**
Macomb   589 sq. mi.
32,913   35,244   37,467   36,653   28,928   28,199
January 25, 1826; organized 1830. Thomas Macdonough (1783–1825). Midshipman 1800; served on *Constellation* and *Philadelphia*; fought Barbary pirates; captain, War of 1812; victorious in battle of Plattsburg on Lake Champlain 1814; received gold medal from Congress and estate from Vermont legislature.

McDowell	**North Carolina**				
Marion	442 sq. mi.				
42,151	35,681	35,135	30,648	26,742	25,720

December 19, 1842. Joseph McDowell (1756–1801). Fought Cherokees 1776; major, North Carolina Militia, in command at battle of King's Mountain 1780; North Carolina House of Commons 1785–88; federal Constitutional Convention 1788–89; North Carolina Senate 1791–95; U.S. representative 1797–99.

McDowell	**West Virginia**				
Welch	535 sq. mi.				
27,329	35,233	49,899	50,666	71,358	98,887

February 20, 1858. James McDowell (1795–1851). Virginia House of Delegates 1830–35 and 1838; governor of Virginia 1842–46; U.S. representative 1846–51.

McDuffie	**Georgia**				
Thomson	260 sq. mi.				
21,231	20,119	18,546	15,276	12,627	11,443

October 18, 1870. George McDuffie (1790–1851). Born in Georgia but made reputation in South Carolina; South Carolina House of Representatives 1818–20; U.S. representative 1821–34; governor of South Carolina 1834–36; U.S. senator 1842–46.

McHenry	**Illinois**				
Woodstock	604 sq. mi.				
260,077	183,241	147,897	111,555	84,210	50,656

January 16, 1836; organized 1837. William McHenry (?–1835). War of 1812; Illinois Constitutional Convention 1818; major, Illinois Mounted Volunteers in Black Hawk War, 1832; Illinois legislature.

McHenry	**North Dakota**				
Towner	1,874 sq. mi.				
5,987	6,528	7,858	8,977	11,099	12,556

January 4, 1873; organized May 14, 1885. James McHenry (?–?). Early settler of Dakota Territory in what became South Dakota; Dakota territorial legislature 1865; Vermillion postmaster 1867–69.

McIntosh	**Georgia**				
Darien	433 sq. mi.				
10,847	8,634	8,046	7,371	6,364	6,008

December 19, 1793. Uncertain. (1) McIntosh family; emigrated from Scotland to Georgia 1736. (2) John Mohr McIntosh (1701–?); led group of Scottish settlers to Georgia 1736; father of Lachlan and grandfather of John McIntosh. (3) Lachlan McIntosh (1727–1806); brigadier general on General Washington's staff; commanded Western Department; established outposts that bolstered U.S. claims to Western lands after Revolutionary War; suspended from service for killing Button Gwinnett in a duel 1777 (see Gwinnett, Georgia); vindicated and promoted to major general. (4) John McIntosh (?–1826); colonel during Revolutionary War and War of 1812.

McIntosh	**North Dakota**				
Ashley	975 sq. mi.				
3,390	4,021	4,800	5,545	6,702	7,590

March 9, 1883; organized October 4, 1884. Edward H. McIntosh (c1822–1901). Dakota territorial legislature 1883; reportedly held up legislation creating counties until one was named for him.

McIntosh	**Oklahoma**				
Eufala	620 sq. mi.				
19,456	16,779	15,562	12,472	12,371	17,829

July 16, 1907. McIntosh family; Creek leaders; descendants of John Mohr McIntosh (see McIntosh (2), Georgia). Family members include: (1) William McIntosh (c1775–1825); tribal leader when Creeks were being moved from Georgia; persuaded Lower Creeks (Cowetas) to cede lands to U.S.; murdered by rival Creeks. (2) Chilly McIntosh (c1800–75); moved party of Creeks from Georgia to site west of the Mississippi River; colonel, 2nd Creek Regiment of Mounted Volunteers in Confederate army. (3) Roley McIntosh (c1790–?); led group of Creeks to Arkansas River; chief of Lower Creeks 1828–59. (4) Daniel N. McIntosh (1822–96); colonel, 1st Creek Regiment of Mounted Volunteers in Confederate army.

McKean	Pennsylvania				
Smethport	982 sq. mi.				
45,936	47,131	50,635	51,915	54,517	56,607

March 26, 1804; organized 1826. Thomas McKean (1734–1817). Delaware Assembly 1752–59; Continental Congress 1774–83; signer of Declaration of Independence 1776; signer of Articles of Confederation 1778; Pennsylvania chief justice 1777–79; governor of Pennsylvania 1799–1808.

McKenzie	North Dakota				
Watford City	2,742 sq. mi.				
5,737	6,383	7,132	6,127	7,296	6,849

March 9, 1883; abolished 1896; recreated May 24, 1901; organized March 16, 1905. Alexander McKenzie (1851–1922). Northern Pacific construction gang leader 1867–72; Burleigh County sheriff 1876–85; instrumental in moving Dakota territorial capital from Yankton to Bismarck.

McKinley	New Mexico				
Gallup	5,449 sq. mi.				
74,798	60,686	56,449	43,208	37,209	27,451

February 23, 1899. William McKinley (1843–1901). Enlisted as private in Union army 1861; brevet major 1865; U.S. representative from Ohio 1877–84 and 1885–91; governor of Ohio 1892–96; 25th president of the U.S. 1897–1901; assassinated September 6, 1901; died September 14, 1901.

McLean	Illinois				
Bloomington	1,184 sq. mi.				
150,433	129,180	119,149	104,389	83,877	76,577

December 25, 1830. John McLean (1791–1830). First U.S. representative from Illinois 1818; Illinois House of Representatives 1820 and Speaker 1826–28; U.S. senator 1823–30.

McLean	Kentucky				
Calhoun	254 sq. mi.				
9,938	9,628	10,090	9,062	9,355	10,021

February 6, 1854. Alney McLean (1779–1841). Kentucky House of Representatives 1812–13; captain, War of 1812; U.S. representative 1815–17 and 1819–21; judge of Kentucky 14th District 1821–41.

McLean	North Dakota				
Washburn	2,110 sq. mi.				
9,311	10,457	12,383	11,251	14,030	18,824

March 8, 1883; organized November 1, 1883. John A. McLean (1849–1916). Construction supplier to Northern Pacific Railroad; mayor of Bismarck 1883; delegation to Washington to open Black Hills to mining.

McLennan	Texas				
Waco	1,042 sq. mi.				
213,517	189,123	170,755	147,553	150,091	130,194

January 22, 1850; organized August 5, 1850. Neil McLennan (c1787–1867). Surveyor; arrived in Texas 1835; settled near Waco 1845.

McLeod	Minnesota				
Glencoe	492 sq. mi.				
34,898	32,030	29,657	27,662	24,401	22,198

March 1, 1856. *Martin McLeod* (1813–60). Fur trader; managed trading posts in western Wisconsin Territory (Minnesota); first Minnesota territorial legislature 1849–53.

McMinn	Tennessee				
Athens	430 sq. mi.				
49,015	42,383	41,878	35,462	33,662	32,024

November 13, 1819. Joseph McMinn (1758–1824). Continental army 1776; Tennessee Constitutional Convention 1796; Tennessee Senate 1796–1812, Speaker 1805–11; governor of Tennessee 1815–21.

McMullen   **Texas**
Tilden   1,113 sq. mi.
851   817   789   1,095   1,116   1,187
February 1, 1858; organized 1877. John McMullen (1785–1853). Established colony of Irish immigrants in Mexican Texas 1828; provisional government of Texas Republic; murdered January 20, 1853.

McNairy   **Tennessee**
Selmer   560 sq. mi.
24,653   22,422   22,525   18,396   18,085   20,390
October 8, 1823. John McNairy (1762–1837). Judge, Territory South of the River Ohio 1790; Tennessee Constitutional Convention 1796; U.S. judge in Tennessee 1797–1834.

McPherson   **Kansas**
McPherson   900 sq. mi.
29,554   27,268   26,855   24,778   24,285   23,670
February 26, 1867; organized 1870. *James Birdseye McPherson* (1828–64). Graduated West Point 1849; 2nd lieutenant of Engineers 1853; rose to brigadier general 1858–63; killed in action at Atlanta July 22, 1864.

McPherson   **Nebraska**
Tryon   859 sq. mi.
533   546   593   623   735   825
March 31, 1887. James Birdseye McPherson.*

McPherson   **South Dakota**
Leola   1,137 sq. mi.
2,904   3,228   4,027   5,022   5,821   7,071
January 8, 1873; organized March 6, 1884. James Birdseye McPherson.*

Meade   **Kansas**
Meade   978 sq. mi.
4,631   4,247   4,788   4,912   5,505   5,710
March 6, 1873; abolished February 21, 1883; recreated March 7, 1885; organized November 4, 1885. *George Gordon Meade* (1815–72). Graduated West Point 1835; Seminole War 1836; Mexican War, battles of Reseca, Palo Alto, and Monterrey 1846; captain 1846; brigadier and major general of Union Volunteers 1861–62; wounded at Glendale 1862; commanded Army of the Potomac, victorious at Gettysburg 1863.

Meade   **Kentucky**
Brandenburg   309 sq. mi.
26,349   24,170   22,854   18,796   18,938   9,422
December 17, 1823. James M. Meade (?–1813). Volunteer; battle of Tippecanoe 1811; appointed as captain 1812; killed at battle of River Raisin January 22, 1813.

Meade   **South Dakota**
Sturgis   3,471 sq. mi.
24,253   21,878   20,717   16,618   12,044   11,516
February 7, 1889. Fort Meade. Established in Black Hills 1878; named for General George Gordon Meade.*

Meagher   **Montana**
White Sulphur Springs   2,392 sq. mi.
1,932   1,819   2,154   2,122   2,616   2,079
November 16, 1867. Thomas Francis Meagher (1823–67). Banished by British to Tasmania for support of Irish independence 1849; escaped to U.S. 1852; brigadier general of Union Volunteers 1862; secretary of Montana Territory 1865; acting governor of Montana Territory 1865–66; presumed to have fallen from a steamboat on the Missouri River and drowned.

Mecklenburg   **North Carolina**
Charlotte   526 sq. mi.

695,454   511,433   404,270   354,656   272,111   197,052
November 3, 1762 (session). Charlotte Sophia of Mecklenburg-Strelitz. (See Charlotte, Florida.)

Mecklenburg   **Virginia**
Boydton   624 sq. mi.
32,380   29,241   29,444   29,426   31,428   33,497
May 26, 1764 (session); effective March 1, 1765. Charlotte Sophia of Mecklenburg-Strelitz. (See Charlotte, Florida.)

Mecosta   **Michigan**
Big Rapids   556 sq. mi.
40,553   37,308   36,961   27,992   21,051   18,968
April 1, 1840; organized February 11, 1859. Mecosta (?–?). Potawatomi chief; signed treaty with U.S. 1836; name is believed to refer the word "bear" in one way or another.

Medina   **Ohio**
Medina   422 sq. mi.
151,095   122,354   113,150   82,717   65,315   40,417
February 18, 1812; organized 1818. Medina, Saudi Arabia. Holy city of Islam.

Medina   **Texas**
Hondo   1,328 sq. mi.
39,304   27,312   23,164   20,249   18,904   17,013
February 12, 1848; organized August 7, 1848. Medina River. Named for Pedro Medina (?–?), Spanish engineer and scholar, by Alonzo de León who led expedition (c1670) using navigation tables published by Medina to determine latitude and longitude.

Meeker   **Minnesota**
Litchfield   609 sq. mi.
22,644   20,846   20,594   18,810   18,887   18,966
February 23, 1856; organized 1866. Bradley B. Meeker (1813–73). Supreme Court of Minnesota Territory 1849–53; Minnesota Constitutional Convention 1857.

Meigs   **Ohio**
Pomeroy   429 sq. mi.
23,072   22,987   23,641   19,799   22,159   23,227
January 21, 1819. *Return Jonathon Meigs* (1764–1825). Indian fighter; Northwest Territory judge 1802–03; chief justice, Ohio Supreme Court 1803–04; judge, Louisiana Territory 1805–06; judge, Michigan Territory 1807–08; U.S. senator from Ohio 1808–10; governor of Ohio 1810–14; U.S. postmaster general 1814–23.

Meigs   **Tennessee**
Decatur   195 sq. mi.
11,086   8,033   7,431   5,219   5,160   6,080
January 20, 1836. Return Jonathon Meigs.*

Mellette   **South Dakota**
White River   1,306 sq. mi.
2,083   2,137   2,249   2,420   2,664   3,046
March 9, 1909; organized May 25, 1911. Arthur C. Mellette (1842–96). Private, Company M, 9th Indiana Infantry; Indiana House of Representatives 1871; editor, *Muncie Times*; governor of Dakota Territory 1889; first governor of South Dakota 1889–93.

Menard   **Illinois**
Petersburg   314 sq. mi.
12,486   11,164   11,700   9,685   9,248   9,639
February 15, 1839. Pierre Menard (1766–1844). Fur trader; lieutenant colonel, Indiana Militia; Indiana Territory legislature 1803–09; first lieutenant governor of Illinois 1818–22.

Menard   **Texas**
Menard   902 sq. mi.
2,360   2,252   2,346   2,646   2,964   4,175
January 22, 1858; organized May 8, 1871. Michel Branaman Menard (1803–56). French Canadian trader; signer of Texas Declaration of Independence 1836; a founder of Galveston 1838; Texas Republic legislature 1840–42.

Mendocino   **California**
Ukiah   3,509 sq. mi.
86,265   80,345   66,738   51,101   51,059   40,854
February 18, 1850; organized 1859. Cape Mendocino. Uncertain origin. (1) Antonio de Mendoza (1490–1552); first viceroy of New Spain (Mexico) 1535–49; sent Coronado expedition to southwest U.S.; viceroy of Peru 1551–52. (2) Lorenzo Suarez de Mendoza (?–?); viceroy of New Spain 1580–83.

Menifee   **Kentucky**
Frenchburg   204 sq. mi.
6,566   5,092   5,117   4,050   4,276   4,789
March 10, 1869. Richard Hickman Menifee (1809–41). Kentucky Commonwealth attorney 1832; Kentucky House of Representatives 1836–37; U.S. representative 1837–39.

Menominee   **Michigan**
Menominee   1,044 sq. mi.
25,326   24,920   26,201   24,587   24,685   25,299
March 15, 1861, as Bleeker; name changed March 19, 1863. Menominee River. Named for *Menominee Indians*; Algonquin linguistic group; lived in northern Michigan and Wisconsin; name means "wild rice people."

Menominee   **Wisconsin**
Keshena   358 sq. mi.
4,562   3,890   3,373   2,607   (a)   (a)
May 1, 1961. Menominee Indians.* County is former Menominee Reservation. [(a) Part of Oconto and Shawano counties.]

Merced   **California**
Merced   1,929 sq. mi.
210,554   178,403   134,560   104,629   90,446   69,780
April 19, 1855. Merced River. Named "El Rio de Nuestra Señora de la Merced" (River of Our Lady of Mercy) by Spanish expedition 1806.

Mercer   **Illinois**
Aledo   561 sq. mi.
16,957   17,290   19,286   17,294   17,149   17,374
January 13, 1825; organized 1835. *Hugh Mercer* (c1725–77). Physician; captain in Braddock's expedition to Fort Duquesne 1756; colonel, 3rd Battalion 1759; colonel, Virginia Militia 1775–76; colonel and brigadier general 1776; mortally wounded at battle of Princeton January 3, 1777; died January 12.

Mercer   **Kentucky**
Harrodsburg   251 sq. mi.
20,817   19,148   19,011   15,960   14,596   14,643
October 17, 1785 (session). Hugh Mercer.*

Mercer   **Missouri**
Princeton   454 sq. mi.
3,757   3,723   4,685   4,910   5,750   7,235
February 14, 1845. Uncertain. (1) Hugh Mercer.* (2) John Francis Mercer (1759–1821); officer in American Revolution 1777–79; Virginia legislature; Continental Congress; represented Maryland at federal Constitutional Convention, walked out in opposition to proposed constitution; Maryland legislature; U.S. representative 1791–94; governor of Maryland 1801–03.

Mercer   **New Jersey**
Trenton   226 sq. mi.
350,761   325,824   307,863   303,968   266,392   229,781
February 22, 1838. Hugh Mercer.*

Mercer   **North Dakota**
Stanton   1,045 sq. mi.
8,644   9,808   9,404   6,175   6,805   8,686
January 14, 1875; organized August 22, 1884. William H. H. Mercer (1844–1901). Union army; early settler in Bismarck; Burleigh County commissioner.

Mercer   **Ohio**
Celina   463 sq. mi.
40,924   39,443   38,334   35,265   32,559   28,311
February 12, 1820; organized 1824. Hugh Mercer.*

Mercer   **Pennsylvania**
Mercer   672 sq. mi.
120,293   121,003   128,299   127,175   127,519   111,954
March 12, 1800; organized 1803. Hugh Mercer.*

Mercer   **West Virginia**
Princeton   420 sq. mi.
62,980   64,980   73,942   63,206   68,206   75,013
March 17, 1837. Hugh Mercer.*

Meriwether   **Georgia**
Greenville   503 sq. mi.
22,534   22,411   21,229   19,461   19,756   21,055
December 24, 1827. David Meriwether (1755–1822). Officer in Continental army; brigadier general, Georgia Militia; Georgia legislature, Speaker; U.S. representative 1801–06.

Merrick   **Nebraska**
Central City   485 sq. mi.
8,204   8,042   8,945   8,751   8,363   8,812
November 4, 1858; organized October 12, 1859. Elvira Merrick De Puy (1828–?). Wife of Henry W. De Puy, member of Nebraska territorial legislature, Speaker, 1860.

Merrimack   **New Hampshire**
Concord   934 sq. mi.
136,225   120,005   98,302   80,925   67,785   63,022
July 1, 1823; effective August 1, 1823. Merrimack River. Indian word, possibly meaning "swift water" or "sturgeon."

Mesa   **Colorado**
Grand Junction   3,328 sq. mi.
116,255   93,145   81,530   54,374   50,715   38,974
February 14, 1883. Grand Mesa. From Spanish word meaning "table"; describes elevated plateaus.

Metcalfe   **Kentucky**
Edmonton   291 sq. mi.
10,037   8,963   9,484   8,177   8,367   9,851
February 1, 1860. Thomas Metcalfe (1780–1855). Captain in War of 1812; Kentucky House of Representatives 1812–16; U.S. representative 1819–28; governor of Kentucky 1828–32; Kentucky Senate 1834; U.S. senator 1848–49.

Miami   **Indiana**
Peru   376 sq. mi.

36,082   36,897   39,820   39,246   38,000   28,201

February 2, 1832; effective April 1, 1832; organized January 2, 1834. *Miami Indians*. Originally lived in Midwest; later moved to Indian Territory (Oklahoma) via Kansas. Origin of name uncertain; most likely from Delaware word *wemiamik,* meaning "all friends," which describes relationship between Delawares and Miamis.

Miami   **Kansas**
Paola   577 sq. mi.
28,351   23,466   21,618   19,254   19,884   19,698
August 30, 1855, as Lykins; name changed June 3, 1861. Miami Indians.*

Miami   **Ohio**
Troy   407 sq. mi.
98,868   93,182   90,381   84,342   72,901   61,309
January 16, 1807. Uncertain. (1) Miami Indians.* (2) Miami River; named for Miami Indians.

Miami-Dade   **Florida**
Miami   1,946 sq. mi.
2,253,362   1,937,094   1,625,781   1,267,792   935,047   495,084
February 4, 1836, as Dade; Dade County and City of Miami consolidated November 13, 1997; name changed December 2, 1997. "Miami" from city of Miami; named from Miami River; Indian word for "very large." "Dade" from Francis Langhorne Dade* (see Dade, Georgia).

Middlesex   **Connecticut**
Middletown   369 sq. mi.
155,071   143,196   129,017   114,816   88,865   67,332
May 2, 1785 (session). Uncertain. (1) Middlesex County, England. (2) Town of Middletown.

Middlesex   **Massachusetts**
East Cambridge   823 sq. mi.
1,465,396   1,398,468   1,367,034   1,397,268   1,238,742   1,064,569
May 10, 1643. Middlesex County, England.

Middlesex   **New Jersey**
New Brunswick   310 sq. mi.
750,162   671,780   595,893   583,813   433,856   264,872
March 1, 1683. Middlesex County, England.

Middlesex   **Virginia**
Saluda   130 sq. mi.
9,932   8,653   7,719   6,295   6,319   6,715
September 21, 1674 (session). Middlesex County, England.

Midland   **Michigan**
Midland   521 sq. mi.
82,874   75,651   73,578   63,769   51,450   35,662
March 2, 1831; organized December 31, 1850; deorganized February 13, 1853; reorganized July 3, 1855. Descriptive of location near geographic center of Michigan's Lower Peninsula.

Midland   **Texas**
Midland   900 sq. mi.
116,009   106,611   82,636   65,433   67,717   25,785
March 4, 1885; organized June 15, 1885. Descriptive of location midway between Fort Worth and El Paso on Texas & Pacific Railway.

Mifflin   **Pennsylvania**
Lewistown   412 sq. mi.

| 46,486 | 46,197 | 46,908 | 45,268 | 44,348 | 43,691 |

September 19, 1789. Thomas Mifflin (1744–1800). Continental Congress 1774–76 and 1782–84, president 1783; major general, Continental army 1779; Speaker, Pennsylvania House of Representatives, 1785–88; federal Constitutional Convention 1787; governor of Pennsylvania 1790–99.

Milam   **Texas**
Cameron   1,017 sq. mi.

| 24,238 | 22,946 | 22,732 | 20,028 | 22,263 | 23,585 |

March 17, 1836; organized 1837. Municipality of Milam. Named for Benjamin R. Milam (1788–1835); War of 1812; traded with Comanches; active in obtaining Mexican independence from Spain and later Texas independence from Mexico; killed during siege of Bexar.

Millard   **Utah**
Fillmore   6,589 sq. mi.

| 12,405 | 11,333 | 8,970 | 6,988 | 7,866 | 9,387 |

October 4, 1851. Millard Fillmore.* (See Fillmore, Minnesota.)

Mille Lacs   **Minnesota**
Milaca   574 sq. mi.

| 22,330 | 18,670 | 18,430 | 15,703 | 14,560 | 15,165 |

May 23, 1857; organized 1860. Mille Lacs Lake. French for "thousand lakes"; a modification of Indian name meaning "all sorts" or "everywhere lake."

Miller   **Arkansas**
Texarkana   624 sq. mi.

| 40,443 | 38,467 | 37,766 | 33,385 | 31,686 | 32,614 |

December 1874. James Miller (1776–1851). U.S. army brevet colonel 1812; brigadier general 1819; governor of Arkansas Territory 1819–25; collector of the Port of Salem, Massachusetts, 1825–49.

Miller   **Georgia**
Colquitt   283 sq. mi.

| 6,383 | 6,280 | 7,038 | 6,397 | 6,908 | 9,023 |

February 26, 1856. Andrew Jackson Miller (1806–56). Attended West Point one year, resigned to become lawyer; Georgia House of Representatives 1836–38; Georgia Senate 1838–56; judge Georgia Superior Court.

Miller   **Missouri**
Tuscumbia   592 sq. mi.

| 23,564 | 20,700 | 18,532 | 15,026 | 13,800 | 13,734 |

February 6, 1837. John Miller (1781–1846). War of 1812, lieutenant colonel, 17th U.S. Infantry; resigned 1818; governor of Missouri 1825–32; U.S. representative 1837–43.

Mills   **Iowa**
Glenwood   437 sq. mi.

| 14,547 | 13,202 | 13,406 | 11,606 | 13,050 | 14,064 |

January 15, 1851. Frederick D. Mills (?–1847). Burlington, Iowa, lawyer 1841; major, U.S. Army 1846; organized company of Iowa Volunteers 1847; died in battle of Churubusco during advance on Mexico City, August 20, 1847.

Mills   **Texas**
Goldthwaite   748 sq. mi.

| 5,151 | 4,531 | 4,477 | 4,212 | 4,467 | 5,999 |

March 15, 1887; organized September 12, 1887. John T. Mills (1817–71). Born in Ireland; established law practice in Texas Republic 1837; successively Texas Republic judge of 3rd, 7th, and 8th Districts.

Milwaukee   **Wisconsin**
Milwaukee   242 sq. mi.

940,164   959,275   964,988   1,054,063   1,036,041   871,047

September 6, 1834; organized August 25, 1835. Milwaukee River. Uncertain Indian derivation; possibly from Potawatomi *meno* (good) and *aki* (land).

Miner   **South Dakota**
Howard   570 sq. mi.
2,884   3,272   3,739   4,454   5,398   6,268

January 8, 1873; organized December 2, 1880. Ephraim Miner and Nelson Miner. Both were members of Dakota Territory legislature when county was created. Ephraim Miner (1833–?); settled in Yankton 1867; surveyor general 1867–70; Dakota territorial legislature 1872–73. Nelson Miner (1827–79); moved to Dakota Territory 1860; organized Company A, Dakota Cavalry; captain 1862–65; Dakota territorial legislature 1869–79.

Mineral   **Colorado**
Creede   876 mi. sq.
831   558   804   786   424   698

March 27, 1893. Descriptive of mineral deposits in the area.

Mineral   **Montana**
Superior   1,220 sq. mi.
3,884   3,315   3,675   2,958   3,037   2,081

August 7, 1914. Descriptive of mineral deposits in the area.

Mineral   **Nevada**
Hawthorne   3,756 sq. mi.
5,071   6,475   6,217   7,051   6,329   5,560

February 10, 1911. Descriptive of mineral deposits in the area.

Mineral   **West Virginia**
Keyser   328 sq. mi.
27,078   26,697   27,234   23,109   22,354   22,333

February 1, 1866. Descriptive of coal and other mineral deposits in the area.

Mingo   **West Virginia**
Williamson   423 sq. mi.
28,253   33,739   37,336   32,780   39,742   47,409

January 30, 1895. Mingo Indians. Detached from Iroquois confederacy c1750; lived in upper Ohio Valley; moved to Indian Territory (Oklahoma) via Kansas 1867.

Minidoka   **Idaho**
Rupert   760 sq. mi.
20,174   19,361   19,718   15,731   14,394   9,785

January 28, 1913. Uncertain. (1) Town of Minidoka. (2) Minidoka Reclamation Project. Both are named from Shoshoni word meaning "broad expanse."

Minnehaha   **South Dakota**
Sioux Falls   810 sq. mi.
148,281   123,809   109,435   95,209   86,575   70,910

April 5, 1862; organized January 4, 1868. Santee Dakota word meaning "waterfall"; popularized in Longfellow's *Song of Hiawatha* as the name of the poem's heroine.

Missaukee   **Michigan**
Lake City   567 sq. mi.
14,478   12,147   10,009   7,126   6,784   7,458

April 1, 1840; organized March 11, 1871. Mesauke (?–?). Ottawa chief; signed treaties with U.S. 1831 and 1833. Name may be from Ottawa *missi* (great) and *aukee* (world, earth, or country).

Mississippi   **Arkansas**
Blytheville   898 sq. mi.
51,979   57,525   59,517   62,060   70,174   82,375
November 1, 1833; effective January 1, 1834. *Mississippi River*. From "Messipi," French rendering of Chippewa (Ojibway) name meaning "great water."

Mississippi   **Missouri**
Charleston   413 sq. mi.
13,427   14,442   15,726   16,647   20,695   22,551
February 14, 1845. Mississippi River.*

Missoula   **Montana**
Missoula   2,598 sq. mi.
95,802   78,687   76,016   58,263   44,663   35,493
February 2, 1865. Salish word of uncertain meaning; most translations involve "water" and "awe."

Mitchell   **Georgia**
Camilla   512 sq. mi.
23,932   20,275   21,114   18,956   19,652   22,528
December 21, 1857. Henry Mitchell (1760–1837). Continental army; wounded at Hanging Rock; brigadier general of Georgia Militia; Georgia legislature.

Mitchell   **Iowa**
Osage   469 sq. mi.
10,874   10,928   12,329   13,108   14,043   13,945
January 15, 1851; organized October 2, 1854. John Mitchell (1815–75). Irish nationalist; arrested and sent to Tasmania 1848; escaped to U.S. 1853; proslavery journalist during Civil War; returned to Ireland.

Mitchell   **Kansas**
Beloit   700 sq. mi.
6,932   7,203   8,117   8,010   8,866   10,320
February 26, 1867; organized 1870. William D. Mitchell (c1841–1865). Private, 2nd Kansas Cavalry 1861; 1st lieutenant, Kentucky Cavalry; killed at Monroe's Crossroads, South Carolina.

Mitchell   **North Carolina**
Bakersville   221 sq. mi.
15,687   14,433   14,428   13,447   13,906   15,143
February 16, 1861. Elisha Mitchell (1793–1857). Professor, University of North Carolina; head of North Carolina's geologic survey; killed from fall while climbing highest peak in eastern U.S. which was later named for him.

Mitchell   **Texas**
Colorado City   910 sq. mi.
9,698   8,016   9,088   9,073   11,255   14,357
August 21, 1876; organized January 10, 1881. Brothers Asa and Eli Mitchell. (1) Asa Mitchell (1795–1865); settled in Austin's colony 1822; battle of Velasco 1832; sergeant, battle of San Jacinto 1836. (2) Eli Mitchell (1797–1870); settled near Velasco 1824; battle of Gonzales 1835.

Mobile   **Alabama**
Mobile   1,233 sq. mi.
399,843   378,643   364,980   317,308   314,301   231,105
August 1, 1812. Mobile Bay, River, and Town. Spanish *maubila* and French *mobile*; possibly derived from Choctaw word for "paddling."

Modoc   **California**
Alturas   3,944 sq. mi.

9,449   9,678   8,610   7,469   8,308   9,678
February 17, 1874. Modoc Indians. Lived in southern Oregon and northern California; Modoc War 1872–73; name may come from Klamath word for "south."

Moffat   **Colorado**
Craig   4,742 sq. mi.
13,184   11,357   13,133   6,525   7,061   5,946
February 27, 1911. David Holliday Moffat (1839–1910). Merchant and railroad builder; Colorado Territory treasurer; president, Rio Grande Railroad 1884–91.

Mohave   **Arizona**
Kingman   13,312 sq. mi.
155,032   93,497   55,865   25,857   7,736   8,510
December 21, 1864. Mojave Indians. Named from *hamol,* meaning "three," and *avi,* meaning "mountain." Clerical error changed spelling of name.

Moniteau   **Missouri**
California   417 sq. mi.
14,827   12,298   12,068   10,742   10,500   10,840
February 14, 1845. Moniteau Creek. French corruption of Indian word for "the deity" or God.

Monmouth   **New Jersey**
Freehold   472 sq. mi.
615,301   553,124   503,173   459,379   334,401   225,327
March 1, 1683. Uncertain. (1) James Scott, Duke of Monmouth and Buccleuch (1649–85); eldest of Charles II's illegitimate children; fought against Dutch and French; claimed right to English throne; executed in Tower of London. (2) Monmouthshire, Wales.

Mono   **California**
Bridgeport   3,044 sq. mi.
12,853   9,956   8,577   4,016   2,213   2,115
April 24, 1861. Mono Indians. From Yokut word *monachi,* meaning "fly people"; Monos used fly pupae from Mono Lake for food and bartering.

Monona   **Iowa**
Onawa   693 sq. mi.
10,020   10,034   11,692   12,069   13,916   16,303
January 15, 1851; organized April 3, 1854. Variation of We-no-nah from Indian legend. (See Winona, Minnesota.)

Monongalia   **West Virginia**
Morgantown   361 sq. mi.
81,866   75,509   75,024   63,714   55,617   60,797
October 7, 1776 (session). Monongahela River. Indian word of unknown meaning. Both spellings are European attempts to approximate Indian name for the river.

Monroe   **Alabama**
Monroeville   1,026 sq. mi.
24,324   23,968   22,651   20,883   22,372   25,732
June 29, 1815. *James Monroe* (1758–1831). Lieutenant, Continental army; wounded at battle of Trenton; Virginia Assembly 1782; Congress of the Confederation 1783–86; U.S. senator 1790–94; U.S. minister to France 1794–96; governor of Virginia 1799–1802 and 1811; U.S. secretary of state in cabinet of President Madison 1811–16; 5th president of U.S. 1817–25.

Monroe   **Arkansas**
Clarendon   607 sq. mi.
10,254   11,333   14,052   15,657   17,327   19,540
November 2, 1829; effective January 1, 1830. James Monroe.*

Monroe **Florida**
Key West 997 sq. mi.
79,589 78,024 63,188 52,586 47,921 29,957
July 3, 1823; effective December 29, 1824. James Monroe.*

Monroe **Georgia**
Forsyth 396 sq. mi.
21,757 17,113 14,610 10,991 10,495 10,523
May 15, 1821. James Monroe.*

Monroe **Illinois**
Waterloo 388 sq. mi.
27,619 22,422 20,117 18,831 15,507 13,282
January 6, 1816. James Monroe.*

Monroe **Indiana**
Bloomington 394 sq. mi.
120,563 108,978 98,785 84,849 59,225 50,080
January 14, 1818; effective April 10, 1819. James Monroe.*

Monroe **Iowa**
Albia 433 sq. mi.
8,016 8,114 9,209 9,357 10,463 11,814
February 17, 1843, as Kishkekosh; organized July 1, 1845; name changed January 19, 1846. James Monroe.*

Monroe **Kentucky**
Tompkinsville 331 sq. mi.
11,756 11,401 12,353 11,642 11,799 13,770
January 19, 1820. James Monroe.*

Monroe **Michigan**
Monroe 551 sq. mi.
145,945 133,600 134,659 118,479 101,120 75,666
July 14, 1817. James Monroe.*

Monroe **Mississippi**
Aberdeen 764 sq. mi.
38,014 36,582 36,404 34,043 33,953 36,543
February 9, 1821. James Monroe.*

Monroe **Missouri**
Paris 646 sq. mi.
9,311 9,104 9,716 9,542 10,688 11,314
January 6, 1831. James Monroe.*

Monroe **New York**
Rochester 659 sq. mi.
735,343 713,968 702,238 711,917 586,387 487,632
February 23, 1821. James Monroe.*

Monroe **Ohio**
Woodsfield 456 sq. mi.
15,180 15,497 17,382 15,739 15,268 15,362
January 29, 1813; organized 1815. James Monroe.*

Monroe   **Pennsylvania**
Stroudsburg   609 sq. mi.
138,687   95,709   69,409   45,422   39,567   33,773
April 1, 1836. James Monroe.*

Monroe   **Tennessee**
Madisonville   635 sq. mi.
38,961   30,541   28,700   23,475   23,316   24,513
November 13, 1819. James Monroe.*

Monroe   **West Virginia**
Union   473 sq. mi.
14,583   12,406   12,873   11,272   11,584   13,123
January 14, 1799. James Monroe.*

Monroe   **Wisconsin**
Sparta   901 sq. mi.
40,899   36,633   35,074   31,610   31,241   31,378
March 21, 1854. James Monroe.*

Montague   **Texas**
Montague   931 sq. mi.
19,117   17,274   17,410   15,326   14,893   17,070
December 24, 1857; organized August 2, 1858. Daniel Montague (1798–1876). Surveyor in Texas Republic; Mexican War 1846–48; fled to Mexico after Civil War.

Montcalm   **Michigan**
Stanton   708 sq. mi.
61,266   53,059   47,555   39,660   35,795   31,013
March 2, 1831; organized March 20, 1850. Louis Joseph, Marquis de Montcalm-Gozon de Saint-Veran (1712–59). Brigadier general in command of French troops in New France (Canada); defeated British at Oswego, Fort William Henry, and Ticonderoga; defeated by British (Wolfe) at Plains of Abraham, Quebec, September 13, 1759; mortally wounded.

Monterey   **California**
Salinas   3,322 sq. mi.
401,762   355,660   290,444   250,071   198,351   130,498
February 18, 1850. Monterey Bay and Town. Named for Gaspar de Zuñiga y Azevedo, Count of Monterey (c1540–1606); viceroy of New Spain (Mexico); ordered Viscaìno expedition which discovered Monterey Bay 1602.

Montezuma   **Colorado**
Cortez   2,037 sq. mi.
23,830   18,672   16,510   12,952   14,024   9,991
April 16, 1889. Montezuma II (1479–1520). Emperor of the Aztecs 1502–20; expanded empire to Honduras; defeated by Spanish under Cortez; executed June 30, 1520.

Montgomery   **Alabama**
Montgomery   790 sq. mi.
223,510   209,085   197,038   167,790   169,210   138,965
December 6, 1816. Lemuel Purnell Montgomery (1786–1814). Officer, War of 1812; killed at battle of Horseshoe Bend.

Montgomery   **Arkansas**
Mount Ida   781 sq. mi.
9,245   7,841   7,771   5,821   5,370   6,680
December 9, 1842. *Richard Montgomery* (1738–75). New York Provincial Congress 1775; brigadier general, Continental army; captured Montreal 1775; killed in unsuccessful assault on Quebec, December 31, 1775.

Montgomery   **Georgia**
Mount Vernon   245 sq. mi.

8,270	7,163	7,011	6,099	6,284	7,901

December 19, 1793. Richard Montgomery.*

Montgomery   **Illinois**
Hillsboro   704 sq. mi.

30,652	30,728	31,686	30,260	31,244	32,460

February 12, 1821. Richard Montgomery.*

Montgomery   **Indiana**
Crawfordsville   505 sq. mi.

37,629	34,436	35,501	33,930	32,089	29,122

December 21, 1822; effective March 1, 1823. Richard Montgomery.*

Montgomery   **Iowa**
Red Oak   424 sq. mi.

11,771	12,076	13,413	12,781	14,467	15,685

January 15, 1851; organized August 5, 1853. Richard Montgomery.*

Montgomery   **Kansas**
Independence   645 sq. mi.

36,252	38,816	42,281	39,949	45,007	46,487

February 26, 1867; organized June 3, 1869. Richard Montgomery.*

Montgomery   **Kentucky**
Mount Sterling   199 sq. mi.

22,554	19,561	20,046	15,364	13,461	13,025

December 14, 1796; effective March 1, 1797. Richard Montgomery.*

Montgomery   **Maryland**
Rockville   496 sq. mi.

873,341	757,027	579,053	522,809	340,928	164,401

September 6, 1776; organized October 1, 1776. Richard Montgomery.*

Montgomery   **Mississippi**
Winona   407 sq. mi.

12,189	12,388	13,366	12,918	13,320	14,470

May 13, 1871. Richard Montgomery.*

Montgomery   **Missouri**
Montgomery City   537 sq. mi.

12,136	11,355	11,537	11,000	11,097	11,555

December 14, 1818. Uncertain. (1) Montgomery County, Kentucky. (2) Richard Montgomery.*

Montgomery   **New York**
Fonda   405 sq. mi.

49,708	51,981	53,439	55,883	57,240	59,594

March 12, 1772, as Tryon; name changed April 2, 1784. Richard Montgomery.*

Montgomery   **North Carolina**
Troy   492 sq. mi.

26,822	23,346	22,469	19,267	18,408	17,260

April 14, 1778 (session). Richard Montgomery.*

Montgomery **Ohio**
Dayton 462 sq. mi.
559,062 573,809 571,697 606,148 527,080 398,441
March 24, 1803. Richard Montgomery.*

Montgomery **Pennsylvania**
Norristown 483 sq. mi.
750,097 678,111 643,621 623,799 516,682 353,068
September 10, 1784. Uncertain. (1) Richard Montgomery.* (2) *John Montgomery* (c1748–94). General, Pennsylvania Militia at battles of Brandywine and Germantown 1777; captain under George Rogers Clark 1778; founded Clarksville; forced by President Washington to abandon participation in French scheme to conquer Florida from Spain; Nickajack expedition 1794; killed by Indians. (3) Montgomeryshire, Wales.

Montgomery **Tennessee**
Clarksville 539 sq. mi.
134,768 100,498 83,342 62,721 55,645 44,186
April 9, 1796. John Montgomery.*

Montgomery **Texas**
Conroe 1,044 sq. mi.
293,768 182,201 128,487 49,479 26,839 24,504
December 14, 1837. Town of Montgomery. Named for Richard Montgomery.*

Montgomery **Virginia**
Christiansburg 388 sq. mi.
83,629 73,913 63,516 47,157 32,923 29,780
October 7, 1776 (session). Richard Montgomery.*

Montmorency **Michigan**
Atlanta 548 sq. mi.
10,315 8,936 7,492 5,247 4,424 4,125
April 1, 1840, as Cheonoquet; name changed March 8, 1843; organized May 21, 1881. Uncertain (1) Francois de Laval-Montmorency (1623–1708); Jesuit priest; ordained 1647; first Roman Catholic bishop of Quebec 1674; Quebec Council 1659. (2) Henri, 2nd Duke de Montmorency (1595–1632); purchased lieutenant-generalship of New France (Canada) c1690; never visited North America; possibly viceroy of New France 1620–24.

Montour **Pennsylvania**
Danville 131 sq. mi.
18,236 17,735 16,675 16,508 16,730 16,001
May 3, 1850. Uncertain. (1) Catherine (or Elizabeth) Montour (c1684–c1752); possible French and Indian ancestry; Indian interpreter of French and English; persuaded Iroquois not to attack settlers 1712. (2) Montour Ridge; mountain ridge named for Catherine Montour.

Montrose **Colorado**
Montrose 2,241 sq. mi.
33,432 24,423 24,352 18,366 18,286 15,220
February 11, 1883. City of Montrose. Named for Sir Walter Scott's *Legend of Montrose*.

Moody **South Dakota**
Flandreau 520 sq. mi.
6,595 6,507 6,692 7,622 8,810 9,252
January 8, 1873. Gideon Curtis Moody (1832–1904). Indiana House of Representatives 1861; Union army, captain through colonel; congressional delegate from Dakota Territory 1867–69 and 1874–75; Dakota Territory Supreme Court 1878–83; U.S. senator from South Dakota 1889–91.

Moore   **North Carolina**
Carthage   698 sq. mi.

74,769	59,013	50,505	39,048	36,733	33,129

April 18, 1784 (session). Alfred Moore (1755–1810). Captain, Continental army; attorney general of North Carolina 1782; U.S. Supreme Court 1799–1804.

Moore   **Tennessee**
Lynchburg   129 sq. mi.

5,740	4,721	4,510	3,568	3,454	3,948

December 14, 1871. William Moore (1786–1871). Tennessee Militia, War of 1812; major general; Tennessee House of Representatives 1825–27.

Moore   **Texas**
Dumas   900 sq. mi.

20,121	17,865	16,575	14,060	14,773	13,349

August 21, 1876; organized July 6, 1892. Edwin Ward Moore (1810–65). Lieutenant, U.S. navy; resigned to command Republic of Texas Navy 1839; raided Mexican coast 1841.

Mora   **New Mexico**
Mora   1,931 sq. mi.

5,180	4,264	4,205	4,673	6,028	8,720

February 1, 1860. Town of Mora. From Spanish *demora,* meaning "to camp" or "to stop over."

Morehouse   **Louisiana**
Bastrop   794 sq. mi.

31,021	31,938	34,803	32,463	33,709	32,038

March 25, 1844. Abraham Morhouse (?–1813). Claimed to be colonel in New York Militia; early settler in northern Louisiana. Letter "e" was added to parish name.

Morgan   **Alabama**
Decatur   582 sq. mi.

111,064	100,043	90,231	77,306	60,454	52,924

February 6, 1818, as Cotaco; name changed June 14, 1821. *Daniel Morgan* (1736–1802). Teamster under General Braddock 1755; lieutenant in Pontiac's War 1764; captain in Dunmore's War 1774; captain, Virginia Riflemen 1775; captured at Quebec 1775; colonel, Virginia Regiment 1776; brigadier general at Saratoga 1780; defeated British at Cowpens 1781; commanded troops against Whiskey Rebellion 1794; U.S. representative from Virginia 1797–99.

Morgan   **Colorado**
Fort Morgan   1,285 sq. mi.

27,171	21,939	22,513	20,105	21,192	18,074

February 19, 1889. Fort Morgan. Named for Christopher A. Morgan (?–1866). Private, 39th Ohio Volunteers 1861; rose to rank of colonel on staff of General Pope; inspector general at St. Louis.

Morgan   **Georgia**
Madison   350 sq. mi.

15,457	12,883	11,572	9,904	10,280	11,899

December 10, 1807. Daniel Morgan.*

Morgan   **Illinois**
Jacksonville   569 sq. mi.

36,616	36,397	37,502	36,174	36,571	35,568

January 31, 1823. Daniel Morgan.*

Morgan   **Indiana**
Martinsville   406 sq. mi.

66,689   55,920   51,999   44,176   33,875   23,726
December 31, 1821; effective February 15, 1822. Daniel Morgan.*

Morgan   **Kentucky**
West Liberty   381 sq. mi.
13,948   11,648   12,103   10,019   11,056   13,624
December 7, 1822. Daniel Morgan.*

Morgan   **Missouri**
Versailles   597 sq. mi.
19,309   15,574   13,807   10,068   9,476   10,207
January 5, 1833. Daniel Morgan.*

Morgan   **Ohio**
McConnelsville   418 sq. mi.
14,897   14,194   14,241   12,375   12,747   12,836
December 29, 1817; organized 1819. Daniel Morgan.*

Morgan   **Tennessee**
Wartburg   522 sq. mi.
19,757   17,300   16,604   13,619   14,304   15,727
October 15, 1817. Daniel Morgan.*

Morgan   **Utah**
Morgan   609 sq. mi.
7,129   5,528   4,917   3,983   2,837   2,519
January 17, 1862. Jedediah Morgan Grant (1816–56). Baptized as Mormon 1833; ordained 1835; missionary in South; counselor to Brigham Young.

Morgan   **West Virginia**
Berkeley Springs   229 sq. mi.
14,943   12,128   10,711   8,547   8,376   8,276
February 9, 1820. Daniel Morgan.*

Morrill   **Nebraska**
Bridgeport   1,424 sq. mi.
5,440   5,423   6,085   5,813   7,057   8,263
November 12, 1908. Charles Henry Morrill (1843–1928). Private, Union army 1863; private secretary to Nebraska Governor Nance 1879; University of Nebraska Board of Regents 1889–99, president 1892; financed geological expeditions throughout Nebraska.

Morris   **Kansas**
Council Grove   697 sq. mi.
6,104   6,198   6,419   6,432   7,392   8,485
August 30, 1855, as Wise; organized and name changed February 11, 1859. Thomas Morris (1776–1844). Ohio House of Representatives 1806–08, 1810, and 1820–21; Ohio Senate 1813–15, 1821–23, 1825–29, and 1831–33; U.S. senator 1833–39; abolitionist; U.S. vice presidential nominee of Liberty Party 1844.

Morris   **New Jersey**
Morristown   469 sq. mi.
470,212   421,353   407,630   383,454   261,620   164,371
March 15, 1739. Lewis Morris (1671–1746). Superior Court of New York and New Jersey 1692, chief justice 1710–38; governor of New Jersey at various times 1703–46.

Morris   **Texas**
Daingerfield   255 sq. mi.

13,048   13,200   14,629   12,310   12,576   9,433

March 6, 1875. William W. Morris (1805–83). District court judge; Texas legislature; interested in railroads in eastern Texas.

Morrison   **Minnesota**
Little Falls   1,125 sq. mi.
31,712   29,604   29,311   26,949   26,641   25,832

February 25, 1856. Brothers Allan and William Morrison. (1) Allan Morrison (1803–77) worked various trading posts; Minnesota territorial legislature. (2) William (1785–1866) also operated trading posts; first recorded visit to Itasca Lake, source of Mississippi River 1804.

Morrow   **Ohio**
Mount Gilead   406 sq. mi.
31,628   27,749   26,480   21,348   19,405   17,168

February 24, 1848. Jeremiah Morrow (1771–1852). Ohio territorial House of Representatives 1801–02; Ohio Senate 1803 and 1827; U.S. representative 1803–13 and 1840–43; U.S. senator 1813–19; governor of Ohio 1822–26; Ohio House of Representatives 1829 and 1835.

Morrow   **Oregon**
Heppner   2,032 sq. mi.
10,995   7,625   7,519   4,465   4,871   4,783

February 16, 1885. Jackson L. Morrow (?–?). Lieutenant in Indian wars; merchant; Oregon legislature 1876 and 1885.

Morton   **Kansas**
Elkhart   730 sq. mi.
3,496   3,480   3,454   3,576   3,354   2,610

February 18, 1886; organized November 18, 1886. *Oliver Hazard Perry Throck Morton* (1823–77). Circuit judge 1852; governor of Indiana 1861–67; U.S. senator 1867–77.

Morton   **North Dakota**
Mandan   1,926 sq. mi.
25,303   23,700   25,177   20,310   20,992   19,295

January 8, 1873; organized February 28, 1881. Oliver Morton.*

Motley   **Texas**
Matador   989 sq. mi.
1,426   1,532   1,950   2,178   2,870   3,963

August 21, 1876; organized February 25, 1891. Dr. Junius William Mottley (1812–36). Signer, Texas Declaration of Independence 1836; killed at battle of San Jacinto April 21, 1836; clerical error caused misspelling of county name.

Moultrie   **Illinois**
Sullivan   336 sq. mi.
14,287   13,930   14,546   13,263   13,635   13,171

February 16, 1843. William Moultrie (1730–1805). South Carolina Militia in Cherokee War 1761; major general, Continental army; South Carolina legislature; governor of South Carolina 1785–87 and 1792–94.

Mountrail   **North Dakota**
Stanley   1,824 sq. mi.
6,631   7,021   7,679   8,437   10,077   9,418

January 4, 1873; abolished November 30, 1892; recreated January 29, 1909. Joseph Mountraille (?–?). Voyageur and mail carrier.

Mower   **Minnesota**
Austin   712 sq. mi.
38,603   37,385   40,390   43,783   48,498   42,277

February 20, 1855; organized March 1, 1856. John E. Mower (1815–79). Minnesota territorial legislature 1854–55; Minnesota House of Representatives 1874–75.

Muhlenberg   **Kentucky**
Greenville   475 sq. mi.
31,839   31,318   32,238   27,537   27,791   32,501
December 14, 1798; effective May 15, 1799. John Peter Gabriel Muhlenberg (1746–1807). Virginia House of Burgesses 1774; Continental army, colonel and brigadier general (1777) major general (1783); Pennsylvania Supreme Executive Council 1785–87; U.S. representative 1789–90, 1793–94, and 1799–1800; U.S. senator 1801–02; collector of Port of Philadelphia 1803–07; extensive land holdings in Kentucky.

Multnomah   **Oregon**
Portland   435 sq. mi.
660,486   583,887   562,640   556,667   522,813   471,537
December 22, 1854. Multnomah Indians; Chinnokan tribe living on island in Columbia River; extinct from disease by 1835. Unknown origin of name.

Murray   **Georgia**
Chatsworth   344 sq. mi.
36,506   26,147   19,685   12,986   10,447   10,676
December 3, 1832. Thomas W. Murray (1790–1832). Georgia legislature 1818, Speaker 1825; nominated for U.S. Congress but died before election.

Murray   **Minnesota**
Slayton   704 sq. mi.
9,165   9,660   11,507   12,508   14,743   14,801
May 23, 1857; organized March 5, 1879. William Pitt Murray (1825–1910). Minnesota territorial legislature 1852–53 and 1857; Minnesota House of Representatives 1863 and 1868; Minnesota Senate 1866–67 and 1875–76.

Murray   **Oklahoma**
Sulphur   418 sq. mi.
12,623   12,042   12,147   10,669   10,622   10,775
July 16, 1907. William Henry "Alfalfa Bill" Murray (1869–1956). President of Oklahoma Constitutional Convention 1906; Oklahoma House of Representatives 1907–09; U.S. representative 1913–17; governor of Oklahoma 1931–35.

Muscatine   **Iowa**
Muscatine   439 sq. mi.
41,722   39,907   40,436   37,181   33,840   32,148
December 7, 1836. Muscatine Island. Large island in Mississippi River; named from Fox word for "prairie."

Muscogee   **Georgia**
Columbus   216 sq. mi.
186,291   179,278   170,108   167,377   158,623   118,028
December 11, 1826; organized December 24, 1827. *Five Civilized Tribes.* Indian name applied to a loose confederation in the southeast U.S. that included Creeks, Choctaws, Chickasaws, Seminoles, and Cherokees.

Muskegon   **Michigan**
Muskegon   509 sq. mi.
170,200   158,983   157,589   157,426   149,943   121,545
February 4, 1859. Muskegon River. From Chippewa name meaning "swampy place."

Muskingum   **Ohio**
Zanesville   665 sq. mi.
84,585   82,068   83,340   77,826   79,159   74,535
January 7, 1804; effective March 1, 1804. Muskingum River. From Delaware word for "swampy land."

Muskogee   **Oklahoma**
Muskogee   814 sq. mi.

| 69,451 | 68,078 | 66,939 | 59,542 | 61,866 | 65,573 |

July 16, 1907. Five Civilized Tribes.*

Musselshell   **Montana**
Roundup   1,867 sq. mi.

| 4,497 | 4,106 | 4,428 | 3,734 | 4,888 | 5,408 |

February 11, 1911. Musselshell River. Descriptive of shells found along the river.

N

Nacogdoches   **Texas**
Nacogdoches   947 sq. mi.

| 59,203 | 54,753 | 46,786 | 36,362 | 28,046 | 30,326 |

March 17, 1836; organized 1837. Mexican department of Nacogdoches. Named for Nacogdoches Indians, one of the major Indian tribes of Texas.

Nance   **Nebraska**
Fullerton   441 sq. mi.

| 4,038 | 4,275 | 4,740 | 5,142 | 5,635 | 6,512 |

February 13, 1879; organized June 21, 1879. Albinus Nance (1848–1911). Private, Illinois Cavalry 1864; Nebraska legislature 1874–78, Speaker 1877; governor of Nebraska 1879–83.

Nantucket   **Massachusetts**
Nantucket   48 sq. mi.

| 9,520 | 6,012 | 5,087 | 3,774 | 3,559 | 3,484 |

June 22, 1695. Nantucket Island. Uncertain Indian derivation; most suggestions refer to water or island.

Napa   **California**
Napa   754 sq. mi.

| 124,279 | 110,765 | 99,199 | 79,140 | 65,890 | 46,603 |

February 18, 1850. Uncertain. Spanish rendering of Napa word for "fish harpoon" or "abundant," among other possibilities.

Nash   **North Carolina**
Nashville   540 sq. mi.

| 87,420 | 76,677 | 67,153 | 59,122 | 61,002 | 59,919 |

November 15, 1777 (session). Francis Nash (c1742–77). North Carolina House of Commons 1764; Assembly 1771 and 1773–75; Provincial Council 1775; Continental army, lieutenant colonel (1775) and brigadier general (1777); mortally wounded at battle of Germantown.

Nassau   **Florida**
Fernandina Beach   652 sq. mi.

| 57,663 | 43,941 | 32,894 | 20,626 | 17,189 | 12,811 |

December 29, 1824. Nassau River. Named for Nassau, capital of Bahama Islands.

Nassau   **New York**
Mineola   287 sq. mi.

| 1,334,544 | 1,287,348 | 1,321,582 | 1,428,080 | 1,300,171 | 672,765 |

April 27, 1898; organized 1899. William Nassau, Prince of Orange, King William III* (see King William, Virginia). Long Island was called Nassau Island during 17th century.

Natchitoches   **Louisiana**
Natchitoches   1,255 sq. mi.

| 39,080 | 36,689 | 39,863 | 35,219 | 35,653 | 38,144 |

April 10, 1805. Natchitoches Indians. Uncertain derivation; most suggestions refer to "eaters" of local fruits.

Natrona   **Wyoming**
Casper   5,340 sq. mi.
66,533   61,226   71,856   51,264   49,623   31,437
March 9, 1888. Descriptive of local deposits of natron or sodium carbonate.

Navajo   **Arizona**
Holbrook   9,953 sq. mi.
97,470   77,658   67,629   47,715   37,994   29,446
March 21, 1895. Navajo Indians. Uncertain Spanish or Indian origin; possibilities include (1) Spanish *nava* (field) and suffix *ajo* (small); (2) pueblo of Navahu, New Mexico; (3) Spanish *navaja,* meaning "knife."

Navarro   **Texas**
Corsicana   1,008 sq. mi.
45,124   39,926   35,323   31,150   34,423   39,916
April 25, 1846; organized July 13, 1846. José Antonio Navarro (1795–1870). Supporter of Mexican independence from Spain, Texas independence from Mexico, and Texas secession from U.S.; Mexican state legislator, favored slavery and Texas independence; signer of Texas Declaration of Independence 1836; Texas Congress; Texas Constitutional Convention 1845.

Nelson   **Kentucky**
Bardstown   423 sq. mi.
37,477   29,710   27,584   23,477   22,168   19,521
October 18, 1784 (session); effective January 1, 1785. *Thomas Nelson* (1738–89). Virginia House of Burgesses 1761 and 1774–75; Continental Congress 1775–77; signer of Declaration of Independence 1776; Virginia Assembly 1779–80; governor of Virginia 1781; commander in chief of Virginia Militia 1779–80.

Nelson   **North Dakota**
Lakota   982 sq. mi.
3,715   4,410   5,233   5,776   7,034   8,090
March 2, 1883; organized June 9, 1883. Nelson E. Nelson (1830–1913). One of first homesteaders in North Dakota; collector of customs at Pembina; Dakota territorial legislature 1883.

Nelson   **Virginia**
Lovingston   472 sq. mi.
14,445   12,778   12,204   11,702   12,752   14,042
December 25, 1807. Thomas Nelson.*

Nemaha   **Kansas**
Seneca   718 sq. mi.
10,717   10,446   11,211   11,825   12,897   14,341
August 30, 1855. *Nemaha River.* Sioux name of unknown meaning; most translations refer to river or stream.

Nemaha   **Nebraska**
Auburn   409 sq. mi.
7,576   7,980   8,367   8,976   9,099   10,973
November 23, 1854, as Forney; name changed March 7, 1855. *Nemaha River.**

Neosho   **Kansas**
Erie   572 sq. mi.
16,997   17,035   18,967   18,812   19,455   20,348
August 30, 1855, as Dorn; name changed June 3, 1861; organized 1864. Neosho River. Unknown Indian origin; most translations refer to river or water.

Neshoba   **Mississippi**
Philadelphia   570 sq. mi.

| 28,684 | 24,800 | 23,789 | 20,802 | 20,927 | 25,730 |

December 23, 1833. Choctaw word meaning "wolf."

Ness   **Kansas**
Ness City   1,075 sq. mi.

| 3,454 | 4,033 | 4,498 | 4,791 | 5,470 | 6,322 |

February 26, 1867; organized 1873; deorganized 1874; reorganized 1880. Noah V. Ness (?–1864). Corporal, Company G, 7th Kansas Cavalry; mortally wounded at Abbeville, Mississippi, August 19, 1864.

Nevada   **Arkansas**
Prescott   620 sq. mi.

| 9,955 | 10,101 | 11,097 | 10,111 | 10,700 | 14,781 |

March 20, 1871. State of Nevada. The shape of the county was thought to match Nevada's; it roughly would if rotated 180°.

Nevada   **California**
Nevada City   958 sq. mi.

| 92,033 | 78,510 | 51,645 | 26,346 | 20,911 | 19,888 |

April 25, 1851; organized May 28, 1851. Town of Nevada City. Spanish for "snow covered."

Newaygo   **Michigan**
White Cloud   842 sq. mi.

| 47,874 | 38,202 | 34,917 | 27,992 | 24,160 | 21,567 |

April 1, 1840; organized January 27, 1851. Uncertain. Could be one of three Indian chiefs, Nuwagon, Naywawgoo (may be same person), or Ningwegon, who signed various treaties with U.S. between 1819 and 1855.

Newberry   **South Carolina**
Newberry   631 sq. mi.

| 36,108 | 33,172 | 31,242 | 29,273 | 29,416 | 31,771 |

March 12, 1785. Uncertain. (1) Captain John Newberry (?–?); served under General Sumter during Revolutionary War. (2) Family or families of early settlers named Newberry or Newbury. (3) Towns in America or England named Newbury.

New Castle   **Delaware**
Wilmington   426 sq. mi.

| 500,265 | 441,946 | 398,115 | 385,856 | 307,446 | 218,879 |

August 8, 1673. Town of New Castle. Name of uncertain origin. (1) Town of Newcastle, England. (2) William Cavendish, Duke of Newcastle (1592–1676); Earl of Newcastle 1628; governor of Prince of Wales (later Charles II); loyalist during English Civil War; elevated to duke by Charles II 1665.

New Hanover   **North Carolina**
Wilmington   199 sq. mi.

| 160,307 | 120,284 | 103,471 | 82,996 | 71,742 | 63,272 |

November 27, 1729 (session). English royal house of Hanover.

New Haven   **Connecticut**
New Haven   606 sq. mi.

| 824,008 | 804,219 | 761,337 | 744,948 | 660,315 | 545,784 |

May 10, 1666 (session). New Haven Colony and City. Descriptive of harbor called Fayre Haven and symbolic of colonists' optimism.

New Kent   **Virginia**
New Kent   210 sq. mi.

| 13,462 | 10,445 | 8,781 | 5,300 | 4,504 | 3,995 |

November 20, 1654 (session). Uncertain. (1) Kent County, England. (2) Kent Island, Maryland; named for Kent, England.

New London   **Connecticut**
New London   666 sq. mi.

259,088   254,957   238,409   230,348   185,745   144,821
May 10, 1666 (session). City of New London. Named for London, England.

New Madrid   **Missouri**
New Madrid   678 sq. mi.
19,760   20,928   22,945   23,420   31,350   39,444
October 1, 1812. Former Spanish colonial district of New Madrid. Named for Madrid, Spain.

Newport   **Rhode Island**
Newport   104 sq. mi.
85,433   87,194   81,383   94,559   81,891   61,539
June 22, 1703, as Rhode Island; name changed June 16, 1729. Town of Newport. Named for village of Newport, Isle of Wight, England.

Newport News   **Virginia**
(Independent City)   68 sq. mi.
180,150   170,045   144,903   138,177   113,662   82,233[a]
1634, as Warwick River; name changed to Warwick 1643; Newport News incorporated as independent city January 16, 1886; Warwick County incorporated as City of Warwick July 16, 1952; merged into City of Newport News July 1, 1958. Uncertain. (1) New Port Newce after port town of Newce, County Cork, Ireland. (2) Sir William Newce (?–1621) and/or Thomas Newce (?–1623); brothers; Thomas succeeded William as superintendent of the London Company's lands in Virginia. (3) Combination of William Newce with Sir Christopher Newport (c1560–1621); British navy and privateer; commanded Jamestown expedition 1607; four subsequent voyages to Virginia between 1608 and 1611; died on expedition to Java for East India Company. [(a) Includes Warwick County (39,875).]

Newton   **Arkansas**
Jasper   823 sq. mi.
8,608   7,666   7,756   5,844   5,963   8,685
December 14, 1842. Thomas Willoughby Newton (1804–53). Arkansas Senate 1844–48; U.S. representative 1845–46.

Newton   **Georgia**
Covington   276 sq. mi.
62,001   41,808   34,489   26,282   20,999   20,185
December 24, 1821. *John Newton* (c1752–80). South Carolina's Revolutionary Army; with friend, William Jasper* (see Jasper, Georgia), rescued American prisoners and captured British guards near Savannah 1775; captured at Charleston; died of small pox 1780.

Newton   **Indiana**
Kentland   402 sq. mi.
14,566   13,551   14,844   11,606   11,502   11,006
February 7, 1835; abolished January 29, 1839; recreated December 8, 1859. John Newton.*

Newton   **Mississippi**
Decatur   578 sq. mi.
21,838   20,291   19,944   18,983   19,517   22,681
February 25, 1836. Isaac Newton (1642–1727). English mathematician and natural philosopher; professor at Cambridge 1669; fellow of Royal Society 1671; knighted by Queen Anne 1705.

Newton   **Missouri**
Neosho   626 sq. mi.
52,636   44,445   40,555   32,901   30,093   28,240
December 30, 1838. John Newton.*

Newton   **Texas**
Newton   933 sq. mi.

15,072   13,569   13,254   11,657   10,372   10,832
April 22, 1846; organized July 13, 1846. John Newton.*

New York   **New York**
New York   23 sq. mi.
1,537,195   1,487,536   1,428,285   1,539,233   1,698,281   1,960,101
November 1, 1683. King James II, Duke of York.* (See Albany, New York.)

Nez Perce   **Idaho**
Lewiston   849 sq. mi.
37,410   33,754   33,220   30,376   27,066   22,658
February 4, 1864. Nez Perce Indians. French for "pierced nose" or from *nez presse,* meaning "pressed nose" or "flattened nose."

Niagara   **New York**
Lockport   523 sq. mi.
219,846   220,756   227,354   235,720   242,269   189,992
March 11, 1808. Niagara River. European rendering of Indian name referring to "bisected bottom lands."

Nicholas   **Kentucky**
Carlisle   197 sq. mi.
6,813   6,725   7,157   6,508   6,677   7,532
December 18, 1799; effective June 1, 1800. George Nicholas (1754–99). Captain; colonel; Virginia House of Delegates 1781; Virginia Constitutional Convention 1788; Kentucky Constitutional Convention 1792; first attorney general of Kentucky.

Nicholas   **West Virginia**
Summersville   649 sq. mi.
26,562   26,775   28,126   22,552   25,414   27,696
January 30, 1818. Wilson Cary Nicholas (1761–1820). Commanded General Washington's Life Guard 1783; Virginia House of Delegates 1784–88, 1789, and 1794–1800; U.S. senator 1799–1804; collector of the Port of Norfolk 1804–07; U.S. representative 1807–09; governor of Virginia 1814–16.

Nicollet   **Minnesota**
Saint Peter   452 sq. mi.
29,771   28,076   26,929   24,518   23,196   20,929
March 5, 1853. Joseph Nicolas Nicollet (1786–1843). French mathematician; emigrated to New Orleans 1832; geographer and explorer; led government exploring and surveying expeditions; made canoe trip from Fort Snelling to Lake Itasca, source of the Mississippi River 1836.

Niobrara   **Wyoming**
Lusk   2,626 sq. mi.
2,407   2,499   2,924   2,924   3,750   4,701
February 14, 1911. Niobrara River. Omaha-Poncah name for river, meaning "water spreading."

Noble   **Indiana**
Albion   411 sq. mi.
46,275   37,877   35,443   31,382   28,162   25,075
February 7, 1835; effective June 1, 1835; organized February 6, 1836; effective March 1, 1836. Uncertain. (1) James Noble (1785–1831); Indiana Constitutional Committee 1816; Indiana House of Representatives 1816; U.S. senator 1816–31. (2) Noah Noble (1794–1844); brother of James; Indiana House of Representatives 1824; governor of Indiana 1831–37.

Noble   **Ohio**
Caldwell   399 sq. mi.
14,058   11,336   11,310   10,428   10,982   11,750
March 11, 1851. Uncertain. (1) James Noble (?–?); pioneer settler. (2) John Noble (?–1831); early settler. (3) John Noble (1802–?); son of John Noble (?–1831); county commissioner. (4) Warren Noble (1820–1903); Ohio legislature 1846–48; U.S. representative 1861–64.

Noble   **Oklahoma**
Perry   732 sq. mi.
11,411   11,045   11,573   10,043   10,376   12,156
1893, as County P; name changed November 6, 1894. John Willock Noble (1831–1912). 3rd Iowa Cavalry 1861; brevet brigadier general 1865; U.S. district attorney for Eastern District of Missouri; 1867; U.S. secretary of the interior 1889–93.

Nobles   **Minnesota**
Worthington   715 sq. mi.
20,832   20,098   21,840   23,208   23,365   22,435
May 23, 1857; organized October 19, 1870. William H. Nobles (1816–76). Minnesota territorial legislature 1854 and 1856; surveyed wagon road intended to go from Minnesota to Rocky Mountains; Union army.

Nodaway   **Missouri**
Maryville   877 sq. mi.
21,912   21,709   21,996   22,467   22,215   24,033
January 2, 1843. Nodaway River. Potawatomi word for "placid."

Nolan   **Texas**
Sweetwater   912 sq. mi.
15,802   16,594   17,359   16,220   18,963   19,808
August 21, 1876; organized January 10, 1881. Phillip Nolan (1771–1801). American filibuster in New Spain (Mexico); involved in James Wilkinson's schemes in western U.S.; built fort near Nacagdoches 1800; killed by Spanish forces 1801.

Nome   **Alaska**
(Census Area)   23,001 sq. mi.
9,196   8,288   6,537   5,749   6,091   6,137
City of Nome. Named for Cape Nome, whose name resulted from a transcription error: a draftsman wrote the notation "? Name" on a manuscript chart for an unnamed cape on the north side of Norton Sound; when transcribed to a British Admiralty chart in 1853, it was written as "C[ape] Nome."

Norfolk   **Massachusetts**
Dedham   400 sq. mi.
650,306   616,087   606,587   605,051   510,256   392,308
March 26, 1793; effective June 20, 1793. Norfolk County, England.

Norfolk   **Virginia**
(Independent City)   54 sq. mi.
234,403   261,229   266,979   307,951   305,872   213,513
February 11, 1845. Norfolk County, England. (Associated counties: Norfolk and Princess Anne [city of Virginia Beach]).

Norman   **Minnesota**
Ada   876 sq. mi.
7,442   7,975   9,379   10,008   11,253   12,909
February 17, 1881. Norwegians, Norsemen, and Normans. Many Minnesota residents are descended from Norwegians.

Northampton   **North Carolina**
Jackson   536 sq. mi.
22,086   20,798   22,584   24,009   26,811   28,432
1741 (session). James Compton, Earl of Northampton (1687–1754).

Northampton   **Pennsylvania**
Easton   374 sq. mi.
267,066   247,105   225,418   214,368   201,412   185,243
October 14, 1751 (session). Northamptonshire, England.

Northampton   **Virginia**
Eastville   207 sq. mi.
13,093   13,061   14,625   14,442   16,966 ·   17,300
1634, as Accawmack; name changed 1643. Uncertain. (1) Northamptonshire, England. (2) Spencer Compton, 2nd Earl of Northampton (1601–43); courtier of Charles I; made Earl of Northampton 1630; killed during English Civil War.

North Slope   **Alaska**
Barrow   88,817 sq. mi.
7,385   5,979   4,199   2,663   2,133   [a]
July 1, 1972. Descriptive of region between Brooks Range and Arctic Ocean. [(a) Part of 2nd and 4th Judicial Districts.]

Northumberland   **Pennsylvania**
Sunbury   460 sq. mi.
94,556   96,771   100,381   99,190   104,138   117,115
March 21, 1772. Northumberland County, England.

Northumberland   **Virginia**
Heathsville   192 sq. mi.
12,259   10,524   9,828   9,239   10,185   10,012
October 12, 1648 (session). Northumberland County, England.

Northwest Arctic   **Alaska**
Kotzebue   35,898 sq. mi.
7,208   6,113   4,831   4,434   3,560   3,692
June 1986. Descriptive of location in northwest Alaska. The Arctic Circle bisects the borough.

Norton   **Kansas**
Norton   878 sq. mi.
5,953   5,947   6,689   7,279   8,035   8,808
February 26, 1867, as Norton; organized 1872; name changed to Billings March 6, 1873; renamed Norton February 19, 1874. Orloff Norton (1837–64). Private, 12th Kansas Volunteer Infantry 1861; 2nd lieutenant, 15th Kansas Volunteer Cavalry 1863; captain; killed at Cave Hill, Arkansas, November 12, 1864.

Norton   **Virginia**
(Independent City)   8 sq. mi.
3,904   4,247   4,757   4,001   4,996   [a]
1954. Eckstein Norton (?–1893). President of Louisville & Nashville Railroad at time of opening of Clinch Valley branch 1891. [(a) Part of Wise County.] (Associated county: Wise.)

Nottoway   **Virginia**
Nottoway   315 sq. mi.
15,725   14,993   14,666   14,260   15,141   15,479
December 22, 1788. Uncertain. (1) Nottoway Indians; Iroquoian tribe in southern Virginia; name given by neighboring Algonquins means "enemy" or "adder." (2) Nottoway River; named for the Nottoways.

Nowata   **Oklahoma**
Nowata   565 sq. mi.
10,569   9,992   11,486   9,773   10,848   12,734
July 16, 1907. Town of Nowata. Named from Delaware word *noweta* or *noweeta*, meaning "welcome."

Noxubee   **Mississippi**
Macon   695 sq. mi.
12,548   12,604   13,212   14,288   16,826   20,022
December 23, 1833. Noxubee River. From Choctow word, approximately "stinking water."

Nuckolls   **Nebraska**
Nelson   575 sq. mi.
5,057   5,786   6,726   7,404   8,217   9,609
January 13, 1860; organized June 27, 1871. Uncertain. (1) Stephen Friel Nuckolls (1825–79); Nebraska territorial legislature 1859; congressional delegate from Wyoming Territory 1869–71; Wyoming territorial legislature 1871. (2) Both Stephen Nuckolls and his brother Lafayette Nuckolls (1835–?); Nebraska territorial legislature at age 19.

Nueces   **Texas**
Corpus Christi   836 sq. mi.
313,645   291,145   268,215   237,544   221,573   165,471
April 18, 1846; organized July 12, 1846. Nueces River. Spanish for "pecans."

Nye   **Nevada**
Tonopah   18,147 sq. mi.
32,485   17,781   9,048   5,599   4,374   3,101
February 16, 1864. James Warren Nye (1814–76). District attorney, Madison County, New York, 1839; president, New York City Metropolitan Board of Police, 1857–60; governor of Nevada Territory 1861–64; U.S. senator from Nevada 1864–73.

O

Oakland   **Michigan**
Pontiac   873 sq. mi.
1,194,156   1,083,592   1,011,793   907,871   690,259   396,001
January 12, 1819; organized March 28, 1820. Descriptive of oak trees in area.

Obion   **Tennessee**
Union City   545 sq. mi.
32,450   31,717   32,781   29,936   26,957   29,056
October 24, 1823. Obion River. Indian word for "many prongs."

O'Brien   **Iowa**
Primghar   573 sq. mi.
15,102   15,444   16,972   17,522   18,840   18,970
January 15, 1851; organized April 7, 1860. William Smith O'Brien (1803–64). British House of Commons 1826–39; leader of Irish independence movement 1848; arrested, sentenced to death 1848; commuted to life imprisonment 1849; transported to Tasmania 1849; fully pardoned 1856.

Ocean   **New Jersey**
Toms River   636 sq. mi.
510,916   433,203   346,038   208,470   108,241   56,622
February 15, 1850. Descriptive of location on Atlantic Ocean.

Oceana   **Michigan**
Hart   540 sq. mi.
26,873   22,454   22,002   17,984   16,547   16,105
March 2, 1831; organized April 7, 1851. Uncertain. (1) Descriptive of location on fresh-water "ocean" of Lake Michigan. (2) From James Harrington's utopian book *The Commonwealth of Oceana* 1656.

Ochiltree   **Texas**
Perryton   918 sq. mi.
9,006   9,128   9,588   9,704   9,380   6,024
August 21, 1876; organized February 21, 1889. William Beck Ochiltree (1811–67). Emigrated to Texas 1840; judge, Texas Republic District Court 1842; secretary of the treasury, Texas Republic, 1844; Texas attorney general 1845; Texas legislature 1855; Texas Constitutional Convention 1861; Provisional Congress of Confederate States 1861; colonel of infantry 1861.

Oconee   **Georgia**
Watkinsville   186 sq. mi.

26,225	17,618	12,427	7,915	6,304	7,009

February 25, 1875. Oconee River. Named for Indian village; Cherokee for "place of springs."

Oconee   **South Carolina**
Walhalla   625 sq. mi.

66,215	57,494	48,611	40,728	40,204	39,050

January 29, 1868. Oconee Indians. Cherokee for "place of springs."

Oconto   **Wisconsin**
Oconto   998 sq. mi.

35,634	30,226	28,947	25,553	25,110	26,238

February 6, 1851; organized 1854. Oconto River. Menominee word for "red river" or "place of the pickerel."

Ogemaw   **Michigan**
West Branch   564 sq. mi.

21,645	18,681	16,436	11,903	9,680	9,345

April 1, 1840; abolished March 7, 1867; recreated March 28, 1873; organized April 27, 1875. Ogemakegato (1794–1840). Chief of Saginaw band of Ojibwas; signed four treaties with U.S. 1819–39; petitioned Congress to reimburse Indians for lands 1832.

Ogle   **Illinois**
Oregon   759 sq. mi.

51,032	45,957	46,338	42,867	38,106	33,429

January 16, 1836; organized 1839. Joseph Ogle (1741–1821). Lieutenant and captain in Illinois Territorial Militia.

Oglethorpe   **Georgia**
Lexington   441 sq. mi.

12,635	9,763	8,929	7,598	7,926	9,958

December 19, 1793. James Edward Oglethorpe (1696–1785). British army 1710; House of Commons 1722; colonized Georgia 1733; defeated Spanish force 1742; returned to England 1743; Georgia charter returned to King George II 1752.

Ohio   **Indiana**
Rising Sun   87 sq. mi.

5,623	5,315	5,114	4,289	4,165	4,223

January 4, 1844; effective May 1, 1844. *Ohio River.* French rendering of Iroquois *oheo, oyo,* or *oyoneri,* meaning "beautiful."

Ohio   **Kentucky**
Hartford   594 sq. mi.

22,916	21,105	21,765	18,790	17,725	20,840

December 17, 1798; effective July 1, 1799. Ohio River.*

Ohio   **West Virginia**
Wheeling   106 sq. mi.

47,427	50,871	61,389	64,197	68,437	71,672

October 7, 1776. Ohio River.*

Okaloosa   **Florida**
Crestwiew   936 sq. mi.

170,498	143,776	109,920	88,187	61,175	27,533

June 3, 1915. Blackwater River. From Choctaw name for the river: *oka,* meaning "water," and *lusa,* meaning "black."

Okanogan   **Washington**
Okanogan   5,268 sq. mi.

39,564   33,350   30,639   25,867   25,520   29,131
February 2, 1888. Uncertain. (1) Okanogan River. (2) Okanagon Lake or Mountains. From Indian word for "rendezvous"; refers to a traditional meeting place near present U.S.–Canada border.

Okeechobee   **Florida**
Okeechobee   774 sq. mi.
35,910   29,627   20,264   11,233   6,424   3,454
May 8, 1917. Lake Okeechobee. From Hitchiti words *oki,* meaning "water," and *chubi,* meaning "big."

Okfuskee   **Oklahoma**
Okemah   625 sq. mi.
11,814   11,551   11,125   10,683   11,706   16,948
July 16, 1907. Okfuskee, Alabama. Former Creek village; largest community in Creek confederacy.

Oklahoma   **Oklahoma**
Oklahoma City   709 sq. mi.
660,448   599,611   568,933   526,805   439,506   325,352
1890. Oklahoma Territory. From Choctaw words *okla,* meaning "people," and *humma,* meaning "red."

Okmulgee   **Oklahoma**
Okmulgee   697 sq. mi.
39,685   36,490   39,169   35,358   36,945   44,561
July 16, 1907. Town of Okmulgee. Creek for "bubbling" or "boiling water."

Oktibbeha   **Mississippi**
Starkville   458 sq. mi.
42,902   38,375   36,018   28,752   26,175   24,569
December 23, 1833. Uncertain. One of two streams named Oktibbeha; Indian name for "fighting water" or "ice therein."

Oldham   **Kentucky**
La Grange   189 sq. mi.
46,178   33,263   27,795   14,687   13,388   11,018
December 15, 1823. William Oldham (1753–91). 1st lieutenant in Nelson's independent rifle company 1776; captain 1776; 5th Pennsylvania Regiment 1777; resigned 1779; member of St. Clair's Militia; killed in battle with Miamis.

Oldham   **Texas**
Vega   1,501 sq. mi.
2,185   2,278   2,283   2,258   1,928   1,672
August 21, 1876; organized June 12, 1881. William Simpson Oldham (1813–68). Arkansas General Assembly 1838–42, Speaker 1842; Arkansas Supreme Court 1844; emigrated to Texas 1849; Texas Secession Convention 1861; Confederate senator from Texas 1861–65.

Oliver   **North Dakota**
Center   724 sq. mi.
2,065   2,381   2,495   2,322   2,610   3,091
March 12, 1885; organized May 18, 1885. Harry S. Oliver (1855–1909). Dakota territorial legislature 1885, chairman on committee of county boundaries; North Dakota legislature 1889–93.

Olmsted   **Minnesota**
Rochester   653 sq. mi.
124,277   106,470   92,006   84,104   65,532   48,228
February 20, 1855. Uncertain. (1) David Olmsted (1822–61); Iowa Constitutional Convention 1846; settled in what became Minnesota Territory 1848; Minnesota territorial legislature 1849–50; proprietor of *Minnesota Democrat* 1853; first mayor of St. Paul 1854. (2) Samuel Baldwin Olmstead (1810–78); Iowa Constitutional Convention 1844; Minnesota territorial legislature 1854.

Oneida **Idaho**
Malad City 1,200 sq. mi.
4,125   3,492   3,258   2,864   3,603   4,387
January 22, 1864. City of Oneida, New York, or Lake Oneida. (See Oneida, New York.)

Oneida **New York**
Utica 1,213 sq. mi.
235,469   250,836   253,466   273,037   264,401   222,855
March 15, 1798. *Oneida Indians*. Lived in central New York state; smallest tribe of Iroquois confederacy; sided with colonists during Revolution; name means "standing stone" or "stone people."

Oneida **Wisconsin**
Rhinelander 1,125 sq. mi.
36,776   31,679   31,216   24,427   22,112   20,648
April 11, 1885. Oneida Indians.* Many Oneidas moved from New York to northern Wisconsin.

Onondaga **New York**
Syracuse 780 sq. mi.
458,336   468,973   463,920   472,746   423,028   341,719
March 5, 1794. Onondaga Indians. Members of Iroquois confederation; main village was capital of confederation; name refers to "hill" or "mountain top."

Onslow **North Carolina**
Jacksonville 767 sq. mi.
150,355   149,838   112,784   102,126   82,706   42,047
1734 (session). Arthur Onslow (1691–1768). English statesman; Hhouse of Commons 1720–61, Speaker 1728–61; chancellor to Queen Caroline (wife of George II) 1729; treasurer of the navy 1734–42.

Ontario **New York**
Canandaigua 644 sq. mi.
100,224   95,101   88,909   78,849   68,070   60,172
January 27, 1789. Lake Ontario. Iroquois for "beautiful lake."

Ontonagon **Michigan**
Ontoganon 1,312 sq. mi.
7,818   8,854   9,861   10,548   10,584   10,282
March 9, 1843; organized January 1, 1853. Ontonagon River. Uncertain Indian origin; translation possibilities include "bowl," "hunting river," and "fishing place."

Orange **California**
Santa Ana 789 sq. mi.
2,846,289   2,410,556   1,932,709   1,420,386   703,925   216,224
March 11, 1889. Descriptive of local orange groves.

Orange **Florida**
Orlando 907 sq. mi.
896,344   677,491   471,016   344,311   263,540   114,950
December 29, 1824, as Mosquito; name unofficially changed to Leigh Read 1842; name changed to Orange January 30, 1845. Descriptive of local orange groves.

Orange **Indiana**
Paoli 400 sq. mi.
19,306   18,409   18,677   16,968   16,877   16,879
December 26, 1815; effective February 1, 1816. Orange County, North Carolina.

Orange   **New York**
Goshen   816 sq. mi.
341,367   307,647   259,603   221,657   183,734   152,255
November 1, 1683; organized 1698. William Nassau, Prince of Orange, King William III* (see King William, Virginia). Title "Orange" belonged to Nassau family from small territory in southern France.

Orange   **North Carolina**
Hillsborough   400 sq. mi.
118,227   93,851   77,055   57,707   42,970   34,435
March 31, 1752 (session). Uncertain. (1) William Nassau, Prince of Orange, King William III.* (2) William V of Orange (1748–1806); grandson of King George II.

Orange   **Texas**
Orange   356 sq. mi.
84,966   80,509   83,838   71,170   60,357   40,567
February 5, 1852; organized March 20, 1852. Descriptive of a specific orange grove near the Neches River.

Orange   **Vermont**
Chelsea   689 sq. mi.
28,226   26,149   22,739   17,676   16,014   17,027
February 22, 1781. Uncertain. (1) Orange County, New York. (2) One of two towns named Orange in Connecticut and Massachusetts. All of these possibilities derive from William Nassau, Prince of Orange, King William III.*

Orange   **Virginia**
Orange   342 sq. mi.
25,881   21,421   18,063   13,792   12,900   12,755
February 1, 1734 (session). *William IV, Prince of Orange* (1711–51). Husband of Princess Anne, eldest daughter of King George II; primary qualification was being a Protestant; physically deformed; served in Holy Roman Empire army.

Orangeburg   **South Carolina**
Orangeburg   1,106 sq. mi.
91,582   84,803   82,276   69,789   68,559   68,726
1769. City of Orangeburg. Named for William IV, Prince of Orange* (see Orange, Virginia).

Oregon   **Missouri**
Alton   791 sq. mi.
10,344   9,470   10,238   9,180   9,845   11,978
February 14, 1845. Oregon Country. Origin of name is uncertain; may be from careless transcription on a map of Ouisconsink (Wisconsin) River in western North America into "Ouariconsint"; Columbia River was initially thought to be the same river.

Orleans   **Louisiana**
New Orleans   181 sq. mi.
484,674   496,938   557,515   593,471   627,525   570,445
April 10, 1805. Uncertain. (1) City of Orleans, France. (2) *Phillippe II, Duke of Orleans* (1674–1723); regent of France during minority of Louis XV 1715–23; prime minister of France 1723.

Orleans   **New York**
Albion   391 sq. mi.
44,171   41,846   38,496   37,305   34,159   29,832
November 12, 1824. Uncertain. (1) City of Orleans, France. (2) French royal house of Orleans; perhaps specifically Louis Phillippe Joseph, Duke of Orleans (1747–93); supported colonists in American Revolution; executed during French Revolution; father of King Louis-Phillippe.

Orleans   **Vermont**
Newport   698 sq. mi.

26,277   24,053   23,440   20,153   20,143   21,190
November 5, 1792; organized 1799. Uncertain. (1) City of Orleans, France. (2) Duke of Orleans.*

Osage   **Kansas**
Lyndon   704 sq. mi.
16,712   15,248   15,319   13,352   12,886   12,811
August 30, 1855, as Weller; organized and name changed February 11, 1859. Marais des Cygnes River. Formerly named Osage River; from Osage Indians* (see Osage, Oklahoma).

Osage   **Missouri**
Linn   606 sq. mi.
13,062   12,018   12,014   10,994   10,867   11,301
January 29, 1841. Osage River. Largest tributary of Missouri River; from Osage Indians* (see Osage, Oklahoma).

Osage   **Oklahoma**
Pawhuska   2,251 sq. mi.
44,437   41,645   39,327   29,750   32,441   33,071
July 16, 1907. *Osage Indians*. Division of Sioux Indians; prairie Indians living in Arkansas, Illinois, Kansas, and Missouri; resettled to Indian Territory (Oklahoma) through series of treaties with U.S.; French corruption of Algonquin *ouasash*, possibly meaning "bone men."

Osborne   **Kansas**
Osborne   892 sq. mi.
4,452   4,867   5,959   6,416   7,506   8,558
February 26, 1867; organized 1871. Vincent B. Osborne (1839–79). Private, Company E, 2nd Kansas Volunteer Infantry, 1861; wounded at Wilson's Creek and discharged 1861; reenlisted as sergeant, Company A, 2nd Kansas Volunteer Cavalry, 1862; sutler at Fort Harker 1865; Kansas legislature 1872.

Osceola   **Florida**
Kissimmee   1,322 sq. mi.
172,493   107,728   49,287   25,267   19,029   11,406
May 12, 1887. *Osceola* (c1804–38). Leader of Seminole Indians; resisted removal to Indian Territory (Oklahoma); captured under flag of truce 1837; died in captivity.

Osceola   **Iowa**
Sibley   399 sq. mi.
7,003   7,267   8,371   8,555   10,064   10,181
January 15, 1851; organized January 1, 1872. Osceola.*

Osceola   **Michigan**
Reed City   566 sq. mi.
23,197   20,146   18,928   14,838   13,595   13,797
April 1, 1840, as Unwattin; name changed March 8, 1843; organized March 17, 1869. Osceola.*

Oscoda   **Michigan**
Mio   565 sq. mi.
9,418   7,842   6,858   4,726   3,447   3,134
April 1, 1840; organized March 10, 1881. Coined Indian word for "pebbly prairie." *Os* from *ossin*, meaning "pebble," and *coda* from *mushcoda*, meaning "prairie."

Oswego   **New York**
Oswego   953 sq. mi.
122,377   121,771   113,901   100,897   86,118   77,181
March 1, 1816. Oswego River. Indian for "flowing out" or "small water into large water" (refering to Lake Ontario).

Otero   **Colorado**
La Junta   1,263 sq. mi.
20,311   20,185   22,567   23,523   24,128   25,275
March 25, 1889. Miguel A. Otero (1829–82). New Mexico territorial legislature 1853; New Mexico Territory congressional delegate; secretary of New Mexico Territory 1861; one of founders of La Junta.

Otero   **New Mexico**
Alamogordo   6,627 sq. mi.
62,298   51,928   44,665   41,097   36,976   14,909
January 30, 1899. Miguel Antonio Otero (1859–1944). Treasurer of city of Las Vegas; probate clerk of San Miguel County; governor of New Mexico Territory 1897–1906; treasurer of New Mexico Territory 1909–11.

Otoe   **Nebraska**
Nebraska City   616 sq. mi.
15,396   14,252   15,183   15,576   16,503   17,056
November 23, 1854, as Pierce; name changed 1855; organized December 1, 1856. Oto Indians. Originally lived near Great Lakes; migrated to Plains by 1700; ceded Nebraska lands to U.S. 1854; resettled in Indian Territory (Oklahoma).

Otsego   **Michigan**
Gaylord   515 sq. mi.
23,301   17,957   14,993   10,422   7,545   6,435
April 1, 1840, as Okkuddo; name changed March 8, 1843; organized March 12, 1875. Otsego County, New York.

Otsego   **New York**
Cooperstown   1,003 sq. mi.
61,676   60,517   59,075   56,181   51,942   50,763
February 16, 1791. Uncertain. (1) Otsego Lake. (2) Town of Otsego. Indian name for the lake, meaning "place of the rock."

Ottawa   **Kansas**
Minneapolis   721 sq. mi.
6,163   5,634   5,971   6,183   6,779   7,265
February 27, 1860; organized 1866. *Ottawa Indians*. Algonquin linguistic family; lived between Ohio and Wisconsin; resettled in Kansas 1836; resettled in Indian Territory (Oklahoma) 1870; Indian name meaning "trader" or "barterer."

Ottawa   **Michigan**
Grand Haven   566 sq. mi.
238,314   187,768   157,174   128,181   98,719   73,751
March 2, 1831; organized December 29, 1837. Ottawa Indians.*

Ottawa   **Ohio**
Port Clinton   255 sq. mi.
40,985   40,029   40,076   37,099   35,323   29,469
March 6, 1840. Ottawa Indians.*

Ottawa   **Oklahoma**
Miami   471 sq. mi.
33,194   30,561   32,870   29,800   28,301   32,218
July 16, 1907. Ottawa Indians.*

Otter Tail   **Minnesota**
Fergus Falls   1,980 sq. mi.
57,159   50,714   51,937   46,097   48,960   51,320
March 18, 1858; organized February 28, 1870. Otter Tail Lake. Named from translation of Indian name descriptive of long, narrow sandbar in the lake.

Ouachita   **Arkansas**
Camden   732 sq. mi.

28,790	30,574	30,541	30,896	31,641	33,051

November 29, 1842. Ouachita River. From Ouachita Indians (see Ouachita, Louisiana).

Ouachita   **Louisiana**
Monroe   611 sq. mi.

147,250	142,191	139,241	115,387	101,663	74,713

April 10, 1805. Ouachita Indians. Clan of Caddoan family living in northeastern Louisiana. Meaning of "Ouachita" uncertain: (1) "black" or "silver water"; (2) French rendering of Choctaw words meaning "hunt" and "big" (see Washita (2), Oklahoma).

Ouray   **Colorado**
Ouray   540 sq. mi.

3,742	2,295	1,925	1,546	1,601	2,103

January 18, 1877, as Uncompahgre; name changed March 2, 1883. Ouray (c1833–80). Chief of Uncompahgre Ute tribe; leader of Ute confederacy; cooperated with U.S.

Outagamie   **Wisconsin**
Appleton   640 sq. mi.

160,971	140,510	128,799	119,356	101,794	81,722

February 17, 1851; organized 1852. Fox Indians. From Chippewa name for Fox Indians; defeated by French 1730.

Overton   **Tennessee**
Livingston   433 sq. mi.

20,118	17,636	17,575	14,866	14,661	17,566

September 11, 1806. John Overton (1766–1833). Tennessee Superior Court 1804–10; Tennessee Supreme Court 1811–16; founder of Memphis 1819.

Owen   **Indiana**
Spencer   385 sq. mi.

21,786	17,281	15,841	12,163	11,400	11,763

December 21, 1818; effective January 1, 1819. *Abraham Owen* (1769–1811). Kentucky legislature; colonel under William Henry Harrison; killed in battle of Tippecanoe November 7, 1811.

Owen   **Kentucky**
Owenton   352 sq. mi.

10,547	9,035	8,924	7,470	8,237	9,755

February 6, 1819. Abraham Owen.*

Owsley   **Kentucky**
Booneville   198 sq. mi.

4,858	5,036	5,709	5,023	5,369	7,324

January 23, 1843. William Owsley (1782–1862). Kentucky legislature; justice of Court of Appeals 1813–28; Kentucky secretary of state; governor of Kentucky 1844–48.

Owyhee   **Idaho**
Murphy   7,678 sq. mi.

10,644	8,392	8,272	6,422	6,375	6,307

December 31, 1863. Owyhee River. Corruption of "Hawaii," in commemoration of Hawaiian trappers killed in the region.

Oxford   **Maine**
South Paris   2,078 sq. mi.

54,755	52,602	48,968	43,457	44,345	44,221

March 4, 1805. Town of Oxford, Massachusetts.

Ozark   **Missouri**
Gainesville   742 sq. mi.
9,542   8,598   7,961   6,226   6,744   8,856
January 29, 1841, as Ozark; name changed to Decatur February 22, 1843; renamed Ozark March 24, 1845. Ozark Mountains. From French *aux arcs,* meaning "with bows"; applied to local Indians.

Ozaukee   **Wisconsin**
Port Washington   232 sq. mi.
82,317   72,831   66,981   54,421   38,441   23,361
March 7, 1853. Sauk Indians. From complete name of Sauks, Osauki-wug, meaning "people of the yellow earth"; defeated with Fox allies in Black Hawk War 1832.

P

Pacific   **Washington**
South Bend   933 sq. mi.
20,984   18,882   17,237   15,796   14,674   16,558
February 4, 1851. Descriptive of location on Pacific Ocean.

Page   **Iowa**
Clarinda   535 sq. mi.
16,976   16,870   19,063   18,507   21,023   23,921
February 24, 1847; organized March 22, 1852. John Page (?–1846). 2nd lieutenant 1818; 1st lieutenant 1819; captain 1831; died at battle of Palo Alto May 8, 1846.

Page   **Virginia**
Luray   311 sq. mi.
23,177   21,690   19,401   16,581   15,572   15,152
March 30, 1831. John Page (1743–1808). Served with Washington in French and Indian Wars 1755; Virginia Constitutional Convention 1776; lieutenant–governor of Virginia 1776–79; colonel; Virginia House of Delegates 1781–83, 1785–88, 1797–98, and 1800–01; U.S. representative 1789–97; governor of Virginia 1802–05.

Palm Beach   **Florida**
West Palm Beach   1,974 sq. mi.
1,131,184   863,518   576,863   348,753   228,106   114,688
April 30, 1909. Town of Palm Beach. Descriptive of palm trees and ocean frontage.

Palo Alto   **Iowa**
Emmetsburg   564 sq. mi.
10,147   10,669   12,721   13,289   14,736   15,891
January 15, 1851; organized December 29, 1858. Battle of Palo Alto. First battle of Mexican War May 8, 1846; U.S. troops commanded by General Zachary Taylor defeated Mexican force over twice as large.

Palo Pinto   **Texas**
Palo Pinto   953 sq. mi.
27,026   25,055   24,062   28,962   20,516   17,154
August 27, 1856; organized April 27, 1857. Palo Pinto Creek. Spanish for "painted trees."

Pamlico   **North Carolina**
Bayboro   337 sq. mi.
12,934   11,372   10,398   9,467   9,850   9,993
February 8, 1872. Pamlico Sound. Named for tribe of Algonquin Indians living in area.

Panola   **Mississippi**
Batesville   684 sq. mi.

34,274 29,996 28,164 26,829 28,791 31,271
February 9, 1836. Cotton. From Choctaw word meaning "cotton."

Panola **Texas**
Carthage 801 sq. mi.
22,756 22,035 20,724 15,894 16,870 19,250
March 30, 1846; organized September 1846. Cotton. From Choctaw word meaning "cotton."

Park **Colorado**
Fairplay 2,201 sq. mi.
14,523 7,174 5,333 2,185 1,822 1,870
November 1, 1861. South Park. Descriptive of an open valley between mountains.

Park **Montana**
Livingston 2,802 sq. mi.
15,694 14,614[a] 12,935[a] 11,261[a] 13,215[a] 12,057[a]
February 23, 1887; effective May 1, 1887. *Yellowstone National Park.* First U.S. national park 1872 (see Yellowstone, Montana). [(a) Includes part of Yellowstone National Park:; 1990, 52; 1980, 66; 1970, 64; 1960, 47; 1950, 58]

Park **Wyoming**
Cody 6,942 sq. mi.
25,786 23,178 21,639 17,752 17,294[a] 15,535[a]
February 15, 1909. Yellowstone National Park.* [(a) Includes portion of Yellowstone National Park: 1960, 420; 1950, 353. Some of the national park's population may have been in the portion included in Teton County.]

Parke **Indiana**
Rockville 445 sq. mi.
17,241 15,410 16,372 14,600 14,804 15,674
January 9, 1821; effective April 2, 1821. Benjamin Parke (1777–1835). Attorney general of Indiana Territory 1804–08; Indiana Territory House of Representatives 1805; congressional delegate from Indiana Territory 1805–08; Indiana Territory judge 1808–17; judge of U.S. District Court of Indiana 1817–35.

Parker **Texas**
Weatherford 904 sq. mi.
88,495 64,785 44,609 33,888 22,880 21,528
December 12, 1855; organized March 11, 1856. Uncertain. (1) Isaac Parker (1793–1883); served in Texas Revolution; Texas Republic legislature 1838–40 and 1841–43; Texas legislature 1846–53. (2) Family of Cynthia Parker (c1825–c1871); captured by Comanches as a child 1836; married Comanche chief Peta Nocona; mother of Quanah Parker, Comanche chief.

Parmer **Texas**
Farwell 882 sq. mi.
10,016 9,863 11,038 10,509 9,583 5,787
August 21, 1876; organized 1907. Martin Parmer (1778–1850). Emigrated to Texas 1825; Fredonia revolt 1827; Texas Republic legislature; Texas Constitutional Convention 1836; signer of Texas Declaration of Independence 1836.

Pasco **Florida**
Dade City 745 sq. mi.
344,765 281,131 193,643 75,955 36,785 20,529
June 2, 1887. Samuel Pasco (1834–1917). Private, Confederate army 1861; wounded and captured at Missionary Ridge 1863; paroled 1865; president of Florida Constitutional Convention 1885; Florida House of Representatives 1886–87; U.S. senator 1887–99.

Pasquotank **North Carolina**
Elizabeth City 227 sq. mi.
34,897 31,298 28,462 26,824 25,630 24,347
1670. Pasquotank Indians. Algonquin tribe; name means "divided tidal water."

Passaic   **New Jersey**
Paterson   185 sq. mi.
489,049   453,060   447,585   460,782   406,618   337,093
February 7, 1837. Passaic River. Indian word referring to "valley."

Patrick   **Virginia**
Stuart   483 sq. mi.
19,407   17,473   17,647   15,282   15,282   15,642
November 26, 1790. Patrick Henry.* (See Henry, Alabama.)

Paulding   **Georgia**
Dallas   313 sq. mi.
81,678   41,611   26,110   17,520   13,101   11,752
December 3, 1832. *John Paulding* (c1758–1818). New York Militia; one of three New York militiamen who captured British major John André, revealing Benedict Arnold's treason September 23, 1780; all three received a silver medal and $200 pension from Congress. (See also Van Wert and Williams, Ohio.)

Paulding   **Ohio**
Paulding   416 sq. mi.
20,293   20,488   21,302   19,329   16,792   15,047
February 12, 1820; organized 1839. John Paulding.*

Pawnee   **Kansas**
Larned   754 sq. mi.
7,233   7,555   8,065   8,484   10,254   11,041
February 26, 1867; organized 1872. Pawnee River. Named for Pawnee Indians* (see Pawnee, Nebraska).

Pawnee   **Nebraska**
Pawnee City   432 sq. mi.
3,087   3,317   3,937   4,473   5,356   6,744
March 6, 1855; organized November 4, 1856. *Pawnee Indians*. Caddoan linguistic family; ranged from Nebraska to Texas; friendly to whites but fought with neighboring tribes; resettled to Indian Territory (Oklahoma) 1870's; name may derive from Apache word for "slave," referring to Pawnees captured in battle.

Pawnee   **Oklahoma**
Pawnee   569 sq. mi.
16,612   15,575   15,310   11,338   10,884   13,616
1893, as County Q; organized and name changed 1895. Pawnee Indians.*

Payette   **Idaho**
Payette   408 sq. mi.
20,578   16,434   15,722   12,401   12,363   11,921
February 28, 1917. Payette River. Named for Francois Payette (?–?); trapper and explorer; postmaster of Hudson's Bay Company's Fort Boise 1835; traded with emigrants on Oregon Trail.

Payne   **Oklahoma**
Stillwater   686 sq. mi.
68,190   61,507   62,435   50,654   44,231   46,430
1890. David L. Payne (1836–84). Union army; Kansas legislature 1864; assistant doorkeeper of U.S. House of Representatives; led illegal groups of settlers into Indian Territory (Oklahoma); nicknamed "the Boomer."

Peach   **Georgia**
Fort Valley   151 sq. mi.
23,668   21,189   19,151   15,990   13,846   11,705
July 18, 1924. Descriptive of peach orchards in region.

Pearl River   **Mississippi**
Poplarville   811 sq. mi.
48,621   38,714   33,795   27,802   22,411   20,641
February 22, 1890. Pearl River. Originally named Riviere des Perles by French after finding pearls in mussels.

Pecos   **Texas**
Fort Stockton   4,764 sq. mi.
16,809   14,675   14,618   13,748   11,957   9,939
May 3, 1871; organized June 13, 1872. Pecos River. Keresan Indian word for "place where there is water"; also the name of a large pueblo in New Mexico.

Pembina   **North Dakota**
Cavalier   1,119 sq. mi.
8,585   9,238   10,399   10,728   12,946   13,990
January 9, 1867; organized August 12, 1867. Pembina trading post. Earliest settlement in Dakota Territory; corruption of Chippewa word meaning "high cranberry bush."

Pemiscot   **Missouri**
Caruthersville   493 sq. mi.
20,047   21,921   24,987   26,373   38,095   45,624
February 19, 1851. Pemiscot Bayou. Indian word for "liquid mud."

Pender   **North Carolina**
Burgaw   871 sq. mi.
41,082   28,855   22,215   18,149   18,508   18,423
February 16, 1875. William Dorsey Pender (1834–63). Graduated West Point 1854; resigned commission in U.S. Army; captain, Confederate army 1861; major general 1863; wounded at Gettysburg; died July 18, 1863.

Pendleton   **Kentucky**
Falmouth   281 sq. mi.
14,390   12,036   10,989   9,949   9,968   9,610
December 13, 1798; organized May 10, 1799. *Edmund Pendleton* (1721–1803). Virginia House of Burgesses 1752–54; Continental Congress 1774–75; president, Committee of Safety, 1775; Virginia House of Delegates 1776–77; president, Virginia Constitutional Convention 1788; president, Virginia Supreme Court of Appeals 1799–1803.

Pendleton   **West Virginia**
Franklin   698 sq. mi.
8,196   8,054   7,910   7,031   8,093   9,313
December 4, 1787; effective May 1, 1788. Edmund Pendleton.*

Pend Oreille   **Washington**
Newport   1,400 sq. mi.
11,732   8,915   8,580   6,025   6,914   7,413
March 1, 1911. Pend d'Oreille Indians. French name meaning "hanging from the ear"; given to Indians for large shell ornaments worn on their ears.

Pennington   **Minnesota**
Thief River Falls   617 sq. mi.
13,584   13,306   15,258   13,266   12,468   12,965
November 23, 1910. Edmund Pennington (1848–1926). Superintendent, Minneapolis, St. Paul, and Sault Ste. Marie Railway Company 1888–89; general manager 1899–1905; president 1909.

Pennington   **South Dakota**
Rapid City   2,776 sq. mi.
88,565   81,343   70,361   59,349   58,195   34,053

January 11, 1875; organized April 19, 1877. John L. Pennington (1821–1900). Alabama Senate 1866–70; governor of Dakota Territory 1874–78; collector of internal revenue of Dakota Territory 1878.

Penobscot   **Maine**
Bangor   3,396 sq. mi.

| 144,919 | 146,601 | 137,015 | 125,393 | 126,346 | 108,198 |

February 15, 1816; effective April 1, 1816. Penobscot River. Named for Penobscot Indians; tribe of Abnaki confederacy; sided with French against English; name means "rocky place" or "rocky river."

Peoria   **Illinois**
Peoria   620 sq. mi.

| 183,433 | 182,827 | 200,466 | 195,318 | 189,044 | 174,347 |

January 13, 1825. Peoria Indians. Member of Illinois Indian confederacy. Origin of name is uncertain; perhaps French rendering of Indian *piwarea,* meaning "carrier" or "packer."

Pepin   **Wisconsin**
Durand   232 sq. mi.

| 7,213 | 7,107 | 7,477 | 7,319 | 7,332 | 7,462 |

February 25, 1858. Lake Pepin. Possible origins of name include (1) Pepin brothers, 17th century explorers; (2) Pepin le Bref (Pepin the Short) (714–768), king of the Franks, father of Charlemagne; (3) Stephen Pepin, Sieur de la Fond; (4) Jean Pepin, early settler.

Perkins   **Nebraska**
Grant   883 sq. mi.

| 3,200 | 3,367 | 3,637 | 3,423 | 4,189 | 4,809 |

November 1887. Charles Elliott Perkins (1840–1907). President of Chicago, Burlington & Quincy Railroad 1881–1901; developed railroad through Nebraska.

Perkins   **South Dakota**
Bison   2,872 sq. mi.

| 3,363 | 3,932 | 4,700 | 4,769 | 5,977 | 6,776 |

November 3, 1908; organized February 9, 1909. Henry E. Perkins (1864–?). Mayor of Sturgis; South Dakota Senate 1903, 1907, and 1911.

Perquimans   **North Carolina**
Hertford   247 sq. mi.

| 11,368 | 10,447 | 9,486 | 8,351 | 9,178 | 9,602 |

1670, as Berkeley; name changed 1681. Perquiman Indians. Algonquin tribe living on north side of Albemarle Sound.

Perry   **Alabama**
Marion   719 sq. mi.

| 11,861 | 12,759 | 15,012 | 15,388 | 17,358 | 20,439 |

December 13, 1819. *Oliver Hazard Perry* (1785–1819). Midshipman 1799; lieutenant 1807; commanded schooner 1809; commanded division of gunboats 1812; constructed fleet of nine vessels on Lake Erie 1813; defeated British in battle of Lake Erie September 10, 1813; sent message to General Harrison "We have met the enemy and they are ours"; commodore 1819; died of yellow fever on diplomatic mission to Venezuela.

Perry   **Arkansas**
Perryville   551 sq. mi.

| 10,209 | 7,969 | 7,266 | 5,634 | 4,927 | 5,978 |

December 18, 1840. Oliver Hazard Perry.*

Perry   **Illinois**
Pinckneyville   441 sq. mi.

| 23,094 | 21,412 | 21,714 | 19,757 | 19,184 | 21,684 |

January 29, 1827. Oliver Hazard Perry.*

Perry   **Indiana**
Tell City   381 sq. mi.

18,899	19,107	19,346	19,075	17,232	17,367

September 7, 1814; effective November 1, 1814. Oliver Hazard Perry.*

Perry   **Kentucky**
Hazard   342 sq. mi.

29,390	30,283	33,763	25,714	34,961	46,566

November 2, 1820. Oliver Hazard Perry.*

Perry   **Mississippi**
New Augusta   647 sq. mi.

12,138	10,865	9,864	9,065	8,745	9,108

February 3, 1820. Oliver Hazard Perry.*

Perry   **Missouri**
Perryville   475 sq. mi.

18,132	16,648	16,784	14,393	14,642	14,890

November 16, 1820. Oliver Hazard Perry.*

Perry   **Ohio**
New Lexington   410 sq. mi.

34,078	31,557	31,032	27,434	27,864	28,999

December 26, 1817. Oliver Hazard Perry.*

Perry   **Pennsylvania**
New Bloomfield   554 sq. mi.

43,602	41,172	35,718	28,615	26,582	24,782

March 22, 1820. Oliver Hazard Perry.*

Perry   **Tennessee**
Linden   415 sq. mi.

7,631	6,612	6,111	5,238	5,273	6,462

November 14, 1818. Oliver Hazard Perry.*

Pershing   **Nevada**
Lovelock   6,037 sq. mi.

6,693	4,336	3,408	2,670	3,199	3,103

March 18, 1919. John Joseph Pershing (1860–1948). Graduated West Point 1886; Apache campaign 1886–87; Sioux campaign 1890–91; Cree campaign 1896; Spanish–American War, Cuba and Philippines, 1898–99; punitive expedition into Mexico against Pancho Villa 1916; commanded American expeditionary force to Europe in World War I 1917; army chief of staff 1921.

Person   **North Carolina**
Roxboro   392 sq. mi.

35,623	30,180	29,164	25,914	26,394	24,361

December 5, 1791 (session). Thomas Person (1733–1800). Justice of the peace 1756 and 1776; sheriff 1762; North Carolina Assembly 1764; Provincial Council 1775; Council of Safety 1776; North Carolina House of Commons 1777–86, 1788–91, 1793–95, and 1797; North Carolina Senate 1787 and 1791; opposed ratification of federal constitution.

Petersburg   **Virginia**
(Independent City)   23 sq. mi.

33,740	38,386	41,055	36,103	36,750	35,054

March 16, 1850. Peter Jones (c1707–c1754). Established trading post named Peter's Point; later named Petersburg. (Associated counties: Chesterfield, Dinwiddie, and Prince George.)

Petroleum   **Montana**
Winnett   1,654 sq. mi.
493   519   655   675   894   1,026
November 24, 1924. Descriptive of local oil fields.

Pettis   **Missouri**
Sedalia   685 sq. mi.
39,403   35,437   36,378   34,137   35,120   31,577
January 26, 1833. Spencer Pettis (1802–31). Missouri secretary of state 1826–28; U.S. representative 1829–31; killed in duel 1831.

Phelps   **Missouri**
Rolla   673 sq. mi.
39,825   35,248   33,633   29,481   25,396   21,504
November 13, 1857. John Smith Phelps (1814–86). Missouri House of Representatives 1840; U.S. representative 1845–63; lieutenant colonel and colonel 1861; military governor of Arkansas 1862; brigadier general 1862; governor of Missouri 1877–81.

Phelps   **Nebraska**
Holdrege   540 sq. mi.
9,747   9,715   9,769   9,553   9,800   9,048
February 11, 1873. William Phelps (1808–?). Steamboat captain on Mississippi and Missouri rivers.

Philadelphia   **Pennsylvania**
Philadelphia   135 sq. mi.
1,517,550   1,585,577   1,688,210   1,948,609   2,002,512   2,071,605
March 10, 1682. City of Philadelphia. Named by William Penn for the site of an ancient Christian church in Asia Minor; from Greek *philadelphos,* meaning "brotherly love."

Phillips   **Arkansas**
Helena   693 sq. mi.
26,445   28,838   34,772   40,046   43,997   46,254
May 1, 1820; effective June 1, 1820. Sylvanus Phillips (1766–1831). Early settler; explored Arkansas River 1798; Arkansas territorial legislature 1820.

Phillips   **Colorado**
Holyoke   688 sq. mi.
4,480   4,189   4,542   4,131   4,440   4,924
March 27, 1889. Rufus O. Phillips (1859–?). Secretary of Lincoln Land Company; active in railroad development.

Phillips   **Kansas**
Phillipsburg   886 sq. mi.
6,001   6,590   7,406   7,888   8,709   9,273
February 26, 1867; organized 1872. William Phillips (?–1856). Free-state martyr; murdered at Leavenworth by proslavery mob September 1, 1856.

Phillips   **Montana**
Malta   5,140 sq. mi.
4,601   5,163   5,367   5,386   6,027   6,334
February 5, 1915. Benjamin D. Phillips (1857–?). Rancher and livestock man; Montana Senate 1898.

Piatt   **Illinois**
Monticello   440 sq. mi.
16,365   15,548   16,581   15,509   14,960   13,970
January 27, 1841. Uncertain. (1) Piatt family; early settlers. (2) Benjamin Piatt (?–?); not an immediate member of Piatt family; attorney general of Illinois Territory 1810–13. (3) James A. Piatt (1789–1838); most prominent member of Piatt family.

Pickaway   **Ohio**
Circleville   502 sq. mi.

52,727	48,255	43,662	40,071	35,855	29,352

January 12, 1810. Piqua Indians. Division of Shawnees; allies of France in French and Indian Wars; name of uncertain origin; may mean "ashes."

Pickens   **Alabama**
Carrollton   881 sq. mi.

20,949	20,699	21,481	20,326	21,882	24,349

December 19, 1820. *Andrew Pickens* (1739–1817). Fought Cherokees 1760 and 1782; captain to brigadier general in Revolutionary War 1779–81; awarded sword by Congress for victory at Cowpens 1781; South Carolina House of Representatives 1781–94 and 1800–12; South Carolina Constitutional Convention 1790; U.S. representative 1793–95; major general of militia 1795.

Pickens   **Georgia**
Jasper   232 sq. mi.

22,983	14,432	11,652	9,620	8,903	8,855

December 5, 1853. Andrew Pickens.*

Pickens   **South Carolina**
Pickens   497 sq. mi.

110,757	93,894	79,292	58,956	46,030	40,058

December 20, 1826. Andrew Pickens.*

Pickett   **Tennessee**
Byrdstown   163 sq. mi.

4,945	4,548	4,358	3,774	4,431	5,093

February 27, 1879. Howard L. Pickett (1847–1914). Tennessee legislature 1879; active in creation of county; moved to Arizona Territory 1882.

Pierce   **Georgia**
Blackshear   343 sq. mi.

15,636	13,328	11,897	9,281	9,678	11,112

December 18, 1857. *Franklin Pierce* (1804–69). New Hampshire House of Representatives 1829–33; U.S. representative 1833–37; U.S. senator 1837–42; colonel and brigadier general in Mexican War 1846–47; 14th president of U.S. 1853–57.

Pierce   **Nebraska**
Pierce   574 sq. mi.

7,857	7,827	8,481	8,493	8,722	9,405

January 26, 1856, as Otoe; name changed 1856; organized September 21, 1870. Franklin Pierce.*

Pierce   **North Dakota**
Rugby   1,018 sq. mi.

4,675	5,052	6,166	6,323	7,394	8,326

March 11, 1887; organized April 11, 1889. Gilbert Ashville Pierce (1839–1901). 2nd lieutenant to colonel, Union army 1861–64; Indiana House of Representatives 1868; assistant financial clerk, U.S. Senate 1869–71; governor of Dakota Territory 1884–87; U.S. senator from North Dakota 1889–91; U.S. minister to Portugal 1893.

Pierce   **Washington**
Tacoma   1,679 sq. mi.

700,820	586,203	485,643	411,027	321,590	275,876

December 22, 1852. Franklin Pierce.*

Pierce   **Wisconsin**
Ellsworth   576 sq. mi.

36,804   32,765   31,149   26,652   22,503   21,448
March 14, 1853. Franklin Pierce.*

Pike   **Alabama**
Troy   671 sq. mi.
29,605   27,595   28,050   25,038   25,987   30,608
December 17, 1821. *Zebulon Montgomery Pike* (1779–1813). Joined army at age fifteen; 1st lieutenant 1799; explored upper Mississippi River 1804; captain 1806; explored Arkansas River, attempted to climb Pikes Peak, 1806; brigadier general 1813; killed during attack on York (Toronto) April 27, 1813, in War of 1812.

Pike   **Arkansas**
Murfreesboro   603 sq. mi.
11,303   10,086   10,373   8,711   7,864   10,032
November 1, 1833; effective December 1, 1833. Zebulon Montgomery Pike.*

Pike   **Georgia**
Zebulon   218 sq. mi.
13,688   10,224   8,937   7,316   7,138   8,459
December 9, 1822; organized December 20, 1824. Zebulon Montgomery Pike.*

Pike   **Illinois**
Pittsfield   830 sq. mi.
17,384   17,577   18,896   19,185   20,552   22,155
January 31, 1821. Zebulon Montgomery Pike.*

Pike   **Indiana**
Petersburg   336 sq. mi.
12,837   12,509   13,465   12,281   12,797   14,995
December 21, 1816; effective February 1, 1817. Zebulon Montgomery Pike.*

Pike   **Kentucky**
Pikeville   788 sq. mi.
68,736   72,583   81,123   61,059   68,264   81,154
December 19, 1821. Zebulon Montgomery Pike.*

Pike   **Mississippi**
Magnolia   409 sq. mi.
38,940   36,882   36,173   31,756   35,063   35,137
December 9, 1815. Zebulon Montgomery Pike.*

Pike   **Missouri**
Bowling Green   673 sq. mi.
18,351   15,969   17,568   16,928   16,706   16,844
December 14, 1818. Zebulon Montgomery Pike.*

Pike   **Ohio**
Waverly   441 sq. mi.
27,695   24,249   22,802   19,114   19,380   14,607
January 4, 1815. Zebulon Montgomery Pike.*

Pike   **Pennsylvania**
Milford   547 sq. mi.
46,302   27,966   18,271   11,818   9,158   8,425
March 26, 1814. Zebulon Montgomery Pike.*

Pima   **Arizona**
Tucson   9,186 sq. mi.

| 843,746 | 666,880 | 531,443 | 351,667 | 265,660 | 141,216 |

December 15, 1864. Pima Indians. Spanish rendering of *pia* or *pim,* meaning "I don't know," the Pimas' repeated response to Spanish inquiries as to tribal name.

Pinal   **Arizona**
Florence   5,370 sq. mi.

| 179,727 | 116,379 | 90,918 | 67,916 | 62,673 | 43,191 |

February 1, 1875. Uncertain. (1) Pinal Apaches. (2) Pinal Mountains. From Spanish word relating to pine, or Apache word for deer.

Pine   **Minnesota**
Pine City   1,411 sq. mi.

| 26,530 | 21,264 | 19,871 | 16,821 | 17,004 | 18,223 |

March 1, 1856; organized April 1, 1857. Uncertain. (1) Descriptive of pine forests in area. (2) Pine River and Pine Lakes.

Pinellas   **Florida**
Clearwater   280 sq. mi.

| 921,482 | 851,659 | 728,531 | 522,329 | 374,665 | 159,249 |

May 23, 1911. Point Pinellas. Southernmost point of Pinellas Peninsula. From Spanish *punta pinal,* meaning "point of pines."

Pipestone   **Minnesota**
Pipestone   466 sq. mi.

| 9,895 | 10,491 | 11,690 | 12,791 | 13,605 | 14,003 |

May 23, 1857, as Rock; name changed September 20, 1862; organized January 27, 1879. Pipestone quarry. Source of red pipestone (catlinite, or steatite), a soft stone used for the bowls of Indian pipes; quarry is sacred to local Indians.

Piscataquis   **Maine**
Dover-Foxcroft   3,966 sq. mi.

| 17,235 | 18,653 | 17,634 | 16,285 | 17,379 | 18,617 |

March 23, 1838; effective April 30, 1838. Piscataquis River. Abnaki word for "river branch" or "little branch stream."

Pitkin   **Colorado**
Aspen   970 sq. mi.

| 14,872 | 12,661 | 10,338 | 6,185 | 2,381 | 1,646 |

February 23, 1881. Frederick Walker Pitkin (1837–86). Lawyer; emigrated to Colorado for his health 1874; governor of Colorado 1879–83.

Pitt   **North Carolina**
Greenville   652 sq. mi.

| 133,798 | 107,924 | 90,146 | 73,900 | 69,942 | 63,789 |

April 24, 1760 (session). William Pitt, Earl of Chatham.* (See Chatham, Georgia.)

Pittsburg   **Oklahoma**
McAlester   1,306 sq. mi.

| 43,953 | 40,581 | 40,524 | 37,521 | 34,360 | 41,031 |

July 16, 1907. Pittsburgh, Pennsylvania. Named for William Pitt, Earl of Chatham (see Chatham, Georgia). The "h" was inadvertently omitted from county name.

Pittsylvania   **Virginia**
Chatham   971 sq. mi.

| 61,745 | 55,655 | 66,147 | 58,789 | 58,296 | 66,096 |

November 6, 1766 (session). William Pitt, Earl of Chatham* (see Chatham, Georgia); combined with Latin *sylva,* meaning "woods."

Piute   **Utah**
Junction   758 sq. mi.
1,435   1,277   1,329   1,164   1,436   1,911
January 16, 1865. Paiute Indians. Nomadic Indians of Great Basin; from Indian *pai,* meaning "water" and *ute,* the name of the tribe.

Placer   **California**
Auburn   1,404 sq. mi.
248,399   172,796   117,247   77,306   56,998   41,649
April 25, 1851; organized May 28, 1851. Placer gold deposits. From Spanish word describing gold deposits on the surface or in streams.

Plaquemines   **Louisiana**
Pointe a la Hache   845 sq. mi.
26,757   25,575   26,049   25,225   22,545   14,239
March 31, 1807. Descriptive of persimmon trees in the area. *Plaquemine* is derived from Maubila word for the fruit.

Platte   **Missouri**
Platte City   420 sq. mi.
73,781   57,867   46,341   32,081   23,350   14,973
December 31, 1838. Platte Purchase. Northwest section of Missouri added to state in 1836; formerly Indian lands. Named for Platte River (see Platte, Nebraska).

Platte   **Nebraska**
Columbus   678 sq. mi.
31,662   29,820   28,852   26,508   23,992   19,910
January 26, 1856. *Platte River.* Tributary of Missouri River; from French for "flat" or "shallow."

Platte   **Wyoming**
Wheatland   2,085 sq. mi.
8,807   8,145   11,975   6,486   7,195   7,925
February 9, 1911. North Platte River. Tributary of Platte River.*

Pleasants   **West Virginia**
Saint Marys   131 sq. mi.
7,514   7,546   8,236   7,274   7,124   6,369
March 29, 1851. James Pleasants (1769–1836). Virginia House of Delegates 1797–1802; U.S. representative 1811–19; U.S. senator 1819–22; governor of Virginia 1822–25.

Plumas   **California**
Quincy   2,554 sq. mi.
20,824   19,739   17,340   11,707   11,620   13,519
March 18, 1854. Feather River. From Spanish name of river, Rio de las Plumas; for the many feathers floating on surface.

Plymouth   **Iowa**
Le Mars   864 sq. mi.
24,849   23,388   24,743   24,312   23,906   23,252
January 15, 1851; organized October 27, 1858. Plymouth Colony, Massachusetts. First permanent European settlement in New England; named for Plymouth, England.

Plymouth   **Massachusetts**
Plymouth   661 sq. mi.
472,822   435,276   405,437   333,314   248,449   189,468
June 2, 1685. Town of Plymouth. (See Plymouth, Iowa.)

Pocahontas   **Iowa**
Pocahontas   578 sq. mi.
8,662   9,525   11,369   12,729   14,234   15,496
January 15, 1851; organized May 11, 1859. *Pocahontas* (c1595–1617). Daughter of Powhatan, chief of Powhatan confederacy in southeastern Virginia (see Powhatan, Virginia); actual name was Matoaka; Pocahontas was nickname meaning "playful girl"; interceded with father to save life of Captain John Smith; married John Rolfe 1614; died in England.

Pocahontas   **West Virginia**
Marlinton   940 sq. mi.
9,131   9,008   9,919   8,870   10,136   12,480
December 21, 1821. Pocahontas.*

Poinsett   **Arkansas**
Harrisburg   758 sq. mi.
25,614   24,664   27,032   26,822   30,834   39,311
February 28, 1838. Joel Roberts Poinsett (1779–1851). South Carolina House of Representatives 1816–20; U.S. representative 1821–25; U.S. minister to Mexico 1825–29; U.S. secretary of war 1837–41; amateur botanist, developed poinsettia from a Mexican flower.

Pointe Coupee   **Louisiana**
New Roads   557 sq. mi.
22,763   22,540   24,045   22,002   22,488   21,841
April 10, 1805. Cut point on the Mississippi River. A "cut point" is created when a river shortens its course by cutting across the neck of a loop; *pointe coupee* is French for "cut point."

Polk   **Arkansas**
Mena   859 sq. mi.
20,229   17,347   17,007   13,297   11,981   14,182
November 30, 1844. *James Knox Polk* (1795–1849). Chief clerk of Tennessee Senate 1821–23; Tennessee House of Representatives 1823–25; U.S. representative 1825–29; governor of Tennessee 1838–41; 11th president of U.S. 1845–49.

Polk   **Florida**
Bartow   1,874 sq. mi.
483,924   405,382   321,652   227,222   185,139   123,997
February 8, 1861. James Knox Polk.*

Polk   **Georgia**
Cedartown   311 sq. mi.
38,127   33,815   32,386   29,656   28,015   30,976
December 20, 1851. James Knox Polk.*

Polk   **Iowa**
Des Moines   569 sq. mi.
374,601   327,140   303,170   286,101   226,315   226,010
January 13, 1846; organized April 6, 1846. James Knox Polk.*

Polk   **Minnesota**
Crookston   1,970 sq. mi.
31,369   32,498   34,844   34,435   36,182   35,900
July 20, 1858; organized February 27, 1879. James Knox Polk.*

Polk   **Missouri**
Bolivar   637 sq. mi.
26,992   21,826   18,822   15,415   13,753   16,062
January 5, 1835. James Knox Polk.*

Polk   **Nebraska**
Osceola   439 sq. mi.
5,639   5,675   6,320   6,468   7,210   8,044
January 26, 1856; organized August 6, 1870. James Knox Polk.*

Polk   **North Carolina**
Columbus   238 sq. mi.
18,324   14,416   12,984   11,735   11,395   11,627
January 18, 1847. William Polk (1758–1834). 2nd lieutenant, 4th South Carolina Mounted Infantry; wounded at Canebrake 1775; major of North Carolina troops at Germantown, Brandywine, and Eutaw Springs; lieutenant colonel, 4th South Carolina Cavalry 1782; North Carolina House of Commons 1785–88 and 1790; supervisor of internal revenue for North Carolina 1791–1808.

Polk   **Oregon**
Dallas   741 sq. mi.
62,380   49,541   45,203   35,349   26,523   26,317
December 22, 1845. James Knox Polk.*

Polk   **Tennessee**
Benton   435 sq. mi.
16,050   13,643   13,602   11,669   12,160   14,074
November 28, 1839. James Knox Polk.*

Polk   **Texas**
Livingston   1,057 sq. mi.
41,133   30,687   24,407   14,457   13,861   16,194
March 30, 1846; organized July 10, 1846. James Knox Polk.*

Polk   **Wisconsin**
Balsam Lake   917 sq. mi.
41,319   34,773   32,351   26,666   24,968   24,944
March 14, 1853. James Knox Polk.*

Pondera   **Montana**
Conrad   1,625 sq. mi.
6,424   6,433   6,731   6,611   7,653   6,392
February 17, 1919. Uncertain. (1) Pend d' Oreille Indians; phonetic rendering of French "Pend d' Oreille"; spelling used to avoid confusion with name "Pend Oreille" for town and county in Idaho and Washington, respectively (see Pend Oreille, Washington). (2) Pondera River.

Pontotoc   **Mississippi**
Pontotoc   497 sq. mi.
26,726   22,237   20,918   17,363   17,232   19,994
February 9, 1836. Town of Pontotoc. Rendering of Chickasaw word meaning "weed prairie."

Pontotoc   **Oklahoma**
Ada   720 sq. mi.
35,143   34,119   32,598   27,867   28,089   30,875
July 16, 1907. Pontotoc County, Chickasaw Nation. Name "Pontotoc" was brought to Oklahoma from Mississippi by Chickasaws (see Pontotoc, Mississippi).

Pope   **Arkansas**
Russellville   812 sq. mi.
54,469   45,883   39,021   28,607   21,177   23,291
November 2, 1829; effective December 25, 1829. John Pope (1770–1845). Kentucky House of Representatives 1802 and 1806–07; U.S. senator 1807–12; Kentucky Senate 1825–29; governor of Arkansas Territory 1829–35; U.S. representative from Kentucky 1837–42.

Pope   **Illinois**
Golconda   371 sq. mi.

| 4,413 | 4,373 | 4,404 | 3,857 | 4,061 | 5,779 |

January 10, 1816. Nathaniel Pope (1784–1850). Secretary of Illinois Territory 1809–16; congressional delegate 1816–18; U.S. judge for District of Illinois 1819–50.

Pope   **Minnesota**
Glenwood   670 sq. mi.

| 11,236 | 10,745 | 11,657 | 11,107 | 11,914 | 12,862 |

February 20, 1862; organized February 28, 1866. John Pope (1823–92). Graduated West Point 1842; 2nd lieutenant in Mexican War under General Zachary Taylor; battle of Buena Vista 1847; explored Red River of the North 1849; explored Rocky Mountains 1854–59; brigadier general 1861; major role in Union loss at Second Bull Run 1862; removed to command of Department of the Northwest; led brutal defeat of Dakotas 1862; retired 1886.

Poquoson   **Virginia**
(Independent City)   16 sq. mi.

| 11,566 | 11,005 | 8,726 | (a) | (a) | (a) |

1976. Indian word meaning "low, flat land." [(a) Part of York County] (Associated county: York.)

Portage   **Ohio**
Ravenna   492 sq. mi.

| 152,061 | 142,585 | 135,856 | 125,868 | 91,798 | 63,954 |

February 10, 1807; effective June 7, 1807. Descriptive of Indian portage between Cuyahoga and Tuscarawas rivers.

Portage   **Wisconsin**
Stevens Point   806 sq. mi.

| 67,182 | 61,405 | 57,420 | 47,541 | 36,964 | 34,858 |

December 7, 1836; organized 1844. Descriptive of Indian portage between Wisconsin and Fox rivers.

Porter   **Indiana**
Valparaiso   418 sq. mi.

| 146,798 | 128,932 | 119,816 | 87,114 | 60,279 | 40,076 |

February 7, 1835; organized January 28, 1836. David Porter (1780–1843). Commanded frigate *Essex* in War of 1812; defeated by British off Valparaiso, Chile, 1813; commanded squadron against Caribbean pirates 1823–25; commander in chief of Mexican navy 1826–29; U.S. consul general to Algiers 1830; U.S. minister to Turkey 1839.

Portsmouth   **Virginia**
(Independent City)   33 sq. mi.

| 100,565 | 103,907 | 104,577 | 110,963 | 114,773 | 80,039 |

March 1, 1858. Portsmouth, England. (Associated county: Norfolk.)

Posey   **Indiana**
Mount Vernon   409 sq. mi.

| 27,061 | 25,968 | 26,414 | 21,740 | 19,214 | 19,818 |

September 7, 1814; effective November 1, 1814. Thomas Posey (1750–1818). Captain of Virginia Regiment 1776–78; major 1778; colonel 1789; Yorktown 1781; brigadier general 1793; Louisiana Senate 1805–06; lieutenant governor of Kentucky; U.S. senator from Louisiana 1812–13; governor of Indiana Territory 1813–16; Indian agent 1816–18.

Pottawatomie   **Kansas**
Westmoreland   844 sq. mi.

| 18,209 | 16,128 | 14,782 | 11,755 | 11,957 | 12,344 |

February 20, 1857. *Potawatomi Indians*. Pushed from Great Lakes region by Indians and Europeans; scattered throughout Midwest by 1800; ceded lands to U.S. 1846; resettled in Indian Territory (Oklahoma); name from Algonquin *pottawatomink* refers to "fire."

Pottawatomie   **Oklahoma**
Shawnee   788 sq. mi.
65,521   58,760   55,239   43,134   41,486   43,517
1891. Potawatomi Indians.*

Pottawattamie   **Iowa**
Council Bluffs   954 sq. mi.
87,704   82,628   86,561   86,991   83,102   69,682
January 15, 1851. Potawatomi Indians.*

Potter   **Pennsylvania**
Coudersport   1,081 sq. mi.
18,080   16,717   17,726   16,395   16,483   16,810
March 26, 1804; organized 1835. James Potter (1729–89). French and Indian Wars; colonel, Pennsylvania Militia 1776–77; wounded at Princeton 1777; brigadier general 1777; major general 1782.

Potter   **South Dakota**
Gettysburg   866 sq. mi.
2,693   3,190   3,674   4,449   4,926   4,688
January 8, 1873, as Ashmore; name changed January 14, 1875; organized December 27, 1883. Joel A. Potter (1825–95). Physician; Dakota territorial legislature 1872; steward of South Dakota State Hospital.

Potter   **Texas**
Amarillo   909 sq. mi.
113,546   97,874   98,637   90,511   115,580   73,366
August 21, 1876; organized September 6, 1887. Robert Potter (c1800–42). U.S. navy 1815–21; North Carolina House of Commons 1826, 1828, and 1834–35; U.S. representative 1829–32; emigrated to Texas 1835; signed Texas Declaration of Independence 1836; Texas Republic secretary of navy 1836; fought at San Jacinto 1836; Texas Congress 1837–41; killed in Regulator–Moderator War, a land feud in east Texas March 2, 1842.

Powder River   **Montana**
Broadus   3,297 sq. mi.
1,858   2,090   2,520   2,862   2,485   2,693
March 7, 1919; effective April 1, 1919. Powder River. Descriptive of gunpowder-colored sand along banks; tributary of Yellowstone River.

Powell   **Kentucky**
Stanton   180 sq. mi.
13,237   11,686   11,101   7,704   6,674   6,812
January 7, 1852. Lazarus Powell (1812–66). Kentucky House of Representatives 1837–39; governor of Kentucky 1851–55; U.S. commissioner to Utah 1858; U.S. senator from Kentucky 1859–65.

Powell   **Montana**
Deer Lodge   2,326 sq. mi.
7,180   6,620   6,958   6,660   7,002   6,301
January 31, 1901. John Wesley Powell (1834–1902). Private, 20th Illinois Volunteers; lost right arm during Shiloh campaign 1862; promoted to major and lieutenant colonel; geologist; explored Grand Canyon 1869; Smithsonian Institute Bureau of Ethnology 1879–1902; director, U.S. Geological Survey 1881–94.

Power   **Idaho**
American Falls   1,406 sq. mi.
7,538   7,086   6,844   4,864   4,111   3,988
January 30, 1913. Descriptive of hydroelectric power generated at American Falls on Snake River.

Poweshiek   **Iowa**
Montezuma   585 sq. mi.

| 18,815 | 19,033 | 19,306 | 18,803 | 19,300 | 19,344 |

February 17, 1843; organized January 24, 1848; effective April 3, 1848. Poweshiek (1797–?). Fox–Mesquaki chief; tried to prevent Black Hawk War 1832; moved Fox from Illinois to Iowa; signed treaties ceding Indian lands 1832–42; expelled to Kansas 1846.

Powhatan   **Virginia**
Powhatan   261 sq. mi.

| 22,377 | 15,328 | 13,062 | 7,696 | 6,747 | 5,556 |

May 5, 1777 (session); effective July 1, 1777. Powhatan (c1550–1618). Chief of Powhatan confederacy in southeastern Virginia; maintained good relations with settlers; named Wahunsonacook, called Powhatan by English after Indian village on James River; father of Pocahontas (see Pocahontas, Iowa). Name is Algonquin for "falls in a river."

Prairie   **Arkansas**
Des Arc   646 sq. mi.

| 9,539 | 9,518 | 10,140 | 10,249 | 10,515 | 13,768 |

November 25, 1846. Grand Prairie. Descriptive of area geography.

Prairie   **Montana**
Terry   1,737 sq. mi.

| 1,199 | 1,383 | 1,836 | 1,752 | 2,318 | 2,377 |

February 5, 1915. Descriptive of local geography.

Pratt   **Kansas**
Pratt   735 sq. mi.

| 9,647 | 9,702 | 10,275 | 10,056 | 12,122 | 12,156 |

February 26, 1867; organized 1879. Caleb Pratt (c1832–1861). Auditor and county clerk of Douglas County; Union army, 2nd lieutenant, Company D, 2nd Kansas, 1861; killed at Wilson's Creek, August 10, 1861.

Preble   **Ohio**
Eaton   425 sq. mi.

| 42,337 | 40,113 | 38,223 | 34,719 | 32,498 | 27,081 |

February 15, 1808; effective March 1, 1808. Edward Preble (1761–1807). Midshipman, Massachusetts Navy; U.S. navy lieutenant 1798; commanded *Essex* 1799, and *Constitution* 1803; bombarded Tripoli against Barbary pirates 1804; forced renewal of treaty with Sultan of Morocco.

Prentiss   **Mississippi**
Booneville   415 sq. mi.

| 25,556 | 23,278 | 24,025 | 20,133 | 17,949 | 19,810 |

April 15, 1870. Sergeant Smith Prentiss (1808–50). Mississippi House of Representatives 1835; U.S. representative 1838–39; various spellings of given name "Sergeant."

Presidio   **Texas**
Marfa   3,856 sq. mi.

| 7,304 | 6,637 | 5,188 | 4,842 | 5,460 | 7,354 |

January 3, 1850; organized 1875. Presidio del Norte. Spanish military post (*presidio*) originally located at junction of Rio Grande and Conchos rivers in Mexico 1759; abandoned and reestablished north of Rio Grande 1767; garrisoned by Spanish troops until 1814.

Presque Isle   **Michigan**
Rogers City   660 sq. mi.

| 14,411 | 13,743 | 14,267 | 12,836 | 13,117 | 11,996 |

April 1, 1840; organized March 31, 1871. Presque Isle Peninsula. Narrow peninsula into Lake Huron; French for "almost an island."

Preston   **West Virginia**
Kingwood   648 sq. mi.

29,334   29,037   30,460   25,455   27,233   31,399
January 19, 1818. James Patton Preston (1774–1843). Virginia Senate 1802; lieutenant colonel of infantry 1812; colonel 1813; wounded at Crysler's Farm, Canada, November 11, 1813; governor of Virginia 1816–19.

Price   **Wisconsin**
Phillips   1,253 sq. mi.
15,822   15,600   15,788   14,520   14,370   16,344
February 26, 1879; organized 1882. William Thompson Price (1824–86). Judge of Jackson County, Wisconsin, 1854 and 1859; Crawford County treasurer 1856–57; Wisconsin Senate 1857, 1870, and 1878–81; Wisconsin legislature 1851 and 1882; U.S. representative 1883–86.

Prince Edward   **Virginia**
Farmville   353 sq. mi.
19,720   17,320   16,456   14,379   14,121   15,398
February 27, 1752 (session). Prince Edward Augustus (1739–67). Grandson of King George II reigning at time county was created; son of Frederick Louis, Prince of Wales; brother of King George III; Duke of York and Albany 1760.

Prince George   **Virginia**
Prince George   266 sq. mi.
33,047   27,394   25,733   29,092   20,270   19,679
December 5, 1700 (session). *Prince George of Denmark* (1653–1708). Son of King Frederick III of Denmark; married Princess Anne of England 1683; denied title of king when wife became Queen Anne; Duke of Cumberland 1689; lord high admiral of England 1702.

Prince George's   **Maryland**
Upper Marlboro   485 sq. mi.
801,515   729,268   665,071   660,567   357,395   194,182
May 20, 1695; organized April 23, 1696. Prince George of Denmark.*

Prince of Wales–Outer Ketchikan   **Alaska**
(Census Area)   7,411 sq. mi.
6,146   6,278   3,822   3,782   1,772[a]   [b]
Prince of Wales Island; named by Captain Vancouver (1793) for George, Prince of Wales (1762–1830); regent during incapacity of George III 1810–20; King George IV of England 1820–30. "Outer Ketchikan" is that part of Ketchikan Census Area not included in Ketchikan Gateway Borough 1963. [(a) Prince of Wales; (b) Part of 1st Judicial District.]

Prince William   **Virginia**
Manassas   338 sq. mi.
280,813   215,686   144,703   111,102   50,164   22,612
February 1, 1727 (Session). Prince William Augustus, Duke of Cumberland (see Cumberland, Kentucky).

Providence   **Rhode Island**
Providence   413 sq. mi.
621,602   596,270   571,349   580,261   568,778   574,973
June 22, 1703, as Providence Plantations; name changed June 16, 1729. Providence Plantations. Roger Williams thanked "God's merciful providence" for delivering him to Narragansett Bay after fleeing Massachusetts 1636.

Prowers   **Colorado**
Lamar   1,640 sq. mi.
14,483   13,347   13,070   13,258   13,296   14,836
April 11, 1889. John W. Prowers (1838–84). Worked at Bent's Fort 1856–63; freighted government supplies from Leavenworth, Kansas, to Fort Union, New Mexico; pioneer cattleman in Arkansas Valley.

Pueblo   **Colorado**
Pueblo   2,389 sq. mi.

141,472   123,051   125,972   118,238   118,707   90,188
November 1, 1861. City of Pueblo. Spanish for "town" or "dwelling;" applied to Native American dwellings in Southwest.

Pulaski   **Arkansas**
Little Rock   771 sq. mi.
361,474   349,660   340,613   287,189   242,980   196,685
December 15, 1818; effective March 1, 1819. *Casimir Pulaski* (1748–79). Polish nobleman; came to America 1777 to aid colonists in Revolution; fought at Brandywine and Germantown 1777; mortally wounded at siege of Savannah, October 9, 1779.

Pulaski   **Georgia**
Hawkinsville   247 sq. mi.
9,588   8,108   8,950   8,066   8,204   8,808
December 13, 1808. Casimir Pulaski.*

Pulaski   **Illinois**
Mound City   201 sq. mi.
7,348   7,523   8,840   8,741   10,490   13,639
March 3, 1843. Casimir Pulaski.*

Pulaski   **Indiana**
Winamac   434 sq. mi.
13,755   12,643   13,258   12,534   12,387   12,493
February 7, 1835; organized February 18, 1839; effective May 6, 1839. Casimir Pulaski.*

Pulaski   **Kentucky**
Somerset   662 sq. mi.
56,217   49,489   45,803   35,234   34,403   38,452
December 10, 1798; effective June 1, 1799. Casimir Pulaski.*

Pulaski   **Missouri**
Waynesville   547 sq. mi.
41,165   41,307   42,011   53,781   46,567   10,392
January 19, 1833. Casimir Pulaski.*

Pulaski   **Virginia**
Pulaski   321 sq. mi.
35,127   34,496   35,229   29,564   27,258   27,758
March 30, 1839. Casimir Pulaski.*

Pushmataha   **Oklahoma**
Antlers   1,397 sq. mi.
11,667   10,997   11,773   9,385   9,088   12,001
July 16, 1907. Pushmataha District of Choctaw Nation. Named for chief Apushmataha (?–1824); supported U.S. in Creek War 1813–14; given rank and dress uniform of brigadier general; ceded Choctaw lands to U.S.; died on mission to Washington after meeting President Monroe 1824; buried in Congressional Cemetery.

Putnam   **Florida**
Palatka   722 sq. mi.
70,423   65,070   50,549   36,290   32,212   23,615
January 13, 1849. Uncertain. (1) Benjamin Putnam (1801–69); fought in 2nd Seminole War; Florida legislature; Speaker of General Assembly 1849; surveyor general of Florida 1849–54. (2) Israel Putnam* (see Putnam, Georgia).

Putnam   **Georgia**
Eatonton   345 sq. mi.

18,812   14,137   10,295   8,394   7,798   7,731

December 10, 1807. *Israel Putnam* (1718–90). Officer in French and Indian Wars 1754–63; Pontiac's War 1764; Connecticut legislature; heard of battle of Lexington while plowing his fields, hurried to Lexington without stopping to change clothes 1775; major general, Continental army 1775–79; commanded at New York and Philadelphia; paralytic stroke ended military service 1779.

Putnam   **Illinois**
Hennepin   160 sq. mi.
6,086   5,730   6,085   5,007   4,570   4,746
January 13, 1825; organized 1831. Israel Putnam.*

Putnam   **Indiana**
Greencastle   480 sq. mi.
36,019   30,315   29,163   26,932   24,927   22,950
December 31, 1821; effective April 1, 1822. Israel Putnam.*

Putnam   **Missouri**
Unionville   518 sq. mi.
5,223   5,079   6,092   5,916   6,999   9,166
February 22, 1843. Israel Putnam.*

Putnam   **New York**
Carmel   231 sq. mi.
95,745   83,941   77,193   56,696   31,722   20,307
June 12, 1812. Israel Putnam.*

Putnam   **Ohio**
Ottawa   484 sq. mi.
34,726   33,819   32,991   31,134   28,331   25,248
February 12, 1820; organized 1834. Israel Putnam.*

Putnam   **Tennessee**
Cookeville   401 sq. mi.
62,315   51,373   47,690   35,487   29,236   29,869
February 2, 1842; abolished 1844; recreated 1854. Israel Putnam.*

Putnam   **West Virginia**
Winfield   346 sq. mi.
51,589   42,835   38,181   27,652   23,561   21,021
March 11, 1848. Israel Putnam.*

Q

Quay   **New Mexico**
Tucumcari   2,875 sq. mi.
10,155   10,823   10,577   10,903   12,279   13,971
February 28, 1903. Matthew Stanley Quay (1833–1904). Lieutenant, 10th Pennsylvania Reserves, 134th Pennsylvania Infantry; awarded Congressional Medal of Honor for bravery at Fredericksburg 1862; colonel 1862; military secretary to governor 1863–65; Pennsylvania House of Representatives 1865–67; secretary of the commonwealth 1872–78 and 1879–82; Pennsylvania treasurer 1885–87; U.S. senator 1887–89 and 1901–04; advocated New Mexico statehood.

Queen Anne's   **Maryland**
Centreville   372 sq. mi.
40,563   33,953   25,508   18,422   16,569   14,579

April 18, 1706; organized 1707. Queen Anne (1665–1714). Second daughter of James II and Anne Hyde; sister of Mary II; married Prince George of Denmark 1683; Queen of England 1702–14; unable to produce heir, of fifteen children only one, Prince William (1689–1700) survived beyond infancy. (See also Fluvanna, Virginia.)

Queens   **New York**
Jamaica   109 sq. mi.

2,229,379	1,951,598	1,891,325	1,986,473	1,809,578	1,550,849

November 1, 1683. Queen Catherine of Braganza (1638–1705). Daughter of the Duke of Braganza who became King John IV of Portugal; wife of Charles II of England 1662; tolerated Charles's many illegitimate children; remained in England following Charles's death (1685) until returning to Portugal 1692.

Quitman   **Georgia**
Georgetown   152 sq. mi.

2,598	2,209	2,357	2,180	2,432	3,015

December 10, 1858. *John Anthony Quitman* (1799–1858). Mississippi House of Representatives 1826–27; chancellor of Mississippi 1828–35; president of Mississippi Senate and acting governor 1835–36; brigadier general of Volunteers 1846; major general, Regular Army 1847; governor of Mississippi 1850–51; U.S. representative 1855–58.

Quitman   **Mississippi**
Marks   405 sq. mi.

10,117	10,490	12,636	15,888	21,019	25,885

February 1, 1877. John Anthony Quitman.*

R

Rabun   **Georgia**
Clayton   371 sq. mi.

15,050	11,648	10,466	8,327	7,456	7,424

December 21, 1819. William Rabun (1771–1819). Georgia Assembly; president of Georgia Senate; governor of Georgia 1817–19; died in office.

Racine   **Wisconsin**
Racine   333 sq. mi.

188,831	175,034	173,132	170,838	141,781	109,585

December 7, 1836. Town of Racine. French for "root"; for numerous roots along banks of Racine River.

Radford   **Virginia**
(Independent City)   10 sq. mi.

15,859	15,940	13,225	11,596	9,371	9,026

1892. Dr. John Blair Radford (1813–72). Prominent resident at time city was incorporated and name changed from Central Depot 1892. (Associated county: Montgomery.)

Rains   **Texas**
Emory   232 sq. mi.

9,139	6,715	4,839	3,752	2,993	4,266

June 9, 1870; organized December 1, 1870. Emory Rains (1800–78). Emigrated to Texas 1826; Texas Republic legislature 1837; delegate to convention that accepted U.S. offer of annexation and drafted state constitution 1845; surveyed area which became Rains County 1869.

Raleigh   **West Virginia**
Beckley   607 sq. mi.

79,220	76,819	86,821	70,080	77,826	96,273

January 23, 1850. Sir Walter Ralegh (c1552–1618). First lord proprietor of Virginia 1584–1603; voyage of discovery and piracy in America with half brother Sir Humphrey Gilbert 1578; favorite of Elizabeth I; knighted 1585; attempted colony on

Roanoke Island 1585, abandoned 1586; second attempt to colonize Roanoke 1587, colony mysteriously disappeared by 1590; participated in victory over Spanish Armada 1588; fell from royal favor after marriage to Elizabeth Throckmorton, one of Elizabeth's maids of honor; stripped of all titles by James I; confined in Tower of London 1603–16; beheaded. (American spelling includes letter "i.")

Ralls   **Missouri**
New London   471 sq. mi.
9,626   8,476   8,911   7,764   8,078   8,686
November 16, 1820. Daniel Ralls (c1785–1820). Missouri Assembly 1820; carried from his sickbed to cast vote for Thomas Hart Benton for U.S. Senate; died one month later.

Ramsey   **Minnesota**
Saint Paul   156 sq. mi.
511,035   485,765   459,784   476,255   422,525   355,332
October 27, 1849; organized March 31, 1851; effective September 1, 1851. *Alexander Ramsey* (1815–1903). Clerk, Pennsylvania House of Representatives 1841; U.S. representative 1843–47; governor of Minnesota Territory 1849; governor of Minnesota 1860–63; U.S. senator 1863–75; U.S. secretary of war 1879–81.

Ramsey   **North Dakota**
Devils Lake   1,185 sq. mi.
12,066   12,681   13,048   12,915   13,443   14,373
January 4, 1873; organized January 25, 1885. Alexander Ramsey.*

Randall   **Texas**
Canyon   914 sq. mi.
104,312   89,673   75,062   53,885   33,913   13,774
August 21, 1876; organized July 27, 1889. Horace Randal (1833–64). Graduated West Point 1854; 2nd lieutenant, infantry; resigned commission 1861; colonel, 28th Texas Cavalry; assigned duties of brigadier general but not officially promoted before being mortally wounded at Jenkin's Ferry, Arkansas, April 30, 1864. (County name is misspelled.)

Randolph   **Alabama**
Wedowee   581 sq. mi.
22,380   19,881   20,075   18,331   19,477   22,513
December 18, 1832. *John Randolph* (1773–1833). Several terms as U.S. representative from Virginia 1799–1833; U.S. senator 1825–26; advocate of Southern interests in Congress; fought duel with Henry Clay April 8, 1826; U.S. minister to Russia 1830–31.

Randolph   **Arkansas**
Pocahontas   652 sq. mi.
18,195   16,558   16,834   12,645   12,520   15,982
October 29, 1835. John Randolph.*

Randolph   **Georgia**
Cuthbert   429 sq. mi.
7,791   8,023   9,599   8,734   11,078   13,804
December 20, 1828. John Randolph.*

Randolph   **Illinois**
Chester   578 sq. mi.
33,893   34,583   35,652   31,379   29,988   31,673
October 5, 1795. Uncertain. (1) Beverly Randolph (1754–97); commanded regiment in Revolutionary War; Virginia House of Delegates; governor of Virginia 1788–91. (2) Edmund Jennings Randolph* (see Randolph, West Virginia).

Randolph   **Indiana**
Winchester   453 sq. mi.

| 27,401 | 27,148 | 29,997 | 28,915 | 28,434 | 27,141 |

January 10, 1818; effective August 10, 1818. Uncertain. (1) Randolph County, North Carolina. (2) Peyton Randolph* (see Randolph, North Carolina). (3) Thomas Randolph (?–1811); cousin of Thomas Jefferson; Virginia legislature; attorney general of Indiana Territory; private, Indiana Militia; killed at Battle of Tippecanoe November 7, 1811.

Randolph   **Missouri**
Huntsville   482 sq. mi.

| 24,663 | 24,370 | 25,460 | 22,434 | 22,014 | 22,918 |

January 22, 1829. John Randolph.*

Randolph   **North Carolina**
Asheboro   787 sq. mi.

| 130,454 | 106,546 | 91,728 | 76,358 | 61,497 | 50,804 |

April 14, 1778 (session). *Peyton Randolph* (1721–75). King's attorney for Virginia 1748; Virginia House of Burgesses 1764–74, Speaker 1766; chairman of Committee of Correspondence 1773; president of Virginia Convention 1774 and 1775; president of Continental Congress 1774 and 1775.

Randolph   **West Virginia**
Elkins   1,040 sq. mi.

| 28,262 | 27,803 | 28,734 | 24,596 | 26,349 | 30,558 |

October 16, 1786 (session); effective May 5, 1787. *Edmund Jennings Randolph* (1753–1813); aide-de-camp to General Washington 1775; Virginia attorney general 1776; Continental Congress 1779–82; governor of Virginia 1786–88; U.S. Constitutional Convention 1788–89; first attorney general of U.S. 1789–94; secretary of state, 1794–95.

Rankin   **Mississippi**
Brandon   775 sq. mi.

| 115,327 | 87,161 | 69,427 | 43,933 | 34,322 | 28,881 |

February 4, 1828. Christopher Rankin (1788–1826). Mississippi territorial legislature 1813; Mississippi Constitutional Convention 1817; U.S. representative 1819–26.

Ransom   **North Dakota**
Lisbon   863 sq. mi.

| 5,890 | 5,921 | 6,698 | 7,102 | 8,078 | 8,876 |

January 4, 1873; organized April 4, 1881. Fort Ransom. Established by General Alfred Terry on the Sheyenne River 1867; abandoned 1872; named for Thomas E. G. Ransom (1834–64); Union army; Fort Donelson, Shiloh, Vicksburg, and Atlanta campaigns; received several combat wounds; brigadier general of Volunteers 1863; died while pursuing Confederate soldiers in Alabama and Georgia 1864.

Rapides   **Louisiana**
Alexandria   1,323 sq. mi.

| 126,337 | 131,556 | 135,282 | 118,078 | 111,351 | 90,648 |

April 10, 1805. Rapids in the Red River. French for "rapids."

Rappahannock   **Virginia**
Washington   267 sq. mi.

| 6,983 | 6,622 | 6,093 | 5,199 | 5,368 | 6,112 |

February 8, 1833. Rappahannock River. Indian name meaning "alternating river" or "river of quick-rising water"; refers to tidal flow of river's estuary at Chesapeake Bay.

Ravalli   **Montana**
Hamilton   2,394 sq. mi.

| 36,070 | 25,010 | 22,493 | 14,409 | 12,341 | 13,101 |

February 16, 1893. Antonio Ravalli (1811–84). Jesuit missionary; arrived in North America 1844; worked among Kalispell Indians at St. Ignatius Mission; missionary to Coeur d'Alene Indians; retired to Santa Clara College, California, 1860; returned to Montana 1863.

Rawlins   **Kansas**
Atwood   1,070 sq. mi.
2,966   3,404   4,105   4,393   5,279   5,728
March 6, 1873; organized March 11, 1881. John Aaron Rawlins (1831–69). Aide-de-camp to General Grant; rose in rank with Grant from major to major general 1861–65; secretary of war 1869.

Ray   **Missouri**
Richmond   569 sq. mi.
23,354   21,971   21,378   17,599   16,075   15,932
November 16, 1820. John Ray (?–1820). Missouri Constitutional Convention 1820; Missouri General Assembly 1820.

Reagan   **Texas**
Big Lake   1,175 sq. mi.
3,326   4,514   4,135   3,239   3,782   3,127
March 7, 1903. John Henninger Reagan (1818–1905). Fought Cherokee Indians 1839; lieutenant colonel of militia 1846; Texas House of Representatives 1847–49; postmaster general of the Confederacy 1861–64; U.S. representative 1875–87; U.S. senator 1887–91.

Real   **Texas**
Leakey   700 sq. mi.
3,047   2,412   2,469   2,013   2,079   2,479
April 3, 1913. Julius Real (1860–1944). County judge and school superintendent 1902–09; Texas Senate 1910–14 and 1924–28.

Red Lake   **Minnesota**
Red Lake Falls   432 sq. mi.
4,299   4,525   5,471   5,388   5,830   6,806
December 24, 1896; organized April 6, 1897. Red Lake River. Runs from Red Lake to the Red River of the North; name is translation of Chippewa name, given for red sunsets rather than iron ore deposits or blood.

Red River   **Louisiana**
Coushatta   389 sq. mi.
9,622   9,387   10,433   9,226   9,978   12,113
March 7, 1871. *Red River*. Descriptive of red color from red clay and sandstone; tributary of Mississippi.

Red River   **Texas**
Clarksville   1,050 sq. mi.
14,314   14,317   16,101   14,298   15,682   21,851
March 17, 1836; organized 1837. Red River.*

Red Willow   **Nebraska**
McCook   717 sq. mi.
11,448   11,705   12,615   12,191   12,940   12,977
February 27, 1873; organized May 27, 1873. Red Willow Creek. Mistranslation of Dakota name "Chashasha Wakpala," meaning "Red Dogwood Creek"; tributary of Republican River.

Redwood   **Minnesota**
Redwood Falls   880 sq. mi.
16,815   17,254   19,341   20,024   21,718   22,127
February 6, 1862; organized February 23, 1865. Redwood River. Descriptive of either red cedar trees, or of red-barked bushes; tributary of Minnesota River.

Reeves   **Texas**
Pecos   2,636 sq. mi.
13,137   15,852   15,801   16,526   17,644   11,745

April 14, 1883; organized November 4, 1884. George R. Reeves (1826–82). Emigrated to Texas 1846; tax collector of Grayson County 1848–50; sheriff of Grayson County 1850–54; Texas House of Representatives 1855–61 and 1873, Speaker 1881–82; Confederate army 1861; colonel 1863.

Refugio   **Texas**
Refugio   770 sq. mi.
7,828   7,976   9,289   9,494   10,975   10,113
March 17, 1836; organized 1837. Mission Nuestra Señora del Refugio (Our Lady of Refuge); founded in 1790's; baptismal records maintained until 1828; buildings in ruins by 1835 from fighting between Americans and Mexico.

Reno   **Kansas**
Hutchinson   1,254 sq. mi.
64,790   62,389   64,983   60,765   59,055   54,058
February 26, 1867; organized 1873. Jesse Lee Reno (1823–62). Graduated West Point 1846; 2nd lieutenant 1847; 1st lieutenant; brevetted for gallantry at Cerro Gordo and Chapultepec; brigadier general of Volunteers 1861; major general 1862; killed at South Mountain during Antietam campaign September 14, 1862.

Rensselaer   **New York**
Troy   654 sq. mi.
152,538   154,429   151,966   152,510   142,585   132,607
February 7, 1791. Van Rensselaer family. The first van Renselaer patroon was Kiliaen van Rensselaer (1580–1644), a stockholder in Dutch West India Company. *Renselaerwyck* was the name of enormous land holdings granted to the van Renselaer family by the Dutch West India Company along the Hudson River.

Renville   **Minnesota**
Olivia   983 sq. mi.
17,154   17,673   20,401   21,139   23,249   23,954
February 20, 1855; organized July 31, 1866. *Joseph Renville* (c1779–1846). Son of French father and Dakota mother; guide and interpreter for Zebulon Pike 1805–06; British captain during War of 1812; trading post at Lac qui Parle 1815; translated Bible into Dakota language.

Renville   **North Dakota**
Mohall   875 sq. mi.
2,610   3,160   3,608   3,828   4,698   5,405
January 4, 1873; abolished November 1892; recreated June 3, 1910. Uncertain. (1) Joseph Renville.* (2) Gabriel Renville (c1824–92); mixed French Canadian and Dakota; nephew of Joseph; friendly to U.S. during Dakota War 1862; resettled from Minnesota to Dakota Reservation in Dakota Territory; chief of Sisseton and Wahpeton bands of Dakotas; supported by U.S.

Republic   **Kansas**
Belleville   716 sq. mi.
5,835   6,482   7,569   8,498   9,768   11,478
February 27, 1860; abolished 1865; recreated 1868; deorganized 1870; reorganized 1878. Republican River. Named for Republican Pawnees (Kitkehahki), one of four bands of Pawnees; their organization was called Pahni Republique by French for acting independently of Pawnees; resettled to Indian Territory (Oklahoma) 1870's.

Reynolds   **Missouri**
Centerville   811 sq. mi.
6,689   6,661   7,230   6,106   5,161   6,918
February 25, 1845. Thomas Reynolds (1796–1844). Clerk of Illinois House of Representatives; chief justice of Illinois Supreme Court 1822–25; Missouri legislature 1828, Speaker 1832; governor of Missouri 1840–44; committed suicide while governor.

Rhea   **Tennessee**
Dayton   316 sq. mi.
28,400   24,344   24,235   17,202   15,863   16,041

November 30, 1807. John Rhea (1753–1832). Ensign, 7th Virginia Regiment 1777; battle of King's Mountain 1780; delegate to North Carolina convention that ratified federal constitution 1789; Tennessee House of Representatives 1796–97; U.S. representative 1803–15 and 1817–23.

Rice   **Kansas**
Lyons   727 sq. mi.
10,761   10,610   11,900   12,320   13,909   15,635
February 26, 1867; organized 1871. Samuel Allen Rice (1828–64). County attorney, Oskaloosa, Iowa, 1853; colonel of Iowa Volunteers 1861; brigadier general 1862; wounded at Jenkin's Ferry, Arkansas, April 30, 1864; died July 6.

Rice   **Minnesota**
Faribault   498 sq. mi.
56,665   49,183   46,087   41,582   38,988   36,235
March 5, 1853; organized October 9, 1855. Henry Mower Rice (1817–94). Negotiated treaties with Indians ceding their lands to U.S. 1847; Minnesota Territory delegate to Congress 1853–57; U.S. senator 1858–63; regent of University of Minnesota 1851–59; treasurer of Ramsey County 1878–84.

Rich   **Utah**
Randolph   1,029 sq. mi.
1,961   1,725   2,100   1,615   1,685   1,673
January 16, 1864, as Richland; name changed January 29, 1868. Charles Coulson Rich (1809–83). Baptized into Mormon faith 1832; military leader during Mormon exodus to Utah 1847; apostle of church 1849; established Mormon colony in San Bernardino, California; Utah legislature 1864–72.

Richardson   **Nebraska**
Falls City   553 sq. mi.
9,531   9,937   11,315   12,277   13,903   16,886
November 23, 1854. William Alexander Richardson (1811–75). Illinois state's attorney 1834–35; Illinois House of Representatives 1836–38 and 1844–46, Speaker 1844; Illinois Senate 1838–42; captain and major during Mexican War; U.S. representative 1847–56, and 1861–63; governor of Nebraska Territory 1858; U.S. senator from Illinois 1863–65.

Richland   **Illinois**
Olney   360 sq. mi.
16,149   16,545   17,587   16,829   16,299   16,889
February 24, 1841. Richland County, Ohio. Origin of early settlers.

Richland   **Louisiana**
Rayville   558 sq. mi.,
20,981   20,629   22,187   21,774   23,824   26,672
September 29, 1868. Descriptive of rich alluvial soils in area.

Richland   **Montana**
Sidney   2,084 sq. mi.
9,667   10,716   12,243   9,837   10,504   10,366
May 27, 1914. Promotional name in hopes of attracting settlers.

Richland   **North Dakota**
Wahpeton   1,437 sq. mi.
17,998   18,148   19,207   18,089   18,824   19,865
January 4, 1873; organized November 25, 1875. Morgan T. Rich (1832–98). Operated ferry across Bois de Sioux River 1868; founder of Wahpeton; county commissioner 1875.

Richland   **Ohio**
Mansfield   497 sq. mi.
128,852   126,137   131,205   129,997   117,761   91,305
January 30, 1808; organized 1813. Descriptive of soil in area.

Richland   **South Carolina**
Columbia   756 sq. mi.
320,677   285,720   269,735   233,868   200,102   142,565
March 12, 1785. Uncertain. (1) Descriptive of rich soil in area. (2) Colonel Thomas Taylor's "Richland Plantation."

Richland   **Wisconsin**
Richland Center   586 sq. mi.
17,924   17,521   17,476   17,079   17,684   19,245
February 18, 1842; organized 1850. Promotional name in hopes of attracting settlers.

Richmond   **Georgia**
Augusta   324 sq. mi.
199,775   189,719   181,629   162,437   135,601   108,876
February 5, 1777. *Charles Lenox, 3rd Duke of Richmond* (1735–1806). General in British army; ambassador extraordinary and minister plenipotentiary to Paris 1766; member of Parliament; supported colonist cause in American Revolution; proposed withdrawal of British troops from America 1778; Knight of the Garter 1782.

Richmond   **New York**
Saint George   58 sq. mi.
443,728   378,977   352,121   295,443   221,991   191,555
November 1, 1683. *Charles Lenox, 1st Duke of Richmond* (1672–1723). Illegitimate child of Charles II; converted to Catholicism 1685; renounced Catholicism 1692; courtier to George I.

Richmond   **North Carolina**
Rockingham   474 sq. mi.
46,564   44,518   45,481   39,889   39,202   39,597
October 18, 1779 (session). Charles Lenox, 3rd Duke of Richmond.*

Richmond   **Virginia**
Warsaw   191 sq. mi.
8,809   7,273   6,952   5,841   6,375   6,189
April 16, 1692 (session). Uncertain. (1) Richmond, England. (2) Charles Lenox, 1st Duke of Richmond.*

Richmond   **Virginia**
(Independent City)   60 sq. mi.
197,790   203,056   219,214   249,621   219,958   230,310
1782. Richmond, England. (Associated counties: Chesterfield and Henrico.)

Riley   **Kansas**
Manhattan   610 sq. mi.
62,843   67,139   63,505   56,788   41,914   33,405
August 30, 1855. Fort Riley. Named for Colonel Bennet Riley (1787–1853); rose from ensign to captain 1813–18; served on frontier against Indians 1823; rose from major to lieutenant colonel 1837–39; brevet colonel for bravery against Seminoles 1840; brevet major general 1847; military governor of California 1849; colonel, 1st Infantry 1850–53.

Ringgold   **Iowa**
Mount Ayr   538 sq. mi.
5,469   5,420   6,112   6,373   7,910   9,528
February 24, 1847; organized January 31, 1855. Samuel Ringgold (1800–46). Graduated West Point 1818; aide to General Winfield Scott; captain 1834; brevet major for service against Florida Indians; died from wounds at battle of Palo Alto 1846.

Rio Arriba   **New Mexico**
Tierra Amarilla   5,858 sq. mi.
41,190   34,365   29,282   25,170   24,193   24,997
January 9, 1852. Upper Rio Grande River area. Spanish for "upper river" or "upstream"; Spain divided colonial New Mexico into three areas: upper, middle, and lower.

Rio Blanco   **Colorado**
Meeker   3,221 sq. mi.

| 5,986 | 5,972 | 6,255 | 4,842 | 5,150 | 4,719 |

March 25, 1889. White River. Hispanicized name of White River.

Rio Grande   **Colorado**
Del Norte   912 sq. mi.

| 12,413 | 10,770 | 10,511 | 10,494 | 11,160 | 12,832 |

February 10, 1874. Rio Grande River. Spanish for "large river."

Ripley   **Indiana**
Versailles   446 sq. mi.

| 26,523 | 24,616 | 24,398 | 21,138 | 20,641 | 18,763 |

December 27, 1816; organized January 14, 1818; effective April 10, 1818. *Eleazar Wheelock Ripley* (1782–1839). Massachusetts House of Representatives 1807 and 1811; Massachusetts Senate 1812; lieutenant colonel 1812; served at Chippewa, Niagara, and Erie in War of 1812; brevet major general 1814; Louisiana Senate 1820; U.S. representative from Louisiana 1835–39.

Ripley   **Missouri**
Doniphan   629 sq. mi.

| 13,509 | 12,303 | 12,458 | 9,803 | 9,096 | 11,414 |

January 5, 1833. Eleazar Wheelock Ripley.*

Ritchie   **West Virginia**
Harrisville   454 sq. mi.

| 10,343 | 10,233 | 11,442 | 10,145 | 10,877 | 12,535 |

February 18, 1843. Thomas Ritchie (1778–1854). Founded *Enquirer* (later *Richmond Enquirer*) in Richmond 1804, editor 1804–45; supported by President Jefferson; editorially supported public funding for public school and development of infrastructure.

Riverside   **California**
Riverside   7,207 sq. mi.

| 1,545,387 | 1,170,413 | 663,923 | 459,074 | 306,191 | 170,046 |

March 11, 1893. City of Riverside. Named for location on Santa Ana River.

Roane   **Tennessee**
Kingston   361 sq. mi.

| 51,910 | 47,227 | 48,425 | 38,881 | 39,133 | 31,665 |

November 6, 1801. Archibald Roane (c1759–1819). Soldier at Yorktown 1781; Tennessee Constitutional Convention 1796; Tennessee Superior Court 1796–1801; governor of Tennessee 1801–03; Tennessee Supreme Court 1815–18.

Roane   **West Virginia**
Spencer   484 sq. mi.

| 15,446 | 15,120 | 15,952 | 14,111 | 15,720 | 18,408 |

March 11, 1856. Spencer Roane (1762–1822). Virginia house of delegates; judge; Virginia Supreme Court of Appeals 1794; friend and supporter of Thomas Jefferson; son in law of Patrick Henry.

Roanoke   **Virginia**
Salem   251 sq. mi.

| 85,778 | 79,332 | 72,945 | 67,339 | 61,693 | 41,486 |

March 30, 1838. *Roanoke River*. River empties into Albemarle Sound, North Carolina, near Roanoke Island; name is Indian for "white shells," "shell money," or "tobacco."

Roanoke   **Virginia**
(Independent City)   43 sq. mi.

| 94,911 | 96,397 | 100,220 | 92,115 | 97,110 | 91,921 |

1884. Roanoke River.* (Associated county: Roanoke.)

Roberts   **South Dakota**
Sisseton   1,101 sq. mi.

10,016	9,914	10,911	11,678	13,190	14,929

March 8, 1883. Samuel G. Roberts (1843–?). Union army during Civil War; lawyer; settled in Fargo, Dakota Territory; Fargo City Council; Dakota territorial legislature 1879–80 and 1883–84.

Roberts   **Texas**
Miami   924 sq. mi.

887	1,025	1,187	967	1,075	1,031

August 21, 1876; organized January 10, 1889. Uncertain. (1) John S. Roberts (1797–1871); battle of Nacogdoches, a prelude to Texas Revolution 1832; signer of Texas Declaration of Independence 1836. (2) Oran Milo Roberts (1815–98); Alabama legislature 1837; Texas Supreme Court 1857; Texas Constitutional Convention 1866; chief justice, Texas Supreme Court 1874; governor of Texas 1879–83. (3) Both John and Oran Roberts.

Robertson   **Kentucky**
Mount Olivet   100 sq. mi.

2,266	2,124	2,265	2,163	2,443	2,881

February 11, 1867. George Robertson (1790–1874). U.S. representative from Kentucky 1817–21; Kentucky House of Representatives 1822–27 and 1848–52, Speaker 1824–27, and 1851–52; Kentucky secretary of state 1824; law professor, Transylvania University 1834–57; court of appeals 1864–71.

Robertson   **Tennessee**
Springfield   476 sq. mi.

54,433	41,494	37,021	29,102	27,335	27,024

April 9, 1796. James Robertson (1742–1814). Explored Watauga Valley 1770; settled at site of Nashville 1779; North Carolina legislature 1785; Tennessee Constitutional Convention 1796; Tennessee Senate 1798.

Robertson   **Texas**
Franklin   855 sq. mi.

16,000	15,511	14,653	14,389	16,157	19,908

December 14, 1837; organized 1838. Sterling Clark Robertson (1785–1842). Major 1812; battle of New Orleans 1815; established Robertson Colony in Texas 1828; signed Texas Declaration of Independence 1836; Republic of Texas Senate 1836 and 1840.

Robeson   **North Carolina**
Lumberton   949 sq. mi.

123,339	105,179	101,610	84,842	89,102	87,769

November 18, 1786 (session). Thomas Robeson (1740–85). North Carolina legislature; North Carolina Provincial Convention 1775–76; battle of Moore's Creek 1776; battle of Elizabethtown 1781; colonel; paid troops out of own funds.

Rock   **Minnesota**
Luverne   483 sq. mi.

9,721	9,806	10,703	11,346	11,864	11,278

May 23, 1857, as Pipestone; name changed February 20, 1862; organized February 7, 1874. Outcrop of quartzite. Enormous (3 square mile) outcrop of reddish-brown quartzite rising above surrounding prairie.

Rock   **Nebraska**
Bassett   1,008 sq. mi.

1,756	2,019	2,383	2,231	2,554	3,026

November 6, 1888; organized January 8, 1889. Rock Creek. Named for building-stone quarry along creek.

Rock   **Wisconsin**
Janesville   720 sq. mi.

152,307	139,510	139,420	131,970	113,913	92,778

December 7, 1836; organized 1839. Uncertain. (1) Large rock near Janesville marked a safe fording site of the Rock River. (2) Rock River; named for the rock.

Rockbridge   **Virginia**
Lexington   600 sq. mi.
20,808   18,350   17,911   16,637   24,039   23,359
October 20, 1777 (session); effective March 1, 1778. Descriptive of natural limestone bridge over Cedar Creek; once owned by Thomas Jefferson.

Rockcastle   **Kentucky**
Mount Vernon   318 sq. mi.
16,582   14,803   13,973   12,305   12,334   13,925
January 8, 1810. Rockcastle River. Named for large rock formations on river's banks; tributary of Cumberland River.

Rockdale   **Georgia**
Conyers   131 sq. mi.
70,111   54,091   36,747   18,152   10,572   8,464
October 18, 1870. Rockdale Church. Named for large subterranean granite deposit underlying north central Georgia.

Rockingham   **New Hampshire**
Brentwood   695 sq. mi.
277,359   245,845   190,345   138,951   99,029   70,059
April 29, 1769. Charles Watson-Wentworth, *Marquis of Rockingham* (1730–82). English army; Knight of the Garter 1760; prime minister 1765–66 and 1782, repealed Stamp Act; sought to avoid armed conflict with American colonists even if it meant losing colonies.

Rockingham   **North Carolina**
Wentworth   566 sq. mi.
91,928   86,064   83,426   72,402   69,629   64,816
November 19, 1785 (session). Marquis of Rockingham.*

Rockingham   **Virginia**
Harrisonburg   851 sq. mi.
67,725   57,482   57,038   47,890   40,485   35,079
October 20, 1777 (session); effective March 1, 1778. Marquis of Rockingham.*

Rock Island   **Illinois**
Rock Island   427 sq. mi.
149,374   148,723   165,968   166,734   150,991   133,558
February 9, 1831; organized 1833. Rock Island. Large island in Mississippi River near mouth of Rock River.

Rockland   **New York**
New City   174 sq. mi.
286,753   265,475   259,530   229,903   136,803   89,276
February 23, 1798. Descriptive of rocky topography in area including Hudson Palisades.

Rockwall   **Texas**
Rockwall   129 sq. mi.
43,080   25,604   14,528   7,046   5,878   6,156
March 1, 1873; organized April 23, 1873. City of Rockwall. Named for a subterranean stone wall discovered beneath proposed town site 1851.

Roger Mills   **Oklahoma**
Cheyenne   1,142 sq. mi.
3,436   4,147   4,799   4,452   5,090   7,395
1892, as County F; name changed November 8, 1892. Roger Quarles Mills (1832–1911). Texas House of Representatives 1859–60; private, Confederate army 1861; rose to colonel, 10th Regiment, Texas Infantry; wounded at Missionary Ridge and Atlanta; U.S. representative 1873–92; U.S. senator 1892–99; favored opening Indian Territory (Oklahoma) to white settlement.

Rogers　　　　　　**Oklahoma**
Claremore　　　　　　675 sq. mi.
70,641　　　55,170　　　46,436　　　28,425　　　20,614　　　19,532
July 16, 1907. Clement V. Rogers (1839–1911). Rancher and stockman; Cherokee Senate; Oklahoma Constitutional Convention 1907; father of humorist Will Rogers.

Rolette　　　　　　**North Dakota**
Rolla　　　　　　　　902 sq. mi.
13,674　　　12,772　　　12,177　　　11,549　　　10,641　　　11,102
January 4, 1873; October 14, 1884. Joseph Rolette (1820–71). Operated American Fur Company trading post at Pembina; Minnesota territorial legislature 1853–57.

Rooks　　　　　　**Kansas**
Stockton　　　　　　888 sq. mi.
5,685　　　6,039　　　7,006　　　7,628　　　9,734　　　9,043
February 26, 1867; organized 1872. John Calvin Rooks (1835–62). Enlisted Union army 1862; wounded at battle of Prairie Grove December 7, 1862; died December 11.

Roosevelt　　　　　　**Montana**
Wolf Point　　　　　　2,356 sq. mi.
10,620　　　10,999　　　10,467　　　10,365　　　11,731　　　9,580
February 18, 1919. *Theodore Roosevelt (1858–1919)*. New York Assembly 1882–84; U.S. Civil Service Commission 1889–95; president, New York Board of Police Commissioners 1895–96; assistant secretary of the navy 1897–98; colonel, Spanish–American War; commanded "Rough Riders"; governor of New York 1899–1900; vice president of U.S. 1901; became president September 14, 1901, upon assassination of President McKinley; 26th president of U.S. 1901–09.

Roosevelt　　　　　　**New Mexico**
Portales　　　　　　2,449 sq. mi.
18,018　　　16,702　　　15,695　　　16,479　　　16,198　　　16,409
February 28, 1903. Theodore Roosevelt.*

Roscommon　　　　　　**Michigan**
Roscommon　　　　　　521 sq. mi.
25,469　　　19,776　　　16,374　　　9,892　　　7,200　　　5,916
April 1, 1840, as Mikenauk; name changed March 8, 1843; organized March 20, 1875. County Roscommon, Ireland.

Roseau　　　　　　**Minnesota**
Roseau　　　　　　　1,663 sq. mi.
16,338　　　15,026　　　12,574　　　11,569　　　12,154　　　14,505
February 28, 1894; organized April 6, 1896. Roseau River and Roseau Lake. French for "reed" or "rush"; descriptive of reeds growing along lakes and streams in area.

Rosebud　　　　　　**Montana**
Forsyth　　　　　　　5,012 sq. mi.
9,383　　　10,505　　　9,899　　　6,032　　　6,187　　　6,570
February 11, 1901. Rosebud Creek. Descriptive of wild roses along banks.

Ross　　　　　　**Ohio**
Chillicothe　　　　　　688 sq. mi.
73,345　　　69,330　　　65,004　　　61,211　　　61,215　　　54,424
August 20, 1798. James Ross (1762–1847). Pennsylvania Constitutional Convention 1789–90; U.S. senator 1794–1803; unsuccessful candidate for governor of Pennsylvania 1799, 1801, and 1808.

Routt　　　　　　**Colorado**
Steamboat Springs　　　2,362 sq. mi.

| 19,690 | 14,088 | 13,404 | 6,592 | 5,900 | 8,940 |

January 29, 1877. John Long Routt (1826–1907). Sheriff of McLean County, Illinois, 1860; aide to General Grant; governor of Colorado Territory 1875–76; governor of Colorado 1876–79 and 1891–93; mayor of Denver 1883.

Rowan   **Kentucky**
Morehead   281 sq. mi.

| 22,094 | 20,353 | 19,049 | 17,010 | 12,808 | 12,708 |

March 15, 1856. John Rowan (1773–1843). Kentucky secretary of state 1804–06; U.S. representative 1807–09; Kentucky House of Representatives 1813–17, 1822, and 1824; court of appeals judge 1819–21; U.S. senator 1825–31.

Rowan   **North Carolina**
Salisbury   511 sq. mi.

| 139,340 | 110,605 | 99,186 | 90,035 | 82,817 | 75,410 |

March 25, 1753 (session). Matthew Rowan (?–1760). North Carolina General Assembly 1729; North Carolina Council 1734–60; justice of the peace 1735 and 1737; surveyor general of North Carolina 1736; acting royal governor 1753–54.

Runnels   **Texas**
Ballinger   1,051 sq. mi.

| 11,495 | 11,294 | 11,872 | 12,108 | 15,016 | 16,771 |

February 1, 1858; organized February 16, 1880. Uncertain. (1) Hardin Richard Runnels (1820–73); Texas legislature 1847–54, Speaker 1853–54; lieutenant governor 1855; governor of Texas 1857–59; Texas Secession Convention 1861; Texas Constitutional Convention 1866. (2) Hiram G. Runnels (1796–1857); Mississippi legislature; governor of Mississippi 1833–35; fought duel with Volney Howard (see Howard, Texas) 1840; moved to Texas 1842; annexation convention 1845; Texas Senate.

Rush   **Indiana**
Rushville   408 sq. mi.

| 18,261 | 18,129 | 19,604 | 20,352 | 20,393 | 19,799 |

December 31, 1821. Benjamin Rush (1745–1813). Physician; Continental Congress from Pennsylvania 1776–77; signer of Declaration of Independence 1776; surgeon general of the army; founder of Pennsylvania Hospital; treasurer of U.S. Mint at Philadelphia 1799–1813.

Rush   **Kansas**
La Crosse   718 sq. mi.

| 3,551 | 3,842 | 4,516 | 5,117 | 6,160 | 7,231 |

February 26, 1867; organized 1874. Alexander Rush (?–1864). Captain, Company H, 2nd Kansas Colored Cavalry; killed at Jenkin's Ferry April 30, 1864.

Rusk   **Texas**
Henderson   924 sq. mi.

| 47,372 | 43,735 | 41,382 | 34,102 | 36,421 | 42,348 |

January 16, 1843; organized February 6, 1843. Thomas Jefferson Rusk (1803–57). Signed Texas Declaration of Independence 1836; Texas Republic secretary of war; battle of San Jacinto 1836; Texas Republic legislature; chief justice of Texas Republic 1838–42; U.S. senator 1846–57, president pro tempore 1857.

Rusk   **Wisconsin**
Ladysmith   913 sq. mi.

| 15,347 | 15,079 | 15,589 | 14,238 | 14,794 | 16,790 |

May 15, 1901, as Gates; name changed June 19, 1905. Jeremiah McLain Rusk (1830–93). Wisconsin Assembly 1862; major, 25th Regiment, Wisconsin Volunteer Infantry 1862; rose from lieutenant colonel to brigadier general 1863–65; U.S. representative 1871–77; governor of Wisconsin 1882–89; U.S. secretary of agriculture 1889–93.

Russell   **Alabama**
Phenix City   641 sq. mi.

| 49,756 | 46,860 | 47,356 | 45,394 | 46,351 | 40,364 |

December 18, 1832. Gilbert Christian Russell (1782–1855). U.S. Army, rose from ensign to colonel 1803–14; served in South and Southwest; honorable discharge 1815.

Russell	**Kansas**				
Russell	885 sq. mi.				
7,370	7,835	8,868	9,428	11,348	13,406

February 26, 1867; organized 1872. Avra P. Russell (1833–62). Established express line from Leavenworth to Pikes Peak; captain, Company K, 2nd Kansas Volunteer Cavalry 1862; wounded at battle of Prairie Grove, December 7, 1862; died December 12; brother, Oscar, was an aide to Confederate General Hindman at Prairie Grove.

Russell	**Kentucky**				
Jamestown	254 sq. mi.				
16,315	14,716	13,708	10,542	11,076	13,717

December 14, 1825. *William Russell* (1758–1825). Lieutenant, Continental army; battle of King's Mountain 1780; Guilford Courthouse 1781; Virginia legislature; lieutenant colonel, Kentucky Mounted Volunteers 1793; Kentucky legislature; colonel 1808; battle of Tippecanoe 1811.

Russell	**Virginia**				
Lebanon	475 sq. mi.				
30,308	28,667	31,761	24,533	26,290	26,818

October 17, 1785 (session); effective May 1, 1786. William Russell.*

Rutherford	**North Carolina**				
Rutherfordton	564 sq. mi.				
62,899	56,918	53,787	47,337	45,091	46,356

April 14, 1779 (session). *Griffith Rutherford* (c1731–1805). North Carolina Provincial Congress 1775; brigadier general, North Carolina Militia 1776; defeated Cherokees 1776; captured at battle of Sanders Creek 1780; North Carolina Senate; Legislative Council of Territory South of the Ohio 1796.

Rutherford	**Tennessee**				
Murfreesboro	619 sq. mi.				
182,023	118,570	84,058	59,428	52,368	40,696

October 25, 1803. Griffith Rutherford.*

Rutland	**Vermont**				
Rutland	933 sq. mi.				
63,400	62,142	58,347	52,637	46,719	45,905

February 22, 1781. Town of Rutland. Uncertain origin: (1) Rutland, Massachusetts; (2) John Manners, 3rd Duke of Rutland (1696–1779); courtier of George II and George III; privy councillor, lord justice of England; developed chess variant named for him.

S

Sabine	**Louisiana**				
Many	865 sq. mi.				
23,459	22,646	25,280	18,638	18,564	20,880

March 7, 1843. *Sabine River*. From Spanish name for river, Rio Sabinas, meaning "River of Cedar Trees"; changed to "Sabine" by French.

Sabine	**Texas**				
Hemphill	490 sq. mi.				
10,469	9,586	8,702	7,187	7,302	8,568

March 17, 1836; organized 1837. Former municipality of Sabine. The Mexican Department of Nacogdoches was composed of districts; the Sabine District was given county status in 1836; named for Sabine River.*

Sac   **Iowa**
Sac City   576 sq. mi.
11,529   12,324   14,118   15,573   17,007   17,518
January 15, 1851; organized April 7, 1856. Sauk Indians.* Variant spelling (see Sauk, Wisconsin).

Sacramento   **California**
Sacramento   966 sq. mi.
1,223,499   1,041,219   783,381   631,498   502,778   277,140
February 18, 1850. Sacramento River. Name originally given to Feather River, a tributary of the Sacramento, by Spanish explorer Gabriel Moraga 1808; name was gradually applied to the main river; Spanish for "sacrament."

Sagadahoc   **Maine**
Bath   254 sq. mi.
35,214   33,535   28,795   23,452   22,793   20,911
April 4, 1854. Lower section of Kennebec River. The section of the Kennebec River below the Androscoggin River was called *sagadahoc* by the Abnaki; means "mouth of the river."

Saginaw   **Michigan**
Saginaw   809 sq. mi.
210,039   211,946   228,059   219,743   190,752   153,515
September 10, 1822; organized February 9, 1835. Saginaw River. From Ojibwa *saging,* meaning "at the mouth."

Saguache   **Colorado**
Saguache   3,168 sq. mi.
5,917   4,619   3,935   3,827   4,473   5,664
December 29, 1866. Saguache Creek. From Ute *saguaguachipa,* meaning "blue earth" or "water at the blue earth"; descriptive of a blue clay deposit near the creek.

Saint Bernard   **Louisiana**
Chalmette   465 sq. mi.
67,229   66,631   64,097   51,185   32,186   11,087
March 31, 1807. Ecclesiastical district of St. Bernard Parish. Named for St. Bernard of Clairvaux (1090–1153); entered monastery 1113; abbot 1115; drew up statutes for Knights Templar 1128; generated support for Second Crusade; canonized 1174.

Saint Charles   **Louisiana**
Hahnville   284 sq. mi.
48,072   42,437   37,259   29,550   21,219   13,363
March 31, 1807. Ecclesiastical district of St. Charles Parish. Named for *St. Carlo Borromeo* (1538–84); nephew of Giovanni Angelo de Medici, Pope Pius IV; appointed by Pius IV as cardinal and archbishop of Milan before being ordained; Council of Trent 1545–63; ordained 1563; in later years gave much of his personal fortune to philanthropy; canonized 1610.

Saint Charles   **Missouri**
Saint Charles   560 sq. mi.
283,883   212,907   144,107   92,954   52,970   29,834
October 1, 1812. Spanish district of St. Charles. Uncertain origin of name. (1) St. Carlo Borromeo.* (2) King Charles IV of Spain (1748–1819); became king 1788; invaded by France 1794; retroceded Louisiana from Spain to France 1801; abdicated after Napoleon occupied Spain 1808; lived in exile 1808–19. (3) King Charles V of France (1338–80); regent of France during captivity of father (John II) by English 1356–64; became king 1364; regained French lands lost to English during Hundred Years' War.

Saint Clair   **Alabama**
Ashville   634 sq. mi.
64,742   50,009   41,205   27,956   25,388   26,687
November 20, 1818. *Arthur St. Clair* (1734–1818). Served under General Wolfe at Quebec 1758; resigned from British army 1762; colonel, Pennsylvania Militia 1776; brigadier general, Continental army 1776–83; surrendered Fort Ticonderoga to Gen-

eral Burgoyne 1777; Continental Congress 1785–87; governor of Northwest Territory 1788–1802; major general 1791; defeated by Miamis at Fort Recovery 1791.

Saint Clair   **Illinois**
Belleville   664 sq. mi.

256,082	262,852	267,531	285,176	262,509	205,995

April 27, 1790. Arthur St. Clair.*

Saint Clair   **Michigan**
Port Huron   724 sq. mi.

164,235	145,607	138,802	120,175	107,201	91,599

March 28, 1820; organized May 8, 1821. St. Clair Township. Origin of name is uncertain: (1) Arthur St. Clair.* (2) Lake St. Clair; named for St. Clare of Assisi (see Santa Clara, California).

Saint Clair   **Missouri**
Osceola   677 sq. mi.

9,652	8,457	8,622	7,667	8,421	10,482

January 16, 1833; organized January 29, 1841. Arthur St. Clair.*

Saint Croix   **Wisconsin**
Hudson   722 sq. mi.

63,155	50,251	43,262	34,354	29,164	25,905

January 9, 1840; deorganized 1843; reorganized 1849. St. Croix River. Derivation of name is uncertain: (1) a cross (French *croix*) was erected at the mouth of the river to memorialize a drowning victim; (2) the drowning victim's name was St. Croix.

Sainte Genevieve   **Missouri**
Sainte Genevieve   502 sq. mi.

17,842	16,037	15,180	12,867	12,116	11,237

October 1, 1812. Spanish district of Ste. Genevieve; made into county by Missouri Territory. Named from town which was named for Ste. Genevieve (422–500); given religious veil by bishop of Paris c437; rallied Parisians to resist Attila the Hun with faith in God; Attila spared Paris and besieged Orleans instead 451; patron saint of Paris.

Saint Francis   **Arkansas**
Forrest City   634 sq. mi.

29,329	28,497	30,858	30,799	33,303	36,841

October 13, 1827; effective December 1, 1827. *St. Francis River*. Tributary of Mississippi River. Named for St. Francis of Assisi (1181–1226); abandoned family wealth to devote life of poverty to God; pilgrimage to Rome 1206; began to attract followers 1209; established Friars Minor, which became Franciscan Order 1210; lacked administrative skills and resigned as head of order 1220; canonized 1228.

Saint Francois   **Missouri**
Farmington   449 sq. mi.

55,641	48,904	42,600	36,818	36,516	35,276

December 19, 1821. St. Francis River.* French spelling.

Saint Helena   **Louisiana**
Greensburg   408 sq. mi.

10,525	9,874	9,827	9,937	9,162	9,013

October 27, 1810. Spanish parish of Santa Helena, West Florida. Named for St. Helena (250–330); mother of Constantine the Great; converted to Christianity 313; made pilgrimage to Holy Land in search of the true cross c325.

Saint James   **Louisiana**
Convent   246 sq. mi.

21,216	20,879	21,495	19,733	18,369	15,334

March 31, 1807. Ecclesiastical district of St. James Parish. Uncertain origin of name: (1) St. James the Greater (?–44); may have been cousin of Jesus; one of first four apostles; became first apostle to be martyred, when he was beheaded on orders of Herod Agrippa. (2) St. James the Less (?–c62) cousin of Jesus; one of the twelve apostles; first bishop of Jerusalem; stoned to death by Pharisees after surviving being thrown from temple roof.

Saint Johns   **Florida**
Saint Augustine   609 sq. mi.

123,135	83,829	51,303	30,727	30,034	24,998

August 12, 1822. St. Johns River. Named for Spanish mission which was named for St. John the Baptist (see Saint John the Baptist, Louisiana).

Saint John the Baptist   **Louisiana**
Laplace   219 sq. mi.

43,044	39,996	31,924	23,813	18,439	14,861

March 31, 1807. Ecclesiastical district of St. John the Baptist Parish. Named for St. John the Baptist (c7 B.C–28 A.D.) lived in desert of Judea; ministered to throngs, requiring them to openly confess sins and be physically baptized; baptized Jesus; beheaded by Herod Antipas at the behest of his wife, Herodias, and Salome, her daughter, who resented John's condemnation of her marriage.

Saint Joseph   **Indiana**
South Bend   457 sq. mi.

265,559	247,052	241,617	245,045	238,614	205,058

January 29, 1830; effective April 1, 1830. *St. Joseph River*. Named for French fort that was named for Mission of St. Joseph founded by Father Allouez. Origin of mission name is uncertain: (1) St. Joseph, husband of Virgin Mary, mother of Jesus; (2) Father Joseph (?–?), a French missionary who was an early settler in area.

Saint Joseph   **Michigan**
Centreville   504 sq. mi.

62,422	58,913	56,083	47,392	42,332	35,071

October 29, 1829. St. Joseph River.*

Saint Landry   **Louisiana**
Opelousas   929 sq. mi.

87,700	80,331	84,128	80,364	81,493	78,476

March 31, 1807. Ecclesiastical district of St. Landry Parish. St. Landry (?–660); Bishop of Paris 650; tradition of founding first hospital in Paris.

Saint Lawrence   **New York**
Canton   2,686 sq. mi.

111,931	111,974	114,254	111,991	111,239	98,897

March 3, 1802. St. Lawrence River. Named for St. Lawrence (?–258); archdeacon and treasurer of Roman Catholic Church c257; tortured and put to death by Roman emperor Valerian.

Saint Louis   **Minnesota**
Duluth   6,225 sq. mi.

200,528	198,213	222,229	220,693	231,588	206,062

March 1, 1856; organized 1857. St. Louis River. Largest stream flowing into Lake Superior. Named for King Louis IX of France (1214–70); became king of France 1226; Treaty of Paris with England 1259; led crusade to Holy Land 1248; captured in Egypt and ransomed; died of plague in Tunis while on a second crusade; canonized 1297.

Saint Louis   **Missouri**
Clayton   508 sq. mi.

1,016,315	993,529	973,896	951,353	703,532	406,349

October 1, 1812. *Spanish district of St. Louis*. Named for city of St. Louis, which was named for Louis XV (1710–74), the reigning French king at the time of settlement, and his patron saint, Louis IX (see St. Louis, Minnesota).

Saint Louis **Missouri**
(Independent City) 62 sq. mi.
348,189 396,685 453,085 622,236 750,026 856,796
March 5, 1877. Spanish district of St. Louis.*

Saint Lucie **Florida**
Fort Pierce 572 sq. mi.
192,695 150,171 87,182 50,836 39,294 20,180
May 24, 1905. Spanish Fort Santa Lucia 1565. Named for St. Lucy of Syracuse (c283–c304); according to legend took vow of virginity as a youth; rejected suitor informed on her to Roman authorities; martyred by a sword thrust down her throat after unsuccessful attempts to burn her.

Saint Martin **Louisiana**
Saint Martinville 740 sq. mi.
48,583 43,978 40,214 32,453 29,063 26,353
March 31, 1807. Ecclesiastical district of St. Martin Parish, from St. Martin church established 1765. Named for St. Martin of Tours (c316–397); converted to Christianity in early teens; served in Roman army; arrested for refusing to fight; fled to France to avoid persecution in eastern Europe 334; bishop of Tours 372; founded monasteries at Liguge and Marmoutier; patron saint of France.

Saint Mary **Louisiana**
Franklin 613 sq. mi.
53,500 58,086 64,253 60,752 48,833 35,848
April 17, 1811. Ecclesiastical district of St. Mary Parish. Named for *St. Mary* (c20 B.C.–?); virgin mother of Jesus; preeminent of all Roman Catholic saints.

Saint Mary's **Maryland**
Leonardtown 361 sq. mi.
86,211 75,974 59,895 47,388 38,915 29,111
February 9, 1637; name changed to Potomac 1654; renamed St. Mary's 1658. Uncertain. (1) St. Mary.* (2) Queen Henrietta Maria (1606–69); daughter of Henry IV of France; Catholic wife of Charles I of England; mother of Charles II and James II.

Saint Tammany **Louisiana**
Covington 854 sq. mi.
191,268 144,508 110,869 63,585 38,643 26,988
October 27, 1810. Tamenend (?–?). Delaware chief in late 17th century; name means "affable"; signed deed ceding land to William Penn 1683; popular with American colonists; called "patron saint" of colonists; not a saint of the Catholic Church and had no connection with Louisiana.

Salem **New Jersey**
Salem 338 sq. mi.
64,285 65,294 64,676 60,346 58,711 49,508
May 17, 1694. Village of New Salem. From Hebrew *shalom,* meaning "peace"; settled by Quakers 1675.

Salem **Virginia**
(Independent City) 15 sq. mi.
24,747 23,756 23,958 21,982 (a) (a)
1968. Salem, New Jersey. [(a) Part of Roanoke County.] (Associated county: Roanoke.)

Saline **Arkansas**
Benton 723 sq. mi.
83,529 64,183 53,161 36,107 28,956 23,816
November 2, 1835. Descriptive of local salt works established 1827.

Saline **Illinois**
Harrisburg 383 sq. mi.

26,733   26,551   28,448   25,721   26,227   33,420
February 25, 1847; abolished 1851; recreated 1852. Descriptive of salt. Uncertain origin of name: (1) Saline Creek; tributary of Ohio River; (2) salt springs and salt deposits in the area.

Saline   **Kansas**
Salina   720 sq. mi.
53,597   49,301   48,905   46,592   54,715   33,409
February 15, 1860. Saline River, tributary of Smoky Hill River. French translation of Indian name Ne Miskua, describing river's salt content.

Saline   **Missouri**
Marshall   756 sq. mi.
23,756   23,523   24,919   24,633   25,148   26,694
November 25, 1820; effective January 1, 1821. Descriptive of local salt springs.

Saline   **Nebraska**
Wilber   575 sq. mi.
13,843   12,715   13,131   12,809   12,542   14,046
March 6, 1855; organized February 18, 1867. Mistaken belief that there were salt deposits in the area.

Salt Lake   **Utah**
Salt Lake City   737 sq. mi.
898,387   725,956   619,066   458,607   383,035   274,895
March 3, 1852, as Great Salt Lake; name changed January 29, 1868. Great Salt Lake. Largest body of water between Great Lakes and Pacific Ocean; high salt content from evaporation.

Saluda   **South Carolina**
Saluda   452 sq. mi.
19,181   16,357   16,150   14,528   14,554   15,924
February 25, 1896. Saluda River. Tributary of Congaree River; Shawnee word for "corn river."

Sampson   **North Carolina**
Clinton   945 sq. mi.
60,161   47,297   49,687   44,954   48,013   49,780
April 18, 1784 (session). John Sampson (?–1784). Sheriff of New Hanvor County 1742; North Carolina Governor's Council; lieutenant colonel of militia 1768.

San Augustine   **Texas**
San Augustine   528 sq. mi.
8,946   7,999   8,785   7,858   7,722   8,837
March 17, 1836; organized 1837. Municipality of San Augustine. Named for *presidio* (fort) San Augustín de Ahumada; founded 1756; abandoned 1771. Presidio named in honor of St. Augustine of Hippo (354–430); born Arelius Augustinius; converted to Christianity 386; ordained 391; bishop 396; wrote doctrines on faith and morals of the Roman Catholic Church.

San Benito   **California**
Hollister   1,389 sq. mi.
53,234   36,697   25,005   18,226   15,396   14,370
February 12, 1874. San Benito (now San Juan) Creek. Named for St. Benedict (c480–547); studied Byzantine monastic orders; lived as hermit for three years; founded monastery at Monte Casino and twelve others; founded Benedictine Order; wrote rules for monastic life. "Benito" is Spanish diminutive of "Benedicto."

San Bernardino   **California**
San Bernardino   20,053 sq. mi.
1,709,434   1,418,380   895,016   684,072   503,591   281,642
April 26, 1853. San Bernardino Mountains. Named for St. Bernardine (1380–1444); Franciscan preacher 1402; preached throughout Italy; declined three bishoprics.

Sanborn **South Dakota**
Woonsocket 569 sq. mi.
2,675 2,833 3,213 3,697 4,641 5,142
March 9, 1883. George W. Sanborn (1832–?). Employed as brakeman by Chicago, Milwaukee & St. Paul Railroad; assistant superintendent of northern division 1869; superintendent of Iowa & Dakota Division 1870; extended railroad throughout eastern Dakota Territory.

Sanders **Montana**
Thompson Falls 2,762 sq. mi.
10,227 8,669 8,675 7,093 6,880 6,983
February 7, 1905. Wilbur Fisk Sanders (1834–1905). Recruited company of infantry and a battery of artillery 1861; 1st lieutenant, 64th Ohio Infantry; Montana Territory House of Representatives 1873–79; U.S. senator 1890–93.

San Diego **California**
San Diego 4,200 sq. mi.
2,813,833 2,498,016 1,861,846 1,357,854 1,033,011 556,808
February 18, 1850. Town of San Diego. Named for San Diego Bay and Mission San Diego de Alcalà, first mission in California 1769. Bay named for St. Didacus (Diego) (1400–63); lay brother in Order of Friars; guardian of Franciscan community on Canary Islands 1445–49; miraculous cures attributed to him; canonized 1588.

Sandoval **New Mexico**
Bernalillo 3,709 sq. mi.
89,908 63,319 34,799 17,492 14,201 12,438
March 10, 1903. Sandoval family. Descendants of Juan de Diós Sandoval Martinez (?–1704); arrived in north-central New Mexico 1792; Juan Sandoval had numerous children, who in turn also had numerous children; prominent Sandovals in area were Alejandro (1845–?) and José Pablo (1850–?), both ranchers and members of New Mexico Territory legislature; other Sandovals were and are businessmen and ranchers in Sandoval County.

Sandusky **Ohio**
Fremont 409 sq. mi.
61,792 61,963 63,267 60,983 56,486 46,114
February 12, 1820. Sandusky River. From Wyandot *otsaandosti* or *sandesti,* meaning "water" or "cool water."

San Francisco **California**
San Francisco 47 sq. mi.
776,733 723,959 678,974 715,674 740,316 775,357
February 18, 1850. City of San Francisco. Named for St. Francis of Assisi (see Saint Francis, Arkansas).

Sangamon **Illinois**
Springfield 868 sq. mi.
188,951 178,386 176,089 161,335 146,539 131,484
January 30, 1821. Sangamon River. From Indian word of uncertain origin; most conjectures involve water, such as, "place of the outlet," "river mouth," or "he pours out."

Sanilac **Michigan**
Sandusky 964 sq. mi.
44,547 39,928 40,789 34,889 32,314 30,837
September 10, 1822; organized December 31, 1849. Sannilac. Indian spirit warrior; from Wyandot legend which was basis of poem *Sannilac* by Henry Whiting 1831.

San Jacinto **Texas**
Coldspring 571 sq. mi.
22,246 16,372 11,434 6,702 6,153 7,172
August 13, 1870; organized December 1, 1870. Battle of San Jacinto. Decisive battle of Texas Revolution April 21, 1836; battle site named from San Jacinto River, which was named for St. Hyacinth because of hyacinths along river banks. St. Hyacinth

(1185–1257); born to Polish nobility; converted to Christianity c1217; entered Dominican Order; missionary activity from Tibet to Denmark; canonized 1594.

San Joaquin   **California**
Stockton   1,399 sq. mi.
563,598   480,628   347,342   290,208   249,989   200,750
February 18, 1850. San Joaquin River. Spanish name for St. Joachim (?–?); father of Virgin Mary.

San Juan   **Colorado**
Silverton   387 sq. mi.
558   745   833   831   849   1,471
January 31, 1876; effective May 1, 1876. San Juan River, Mountains, and region. Named from San Juan Pueblo in northwest New Mexico, which was named for St. John the Baptist (see Saint John the Baptist, Louisiana).

San Juan   **New Mexico**
Aztec   5,514 sq. mi.
113,801   91,605   81,433   52,517   53,306   18,292
February 24, 1887. *San Juan River*. Named for St. John the Baptist (see Saint John the Baptist, Louisiana).

San Juan   **Utah**
Monticello   7,820 sq. mi.
14,413   12,621   12,253   9,606   9,040   5,315
February 17, 1880. San Juan River.*

San Juan   **Washington**
Friday Harbor   175 sq. mi.
14,077   10,035   7,838   3,856   2,872   3,245
October 31, 1873. San Juan Island. Named for St. John the Baptist (see Saint John the Baptist, Louisiana).

San Luis Obispo   **California**
San Luis Obispo   3,304 sq. mi.
246,681   217,162   155,435   105,690   81,044   51,417
February 18, 1850. Mission San Luis Obispo de Tolosa. Mission founded 1772 by Junipero Serra. Named for St. Louis of Toulouse (1274–97); son of the King of Naples and Sicily; joined Friars Minor (Franciscans); bishop of Toulouse 1297; canonized 1317.

San Mateo   **California**
Redwood City   449 sq. mi.
707,161   649,623   587,329   556,234   444,387   235,659
April 19, 1856. San Mateo Creek. Named for St. Matthew (?–?); Roman tax collector; became one of Christ's twelve disciples; author of the first gospel of the Bible; preached in Ethiopia.

San Miguel   **Colorado**
Telluride   1,287 sq. mi.
6,594   3,653   3,192   1,949   2,944   2,693
November 1, 1883. San Miguel River and Mountains. Uncertain; Spanish name for any one of many St. Michaels; most likely Archangel Michael, one of four great angels in Old Testament and military leader in war between God and Satan in Book of Revelations.

San Miguel   **New Mexico**
Las Vegas   4,717 sq. mi.
30,126   25,743   22,751   21,951   23,468   26,512
January 9, 1852. Town of San Miguel del Bado. Named for Archangel Michael (see San Miguel, Colorado).

San Patricio   **Texas**
Sinton   692 sq. mi.
67,138   58,749   58,013   47,288   45,021   35,842

March 17, 1836; organized 1847. Town of San Patricio. Named for St. Patrick (389–461); born to Christian family in Roman Britain; kidnapped by pirates and taken to Ireland 405; escaped to Britain 411; returned to Ireland as missionary bishop 432; led conversion of Ireland to Christianity; patron saint of Ireland.

Sanpete   **Utah**
Manti   1,588 sq. mi.

| 22,763 | 16,259 | 14,620 | 10,976 | 11,053 | 13,891 |

March 3, 1852. San Pitch Valley. From division of Utes named *sampitches* or *sampichya,* among other variables; may also be name of a Ute chief. County originally named San Pete.

San Saba   **Texas**
San Saba   1,134 sq. mi.

| 6,186 | 5,401 | 6,204 | 5,540 | 6,381 | 8,666 |

February 1, 1856; organized May 3, 1856. San Saba River. Named for St. Sabbas (439–532); preached in Judaean wilderness; founded several monasteries and hospices; abbot of monastery near Jerusalem.

Santa Barbara   **California**
Santa Barbara   2,737 sq. mi.

| 399,347 | 369,608 | 298,694 | 264,324 | 168,962 | 98,220 |

February 18, 1850. Town of Santa Barbara. Named for Santa Barbara Channel and Mission, which were named for St. Barbara (?–c235); child of Roman official, Dioscorus, whose duties included persecution of Christians; Barbara converted to Christianity and vowed to rule her life according to the gospels; refused to renounce Christianity to her father who personally beheaded her.

Santa Clara   **California**
San Jose   1,291 sq. mi.

| 1,682,585 | 1,497,577 | 1,295,071 | 1,064,714 | 642,315 | 290,547 |

February 18, 1850. Mission Santa Clara de Asís; founded 1777. Named for St. Clare (1194–1253); born in Assisi; friend and follower of St. Francis of Assisi; entered Benedictine convent 1212; abbess of San Damiano convent 1213–53; founded Order of Poor Ladies (Poor Clares); canonized 1255.

Santa Cruz   **Arizona**
Nogales   1,238 sq. mi.

| 38,381 | 29,676 | 20,459 | 13,966 | 10,808 | 9,344 |

March 15, 1899. Santa Cruz River. Spanish for "holy cross."

Santa Cruz   **California**
Santa Cruz   445 sq. mi.

| 255,602 | 229,734 | 188,141 | 123,790 | 84,219 | 66,534 |

February 18, 1850, as Branciforte; name changed April 5, 1850. Mission Santa Cruz. Named for Santa Cruz Creek; Spanish for "holy cross."

Santa Fe   **New Mexico**
Santa Fe   1,909 sq. mi.

| 129,292 | 98,928 | 75,360 | 53,756 | 44,970 | 38,153 |

January 9, 1852. City of Santa Fe. Established as La Villa Real de Santa Fe (The Royal Town of the Holy Faith) 1609; named after town in Spain founded by Ferdinand and Isabella to celebrate Spain's victory over the Moors 1492.

Santa Rosa   **Florida**
Milton   1,017 sq. mi.

| 117,743 | 81,608 | 55,988 | 37,741 | 29,547 | 18,554 |

February 18, 1842. Santa Rosa Island. Named for St. Rose of Viterbo (1234–52); her life story is mostly legend; performed miracle at age three; began preaching at age ten; denounced Emperor Frederick II for harassing the pope; banished from Viterbo; canonized 1457.

Sarasota   **Florida**
Sarasota   572 sq. mi.

325,957   277,776   202,251   120,413   76,895   28,827

May 14, 1921. Uncertain; either city of Sarasota or Sarasota Bay. Derivation of the name "Sarasota" is also unknown; numerous theories range from various Spanish or Indian words concerning vegetation, or dancing, to a legend that Hernando de Soto had a daughter named Sara.

Saratoga   **New York**
Ballston Spa   812 sq. mi.
200,635   181,276   153,759   121,679   89,096   74,869

February 7, 1791. Uncertain; most likely named for the battle of Saratoga in which British forces under General Burgoyne surrendered to Americans under General Gates October 17, 1777. The meaning of the Indian name "Saratoga" is uncertain; leading contenders are "beaver place" or "side hill."

Sargent   **North Dakota**
Forman   859 sq. mi.
4,366   4,549   5,512   5,937   6,856   7,616

March 3, 1883; organized October 8, 1883. Homer E. Sargent (1822–c1901). General manager of Northern Pacific Railroad 1879–81; invested in land in northern Dakota Territory.

Sarpy   **Nebraska**
Papillion   241 sq. mi.
122,595   102,583   86,015   63,696   31,281   15,693

February 7, 1857; organized June 19, 1857. Peter A. Sarpy (1805–65). Fur trader for American Fur Company on Platte River system; operated trading post at mouth of Platte River; quartermaster, Nebraska Volunteer Regiment 1855.

Sauk   **Wisconsin**
Baraboo   838 sq. mi.
55,225   46,975   43,469   39,057   36,179   38,120

January 11, 1840; organized 1844. *Sauk Indians.* Originally in Great Lakes region; declared war against U.S. under Chief Black Hawk; defeated at Bad Axe, Wisconsin August 2, 1832; united with Fox; moved to Illinois and Iowa; resettled in Indian Territory (Oklahoma); name from "yellow earth" from which the Sauk believed they were created.

Saunders   **Nebraska**
Wahoo   754 sq. mi.
19,830   18,285   18,716   17,018   17,720   16,923

January 26, 1856, as Calhoun; name changed January 8, 1862; organized November 10, 1866. Alvin Saunders (1817–99). Iowa Constitutional Convention 1846; Iowa Senate 1854–56 and 1858–60; governor of Nebraska Territory 1861–67; U.S. senator from Nebraska 1877–83.

Sawyer   **Wisconsin**
Hayward   1,256 sq. mi.
16,196   14,181   12,843   9,670   9,475   10,323

March 10, 1883; organized 1885. Philetus Sawyer (1861–1900). Wisconsin assembly 1857 and 1861; mayor of Oshkosh 1863–64; U.S. representative 1865–75; U.S. senator 1881–93.

Schenectady   **New York**
Schenectady   206 sq. mi.
146,555   149,285   149,946   160,979   152,896   142,497

March 7, 1809. City of Schenectady. City named from Dutch *skonowe,* meaning "flat land," or from Dutch *schoonehetstede,* meaning "beautiful town."

Schleicher   **Texas**
Eldorado   1,311 sq. mi.
2,935   2,990   2,820   2,277   2,791   2,852

April 1, 1887; organized 1901. Gustav Schleicher (1823–79). Emigrated from Germany 1850; Texas House of Representatives 1853–54; Texas Senate 1859–61; captain of engineers, Confederate army 1861–65; U.S. representative 1875–79.

Schley   **Georgia**
Ellaville   168 sq. mi.
3,766   3,588   3,433   3,097   3,256   4,036
December 22, 1857. William Schley (1786–1858). Judge of superior court 1825–28; Georgia House of Representatives 1830; U.S. representative 1833–35; governor of Georgia 1835–37.

Schoharie   **New York**
Schoharie   622 sq. mi.
31,582   31,859   29,710   24,750   22,616   22,703
April 6, 1795. Town of Schoharie. Derived from the Mohawk name for Schoharie Creek, meaning "driftwood."

Schoolcraft   **Michigan**
Manistique   1,178 sq. mi.
8,903   8,302   8,575   8,226   8,953   9,148
March 9, 1843; organized March 23, 1871. *Henry Rowe Schoolcraft* (1793–1864). Explored Arkansas and Missouri 1818–20; explored upper Mississippi and Lake Superior 1820–22; Michigan territorial legislature 1828–32; ethnologist and author of numerous books on Indians; Michigan superintendent of Indian affairs 1836–41; created the names of many Michigan counties by combining unrelated Indian and Latin words.

Schuyler   **Illinois**
Rushville   437 sq. mi.
7,189   7,498   8,365   8,135   8,746   9,613
January 13, 1825. *Philip John Schuyler* (1733–1804). Captain, British army 1755; major 1758; worked in England to settle colonial claims 1758–63; Continental Congress 1775–77 and 1778–81; major general, Continental army 1775; resigned 1779; New York Senate 1780–84, 1786–90, and 1792–97; U.S. senator 1789–91 and 1797–98.

Schuyler   **Missouri**
Lancaster   308 sq. mi.
4,170   4,236   4,979   4,665   5,052   5,760
February 14, 1845. Philip John Schuyler.*

Schuyler   **New York**
Watkins Glen   329 sq. mi.
19,224   18,662   17,686   16,737   15,044   14,182
April 17, 1854. Philip John Schuyler.*

Schuylkill   **Pennsylvania**
Pottsville   778 sq. mi.
150,336   152,585   160,630   160,089   173,027   200,577
March 1, 1811. Schuylkill River. Named from Dutch *schuilplaats,* meaning "hiding place."

Scioto   **Ohio**
Portsmouth   612 sq. mi.
79,195   80,327   84,545   76,951   84,216   82,910
March 24, 1803; effective May 1, 1803. Scioto River. From Wyandot *ochskonto*; the first part of the name refers to deer, the second part is unknown but may refer to river.

Scotland   **Missouri**
Memphis   438 sq. mi.
4,983   4,822   5,415   5,499   6,484   7,332
January 29, 1841. Scotland, United Kingdom.

Scotland   **North Carolina**
Laurinburg   319 sq. mi.
35,998   33,754   32,273   26,929   25,183   26,336
February 20, 1899. Scotland, United Kingdom.

Scott   **Arkansas**
Waldron   894 sq. mi.
10,996   10,205   9,685   8,207   7,297   10,057
November 5, 1833; effective December 1, 1833. Andrew Scott (1788–1851). Judge, Superior Court of Arkansas Territory 1819–21; killed one man in a duel and another in a fight over an election defeat 1828; Arkansas Constitutional Convention 1836.

Scott   **Illinois**
Winchester   251 sq. mi.
5,537   5,644   6,142   6,096   6,377   7,245
February 16, 1839. Scott County, Kentucky.

Scott   **Indiana**
Scottsburg   190 sq. mi.
22,960   20,991   20,422   17,144   14,643   11,519
January 12, 1820; effective February 1, 1820. *Charles Scott* (1733–1813). British army during French and Indian Wars; colonel Continental army 1776; brigadier general 1777; captured 1780; released at end of war 1781; guide for General St. Clair; battle of Fallen Timbers 1794; governor of Kentucky 1808–12.

Scott   **Iowa**
Davenport   458 sq. mi.
158,668   150,979   160,022   142,687   119,067   100,698
December 21, 1837. *Winfield Scott* (1786–1866). Captain, Virginia Light Artillery 1808; lieutenant colonel 1812; colonel 1813; brigadier general 1814; brevet major general for services at Chippewa and Niagara Falls 1814; awarded gold medal by Congress 1814; commander in chief of U.S. army 1841–61; captured Vera Cruz 1847; occupied Mexico City 1848; lieutenant general 1852; Whig Party candidate for president, lost to Franklin Pierce, 1852.

Scott   **Kansas**
Scott City   718 sq. mi.
5,120   5,289   5,782   5,606   5,228   4,921
March 6, 1873; organized January 29, 1886. Winfield Scott.*

Scott   **Kentucky**
Georgetown   285 sq. mi.
33,061   23,867   21,813   17,948   15,376   15,141
June 22, 1792; effective September 1, 1792. Charles Scott.*

Scott   **Minnesota**
Shakopee   357 sq. mi.
89,498   57,846   43,784   32,423   21,909   16,486
March 5, 1853. Winfield Scott.*

Scott   **Mississippi**
Forest   609 sq. mi.
28,423   24,137   24,556   21,369   21,187   21,681
December 23, 1833. Abraham M. Scott (1785–1833). Fought Creeks 1811; Mississippi Constitutional Convention 1817; Mississippi Senate 1822 and 1826–27; lieutenant governor 1828–30; governor of Mississippi 1832–33; died in office.

Scott   **Missouri**
Benton   421 sq. mi.
40,422   39,376   39,647   33,250   32,748   32,842
December 28, 1821. John Scott (c1782–1861). Missouri Territory delegate to Congress 1815–20; U.S. representative 1821–27.

Scott   **Tennessee**
Huntsville   532 sq. mi.
21,127   18,358   19,259   14,762   15,413   17,362
December 17, 1849. Winfield Scott.*

Scott   **Virginia**
Gate City   537 sq. mi.

23,403	23,204	25,068	24,376	25,813	27,640

November 24, 1814. Winfield Scott.*

Scotts Bluff   **Nebraska**
Gering   739 sq. mi.

36,951	36,025	38,344	36,432	33,809	33,939

November 6, 1888; organized January 28, 1889. Scotts Bluff Butte. Landmark on the Oregon Trail; rises 800 feet above surrounding plain; named for Hiram Scott (c1805–c1828); fell ill during a fur trading expedition and was left alone to die; bones later found near Scotts Bluff were declared to be his.

Screven   **Georgia**
Sylvania   648 sq. mi.

15,374	13,842	14,043	12,591	14,919	18,000

December 14, 1793. James Screven (c1744–78). Georgia Provincial Congress 1775; captain, 3rd Georgia Rangers 1776; brigadier general 1778; mortally wounded near Midway Church, Georgia.

Scurry   **Texas**
Snyder   903 sq. mi.

16,361	18,634	18,192	15,760	20,369	22,779

August 21, 1876; organized 1884. Uncertain. (1) William Richardson Scurry (1811–62); joined Texas Army 1836; battle of San Jacinto 1836; Republic of Texas House of Representatives 1842–44; U.S. representative 1851–53; adjutant general on staff of General Albert Sidney Johnston 1861. (2) William Read Scurry (1821–64); rose from private to major during Mexican War; Texas Secession Convention 1861; lieutenant colonel, 4th Texas Cavalry 1861; commanded Confederate forces at Glorietta Pass 1862; mortally wounded at Jenkin's Ferry April 30, 1864.

Searcy   **Arkansas**
Marshall   667 sq. mi.

8,261	7,841	8,847	7,731	8,124	10,424

December 13, 1838. Richard Searcy (?–1832). Judge, Arkansas Territory 1823; two time unsuccessful candidate for territorial delegate to Congress 1828 and 1832.

Sebastian   **Arkansas**
Fort Smith   536 sq. mi.

115,071	99,590	95,172	79,237	66,685	64,202

January 6, 1851. William King Sebastian (1812–65). Arkansas Circuit Court judge 1840–43; Arkansas Supreme Court 1843–45; Arkansas Senate 1846–47; U.S. senator 1848–61; expelled from Senate 1861; Senate posthumously revoked expulsion and compensated family.

Sedgwick   **Colorado**
Julesburg   548 sq. mi.

2,747	2,690	3,266	3,405	4,242	5,095

April 9, 1889. Fort Sedgwick. Founded near South Platte River 1864, as Camp Rankin; name changed to Fort Sedgwick 1865. Named for *John Sedgwick* (1813–64); graduated West Point 1837; Mexican War; commanded Fort Wise 1859–60; brigadier general of Volunteers 1861; major general 1862; killed at Spotsylvania May 9, 1864.

Sedgwick   **Kansas**
Wichita   999 sq. mi.

452,869	403,662	366,531	350,694	343,231	222,290

February 26, 1867; organized 1870. John Sedgwick.*

Seminole   **Florida**
Sanford   308 sq. mi.

365,196	287,529	179,752	83,692	54,947	26,883

April 25, 1913. *Seminole Indians*. Evolved as a distinct tribe from group of Oconees who migrated to Florida during the middle of the 18th century; combined with Florida Indians and runaway slaves; fiercely resisted attempted removal to Indian Territory (Oklahoma) during Second Seminole War 1835–42. Suggestions for origin of name include (1) Creek *simanole* or *siminole,* meaning "runaways" or "those who separate"; (2) Creek *ishti semoli,* meaning "wild men"; (3) Spanish *cimarron,* meaning "wild," "unruly," or "runaway slave."

Seminole   **Georgia**
Donalsonville   238 sq. mi.
9,369   9,010   9,057   7,059   6,802   7,904
July 8, 1920. Seminole Indians.*

Seminole   **Oklahoma**
Wewoka   633 sq. mi.
24,894   25,412   27,473   25,144   28,066   40,672
July 16, 1907. Seminole Indians.*

Seneca   **New York**
Waterloo   325 sq. mi.
33,342   33,683   33,733   35,083   31,984   29,253
March 24, 1804. *Seneca Indians*. Largest tribe of Iroquois confederation. *Seneca* has various translations, most of which involve "stone."

Seneca   **Ohio**
Tiffin   551 sq. mi.
58,683   59,733   61,901   60,696   59,326   52,978
February 12, 1820; organized 1824. Seneca Indians.*

Sequatchie   **Tennessee**
Dunlap   266 sq. mi.
11,370   8,863   8,605   6,331   5,915   5,685
December 9, 1857. Sequatchie River Valley. Named for an Indian chief who signed treaties with whites; nothing more is known of him.

Sequoyah   **Oklahoma**
Sallisaw   674 sq. mi.
38,972   33,828   30,749   23,370   18,001   19,773
July 16, 1907. Sequoya (c1770–1843). Developed a list of about eighty-six syllables for writing the Cherokee language; symbols developed by Sequoya were used to translate parts of the Bible and to print an Indian newspaper, *The Phoenix*; taught school in Indian Territory (Oklahoma).

Sevier   **Arkansas**
De Queen   564 sq. mi.
15,757   13,637   14,060   11,272   10,156   12,293
October 17, 1828; effective November 1, 1828. Ambrose Hundley Sevier (1801–48). Arkansas Territory House of Representatives 1823–27; delegate to Congress 1828–36; U.S. senator 1836–48; U.S. minister to Mexico 1848.

Sevier   **Tennessee**
Sevierville   592 sq. mi.
71,170   51,043   41,418   28,241   24,251   23,375
September 27, 1794. John Sevier (1745–1815). Captain of Colonial Militia under Washington in Governor Dunmore's War against Indians 1773 and 1774; only governor of proclaimed state of Franklin 1785–88; U.S. representative from North Carolina 1789–91; brigadier general of Militia for Territory South of the Ohio 1791; governor of Tennessee 1796–1801 and 1803–09; U.S. representative 1811–15.

Sevier   **Utah**
Richfield   1,910 sq. mi.

18,842   15,431   14,727   10,103   10,565   12,072
January 16, 1865. Sevier River. Named Rio Severo (Severe River) by Spanish explorers; Americans later turned *severo* into a well-known proper name.

Seward   **Kansas**
Liberal   640 sq. mi.
22,510   18,743   17,071   15,744   15,930   9,972
March 6, 1873; organized February 18, 1886. *William Henry Seward* (1801–72). New York Senate 1830–34; governor of New York 1838–42; U.S. senator 1849–61; U.S. secretary of state 1861–69; negotiated treaty with Russia for purchase of Alaska 1867.

Seward   **Nebraska**
Seward   575 sq. mi.
16,496   15,450   15,789   14,460   13,581   13,155
March 6, 1855, as Greene; name changed January 3, 1862; organized February 9, 1866. William Henry Seward.*

Shackelford   **Texas**
Albany   914 sq. mi.
3,302   3,316   3,915   3,323   3,990   5,001
February 1, 1858; organized September 12, 1874. John Shackelford (1790–1857). General Jackson's staff, War of 1812; Alabama Senate 1822–24; raised company of Alabama Volunteers called "Red Rovers" for Texas Revolution 1835; Goliad campaign 1836; captured at Coleto; survived Goliad massacre because he was a physician attending to wounded; returned to Alabama 1836.

Shannon   **Missouri**
Eminence   1,004 sq. mi.
8,324   7,613   7,885   7,196   7,087   8,377
January 29, 1841. George Shannon (1787–1836). Private in Lewis and Clark expedition 1804–06; Missouri Senate; U.S. attorney for Missouri.

Shannon   **South Dakota**
(Unorganized)   2,094 sq. mi.
12,466   9,902   11,323   8,198   6,000   5,669
January 11, 1875; attached to Fall River County. Peter C. Shannon (1821–99). Chief justice of Dakota Territory 1873–82.

Sharkey   **Mississippi**
Rolling Fork   428 sq. mi.
6,580   7,066   7,964   8,937   10,738   12,903
March 29, 1876. William Lewis Sharkey (1798–1873). Mississippi House of Representatives 1828–29; Mississippi Supreme Court 1832; trustee, University of Mississippi 1844–65; provisional Reconstruction governor of Mississippi 1865; elected to U.S. Senate but denied seat 1865.

Sharp   **Arkansas**
Ash Flat   604 sq. mi.
17,119   14,109   14,607   8,233   6,319   8,999
July 18, 1868. Ephraim Sharp (1833–?). Lieutenant, Company L, Tappen's brigade; battle of Prairie Grove 1862; Arkansas legislature 1868.

Shasta   **California**
Redding   3,785 sq. mi.
163,256   147,036   115,715   77,640   59,468   36,413
February 18, 1850. Mount Shasta. Named Mount Sastise by Peter Skene Ogden for Shastika Indians 1827.

Shawano   **Wisconsin**
Shawano   893 sq. mi.
40,664   37,157   35,928   32,650   34,351   35,249

February 16, 1853 as Shawanaw; organized 1860; spelling changed 1864. Uncertain. (1) Lake Shawano. (2) Indian chief whose name was similar to "Shawano." *Shawano* is a Chippewa word of various translations, most of which mean "south" or "southern."

Shawnee   **Kansas**
Topeka   550 sq. mi.

169,871	160,976	154,916	155,322	141,286	105,418

August 30, 1855. Shawnee Indians. Algonquin linguistic family; related to Delawares; first encountered by Europeans in Ohio River Valley; sided with French in French and Indian Wars; hostile to U.S.; driven westward to Kansas; ceded lands and removed to Indian Territory (Oklahoma) 1854.

Sheboygan   **Wisconsin**
Sheboygan   514 sq. mi.

112,646	103,877	100,935	96,660	86,484	80,631

December 7, 1836; organized 1846. Sheboygan River. Uncertain origin; *he* may be Ojibwa word meaning "big," and *boygan* means "pipe"; most other suggestions also refer to water or channels.

Shelby   **Alabama**
Columbiana   795 sq. mi.

143,293	99,358	66,298	38,037	32,132	30,362

February 7, 1818. *Isaac Shelby* (1750–1826). Virginia legislature; Revolutionary War; King's Mountain 1780; North Carolina legislature 1781–82; governor of Kentucky 1792–96 and 1812–16; led Kentucky Volunteers in War of 1812; battle of Thames River 1813; declined President Monroe's nomination for secretary of war 1817.

Shelby   **Illinois**
Shelbyville   759 sq. mi.

22,893	22,261	23,923	22,589	23,404	24,434

January 23, 1827. Uncertain. (1) Isaac Shelby.* (2) Shelby County, Kentucky.

Shelby   **Indiana**
Shelbyville   413 sq. mi.

43,445	40,307	39,887	37,797	34,093	28,026

December 31, 1821; effective April 1, 1822. Isaac Shelby.*

Shelby   **Iowa**
Harlan   591 sq. mi.

13,173	13,230	15,043	15,528	15,825	15,942

January 15, 1851; organized January 12, 1853; effective March 7, 1853. Isaac Shelby.*

Shelby   **Kentucky**
Shelbyville   384 sq. mi.

33,337	24,824	23,328	18,999	18,493	17,912

June 23, 1792; effective September 1, 1792. Isaac Shelby.*

Shelby   **Missouri**
Shelbyville   501 sq. mi.

6,799	6,942	7,826	7,906	9,063	9,730

January 2, 1835. Isaac Shelby.*

Shelby   **Ohio**
Sidney   409 sq. mi.

47,910	44,915	43,089	37,748	33,586	28,488

January 7, 1819. Isaac Shelby.*

Shelby   **Tennessee**
Memphis   755 sq. mi.

897,472   826,330   777,113   722,014   627,019   482,393
November 24, 1819. Isaac Shelby.*

Shelby   **Texas**
Center   794 sq. mi.
25,224   22,034   23,084   19,672   20,479   23,479
March 17, 1836; organized 1837. Municipality of Shelby; formerly Mexican municipality of Tenahaw; named for Isaac Shelby.*

Shenandoah   **Virginia**
Woodstock   512 sq. mi.
35,075   31,636   27,559   22,852   21,825   21,169
March 24, 1772, as Dunmore; effective May 15, 1772; name changed February 1, 1778. Shenandoah River. Indian word for "sprucey stream."

Sherburne   **Minnesota**
Elk River   436 sq. mi.
64,417   41,945   29,908   18,344   12,861   10,661
February 25, 1856; organized March 6, 1862. Moses Sherburne (1808–68). Maine legislature; associate justice, Minnesota Territory Supreme Court 1853–57; Minnesota Constitutional Convention 1857.

Sheridan   **Kansas**
Hoxie   896 sq. mi.
2,813   3,043   3,544   3,859   4,267   4,607
March 6, 1873; organized 1880. *Philip Henry Sheridan* (1831–88). Graduated West Point 1853; brevet 2nd lieutenant of Infantry 1853; 1st lieutenant and captain 1861; colonel, 2nd Michigan Cavalry 1862; brigadier general of Volunteers 1862; major general 1863; brigadier general, U.S. Army 1864; commander of the army; blocked Lee's escape at Appomattox 1865; lieutenant general 1869; army commander in chief 1884–88.

Sheridan   **Montana**
Plentywood   1,677 sq. mi.
4,105   4,732   5,414   5,779   6,458   6,674
March 24, 1913. Philip Henry Sheridan.*

Sheridan   **Nebraska**
Rushville   2,441 sq. mi.
6,198   6,750   7,544   7,285   9,049   9,539
February 25, 1885; organized July 25, 1885. Philip Henry Sheridan.*

Sheridan   **North Dakota**
McClusky   972 sq. mi.
1,710   2,148   2,819   3,232   4,350   5,253
January 4, 1873; abolished 1892; recreated December 24, 1908. Philip Henry Sheridan.*

Sheridan   **Wyoming**
Sheridan   2,523 sq. mi.
26,560   23,562   25,048   17,852   18,989   20,185
March 9, 1888; organized May 11, 1888. Town of Sheridan. Named for Philip Henry Sheridan.*

Sherman   **Kansas**
Goodland   1,056 sq. mi.
6,760   6,926   7,759   7,792   6,682   7,373
March 6, 1873; organized September 20, 1886. *William Tecumseh Sherman* (1820–91). Graduated West Point 1840; 2nd lieutenant 1840; 1st lieutenant 1841; brevet captain for service in California during Mexican War 1848; captain 1850; resigned 1853; recommissioned colonel 1861; brigadier general of Volunteers 1861; major general 1862–64; March to the Sea 1864;

only person to receive two Thanks of Congress during the Civil War, for actions at Chattanooga and Atlanta; commander of the army 1869.

Sherman   **Nebraska**
Loup City   566 sq. mi.
3,318   3,718   4,226   4,725   5,382   6,421
March 1, 1871; organized April 1, 1873. William Tecumseh Sherman.*

Sherman   **Oregon**
Moro   823 sq. mi.
1,934   1,918   2,172   2,139   2,446   2,271
February 25, 1889. William Tecumseh Sherman.*

Sherman   **Texas**
Stratford   923 sq. mi.
3,186   2,858   3,174   3,657   2,605   2,443
August 21, 1876; organized June 13, 1889. Sidney Sherman (1805–73). Raised company of Kentucky Volunteers for Texas Revolution; elected colonel; battle of San Jacinto 1836; major general of Texas Militia; Republic of Texas legislature 1842; Texas legislature 1852–53.

Shiawassee   **Michigan**
Corunna   539 sq. mi.
71,687   69,770   71,140   63,075   53,446   45,967
September 10, 1822; organized March 13, 1837. Shiawassee River. Indian word of unknown meaning; possibilities include both "twisting" and "straight."

Shoshone   **Idaho**
Wallace   2,634 sq. mi.
13,771   13,931   19,226   19,718   20,876   22,806
February 4, 1864. Shoshoni Indians. Lived in Snake River region. Name from *shawnt,* meaning "abundance" and *shaw-nip,* meaning "grass."

Sibley   **Minnesota**
Gaylord   589 sq. mi.
15,356   14,366   15,448   15,845   16,228   15,816
March 5, 1853; organized March 2, 1854. Henry Hastings Sibley (1811–91). American Fur Company agent in Minnesota 1834; congressional delegate from Wisconsin Territory 1848–49; delegate from Minnesota Territory 1849–53; Minnesota Territory legislature 1855; governor of Minnesota 1858–60; brigadier general of Volunteers 1862–63; suppressed Dakota Indian uprising, hanged thirty-eight Indians 1862; brevet major general 1863.

Sierra   **California**
Downieville   953 sq. mi.
3,555   3,318   3,073   2,365   2,247   2,410
April 16, 1852. Sierra Nevada Mountains. Named by Spanish explorer Pedro Font for a mountain range in Spain 1776. *Sierra* is Spanish for "mountain" or "mountain range"; *nevada* means "snow covered."

Sierra   **New Mexico**
Truth or Consequences   4,180 sq. mi.
13,270   9,912   8,454   7,189   6,409   7,186
April 3, 1884. Uncertain. (1) Caballo Mountains. (2) Black Mountains. Both are within the county. *Sierra* is Spanish for "mountain" or "mountain range."

Silver Bow   **Montana**
Butte   718 sq. mi.
34,606   33,941   38,092   41,981   46,454   48,422
February 16, 1881. Silver Bow Creek. Named by miners; the origin of the name is lost in legend.

Simpson   **Kentucky**
Franklin   236 sq. mi.
16,405   15,145   14,673   13,054   11,548   11,678
January 28, 1819. John Simpson (?–1813). Served under General Wayne at battle of Fallen Timbers 1794; Kentucky House of Representatives 1807–11, Speaker 1810–11; elected to U.S. House of Representatives but was commissioned as a captain at the start of War of 1812; killed at battle of River Raisin, January 22, 1813.

Simpson   **Mississippi**
Mendenhall   589 sq. mi.
27,639   23,953   23,441   19,947   20,454   21,819
January 23, 1824. Josiah Simpson (?–1817). Mississippi Territory judge; Constitutional Convention 1817.

Sioux   **Iowa**
Orange City   768 sq. mi.
31,589   29,903   30,813   27,996   26,375   26,381
January 15, 1851; organized January 1, 1860. *Sioux Indians*. The word *sioux* comes from the ending of a Chippewa–French derogatory name for the Dakotas, Nadouaissiou, meaning "like adders" or "snakes," identifying the Dakotas as enemies. (See Dakota, Minnesota.)

Sioux   **Nebraska**
Harrison   2,067 sq. mi.
1,475   1,549   1,845   2,034   2,575   3,124
February 19, 1877; organized September 20, 1886. Sioux Indians.*

Sioux   **North Dakota**
Fort Yates   1,094 sq. mi.
4,044   3,761   3,620   3,632   3,662   3,696
September 3, 1914. Sioux Indians.*

Siskiyou   **California**
Yreka   6,287 sq. mi.
44,301   43,531   39,732   33,225   32,885   30,733
March 22, 1852. Siskiyou Mountains. The derivation of the name is uncertain: (1) a Cree and Chinook word meaning "bobtailed horse"; (2) corruption of French *six cailloux,* meaning "six stones," to describe a ford across a stream.

Sitka   **Alaska**
Sitka   2,874 sq. mi.
8,835   8,588   7,803   6,109   6,690   [a]
December, 1971. Town of Sitka. Tlingit name believed to mean "by the sea" or "on Shi," the Tlingit name for Baranof Island. [(a) Part of 1st Judicial District.]

Skagit   **Washington**
Mount Vernon   1,735 sq. mi.
102,979   79,555   64,138   52,381   51,350   43,273
November 28, 1883. Uncertain. Many geographic features in the area are named after the Skagit Indians with various spellings; any one or more could be the source of the county's name. The derivation of the name "Skagit" is unknown.

Skagway-Hoonah-Angoon   **Alaska**
(Census Area)   7,896 sq. mi.
3,436   4,385[a]   3,478[a]   2,660[a]   2,945[b]   [c]
"Skagway" is from Skagway River, from Tlingit word *schkaguè,* meaning "home of the north wind." "Hoonah" is from Huna, a Tlingit village. "Angoon" is from Tlingit village of Augoon. [(a) Skagway-Yakutat-Angoon; (b) Lynn Canal–Icy Straits; (c) part of 1st Judicial District.]

Skamania   **Washington**
Stevenson   1,656 sq. mi.

9,872	8,289	7,919	5,845	5,207	4,788

March 9, 1854. Indian word for "swift river."

Slope   **North Dakota**
Amidon   1,218 sq. mi.

767	907	1,157	1,484	1,893	2,315

November 3, 1914; organized January 14, 1915. Missouri Slope. Name given to the general eastward slope of North Dakota west of the Missouri River.

Smith   **Kansas**
Smith Center   895 sq. mi.

4,536	5,078	5,947	6,757	7,776	8,846

February 26, 1867; organized 1872. James Nelson Smith (1837–64). Major, 2nd Colorado Volunteers; served in Arkansas and Missouri; killed at battle of the Little Blue October 23, 1864.

Smith   **Mississippi**
Raleigh   636 sq. mi.

16,182	14,798	15,077	13,561	14,303	16,740

December 23, 1833. David Smith (1753–1835). Private in Revolutionary War; King's Mountain 1780; Cowpens and Eutaw Springs 1781; major, Kentucky Militia; moved to Mississippi 1822.

Smith   **Tennessee**
Carthage   314 sq. mi.

17,712	14,143	14,935	12,509	12,059	14,098

October 26, 1799. Daniel Smith (1748–1818). Surveyor of Augusta County, Virginia, 1773; colonel in Revolutionary War; secretary of the Territory South of the Ohio River 1790–96; Tennessee Constitutional Convention 1796; mapped Tennessee; general, Tennessee Militia; U.S. senator 1798–99 and 1805–09.

Smith   **Texas**
Tyler   928 sq. mi.

174,706	151,309	128,366	97,096	86,350	74,701

April 11, 1846; organized July 10, 1846. James Smith (1792–1855). War of 1812; moved to Texas 1835; organized cavalry troop 1836; rose from captain to colonel 1836; Texas brigadier general in charge of northwest frontier 1841; commanded Texas troops in suppressing Regulator–Moderator War 1844; Texas House of Representatives 1846–47.

Smyth   **Virginia**
Marion   452 sq. mi.

33,081	32,370	33,366	31,349	31,066	30,187

February 23, 1832. Alexander Smyth (1765–1830). Served nine nonconsecutive terms in Virginia House of Delegates between 1792 and 1827; Virginia Senate 1808–09; colonel, U.S. Army Rifleman Regiment 1808–12; inspector general with rank of brigadier general 1812–13; U.S. representative 1817–24 and 1827–30.

Snohomish   **Washington**
Everett   2,089 sq. mi.

606,024	465,642	337,720	265,236	172,199	111,580

January 14, 1861. Snohomish Indians. Unknown meaning; Indian suffix *mish* means "people."

Snyder   **Pennsylvania**
Middleburg   331 sq. mi.

37,546	36,680	33,584	29,269	25,922	22,912

March 2, 1855. Simon Snyder (1759–1819). Pennsylvania Constitutional Convention 1789–90; Pennsylvania Assembly 1797–1807, Speaker 1802–07; Pennsylvania Senate 1817.

Socorro   **New Mexico**
Socorro   6,646 sq. mi.

18,078   14,764   12,566   9,763   10,168   9,670

January 9, 1852. Town of Socorro. Name given to nearby Indian pueblo by Don Juan de Oñate 1598, for food and aid, i.e., succor (Spanish *socorro*), given to starving colonists by Indians.

Solano   **California**
Fairfield   829 sq. mi.
394,542   340,421   235,203   169,941   134,597   104,833

February 18, 1850. Francisco Solano (?–?). Chief of Suisun and Soscol Indians; defeated by Mexican general Vallejo 1835; given name Solano when he was baptized at Mission San Francisco Solano; prevented Indian raid on the mission.

Somerset   **Maine**
Skowhegan   3,927 sq. mi.
50,888   49,767   45,028   40,597   39,749   39,785

March 1, 1809. Somersetshire, England.

Somerset   **Maryland**
Princess Anne   327 sq. mi.
24,747   23,440   19,188   18,924   19,623   20,745

August 22, 1666. Mary Arundell Somerset (?–?). Wife of Sir John Somerset; sister of Anne Arundell Calvert (see Anne Arundel, Maryland); sister-in-law of Cecil Calvert (see Cecil and Calvert, Maryland).

Somerset   **New Jersey**
Somerville   305 sq. mi.
297,490   240,279   203,129   198,372   143,913   99,052

May 1688; organized 1714. Somersetshire, England.

Somerset   **Pennsylvania**
Somerset   1,075 sq. mi.
80,023   78,218   81,243   76,037   77,450   81,813

April 17, 1795. Town of Somerset. Named for Somersetshire, England.

Somervell   **Texas**
Glen Rose   187 sq. mi.
6,809   5,360   4,154   2,793   2,577   2,542

March 13, 1875. Alexander Somervell (1796–1854). Moved to Austin's second colony 1832; lieutenant colonel at San Jacinto 1836; Republic of Texas secretary of war 1836; brigadier general 1839; commanded Somervell expedition into Mexico 1842.

Sonoma   **California**
Santa Rosa   1,576 sq. mi.
458,614   388,222   299,681   204,885   147,375   103,405

February 18 1850. Town of Sonoma. Name given by Spanish to local Indians; *tso* is local Indian word for "earth"; *noma* means "village"; the names of many local Indian villages ended in "tsonoma."

Southampton   **Virginia**
Courtland   600 sq. mi.
17,482   17,550   18,731   18,582   27,195   26,522

April 30, 1749. Southampton Hundred. *Henry Wriothesley, 3rd Earl of Southampton* (1573–1624); patron of Shakespeare; imprisoned in Tower of London by Elizabeth I 1601; released by James I; Virginia Company's council 1609–24, treasurer 1620–24. "Hundreds" were political subdivisions created in early Virginia that contained 100 families or could produce 100 fighting men.

Southeast Fairbanks   **Alaska**
(Census Area)   24,815 sq. mi.
6,174   5,913   5,676   4,179   (a)   (b)

Southeastern section of Fairbanks census area remaining when borough of Fairbanks North Star was created 1964 (see Fairbanks North Star, Alaska). [(a) Part of Fairbanks; (b) part of 4th Judicial District.]

Spalding   **Georgia**
Griffin   198 sq. mi.
58,417   54,457   47,899   39,514   35,404   31,045
December 20, 1851. Thomas Spalding (1774–1851). Georgia House of Representatives 1794; Georgia Constitutional Convention 1798; Georgia Senate 1804; U.S. representative 1805–06; Florida–Georgia Boundary Commission 1826.

Spartanburg   **South Carolina**
Spartanburg   811 sq. mi.
253,791   226,800   201,861   173,724   156,830   150,349
March 12, 1785. Spartan Regiment of South Carolina Militia. Named for military reputation of Sparta, ancient Greece; fought at Cedar Spring and Musgrove's Mill 1780; Cowpens 1781.

Spencer   **Indiana**
Rockport   399 sq. mi.
20,391   19,490   19,361   17,134   16,074   16,174
January 10, 1818; effective February 1, 1818. *Spear Spencer* (?–1811); also Spier Spencer. Sheriff of Harrison County, Indiana; captain of Mounted Riflemen; killed at battle of Tippecanoe November 7, 1811.

Spencer   **Kentucky**
Taylorsville   186 sq. mi.
11,766   6,801   5,929   5,488   5,680   6,157
January 7, 1824. Spear Spencer.*

Spink   **South Dakota**
Redfield   1,504 sq. mi.
7,454   7,981   9,201   10,595   11,706   12,204
January 8, 1873; organized August 1, 1879. Solomon Lewis Spink (1831–81). Illinois House of Representatives 1864; secretary of Dakota Territory 1865–69; acting governor 1866–67; congressional delegate 1869–71.

Spokane   **Washington**
Spokane   1,764 sq. mi.
417,939   361,364   341,835   287,487   278,333   221,561
January 29, 1858, as Shoshone; name changed 1860; abolished 1864; recreated 1879. Spokane Indians. Dominant tribe in a confederacy in eastern Washington; name means "chief" or "child of the sun."

Spotsylvania   **Virginia**
Spotsylvania   401 sq. mi.
90,395   57,403   34,435   16,424   13,819   11,920
November 2, 1720 (session). Alexander Spotswood (1676–1740). Lieutenant colonel, battle of Blenheim in War of Spanish Succession 1704; lieutenant governor of Virginia 1710–22, acting governor in permanent absence of governor; deputy postmaster general of American colonies 1730–39. Combined with Latin *sylva,* meaning "woods."

Stafford   **Kansas**
Saint John   792 sq. mi.
4,789   5,365   5,694   5,943   7,451   8,816
February 26, 1867; organized 1879. Lewis Stafford (?–1863). Captain, Company E, 1st Kansas Volunteer Infantry 1861; battle of Wilson's Creek 1861; accidentally killed at Young's Point, Louisiana, January 31, 1863.

Stafford   **Virginia**
Stafford   270 sq. mi.
92,446   61,236   40,470   24,587   16,876   11,902
June 5, 1666 (session). Staffordshire, England.

Stanislaus   **California**
Modesto   1,494 sq. mi.

446,997   370,522   265,900   194,506   157,294   127,231

April 1, 1854. Stanislaus River. Estanislao (?–?); Indian chief whose Christian name honored one of two Polish saints named Stanislas; ran away from Mission San José c1828; leader of escaped Indian neophytes that harassed settlements and missions; defeated by General Vallejo 1829; surrendered to Father Duran at Mission San José.

Stanley   **South Dakota**
Fort Pierre   1,443 sq. mi.
2,772   2,453   2,533   2,457   4,085   2,055

January 8, 1873; organized April 23, 1890. David Sloane Stanley (1828–1902). Graduated West Point 1852; rose from 2nd lieutenant to captain 1852–61; battle of Wilson's Creek 1861; brigadier general of Volunteers 1861; major general 1862; battle of Franklin 1864 (awarded Congressional Medal of Honor 1893); brevet major general 1865; served in western Indian campaigns 1866–74; commandant of Fort Sully, Dakota Territory; brigadier general 1884; brevet major general 1892; governor of U.S. Soldiers' Home 1893–98.

Stanly   **North Carolina**
Albemarle   395 sq. mi.
58,100   51,765   48,517   42,822   40,873   37,130

January 11, 1841. John Stanly (1774–1834). North Carolina House of Commons 1798–99 and various terms 1812–26; U.S. representative 1801–03 and 1809–11.

Stanton   **Kansas**
Johnson   680 sq. mi.
2,406   2,333   2,339   2,287   2,108   2,263

March 6, 1873; organized March 5, 1887. *Edwin McMasters Stanton* (1814–69). U.S. attorney general 1860–61; U.S. secretary of war 1862–68; died four days after receiving appointment to U.S. Supreme Court.

Stanton   **Nebraska**
Stanton   430 sq. mi.
6,455   6,244   6,549   5,758   5,783   6,387

March 6, 1855, as Izard; name changed January 10, 1862; organized January 23, 1867. Edwin McMasters Stanton.*

Stark   **Illinois**
Toulon   288 sq. mi.
6,332   6,534   7,389   7,510   8,152   8,721

March 2, 1839. *John Stark* (1728–1822). Lieutenant, French and Indian War 1755; colonel, New Hampshire Regiment 1775; Bunker Hill 1775; Trenton 1776; Bennington and Princeton 1777; brigadier general 1777; commanded Northern District 1778.

Stark   **North Dakota**
Dickinson   1,338 sq. mi.
22,636   22,832   23,697   19,613   18,451   16,317

February 10, 1879; organized May 25, 1882. George Stark (?–?). Helped to reorganize Northern Pacific Railroad from bankruptcy 1873; vice president, Northern Pacific Railroad 1875–79; promoted settlement in Dakota Territory.

Stark   **Ohio**
Canton   576 sq. mi.
378,098   367,585   378,823   372,210   340,345   283,194

February 13, 1808; organized January 1, 1809. John Stark.*

Starke   **Indiana**
Knox   309 sq. mi.
23,556   22,747   21,997   19,280   17,911   15,282

February 7, 1835; organized January 15, 1850. John Stark.* Letter "e" added to county name.

Starr   **Texas**
Rio Grande City   1,223 sq. mi.

53,597   40,518   27,266   17,707   17,137   13,948

February 10, 1848; organized August 7, 1848. James Harper Starr (1809–90). Physician and surgeon; Texas Republic secretary of treasury 1839; promoted settlement in Texas; various civilian positions in Confederacy.

Staunton   **Virginia**
(Independent City)   20 sq. mi.
23,853   24,461   21,857   24,504   22,232   19,927

January 16, 1908. Rebecca Staunton (c1690–1775). Wife of Sir William Gooch, governor of Virginia (see Goochland, Virginia). (Associated county: Augusta.)

Stearns   **Minnesota**
Saint Cloud   1,345 sq. mi.
133,166   118,791   108,161   95,400   80,345   70,681

February 20, 1855; organized March 3, 1855. Charles Thomas Stearns (1807–98). Minnesota territorial legislature 1854–55. County was intended to be named for Isaac Stevens (see Stevens, Minnesota) but due to clerical error it was named after Stearns, who was in the legislature at the time.

Steele   **Minnesota**
Owatonna   430 sq. mi.
33,680   30,729   30,328   26,931   25,029   21,155

February 20, 1855; organized February 29, 1856. *Franklin Steele* (1813–80). Made fortune in lumber business; acquired large land holdings in Minnesota and Dakota Territory; first Board of Regents, University of Minnesota 1851.

Steele   **North Dakota**
Finley   712 sq. mi.
2,258   2,420   3,106   3,749   4,719   5,145

March 8, 1883; organized June 13, 1883. Uncertain. (1) Franklin Steele.* (2) Edward H. Steele (1846–99); associated with Franklin Steele in Red River Land Company; actively lobbied for creation of county.

Stephens   **Georgia**
Toccoa   179 sq. mi.
25,435   23,257   21,763   20,331   18,391   16,647

August 18, 1905. *Alexander Hamilton Stephens* (1812–83). Georgia House of Representatives 1836–41; Georgia Senate 1842; U.S. representative 1843–59 and 1873–82; opposed secession but remained loyal to Georgia; Montgomery Convention 1861; vice president of Confederacy 1861–65; elected to U.S. Senate but denied seat 1866; governor of Georgia 1882–83.

Stephens   **Oklahoma**
Duncan   874 sq. mi.
43,182   42,299   43,419   35,902   37,990   34,071

July 16, 1907. John Hall Stephens (1847–1924). Texas Senate 1886–88; U.S. representative 1897–1917; promoted Oklahoma statehood.

Stephens   **Texas**
Breckenridge   895 sq. mi.
9,674   9,010   9,926   8,414   8,885   10,597

January 22, 1858, as Buchanan; name changed December 17, 1861; organized August 21, 1876. Alexander Hamilton Stephens.*

Stephenson   **Illinois**
Freeport   564 sq. mi.
48,979   48,052   49,536   48,861   46,207   41,595

March 4, 1837. Benjamin Stephenson (?–1822). Adjutant general of Illinois Territory 1813; colonel, War of 1812; congressional delegate 1814–16; Illinois Constitutional Committee 1818.

Sterling   **Texas**
Sterling City   923 sq. mi.

| 1,393 | 1,438 | 1,206 | 1,056 | 1,177 | 1,282 |

March 4, 1891; organized June 3, 1891. W. S. Sterling (?–?). First settler in region; buffalo hunter.

Steuben **Indiana**
Angola 309 sq. mi.

| 33,214 | 27,446 | 24,694 | 20,159 | 17,184 | 17,087 |

February 7, 1835; organized January 18, 1837; effective May 1, 1837. *Friedrich Wilhelm Ludolf Gerhard Augustin von Steuben* (1730–94). Prussian army during Seven Years' War 1756–63; aide-de-camp to Frederick the Great; arrived in America to serve in Continental army 1777; inspector general; trained troops at Valley Forge; major general at Monmouth and Yorktown; became U.S. citizen.

Steuben **New York**
Bath 1,393 sq. mi.

| 98,726 | 99,088 | 99,217 | 99,546 | 97,691 | 91,439 |

March 18, 1796. Friedrich von Steuben.*

Stevens **Kansas**
Hugoton 728 sq. mi.

| 5,463 | 5,048 | 4,736 | 4,198 | 4,400 | 4,516 |

March 6, 1873; organized August 3, 1886. Thaddeus Stevens (1792–68). Pennsylvania House of Representatives 1833–35, 1837, and 1841; Constitutional Convention 1838; U.S. representative 1849–53 and 1850–68; led Radical Republicans in imposing Reconstruction on the South following Civil War; led impeachment of President Johnson.

Stevens **Minnesota**
Morris 562 sq. mi.

| 10,053 | 10,634 | 11,322 | 11,218 | 11,262 | 11,106 |

February 20, 1862; organized December 31, 1871. *Isaac Ingalls Stevens* (1818–62). Graduated West Point at head of class 1839; staff of General Scott in Mexican War; wounded at Mexico City; brevet captain and major; initiated survey of railroad route between Minnesota and Washington Territory 1853; governor of Washington Territory 1853–57; congressional delegate 1857–61; reentered Union army as colonel 1861; major general of Volunteers 1862; killed at battle of Chantilly September 1, 1862.

Stevens **Washington**
Colville 2,478 sq. mi.

| 40,066 | 30,948 | 28,979 | 17,405 | 17,884 | 18,580 |

January 20, 1863. Isaac Ingalls Stevens.*

Stewart **Georgia**
Lumpkin 459 sq. mi.

| 5,252 | 5,654 | 5,896 | 6,511 | 7,371 | 9,194 |

December 23, 1830. Daniel Stewart (1759–1829). General, Continental army; brigadier general of Cavalry, War of 1812; Seminole War 1817–18.

Stewart **Tennessee**
Dover 458 sq. mi.

| 12,370 | 9,479 | 8,665 | 7,319 | 7,851 | 9,175 |

November 1, 1803. Duncan Stewart (1752–1815). North Carolina House of Commons 1789–90; moved to Tennessee c1800; Tennessee Senate 1801–07; moved to Mississippi c1808.

Stillwater **Montana**
Columbus 1,795 sq. mi.

| 8,195 | 6,536 | 5,598 | 4,632 | 5,526 | 5,416 |

March 24, 1913. Stillwater River. Tributary of the Yellowstone; the name is inappropriate to the river; for most of its seventy miles it is a fast-moving stream.

Stoddard **Missouri**
Bloomfield 827 sq. mi.

| 29,705 | 28,895 | 29,009 | 25,771 | 29,490 | 33,463 |

January 2, 1835. Amos Stoddard (1762–1813). Revolutionary War 1779–83; Massachusetts legislature 1797; returned to army as captain of artillery 1798; received formal transfer of Upper Louisiana (Missouri Territory) from France to U.S. after receiving transfer from Spain to France the previous day 1804; major 1807; killed during siege of Fort Meigs, War of 1812.

Stokes   **North Carolina**
Danbury   452 sq. mi.

| 44,711 | 37,223 | 33,086 | 23,782 | 22,314 | 21,520 |

November 2, 1789 (session). John Stokes (1756–90). Ensign, 6th Virginia Regiment 1776; rose from 2nd lieutenant to captain 1776–78; wounded and captured at Waxhaw Massacre 1780; exchanged 1783; North Carolina Senate 1786–87; North Carolina House of Representatives 1789; appointed U.S. district judge, died on way to first court session.

Stone   **Arkansas**
Mountain View   607 sq. mi.

| 11,499 | 9,775 | 9,022 | 6,838 | 6,294 | 7,662 |

April 21, 1873. Descriptive of local geology.

Stone   **Mississippi**
Wiggins   445 sq. mi.

| 13,622 | 10,750 | 9,716 | 8,101 | 7,013 | 6,264 |

April 3, 1916. John Marshall Stone (1830–1900). Rose from captain to colonel of Mississippi Rifles 1861; Mississippi Senate 1870–76; acting governor 1876–82; governor of Mississippi 1890–96.

Stone   **Missouri**
Galena   463 sq. mi.

| 28,658 | 19,078 | 15,587 | 9,921 | 8,176 | 9,748 |

February 10, 1851. Uncertain. (1) William Stone (?–?); judge. (2) Family of early settlers. (3) Descriptive of the local geology.

Stonewall   **Texas**
Aspermont   919 sq. mi.

| 1,693 | 2,013 | 2,406 | 2,397 | 3,017 | 3,679 |

August 21, 1876; organized 1888. *Thomas Jonathon "Stonewall" Jackson* (1824–63). Graduated West Point 1846; brevet 2nd lieutenant 1846; 1st lieutenant, brevet captain, and major 1847; Mexican War battles of Vera Cruz, Chapultepec, and Contreras; resigned 1852; professor of artillery, Virginia Military Institute 1852–61; colonel, Virginia Volunteers 1861; given nickname at first battle of Bull Run 1861; rose from brigadier general to lieutenant general 1862; mortally wounded by own troops at Chancellorville, died May 10, 1863.

Storey   **Nevada**
Virginia City   263 sq. mi.

| 3,399 | 2,526 | 1,503 | 695 | 568 | 671 |

November 25, 1861. Edward F. Storey (1828–60). Lieutenant, Mexican War; miner, Comstock Lode 1859; raised rifle company to pursue marauding Paiutes; killed in battle near Pyramid Lake.

Story   **Iowa**
Nevada   573 sq. mi.

| 79,981 | 74,252 | 72,326 | 62,783 | 49,327 | 44,294 |

January 13, 1846; organized June 1, 1853. Joseph Story (1779–1845). Massachusetts House of Representatives 1805–07; U.S. representative 1808–09; associate justice, U.S. Supreme Court 1811–45.

Strafford   **New Hampshire**
Dover   369 sq. mi.

| 112,233 | 104,233 | 85,408 | 70,431 | 59,799 | 51,567 |

April 29, 1769; organized 1773. Thomas Wentworth, Earl of Strafford (1593–1641). British House of Commons 1614; court favorite of Charles I; made 1st Earl of Strafford 1640; impeached by enemies in Parliament and sent to Tower of London 1640; executed.

Stutsman   **North Dakota**
Jamestown   2,221 sq. mi.
21,908   22,241   24,154   23,550   25,137   24,158
January 4, 1873; organized June 10, 1873. Enos Stutsman (1826–74). Various terms in Dakota Territory legislature 1862–74; U.S. customs agent 1866–67.

Sublette   **Wyoming**
Pinedale   4,883 sq. mi.
5,920   4,843   4,548   3,755   3,778   2,481
February 15, 1921. William Lewis Sublette (1799–1845). Trapper in Rocky Mountains 1823–32; founder of Rocky Mountain Fur Company 1826; established trading post which became Fort Laramie 1834.

Suffolk   **Massachusetts**
Boston   59 sq. mi.
689,807   663,906   650,142   735,190   791,329   896,615
May 10, 1643. Suffolk County, England.

Suffolk   **New York**
Riverhead   912 sq. mi.
1,419,369   1,321,864   1,284,231   1,124,950   666,784   276,129
November 1, 1683. Suffolk County, England.

Suffolk   **Virginia**
(Independent City)   400 sq. mi.
63,677   52,141   47,621   45,024[a]   43,975[a]   37,577[a]
1637, as Upper Norfolk; name changed to Nansemond 1642; incorporated as City of Nansemond 1972; merged with City of Suffolk 1974. Suffolk, England. [(a) Includes Nansemond County: 1970, 35,166; 1960, 31,366; 1950, 25,238. (Associated county: Nansemond.)]

Sullivan   **Indiana**
Sullivan   447 sq. mi.
21,751   18,993   21,107   19,889   21,721   23,667
December 30, 1816; effective January 15, 1817. Uncertain. (1) Daniel Sullivan (?–1790); settled near Vincennes 1786; conducted raids against local Indians; killed by Indians while traveling from Vincennes to Louisville. (2) John Sullivan* (see Sullivan, New Hampshire).

Sullivan   **Missouri**
Milan   651 sq. mi.
7,219   6,326   7,434   7,572   8,783   11,299
February 17, 1843, as Highland; name changed and organized February 14, 1845. Sullivan County, Tennessee.

Sullivan   **New Hampshire**
Newport   537 sq. mi.
40,458   38,592   36,063   30,949   28,067   26,441
July 5, 1827. *John Sullivan* (1740–95). Continental Congress from New Hampshire 1774–75 and 1780–81; brigadier general and major general, Continental army 1775–80; attorney general of New Hampshire 1782–86; president (governor) of New Hampshire 1786–88 and 1789–90; federal Constitutional Convention 1787; Speaker, New Hampshire House of Representatives; judge, U.S. District Court 1789–95.

Sullivan   **New York**
Monticello   970 sq. mi.
73,966   69,277   65,155   52,580   45,272   40,731
March 27, 1809; effective September 4, 1827. John Sullivan.*

Sullivan   **Pennsylvania**
Laporte   450 sq. mi.

6,556   6,104   6,349   5,961   6,251   6,745
March 15, 1847. John Sullivan.*

Sullivan   **Tennessee**
Blountsville   413 sq. mi.
153,048   143,596   143,968   127,329   114,139   95,063
October 18, 1779 (session). John Sullivan.*

Sully   **South Dakota**
Onida   1,007 sq. mi.
1,556   1,589   1,990   2,362   2,607   2,713
January 8, 1873; organized April 19, 1883. Uncertain. (1) Alfred Sully (1821–79); graduated West Point 1841; fought against Sioux and Seminoles; 1st lieutenant, Mexican War 1847; captain 1852; major 1862; brigadier general of Volunteers 1862; Antietam 1862; sent west to fight Indians 1863; brevet major general of Volunteers 1863; mustered out of Volunteer Army 1866 continued as colonel in Regular Army. (2) Fort Sully; named for Alfred Sully; established near Pierre by Sully 1863; moved up Missouri River 1866; abandoned 1894.

Summers   **West Virginia**
Hinton   361 sq. mi.
12,999   14,204   15,875   13,213   15,640   19,183
February 27, 1871. George William Summers (1804–68). Virginia House of Delegates 1830–32 and 1834–36; U.S. representative 1831–45; voted against Virginia secession 1861.

Summit   **Colorado**
Breckenridge   608 sq. mi.
23,548   12,881   8,848   2,665   2,073   1,135
November 1, 1861. Descriptive of mountainous terrain.

Summit   **Ohio**
Akron   413 sq. mi.
542,899   514,990   524,472   553,371   513,569   410,032
March 3, 1840. Highest elevation on Ohio Canal; on divide between Lake Erie and Ohio River.

Summit   **Utah**
Coalville   1,871 sq. mi.
29,736   15,518   10,198   5,879   5,673   6,745
January 13, 1854. Descriptive of divide between Green River and the Great Basin.

Sumner   **Kansas**
Wellington   1,182 sq. mi.
25,946   25,841   24,928   23,553   25,316   23,646
February 26, 1867; organized November 7, 1871. Charles Sumner (1811–74). U.S. senator from Massachusetts 1851–74; ardent foe of extending slavery into Kansas; severely caned by South Carolina representative Preston Brooks (see Brooks, Georgia) following speech "The Crime Against Kansas" 1856.

Sumner   **Tennessee**
Gallatin   529 sq. mi.
130,449   103,281   85,790   56,106   36,217   33,533
November 18, 1786 (session). Jethro Sumner (c1733–85). Virginia Militia, French and Indian Wars 1755–61; commanded Fort Bedford 1760; colonel, North Carolina 3rd Battalion 1776; brigadier general 1780–83.

Sumter   **Alabama**
Livingston   905 sq. mi.
14,798   16,174   16,908   16,974   20,041   23,610

December 18, 1832. *Thomas Sumter* (1734–1832). Lieutenant colonel, 6th Continental Regiment; brigadier general of militia 1780; voted Thanks of Congress 1781; South Carolina Senate 1781–82; U.S. representative 1789–93 and 1797–1801; U.S. senator 1801–10.

Sumter   **Florida**
Bushnell   546 sq. mi.

53,345	31,577	24,272	14,839	11,869	11,330

January 8, 1853. Thomas Sumter.*

Sumter   **Georgia**
Americus   485 sq. mi.

33,200	30,228	29,360	26,931	24,652	24,208

December 26, 1831. Thomas Sumter.*

Sumter   **South Carolina**
Sumter   665 sq. mi.

104,646	102,637	88,243	79,425	74,941	57,634

1798, as judicial district; converted to county 1868. Thomas Sumter.*

Sunflower   **Mississippi**
Indianola   694 sq. mi.

34,369	32,867	34,844	37,047	45,750	56,031

February 15, 1844. Sunflower River. Tributary of Yazoo River.

Surry   **North Carolina**
Dobson   537 sq. mi.

71,219	61,704	59,449	51,415	48,205	45,593

December 5, 1770 (session). Uncertain. (1) An unspecified lord (or earl) of Surry (or Surrey) who opposed taxation of American colonies. (2) Surrey County, England.

Surry   **Virginia**
Surry   279 sq. mi.

6,829	6,145	6,046	5,882	6,220	6,220

1652. Surrey County, England.

Susquehanna   **Pennsylvania**
Montrose   823 sq. mi.

42,238	40,380	37,876	34,344	33,137	31,970

February 21, 1810; organized 1812. Susquehanna River. Name is of uncertain Indian origin; may be from *sisku,* meaning "mud," and *hanne,* meaning "river."

Sussex   **Delaware**
Georgetown   938 sq. mi.

156,638	113,229	98,004	80,356	73,195	61,336

August 8, 1673, as Hoarkill; name changed to Deale 1681; name changed to Sussex December 4, 1682. Sussex County, England. Named by William Penn for his home county in England.

Sussex   **New Jersey**
Newton   521 sq. mi.

144,166	130,943	116,119	77,528	49,255	34,423

May 16, 1753 (session). Sussex County, England.

Sussex   **Virginia**
Sussex   491 sq. mi.

12,504   10,248   10,874   11,464   12,411   12,785
February 27, 1752 (session). Sussex County, England.

Sutter   **California**
Yuba City   603 sq. mi.
78,930   64,415   52,246   41,935   33,380   26,239
February 18, 1850. John Augustus Sutter (1803–80). Became Mexican citizen after arriving in California 1839; received land grant at present site of Sacramento; gold discovered on his property, leading to his financial ruin as workers deserted him and squatters took over his land 1848; received pension from California.

Sutton   **Texas**
Sonora   1,454 sq. mi.
4,077   4,135   5,130   3,175   3,738   3,746
April 1, 1887; organized November 4, 1890. John Schuyler Sutton (c1821–62). 2nd lieutenant, Republic of Texas Army 1839; captured on Santa Fe expedition 1841; released 1842; private, Texas Mounted Rifles in Mexican War; Monterrey and Mexico City campaigns; lieutenant colonel, 7th Texas Cavalry 1861; wounded at battle of Valverde, New Mexico Territory, February 21, 1862; died next day after refusing to have leg amputated.

Suwanee   **Florida**
Live Oak   688 sq. mi.
34,844   26,780   22,287   15,559   14,961   16,986
December 21, 1858. Suwanee River. Origin of name is unknown; possibilities include (1) Indian word *suwani,* meaning "echo"; (2) corruption of Spanish "San Juan," after a 17th-century mission in area; (3) Indian words meaning "long winding river."

Swain   **North Carolina**
Bryson City   528 sq. mi.
12,968   11,268   10,283   7,861   8,387   9,921
February 24, 1871. David Lowrie Swain (1801–68). North Carolina House of Commons 1824–30; governor of North Carolina 1832–35; president, University of North Carolina 1835–68; declined offer to serve in Confederate Senate 1863.

Sweet Grass   **Montana**
Big Timber   1,855 sq. mi.
3,609   3,154   3,216   2,980   3,290   3,621
March 5, 1895. Uncertain. (1) Descriptive of local vegetation. (2) Sweet Grass River, which was named for the local grasses.

Sweetwater   **Wyoming**
Green River   10,425 sq. mi.
37,613   38,823   41,723   18,391   17,920   22,017
December 27, 1867, as Carter; organized January 3, 1868; name changed December 13, 1869. Sweetwater River. Named for palatable water, compared to that found elsewhere along the Oregon Trail.

Swift   **Minnesota**
Benson   744 sq. mi.
11,956   10,724   12,920   13,177   14,936   15,837
February 18, 1870; organized April 6, 1897. Henry Adoniram Swift (1823–69). Minnesota Senate 1862–63 and 1864–65; as president of the Senate became governor of Minnesota following resignation of Alexander Ramsey 1863–64; registrar, U.S. Land Office 1865–69.

Swisher   **Texas**
Tulia   900 sq. mi.
8,378   8,133   9,723   10,373   10,607   8,249
August 21, 1876; organized July 17, 1890. James Gibson Swisher (1795–1864). Private, Tennessee Militia 1813–14; private, U.S. Mounted Rangers 1814–15; moved to Texas 1833; captain of Volunteers at siege of Bexar 1835; resigned from Texas Army 1836; signer of Texas Declaration of Independence 1836.

Switzerland		Indiana			
Vevay		221 sq. mi.			
9,065	7,738	7,153	6,306	7,092	7,599

September 7, 1814; effective October 1, 1814. Country of Switzerland.

T

Talbot		Georgia			
Talbotton		393 sq. mi.			
6,498	6,524	6,536	6,625	7,127	7,687

December 14, 1827. Matthew Talbot (?–1827). Georgia Constitutional Convention 1798; Georgia Senate 1808–23, president 1818–23; interim governor of Georgia 1819.

Talbot		Maryland			
Easton		269 sq. mi.			
33,812	30,549	25,604	23,682	21,578	19,428

February 18, 1662. Uncertain. (1) Either one of two women from the Talbot family related to Cecilius Calvert (see Cecil, Maryland) by marriage: (a) Grace Calvert Talbot (1614–72); daughter of George Calvert, 1st Lord Baltimore, and sister of Cecilius, 2nd Lord Baltimore; married Robert Talbot of County Kildare, Ireland; (b) Frances Arundell Talbot (?–?); sister of Anne Arundell Calvert, wife of Cecilius Calvert. (2) Named for the Talbot family in general; numerous members were related to Cecilius Calvert by blood or marriage.

Taliaferro		Georgia			
Crawfordville		195 sq. mi.			
2,077	1,915	2,032	2,423	3,370	4,515

December 24, 1825. Benjamin Taliaferro (1750–1821). Lieutenant, Revolutionary War; captured at Charleston 1780; Georgia Senate, president; Georgia Constitutional Convention 1798; U.S. representative 1799–1802; judge of superior court.

Talladega		Alabama			
Talladega		740 sq. mi.			
80,321	74,107	73,826	65,280	65,495	63,639

December 18, 1832. Battle of Talladega. Andrew Jackson defeated Creeks November, 1813; battle named for Muskogee village of Talatigi; *atigi* or *teka* means "border," and *talwa* or *talla* means "town"; the village was near a tribal boundary.

Tallahatchie		Mississippi			
Charleston		644 sq. mi.			
14,903	15,210	17,157	19,338	24,081	30,486

December 23, 1833. Tallahatchie River. Named from Choctaw *tali,* meaning "rock," and *hacha,* meaning "river."

Tallapoosa		Alabama			
Dadeville		718 sq. mi.			
41,475	38,826	38,676	33,840	35,007	35,074

December 18, 1832. Tallapoosa River. Origin of name is unknown; disparate possibilities include Creek for "cat town," "swift current," or "newcomer."

Tama		Iowa			
Toledo		721 sq. mi.			
18,103	17,419	19,533	20,147	21,413	21,688

February 17, 1843; organized July 4, 1853. Tama (c1780–c1833). Fox chief; negotiated treaties with U.S. 1824, 1825, and 1832; name believed to mean "sudden crash of thunder."

Taney		Missouri			
Forsyth		632 sq. mi.			
39,703	25,561	20,467	13,023	10,238	9,863

January 6, 1837. Roger Brooke Taney (1777–1864). Maryland Senate; U.S. attorney general 1831–33; U.S. treasurer 1833–34; chief justice of U.S. 1836–64, presided over Dred Scott case 1857.

Tangipahoa   **Louisiana**
Amite   790 sq. mi.
100,588   85,709   80,698   65,873   59,434   53,218
March 6, 1869. Tangipahoa Indians. Meaning of name is uncertain but most suggestions involve corn or maize in one way or another.

Taos   **New Mexico**
Taos   2,203 sq. mi.
29,979   23,118   19,456   17,516   15,934   17,146
January 9, 1852. Taos Pueblo. Spanish attempt at Indian name Towi, or Tuota.

Tarrant   **Texas**
Fort Worth   863 sq. mi.
1,446,219   1,170,103 860,880   716,317   538,495   361,253
December 20, 1849; organized August 5, 1850. Edward H. Tarrant (1796–1858). Battle of New Orleans 1815; Texas Rangers 1835; Texas Republic Congress 1837–38; brigadier general, Texas Army 1841; battle of Village Creek 1841; Texas Constitutional Convention 1845; Texas legislature 1846.

Tate   **Mississippi**
Senatobia   404 sq. mi.
25,370   21,432   20,119   18,544   18,138   18,011
April 15, 1873. Uncertain. (1) Thomas Simpson Tate (?–c1881); trustee, Free Land & Colonization Company of De Soto County 1868; influential in creating Tate County from De Soto County 1873; Mississippi legislature. (2) Tate family; prominent in northwestern Mississippi.

Tattnall   **Georgia**
Reidsville   484 sq. mi.
22,305   17,722   18,134   16,557   15,837   15,939
December 5, 1801. Josiah Tattnall (1764–1803). Revolutionary War under General Wayne 1782; Georgia House of Representatives 1795 and 1796; U.S. senator 1796–99; colonel and brigadier general, Georgia Regiment 1801; governor of Georgia 1801–02.

Taylor   **Florida**
Perry   1,042 sq. mi.
19,256   17,111   16,532   13,641   13,168   10,416
December 23, 1856. *Zachary Taylor* (1784–1850). 1st lieutenant, U.S. Army 1808; captain 1810; major War of 1812; lieutenant colonel 1829; defeated Seminoles at Lake Okeechobee 1837; brevet brigadier general 1837; Mexican War victories in battles of Palo Alto and Resaca de la Palma 1846; captured Matamoros and Monterrey; defeated Santa Anna at battle of Buena Vista 1847; 12th president of the U.S. 1849–50; died in office July 9, 1850.

Taylor   **Georgia**
Butler   377 sq. mi.
8,815   7,642   7,902   7,865   8,311   9,113
January 15, 1852. Zachary Taylor.*

Taylor   **Iowa**
Bedford   534 sq. mi.
6,958   7,114   8,353   8,790   10,288   12,420
February 24, 1847; organized February 26, 1851. Zachary Taylor.*

Taylor   **Kentucky**
Campbellsville   270 sq. mi.

22,927   21,146   21,178   17,138   16,285   14,403
January 13, 1848. Zachary Taylor.*

Taylor   **Texas**
Abeline   916 sq. mi.
126,555   119,655   110,932   97,853   101,078   63,370
February 1, 1858; organized July 3, 1878. Uncertain, although in 1954 the Texas legislature declared the county was named for three Taylor brothers who died at the Alamo: Edward Taylor (1812–36), George Taylor (1816–36), and James Taylor (1814–36) were all privates serving as Riflemen at the Alamo March 6, 1836. Before the legislature's action other contenders included a fourth, unrelated Taylor who died at the Alamo and three Taylors in the legislature at the time the county was created.

Taylor   **West Virginia**
Grafton   173 sq. mi.
16,089   15,144   16,584   13,878   15,010   18,422
January 19, 1844. John Taylor (1753–1824). Major and colonel in Revolutionary War; Virginia House of Delegates 1779–85 and 1796–1800; U.S. senator 1791–95, 1803–04, and 1822–24.

Taylor   **Wisconsin**
Medford   975 sq. mi.
19,680   18,901   18,817   16,958   17,843   18,456
March 4, 1875. William Robert Taylor (1820–1909). Wisconsin legislature; trustee for the state hospital for the insane 1860–74; governor of Wisconsin 1874–76.

Tazewell   **Illinois**
Pekin   649 sq. mi.
128,485   123,692   132,078   118,649   99,789   76,165
January 31, 1827. Littleton Waller Tazewell (1774–1860). Virginia House of Delegates 1796–1800 and 1816; U.S. representative 1800–01; U.S. senator 1824–32; governor of Virginia 1834–36.

Tazewell   **Virginia**
Tazewell   520 sq. mi.
44,598   45,960   50,511   39,816   44,791   47,512
December 7, 1799 (session). Henry Tazewell (1753–99). Virginia House of Burgesses 1775; Virginia Constitutional Convention 1775–76; Virginia Supreme court 1785–93, chief justice 1785–93; U.S. senator 1794–99.

Tehama   **California**
Red Bluff   2,951 sq. mi.
56,039   49,625   38,888   29,517   25,305   19,276
April 9, 1856. Village of Tehama. Indian word of uncertain meaning; possibilities include (1) "high water" or "low land"; (2) "salmon"; (3) a specific ford of the Sacramento River; (4) "plains" or "prairie."

Telfair   **Georgia**
McRae   441 sq. mi.
11,794   11,000   11,445   11,381   11,715   13,221
December 10, 1807. Edward Telfair (1735–1807). Georgia Council of Safety 1775 and 1776; Georgia Provisional Congress 1776; Continental Congress 1777–79 and 1780–83; signer of Articles of Confederation 1781; governor of Georgia 1786 and 1790–93; federal Constitutional Convention 1787.

Teller   **Colorado**
Cripple Creek   557 sq. mi.
20,555   12,468   8,034   3,316   2,495   2,754
March 23, 1899. Henry Moore Teller (1830–1914). Major general, Colorado Militia 1862–64; U.S. senator 1876–82 and 1885–1909; U.S. secretary of interior 1882–85.

Tensas   **Louisiana**
Saint Joseph   602 sq. mi.

6,618	7,103	8,525	9,732	11,796	13,209

March 17, 1843. Taensa Indians. Large tribe encountered on Mississippi River by La Salle 1682.

Terrebonne   **Louisiana**
Houma   1,255 sq. mi.

104,503	96,982	94,393	76,049	60,771	43,328

March 22, 1822. Uncertain. Name is French for "good earth" and may simply be a description of the area. Other offerings include (1) a parish in Canada; (2) corruption of "Derbonne" or "Derbene," name of an early settler; (3) Bayou Terrebonne; or (4) Terrebonne Bay.

Terrell   **Georgia**
Dawson   335 sq. mi.

10,970	10,653	12,017	11,416	12,742	14,314

February 16, 1856. William Terrell (1778–1855). Physician; Georgia House of Representatives 1810–13; U.S. representative 1817–21.

Terrell   **Texas**
Sanderson   2,358 sq. mi.

1,081	1,410	1,595	1,940	2,600	3,189

April 8, 1905. Alexander Watkins Terrell (1827–1912). District judge 1857–62; major, 1st Texas Cavalry 1861; lieutenant colonel, Terrell's Cavalry Battalion 1863; colonel, Terrell's Cavalry Regiment 1863; assigned duties of brigadier general but war ended before official promotion 1865; fled to Mexico 1866; served under Emperor Maximilian; Texas legislature 1875–82; U.S. minister to Turkey 1893–97.

Terry   **Texas**
Brownfield   890 sq. mi.

12,761	13,218	14,581	14,118	16,286	13,107

August 21, 1876; organized July 5, 1904. Benjamin Franklin Terry (1821–61). Delegate to Texas Secession Convention 1861; colonel, 8th Texas Cavalry; first battle of Bull Run 1861; killed in skirmish at Rowlett's Station, Kentucky, December 17, 1861.

Teton   **Idaho**
Driggs   450 sq. mi.

5,999	3,439	2,897	2,351	2,639	3,204

January 26, 1915. *Teton Mountains*, Wyoming. Three mountain peaks resembling female breasts; named Les Trois Tetons (The Three Breasts) by French Canadian trappers.

Teton   **Montana**
Choteau   2,273 sq. mi.

6,445	6,271	6,491	6,116	7,295	7,232

February 7, 1893. Teton River and Teton Peak. Teton Peak named for resemblance to female breast; this peak is not part of Teton Mountain Range in Wyoming (see Teton, Idaho).

Teton   **Wyoming**
Jackson   4,008 sq. mi.

18,251	11,172	9,355	4,823	3,062[a]	2,593[a]

February 15, 1921. Teton Mountains.* County includes Les Trois Tetons (see Teton, Idaho). [(a) See note (a) at Park County, Wyoming]

Texas   **Missouri**
Houston   1,179 sq. mi.

23,003	21,476	21,070	18,320	17,758	18,992

February 17, 1843, as Ashley; name changed February 14, 1845. Republic of *Texas*. Named from the Indian confederacy Texia, meaning "allies" or "friends"; Spanish form was Tejas.

Texas	**Oklahoma**				
Guymon	2,037 sq. mi.				
20,107	16,419	17,727	16,352	14,162	14,235

July 16, 1907. State of Texas.* (See Texas, Missouri).

Thayer	**Nebraska**				
Hebron	575 sq. mi.				
6,055	6,635	7,582	7,779	9,118	10,563

January 26, 1856, as Jefferson; abolished 1867; recreated as Thayer January 26, 1871; organized December 30, 1871. John Milton Thayer (1820–1906). Brigadier general and major general 1855–61; Nebraska Territory Senate 1860; Nebraska Constitutional Convention 1860; colonel, 1st Nebraska Volunteers Regiment 1861; rose from brigadier general to major general of Volunteers 1861–65; U.S. senator 1867–71; governor of Wyoming Territory 1875–78; governor of Nebraska 1887–92.

Thomas	**Georgia**				
Thomasville	548 sq. mi.				
42,737	38,986	38,098	34,515	34,319	33,932

December 23, 1825. Jett Thomas (1776–1817). Captain of artillery, War of 1812, under General Floyd (see Floyd, Georgia); major general, Georgia Militia; built state capitol at Milledgeville 1807.

Thomas	**Kansas**				
Colby	1,075 sq. mi.				
8,180	8,258	8,451	7,501	7,358	7,572

March 6, 1873; organized October 8, 1885. *George Henry Thomas* (1816–70). Graduated West Point 1840; rose from 2nd lieutenant to colonel 1840–61; Seminole and Mexican wars; born in Virginia but remained loyal to Union; brigadier general and major general of Volunteers 1861; succeeded Grant in command of Army of the Tennessee 1862; brigadier general, Regular Army 1863; major general 1864; drove Confederates from Tennessee at battle of Nashville 1864; received Thanks of Congress 1865.

Thomas	**Nebraska**				
Thedford	713 sq. mi.				
729	851	973	954	1,078	1,206

March 31, 1887; organized October 7, 1887. George Henry Thomas.*

Throckmorton	**Texas**				
Throckmorton	912 sq. mi.				
1,850	1,880	2,053	2,205	2,767	3,618

January 13, 1858; organized March 18, 1879. William Edward Throckmorton (1795–1843). Physician; early settler in northern Texas; naming was a compliment to his son, James Webb Throckmorton, governor of Texas and U.S. representative.

Thurston	**Nebraska**				
Pender	394 sq. mi.				
7,171	6,936	7,186	6,942	7,237	8,590

March 7, 1855, as Blackbird; name changed March 28, 1889; organized April 1, 1889. John Mellen Thurston (1847–1916). Omaha City Council 1872–74; Nebraska legislature 1875–77; solicitor general, Union Pacific Railroad 1888; U.S. senator 1895–1901; chairman, Republican National Convention 1896.

Thurston	**Washington**				
Olympia	727 sq. mi.				
207,355	161,238	124,264	76,894	55,049	44,884

January 12, 1852. Samuel Royal Thurston (1816–51). Editor, *Iowa Gazette*; congressional delegate from Oregon Territory 1849–51; term ended March 3, died at sea while returning from Washington, D.C., April 9, 1851.

Tift	**Georgia**				
Tifton	265 sq. mi.				
38,407	34,998	32,862	27,288	23,487	22,645

August 17, 1905. Nelson Tift (1810–77). Colonel, Baker County Militia 1840; Georgia House of Representatives 1841, 1847, and 1851–52; editor, *Albany Patriot* 1845–58; captain, Confederate navy 1861–65; U.S. representative 1868–69.

Tillamook   **Oregon**
Tillamook   1,102 sq. mi.
24,262   21,570   21,164   17,930   18,955   18,606
December 15, 1853. Tillamook Indians. Large tribe of Salishan linguistic group; encountered by Lewis and Clark 1805–06; population rapidly dwindled from European diseases.

Tillman   **Oklahoma**
Frederick   872 sq. mi.
9,287   10,384   12,398   12,901   14,654   17,598
July 16, 1907. Benjamin Ryan Tillman (1847–1918). Governor of South Carolina 1890–94; founder of Clemson Agricultural and Mechanical College 1893; U.S. senator 1895–1918. Uncertain as to why an Oklahoma county was named for a South Carolina politician.

Tioga   **New York**
Owego   519 sq. mi.
51,784   52,337   49,812   46,513   37,802   30,166
February 16, 1791. *Tioga River*. Tributary of Chemung River. Named from Indian name meaning "at the forks," given to confluence of Chemung and Susquehanna rivers.

Tioga   **Pennsylvania**
Wellsboro   1,134 sq. mi.
41,373   41,126   40,973   39,691   36,614   35,474
March 26, 1804; organized 1812. Tioga River.*

Tippah   **Mississippi**
Ripley   458 sq. mi.
20,826   19,523   18,739   15,852   15,093   17,522
February 9, 1836. Tippah Creek. From Choctaw *bok tapa,* meaning "separated creek"; refers to the four branches of Tippah Creek.

Tippecanoe   **Indiana**
Lafayette   500 sq. mi.
148,955   130,598   121,702   109,378   89,122   74,473
January 20, 1826; effective March 1, 1826. Uncertain. (1) Tippecanoe River; uncertain origin; may be corruption of Potawatomie *ketapekonnong,* meaning "town" or "place." (2) Battle of Tippecanoe; November 7, 1811, near confluence of Tippecanoe and Wabash rivers; General William Henry Harrison defeated Shawnees led by Tenskwatawa the Prophet.

Tipton   **Indiana**
Tipton   260 sq. mi.
16,577   16,119   16,819   16,650   15,856   15,566
January 15, 1844; effective May 1, 1844. John Tipton (1786–1839). Private, Indiana Militia 1807; ensign 1811; promoted to captain during battle of Tippecanoe 1811; major general of militia; Indiana House of Representatives 1819–23; U.S. senator 1832–39.

Tipton   **Tennessee**
Covington   459 sq. mi.
51,271   37,568   32,930   28,001   28,564   29,782
October 29, 1823. Jacob Tipton (?–1791). Captain of Tennessee company under General St. Clair against Indians on northwest frontier; killed in combat near Fort Wayne November 4, 1791.

Tishomingo   **Mississippi**
Iuka   424 sq. mi.
19,163   17,683   18,434   14,940   13,889   15,544

February 9, 1836. Tishomingo (c1737–c1837). Chief of Chickasaw Nation; personally acquainted with presidents Washington, Jefferson, Monroe, and Jackson; signed treaty ceding Chickasaw lands east of Mississippi River 1832; died en route to Indian Territory (Oklahoma); name means "warrior chief."

Titus **Texas**
Mount Pleasant 411 sq. mi.

| 28,118 | 24,009 | 21,442 | 16,702 | 16,785 | 17,302 |

May 11, 1846; organized July 13, 1846. Andrew Jackson Titus (1823–55). Mexican War; Texas legislature 1851–52; worked for annexation of Texas to U.S.

Todd **Kentucky**
Elkton 376 sq. mi.

| 11,971 | 10,940 | 11,874 | 10,823 | 11,364 | 12,890 |

December 30, 1819. John Todd (1750–82). Lord Dunmore's War 1774; Virginia legislature 1777; acquired huge tracts of land in Kentucky and Tennessee; killed at battle of Blue Licks, Kentucky, August 19, 1782.

Todd **Minnesota**
Long Prairie 942 sq. mi.

| 24,426 | 23,363 | 24,991 | 22,114 | 23,119 | 25,420 |

February 20, 1855; organized March 1, 1856. *John Blair Smith Todd* (1814–72). Graduated West Point 1837; Seminole Wars 1837–42; captain 1843; Mexican War 1846–47; commander, Fort Ripley, Minnesota Territory, 1849–56; brigadier general of Volunteers 1861–62; congressional delegate from Dakota Territory 1861–65; Dakota Territory legislature, Speaker 1877–67.

Todd **South Dakota**
(Unorganized) 1,388 sq. mi.

| 9,050 | 8,352 | 7,328 | 6,606 | 4,661 | 4,758 |

March 9, 1909; attached to Tripp County. John Blair Smith Todd.*

Tolland **Connecticut**
Rockville 410 sq. mi.

| 136,364 | 128,699 | 114,823 | 103,440 | 68,737 | 44,709 |

October 13, 1785 (session). Town of Tolland. Named for Tolland, Somersetshire, England.

Tom Green **Texas**
San Angelo 1,522 sq. mi.

| 104,010 | 98,458 | 84,784 | 71,047 | 64,630 | 58,929 |

March 13, 1874; organized January 5, 1875. Thomas Green (1814–64). Private, Texas Army 1836; battle of San Jacinto 1836; Texas legislature; captain, Mexican War; colonel, Confederate army 1861; brigadier general 1863; killed at battle of Blair's Landing April 12, 1864.

Tompkins **New York**
Ithaca 476 sq. mi.

| 96,501 | 94,097 | 87,085 | 76,879 | 66,164 | 59,122 |

April 7, 1817. Daniel D. Tompkins (1774–1825). New York Constitutional Conventions 1801 and 1821; justice, New York Supreme Court 1804–07; governor of New York 1807–17; U.S. vice president 1817–25.

Tooele **Utah**
Tooele 6,930 sq. mi.

| 40,735 | 26,601 | 26,033 | 21,545 | 17,868 | 14,636 |

March 3, 1852. Tooele Valley. Origin of name is uncertain: (1) Indian origin, possibly for a chief, derived from "black bear" or "bear"; (2) descriptive of bulrushes or "tules" growing in the region.

Toole **Montana**
Shelby 1,911 sq. mi.

| 5,267 | 5,046 | 5,559 | 5,839 | 7,904 | 6,867 |

May 7, 1914. Joseph Kemp Toole (1851–1929). Montana Territory legislature 1879–81; president, Montana Territorial Council 1881–83; Montana Constitutional Conventions 1884 and 1889; congressional delegate 1885–89; governor of Montana 1889–93 and 1901–08.

Toombs   **Georgia**
Lyons   367 sq. mi.

| 26,067 | 24,072 | 22,592 | 19,151 | 16,837 | 17,382 |

August 18, 1905. Robert Augustus Toombs (1810–85). Captain under General Scott in Creek War 1836; Georgia House of Representatives 1837–40 and 1841–44; U.S. representative 1845–53; U.S. senator 1853–61; Confederate secretary of state 1861; brigadier general 1861–63.

Torrance   **New Mexico**
Estancia   3,345 sq. mi.

| 16,911 | 10,285 | 7,491 | 5,290 | 6,497 | 8,012 |

March 16, 1903. Francis J. Torrance (?–?). Railroad developer; established New Mexico Central Railroad, linking town of Torrance to national railroads 1900.

Towner   **North Dakota**
Cando   1,025 sq. mi.

| 2,876 | 3,627 | 4,052 | 4,645 | 5,624 | 6,360 |

March 8, 1883; organized January 24, 1884. Oscar M. Towner (1842–97). Some dispute as to whether or not Towner graduated from West Point and served in Confederate army; it is known he raised cattle and served in Dakota Territory legislature at the time county was created.

Towns   **Georgia**
Hiawassee   167 sq. mi.

| 9,319 | 6,754 | 5,638 | 4,565 | 4,538 | 4,803 |

March 6, 1856. George Washington Bonaparte Towns (1801–54). Georgia House of Representatives 1829–30; Georgia Senate 1832–34; U.S. representative 1835–36, 1837–39; and 1846–47; governor of Georgia 1847–51.

Traill   **North Dakota**
Hillsboro   862 sq. mi.

| 8,477 | 8,752 | 9,624 | 9,571 | 10,583 | 11,359 |

January 12, 1875. Walter S. Traill (1847–1933). Clerk for Hudson's Bay Company 1866–75; escaped to Dakota Territory during Red River Rebellion 1869; supervised liquidation of Hudson's Bay Company in Red River region 1875; grain merchant and farmer in Minnesota, Montana, and British Columbia.

Transylvania   **North Carolina**
Brevard   378 sq. mi.

| 29,334 | 25,520 | 23,417 | 19,713 | 16,372 | 15,194 |

February 15, 1861. Descriptive. Latin derivation from *trans,* meaning "across," and *sylva,* meaning "woods" or "forest."

Traverse   **Minnesota**
Wheaton   574 sq. mi.

| 4,134 | 4,463 | 5,542 | 6,254 | 7,503 | 8,053 |

February 20, 1862; organized February 14, 1881. Lake Traverse. Uncertain origin of name. (1) French translation of Dakota name into Lac Travers, meaning "crossways," referring to northeast–southwest orientation of Lake Traverse in relation to northwest–southeast orientation of Big Stone Lake and Lac qui Parle. (2) In early days of settlement the Minnesota River would reverse direction during high floods, flowing northward into Lake Traverse and drainage of the Red River of the North rather than southward toward the Mississippi River.

Travis   **Texas**
Austin   989 sq. mi.

| 812,280 | 576,407 | 419,573 | 295,516 | 212,136 | 160,980 |

January 25, 1840; organized April 8, 1843. William Barret Travis (1809–36). Major and lieutenant colonel of artillery 1835; led expedition against Mexican fort at Anahuac 1835; commanded Texas garrison at the Alamo March 6, 1836.

Treasure   **Montana**
Hysham   979 sq. mi.

861	874	981	1,069	1,345	1,402

February 7, 1919. Promotional name.

Trego   **Kansas**
WaKeeney   888 sq. mi.

3,319	3,694	4,165	4,436	5,473	5,868

February 26, 1867; organized 1879. Edward P. Trego (?–1863). Captain, Company H, 8th Kansas Volunteer Infantry; killed at Chickamauga September 19, 1863.

Trempealeau   **Wisconsin**
Whitehall   734 sq. mi.

27,010	25,263	26,158	23,344	23,377	23,730

January 27, 1854; organized 1855. Trempealeau River. From French translation of Indian name meaning "mountain soaked in water" into *la montagne qui trempe a l'eau,* after a large island in the river.

Treutlen   **Georgia**
Soperton   201 sq. mi.

6,854	5,994	6,087	5,647	5,874	6,522

August 21, 1917. John Adam Treutlen (1726–1783). Georgia Commons; Georgia Provincial Congress 1775; governor of Georgia 1777–78.

Trigg   **Kentucky**
Cadiz   443 sq. mi.

12,597	10,361	9,384	8,620	8,870	9,683

January 27, 1820. Stephen Trigg (1742–82). Virginia legislature; trustee, Transylvania University; colonel of militia 1781; killed at battle of Blue Licks August 17, 1782.

Trimble   **Kentucky**
Bedford   149 sq. mi.

8,125	6,090	6,253	5,349	5,102	5,148

February 9, 1837. Robert Trimble (1777–1828). Kentucky legislature 1803; judge, court of appeals 1808; chief justice of Kentucky 1810; U.S. district judge 1816–26; U.S. Supreme Court 1826–28.

Trinity   **California**
Weaverville   3,179 sq. mi.

13,022	13,063	11,858	7,615	9,706	5,087

February 18, 1850. Trinity River (California). Named in mistaken belief that it flowed into Trinidad Bay. Spanish "Trinidad" refers to the Holy Trinity of the Christian faith.

Trinity   **Texas**
Groveton   693 sq. mi.

13,779	11,445	9,450	7,628	7,539	10,040

February 11, 1850; organized April 1, 1850. Trinity River (Texas). Flows into Trinity Bay, an arm of Galveston Bay. Spanish "Trinidad" refers to the Holy Trinity of the Christian faith.

Tripp   **South Dakota**
Winner   1,614 sq. mi.

6,430	6,924	7,268	8,171	8,761	9,139

January 8, 1873; organized June 15, 1909. Bartlett Tripp (1842–1911). President, South Dakota Constitutional Convention 1883; chief justice of Dakota Territory 1886–89; U.S. minister to Austria-Hungary 1893–97.

Troup   **Georgia**
La Grange   414 sq. mi.
58,779   55,536   50,003   44,466   47,189   49,841
December 11, 1826. George Michael Troup (1780–1856). Georgia House of Representatives 1803–05; U.S. representative 1807–15; U.S. senator 1816–18 and 1829–33; governor of Georgia 1823–27.

Trousdale   **Tennessee**
Hartsville   114 sq. mi.
7,259   5,920   6,137   5,155   4,914   5,520
June 21, 1870. William Trousdale (1790–1872). Creek War 1813; lieutenant under General Jackson at New Orleans 1815; Tennessee legislature 1835; major general of Volunteers in Seminole War 1836; Mexican War, wounded at Chapultepec 1847; brevet brigadier general; governor of Tennessee 1849–51; U.S. minister to Brazil 1852–57.

Trumbull   **Ohio**
Warren   616 sq. mi.
225,116   227,813   241,862   232,579   208,526   158,915
July 10, 1800. Jonathon Trumbull (1740–1809). Connecticut legislature; paymaster, Continental army 1776–80; secretary and aide-de-camp to Washington 1780–83; U.S. representative 1789–95; U.S. senator 1795–96; lieutenant governor 1769–76; governor of Connecticut 1776–84 and 1789–1809; ceded Connecticut's Western Reserve in northeastern Ohio to U.S.

Tucker   **West Virginia**
Parsons   419 sq. mi.
7,321   7,728   8,675   7,447   7,750   10,600
March 7, 1856. Henry St. George Tucker (1780–1848). Cavalry captain, War of 1812; U.S. representative from Virginia 1815–19; chancellor of 4th Judicial District of Virginia 1824–31; president of Virginia Court of Appeals 1831–41; professor of law, University of Virginia 1841–45.

Tulare   **California**
Visalia   4,824 sq. mi.
368,021   311,921   245,738   188,322   168,403   149,264
April 20, 1852. Tule marshlands. From the cattails and bulrushes growing in the area; from Aztec *tullin* or *tollin*.

Tulsa   **Oklahoma**
Tulsa   570 sq. mi.
563,299   503,341   470,593   401,663   346,038   251,686
1905. City of Tulsa. Named from Tulsey Town or Tullahassee, a village in Alabama that had been the Creek's home before their forced removal to Indian Territory (Oklahoma) 1836.

Tunica   **Mississippi**
Tunica   455 sq. mi.
9,227   8,164   9,652   11,854   16,826   21,664
February 9, 1836. Tunica Indians. A small tribe living near the junction of the Yazoo and Mississippi rivers; Indian for "the people."

Tuolumne   **California**
Sonora   2,235 sq. mi.
54,501   48,456   33,928   22,169   14,404   12,584
February 18, 1850. Tuolumne Indians. Collective name for a group of tribes. One village was on a steep, rocky precipice. *Tuol* is remnant of the Indian word for "a village of stone caves," and *umne* means "people" or "tribe."

Turner   **Georgia**
Ashburn   286 sq. mi.
9,504   8,703   9,510   8,790   8,439   10,479

August 18, 1905; effective January 1, 1906. Henry Gray Turner (1839–1904). Rose from private to captain, Confederate army 1861–65; wounded at Gettysburg 1863; Georgia House of Representatives 1874–76, 1878, and 1879; U.S. representative 1881–97; justice of Georgia Supreme Court 1903.

Turner   **South Dakota**
Parker   617 sq. mi.

8,849	8,576	9,255	9,872	11,159	12,100

January 13, 1871. John W. Turner (1800–83). Michigan General Assembly 1851; Dakota Territory legislature 1865–66 and 1872; superintendent of public instruction 1870–71.

Tuscaloosa   **Alabama**
Tuscaloosa   1,324 sq. mi.

164,875	150,522	137,541	116,029	109,047	94,092

February 6, 1818. Tuscaloosa. Choctaw name for their chiefs, meaning "black warrior," or may have been a particular chief.

Tuscarawas   **Ohio**
New Philadelphia   568 sq. mi.

90,914	84,090	84,614	77,211	76,789	70,320

February 13, 1808; effective March 15, 1808. Tuscarawas River. From Tuscarowa Indians; members of Iroquois confederacy. The river was named for a Tuscarowa village on its banks.

Tuscola   **Michigan**
Caro   812 sq. mi.

58,266	55,498	56,961	48,603	43,305	38,258

April 1, 1840; organized March 2, 1850. Coined word. From Indian words *dusinagon,* meaning "level," and *cola,* meaning "land."

Twiggs   **Georgia**
Jeffersonville   360 sq. mi.

10,590	9,806	9,354	8,222	7,935	8,308

December 14, 1809. John Twiggs (1750–1816). Brigadier general, Revolutionary War; negotiated treaties with Creeks 1783; major general, Georgia Militia against the Creeks.

Twin Falls   **Idaho**
Twin Falls   1,925 sq. mi.

64,284	53,580	52,927	41,807	41,842	40,979

February 21, 1907. Twin falls in the Snake River. The Snake River is divided by a large rock formation that splits the falls.

Tyler   **Texas**
Woodville   923 sq. mi.

20,871	16,646	16,223	12,417	10,666	11,292

April 3, 1846; organized July 13, 1846. John Tyler (1790–1862). Virginia House of Delegates 1811–16 and 1823–25; U.S. representative 1817–21; governor of Virginia 1825–27; U.S. senator 1827–36; U.S. vice president 1841; 10th president of the U.S. on death of President Harrison 1841–45; Confederate Provisional Congress 1861.

Tyler   **West Virginia**
Middlebourne   258 sq. mi.

9,592	9,796	11,320	9,929	10,026	10,535

December 6, 1814. John Tyler (1747–1813). Virginia House of Delegates 1777–1785, Speaker 1781–85; judge, Virginia General Court 1789–1808; governor of Virginia 1808–11; father of President John Tyler.

Tyrrell   **North Carolina**
Columbia   390 sq. mi.

4,149	3,856	3,975	3,806	4,520	5,048

November 27, 1729 (session). John Tyrrell (1685–1729). One of eight lords proprietor of Carolina; purchased proprietorship 1725.

U

Uinta   **Wyoming**
Evanston   2,082 sq. mi.
19,742   18,705   13,021   7,100   7,484   7,331
December 1, 1869. Uncertain. (1) *Uinta Indians*; subtribe of Ute Indians; dislocated by early Mormon settlers. (2) Uintah Mountains; in Utah just south of Wyoming; named for Uinta Utes. (See Utah, Utah.)

Uintah   **Utah**
Vernal   4,477 sq. mi.
25,224   22,211   20,506   12,684   11,582   10,300
February 18, 1880. Uinta Indians.*

Ulster   **New York**
Kingston   1,126 sq. mi.
177,749   165,304   158,158   141,241   118,804   92,621
November 1, 1683. James II. (See Albany, New York.) Named Earl of Ulster for his Irish lands 1672.

Umatilla   **Oregon**
Pendleton   3,215 sq. mi.
70,548   59,249   58,861   44,923   44,352   41,703
September 27, 1862. Umatilla River. Tributary of Columbia River; named for Umatilla Indians, a group of tribes encountered by Lewis and Clark 1805.

Unicoi   **Tennessee**
Erwin   186 sq. mi.
17,667   16,549   16,362   15,254   15,082   15,886
March 23, 1875. Unaka Mountains. From Indian word for "white"; also *unicoy*.

Union   **Arkansas**
El Dorado   1,039 sq. mi.
45,629   46,719   48,573   45,428   49,518   49,686
November 2, 1829. The United States.

Union   **Florida**
Lake Butler   240 sq. mi.
13,442   10,252   10,166   8,112   6,043   8,906
May 20, 1921. In recognition of united opinion for creation of county.

Union   **Georgia**
Blairsville   323 sq. mi.
17,289   11,993   9,390   6,811   6,510   7,318
December 3, 1832. The United States. Named to show local opposition to secession movement over Nullification.

Union   **Illinois**
Jonesboro   416 sq. mi.
18,293   17,619   17,765   16,071   17,645   20,500
January 2, 1818. A local revival meeting. Two rival denominations, Baptist and Dunker (German Baptist), held a joint revival known locally as the "union meeting" shortly before county was created.

Union   **Indiana**
Liberty   162 sq. mi.
7,349   6,976   6,860   6,582   6,457   6,412
January 5, 1821; effective February 1, 1821. Uncertain. (1) The United States. (2) Town of Union. (3) New county consisted of a union of land from three counties. (4) A futile hope to avoid a dispute as to location of the county seat.

Union   **Iowa**
Creston   424 sq. mi.

| 12,309 | 12,750 | 13,858 | 13,557 | 13,712 | 15,651 |

January 15, 1851; organized January 12, 1853; effective May 1, 1853. Preservation of the Union. Hopes for avoiding a national split over slavery were raised following Compromise of 1850.

Union   **Kentucky**
Morganfield   345 sq. mi.

| 15,637 | 16,557 | 17,821 | 15,882 | 14,537 | 14,893 |

January 15, 1811. Uncertain. (1) Kentucky motto "United We Stand. Divided We Fall." (2) The United States. (3) Desire to preserve national union over sectional differences about issues leading to War of 1812. (4) United opinion that county should be created.

Union   **Louisiana**
Farmerville   878 sq. mi.

| 22,803 | 20,690 | 21,167 | 18,447 | 17,624 | 19,141 |

March 13, 1839. Uncertain. (1) The United States. (2) Patriotic sentiment. (3) Daniel Webster's phrase "Liberty and Union, now and forever, one and inseparable" was popular in the South at the time the parish was created.

Union   **Mississippi**
New Albany   415 sq. mi.

| 25,362 | 22,085 | 21,741 | 19,096 | 18,904 | 20,262 |

July 7, 1870. The United States.

Union   **New Jersey**
Elizabeth   103 sq. mi.

| 522,541 | 493,819 | 504,094 | 543,116 | 504,255 | 398,138 |

March 19, 1857. Uncertain. (1) Town of Union. (2) Preservation of the Union in face of approaching Civil War. (3) United effort of communities in establishing new county's government.

Union   **New Mexico**
Clayton   3,830 sq. mi.

| 4,174 | 4,124 | 4,725 | 4,925 | 6,068 | 7,372 |

February 23, 1893. United opinion for creating county.

Union   **North Carolina**
Monroe   637 sq. mi.

| 123,677 | 84,211 | 70,380 | 54,714 | 44,670 | 42,034 |

December 19, 1842. Uncertain. (1) The American federal union which was moving toward civil war. (2) Compromise name instead of Clay or Jackson, which being advocated by Whigs and Democrats, respectively.

Union   **Ohio**
Marysville   437 sq. mi.

| 40,909 | 31,969 | 29,536 | 23,786 | 22,853 | 20,687 |

January 10, 1820; effective April 1, 1820. Uncertain. Majority opinion leans toward the view that the county was created from the union of land from four counties.

Union   **Oregon**
La Grande   2,037 sq. mi.

| 24,530 | 23,598 | 23,921 | 19,377 | 18,180 | 17,962 |

October 14, 1864. Uncertain. (1) Town of Union. (2) Union army.

Union   **Pennsylvania**
Lewisburg   317 sq. mi.

| 41,624 | 36,176 | 32,870 | 28,603 | 25,646 | 23,150 |

March 22, 1813. The United States.

Union   **South Carolina**
Union   514 sq. mi.
29,881   30,337   30,751   29,230   30,015   31,334
March 12, 1785. Union Church. Unified congregation of Protestant denominations.

Union   **South Dakota**
Elk Point   460 sq. mi.
12,584   10,189   10,938   9,643   10,197   10,792
April 10, 1862, as Cole; name changed 1864. Union side in the Civil War.

Union   **Tennessee**
Maynardville   224 sq. mi.
17,808   13,694   11,707   9,072   8,498   8,670
January 3, 1850. Uncertain. (1) Preservation of federal union in face of approaching division over slavery. (2) Union of lands taken from surrounding counties to create new county.

Upshur   **Texas**
Gilmer   588 sq. mi.
35,291   31,370   28,595   20,976   19,793   20,822
April 27, 1846; organized July 13, 1846. *Abel Parker Upshur* (1791–1844). Virginia legislature 1825; judge, Virginia courts 1826–41; U.S. secretary of navy 1841–43; U.S. secretary of state 1843–44; killed by explosion of gun being demonstrated on USS *Princeton* in presence of President Tyler February 28, 1844.

Upshur   **West Virginia**
Buckhannon   355 sq. mi.
23,404   22,867   23,427   19,092   18,292   19,242
March 26, 1851. Abel Parker Upshur.*

Upson   **Georgia**
Thomaston   325 sq. mi.
27,597   26,300   25,998   23,505   23,800   25,078
December 15, 1824. Stephen Upson (1784–1824). Trustee, University of Georgia; Georgia legislature 1820–24.

Upton   **Texas**
Rankin   1,242 sq. mi.
3,404   4,447   4,619   4,697   6,239   5,307
February 26, 1887; organized 1910. John Cunningham Upton and William Felton Upton; brothers. (1) John Upton (1828–62); lieutenant colonel, Hood's Texas brigade 1861; killed at Manassas August 30, 1862. (2) William Upton (1832–87); captain, Hood's Texas Brigade 1861; rose to lieutenant colonel during Civil War; Texas legislature 1866 and 1879–85.

Utah   **Utah**
Provo   1,998 sq. mi.
368,536   263,590   218,106   137,776   106,991   81,912
March 3, 1852. Ute Indians. Three Shoshone subtribes of hunters and gatherers that became nomadic hunters with the introduction of horses; nicknamed "Utes" by Apaches and Navajos, meaning "hill dwellers"; tribal name written as "Yutta" by Spanish; spelled "Utah" by Fremont in naming the lake and river 1844.

Uvalde   **Texas**
Uvalde   1,557 sq. mi.
25,926   23,340   22,441   17,348   16,814   16,015
February 8, 1850; organized April 21, 1856. Uvalde Canyon. Named for Juan de Ugalde (1729–1816); Spanish military officer; served in Europe and Peru; arrived in New Spain (Mexico) 1777; governor of Coahuila and Texas 1777; fought Apaches in Texas 1779–83, 1787, and 1789; colonel, Mexican army 1783–86.

V

Valdez-Cordova   **Alaska**
(Census Area)   34,319 sq. mi.
10,195   9,952   8,348   4,955[a]   4,603[a]   [b]
Port of Valdez. Named for Spanish naval officer Antonio Valdès y Basan; sponsored survey of Alaska's coast 1791. Town of Cordova; Puerto Cordova (now Orca Bay); named by Spanish explorer Salvador Fidalgo, 1790, in honor of his voyage's sponsor Antonio Marìa Bucareli . . . Villacis y Cordova, viceroy of New Spain (Mexico). [(a) Valdez-Chitina-Whittier includes Cordova-McCarthy; (b) part of 3rd Judicial District.]

Valencia   **New Mexico**
Los Lunas   1,068 sq. mi.
66,152   45,235   61,115   40,539   39,085   22,481
January 9, 1852. Village of Valencia. Named for several generations of Valencia families dating from the 16th century. Leading candidates for village name are (1) Francisco de Valencia; lieutenant general in Rio Abajo area of New Mexico; (2) Juan de Valencia, whose hacienda was on the site of the village of Valencia.

Valley   **Idaho**
Cascade   3,678 sq. mi.
7,651   6,109   5,604   3,609   3,663   4,270
February 26, 1917. Long Valley.

Valley   **Montana**
Glasgow   4,921 sq. mi.
7,675   8,239   10,250   11,471   17,080   11,353
February 6, 1893. Milk River and Missouri River valleys.

Valley   **Nebraska**
Ord   568 sq. mi.
4,647   5,169   5,633   5,783   6,590   7,252
March 1, 1871; organized June 23, 1873. Descriptive of valleys and bottom lands in the area.

Val Verde   **Texas**
Del Rio   3,170 sq. mi.
44,856   38,721   35,910   27,471   24,461   16,635
February 20, 1885; organized May 2, 1885. Battle of Valverde. Civil War battle in New Mexico Territory February 21, 1862; Spanish for "green valley."

Van Buren   **Arkansas**
Clinton   712 sq. mi.
16,192   14,008   13,357   8,275   7,228   9,687
November 11, 1833. *Martin Van Buren* (1782–1862). New York Senate 1813–20; attorney general of New York 1815–19; New York Constitutional Convention 1821; U.S. senator 1821–28; governor of New York 1828–29; U.S. secretary of state 1829–31; U.S. vice president 1833–37; 8th president of the U.S. 1837–41.

Van Buren   **Iowa**
Keosauqua   485 sq. mi.
7,809   7,676   8,626   8,643   9,778   11,007
December 7, 1836. Martin Van Buren.*

Van Buren   **Michigan**
Paw Paw   611 sq. mi.
76,263   70,060   66,814   56,173   48,395   39,184
October 29, 1829; organized April 3, 1837. Martin Van Buren.*

Van Buren   **Tennessee**
Spencer   273 sq. mi.
5,508   4,846   4,728   3,758   3,671   3,985
January 3, 1840. Martin Van Buren.*

Vance   **North Carolina**
Henderson   254 sq. mi.
42,954   38,892   36,748   32,691   32,002   32,101
March 5, 1881. Zebulon Baird Vance (1830–94). Prosecuting attorney; Buncombe County 1852; North Carolina House of Commons 1854; U.S. representative 1858–61; rose from captain to colonel, Confederate army 1861; governor of North Carolina 1862–65 and 1877–79; elected to U.S. Senate but denied seat 1870; U.S. senator 1879–94.

Vanderburgh   **Indiana**
Evansville   235 sq. mi.
171,922   165,058   167,515   168,772   165,794   160,422
January 7, 1818; effective February 1, 1818. Henry Vanderburgh (1760–1812). Captain, Continental army; Northwest Territory Legislative Council; judge, Indiana Territory 1800–12.

Van Wert   **Ohio**
Van Wert   410 sq. mi.
29,659   30,464   30,458   29,194   28,840   26,971
February 12, 1820; organized 1837. Isaac Van Wart (c1758–1828). One of three captors of British major André (see Paulding, Georgia).

Van Zandt   **Texas**
Canton   849 sq. mi.
48,140   37,944   31,426   22,155   19,091   22,593
March 20, 1848. Isaac Van Zandt (1813–47). Texas House of Representatives 1840–42; Texas charge d'affaires to U.S. 1842; Texas Constitutional Convention 1842; died of yellow fever while campaigning for governor.

Venango   **Pennsylvania**
Franklin   675 sq. mi.
57,565   59,381   64,444   62,353   65,295   65,328
March 12, 1800; organized 1805. Uncertain. (1) Venango River (now French Creek). (2) Indian village at the mouth of French Creek. *Venango* is an Indian word describing a "rude sculpture" carved on a tree near the river.

Ventura   **California**
Ventura   1,845 sq. mi.
753,197   669,016   529,174   376,430   199,138   114,647
March 22, 1872. City of Ventura. Named for Mission San Buenaventura (Spanish for "good fortune") which was named for St. Bonaventure (1221–74); member of Friars Minor (Franciscan Order) 1238, minister general 1257–74; declined bishopric 1265; compelled to become cardinal–bishop 1273; led reconciliation with Greek Church; canonized 1482.

Vermilion   **Illinois**
Danville   899 sq. mi.
83,919   88,257   95,222   97,047   96,176   87,079
January 18, 1826. *Vermilion River*. Tributary of Wabash River. Named for reddish-orange color of river caused by fine red soils along river.

Vermilion   **Louisiana**
Abbeville   1,174 sq. mi.
53,807   50,055   48,458   43,071   38,855   36,929
March 25, 1844. Vermilion River* and Vermilion Bay. Descriptive of red color of water from river bluffs.

Vermillion   **Indiana**
Newport   257 sq. mi.

| 16,788 | 16,773 | 18,229 | 16,793 | 17,683 | 19,723 |

January 2, 1824; effective February 1, 1824. Vermilion River.* (French spelling with double "l.")

Vernon   **Louisiana**
Leesville   1,328 sq. mi.

| 52,531 | 61,961 | 53,475 | 53,794 | 18,301 | 18,874 |

March 30, 1871. Uncertain. (1) Mount Vernon,* home of George Washington (see Vernon, Wisconsin); (2) a popular teacher whose name was chosen as a compromise; (3) a race horse; (4) a mule named Vernon who happened by during a whiskey-inspired meeting for naming the parish.

Vernon   **Missouri**
Nevada   834 sq. mi.

| 20,454 | 19,041 | 19,806 | 19,065 | 20,540 | 22,685 |

February 17, 1851; abolished 1852; recreated February 27, 1855. Miles Vernon (1786–1866). War of 1812; battle of New Orleans 1815; Tennessee legislature; Missouri Senate 1850–61; favored Missouri secession 1861.

Vernon   **Wisconsin**
Viroqua   795 sq. mi.

| 28,056 | 25,617 | 25,642 | 24,557 | 25,663 | 27,906 |

March 1, 1851, as Bad Ax; name changed March 22, 1862. *Mount Vernon.* Home of George Washington; named for Admiral Edward Vernon of the British navy, commanding officer of Lawrence Washington, George's half-brother.

Victoria   **Texas**
Victoria   883 sq. mi.

| 84,088 | 74,361 | 68,807 | 53,766 | 46,475 | 31,241 |

March 17, 1836; organized 1837. Municipality of Victoria. Named for Guadalupe Victoria (1786–1843); born Juan Manuel Felix Fernandez; changed name to Guadalupe to honor Mexico's patron saint and to Victoria for desired victory of fight for Mexican independence against Spain; first president of Mexico 1825–29.

Vigo   **Indiana**
Terre Haute   403 sq. mi.

| 105,848 | 106,107 | 112,385 | 114,528 | 108,458 | 105,160 |

January 21, 1818; effective February 15, 1818. Joseph María Francesco Vigo (1747–1836). Private in Spanish army; fur trader 1772; provided supplies for George Rogers Clark; joined Clark in capture of British garrison at Vincennes 1779.

Vilas   **Wisconsin**
Eagle River   874 sq. mi.

| 21,033 | 17,707 | 16,535 | 10,958 | 9,332 | 9,363 |

April 12, 1893. William Freeman Vilas (1840–1908). Rose from captain to lieutenant colonel, 23rd Wisconsin Volunteer Infantry 1861–65; University of Wisconsin law professor 1868–85 and 1889–92, regent 1880–85 and 1898–1905; U.S. postmaster general 1885–88; U.S. secretary of interior 1888–89; U.S. senator 1891–97.

Vinton   **Ohio**
McArthur   414 sq. mi.

| 12,806 | 11,098 | 11,584 | 9,420 | 10,274 | 10,759 |

March 23, 1850. Samuel Finley Vinton (1792–1862). U.S. representative from Ohio 1823–37 and 1843–51; president, Toledo & Cleveland Railroad 1853–54.

Virginia Beach   **Virginia**
(Independent City)   248 sq. mi.

| 425,257 | 393,069 | 262,199 | 172,106 | 84,215[a] | 42,277[b] |

1691, as Princess Anne; Virginia Beach incorporated 1952; Princess Anne County annexed by Virginia Beach January 1, 1963. Descriptive of location on Atlantic Ocean. [(a) Includes Princess Anne County (76,124); (b) Princess Anne County. (Associated county: Princess Anne.)]

Volusia   **Florida**
De Land   1,103 sq. mi.

| 443,343 | 370,712 | 258,762 | 169,487 | 125,319 | 74,229 |

December 29, 1854. Settlement of Volusia Landing on St. Johns River. Uncertain origin of name: (1) early settler named Volus; (2) Belgian or Frenchman named Veluche; (3) nearby plantation named Volusia.

W

Wabash   **Illinois**
Mount Carmel   223 sq. mi.

| 12,937 | 13,111 | 13,713 | 12,841 | 14,047 | 14,651 |

December 27, 1824. *Wabash River.* Uncertain origin of name. (1) French renderings *oubadhei* or *ouabachi* of Indian *wahbahshikki,* meaning "pure white" or "white stone river," for river's limestone bed. (2) Indian *wabashkisibi,* meaning "bog river."

Wabash   **Indiana**
Wabash   413 sq. mi.

| 34,960 | 35,069 | 36,640 | 35,553 | 32,605 | 29,047 |

February 2, 1832; organized January 22, 1835; effective March 1, 1853. Wabash River.*

Wabasha   **Minnesota**
Wabasha   525 sq. mi.

| 21,610 | 19,744 | 19,335 | 17,224 | 17,007 | 16,878 |

October 27, 1849; organized March 5, 1853. Town of Wabasha. Named for hereditary line of Dakota chiefs named Wapashaw, a title bestowed by French explorers meaning "red leaf" from the oak trees in the area.

Wabaunsee   **Kansas**
Alma   797 sq. mi.

| 6,885 | 6,603 | 6,867 | 6,397 | 6,648 | 7,212 |

August 30, 1855, as Richardson; organized and name changed February 11, 1859. Wabaunsee (?–?). Potawatomie chief; led massacre of U.S. troops at Fort Dearborn 1812; allied with Illinois Militia in Black Hawk War 1832; granted land in Illinois, later moved to Iowa. Translation of "Wabaunsee" is given as "dawn of day" or "foggy," supposedly related to conditions at the time of his more famous warrior exploits.

Wade Hampton   **Alaska**
(Census Area)   17,194 sq. mi.

| 7,028 | 5,791 | 4,665 | 3,917 | 3,128 | (a) |

Uncertain. (1) Wade Hampton (see Hampton, South Carolina). Hampton's son-in-law, John Randolph Tucker, judge of Alaska's 2nd Judicial Division, created new recorder's district from Kuskokwim District and named it for his father-in-law 1913. (2) Wade Hampton and Frederick Coate Wade (1860–1924); lawyer and junior councilor at 1903 Alaska tribunal; original spelling was Wade-Hampton District, indicating separate components of the name. [(a) Part of 2nd Judicial Division.]

Wadena   **Minnesota**
Wadena   535 sq. mi.

| 13,713 | 13,154 | 14,192 | 12,412 | 12,199 | 12,806 |

June 11, 1858; organized February 17, 1881. Wadena trading post. Chippewa for "village" or "little round hill."

Wagoner   **Oklahoma**
Wagoner   563 sq. mi.

| 57,491 | 47,883 | 41,801 | 22,163 | 15,673 | 16,741 |

July 16 1907. Town of Wagoner. Named for Henry Samuel "Bigfoot" Wagoner (?–?); dispatcher for Missouri, Kansas & Texas Railroad; ordered a switch to be placed between Gibson Station and Lelietta which became known as Wagoner's Switch.

Wahkiakum   **Washington**
Cathlamet   264 sq. mi.

| 3,824 | 3,327 | 3,832 | 3,592 | 3,462 | 3,835 |

April 24, 1854. Wahkiakum Indians. Named for Chief Wakaiyakam who led separation of Wahkiakums from Chinooks.

Wake   **North Carolina**
Raleigh   832 sq. mi.
627,846   423,380   301,327   228,453   169,082   136,450
December 5, 1770 (session). Margaret Wake Tryon (1733–1819). Name chosen by Governor Tryon to honor his wife; lived in North Carolina 1764–71.

Wakulla   **Florida**
Crawfordville   607 sq. mi.
22,863   14,202   10,887   6,308   5,257   5,258
March 11, 1843. Wakulla Springs. Indian corruption of Spanish "Guacara," the phonetic spelling of the Indian name of uncertain meaning; popular guess is that it means "mystery."

Waldo   **Maine**
Belfast   730 sq. mi.
36,280   33,018   28,414   23,382   22,632   21,687
February 7, 1827; effective July 3, 1827. Samuel Waldo (1695–1759). Boston merchant and land speculator; mast-agent responsible for obtaining New England white pines for the British navy; opened land for settlers known as Waldo Patent 1740; brigadier general in King George's War 1745.

Walker   **Alabama**
Jasper   794 sq. mi.
70,713   67,670   68,660   56,246   54,211   63,769
December 26, 1823. John Walker (1783–1823). Mississippi and Alabama territorial legislatures; Alabama Constitutional Convention 1819; U.S. Senate 1819–23.

Walker   **Georgia**
LaFayette   447 sq. mi.
61,053   58,340   56,470   50,691   45,264   38,198
December 18, 1833. Freeman Walker (1780–1827). Georgia House of Representatives 1807–11; mayor of Augusta 1818–19 and 1823; U.S. senator 1819–21.

Walker   **Texas**
Huntsville   787 sq. mi.
61,758   50,917   41,789   27,680   21,475   20,163
April 6, 1846; organized July 18, 1846. Originally in honor of Robert James Walker; changed by legislature to Samuel Hamilton Walker December 10, 1863, because of Robert Walker's Union sympathies. (1) Robert Walker (1801–69); U.S. senator from Mississippi 1835–45, introduced resolution for annexation of Texas; U.S. secretary of treasury 1845–49; governor of Kansas Territory 1857; U.S. financial agent in Europe 1863–64. (2) Samuel Walker (c1810–1847); Texas Rangers 1836; Walker-Colt revolver used in Texas was result of design suggestions offered to Samuel Colt; served under General Taylor in Mexican War; killed at Huamantla October 9, 1847.

Wallace   **Kansas**
Sharon Springs   914 sq. mi.
1,749   1,821   2,045   2,215   2,069   2,508
March 2, 1868; organized January 5, 1889. William Harvey Lamb Wallace (1821–62). Rose from private to 1st lieutenant, Illinois Infantry in Mexican War; mustered out 1847; recommissioned colonel, Illinois Infantry 1861; brigadier general 1862; died of wounds received at Shiloh.

Walla Walla   **Washington**
Walla Walla   1,271 sq. mi.
55,180   48,439   47,435   42,176   42,195   40,135
April 25, 1854. Nez Perce word of uncertain meaning but all suggestions refer to some form of water.

Waller   **Texas**
Hempstead   514 sq. mi.

| 32,663 | 23,390 | 19,798 | 14,285 | 12,071 | 11,961 |

April 28, 1873; organized August 16, 1873. Edwin Waller (1800–83). Texas Declaration of Independence 1836; first mayor of Austin 1840; appointed Texas postmaster general but served only two days 1839; chief justice, Austin County 1844–56; Secession Convention 1861.

Wallowa   **Oregon**
Enterprise   3,145 sq. mi.

| 7,226 | 6,911 | 7,273 | 6,247 | 7,102 | 7,264 |

February 11, 1887. Wallowa Lake and River. From Nez Perce *lacallas*, a tripod structure for trapping fish.

Walsh   **North Dakota**
Grafton   1,282 sq. mi.

| 12,389 | 13,840 | 15,371 | 16,251 | 17,997 | 18,859 |

February 18, 1881. George H. Walsh (1845–1913). Union army 1862–65; Dakota Territory legislature 1879–89; North Dakota legislature 1889–93.

Walthall   **Mississippi**
Tylertown   404 sq. mi.

| 15,156 | 14,352 | 13,761 | 12,500 | 13,512 | 15,563 |

March 16, 1910; organized 1914. Edward Cary Walthall (1831–98). Rose from 1st lieutenant to major general, Confederate army 1861–65; wounded in defense of Lookout Mountain 1864; U.S. senator 1885–98.

Walton   **Florida**
De Funiak Springs   1,058 sq. mi.

| 40,601 | 27,760 | 21,300 | 16,087 | 15,576 | 14,725 |

December 29, 1824. George Walton (?–?). Colonel and aide to General Jackson; governor of West Florida 1821–22; secretary of Florida Territory 1822–26.

Walton   **Georgia**
Monroe   329 sq. mi.

| 60,687 | 38,586 | 31,211 | 23,404 | 20,481 | 20,230 |

December 15, 1818. George Walton (1750–1804). Delegate to Continental Congress 1776–81; signer of Declaration of Independence 1776; colonel of militia; wounded and captured at Savannah; governor of Georgia 1779–80 and 1783; chief justice of Georgia 1783–86 and 1793; U.S. senator 1795–96; circuit court judge 1799–1804.

Walworth   **South Dakota**
Selby   708 sq. mi.

| 5,974 | 6,087 | 7,011 | 7,842 | 8,097 | 7,648 |

January 8, 1873; organized March 28, 1883. Walworth County, Wisconsin.

Walworth   **Wisconsin**
Elkhorn   555 sq. mi.

| 93,759 | 75,000 | 71,507 | 63,444 | 52,368 | 41,584 |

December 7, 1836; organized 1839. Reuben Hyde Walworth (1788–1867). Colonel, aide-de-camp to General Mooers, War of 1812; U.S. representative from New York 1821–23; district judge of New York 1823–28; nominated to U.S. Supreme Court by President Tyler but not confirmed by Senate 1844; national leader of temperance movement.

Wapello   **Iowa**
Ottumwa   432 sq. mi.

| 36,051 | 35,687 | 40,241 | 42,149 | 46,126 | 47,397 |

February 17, 1843; organized February 13, 1844; effective March 1, 1844. Wapello (1787–1842). Fox Indian chief; led peaceful and ineffective resistance to European encroachment; moved village around Iowa several times; signed five treaties with U.S. 1822–37.

Ward   **North Dakota**
Minot   2,013 sq. mi.

58,795   57,921   58,392   58,560   47,072   34,782
April 14, 1885; organized November 23, 1885. Mark Ward (1844–1902). Dakota Territory legislature, chairman of committee on counties 1885.

Ward   **Texas**
Monahans   835 sq. mi.
10,909   13,115   13,976   13,019   14,917   13,346
February 26, 1887; organized March 29, 1892. Thomas William Ward (1807–72). Lost leg during siege of Bexar 1835; commissioner, Texas Land Office 1841–48; mayor of Austin 1840, 1853, and 1865; U.S. consul to Panama 1840, 1853, and 1865; opposed secession 1861; collector of customs at Corpus Christi 1865–69.

Ware   **Georgia**
Waycross   902 sq. mi.
35,483   35,471   37,180   33,525   34,219   30,289
December 15, 1824. Nicholas Ware (1769–1824). Georgia legislature 1808–11 and 1814–15; mayor of Augusta 1819–21; U.S. senator 1821–24.

Warren   **Georgia**
Warrenton   286 sq. mi.
6,336   6,078   6,583   6,669   7,360   8,779
December 19, 1793. *Joseph Warren* (1741–75). Physician; president of Massachusetts Provisional Congress 1775; major general, Continental army 1775; killed at Breed's Hill (Bunker Hill) June 17, 1775.

Warren   **Illinois**
Monmouth   543 sq. mi.
18,735   19,181   21,943   21,595   21,587   21,981
January 13, 1825; organized 1831. Joseph Warren.*

Warren   **Indiana**
Williamsport   365 sq. mi.
8,419   8,176   8,976   8,705   8,545   8,535
January 19, 1827; effective March 1, 1827. Joseph Warren.*

Warren   **Iowa**
Indianola   572 sq. mi.
40,671   36,033   34,878   27,432   20,829   17,758
January 13, 1846; organized February 10, 1849. Joseph Warren.*

Warren   **Kentucky**
Bowling Green   545 sq. mi.
92,522   76,673   71,828   57,432   45,491   42,758
December 14, 1796; effective March 1, 1797. Joseph Warren.*

Warren   **Mississippi**
Vicksburg   587 sq. mi.
49,644   47,880   51,627   44,981   42,206   39,616
December 22, 1809. Joseph Warren.*

Warren   **Missouri**
Warrenton   431 sq. mi.
24,525   19,534   14,900   9,699   8,750   7,666
January 5, 1833. Joseph Warren.*

Warren   **New Jersey**
Belvidere   358 sq. mi.

102,437   91,607   84,429   73,879   63,220   54,374
November 20, 1824. Joseph Warren.*

Warren   **New York**
Lake George   869 sq. mi.
63,303   59,209   54,854   49,402   44,002   39,205
March 12, 1813. Joseph Warren.*

Warren   **North Carolina**
Warrenton   429 sq. mi.
19,972   17,265   16,232   15,810   19,652   23,539
April 14, 1779 (session). Joseph Warren.*

Warren   **Ohio**
Lebanon   400 sq. mi.
158,383   113,909   99,276   84,925   65,711   38,505
March 24, 1803. Joseph Warren.*

Warren   **Pennsylvania**
Warren   883 sq. mi.
43,863   45,050   47,449   47,682   45,582   42,698
March 12, 1800; organized 1819. Joseph Warren.*

Warren   **Tennessee**
McMinnville   433 sq. mi.
38,276   32,992   32,653   26,972   23,102   22,271
November 26, 1807. Joseph Warren.*

Warren   **Virginia**
Front Royal   214 sq. mi.
31,584   26,142   21,200   15,301   14,655   14,801
March 9, 1836. Joseph Warren.*

Warrick   **Indiana**
Boonville   384 sq. mi.
52,383   44,920   41,474   27,972   23,577   21,527
March 9, 1813; effective April 1, 1813. Jacob Warrick (?–1811). Captain under General Harrison; mortally wounded at battle of Tippecanoe November 7, 1811.

Wasatch   **Utah**
Heber City   1,177 sq. mi.
15,215   10,089   8,523   5,863   5,308   5,574
January 17, 1862. Wasatch Mountains. Derived from Ute word meaning "a low pass over a high range."

Wasco   **Oregon**
The Dalles   2,381 sq. mi.
23,791   21,683   21,732   20,133   20,205   15,552
January 11, 1854. Wasco Indians. Name is from Indian word for "horn basin," a cup or small bowl made of horn.

Waseca   **Minnesota**
Waseca   423 sq. mi.
19,526   18,079   18,448   16,663   16,041   14,957
February 27, 1857. Dakota word meaning "fertile"; descriptive of local soil.

Washakie   **Wyoming**
Worland   2,240 sq. mi.

| 8,289 | 8,388 | 9,496 | 7,569 | 8,883 | 7,252 |

February 9, 1911. Washakie (c1804–1900). Shoshoni chief; assisted emigrants on Oregon Trail; at age 70 took six scalps to prove he was not too old to rule; converted to Christianity 1897; name means "rawhide rattle."

Washburn   **Wisconsin**
Shell Lake   810 sq. mi.

| 16,036 | 13,772 | 13,174 | 10,601 | 10,301 | 11,665 |

March 27, 1883. Cadwallader Colden Washburn (1818–82). U.S. representative from Wisconsin 1855–61 and 1867–71; rose from colonel to major general, 2nd Regiment Wisconsin Volunteer Cavalry 1862–65; governor of Wisconsin 1872–73.

Washington   **Alabama**
Chatom   1,081 sq. mi.

| 18,097 | 16,694 | 16,821 | 16,241 | 15,372 | 15,612 |

June 4, 1800. *George Washington* (1732–99). Surveyor; served with General Braddock in French and Indian Wars; assumed command of Continental Armies 1775; successfully conducted Revolutionary War, ending with surrender of Cornwallis at Yorktown October 19, 1781; resigned commission 1783; presided over federal Constitutional Convention 1787; 1st president of the U.S. 1789–97; accepted commission as lieutenant general and commander in chief when war with France threatened 1798.

Washington   **Arkansas**
Fayetteville   950 sq. mi.

| 157,715 | 113,409 | 100,494 | 77,370 | 55,797 | 49,979 |

October 17, 1828; effective November 1, 1828. George Washington.*

Washington   **Colorado**
Akron   2,521 sq. mi.

| 4,926 | 4,812 | 5,304 | 5,550 | 6,625 | 7,520 |

February 9, 1887. George Washington.*

Washington   **Florida**
Chipley   580 sq. mi.

| 20,973 | 16,919 | 14,509 | 11,453 | 11,249 | 11,888 |

December 9, 1825. George Washington.*

Washington   **Georgia**
Sandersville   680 sq. mi.

| 21,176 | 19,112 | 18,842 | 17,480 | 18,903 | 21,012 |

February 25, 1784. George Washington.*

Washington   **Idaho**
Weiser   1,456 sq. mi.

| 9,977 | 8,550 | 8,803 | 7,633 | 8,378 | 8,576 |

February 20, 1879. George Washington.*

Washington   **Illinois**
Nashville   563 sq. mi.

| 15,148 | 14,965 | 15,472 | 13,780 | 13,569 | 14,460 |

January 2, 1818. George Washington.*

Washington   **Indiana**
Salem   514 sq. mi.

| 27,223 | 23,717 | 21,932 | 19,278 | 17,819 | 16,520 |

December 21, 1813; effective January 17, 1814. George Washington.*

Washington   **Iowa**
Washington   569 sq. mi.

20,670   19,612   20,141   18,967   19,406   19,557
January 16, 1837, as Slaughter; organized January 18, 1838; name changed January 25, 1839. George Washington.*

Washington   **Kansas**
Washington   898 sq. mi.
6,483   7,073   8,543   9,249   10,739   12,977
February 20, 1857. George Washington.*

Washington   **Kentucky**
Springfield   301 sq. mi.
10,916   10,441   10,764   10,728   11,168   12,777
June 22, 1792; effective September 1, 1792. George Washington.*

Washington   **Louisiana**
Franklinton   670 sq. mi.
43,926   43,185   44,207   41,987   44,015   38,371
March 6, 1819. George Washington.*

Washington   **Maine**
Machias   2,568 sq. mi.
33,941   35,308   34,963   29,859   32,908   35,187
June 25, 1789; effective May 1, 1790. George Washington.*

Washington   **Maryland**
Hagerstown   458 sq. mi.
131,923   121,393   113,086   103,829   91,219   78,886
September 6, 1776; effective October 1, 1776. George Washington.*

Washington   **Minnesota**
Stillwater   392 sq. mi.
201,130   145,896   113,571   82,948   52,432   34,544
October 27, 1849; organized March 31, 1851; effective September 1, 1851. George Washington.*

Washington   **Mississippi**
Greenville   724 sq. mi.
62,977   67,935   72,344   70,581   78,638   70,504
January 29, 1827. George Washington.*

Washington   **Missouri**
Potosi   760 sq. mi.
23,344   20,380   17,983   15,086   14,346   14,689
August 21, 1813. George Washington.*

Washington   **Nebraska**
Blair   390 sq. mi.
18,780   16,607   15,508   13,310   12,103   11,511
November 23, 1854. George Washington.*

Washington   **New York**
Fort Edward   835 sq. mi.
61,042   59,330   54,795   52,725   48,476   47,144
March 12, 1772, as Charlotte; name changed April 2, 1784. George Washington.*

Washington   **North Carolina**
Plymouth   348 sq. mi.

13,723   13,997   14,801   14,038   13,488   13,180
November 15, 1799 (session). George Washington.*

Washington   **Ohio**
Marietta   635 sq. mi.
63,251   62,254   64,266   57,160   51,689   44,407
July 27, 1788. George Washington.*

Washington   **Oklahoma**
Bartlesville   417 sq. mi.
48,996   48,066   48,113   42,277   42,347   32,880
July 16, 1907. George Washington.*

Washington   **Oregon**
Hillsboro   724 sq. mi.
445,342   311,554   245,808   157,920   92,237   61,269
July 5, 1843, as Twality; name changed September 3, 1849. George Washington.*

Washington   **Pennsylvania**
Washington   857 sq. mi.
202,897   204,584   217,074   210,876   217,271   209,628
March 28, 1781. George Washington.*

Washington   **Rhode Island**
Wakefield   333 sq. mi.
123,546   110,006   93,317   83,586   59,054   48,542
June 3, 1729, as King's; name changed October 29, 1781. George Washington.*

Washington   **Tennessee**
Jonesborough   326 sq. mi.
107,198   92,315   88,755   73,924   64,832   59,971
November 15, 1777 (session). George Washington.*

Washington   **Texas**
Brenham   609 sq. mi.
30,373   26,154   21,998   18,842   19,145   20,542
March 17, 1836; organized 1837. Municipality of Washington on the Brazos. Settled in Mexican Texas 1834; established as municipality 1835; named for Washington, Georgia, which was named for George Washington.*

Washington   **Utah**
Saint George   2,427 sq. mi.
90,354   48,560   26,065   13,669   10,271   9,836
March 3, 1852. George Washington.*

Washington   **Vermont**
Montpelier   689 sq. mi.
58,039   54,928   52,393   47,659   42,860   42,870
November 1, 1810, as Jefferson; organized October 16, 1811; effective December 1, 1811; name changed November 8, 1814. George Washington.*

Washington   **Virginia**
Abingdon   563 sq. mi.
51,103   45,887   46,487   40,835   38,076   37,536
October 7, 1776 (session). George Washington.*

Washington   **Wisconsin**
West Bend   431 sq. mi.
117,493   95,328   84,848   63,839   46,119   33,902
December 7, 1836; organized August 13, 1840; effective September 28, 1840. George Washington.*

Washita   **Oklahoma**
Cordell   1,003 sq. mi.
11,508   11,441   13,798   12,141   18,121   17,657
1892, as County H; organized and name changed 1900. Washita River. Tributary of Red River. Uncertain origin of name: (1) related to Indian word for "water with painted face," a reference to the red silt carried in the river; (2) anglicized rendering of Choctaw words for "hunt" and "big" (see Ouachita (2), Louisiana); (3) from French "Faux Ouachita," meaning "False Ouachita," to distinguish this river from Ouachita River in Arkansas.

Washoe   **Nevada**
Reno   6,342 sq. mi.
339,486   254,667   193,623   121,068   84,743   50,205
November 25, 1861. Washo Indians. American rendering of the tribal name Washiu, meaning "people."

Washtenaw   **Michigan**
Ann Arbor   710 sq. mi.
322,895   282,937   264,748   234,103   172,440   134,606
September 10, 1822; organized November 20, 1826. Grand River. "Washtenong" is Chippewa name for the Grand River. Name is of uncertain origin; may mean "river that is far off."

Watauga   **North Carolina**
Boone   313 sq. mi.
42,695   36,952   31,666   23,404   17,529   18,342
January 27, 1849. Watauga River. May be named from an Indian tribe or a village on the river.

Watonwan   **Minnesota**
Saint James   435 sq. mi.
11,876   11,682   12,361   13,298   14,460   13,881
February 25, 1860; organized June 15, 1871. Watonwan Township. County created from Watonwan Township, Blue Earth County; township named for Watonwan River, which is an anglicized version of Indian word of unknown origin; most guesses refer to fish or seeing.

Waukesha   **Wisconsin**
Waukesha   556 sq. mi.
360,767   304,715   280,326   231,365   158,249   85,901
January 31, 1846. Uncertain. Indian word *wauk-tsha,* meaning "fox"; county name may be from the Fox Indians, Fox River, or the animal.

Waupaca   **Wisconsin**
Waupaca   751 sq. mi.
51,731   46,104   42,831   37,780   35,340   35,056
February 17, 1851; organized 1852. Waupaca River. Uncertain origin; guesses range from "white sand bottom" to "our brave young hero."

Waushara   **Wisconsin**
Wautoma   626 sq. mi.
23,154   19,385   18,526   14,795   13,497   13,920
February 15, 1851; organized 1852. Contrived, pseudo-Indian name of unknown translation; one suggestion is "good land river."

Wayne   **Georgia**
Jesup   645 sq. mi.

26,565   22,356   20,750   17,858   17,921   14,248

May 11, 1803. *Anthony Wayne* (1745–96). Pennsylvania House of Representatives 1774–75; colonel, 4th Pennsylvania Regiment; wounded at battle of Three Rivers 1776; brigadier general 1777; Valley Forge 1777–78; captured Stony Point 1779; awarded Thanks of Congress and gold medal 1779; brevet major general 1783; retired from army 1784; Pennsylvania Assembly 1784; U.S. representative from Georgia 1791–92; major general and general-in-chief of Army, defeated Indians at battle of Fallen Timbers 1794; nicknamed "Mad Anthony" for daring exploits.

Wayne　　　　　　**Illinois**
Fairfield　　　　　　714 sq. mi.
17,151   17,241   18,059   17,004   19,008   20,933
March 26, 1819. Anthony Wayne.*

Wayne　　　　　　**Indiana**
Richmond　　　　　　404 sq. mi.
71,097   71,951   76,058   79,109   74,039   68,566
November 27, 1810; effective February 1, 1811. Anthony Wayne.*

Wayne　　　　　　**Iowa**
Corydon　　　　　　526 sq. mi.
6,730   7,067   8,199   8,405   9,800   11,737
January 13, 1846; organized January 27, 1851. Anthony Wayne.*

Wayne　　　　　　**Kentucky**
Monticello　　　　　　459 sq. mi.
19,923   17,468   17,022   14,268   14,700   16,475
December 18, 1800. Anthony Wayne.*

Wayne　　　　　　**Michigan**
Detroit　　　　　　614 sq. mi.
2,061,162   2,111,687   2,337,891   2,666,751   2,666,297   2,435,235
November 21, 1815. Anthony Wayne.*

Wayne　　　　　　**Mississippi**
Waynesboro　　　　　　810 sq. mi.
21,216   19,517   19,135   16,650   16,258   17,010
December 21, 1809. Anthony Wayne.*

Wayne　　　　　　**Missouri**
Greenville　　　　　　761 sq. mi.
13,259   11,543   11,277   8,546   8,638   10,514
December 11, 1818. Anthony Wayne.*

Wayne　　　　　　**Nebraska**
Wayne　　　　　　443 sq. mi.
9,851   9,364   9,858   10,400   9,959   10,129
March 4, 1871. Anthony Wayne.*

Wayne　　　　　　**New York**
Lyons　　　　　　604 sq. mi.
93,765   89,123   84,581   79,404   67,989   57,323
April 11, 1823. Anthony Wayne.*

Wayne　　　　　　**North Carolina**
Goldsboro　　　　　　553 sq. mi.

113,329   104,666   97,054   85,408   82,059   64,267
October 18, 1779 (session). Anthony Wayne.*

Wayne   **Ohio**
Wooster   555 sq. mi.
111,564   101,461   97,408   87,123   75,497   58,716
February 13, 1808; organized 1812. Anthony Wayne.*

Wayne   **Pennsylvania**
Honesdale   729 sq. mi.
47,722   39,944   35,237   29,581   28,237   28,478
March 21, 1798. Anthony Wayne.*

Wayne   **Tennessee**
Waynesboro   734 sq. mi.
16,842   13,935   13,946   12,365   11,908   13,864
November 24, 1817. Anthony Wayne.*

Wayne   **Utah**
Loa   2,460 sq. mi.
2,509   2,177   1,911   1,483   1,728   2,205
March 10, 1892. Wayne C. Robison (1885–96). Son of Utah legislator Willis Robison; accidentally killed by horse at age eleven.

Wayne   **West Virginia**
Wayne   506 sq. mi.
42,903   41,636   46,021   37,581   38,977   38,696
January 18, 1842. Anthony Wayne.*

Waynesboro   **Virginia**
(Independent City)   15 sq. mi.
19,520   18,549   15,329   16,707   15,694   12,357
February 1948. Anthony Wayne.* (Associated county: Augusta.)

Weakley   **Tennessee**
Dresden   580 sq. mi.
34,895   31,972   32,896   28,827   24,227   27,962
October 21, 1823. Robert Weakley (1764–1845). Revolutionary War 1780; North Carolina House of Representatives 1796; U.S. representative from Tennessee 1809–11; Tennessee Senate 1823–24, Speaker; Tennessee Constitutional Convention 1834.

Webb   **Texas**
Laredo   3,357 sq. mi.
193,117   133,239   99,258   72,859   64,791   56,141
January 28, 1848; organized March 16, 1848. James Webb (1792–1856). War of 1812; U.S. district judge, Florida Territory; Texas Republic attorney general 1839–41; Texas legislature 1841–45; Constitutional Convention 1845; Texas secretary of state 1850–51; judge, 14th Judicial District 1854–56; reporter, Texas Supreme Court 1846–49.

Weber   **Utah**
Ogden   576 sq. mi.
196,533   158,330   144,616   126,278   110,744   83,319
March 3, 1852. Weber River. Named for John Weber (1779–1859); Danish sea captain; lived in Ste. Genevieve, Missouri, 1807; explorer and fur trapper in American West.

Webster   **Georgia**
Preston   210 sq. mi.
2,390   2,263   2,341   2,362   3,247   4,081

December 16, 1853 as Kinchafoonee; name changed February 21, 1856. *Daniel Webster* (1782–1852). U.S. representative from New Hampshire 1813–17 and Massachusetts 1823–27; Massachusetts Constitutional Convention 1820; U.S. senator 1827–41 and 1845–50; U.S. secretary of state 1841–43 and 1850–52.

Webster   **Iowa**
Fort Dodge   715 sq. mi.
40,235   40,342   45,953   48,391   47,810   44,241
January 15, 1851, as Risley; organized and name changed January 12, 1853; effective March 1, 1853. Daniel Webster.*

Webster   **Kentucky**
Dixon   335 sq. mi.
14,120   13,955   14,832   13,282   14,244   15,555
February 29, 1860. Daniel Webster.*

Webster   **Louisiana**
Minden   595 sq. mi.
41,831   41,989   43,631   39,939   39,701   35,704
February 27, 1871. Daniel Webster.*

Webster   **Mississippi**
Walthall   422 sq. mi.
10,294   10,222   10,300   10,047   10,580   11,607
April 6, 1874, as Sumner; name changed January 20, 1882. Daniel Webster.*

Webster   **Missouri**
Marshfield   593 sq. mi.
31,045   23,753   20,414   15,562   13,753   15,072
March 3, 1855. Daniel Webster.*

Webster   **Nebraska**
Red Cloud   575 sq. mi.
4,061   4,279   4,858   6,477   6,224   7,395
February 16, 1867; organized July 5, 1871. Daniel Webster.*

Webster   **West Virginia**
Webster Springs   556 sq. mi.
9,719   10,729   12,245   9,809   13,719   17,888
January 10, 1860. Daniel Webster.*

Weld   **Colorado**
Greeley   3,992 sq. mi.
180,936   131,821   123,438   89,297   72,344   67,504
November 1, 1861. Lewis Ledyard Weld (1833–65). Abolitionist in Kansas Territory; secretary of Colorado Territory 1860; captain, U.S. 7th Colored Troops 1861; major, 41st Colored Infantry; lieutenant colonel; died of illness.

Wells   **Indiana**
Bluffton   370 sq. mi.
27,600   25,948   25,401   23,821   21,220   19,564
February 7, 1835; organized February 2, 1837; effective May 1, 1837. William Wells (c1766–1812). Kidnapped and raised by Miamis 1774; favorite of Chief Little Turtle; fought against Americans; interpreter during treaty negotiations; became concerned about possibility of killing Kentucky relatives in battle; joined U.S. army; captain under Generals Wayne and Harrison; maintained ties with Miamis; killed by Potawatamies on mission with Miamis to rescue Fort Dearborn (Chicago).

Wells   **North Dakota**
Fessenden   1,271 sq. mi.

5,102   5,864   6,979   7,847   9,237   10,417

January 4, 1873, as Gingras; name changed February 26, 1881. Edward P. Wells (1847–1936). Merchant in Milwaukee and Minneapolis 1864–78; banker in Jamestown, Dakota Territory, 1880–1901; Dakota Territory legislature 1881.

West Baton Rouge   **Louisiana**
Port Allen   191 sq. mi.
21,601   19,419   19,086   16,864   14,796   11,738

March 31, 1807, as Baton Rouge; name changed 1812. (See East Baton Rouge, Louisiana).

West Carroll   **Louisiana**
Oak Grove   359 sq. mi.
12,314   12,093   12,922   13,028   14,177   17,248

March 28, 1877. Charles Carroll (see Carroll, Arkansas).

Westchester   **New York**
White Plaines   433 sq. mi.
923,459   874,866   866,599   894,104   808,891   625,816

November 1, 1683. Township of Westchester. Named for Chester, England.

West Feliciana   **Louisiana**
Saint Francisville   406 sq. mi.
15,111   12,915   12,186   11,376   12,395   10,169

February 17, 1824. Feliciana Parish (see East Feliciana, Louisiana).

Westmoreland   **Pennsylvania**
Greensburg   1,025 sq. mi.
369,993   370,321   392,294   376,935   352,629   313,179

February 26, 1773. *Westmoreland County, England.*

Westmoreland   **Virginia**
Montross   229 sq. mi.
16,718   15,480   14,041   12,142   11,042   10,148

July 5, 1653 (session). Westmoreland County, England.*

Weston   **Wyoming**
Newcastle   2,398 sq. mi.
6,644   6,518   7,106   6,307   7,929   6,733

March 12, 1890. Uncertain. (1) John B. Weston (?–?); geologist and surveyor for Newcastle Coal Company; discovered rich anthracite coal deposits in the area 1878. (2) Jefferson B. Weston (1831–95); founder of Beatrice, Nebraska, 1857; Nebraska state auditor 1873–79; president of Beatrice National Bank; helped finance construction of Chicago, Burlington, and Quincy RR. (Confusion between John B. and Jefferson B. Weston is such that some attributes given to one may belong to the other.)

Wetzel   **West Virginia**
New Martinsville   359,sq. mi.
17,693   19,258   21,874   20,314   19,347   20,154

January 10, 1846. Lewis Wetzel (1764–1808). Captured with his brother and taken to Ohio by Indians c1776; devoted his life to fighting Indians; known for his excessive brutality even for frontier times.

Wexford   **Michigan**
Cadillac   565 sq. mi.
30,484   26,360   25,102   19,717   18,466   18,628

April 1, 1840, as Kautawaubet; name changed March 8, 1843; organized March 30, 1869. County Wexford, Ireland.

Wharton   **Texas**
Wharton   1,090 sq. mi.

41,188   39,955   40,242   36,729   38,152   36,077

April 3, 1846. Wharton brothers. (1) William Harris Wharton (1802–39); immigrated to Texas 1829; authored petition requesting Mexican statehood for Texas 1832; siege of Bexar (San Antonio) 1835; commissioner to seek aid from U.S. 1835; Texas Republic minister to U.S. 1836–37; captured by Mexican navy while returning from Washington 1837; escaped 1837; Texas Senate 1838. (2) John Austin Wharton (1806–38); joined his brother in Texas 1833; leader in Texas independence movement; general council of provisional government 1835; adjutant general to General Houston; cited for bravery at battle of San Jacinto 1836; Texas secretary of war; Texas legislature 1836–37.

Whatcom   Washington
Bellingham   2,120 sq. mi.
166,814   127,780   106,701   81,950   70,317   66,733

March 9, 1854. Uncertain. (1) Whatcom Falls or Whatcom Creek; from Indian word meaning "noisy water." (2) A chief named Whatcom.

Wheatland   Montana
Harlowton   1,423 sq. mi.
2,259   2,246   2,359   2,529   3,026   3,187

February 22, 1917. Descriptive of local wheat-producing farmland.

Wheeler   Georgia
Alamo   298 sq. mi.
6,179   4,903   5,155   4,596   5,342   6,712

August 14, 1912. Joseph Wheeler (1836–1906). Graduated West Point 1859; commissioned in Confederate army 1861; rose from 1st lieutenant to lieutenant general 1861–65; senior cavalry general of Confederate army; Atlanta campaign 1864; ineffectual resistance to Sherman's March to the Sea 1864; prisoner for one month 1865; U.S. representative from Alabama 1881–82 and 1885–1900; major general of Volunteers, Spanish–American War 1898; negotiated Spanish surrender in Cuba 1898; Tarlac campaign in Philippines 1899–1900; brigadier general, Regular Army 1900.

Wheeler   Nebraska
Bartlett   575 sq. mi.
886   948   1,060   1,054   1,297   1,526

February 17, 1877; organized April 11, 1881. Daniel H. Wheeler (1834–1912). Merchant; Cass County clerk; Cass County judge 1864; secretary Nebraska board of agriculture 1868–81; Nebraska senate 1873–77; Omaha city council.

Wheeler   Oregon
Fossil   1,715 sq. mi.
1,547   1,396   1,513   1,849   2,722   3,313

February 17, 1899. Henry H. Wheeler (1826–1915). Drove ox team from Wisconsin to California 1857; owner and operator of stagecoach line between The Dalles and Canyon City; frequently robbed by Indians and bandits; rancher in Wheeler County area 1878–1904.

Wheeler   Texas
Wheeler   914 sq. mi.
5,284   5,879   7,137   6,434   7,947   10,317

August 21, 1876; organized April 12, 1879. Royal Tyler Wheeler (1810–64). Texas district attorney 1842; district judge 1844; Texas Supreme Court 1854, chief justice 1857–64; professor of law, Austin College 1858.

White   Arkansas
Searcy   1,034 sq. mi.
67,165   54,676   50,835   39,253   32,745   38,040

October 23, 1835; effective December 1, 1835. Uncertain. (1) Hugh Lawson White (1773–1840); fought Cherokees; Tennessee Supreme Court 1801–07 and 1809–15; Tennessee Senate 1807–09 and 1817–25; U.S. senator 1825–40; candidate for U.S. president 1836. (2) White River; tributary of Mississippi; known for its clear, transparent water from springs.

White   Georgia
Cleveland   242 sq. mi.

| 19,944 | 13,006 | 10,120 | 7,742 | 6,935 | 5,951 |

December 22, 1857. Uncertain. (1) David T. White (1812–71). Georgia legislature. (2) John White (?–?); British naval surgeon; rose from captain to colonel, Continental army; during siege of Savannah captured over 100 British troops with only six men by convincing them that they were surrounded by a superior force.

White   Illinois
Carmi   495 sq. mi.

| 15,371 | 16,522 | 17,864 | 17,312 | 19,373 | 20,935 |

December 9, 1815. Uncertain. (1) Isaac White* (see White, Indiana). (2) Leonard White (?–?); militia captain under Colonel Isaac White; colonel 1811; Illinois Constitutional Convention 1818; Illinois Senate 1820s; secretary of Senate 1834–36.

White   Indiana
Monticello   505 sq. mi.

| 25,267 | 23,265 | 23,867 | 20,995 | 19,709 | 18,042 |

February 1, 1834; effective April 1, 1834. *Isaac White* (c1776–1811); militia captain 1806; colonel 1809; killed at battle of Tippecanoe November 7, 1811.

White   Tennessee
Sparta   377 sq. mi.

| 23,102 | 20,090 | 19,567 | 17,088 | 15,577 | 16,204 |

September 11, 1806. John White (?–1846). Continental army, battles of Brandywine and Germantown 1777; early squatter in central Tennessee, eventually purchased the land.

White Pine   Nevada
Ely   8,876 sq. mi.

| 9,181 | 9,264 | 8,167 | 10,150 | 9,808 | 9,424 |

March 2, 1869; effective April 1, 1869. White Pine Mining District. Established after discovery of silver, copper, and lead in White Mountains 1865.

Whiteside   Illinois
Morrison   685 sq. mi.

| 60,653 | 60,186 | 65,979 | 62,877 | 59,887 | 49,336 |

January 16, 1836; organized 1840. Samuel Whiteside (?–?). Moved to Illinois c1806; captain, Mounted Rifles 1812; captain of Rangers 1813; honorably discharged 1814; brigadier general, Illinois Volunteers 1832; Black Hawk War 1832; Illinois legislature.

Whitfield   Georgia
Dalton   290 sq. mi.

| 83,525 | 72,462 | 65,789 | 55,108 | 42,109 | 34,432 |

December 30, 1851. George Whitefield (1714–70). Church of England clergyman; missionary in America c1738; established Bethesda Orphanage, Savannah, 1740; resided in England but visited America often. Letter "e" omitted from county name.

Whitley   Indiana
Columbia City   336 sq. mi.

| 30,707 | 27,651 | 26,215 | 23,395 | 20,954 | 18,828 |

February 7, 1835; organized February 17, 1838; effective April 1, 1838. *William Whitley* (1749–1813). Explored Kentucky 1775–80; Indian fighter; referred to as captain, major, and colonel; volunteered as private in Kentucky Militia for War of 1812 at age sixty-three; killed at battle of the River Thames 1813.

Whitley   Kentucky
Williamsburg   440 sq. mi.

| 35,865 | 33,326 | 33,396 | 24,145 | 25,815 | 31,940 |

January 17, 1818. William Whitley.*

Whitman   Washington
Colfax   2,159 sq. mi.

| 40,740 | 38,775 | 40,103 | 37,900 | 31,263 | 32,469 |

November 29, 1871. Marcus Whitman (1802–47). Physician and missionary; with wife, Narcissa, established mission near Walla Walla; encouraged settlement of Oregon Territory by Americans to counter British claims to region; Whitmans and twelve others massacred by Cayuse Indians November 29, 1847.

Wibaux   **Montana**
Wibaux   889 sq. mi.

| 1,068 | 1,191 | 1,476 | 1,465 | 1,698 | 1,907 |

August 17, 1914. Uncertain. (1) Town of Wibaux; named for Pierre Wibaux. (2) Pierre Wibaux (1858–?); member of wealthy French family; settled in eastern Montana 1883; convinced Northern Pacific Railroad to build stockyards near his ranch; owned land in Texas and North Dakota; invested in gold mines.

Wichita   **Kansas**
Leoti   719 sq. mi.

| 2,531 | 2,758 | 3,041 | 3,274 | 2,765 | 2,640 |

March 6, 1873; organized December 24, 1886. *Wichita Indians*. Part of Indian Confederacy occupying southern plains; encountered by Coronado 1541; population diminished during 19th century from small pox, American encroachment, and Osage raids; resettled in Indian Territory (Oklahoma) by 1860's. Meaning of name is uncertain; may refer to Wichita practice of painting their faces.

Wichita   **Texas**
Wichita Falls   628 sq. mi.

| 131,664 | 122,378 | 121,082 | 121,862 | 123,528 | 98,493 |

February 1, 1858; organized June 21, 1882. Wichita River. Tributary of Red River; named for Wichita Indians.*

Wicomico   **Maryland**
Salisbury   377 sq. mi.

| 84,644 | 74,339 | 64,540 | 54,236 | 49,050 | 39,641 |

August 17, 1867. Wicomico River. From Indian word rendered by English as *wicko-mekee*, meaning "where houses are built."

Wilbarger   **Texas**
Vernon   971 sq. mi.

| 14,676 | 15,121 | 15,931 | 15,355 | 17,748 | 20,552 |

February 1, 1858; organized October 10, 1881. Wilbarger brothers. (1) Josiah Pugh Wilbarger (1801–45); moved to Texas 1827; teacher, surveyor, and farmer; survived scalping 1833. (2) Mathias Wilbarger (c1807–1853); immigrated to Texas 1829; settled near his brother Josiah.

Wilcox   **Alabama**
Camden   889 sq. mi.

| 13,183 | 13,568 | 14,755 | 16,303 | 18,739 | 23,476 |

December 13, 1819. Joseph M. Wilcox (1791–1814). Lieutenant in Creek War; captured and scalped 1814.

Wilcox   **Georgia**
Abbeville   380 sq. mi.

| 8,577 | 7,008 | 7,682 | 6,998 | 7,905 | 10,167 |

December 22, 1857. Uncertain; Wilcox father or son. (1) John Wilcox (?–?); captain in battles with Indians in Georgia; early settler in south-central Georgia; father of Mark Wilcox. (2) Mark Wilcox (c1800–50); sheriff, Telfair County; Georgia legislature; major general, Georgia Militia.

Wilkes   **Georgia**
Washington   471 sq. mi.

| 10,687 | 10,597 | 10,951 | 10,184 | 10,961 | 12,388 |

February 5, 1777. *John Wilkes* (1727–97). Member of British parliament; imprisoned for his fervent opposition to British colonial policies in America.

Wilkes   **North Carolina**
Wilkesboro   757 sq. mi.

65,632   59,393   58,657   49,524   45,269   45,243
November 15, 1777 (session). John Wilkes.*

Wilkin   **Minnesota**
Breckenridge   751 sq. mi.
7,138   7,516   8,454   9,389   10,650   10,567
March 18, 1858, as Toombs; name changed to Andy Johnson March 18, 1862; name changed to Wilkin March 6, 1868; organized March 4, 1872. Alexander Wilkin (1820–64). Infantry captain 1847; resigned 1848; secretary of Minnesota Territory 1851–53; U.S. marshal for Minnesota; captain, 1st Minnesota Infantry 1861; rose from major to colonel, 2nd Minnesota Infantry 1862; killed at battle of Tupelo July 14, 1864.

Wilkinson   **Georgia**
Irwinton   447 sq. mi.
10,220   10,228   10,368   9,393   9,250   9,781
May 11, 1803; organized December 1805. *James Wilkinson* (1757–1825). Captain, Continental army; served under Generals Arnold, Gates, and Washington; negotiated treaty with Creeks ceding land to Georgia; civil and military governor of Louisiana Territory 1805–07; involved in intrigue to make southwest U.S. part of Spain; found innocent by court-martial 1811; brevet major general, commanded attacks against Canada in War of 1812; relieved for poor performance at Montreal; died in Mexico City seeking Spanish land grant in Texas.

Wilkinson   **Mississippi**
Woodville   677 sq. mi.
10,312   9,678   10,021   11,099   13,235   14,116
January 30, 1802. James Wilkinson.*

Will   **Illinois**
Joliet   837 sq. mi.
502,266   357,313   324,460   249,498   191,617   134,336
January 12, 1836. Conrad Will (c1778–1835). Physician; Illinois Constitutional Convention 1818; Illinois Senate 1818–19 and 1827–35; Illinois Assembly 1819–27.

Willacy   **Texas**
Raymondville   597 sq. mi.
20,082   17,705   17,495   15,570   20,084   20,920
March 11, 1911; organized 1912. John G. Willacy (c1859–1943). Texas legislature 1899–1914; Texas tax commissioner 1921–25.

Williams   **North Dakota**
Williston   2,070 sq. mi.
19,761   21,129   22,237   19,301   22,051   16,442
November 30, 1892. Erastus A. Williams (1850–1930). Immigrated to Dakota Territory 1871; involved in extension of Northern Pacific Railroad across Dakota Territory; Dakota Territory legislature 1872–1889; North Dakota Constitutional Convention 1889; North Dakota legislature 1889–97, Speaker 1897.

Williams   **Ohio**
Bryan   422 sq. mi.
39,188   36,956   36,369   33,669   29,968   26,202
February 12, 1820; organized 1824. David Williams (1754–1831). One of three captors of British major André (see Paulding, Georgia).

Williamsburg   **South Carolina**
Kingstree   934 sq. mi.
37,217   36,815   38,226   34,243   40,932   43,807
March 12, 1785; abolished 1800; recreated 1802. Williamsburg Township. The source of the township's name is uncertain. (1) William III* (see King William, Virginia). (2) William IV, Prince of Orange (see Orange, Virginia).

Williamsburg   **Virginia**
(Independent City)   9 sq. mi.

| 11,998 | 11,530 | 9,870 | 9,069 | 6,832 | 6,735 |

1884. William III* (see King William, Virginia). (Associated counties: James City and York.)

Williamson   **Illinois**
Marion   423 sq. mi.

| 61,296 | 57,733 | 56,538 | 49,021 | 46,117 | 48,621 |

February 28, 1839. Williamson County, Tennessee.

Williamson   **Tennessee**
Franklin   583 sq. mi.

| 126,638 | 81,021 | 58,108 | 34,330 | 25,267 | 24,307 |

October 26, 1799. Hugh Williamson (1735–1819). Theologian, mathematician, astronomer, and physician; surgeon general to North Carolina troops 1779–82; North Carolina House of Commons 1782; Continental Congress 1782–85, 1787, and 1788; federal Constitution Convention 1787; U.S. representative 1789–93.

Williamson   **Texas**
Georgetown   1,123 sq. mi.

| 249,967 | 139,551 | 76,521 | 37,305 | 35,044 | 38,853 |

March 13, 1848; organized August 7, 1848. Robert McAlpin Williamson (c1806–59). Editor of newspaper *The Cotton Plant* 1829–31; major ,Texas Army 1835; battle of San Jacinto 1836; district judge and member of Texas Supreme Court 1836; Texas Republic legislature 1841; Texas state legislature 1845–50.

Wilson   **Kansas**
Fredonia   574 sq. mi.

| 10,332 | 10,289 | 12,128 | 11,317 | 13,077 | 14,815 |

August 30, 1855; organized 1864. Hiero T. Wilson (1806–?). Sutler (provisioner) of Fort Scott, Kansas, 1843; merchant and Indian trader; Lecompton Constitutional Convention; Kansas legislature 1855.

Wilson   **North Carolina**
Wilson   371 sq. mi.

| 73,814 | 66,061 | 63,132 | 57,486 | 57,716 | 54,506 |

February 13, 1855. Louis D. Wilson (1789–1847). North Carolina legislature 1815–46; challenged to back up his support for war with Mexico, resigned legislature and joined army at age fifty-seven, 1846; rose from captain to colonel 1846–47; died of fever at Vera Cruz.

Wilson   **Tennessee**
Lebanon   571 sq. mi.

| 88,809 | 67,675 | 56,064 | 36,999 | 27,668 | 26,318 |

October 26, 1799. David Wilson (1752–c1804). Major in Revolutionary War; Speaker, Territory South of the Ohio Assembly 1794.

Wilson   **Texas**
Floresville   807 sq. mi.

| 32,408 | 22,650 | 16,756 | 13,041 | 13,267 | 14,672 |

February 13, 1860; organized August 6, 1860; name changed to Cibilo 1869; renamed Wilson 1874. James Charles Wilson (1816–61). Somervell punitive expedition into Mexico 1842; captured during Mier expedition into Mexico 1843; escaped execution 1843; Texas Senate 1851–52.

Winchester   **Virginia**
(Independent City)   9 sq. mi.

| 23,585 | 21,947 | 20,217 | 14,643 | 15,110 | 13,841 |

1874. Winchester, England. (Associated county: Frederick.)

Windham   **Connecticut**
Willamantic   513 sq. mi.

109,091	102,525	92,312	84,515	68,572	61,759

May 12, 1726 (session). Town of Windham. Named for either of two towns in England: Windham, Sussex, or Wymondham (pronounced as "Windham"), Norfolk.

Windham   **Vermont**
Newfane   789 sq. mi.

44,216	41,588	36,933	33,074	29,776	28,749

February 22, 1781. Uncertain. (1) Windham County, Connecticut. (2) Town of Windham, Connecticut.

Windsor   **Vermont**
Woodstock   971 sq. mi.

57,418	54,055	51,030	44,082	42,483	40,885

February 22, 1781. Town of Windsor, New Hampshire grant (Vermont); origin of name uncertain. (1) John Stuart, Earl of Windsor (1713–92); Scottish peer; friend and virtual prime minister of George III; British secretary of state 1761. (2) Windsor, Connecticut. (3) Windsor Castle, official residence of British sovereigns.

Winkler   **Texas**
Kermit   841 sq. mi.

7,173	8,626	9,944	9,640	13,652	10,064

February 26, 1887; organized April 5, 1910. Clinton McKamy Winkler (1827–82). Texas legislature 1848; captain, Confederate army 1861; rose from major to lieutenant colonel 1862–63; wounded at Gettysburg 1863; judge, Court of Civil Appeals 1876–82.

Winn   **Louisiana**
Winnfield   950 sq. mi.

16,894	16,269	17,253	16,369	16,034	16,119

February 24, 1852. Walter O. Winn (?–?). Founder of seminary that became Louisiana State University; Louisiana legislature.

Winnebago   **Illinois**
Rockford   514 sq. mi.

278,418	252,913	250,884	246,623	209,765	152,385

January 16, 1836. *Winnebago Indians.* Lived in Illinois–Wisconsin area; fought on British side in American Revolution and War of 1812; forced many times by treaties and warfare to relocate, winding up on a reservation in Nebraska. From Algonquin name for them meaning "stinking water"; or possibly refers to earlier home in Canada and means "people of the sea."

Winnebago   **Iowa**
Forest City   400 sq. mi.

11,723	12,122	13,010	12,990	13,099	13,450

February 20, 1847; organized November 1, 1857. Winnebago Indians.*

Winnebago   **Wisconsin**
Oshkosh   439 sq. mi.

156,763	140,320	131,703	129,931	107,928	91,103

January 6, 1840; organized February 16, 1842; effective April 4, 1842. Uncertain. (1) Winnebago Indians.* (2) Lake Winnebago, which was named for the Winnebagos.

Winneshiek   **Iowa**
Decorah   690 sq. mi.

21,310	20,847	21,876	21,758	21,651	21,639

February 20, 1847; organized January 15, 1851; effective March 1, 1851. Winneshiek (1812–c1872). Winnebago chief; supported Chief Black Hawk in Black Hawk War 1832; forced by U.S. to move from Wisconsin to Iowa, Minnesota, South Dakota, and Nebraska 1840–59.

Winona   **Minnesota**
Winona   626 sq. mi.

49,985	47,828	46,256	44,409	40,937	39,841

February 23, 1854. Village of Winona. Named for We-no-nah, the name Dakotas gave to first-born daughters; also from a legendary *We-no-nah*, who dove to her death in Lake Pepin rather than marry a man not of her choosing.

Winston   **Alabama**
Double Springs   614 sq. mi.
24,843   22,053   21,953   16,654   14,858   18,250
February 12, 1850, as Hancock; name changed January 22, 1858. John Anthony Winston (1812–71). Alabama Assembly 1840–45; Alabama Senate 1845, 1851, and 1867; colonel, 1st Alabama Volunteers 1846; governor of Alabama 1853–57; Confederate army.

Winston   **Mississippi**
Louisville   607 sq. mi.
20,160   19,433   19,474   18,406   19,246   22,231
December 23, 1833. Louis Winston (1784–1824). Militia colonel; secretary, Mississippi Constitutional Convention 1817; circuit court judge 1821–24.

Wirt   **West Virginia**
Elizabeth   233 sq. mi.
5,873   5,192   4,922   4,154   4,391   5,119
January 19, 1848. William Wirt (1774–1838). Prosecuted case against Aaron Burr 1807; Virginia House of Delegates 1808; captain of artillery 1812; U.S. attorney for Virginia 1816; U.S. attorney general 1817–29; Anti-Masonic presidential candidate against Andrew Jackson 1832.

Wise   **Texas**
Decatur   905 sq. mi.
48,793   34,679   26,575   19,687   17,012   16,141
January 23, 1856; organized May 5, 1856. *Henry Alexander Wise* (1806–76). U.S. representative from Virginia 1833–44; U.S. minister to Brazil 1844–47; Virginia Constitutional Convention 1850; governor of Virginia 1856–60; Virginia Secession Convention 1861; brigadier general and major general, Confederate army 1861–65.

Wise   **Virginia**
Wise   404 sq. mi.
40,123   39,573   43,863   35,947   43,579   56,336
February 16, 1856. Henry Alexander Wise.*

Wolfe   **Kentucky**
Campton   223 sq. mi.
7,065   6,503   6,698   5,669   6,534   7,615
March 5, 1860. Nathaniel Wolfe (1810–65). Commonwealth attorney for Jefferson County 1839–52; Kentucky Senate 1853–55; Kentucky House of Representatives 1859–61 and 1861–63; advocate of Kentucky neutrality in Civil War.

Wood   **Ohio**
Bowling Green   617 sq. mi.
121,065   113,269   107,372   89,722   72,596   59,605
February 12, 1820. Eleazer Derby Wood (1783–1814). Graduated West Point; captain, War of 1812; built Fort Meigs 1813; withstood British siege 1813; battle of Thames River; lieutenant colonel; killed in combat near Niagara.

Wood   **Texas**
Quitman   650 sq. mi.
36,752   29,380   24,697   18,859   17,653   21,308
February 5, 1850; organized August 5, 1850. George Tyler Wood (1795–1856). Battle of Horseshoe Bend, Creek Indian War 1814; Georgia Assembly 1837–38; Texas Constitutional Convention 1845; colonel, Texas Mounted Volunteers, battle of Monterrey 1846; Texas Senate 1846; governor of Texas 1847–49.

Wood   **West Virginia**
Parkersburg   367 sq. mi.

87,986   86,915   93,648   86,818   78,331   66,540
December 21, 1798. James Wood (1741–1813). French and Indian Wars; captain 1764; Virginia House of Burgesses 1775; colonel, 8th Regiment, Virginia Militia 1776; battle of Brandywine 1777; brigadier general, Virginia Militia 1783; Virginia Executive Council 1784; governor of Virginia 1796–99.

Wood   **Wisconsin**
Wisconsin Rapids   793 sq. mi.
75,555   73,605   72,799   65,362   59,105   50,500
March 29, 1856. Joseph Wood (1811–90). Operated boat on Erie Canal 1830–36; Wisconsin commissioner of state lands 1848–52; Wisconsin legislature 1856; judge of Wood County 1857–58.

Woodbury   **Iowa**
Sioux City   873 sq. mi.
103,877   98,276   100,884   103,052   107,849   103,917
January 15, 1851, as Wahkaw; name changed January 22, 1853; organized March 7, 1853. Levi Woodbury (1789–1851). Governor of New Hampshire 1823–24; New Hampshire House of Representatives 1825; U.S. senator 1825–31 and 1841–45; U.S. secretary of the navy 1831–34; U.S. secretary of the treasury 1834–41; U.S. Supreme Court 1845–51.

Woodford   **Illinois**
Eureka   528 sq. mi.
35,469   32,653   33,320   28,012   24,579   21,335
February 27, 1841. Woodford County, Kentucky.

Woodford   **Kentucky**
Versailles   191 sq. mi.
23,208   19,955   17,778   14,434   11,913   11,212
November 12, 1788; effective May 1, 1789. William Woodford (1735–80). French and Indian Wars 1755; colonel, 2nd Virginia Regiment 1775; brigadier general, Continental army 1777; wounded at Brandywine 1777; captured at Charleston 1780; died in captivity 1780.

Woodruff   **Arkansas**
Augusta   587 sq. mi.
8,741   9,520   11,222   11,566   13,954   18,957
November 26, 1862. William E. Woodruff (1795–1885). War of 1812; established *Arkansas Gazette* 1818; Arkansas treasurer 1836–38; Little Rock postmaster 1845; founded *Arkansas Democrat* 1850.

Woods   **Oklahoma**
Alva   1,287 sq. mi.
9,089   9,103   10,923   11,920   11,932   14,526
1893, as County M; name changed November 6, 1894. Samuel N. Wood (1825–91). Abolitionist in Kansas Territory 1854; part owner of *Kansas Tribune*; Kansas Territory legislature; Kansas Senate; assassinated 1891. ("S" at end of county name is a clerical error.)

Woodson   **Kansas**
Yates Center   501 sq. mi.
3,788   4,116   4,600   4,789   5,423   6,711
August 30, 1855; organized 1858. Daniel Woodson (1824–94). Secretary of Kansas Territory 1854–57; acting governor on many occasions; proslavery sympathizer.

Woodward   **Oklahoma**
Woodward   1,242 sq. mi.
18,486   18,976   21,172   15,537   13,902   14,383
1893, as County N; name changed November 6, 1894. City of Woodward. Named for Brinton W. Woodward (?–?); director of Santa Fe Railroad; city grew around train depot where railroad intersected an army road 1887.

Worcester   **Maryland**
Snow Hill   473 sq. mi.

46,543	35,028	30,889	24,442	23,733	23,148

October 29, 1742. Uncertain. (1) Edward Somerset, Earl of Worcester (1553–1628); court favorite of Elizabeth I and James I; became 4th Earl of Somerset 1589; Elizabeth's master of the horse 1601; great chamberlain at coronation of Charles I 1625. (2) Edward Somerset, Earl of Worcester (1601–67); 6th Earl of Somerset 1646; served Charles I in South Wales and Ireland as general and admiral. (3) Worcester, England.

Worcester   **Massachusetts**
Worcester   1,513 sq. mi.

750,963	709,705	646,352	637,969	583,228	546,401

April 5, 1731; effective July 10, 1731. Worcester, England.

Worth   **Georgia**
Sylvester   570 sq. mi.

21,967	19,745	18,064	14,770	16,682	19,357

December 20, 1853. *William Jenkins Worth* (1794–1849). 1st lieutenant, U.S. Infantry 1813; captain 1814; brevet captain for bravery at Chippewa 1814; lieutenant colonel 1814–24; commandant of West Point cadets 1820–28; major 1824; colonel 1838; Seminole War 1838; brevet major general for heroism in Mexican War 1846; awarded sword by Congress 1847.

Worth   **Iowa**
Northwood   400 sq. mi.

7,909	7,991	9,075	8,968	10,259	11,068

January 15, 1851; organized October 13, 1857. William Jenkins Worth.*

Worth   **Missouri**
Grant City   267 sq. mi.

2,382	2,440	3,008	3,359	3,936	5,120

February 6, 1861. William Jenkins Worth.*

Wrangell-Petersburg   **Alaska**
(Census Area)   5,835 sq. mi.

6,684	7,042	6,167	4,913	4,181 [a]

Wrangell Island; named for Russian admiral Baron Ferdinand Petrovich von Vrangelya (?–?); manager of Russian–American Fur Company 1830–36. Town of Petersburg; named for Peter Bushman (?–?); established salmon cannery and sawmill 1897–99. [(a) Part of 1st Judicial District.]

Wright   **Iowa**
Clarion   581 sq. mi.

14,334	14,269	16,319	17,294	19,447	19,652

January 15, 1851; organized October 1, 1855. Joseph Albert Wright and Silas Wright; neither was closely associated with Iowa. (1) Joseph Wright (1810–67); Indiana House of Representatives 1833; Indiana Senate 1840; U.S. representative 1843–45; governor of Indiana 1849–57; U.S. minister to Prussia 1857–61 and 1865–67; U.S. senator 1862–63. (2) Silas Wright* (see Wright, Minnesota).

Wright   **Minnesota**
Buffalo   661 sq. mi.

89,986	68,710	58,681	38,933	29,935	27,716

February 20, 1855. *Silas Wright* (1795–1847). New York Senate 1824–27; brigadier general, New York Militia 1827; U.S. representative 1827–29; New York state comptroller 1829–33; U.S. Senator 1833–45; declined nomination to run for U.S. vice president with James Polk 1844; governor of New York 1844–46.

Wright   **Missouri**
Hartville   682 sq. mi.

17,955	16,758	16,188	13,667	14,183	15,834

January 29, 1841. Silas Wright.*

Wyandot   **Ohio**
Upper Sandusky   406 sq. mi.

| 22,908 | 22,254 | 22,651 | 21,826 | 21,648 | 19,785 |

February 3, 1845. *Wyandot Indians*. Name given to surviving members of Huron tribe (see Huron, Michigan); called themselves "Wendat;" most suggested translations refer to living near water.

Wyandotte   **Kansas**
Kansas City   151 sq. mi.

| 157,882 | 161,993 | 172,335 | 186,845 | 185,495 | 165,318 |

January 29, 1859. Wyandot Indians.*

Wyoming   **New York**
Warsaw   593 sq. mi.

| 43,424 | 42,507 | 39,895 | 37,688 | 34,793 | 32,822 |

May 19, 1841. Village of M'chewomink. Indian name meaning "on the broad plain," rendered by English as "Wyoming;" name perpetuated by Thomas Campbell poem "Gertrude of Wyoming" 1809.

Wyoming   **Pennsylvania**
Tunkhannock   397 sq. mi.

| 28,080 | 28,076 | 26,433 | 19,082 | 16,813 | 16,766 |

April 4, 1842. *Wyoming Valley*. Named for Indian village; site of massacre of settlers by Indian allies of British 1757 (see Wyoming, New York).

Wyoming   **West Virginia**
Pineville   501 sq. mi.

| 25,708 | 28,990 | 35,993 | 30,095 | 34,836 | 37,540 |

January 26, 1850. Wyoming Valley.*

Wythe   **Virginia**
Wytheville   463 sq. mi.

| 27,599 | 25,466 | 25,522 | 22,139 | 21,975 | 23,327 |

December 1, 1789; effective May 1, 1790. George Wythe (1726–1806). Virginia House of Burgesses 1758–68, clerk 1768–75; Virginia Committee of Correspondence 1759; Continental Congress 1775–77; signer, Declaration of Independence 1776; professor of law, William & Mary College 1779–91; federal Constitutional Convention 1787.

Y

Yadkin   **North Carolina**
Yadkinville   336 sq. mi.

| 36,348 | 30,488 | 28,439 | 24,599 | 22,804 | 22,133 |

December 28, 1850. Yadkin River. Unknown Indian origin; Yadkin River was a neutral zone where a tribe's women, children, and old men could be safely left during battles.

Yakima   **Washington**
Yakima   4,296 sq. mi.

| 222,581 | 188,823 | 172,508 | 144,971 | 145,112 | 135,723 |

January 21, 1865. Yakima Indians. Yakima word for "black bear."

Yakutat   **Alaska**
Yakutat   7,650 sq. mi.

| 808 | (a) | (a) | (b) | (b) | (c) |

September, 1992. Town of Yakutat. Yakutat Bay given various names by European explorers; name reverted to Tlingit name from *yak,* meaning "ocean," and *tat,* meaning "saltwater estuary"; also possibly from Tlingit word meaning "place where canoes rest." [(a) Part of Skagway-Yakutat-Angoon and Valdez-Cordova Census Areas; (b) part of Skagway-Yakutat and Valdez-Chitina-Whittier Census Areas; (c) part of 1st and 3rd Judicial Districts.]

Yalobusha **Mississippi**
Water Valley 467 sq. mi.
13,051 12,033 13,139 11,915 12,502 15,191
December 23, 1833. Yalobusha River. "Tadpole place," from Choctaw words *yaluba,* meaning "tadpoles," and *asha,* meaning "to be there."

Yamhill **Oregon**
McMinnville 716 sq. mi.
84,992 65,551 55,332 40,213 32,478 33,484
July 5, 1843. Yamel Indians. One of sixteen tribes of Kalapuyan family. Name of unknown origin.

Yancey **North Carolina**
Burnsville 312 sq. mi.
17,774 15,419 14,934 12,629 14,008 16,306
1833. Bartlett Yancey (1785–1828). U.S. representative from North Carolina 1813–17; North Carolina Senate 1817–27; declined appointment as U.S. minister to Peru 1826.

Yankton **South Dakota**
Yankton 522 sq. mi.
21,652 19,252 18,952 19,039 17,551 16,804
April 10, 1862. Town of Yankton. Named for Yankton Indians; major division of the Sioux (Dakota) Indians; from corruption of Sioux word *ihanktonwan,* meaning "end village."

Yates **New York**
Penn Yan 338 sq. mi.
24,621 22,810 21,459 19,831 18,614 17,615
February 5, 1823. Joseph Christopher Yates (1768–1837). Mayor of Schenectady 1798; New York Senate 1805; New York Supreme Court 1808–22; governor of New York 1823–24.

Yavapai **Arizona**
Prescott 8,123 sq. mi.
167,517 107,714 68,145 36,733 28,912 24,991
December 21, 1864. Yavapai Indians. Apache–Mojave tribe; name of uncertain origin. (1) From their name for themselves; *enyaeva,* meaning sun, and *pai,* meaning people. (2) Apache *yava,* meaning "hill," and Spanish *país,* meaning "country." (3) From *ya mouth pai,* meaning "talking people." (4) *Nya va pi,* meaning "east" or "sun people."

Yazoo **Mississippi**
Yazoo City 919 sq. mi.
28,149 25,506 27,349 27,304 31,653 35,712
January 21, 1823. Uncertain. (1) Yazoo River; tributary of Mississippi; named for Yazoo Indians. (2) Yazoo Indians; name means "to blow on an instrument."

Yell **Arkansas**
Danville 928 sq. mi.
21,139 17,759 17,026 14,208 11,940 14,057
December 5, 1840. Archibald Yell (1797–1847). Creek Indian wars; battle of New Orleans 1815; Arkansas Territory judge 1832–35; U.S. representative 1836–39 and 1845–46; governor of Arkansas 1840–44; colonel, 1st Arkansas Volunteer Cavalry 1846; killed at battle of Buena Vista February 22, 1847.

Yellow Medicine **Minnesota**
Granite Falls 758 sq. mi.
11,080 11,684 13,653 14,418 15,523 16,279

March 6, 1871; organized February 25, 1874. Yellow Medicine River. Tributary of Minnesota River; local Indians used the yellow root of the moonseed vine as a medicine.

Yellowstone   **Montana**
Billings   2,635 sq. mi.
129,352   113,419   108,035   87,367   79,016   55,875
February 26, 1883; effective May 1, 1883. Yellowstone River. Tributary of Missouri River; named Roche Jaune (Yellow Rock) by French for yellow rocks along its banks.

Yoakum   **Texas**
Plains   800 sq. mi.
7,322   8,786   8,299   7,344   8,032   4,339
August 21, 1876; organized 1907. Henderson King Yoakum (1810–56). Graduated West Point 1832; resigned 1833; captain, Tennessee Mounted Militia 1836; mayor of Murfreesboro 1837; colonel, Tennessee Infantry in Cherokee War 1838; Tennessee Senate 1839; enlisted as private in Mexican War 1846; 1st lieutenant 1846; battle of Monterrey 1846; wrote *History of Texas* 1855.

Yolo   **California**
Woodland   1,013 sq. mi.
168,660   141,092   113,374   91,788   65,727   40,640
February 18, 1850. Yolo Indians. Corruption of Indian word *yoloy* or *yodoi,* meaning "place abounding with rushes."

York   **Maine**
Alfred   991 sq. mi.
186,742   164,587   139,666   111,576   99,402   93,541
November 20, 1652; abolished 1664; recreated 1668; abolished 1680; recreated 1691. Uncertain. (1) Town of York, Maine; named for town of York, Yorkshire, England. (2) York and Yorkshire, England. (3) King James II, Duke of York and Albany (see Albany, New York).

York   **Nebraska**
York   576 sq. mi.
14,598   14,428   14,798   13,685   13,724   14,346
March 13, 1855; organized January 4, 1870. Uncertain. (1) England's royal house of York; 1st Duke of York was Edmund de Langley (1341–1402), fifth son of Edward III; title "Duke of York" given to second son of English royal family. (2) King James II, Duke of York and Albany (see Albany, New York). (3) York and Yorkshire, England. (4) York County, Pennsylvania.

York   **Pennsylvania**
York   904 sq. mi.
381,751   339,574   312,963   272,603   238,336   202,737
October 14, 1748 (session). Town of York, Pennsylvania. Uncertain. (1) York and Yorkshire, England. (2) King James II, Duke of York and Albany (see Albany, New York).

York   **South Carolina**
York   682 sq. mi.
164,614   131,497   106,720   85,216   78,760   71,596
March 12, 1785. York County, Pennsylvania.

York   **Virginia**
Yorktown   106 sq. mi.
56,297   42,422   35,463   33,203   21,583   11,750
1634, as Charles River; name changed 1642. Uncertain. (1) King James II, Duke of York and Albany (see Albany, New York). (2) Yorkshire, England.

Young   **Texas**
Graham   922 sq. mi.
17,943   18,126   19,083   15,400   17,254   16,810

February 2, 1856; organized April 27, 1874. William Cocke Young (1812–62). Sheriff, Red River County, Texas, 1837; district attorney 1844; Texas Constitutional Convention 1845; Mexican War 1846; U.S. marshal at Shawneetown, Illinois, 1851; colonel, organized and commanded 11th Texas Cavalry Regiment 1861; killed by outlaws October 16, 1862.

Yuba   **California**
Marysville   631 sq. mi.
60,219   58,228   49,733   44,736   33,859   24,420
February 18, 1850. Yuba River. Named for Maidu Indians and their village; "Yuba" evolved from the Indian's name for themselves.

Yukon-Koyukuk   **Alaska**
(Census area)   145,900 sq. mi.
6,551   8,478   7,873   6,436[a]   5,716[a]   [b]
Yukon River; Athabascan *yukonna,* meaning "great river." Koyukuk River; tributary of Yukon; unknown origin, may be Russian adaptation of Athabascan word for "big mountain." [(a) Includes Upper Yukon Census Division; (b) part of 4th Judicial District.]

Yuma   **Arizona**
Yuma   5,514 sq. mi.
160,026   106,895   90,554   60,827   46,235   28,006
December 21, 1864. Yuma Indians. Uncertain origin; suggestions include (1) *yahmayo,* meaning "son of chief" or "captain"; may be result of misunderstanding by Spanish explorers; (2) Spanish *humo,* meaning "smoke"; refers to large, smoky fires built by Yumas in hopes of causing rain.

Yuma   **Colorado**
Wray   2,366 sq. mi.
9,841   8,954   9,682   8,544   8,912   10,827
March 15, 1889. Town of Yuma. From Yuma Switch railroad siding; named for a Yuma Indian laborer from Arizona who died and was buried near switch (see Yuma, Arizona).

Z

Zapata   **Texas**
Zapata   997 sq. mi.
12,182   9,279   6,628   4,352   4,393   4,405
January 22, 1858; organized April 26, 1858. Antonio Zapata (?–1840). Led revolt against Mexican president Santa Anna; declared Republic of Rio Grande independent of Mexico 1840; captured and beheaded March 15, 1840; head displayed on pike at Guerrero as warning to other would-be revolutionaries.

Zavala   **Texas**
Crystal City   1,298 sq. mi.
11,600   12,162   11,666   11,370   12,696   11,281
February 1, 1858; organized February 25, 1884. Manuel Lorenzo Justiniano de Zavala y Sáenz (1788–1836). Political leader in Yucatán after Mexican independence from Spain; Mexican congress 1823–34; Mexican senate 1825–26; governor of state of Mexico 1826–28 and 1832–33; licensed to settle 500 families in Mexican Texas 1829; exiled to New York and Europe 1830–32; Mexican minister to France 1834; signer, Texas Declaration of Independence 1836; ad interim vice president of Texas Republic 1836; died of exposure following boating accident.

Ziebach   **South Dakota**
Dupree   1,962 sq. mi.
2,519   2,220   2,308   2,221   2,495   2,606
February 1, 1911. Francis Marion Ziebach (1830–1929). Founded *Yankton Dakotaon* (or *Weekly Dakotian*) 1861; captain, Company A, Dakota Militia 1862; Dakota Territory legislature 1883–84; South Dakota Constitutional Convention 1883.

Appendix A:
Dates of County Creation

A number of variables are involved in determining the date a county was created. Is it the date county was created by legislation? Is it the date the legislation was signed by the governor or, in the case of colonial counties, signed by the king or viceroy? Is it the date county government began to function? Was such functioning a meeting or an election? All of these possibilities have been used to establish the date various counties were created.

The dates for counties created during the colonial period are the most nebulous. In some cases no date can be found in the legislative record, but elsewhere the county may be mentioned as an accomplished fact. Often the only date that can be positively associated with the creation of a colonial county is the convening date of the legislative session during which the county was created. In these cases, "Sess." is included after the date given. The county, of course, would have been created sometime after the beginning date of the session.

The date given for an independent city (indicated by IC) is not the date the city was founded but the date the city achieved independent status. An exception to this is in Virginia, where the independent cities of Chesapeake, Hampton, Newport News, Suffolk, and Virginia Beach were merged with the counties of Norfolk, Elizabeth City, Warwick, Nansemond, and Princess Anne, respectively. The date given for these five Virginia independent cities is the date its predecessor county was created. (The cities of Norfolk and Portsmouth were created from portions of Norfolk County before its merger into the city of Chesapeake.) The same exception applies to Carson City, Nevada, which was merged with Ormsby County.

County	State	Date	
Charles City	Virginia	1634	
Hampton (IC)	Virginia	1634	
Henrico	Virginia	1634	
Isle of Wight	Virginia	1634	
James City	Virginia	1634	
Newport News (IC)	Virginia	1634	
Northampton	Virginia	1634	
York	Virginia	1634	
Saint Mary's	Maryland	February 9, 1637	
Suffolk (IC)	Virginia	1637	
Kent	Maryland	August 2, 1642	
Essex	Massachusetts	May 10, 1643	
Middlesex	Massachusetts	May 10, 1643	
Suffolk	Massachusetts	May 10, 1643	
Northumberland	Virginia	October 12, 1648	Sess.
Anne Arundel	Maryland	April 9, 1650	

Gloucester	Virginia	1651	
York	Maine	November 20, 1652	
Lancaster	Virginia	1652	
Surry	Virginia	1652	
Westmoreland	Virginia	July 5, 1653	Sess.
Calvert	Maryland	July 3, 1654	
New Kent	Virginia	November 20, 1654	Sess.
Charles	Maryland	July 10, 1658	
Accomack	Virginia	1661	
Talbot	Maryland	February 18, 1662	
Hampshire	Massachusetts	May 7, 1662	
Fairfield	Connecticut	May 10, 1666	Sess.
Hartford	Connecticut	May 10, 1666	Sess.
New Haven	Connecticut	May 10, 1666	Sess.
New London	Connecticut	May 10, 1666	Sess.
Stafford	Virginia	June 5, 1666	Sess.
Somerset	Maryland	August 22, 1666	
Dorchester	Maryland	February 16, 1669	
Chowan	North Carolina	1670	
Currituck	North Carolina	1670	
Pasquotank	North Carolina	1670	
Perquimans	North Carolina	1670	
New Castle	Delaware	August 8, 1673	
Sussex	Delaware	August 8, 1673	
Middlesex	Virginia	September 21, 1674	Sess.
Cecil	Maryland	December 31, 1674	
Kent	Delaware	1680	
Bucks	Pennsylvania	March 10, 1682	
Chester	Pennsylvania	March 10, 1682	
Philadelphia	Pennsylvania	March 10, 1682	
Colleton	South Carolina	1682	
Bergen	New Jersey	March 1, 1683	
Essex	New Jersey	March 1, 1683	
Middlesex	New Jersey	March 1, 1683	
Monmouth	New Jersey	March 1, 1683	
Albany	New York	November 1, 1683	
Dutchess	New York	November 1, 1683	
Kings	New York	November 1, 1683	
New York	New York	November 1, 1683	
Orange	New York	November 1, 1683	
Queens	New York	November 1, 1683	

Richmond	New York	November 1, 1683	
Suffolk	New York	November 1, 1683	
Ulster	New York	November 1, 1683	
Westchester	New York	November 1, 1683	
Barnstable	Massachusetts	June 2, 1685	
Bristol	Massachusetts	June 2, 1685	
Plymouth	Massachusetts	June 2, 1685	
Gloucester	New Jersey	May 28, 1686	
Somerset	New Jersey	May 1688	
King and Queen	Virginia	April 16, 1691	Sess.
Chesapeake (IC)	Virginia	1691	
Virginia Beach (IC)	Virginia	April 16, 1691	Sess.
Essex	Virginia	April 16, 1692	Sess.
Richmond	Virginia	April 16, 1692	Sess.
Cape May	New Jersey	November 12, 1692	
Burlington	New Jersey	May 17, 1694	
Salem	New Jersey	May 17, 1694	
Prince George's	Maryland	May 20, 1695	
Dukes	Massachusetts	June 22, 1695	
Nantucket	Massachusetts	June 22, 1695	
Baltimore	Maryland	June 30, 1695	
King William	Virginia	December 5, 1700	Sess.
Prince George	Virginia	December 5, 1700	Sess.
Newport	Rhode Island	June 22, 1703	
Providence	Rhode Island	June 22, 1703	
Craven	North Carolina	December 3, 1705	
Beaufort	North Carolina	December 3, 1705	
Hyde	North Carolina	December 3, 1705	
Queen Anne's	Maryland	April 18, 1706	
Hunterdon	New Jersey	March 13, 1714	
Brunswick	Virginia	November 2, 1720	Sess.
Hanover	Virginia	November 2, 1720	Sess.
King George	Virginia	November 2, 1720	Sess.
Spotsylvania	Virginia	November 2, 1720	Sess.
Bertie	North Carolina	October 2, 1722	Sess.
Carteret	North Carolina	1722	
Windham	Connecticut	May 12, 1726	Sess.
Caroline	Virginia	February 1, 1727	Sess.
Goochland	Virginia	February 1, 1727	Sess.

Prince William	Virginia	February 1, 1727	Sess.
Lancaster	Pennsylvania	October 14, 1728	Sess.
Washington	Rhode Island	June 3, 1729	
New Hanover	North Carolina	November 27, 1729	Sess.
Tyrrell	North Carolina	November 27, 1729	Sess.
Worcester	Massachusetts	April 5, 1731	
Amelia	Virginia	February 1, 1734	Sess.
Orange	Virginia	February 1, 1734	Sess.
Bladen	North Carolina	1734	Sess.
Onslow	North Carolina	1734	Sess.
Augusta	Virginia	August 1, 1738	Sess.
Frederick	Virginia	August 1, 1738	Sess.
Morris	New Jersey	March 15, 1739	
Edgecombe	North Carolina	April 4, 1741	
Northampton	North Carolina	1741	Sess.
Fairfax	Virginia	May 6, 1742	Sess.
Louisa	Virginia	May 6, 1742	Sess.
Worcester	Maryland	October 29, 1742	
Albemarle	Virginia	May 6, 1744	Sess.
Lunenburg	Virginia	May 6, 1745	Sess.
Granville	North Carolina	June 28, 1746	Sess.
Johnston	North Carolina	June 28, 1746	Sess.
Bristol	Rhode Island	February 17, 1747	
Cumberland	New Jersey	January 19, 1748	
Culpeper	Virginia	March 23, 1748	
Frederick	Maryland	June 10, 1748	
York	Pennsylvania	October 14, 1748	Sess.
Anson	North Carolina	March 17, 1749	Sess.
Duplin	North Carolina	March 17, 1749	Sess.
Cumberland	Virginia	March 23, 1749	
Southampton	Virginia	March 30, 1749	
Chesterfield	Virginia	May 1, 1749	
Cumberland	Pennsylvania	January 27, 1750	
Kent	Rhode Island	June 11, 1750	
Berks	Pennsylvania	October 14, 1751	Sess.
Litchfield	Connecticut	October 14, 1751	Sess.
Northampton	Pennsylvania	October 14, 1751	Sess.
Bedford	Virginia	February 27, 1752	Sess.

Dinwiddie	Virginia	February 27, 1752	Sess.
Halifax	Virginia	February 27, 1752	Sess.
Hampshire	West Virginia	February 27, 1752	Sess.
Prince Edward	Virginia	February 27, 1752	Sess.
Sussex	Virginia	February 27, 1752	Sess.
Orange	North Carolina	March 31, 1752	Sess.
Rowan	North Carolina	March 25, 1753	Sess.
Sussex	New Jersey	May 16, 1753	Sess.
Cumberland	North Carolina	February 19, 1754	Sess.
Halifax	North Carolina	December 12, 1754	Sess.
Hertford	North Carolina	December 12, 1754	Sess.
Loudoun	Virginia	March 25, 1757	Sess.
Amherst	Virginia	September 14, 1758	Sess.
Buckingham	Virginia	September 14, 1758	Sess.
Fauquier	Virginia	September 14, 1758	Sess.
Pitt	North Carolina	April 24, 1760	Sess.
Berkshire	Massachusetts	May 28, 1760	Sess.
Cumberland	Maine	May 28, 1760	Sess.
Lincoln	Maine	May 28, 1760	Sess.
Mecklenburg	North Carolina	November 3, 1762	Sess.
Brunswick	North Carolina	January 30, 1764	Sess.
Charlotte	Virginia	May 26, 1764	Sess.
Mecklenburg	Virginia	May 26, 1764	Sess.
Pittsylvania	Virginia	November 6, 1766	Sess.
Cheshire	New Hampshire	April 29, 1769	
Grafton	New Hampshire	April 29, 1769	
Hillsborough	New Hampshire	April 29, 1769	
Rockingham	New Hampshire	April 29, 1769	
Strafford	New Hampshire	April 29, 1769	
Botetourt	Virginia	November 7, 1769	Sess.
Charleston	South Carolina	1769	
Georgetown	South Carolina	1769	
Orangeburg	South Carolina	1769	
Chatham	North Carolina	December 5, 1770	Sess.
Guilford	North Carolina	December 5, 1770	Sess.
Surry	North Carolina	December 5, 1770	Sess.
Wake	North Carolina	December 5, 1770	Sess.
Bedford	Pennsylvania	March 9, 1771	
Berkeley	West Virginia	February 10, 1772	Sess.
Montgomery	New York	March 12, 1772	
Washington	New York	March 12, 1772	
Northumberland	Pennsylvania	March 21, 1772	
Shenandoah	Virginia	March 24, 1772	

Westmoreland	Pennsylvania	February 26, 1773	
Caroline	Maryland	December 5, 1773	
Harford	Maryland	March 2, 1774	
Martin	North Carolina	March 2, 1774	
Montgomery	Maryland	September 6, 1776	
Washington	Maryland	September 6, 1776	
Henry	Virginia	October 7, 1776	Sess.
Monongalia	West Virginia	October 7, 1776	Sess.
Montgomery	Virginia	October 7, 1776	Sess.
Ohio	West Virginia	October 7, 1776	
Washington	Virginia	October 7, 1776	Sess.
Burke	Georgia	February 5, 1777	
Camden	Georgia	February 5, 1777	
Chatham	Georgia	February 5, 1777	
Effingham	Georgia	February 5, 1777	
Glynn	Georgia	February 5, 1777	
Liberty	Georgia	February 5, 1777	
Richmond	Georgia	February 5, 1777	
Wilkes	Georgia	February 5, 1777	
Burke	North Carolina	April 8, 1777	
Camden	North Carolina	April 8, 1777	
Caswell	North Carolina	April 8, 1777	
Fluvanna	Virginia	May 5, 1777	Sess.
Powhatan	Virginia	May 5, 1777	Sess.
Greenbrier	West Virginia	October 20, 1777	Sess.
Rockbridge	Virginia	October 20, 1777	Sess.
Rockingham	Virginia	October 20, 1777	Sess.
Nash	North Carolina	November 15, 1777	Sess.
Washington	Tennessee	November 15, 1777	Sess.
Wilkes	North Carolina	November 15, 1777	Sess.
Franklin	North Carolina	April 14, 1778	Sess.
Gates	North Carolina	April 14, 1778	Sess.
Jones	North Carolina	April 14, 1778	Sess.
Lincoln	North Carolina	April 14, 1778	Sess.
Montgomery	North Carolina	April 14, 1778	Sess.
Randolph	North Carolina	April 14, 1778	Sess.
Bennington	Vermont	February 11, 1779	Sess.
Rutherford	North Carolina	April 14, 1779	Sess.
Warren	North Carolina	April 19, 1779	Sess.
Richmond	North Carolina	October 18, 1779	Sess.
Sullivan	Tennessee	October 18, 1779	Sess.
Wayne	North Carolina	October 18, 1779	Sess.
Fayette	Kentucky	May 1, 1780	Sess.
Jefferson	Kentucky	May 1, 1780	Sess.
Lincoln	Kentucky	May 1, 1780	Sess.
Greensville	Virginia	October 16, 1780	Sess.
Orange	Vermont	February 22, 1781	
Rutland	Vermont	February 22, 1781	

Windham	Vermont	February 22, 1781	
Windsor	Vermont	February 22, 1781	
Washington	Pennsylvania	March 28, 1781	
Campbell	Virginia	November 5, 1781	Sess.
Richmond (IC)	Virginia	1782	
Davidson	Tennessee	April 18, 1783	Sess.
Greene	Tennessee	April 18, 1783	Sess.
Fayette	Pennsylvania	September 26, 1783	
Franklin	Georgia	February 25, 1784	
Washington	Georgia	February 25, 1784	
Moore	North Carolina	April 18, 1784	Sess.
Sampson	North Carolina	April 18, 1784	Sess.
Harrison	West Virginia	May 3, 1784	Sess.
Franklin	Pennsylvania	September 9, 1784	
Montgomery	Pennsylvania	September 10, 1784	
Nelson	Kentucky	October 18, 1784	Sess.
Dauphin	Pennsylvania	March 4, 1785	
Abbeville	South Carolina	March 12, 1785	
Beaufort	South Carolina	March 12, 1785	
Chester	South Carolina	March 12, 1785	
Chesterfield	South Carolina	March 12, 1785	
Clarendon	South Carolina	March 12, 1785	
Darlington	South Carolina	March 12, 1785	
Edgefield	South Carolina	March 12, 1785	
Fairfield	South Carolina	March 12, 1785	
Lancaster	South Carolina	March 12, 1785	
Laurens	South Carolina	March 12, 1785	
Lexington	South Carolina	March 12, 1785	
Marlboro	South Carolina	March 12, 1785	
Newberry	South Carolina	March 12, 1785	
Richland	South Carolina	March 12, 1785	
Spartanburg	South Carolina	March 12, 1785	
Union	South Carolina	March 12, 1785	
Williamsburg	South Carolina	March 12, 1785	
York	South Carolina	March 12, 1785	
Middlesex	Connecticut	May 2, 1785	Sess.
Tolland	Connecticut	October 13, 1785	Sess.
Bourbon	Kentucky	October 17, 1785	Sess.
Franklin	Virginia	October 17, 1785	Sess.
Hardy	West Virginia	October 17, 1785	Sess.
Madison	Kentucky	October 17, 1785	Sess.
Mercer	Kentucky	October 17, 1785	Sess.
Russell	Virginia	October 17, 1785	Sess.
Addison	Vermont	October 18, 1785	
Rockingham	North Carolina	November 19, 1785	Sess.
Greene	Georgia	February 3, 1786	
Greenville	South Carolina	March 22, 1786	
Columbia	New York	April 4, 1786	
Luzerne	Pennsylvania	September 25, 1786	
Randolph	West Virginia	October 16, 1786	Sess.

Hawkins	Tennessee	November 18, 1786	Sess.
Robeson	North Carolina	November 18, 1786	Sess.
Sumner	Tennessee	November 18, 1786	Sess.
Huntingdon	Pennsylvania	September 20, 1787	
Chittenden	Vermont	October 22, 1787	
Pendleton	West Virginia	December 4, 1787	
Clinton	New York	March 17, 1788	
Washington	Ohio	July 27, 1788	
Allegheny	Pennsylvania	September 24, 1788	
Iredell	North Carolina	November 3, 1788	Sess.
Mason	Kentucky	November 5, 1788	
Woodford	Kentucky	November 12, 1788	
Kanawha	West Virginia	November 14, 1788	
Nottoway	Virginia	December 22, 1788	
Ontario	New York	January 27, 1789	
Hancock	Maine	June 25, 1789	
Washington	Maine	June 25, 1789	
Mifflin	Pennsylvania	September 19, 1789	
Delaware	Pennsylvania	September 26, 1789	
Stokes	North Carolina	November 2, 1789	Sess.
Wythe	Virginia	December 1, 1789	
Allegany	Maryland	December 25, 1789	
Hamilton	Ohio	January 2, 1790	
Saint Clair	Illinois	April 27, 1790	
Knox	Indiana	June 20, 1790	
District of Columbia		July 16, 1790	
Patrick	Virginia	November 26, 1790	
Columbia	Georgia	December 10, 1790	
Elbert	Georgia	December 10, 1790	
Bath	Virginia	December 14, 1790	
Mathews	Virginia	December 16, 1790	
Rensselaer	New York	February 7, 1791	
Saratoga	New York	February 7, 1791	
Herkimer	New York	February 16, 1791	
Otsego	New York	February 16, 1791	
Tioga	New York	February 16, 1791	
Kershaw	South Carolina	February 19, 1791	
Buncombe	North Carolina	December 5, 1791	Sess.
Lenoir	North Carolina	December 5, 1791	Sess.
Person	North Carolina	December 5, 1791	Sess.
Jefferson	Tennessee	June 11, 1792	
Knox	Tennessee	June 11, 1792	
Scott	Kentucky	June 22, 1792	
Washington	Kentucky	June 22, 1792	
Shelby	Kentucky	June 23, 1792	
Logan	Kentucky	June 28, 1792	Sess.
Lee	Virginia	October 25, 1792	
Caledonia	Vermont	November 5, 1792	
Essex	Vermont	November 5, 1792	

Franklin	Vermont	November 5, 1792	
Orleans	Vermont	November 5, 1792	
Grayson	Virginia	November 7, 1792	
Cabarrus	North Carolina	November 15, 1792	Sess.
Madison	Virginia	December 4, 1792	Sess.
Clark	Kentucky	December 6, 1792	
Hardin	Kentucky	December 15, 1792	
Green	Kentucky	December 20, 1792	
Norfolk	Massachusetts	March 26, 1793	
Screven	Georgia	December 14, 1793	
Hancock	Georgia	December 17, 1793	
Bryan	Georgia	December 19, 1793	
McIntosh	Georgia	December 19, 1793	
Montgomery	Georgia	December 19, 1793	
Oglethorpe	Georgia	December 19, 1793	
Warren	Georgia	December 19, 1793	
Harrison	Kentucky	December 21, 1793	
Onondaga	New York	March 5, 1794	
Sevier	Tennessee	September 27, 1794	
Franklin	Kentucky	December 7, 1794	
Campbell	Kentucky	December 17, 1794	
Schoharie	New York	April 6, 1795	
Lycoming	Pennsylvania	April 13, 1795	
Somerset	Pennsylvania	April 17, 1795	
Blount	Tennessee	July 11, 1795	
Randolph	Illinois	October 5, 1795	
Bulloch	Georgia	February 8, 1796	
Greene	Pennsylvania	February 9, 1796	
Jackson	Georgia	February 11, 1796	
Jefferson	Georgia	February 20, 1796	
Lincoln	Georgia	February 20, 1796	
Steuben	New York	March 18, 1796	
Carter	Tennessee	April 9, 1796	
Montgomery	Tennessee	April 9, 1796	
Robertson	Tennessee	April 9, 1796	
Grainger	Tennessee	April 22, 1796	
Brooke	West Virginia	November 30, 1796	
Bullitt	Kentucky	December 13, 1796	
Christian	Kentucky	December 13, 1796	
Bracken	Kentucky	December 14, 1796	
Montgomery	Kentucky	December 14, 1796	
Warren	Kentucky	December 14, 1796	
Garrard	Kentucky	December 17, 1796	
Baltimore (IC)	Maryland	December 31, 1796	
Delaware	New York	March 10, 1797	
Adams	Ohio	July 10, 1797	
Jefferson	Ohio	July 27, 1797	
Cocke	Tennessee	October 9, 1797	
Fleming	Kentucky	February 10, 1798	

Rockland	New York	February 23, 1798	
Chenango	New York	March 15, 1798	
Oneida	New York	March 15, 1798	
Wayne	Pennsylvania	March 21, 1798	
Ross	Ohio	August 20, 1798	
Pulaski	Kentucky	December 10, 1798	
Boone	Kentucky	December 13, 1798	
Livingston	Kentucky	December 13, 1798	
Pendleton	Kentucky	December 13, 1798	
Cumberland	Kentucky	December 14, 1798	
Gallatin	Kentucky	December 14, 1798	
Henry	Kentucky	December 14, 1798	
Muhlenberg	Kentucky	December 14, 1798	
Ohio	Kentucky	December 17, 1798	
Jessamine	Kentucky	December 19, 1798	
Barren	Kentucky	December 20, 1798	
Henderson	Kentucky	December 21, 1798	
Wood	West Virginia	December 21, 1798	
Barnwell	South Carolina	1798	
Marion	South Carolina	1798	
Sumter	South Carolina	1798	
Monroe	West Virginia	January 14, 1799	
Kennebec	Maine	February 20, 1799	
Essex	New York	March 1, 1799	
Cayuga	New York	March 8, 1799	
Adams	Mississippi	April 2, 1799	
Jefferson	Mississippi	April 2, 1799	
Smith	Tennessee	October 26, 1799	
Williamson	Tennessee	October 26, 1799	
Wilson	Tennessee	October 26, 1799	
Washington	North Carolina	November 15, 1799	Sess.
Ashe	North Carolina	November 18, 1799	Sess.
Greene	North Carolina	November 18, 1799	Sess.
Tazewell	Virginia	December 7, 1799	Sess.
Breckinridge	Kentucky	December 9, 1799	
Floyd	Kentucky	December 13, 1799	
Nicholas	Kentucky	December 18, 1799	
Knox	Kentucky	December 19, 1799	
Adams	Pennsylvania	January 22, 1800	
Centre	Pennsylvania	February 13, 1800	
Armstrong	Pennsylvania	March 12, 1800	
Beaver	Pennsylvania	March 12, 1800	
Butler	Pennsylvania	March 12, 1800	
Crawford	Pennsylvania	March 12, 1800	
Erie	Pennsylvania	March 12, 1800	
Mercer	Pennsylvania	March 12, 1800	
Venango	Pennsylvania	March 12, 1800	
Warren	Pennsylvania	March 12, 1800	
Greene	New York	March 25, 1800	
Washington	Alabama	June 4, 1800	
Trumbull	Ohio	July 10, 1800	
Clermont	Ohio	December 6, 1800	
Fairfield	Ohio	December 9, 1800	

Wayne	Kentucky	December 18, 1800
Jefferson	West Virginia	January 8, 1801
Clark	Indiana	February 3, 1801
Belmont	Ohio	September 7, 1801
Claiborne	Tennessee	October 29, 1801
Anderson	Tennessee	November 6, 1801
Jackson	Tennessee	November 6, 1801
Roane	Tennessee	November 6, 1801
Clarke	Georgia	December 5, 1801
Tattnall	Georgia	December 5, 1801
Adair	Kentucky	December 11, 1801
Horry	South Carolina	December 19, 1801
Claiborne	Mississippi	January 27, 1802
Wilkinson	Mississippi	January 30, 1802
Saint Lawrence	New York	March 3, 1802
Genesee	New York	March 30, 1802
Grand Isle	Vermont	November 9, 1802
Dearborn	Indiana	March 7, 1803
Butler	Ohio	March 24, 1803
Greene	Ohio	March 24, 1803
Montgomery	Ohio	March 24, 1803
Scioto	Ohio	March 24, 1803
Warren	Ohio	March 24, 1803
Columbiana	Ohio	March 25, 1803
Gallia	Ohio	March 25, 1803
Franklin	Ohio	March 30, 1803
Indiana	Pennsylvania	March 30, 1803
Baldwin	Georgia	May 11, 1803
Wayne	Georgia	May 11, 1803
Wilkinson	Georgia	May 11, 1803
Dickson	Tennessee	October 25, 1803
Rutherford	Tennessee	October 25, 1803
Stewart	Tennessee	November 1, 1803
Greenup	Kentucky	December 12, 1803
Coos	New Hampshire	December 24, 1803
Mason	West Virginia	January 2, 1804
Muskingum	Ohio	January 7, 1804
Seneca	New York	March 24, 1804
Cambria	Pennsylvania	March 26, 1804
Clearfield	Pennsylvania	March 26, 1804
Jefferson	Pennsylvania	March 26, 1804
McKean	Pennsylvania	March 26, 1804
Potter	Pennsylvania	March 26, 1804
Tioga	Pennsylvania	March 26, 1804
Highland	Ohio	February 18, 1805
Athens	Ohio	February 20, 1805
Champaign	Ohio	February 20, 1805
Oxford	Maine	March 4, 1805
Jefferson	New York	March 28, 1805
Lewis	New York	March 28, 1805

Acadia	Louisiana	April 10, 1805
Concordia	Louisiana	April 10, 1805
Iberville	Louisiana	April 10, 1805
Lafourche	Louisiana	April 10, 1805
Natchitoches	Louisiana	April 10, 1805
Orleans	Louisiana	April 10, 1805
Ouachita	Louisiana	April 10, 1805
Pointe Coupee	Louisiana	April 10, 1805
Rapides	Louisiana	April 10, 1805
Geauga	Ohio	December 31, 1805
Giles	Virginia	January 16, 1806
Madison	New York	March 21, 1806
Broome	New York	March 28, 1806
Allegany	New York	April 7, 1806
Campbell	Tennessee	September 11, 1806
Overton	Tennessee	September 11, 1806
White	Tennessee	September 11, 1806
Casey	Kentucky	November 14, 1806
Clay	Kentucky	December 2, 1806
Lewis	Kentucky	December 2, 1806
Hopkins	Kentucky	December 9, 1806
Miami	Ohio	January 16, 1807
Ashtabula	Ohio	February 10, 1807
Cuyahoga	Ohio	February 10, 1807
Portage	Ohio	February 10, 1807
Ascension	Louisiana	March 31, 1807
Assumption	Louisiana	March 31, 1807
Avoyelles	Louisiana	March 31, 1807
Plaquemines	Louisiana	March 31, 1807
Saint Bernard	Louisiana	March 31, 1807
Saint Charles	Louisiana	March 31, 1807
Saint James	Louisiana	March 31, 1807
Saint John the Baptist	Louisiana	March 31, 1807
Saint Landry	Louisiana	March 31, 1807
Saint Martin	Louisiana	March 31, 1807
West Baton Rouge	Louisiana	March 31, 1807
Maury	Tennessee	November 16, 1807
Warren	Tennessee	November 26, 1807
Bledsoe	Tennessee	November 30, 1807
Rhea	Tennessee	November 30, 1807
Bedford	Tennessee	December 3, 1807
Franklin	Tennessee	December 3, 1807
Hickman	Tennessee	December 3, 1807
Jasper	Georgia	December 10, 1807
Jones	Georgia	December 10, 1807
Laurens	Georgia	December 10, 1807
Morgan	Georgia	December 10, 1807
Putnam	Georgia	December 10, 1807
Telfair	Georgia	December 10, 1807
Nelson	Virginia	December 25, 1807
Estill	Kentucky	January 27, 1808
Knox	Ohio	January 30, 1808
Licking	Ohio	January 30, 1808

Richland	Ohio	January 30, 1808
Delaware	Ohio	February 10, 1808
Stark	Ohio	February 13, 1808
Tuscarawas	Ohio	February 13, 1808
Wayne	Ohio	February 13, 1808
Preble	Ohio	February 15, 1808
Cattaraugus	New York	March 11, 1808
Chautauqua	New York	March 11, 1808
Franklin	New York	March 11, 1808
Niagara	New York	March 11, 1808
Catahoula	Louisiana	March 23, 1808
Cortland	New York	April 8, 1808
Harrison	Indiana	October 11, 1808
Madison	Alabama	December 13, 1808
Pulaski	Georgia	December 13, 1808
Columbus	North Carolina	December 15, 1808
Haywood	North Carolina	December 15, 1808
Cabell	West Virginia	January 2, 1809
Darke	Ohio	January 3, 1809
Caldwell	Kentucky	January 13, 1809
Huron	Ohio	February 7, 1809
Amite	Mississippi	February 24, 1809
Somerset	Maine	March 1, 1809
Schenectady	New York	March 7, 1809
Sullivan	New York	March 27, 1809
Humphreys	Tennessee	October 19, 1809
Giles	Tennessee	November 14, 1809
Lincoln	Tennessee	November 14, 1809
Twiggs	Georgia	December 14, 1809
Baldwin	Alabama	December 21, 1809
Franklin	Mississippi	December 21, 1809
Wayne	Mississippi	December 21, 1809
Warren	Mississippi	December 22, 1809
Rockcastle	Kentucky	January 8, 1810
Pickaway	Ohio	January 12, 1810
Butler	Kentucky	January 18, 1810
Grayson	Kentucky	January 25, 1810
Coshocton	Ohio	January 31, 1810
Guernsey	Ohio	January 31, 1810
Madison	Ohio	February 16, 1810
Clinton	Ohio	February 19, 1810
Fayette	Ohio	February 19, 1810
Bradford	Pennsylvania	February 21, 1810
Susquehanna	Pennsylvania	March 21, 1810
Saint Helena	Louisiana	October 27, 1810
Saint Tammany	Louisiana	October 27, 1810
Washington	Vermont	November 1, 1810
Jefferson	Indiana	November 23, 1810
Franklin	Indiana	November 27, 1810
Wayne	Indiana	November 27, 1810
East Baton Rouge	Louisiana	December 22, 1810
Bath	Kentucky	January 15, 1811
Union	Kentucky	January 15, 1811

Schuylkill	Pennsylvania	March 1, 1811
Saint Mary	Louisiana	April 17, 1811
Franklin	Massachusetts	June 24, 1811
Madison	Georgia	December 5, 1811
Greene	Mississippi	December 9, 1811
Marion	Mississippi	December 9, 1811
Medina	Ohio	February 18, 1812
Hampden	Massachusetts	February 25, 1812
Lehigh	Pennsylvania	March 6, 1812
Putnam	New York	June 12, 1812
Mobile	Alabama	August 1, 1812
Gallatin	Illinois	September 14, 1812
Johnson	Illinois	September 14, 1812
Madison	Illinois	September 14, 1812
Cape Girardeau	Missouri	October 1, 1812
New Madrid	Missouri	October 1, 1812
Saint Charles	Missouri	October 1, 1812
Sainte Genevieve	Missouri	October 1, 1812
Saint Louis	Missouri	October 1, 1812
Clarke	Alabama	December 10, 1812
Emanuel	Georgia	December 10, 1812
Hancock	Mississippi	December 18, 1812
Jackson	Mississippi	December 18, 1812
Harrison	Ohio	January 12, 1813
Monroe	Ohio	January 29, 1813
Lebanon	Pennsylvania	February 16, 1813
Gibson	Indiana	March 9, 1813
Warrick	Indiana	March 9, 1813
Warren	New York	March 12, 1813
Columbia	Pennsylvania	March 22, 1813
Union	Pennsylvania	March 22, 1813
Washington	Missouri	August 21, 1813
Washington	Indiana	December 21, 1813
Arkansas	Arkansas	December 31, 1813
Pike	Pennsylvania	March 26, 1814
Perry	Indiana	September 7, 1814
Posey	Indiana	September 7, 1814
Switzerland	Indiana	September 7, 1814
Scott	Virginia	November 24, 1814
Edwards	Illinois	November 28, 1814
Tyler	West Virginia	December 6, 1814
Lawrence	Mississippi	December 22, 1814
Pike	Ohio	January 4, 1815
Allen	Kentucky	January 11, 1815
Daviess	Kentucky	January 14, 1815
Lawrence	Arkansas	January 15, 1815
Monroe	Alabama	June 29, 1815
Wayne	Michigan	November 21, 1815
Pike	Mississippi	December 9, 1815
White	Illinois	December 9, 1815
Jackson	Indiana	December 18, 1815

Lawrence	Ohio	December 21, 1815
Orange	Indiana	December 26, 1815
Monroe	Illinois	January 6, 1816
Jackson	Illinois	January 10, 1816
Pope	Illinois	January 10, 1816
Jackson	Ohio	January 12, 1816
Howard	Missouri	January 13, 1816
Penobscot	Maine	February 15, 1816
Oswego	New York	March 1, 1816
Hamilton	New York	April 12, 1816
Montgomery	Alabama	December 6, 1816
Lewis	West Virginia	December 18, 1816
Pike	Indiana	December 21, 1816
Daviess	Indiana	December 24, 1816
Jennings	Indiana	December 27, 1816
Ripley	Indiana	December 27, 1816
Sullivan	Indiana	December 30, 1816
Crawford	Illinois	December 31, 1816
Bond	Illinois	January 4, 1817
Tompkins	New York	April 7, 1817
Monroe	Michigan	July 14, 1817
Morgan	Tennessee	October 15, 1817
Lawrence	Tennessee	October 21, 1817
Marion	Tennessee	November 20, 1817
Wayne	Tennessee	November 24, 1817
Dubois	Indiana	December 20, 1817
Clark	Ohio	December 26, 1817
Perry	Ohio	December 26, 1817
Brown	Ohio	December 27, 1817
Morgan	Ohio	December 29, 1817
Logan	Ohio	December 30, 1817
Franklin	Illinois	January 2, 1818
Union	Illinois	January 2, 1818
Washington	Illinois	January 2, 1818
Hocking	Ohio	January 3, 1818
Lawrence	Indiana	January 7, 1818
Vanderburgh	Indiana	January 7, 1818
Randolph	Indiana	January 10, 1818
Spencer	Indiana	January 10, 1818
Monroe	Indiana	January 14, 1818
Macomb	Michigan	January 15, 1818
Whitley	Kentucky	January 17, 1818
Preston	West Virginia	January 19, 1818
Vigo	Indiana	January 21, 1818
Crawford	Indiana	January 29, 1818
Nicholas	West Virginia	January 30, 1818
Blount	Alabama	February 6, 1818
Franklin	Alabama	February 6, 1818
Lauderdale	Alabama	February 6, 1818
Lawrence	Alabama	February 6, 1818
Limestone	Alabama	February 6, 1818
Marengo	Alabama	February 6, 1818

Morgan	Alabama	February 6, 1818
Tuscaloosa	Alabama	February 6, 1818
Bibb	Alabama	February 7, 1818
Shelby	Alabama	February 7, 1818
Dallas	Alabama	February 9, 1818
Conecuh	Alabama	February 13, 1818
Marion	Alabama	February 13, 1818
Brown	Wisconsin	October 26, 1818
Crawford	Wisconsin	October 26, 1818
Mackinac	Michigan	October 26, 1818
Perry	Tennessee	November 14, 1818
Saint Clair	Alabama	November 20, 1818
Autauga	Alabama	November 21, 1818
Jefferson	Missouri	December 8, 1818
Franklin	Missouri	December 11, 1818
Wayne	Missouri	December 11, 1818
Lincoln	Missouri	December 14, 1818
Madison	Missouri	December 14, 1818
Montgomery	Missouri	December 14, 1818
Pike	Missouri	December 14, 1818
Appling	Georgia	December 15, 1818
Clark	Arkansas	December 15, 1818
Early	Georgia	December 15, 1818
Gwinnett	Georgia	December 15, 1818
Habersham	Georgia	December 15, 1818
Hall	Georgia	December 15, 1818
Hempstead	Arkansas	December 15, 1818
Irwin	Georgia	December 15, 1818
Pulaski	Arkansas	December 15, 1818
Walton	Georgia	December 15, 1818
Cooper	Missouri	December 17, 1818
Owen	Indiana	December 21, 1818
Fayette	Indiana	December 28, 1818
Floyd	Indiana	January 2, 1819
Shelby	Ohio	January 7, 1819
Oakland	Michigan	January 12, 1819
Meigs	Ohio	January 21, 1819
Harlan	Kentucky	January 28, 1819
Hart	Kentucky	January 28, 1819
Simpson	Kentucky	January 28, 1819
Covington	Mississippi	February 5, 1819
Owen	Kentucky	February 6, 1819
Alexander	Illinois	March 4, 1819
Washington	Louisiana	March 6, 1819
Clark	Illinois	March 22, 1819
Jefferson	Illinois	March 26, 1819
Wayne	Illinois	March 26, 1819
Hamilton	Tennessee	October 25, 1819
Hardin	Tennessee	November 13, 1819
McMinn	Tennessee	November 13, 1819
Monroe	Tennessee	November 13, 1819
Shelby	Tennessee	November 24, 1819
Butler	Alabama	December 13, 1819
Greene	Alabama	December 13, 1819

Henry	Alabama	December 13, 1819
Jackson	Alabama	December 13, 1819
Jefferson	Alabama	December 13, 1819
Perry	Alabama	December 13, 1819
Wilcox	Alabama	December 13, 1819
Rabun	Georgia	December 21, 1819
Todd	Kentucky	December 30, 1819
Union	Ohio	January 10, 1820
Scott	Indiana	January 12, 1820
Martin	Indiana	January 17, 1820
Monroe	Kentucky	January 19, 1820
Trigg	Kentucky	January 27, 1820
Perry	Mississippi	February 3, 1820
Morgan	West Virginia	February 9, 1820
Allen	Ohio	February 12, 1820
Crawford	Ohio	February 12, 1820
Grant	Kentucky	February 12, 1820
Hancock	Ohio	February 12, 1820
Hardin	Ohio	February 12, 1820
Henry	Ohio	February 12, 1820
Marion	Ohio	February 12, 1820
Mercer	Ohio	February 12, 1820
Paulding	Ohio	February 12, 1820
Putnam	Ohio	February 12, 1820
Sandusky	Ohio	February 12, 1820
Seneca	Ohio	February 12, 1820
Van Wert	Ohio	February 12, 1820
Williams	Ohio	February 12, 1820
Wood	Ohio	February 12, 1820
Perry	Pennsylvania	March 22, 1820
Saint Clair	Michigan	March 28, 1820
Phillips	Arkansas	May 1, 1820
Crawford	Arkansas	October 18, 1820
Independence	Arkansas	October 23, 1820
Perry	Kentucky	November 2, 1820
Boone	Missouri	November 16, 1820
Chariton	Missouri	November 16, 1820
Cole	Missouri	November 16, 1820
Lafayette	Missouri	November 16, 1820
Perry	Missouri	November 16, 1820
Ralls	Missouri	November 16, 1820
Ray	Missouri	November 16, 1820
Callaway	Missouri	November 25, 1820
Gasconade	Missouri	November 25, 1820
Saline	Missouri	November 25, 1820
Pickens	Alabama	December 19, 1820
Greene	Indiana	January 5, 1821
Union	Indiana	January 5, 1821
Bartholomew	Indiana	January 8, 1821
Parke	Indiana	January 9, 1821
Lawrence	Illinois	January 16, 1821
Greene	Illinois	January 20, 1821
Sangamon	Illinois	January 30, 1821

Pike	Illinois	January 31, 1821
Hamilton	Illinois	February 8, 1821
Monroe	Mississippi	February 9, 1821
Hinds	Mississippi	February 12, 1821
Montgomery	Illinois	February 12, 1821
Fayette	Illinois	February 14, 1821
Livingston	New York	February 23, 1821
Monroe	New York	February 23, 1821
Erie	New York	April 2, 1821
Dooly	Georgia	May 15, 1821
Fayette	Georgia	May 15, 1821
Henry	Georgia	May 15, 1821
Houston	Georgia	May 15, 1821
Monroe	Georgia	May 15, 1821
Escambia	Florida	July 21, 1821
Carroll	Tennessee	November 7, 1821
Henderson	Tennessee	November 7, 1821
Henry	Tennessee	November 7, 1821
Madison	Tennessee	November 7, 1821
Covington	Alabama	December 7, 1821
Lawrence	Kentucky	December 14, 1821
Pike	Alabama	December 17, 1821
Calloway	Kentucky	December 19, 1821
Graves	Kentucky	December 19, 1821
Hickman	Kentucky	December 19, 1821
Pike	Kentucky	December 19, 1821
Saint Francois	Missouri	December 19, 1821
Pocahontas	West Virginia	December 21, 1821
Newton	Georgia	December 24, 1821
Scott	Missouri	December 28, 1821
Decatur	Indiana	December 31, 1821
Henry	Indiana	December 31, 1821
Marion	Indiana	December 31, 1821
Morgan	Indiana	December 31, 1821
Putnam	Indiana	December 31, 1821
Rush	Indiana	December 31, 1821
Shelby	Indiana	December 31, 1821
Clay	Missouri	January 2, 1822
Alleghany	Virginia	January 5, 1822
Terrebonne	Louisiana	March 22, 1822
Duval	Florida	August 12, 1822
Jackson	Florida	August 12, 1822
Saint Johns	Florida	August 12, 1822
Lapeer	Michigan	September 10, 1822
Lenawee	Michigan	September 10, 1822
Saginaw	Michigan	September 10, 1822
Sanilac	Michigan	September 10, 1822
Shiawassee	Michigan	September 10, 1822
Washtenaw	Michigan	September 10, 1822
Morgan	Kentucky	December 7, 1822
Bibb	Georgia	December 9, 1822
Crawford	Georgia	December 9, 1822
Davidson	North Carolina	December 9, 1822
DeKalb	Georgia	December 9, 1822

Pike	Georgia	December 9, 1822
Marion	Missouri	December 14, 1822
Montgomery	Indiana	December 21, 1822
Lorain	Ohio	December 26, 1822
Johnson	Indiana	December 31, 1822
Edgar	Illinois	January 3, 1823
Madison	Indiana	January 4, 1823
Hamilton	Indiana	January 8, 1823
Lafayette	Louisiana	January 17, 1823
Copiah	Mississippi	January 21, 1823
Yazoo	Mississippi	January 21, 1823
Marion	Illinois	January 24, 1823
Fulton	Illinois	January 28, 1823
Morgan	Illinois	January 31, 1823
Yates	New York	February 5, 1823
Wayne	New York	April 11, 1823
Gadsden	Florida	June 24, 1823
Merrimack	New Hampshire	July 1, 1823
Monroe	Florida	July 3, 1823
McNairy	Tennessee	October 8, 1823
Dyer	Tennessee	October 16, 1823
Hardeman	Tennessee	October 16, 1823
Gibson	Tennessee	October 21, 1823
Weakley	Tennessee	October 21, 1823
Obion	Tennessee	October 24, 1823
Chicot	Arkansas	October 25, 1823
Tipton	Tennessee	October 29, 1823
Haywood	Tennessee	November 3, 1823
Fentress	Tennessee	November 28, 1823
Decatur	Georgia	December 8, 1823
Oldham	Kentucky	December 15, 1823
Allen	Indiana	December 17, 1823
Meade	Kentucky	December 17, 1823
Hendricks	Indiana	December 20, 1823
Walker	Alabama	December 26, 1823
Vermillion	Indiana	January 2, 1824
Spencer	Kentucky	January 7, 1824
Logan	West Virginia	January 12, 1824
Holmes	Ohio	January 20, 1824
Simpson	Mississippi	January 23, 1824
East Feliciana	Louisiana	February 17, 1824
West Feliciana	Louisiana	February 17, 1824
Fayette	Tennessee	September 29, 1824
Orleans	New York	November 12, 1824
Warren	New Jersey	November 20, 1824
Upson	Georgia	December 15, 1824
Ware	Georgia	December 15, 1824
McCracken	Kentucky	December 17, 1824
Fayette	Alabama	December 20, 1824
Dale	Alabama	December 22, 1824
Clay	Illinois	December 23, 1824
Clinton	Illinois	December 27, 1824
Wabash	Illinois	December 27, 1824

Alachua	Florida	December 29, 1824
Leon	Florida	December 29, 1824
Nassau	Florida	December 29, 1824
Orange	Florida	December 29, 1824
Walton	Florida	December 29, 1824
Calhoun	Illinois	January 10, 1825
Edmonson	Kentucky	January 12, 1825
Adams	Illinois	January 13, 1825
Hancock	Illinois	January 13, 1825
Henry	Illinois	January 13, 1825
Knox	Illinois	January 13, 1825
Mercer	Illinois	January 13, 1825
Peoria	Illinois	January 13, 1825
Putnam	Illinois	January 13, 1825
Schuyler	Illinois	January 13, 1825
Warren	Illinois	January 13, 1825
Jefferson	Louisiana	February 11, 1825
Clay	Indiana	February 12, 1825
Conway	Arkansas	October 20, 1825
Crittenden	Arkansas	October 22, 1825
Izard	Arkansas	October 27, 1825
Washington	Florida	December 9, 1825
Baker	Georgia	December 12, 1825
Laurel	Kentucky	December 12, 1825
Russell	Kentucky	December 14, 1825
Fountain	Indiana	December 20, 1825
Lowndes	Georgia	December 23, 1825
Thomas	Georgia	December 23, 1825
Butts	Georgia	December 24, 1825
Taliaferro	Georgia	December 24, 1825
Vermilion	Illinois	January 18, 1826
Tippecanoe	Indiana	January 20, 1826
Jones	Mississippi	January 24, 1826
McDonough	Illinois	January 25, 1826
Carroll	Georgia	December 11, 1826
Coweta	Georgia	December 11, 1826
Lee	Georgia	December 11, 1826
Muscogee	Georgia	December 11, 1826
Troup	Georgia	December 11, 1826
Jackson	Missouri	December 15, 1826
Anderson	South Carolina	December 20, 1826
Pickens	South Carolina	December 20, 1826
Chippewa	Michigan	December 22, 1826
Jefferson	Florida	January 6, 1827
Anderson	Kentucky	January 16, 1827
Warren	Indiana	January 19, 1827
Shelby	Illinois	January 23, 1827
Delaware	Indiana	January 26, 1827
Hancock	Indiana	January 26, 1827
Perry	Illinois	January 29, 1827
Washington	Mississippi	January 29, 1827
Tazewell	Illinois	January 31, 1827

Waldo	Maine	February 7, 1827
Jo Daviess	Illinois	February 17, 1827
Sullivan	New Hampshire	July 5, 1827
Saint Francis	Arkansas	October 13, 1827
Lafayette	Arkansas	October 15, 1827
Harris	Georgia	December 14, 1827
Talbot	Georgia	December 14, 1827
Marion	Georgia	December 24, 1827
Meriwether	Georgia	December 24, 1827
Hamilton	Florida	December 26, 1827
Madison	Florida	December 26, 1827
Carroll	Indiana	January 7, 1828
Madison	Mississippi	January 29, 1828
Rankin	Mississippi	February 4, 1828
Claiborne	Louisiana	March 13, 1828
Sevier	Arkansas	October 17, 1828
Washington	Arkansas	October 17, 1828
Cass	Indiana	December 18, 1828
Randolph	Georgia	December 20, 1828
Macon	North Carolina	1828
Hancock	Kentucky	January 3, 1829
Macoupin	Illinois	January 17, 1829
Macon	Illinois	January 19, 1829
Randolph	Missouri	January 22, 1829
Crawford	Missouri	January 23, 1829
Iowa	Wisconsin	October 9, 1829
Barry	Michigan	October 29, 1829
Berrien	Michigan	October 29, 1829
Branch	Michigan	October 29, 1829
Calhoun	Michigan	October 29, 1829
Cass	Michigan	October 29, 1829
Eaton	Michigan	October 29, 1829
Hillsdale	Michigan	October 29, 1829
Ingham	Michigan	October 29, 1829
Jackson	Michigan	October 29, 1829
Kalamazoo	Michigan	October 29, 1829
Saint Joseph	Michigan	October 29, 1829
Van Buren	Michigan	October 29, 1829
Hot Spring	Arkansas	November 2, 1829
Jefferson	Arkansas	November 2, 1829
Monroe	Arkansas	November 2, 1829
Pope	Arkansas	November 2, 1829
Union	Arkansas	November 2, 1829
Jackson	Arkansas	November 5, 1829
Lowndes	Alabama	January 20, 1830
Boone	Indiana	January 29, 1830
Clinton	Indiana	January 29, 1830
Elkhart	Indiana	January 29, 1830
Saint Joseph	Indiana	January 29, 1830
Lowndes	Mississippi	January 30, 1830
Heard	Georgia	December 22, 1830
Stewart	Georgia	December 23, 1830

Coles	Illinois	December 25, 1830
McLean	Illinois	December 25, 1830
Monroe	Missouri	January 6, 1831
Audrain	Missouri	January 12, 1831
Cook	Illinois	January 15, 1831
Floyd	Virginia	January 15, 1831
La Salle	Illinois	January 15, 1831
Rock Island	Illinois	February 9, 1831
Grant	Indiana	February 10, 1831
Effingham	Illinois	February 15, 1831
Jasper	Illinois	February 15, 1831
Fayette	West Virginia	February 28, 1831
Jackson	West Virginia	March 1, 1831
Allegan	Michigan	March 2, 1831
Arenac	Michigan	March 2, 1831
Clinton	Michigan	March 2, 1831
Gladwin	Michigan	March 2, 1831
Gratiot	Michigan	March 2, 1831
Ionia	Michigan	March 2, 1831
Isabella	Michigan	March 2, 1831
Juniata	Pennsylvania	March 2, 1831
Kent	Michigan	March 2, 1831
Midland	Michigan	March 2, 1831
Montcalm	Michigan	March 2, 1831
Oceana	Michigan	March 2, 1831
Ottawa	Michigan	March 2, 1831
Page	Virginia	March 30, 1831
Cherokee	Georgia	December 26, 1831
Sumter	Georgia	December 26, 1831
LaPorte	Indiana	January 9, 1832
Huntington	Indiana	February 2, 1832
LaGrange	Indiana	February 2, 1832
Miami	Indiana	February 2, 1832
Wabash	Indiana	February 2, 1832
Columbia	Florida	February 4, 1832
Franklin	Florida	February 8, 1832
Livingston	Louisiana	February 10, 1832
Smyth	Virginia	February 23, 1832
Bartow	Georgia	December 3, 1832
Cobb	Georgia	December 3, 1832
Floyd	Georgia	December 3, 1832
Forsyth	Georgia	December 3, 1832
Gilmer	Georgia	December 3, 1832
Lumpkin	Georgia	December 3, 1832
Murray	Georgia	December 3, 1832
Paulding	Georgia	December 3, 1832
Union	Georgia	December 3, 1832
Barbour	Alabama	December 18, 1832
Calhoun	Alabama	December 18, 1832
Chambers	Alabama	December 18, 1832
Coosa	Alabama	December 18, 1832
Macon	Alabama	December 18, 1832
Randolph	Alabama	December 18, 1832

Russell	Alabama	December 18, 1832
Sumter	Alabama	December 18, 1832
Talladega	Alabama	December 18, 1832
Tallapoosa	Alabama	December 18, 1832
Carroll	Ohio	December 25, 1832
Carroll	Missouri	January 2, 1833
Clinton	Missouri	January 2, 1833
Greene	Missouri	January 2, 1833
Lewis	Missouri	January 2, 1833
Morgan	Missouri	January 5, 1833
Ripley	Missouri	January 5, 1833
Warren	Missouri	January 5, 1833
Saint Clair	Missouri	January 16, 1833
Pulaski	Missouri	January 19, 1833
Pettis	Missouri	January 26, 1833
Rappahannock	Virginia	February 8, 1833
Holmes	Mississippi	February 19, 1833
Champaign	Illinois	February 20, 1833
Iroquois	Illinois	February 26, 1833
Livingston	Michigan	March 21, 1833
Carroll	Arkansas	November 1, 1833
Mississippi	Arkansas	November 1, 1833
Pike	Arkansas	November 1, 1833
Greene	Arkansas	November 5, 1833
Scott	Arkansas	November 5, 1833
Van Buren	Arkansas	November 11, 1833
Johnson	Arkansas	November 16, 1833
Walker	Georgia	December 18, 1833
Attala	Mississippi	December 23, 1833
Carroll	Mississippi	December 23, 1833
Choctaw	Mississippi	December 23, 1833
Clarke	Mississippi	December 23, 1833
Jasper	Mississippi	December 23, 1833
Kemper	Mississippi	December 23, 1833
Lauderdale	Mississippi	December 23, 1833
Leake	Mississippi	December 23, 1833
Neshoba	Mississippi	December 23, 1833
Noxubee	Mississippi	December 23, 1833
Oktibbeha	Mississippi	December 23, 1833
Scott	Mississippi	December 23, 1833
Smith	Mississippi	December 23, 1833
Tallahatchie	Mississippi	December 23, 1833
Winston	Mississippi	December 23, 1833
Yalobusha	Mississippi	December 23, 1833
Yancey	North Carolina	1833
Hillsborough	Florida	January 25, 1834
Marion	Kentucky	January 25, 1834
White	Indiana	February 1, 1834
Des Moines	Iowa	September 6, 1834
Dubuque	Iowa	September 6, 1834
Milwaukee	Wisconsin	September 6, 1834
Henry	Missouri	December 13, 1834
Johnson	Missouri	December 13, 1834

Shelby	Missouri	January 2, 1835
Stoddard	Missouri	January 2, 1835
Benton	Missouri	January 3, 1835
Barry	Missouri	January 5, 1835
Polk	Missouri	January 5, 1835
Adams	Indiana	February 7, 1835
DeKalb	Indiana	February 7, 1835
Fulton	Indiana	February 7, 1835
Jasper	Indiana	February 7, 1835
Jay	Indiana	February 7, 1835
Kosciusko	Indiana	February 7, 1835
Marshall	Indiana	February 7, 1835
Newton	Indiana	February 7, 1835
Noble	Indiana	February 7, 1835
Porter	Indiana	February 7, 1835
Pulaski	Indiana	February 7, 1835
Starke	Indiana	February 7, 1835
Steuben	Indiana	February 7, 1835
Wells	Indiana	February 7, 1835
Whitley	Indiana	February 7, 1835
Cass	Missouri	March 3, 1835
Marshall	West Virginia	March 12, 1835
Genesee	Michigan	March 28, 1835
Lucas	Ohio	June 20, 1835
White	Arkansas	October 23, 1835
Lamoille	Vermont	October 26, 1835
Randolph	Arkansas	October 29, 1835
Saline	Arkansas	November 2, 1835
Marion	Arkansas	November 3, 1835
Lauderdale	Tennessee	November 24, 1835
Benton	Tennessee	December 19, 1835
Johnson	Tennessee	January 2, 1836
Coffee	Tennessee	January 8, 1836
Cherokee	Alabama	January 9, 1836
DeKalb	Alabama	January 9, 1836
Marshall	Alabama	January 9, 1836
Will	Illinois	January 12, 1836
Braxton	West Virginia	January 15, 1836
Kane	Illinois	January 16, 1836
McHenry	Illinois	January 16, 1836
Ogle	Illinois	January 16, 1836
Whiteside	Illinois	January 16, 1836
Winnebago	Illinois	January 16, 1836
Meigs	Tennessee	January 20, 1836
Lake	Indiana	January 28, 1836
Cannon	Tennessee	January 31, 1836
Brown	Indiana	February 4, 1836
Miami-Dade	Florida	February 4, 1836
Bolivar	Mississippi	February 9, 1836
Chickasaw	Mississippi	February 9, 1836
Coahoma	Mississippi	February 9, 1836
DeSoto	Mississippi	February 9, 1836
Itawamba	Mississippi	February 9, 1836
Lafayette	Mississippi	February 9, 1836

Marshall	Mississippi	February 9, 1836
Panola	Mississippi	February 9, 1836
Pontotoc	Mississippi	February 9, 1836
Tippah	Mississippi	February 9, 1836
Tishomingo	Mississippi	February 9, 1836
Tunica	Mississippi	February 9, 1836
Bradley	Tennessee	February 10, 1836
Clinton	Kentucky	February 20, 1836
Marshall	Tennessee	February 20, 1836
Newton	Mississippi	February 25, 1836
Clarke	Virginia	March 8, 1836
Warren	Virginia	March 9, 1836
Austin	Texas	March 17, 1836
Bastrop	Texas	March 17, 1836
Bexar	Texas	March 17, 1836
Brazoria	Texas	March 17, 1836
Colorado	Texas	March 17, 1836
Goliad	Texas	March 17, 1836
Gonzales	Texas	March 17, 1836
Harris	Texas	March 17, 1836
Jackson	Texas	March 17, 1836
Jasper	Texas	March 17, 1836
Jefferson	Texas	March 17, 1836
Liberty	Texas	March 17, 1836
Matagorda	Texas	March 17, 1836
Milam	Texas	March 17, 1836
Nacogdoches	Texas	March 17, 1836
Red River	Texas	March 17, 1836
Refugio	Texas	March 17, 1836
Sabine	Texas	March 17, 1836
San Augustine	Texas	March 17, 1836
San Patricio	Texas	March 17, 1836
Shelby	Texas	March 17, 1836
Victoria	Texas	March 17, 1836
Washington	Texas	March 17, 1836
Chemung	New York	March 29, 1836
Monroe	Pennsylvania	April 1, 1836
Benton	Arkansas	September 30, 1836
Madison	Arkansas	September 30, 1836
Calumet	Wisconsin	December 7, 1836
Dane	Wisconsin	December 7, 1836
Dodge	Wisconsin	December 7, 1836
Fond du Lac	Wisconsin	December 7, 1836
Henry	Iowa	December 7, 1836
Jefferson	Wisconsin	December 7, 1836
Lee	Iowa	December 7, 1836
Louisa	Iowa	December 7, 1836
Manitowoc	Wisconsin	December 7, 1836
Marquette	Wisconsin	December 7, 1836
Muscatine	Iowa	December 7, 1836
Portage	Wisconsin	December 7, 1836
Racine	Wisconsin	December 7, 1836
Rock	Wisconsin	December 7, 1836
Sheboygan	Wisconsin	December 7, 1836
Van Buren	Iowa	December 7, 1836

Walworth	Wisconsin	December 7, 1836
Washington	Wisconsin	December 7, 1836
Grant	Wisconsin	December 8, 1836
Green	Wisconsin	December 8, 1836
Clark	Missouri	December 16, 1836
Davie	North Carolina	December 20, 1836
Caldwell	Missouri	December 29, 1836
Daviess	Missouri	December 29, 1836
Linn	Missouri	January 6, 1837
Livingston	Missouri	January 6, 1837
Macon	Missouri	January 6, 1837
Taney	Missouri	January 6, 1837
Washington	Iowa	January 16, 1837
Carroll	Maryland	January 19, 1837
Miller	Missouri	February 6, 1837
Atlantic	New Jersey	February 7, 1837
Passaic	New Jersey	February 7, 1837
Trimble	Kentucky	February 9, 1837
Livingston	Illinois	February 27, 1837
Bureau	Illinois	February 28, 1837
Cass	Illinois	March 3, 1837
Boone	Illinois	March 4, 1837
DeKalb	Illinois	March 4, 1837
Stephenson	Illinois	March 4, 1837
Mercer	West Virginia	March 17, 1837
Houston	Texas	June 12, 1837
DeKalb	Tennessee	December 11, 1837
Fannin	Texas	December 14, 1837
Fayette	Texas	December 14, 1837
Macon	Georgia	December 14, 1837
Montgomery	Texas	December 14, 1837
Robertson	Texas	December 14, 1837
Franklin	Arkansas	December 19, 1837
Benton	Iowa	December 21, 1837
Buchanan	Iowa	December 21, 1837
Cedar	Iowa	December 21, 1837
Clayton	Iowa	December 21, 1837
Clinton	Iowa	December 21, 1837
Delaware	Iowa	December 21, 1837
Fayette	Iowa	December 21, 1837
Jackson	Iowa	December 21, 1837
Johnson	Iowa	December 21, 1837
Jones	Iowa	December 21, 1837
Keokuk	Iowa	December 21, 1837
Linn	Iowa	December 21, 1837
Scott	Iowa	December 21, 1837
Dade	Georgia	December 25, 1837
Fort Bend	Texas	December 29, 1837
Caddo	Louisiana	January 18, 1838
Madison	Louisiana	January 19, 1838
Greene	Virginia	January 24, 1838
Calhoun	Florida	January 26, 1838
Carroll	Kentucky	February 9, 1838

Carter	Kentucky	February 9, 1838
Blackford	Indiana	February 15, 1838
Mercer	New Jersey	February 22, 1838
Poinsett	Arkansas	February 28, 1838
Caldwell	Louisiana	March 6, 1838
Erie	Ohio	March 15, 1838
Franklin	Maine	March 20, 1838
Piscataquis	Maine	March 23, 1838
Roanoke	Virginia	March 30, 1838
Fulton	New York	April 18, 1838
Galveston	Texas	May 15, 1838
Desha	Arkansas	December 12, 1838
Searcy	Arkansas	December 13, 1838
Henderson	North Carolina	December 15, 1838
Chattooga	Georgia	December 28, 1838
Newton	Missouri	December 30, 1838
Buchanan	Missouri	December 31, 1838
Platte	Missouri	December 31, 1838
Cherokee	North Carolina	January 4, 1839
Marshall	Illinois	January 19, 1839
Jefferson	Iowa	January 21, 1839
Harrison	Texas	January 28, 1839
Brown	Illinois	February 1, 1839
Breathitt	Kentucky	February 8, 1839
DuPage	Illinois	February 9, 1839
Christian	Illinois	February 15, 1839
Logan	Illinois	February 15, 1839
Menard	Illinois	February 15, 1839
Scott	Illinois	February 16, 1839
Carroll	Illinois	February 22, 1839
Lee	Illinois	February 27, 1839
Jersey	Illinois	February 28, 1839
Williamson	Illinois	February 28, 1839
De Witt	Illinois	March 1, 1839
Lake	Illinois	March 1, 1839
Hardin	Illinois	March 2, 1839
Stark	Illinois	March 2, 1839
Clarion	Pennsylvania	March 11, 1839
Union	Louisiana	March 13, 1839
Aroostook	Maine	March 16, 1839
Pulaski	Virginia	March 30, 1839
Clinton	Pennsylvania	June 21, 1839
Polk	Tennessee	November 28, 1839
Van Buren	Tennessee	January 3, 1840
Winnebago	Wisconsin	January 6, 1840
Saint Croix	Wisconsin	January 9, 1840
Sauk	Wisconsin	January 11, 1840
Travis	Texas	January 25, 1840
Kenton	Kentucky	January 29, 1840
Benton	Indiana	February 18, 1840
Hudson	New Jersey	February 22, 1840
Summit	Ohio	March 3, 1840
Lake	Ohio	March 6, 1840

Ottawa	Ohio	March 6, 1840
Calcasieu	Louisiana	March 24, 1840
Alcona	Michigan	April 1, 1840
Alpena	Michigan	April 1, 1840
Antrim	Michigan	April 1, 1840
Charlevoix	Michigan	April 1, 1840
Cheboygan	Michigan	April 1, 1840
Clare	Michigan	April 1, 1840
Crawford	Michigan	April 1, 1840
Emmet	Michigan	April 1, 1840
Huron	Michigan	April 1, 1840
Iosco	Michigan	April 1, 1840
Kalkaska	Michigan	April 1, 1840
Lake	Michigan	April 1, 1840
Leelanau	Michigan	April 1, 1840
Manistee	Michigan	April 1, 1840
Mason	Michigan	April 1, 1840
Mecosta	Michigan	April 1, 1840
Missaukee	Michigan	April 1, 1840
Montmorency	Michigan	April 1, 1840
Newaygo	Michigan	April 1, 1840
Ogemaw	Michigan	April 1, 1840
Osceola	Michigan	April 1, 1840
Oscoda	Michigan	April 1, 1840
Otsego	Michigan	April 1, 1840
Presque Isle	Michigan	April 1, 1840
Roscommon	Michigan	April 1, 1840
Tuscola	Michigan	April 1, 1840
Wexford	Michigan	April 1, 1840
Yell	Arkansas	December 5, 1840
Bowie	Texas	December 17, 1840
Lamar	Texas	December 17, 1840
Bradley	Arkansas	December 18, 1840
Perry	Arkansas	December 18, 1840
Belknap	New Hampshire	December 22, 1840
Carroll	New Hampshire	December 22, 1840
Caldwell	North Carolina	January 11, 1841
Cleveland	North Carolina	January 11, 1841
Stanly	North Carolina	January 11, 1841
Henderson	Illinois	January 20, 1841
Mason	Illinois	January 20, 1841
Piatt	Illinois	January 27, 1841
Adair	Missouri	January 29, 1841
Andrew	Missouri	January 29, 1841
Bates	Missouri	January 29, 1841
Camden	Missouri	January 29, 1841
Dade	Missouri	January 29, 1841
Dallas	Missouri	January 29, 1841
Grundy	Missouri	January 29, 1841
Holt	Missouri	January 29, 1841
Jasper	Missouri	January 29, 1841
Osage	Missouri	January 29, 1841
Ozark	Missouri	January 29, 1841
Scotland	Missouri	January 29, 1841

Shannon	Missouri	January 29, 1841
Wright	Missouri	January 29, 1841
Brazos	Texas	January 30, 1841
Harrison	Mississippi	February 5, 1841
Grundy	Illinois	February 7, 1841
Gentry	Missouri	February 12, 1841
Kendall	Illinois	February 19, 1841
Richland	Illinois	February 24, 1841
Woodford	Illinois	February 27, 1841
Wyoming	New York	May 19, 1841
Coffee	Alabama	December 29, 1841
Marion	West Virginia	January 14, 1842
Carroll	Virginia	January 17, 1842
Macon	Tennessee	January 18, 1842
Wayne	West Virginia	January 18, 1842
Crittenden	Kentucky	January 26, 1842
Putnam	Tennessee	February 2, 1842
Marshall	Kentucky	February 12, 1842
Ballard	Kentucky	February 15, 1842
Boyle	Kentucky	February 15, 1842
Richland	Wisconsin	February 18, 1842
Santa Rosa	Florida	February 18, 1842
Letcher	Kentucky	March 3, 1842
Wyoming	Pennsylvania	April 4, 1842
Ouachita	Arkansas	November 29, 1842
Montgomery	Arkansas	December 9, 1842
Catawba	North Carolina	December 12, 1842
Newton	Arkansas	December 14, 1842
McDowell	North Carolina	December 19, 1842
Union	North Carolina	December 19, 1842
Fulton	Arkansas	December 21, 1842
Nodaway	Missouri	January 2, 1843
Rusk	Texas	January 16, 1843
Owsley	Kentucky	January 23, 1843
Massac	Illinois	February 8, 1843
Moultrie	Illinois	February 16, 1843
Appanoose	Iowa	February 17, 1843
Black Hawk	Iowa	February 17, 1843
Davis	Iowa	February 17, 1843
Iowa	Iowa	February 17, 1843
Mahaska	Iowa	February 17, 1843
Monroe	Iowa	February 17, 1843
Poweshiek	Iowa	February 17, 1843
Sullivan	Missouri	February 17, 1843
Tama	Iowa	February 17, 1843
Texas	Missouri	February 17, 1843
Wapello	Iowa	February 17, 1843
Ritchie	West Virginia	February 18, 1843
Putnam	Missouri	February 22, 1843
Atchison	Missouri	February 23, 1843
Bossier	Louisiana	February 24, 1843
Hernando	Florida	February 24, 1843
Johnson	Kentucky	February 24, 1843

Franklin	Louisiana	March 1, 1843
Cumberland	Illinois	March 2, 1843
Barbour	West Virginia	March 3, 1843
Pulaski	Illinois	March 3, 1843
Larue	Kentucky	March 4, 1843
Sabine	Louisiana	March 7, 1843
Delta	Michigan	March 9, 1843
Marquette	Michigan	March 9, 1843
Ontonagon	Michigan	March 9, 1843
Schoolcraft	Michigan	March 9, 1843
Wakulla	Florida	March 11, 1843
Carbon	Pennsylvania	March 13, 1843
Tensas	Louisiana	March 17, 1843
De Soto	Louisiana	April 1, 1843
Elk	Pennsylvania	April 18, 1843
Clackamas	Oregon	July 5, 1843
Marion	Oregon	July 5, 1843
Washington	Oregon	July 5, 1843
Yamhill	Oregon	July 5, 1843
Lewis	Tennessee	December 21, 1843
Ohio	Indiana	January 4, 1844
Hancock	Tennessee	January 7, 1844
Howard	Indiana	January 15, 1844
Tipton	Indiana	January 15, 1844
Taylor	West Virginia	January 19, 1844
Issaquena	Mississippi	January 23, 1844
Grundy	Tennessee	January 29, 1844
Sunflower	Mississippi	February 15, 1844
Camden	New Jersey	March 13, 1844
Brevard	Florida	March 14, 1844
Marion	Florida	March 14, 1844
Morehouse	Louisiana	March 25, 1844
Vermilion	Louisiana	March 25, 1844
Clatsop	Oregon	June 22, 1844
Clark	Washington	June 27, 1844
Polk	Arkansas	November 30, 1844
Dallas	Arkansas	January 1, 1845
Fulton	Kentucky	January 15, 1845
Chippewa	Wisconsin	February 3, 1845
Gilmer	West Virginia	February 3, 1845
Wyandot	Ohio	February 3, 1845
Doddrodge	West Virginia	February 4, 1845
Appomattox	Virginia	February 8, 1845
Norfolk (IC)	Virginia	February 11, 1845
Cedar	Missouri	February 14, 1845
Dunklin	Missouri	February 14, 1845
Harrison	Missouri	February 14, 1845
Hickory	Missouri	February 14, 1845
Knox	Missouri	February 14, 1845
Lawrence	Missouri	February 14, 1845
Mercer	Missouri	February 14, 1845
Mississippi	Missouri	February 14, 1845
Moniteau	Missouri	February 14, 1845

Oregon	Missouri	February 14, 1845
Schuyler	Missouri	February 14, 1845
Bayfield	Wisconsin	February 19, 1845
DeKalb	Missouri	February 25, 1845
Reynolds	Missouri	February 25, 1845
Jackson	Louisiana	February 27, 1845
Defiance	Ohio	March 4, 1845
Levy	Florida	March 10, 1845
Houghton	Michigan	March 19, 1845
Marion	Iowa	June 10, 1845
Decatur	Tennessee	November, 1845
Crockett	Tennessee	December 20, 1845
Lewis	Washington	December 21, 1845
Polk	Oregon	December 22, 1845
Wetzel	West Virginia	January 10, 1846
Boone	Iowa	January 13, 1846
Clarke	Iowa	January 13, 1846
Dallas	Iowa	January 13, 1846
Decatur	Iowa	January 13, 1846
Jasper	Iowa	January 13, 1846
Lucas	Iowa	January 13, 1846
Madison	Iowa	January 13, 1846
Marshall	Iowa	January 13, 1846
Polk	Iowa	January 13, 1846
Story	Iowa	January 13, 1846
Warren	Iowa	January 13, 1846
Wayne	Iowa	January 13, 1846
Lafayette	Wisconsin	January 31, 1846
Waukesha	Wisconsin	January 31, 1846
Columbia	Wisconsin	February 3, 1846
Mahoning	Ohio	February 16, 1846
Ashland	Ohio	February 24, 1846
Blair	Pennsylvania	February 26, 1846
Grayson	Texas	March 17, 1846
Leon	Texas	March 17, 1846
Anderson	Texas	March 24, 1846
Burleson	Texas	March 24, 1846
Comal	Texas	March 24, 1846
DeWitt	Texas	March 24, 1846
Hopkins	Texas	March 25, 1846
Dallas	Texas	March 30, 1846
Guadalupe	Texas	March 30, 1846
Panola	Texas	March 30, 1846
Polk	Texas	March 30, 1846
Collin	Texas	April 3, 1846
Tyler	Texas	April 3, 1846
Wharton	Texas	April 3, 1846
Calhoun	Texas	April 4, 1846
Grimes	Texas	April 6, 1846
Lavaca	Texas	April 6, 1846
Walker	Texas	April 6, 1846
Cherokee	Texas	April 11, 1846
Denton	Texas	April 11, 1846
Hunt	Texas	April 11, 1846

Limestone	Texas	April 11, 1846
Smith	Texas	April 11, 1846
Nueces	Texas	April 18, 1846
Angelina	Texas	April 22, 1846
Newton	Texas	April 22, 1846
Cass	Texas	April 25, 1846
Navarro	Texas	April 25, 1846
Henderson	Texas	April 27, 1846
Upshur	Texas	April 27, 1846
Titus	Texas	May 11, 1846
Prairie	Arkansas	November 25, 1846
Drew	Arkansas	November 26, 1846
Gaston	North Carolina	December 21, 1846
Alexander	North Carolina	January 15, 1847
Polk	North Carolina	January 18, 1847
Allamakee	Iowa	February 20, 1847
Winnebago	Iowa	February 20, 1847
Winneshiek	Iowa	February 20, 1847
Fremont	Iowa	February 24, 1847
Page	Iowa	February 24, 1847
Ringgold	Iowa	February 24, 1847
Taylor	Iowa	February 24, 1847
Saline	Illinois	February 25, 1847
Boone	West Virginia	March 11, 1847
Arlington	Virginia	March 13, 1847
Sullivan	Pennsylvania	March 15, 1847
Highland	Virginia	March 19, 1847
Benton	Oregon	December 23, 1847
Linn	Oregon	December 28, 1847
Choctaw	Alabama	December 29, 1847
Holmes	Florida	January 8, 1848
Taylor	Kentucky	January 13, 1848
Hancock	West Virginia	January 15, 1848
Wirt	West Virginia	January 19, 1848
Webb	Texas	January 28, 1848
Starr	Texas	February 10, 1848
Cameron	Texas	February 12, 1848
Medina	Texas	February 12, 1848
Auglaize	Ohio	February 14, 1848
Gillespie	Texas	February 23, 1848
Morrow	Ohio	February 24, 1848
Kaufman	Texas	February 26, 1848
Hays	Texas	March 1, 1848
Caldwell	Texas	March 6, 1848
Adams	Wisconsin	March 11, 1848
Putnam	West Virginia	March 11, 1848
Williamson	Texas	March 13, 1848
Bienville	Louisiana	March 14, 1848
Cooke	Texas	March 20, 1848
Van Zandt	Texas	March 20, 1848
Forest	Pennsylvania	April 11, 1848
Ashley	Arkansas	November 30, 1848

Putnam	Florida	January 13, 1849
Forsyth	North Carolina	January 16, 1849
Watauga	North Carolina	January 27, 1849
Alamance	North Carolina	January 29, 1849
Laclede	Missouri	February 24, 1849
Butler	Missouri	February 27, 1849
McDonald	Missouri	March 3, 1849
Hampton	Virginia	March 19, 1849
Lawrence	Pennsylvania	March 20, 1849
Benton	Minnesota	October 27, 1849
Dakota	Minnesota	October 27, 1849
Itasca	Minnesota	October 27, 1849
Kittson	Minnesota	October 27, 1849
Ramsey	Minnesota	October 27, 1849
Wabasha	Minnesota	October 27, 1849
Washington	Minnesota	October 27, 1849
Scott	Tennessee	December 17, 1849
Ellis	Texas	December 20, 1849
Tarrant	Texas	December 20, 1849
El Paso	Texas	January 3, 1850
Presidio	Texas	January 3, 1850
Union	Tennessee	January 3, 1850
Bell	Texas	January 22, 1850
McLennan	Texas	January 22, 1850
Raleigh	West Virginia	January 23, 1850
Wyoming	West Virginia	January 26, 1850
Falls	Texas	January 28, 1850
Kinney	Texas	January 28, 1850
Kenosha	Wisconsin	January 30, 1850
Iron	Utah	January 31, 1850
Wood	Texas	February 5, 1850
Uvalde	Texas	February 8, 1850
Marathon	Wisconsin	February 9, 1850
Trinity	Texas	February 11, 1850
Winston	Alabama	February 12, 1850
Gordon	Georgia	February 13, 1850
Clinch	Georgia	February 14, 1850
Ocean	New Jersey	February 15, 1850
Butte	California	February 18, 1850
Calaveras	California	February 18, 1850
Colusa	California	February 18, 1850
Contra Costa	California	February 18, 1850
El Dorado	California	February 18, 1850
Los Angeles	California	February 18, 1850
Marin	California	February 18, 1850
Mariposa	California	February 18, 1850
Mendocino	California	February 18, 1850
Monterey	California	February 18, 1850
Napa	California	February 18, 1850
Sacramento	California	February 18, 1850
San Diego	California	February 18, 1850
San Francisco	California	February 18, 1850
San Joaquin	California	February 18, 1850

San Luis Obispo	California	February 18, 1850
Santa Barbara	California	February 18, 1850
Santa Clara	California	February 18, 1850
Santa Cruz	California	February 18, 1850
Shasta	California	February 18, 1850
Solano	California	February 18, 1850
Sonoma	California	February 18, 1850
Sutter	California	February 18, 1850
Trinity	California	February 18, 1850
Tuolumne	California	February 18, 1850
Yolo	California	February 18, 1850
Yuba	California	February 18, 1850
Fulton	Ohio	February 28, 1850
Petersburg (IC)	Virginia	March 16, 1850
Vinton	Ohio	March 23, 1850
Fulton	Pennsylvania	April 19, 1850
Montour	Pennsylvania	May 3, 1850
Freestone	Texas	September 6, 1850
Calhoun	Arkansas	December 6, 1850
Yadkin	North Carolina	December 28, 1850
Sebastian	Arkansas	January 6, 1851
Adair	Iowa	January 15, 1851
Adams	Iowa	January 15, 1851
Audubon	Iowa	January 15, 1851
Bremer	Iowa	January 15, 1851
Buena Vista	Iowa	January 15, 1851
Butler	Iowa	January 15, 1851
Calhoun	Iowa	January 15, 1851
Carroll	Iowa	January 15, 1851
Cass	Iowa	January 15, 1851
Cerro Gordo	Iowa	January 15, 1851
Cherokee	Iowa	January 15, 1851
Chickasaw	Iowa	January 15, 1851
Clay	Iowa	January 15, 1851
Crawford	Iowa	January 15, 1851
Dickinson	Iowa	January 15, 1851
Emmet	Iowa	January 15, 1851
Floyd	Iowa	January 15, 1851
Franklin	Iowa	January 15, 1851
Greene	Iowa	January 15, 1851
Grundy	Iowa	January 15, 1851
Guthrie	Iowa	January 15, 1851
Hancock	Iowa	January 15, 1851
Hardin	Iowa	January 15, 1851
Harrison	Iowa	January 15, 1851
Howard	Iowa	January 15, 1851
Humboldt	Iowa	January 15, 1851
Ida	Iowa	January 15, 1851
Kossuth	Iowa	January 15, 1851
Lyon	Iowa	January 15, 1851
Mills	Iowa	January 15, 1851
Mitchell	Iowa	January 15, 1851
Monona	Iowa	January 15, 1851
Montgomery	Iowa	January 15, 1851

O'Brien	Iowa	January 15, 1851
Osceola	Iowa	January 15, 1851
Palo Alto	Iowa	January 15, 1851
Plymouth	Iowa	January 15, 1851
Pocahontas	Iowa	January 15, 1851
Pottawattamie	Iowa	January 15, 1851
Sac	Iowa	January 15, 1851
Shelby	Iowa	January 15, 1851
Sioux	Iowa	January 15, 1851
Union	Iowa	January 15, 1851
Webster	Iowa	January 15, 1851
Woodbury	Iowa	January 15, 1851
Worth	Iowa	January 15, 1851
Wright	Iowa	January 15, 1851
Madison	North Carolina	January 27, 1851
Lane	Oregon	January 28, 1851
Jackson	North Carolina	January 29, 1851
Pacific	Washington	February 4, 1851
Oconto	Wisconsin	February 6, 1851
Dent	Missouri	February 10, 1851
Stone	Missouri	February 10, 1851
Door	Wisconsin	February 11, 1851
Waushara	Wisconsin	February 15, 1851
Outagamie	Wisconsin	February 17, 1851
Vernon	Missouri	February 17, 1851
Waupaca	Wisconsin	February 17, 1851
Pemiscot	Missouri	February 19, 1851
Bollinger	Missouri	March 1, 1851
La Crosse	Wisconsin	March 1, 1851
Vernon	Wisconsin	March 1, 1851
Noble	Ohio	March 11, 1851
Craig	Virginia	March 21, 1851
Upshur	West Virginia	March 26, 1851
Pleasants	West Virginia	March 29, 1851
Cass	Minnesota	March 31, 1851
Chisago	Minnesota	March 31, 1851
Grand Traverse	Michigan	April 7, 1851
Nevada	California	April 25, 1851
Placer	California	April 25, 1851
Baltimore (IC)	Maryland	July 4, 1851
Howard	Maryland	July 4, 1851
Millard	Utah	October 4, 1851
Polk	Georgia	December 20, 1851
Spalding	Georgia	December 20, 1851
Whitfield	Georgia	December 30, 1851
Douglas	Oregon	January 7, 1852
Powell	Kentucky	January 7, 1852
Bernalillo	New Mexico	January 9, 1852
Dona Ana	New Mexico	January 9, 1852
Rio Arriba	New Mexico	January 9, 1852
San Miguel	New Mexico	January 9, 1852
Santa Fe	New Mexico	January 9, 1852
Socorro	New Mexico	January 9, 1852
Taos	New Mexico	January 9, 1852

Valencia	New Mexico	January 9, 1852
Jackson	Oregon	January 12, 1852
Thurston	Washington	January 12, 1852
Taylor	Georgia	January 15, 1852
Hidalgo	Texas	January 24, 1852
Burnet	Texas	February 5, 1852
Orange	Texas	February 5, 1852
Winn	Louisiana	February 24, 1852
Davis	Utah	March 3, 1852
Juab	Utah	March 3, 1852
Salt Lake	Utah	March 3, 1852
Sanpete	Utah	March 3, 1852
Tooele	Utah	March 3, 1852
Utah	Utah	March 3, 1852
Washington	Utah	March 3, 1852
Weber	Utah	March 3, 1852
Hennepin	Minnesota	March 6, 1852
Calhoun	Mississippi	March 8, 1852
Siskiyou	California	March 22, 1852
Kewaunee	Wisconsin	April 16, 1852
Sierra	California	April 16, 1852
Tulare	California	April 20, 1852
Lynchburg (IC)	Virginia	August 27, 1852
Columbia	Arkansas	December 17, 1852
Jefferson	Washington	December 22, 1852
King	Washington	December 22, 1852
Pierce	Washington	December 22, 1852
Alexandria (IC)	Virginia	1852
Island	Washington	January 6, 1853
Sumter	Florida	January 8, 1853
Madison	Texas	January 27, 1853
Hill	Texas	February 7, 1853
Jackson	Wisconsin	February 11, 1853
Kankakee	Illinois	February 11, 1853
Shawano	Wisconsin	February 16, 1853
Blue Earth	Minnesota	March 5, 1853
Fillmore	Minnesota	March 5, 1853
Goodhue	Minnesota	March 5, 1853
Le Seuer	Minnesota	March 5, 1853
Nicollet	Minnesota	March 5, 1853
Rice	Minnesota	March 5, 1853
Scott	Minnesota	March 5, 1853
Sibley	Minnesota	March 5, 1853
Ozaukee	Wisconsin	March 7, 1853
Pierce	Wisconsin	March 14, 1853
Polk	Wisconsin	March 14, 1853
Alameda	California	March 25, 1853
San Bernardino	California	April 26, 1853
Humboldt	California	May 12, 1853
Buffalo	Wisconsin	July 6, 1853
Clark	Wisconsin	July 6, 1853
Catoosa	Georgia	December 5, 1853
Pickens	Georgia	December 5, 1853
Hart	Georgia	December 7, 1853

Dougherty	Georgia	December 15, 1853
Tillamook	Oregon	December 15, 1853
Webster	Georgia	December 16, 1853
Fulton	Georgia	December 20, 1853
Worth	Georgia	December 20, 1853
Coos	Oregon	December 22, 1853
Wasco	Oregon	January 11, 1854
Summit	Utah	January 13, 1854
Lyon	Kentucky	January 14, 1854
Columbia	Oregon	January 16, 1854
Fannin	Georgia	January 21, 1854
Trempealeau	Wisconsin	January 27, 1854
Dunn	Wisconsin	February 3, 1854
Bosque	Texas	February 4, 1854
Coryell	Texas	February 4, 1854
Karnes	Texas	February 4, 1854
McLean	Kentucky	February 6, 1854
Coffee	Georgia	February 9, 1854
Douglas	Wisconsin	February 9, 1854
Chattahoochee	Georgia	February 13, 1854
Johnson	Texas	February 13, 1854
Clay	Georgia	February 16, 1854
Charlton	Georgia	February 18, 1854
Calhoun	Georgia	February 20, 1854
Houston	Minnesota	February 23, 1854
Winona	Minnesota	February 23, 1854
Skamania	Washington	March 9, 1854
Whatcom	Washington	March 9, 1854
Mason	Washington	March 13, 1854
Androscoggin	Maine	March 18, 1854
Plumas	California	March 18, 1854
Monroe	Wisconsin	March 21, 1854
Stanislaus	California	April 1, 1854
Sagadahoc	Maine	April 4, 1854
Grays Harbor	Washington	April 14, 1854
Schuyler	New York	April 17, 1854
Cowlitz	Washington	April 21, 1854
Wahkiakum	Washington	April 24, 1854
Walla Walla	Washington	April 25, 1854
Clallam	Washington	April 26, 1854
Amador	California	May 11, 1854
Cass	Nebraska	November 3, 1854
Burt	Nebraska	November 23, 1854
Dodge	Nebraska	November 23, 1854
Douglas	Nebraska	November 23, 1854
Nemaha	Nebraska	November 23, 1854
Otoe	Nebraska	November 23, 1854
Richardson	Nebraska	November 23, 1854
Washington	Nebraska	November 23, 1854
Multnomah	Oregon	December 22, 1854
Volusia	Florida	December 29, 1854
Manatee	Florida	January 9, 1855
Harnett	North Carolina	February 7, 1855

Wilson	North Carolina	February 13, 1855
Brown	Minnesota	February 20, 1855
Carver	Minnesota	February 20, 1855
Dodge	Minnesota	February 20, 1855
Faribault	Minnesota	February 20, 1855
Freeborn	Minnesota	February 20, 1855
Lake	Minnesota	February 20, 1855
Mower	Minnesota	February 20, 1855
Olmsted	Minnesota	February 20, 1855
Renville	Minnesota	February 20, 1855
Stearns	Minnesota	February 20, 1855
Steele	Minnesota	February 20, 1855
Todd	Minnesota	February 20, 1855
Wright	Minnesota	February 20, 1855
Johnson	Nebraska	March 2, 1855
Maries	Missouri	March 2, 1855
Snyder	Pennsylvania	March 2, 1855
Webster	Missouri	March 3, 1855
Lancaster	Nebraska	March 6, 1855
Pawnee	Nebraska	March 6, 1855
Saline	Nebraska	March 6, 1855
Seward	Nebraska	March 6, 1855
Stanton	Nebraska	March 6, 1855
Dakota	Nebraska	March 7, 1855
Thurston	Nebraska	March 7, 1855
York	Nebraska	March 13, 1855
Buffalo	Nebraska	March 14, 1855
Cuming	Nebraska	March 16, 1855
Gage	Nebraska	March 16, 1855
Merced	California	April 19, 1855
Allen	Kansas	August 30, 1855
Anderson	Kansas	August 30, 1855
Atchison	Kansas	August 30, 1855
Bourbon	Kansas	August 30, 1855
Brown	Kansas	August 30, 1855
Butler	Kansas	August 30, 1855
Cherokee	Kansas	August 30, 1855
Coffey	Kansas	August 30, 1855
Doniphan	Kansas	August 30, 1855
Douglas	Kansas	August 30, 1855
Franklin	Kansas	August 30, 1855
Geary	Kansas	August 30, 1855
Greenwood	Kansas	August 30, 1855
Jackson	Kansas	August 30, 1855
Jefferson	Kansas	August 30, 1855
Johnson	Kansas	August 30, 1855
Leavenworth	Kansas	August 30, 1855
Linn	Kansas	August 30, 1855
Lyon	Kansas	August 30, 1855
Marion	Kansas	August 30, 1855
Marshall	Kansas	August 30, 1855
Miami	Kansas	August 30, 1855
Morris	Kansas	August 30, 1855
Nemaha	Kansas	August 30, 1855
Neosho	Kansas	August 30, 1855

Osage	Kansas	August 30, 1855
Riley	Kansas	August 30, 1855
Shawnee	Kansas	August 30, 1855
Wabaunsee	Kansas	August 30, 1855
Wilson	Kansas	August 30, 1855
Woodson	Kansas	August 30, 1855
Cumberland	Tennessee	November 16, 1855
Barton	Missouri	December 12, 1855
Parker	Texas	December 12, 1855
Liberty	Florida	December 15, 1855
Curry	Oregon	December 18, 1855
Beaver	Utah	January 5, 1856
Box Elder	Utah	January 5, 1856
Cache	Utah	January 5, 1856
Josephine	Oregon	January 22, 1856
Wise	Texas	January 23, 1856
Atascosa	Texas	January 25, 1856
Comanche	Texas	January 25, 1856
Erath	Texas	January 25, 1856
Bandera	Texas	January 26, 1856
Butler	Nebraska	January 26, 1856
Dixon	Nebraska	January 26, 1856
Fillmore	Nebraska	January 26, 1856
Haralson	Georgia	January 26, 1856
Jefferson	Nebraska	January 26, 1856
Kerr	Texas	January 26, 1856
Madison	Nebraska	January 26, 1856
Pierce	Nebraska	January 26, 1856
Platte	Nebraska	January 26, 1856
Polk	Nebraska	January 26, 1856
Saunders	Nebraska	January 26, 1856
Thayer	Nebraska	January 26, 1856
Lampasas	Texas	February 1, 1856
Llano	Texas	February 1, 1856
San Saba	Texas	February 1, 1856
Live Oak	Texas	February 2, 1856
Maverick	Texas	February 2, 1856
Young	Texas	February 2, 1856
Terrell	Georgia	February 16, 1856
Wise	Virginia	February 16, 1856
Meeker	Minnesota	February 23, 1856
Berrien	Georgia	February 25, 1856
Colquitt	Georgia	February 25, 1856
Morrison	Minnesota	February 25, 1856
Sherburne	Minnesota	February 25, 1856
Miller	Georgia	February 26, 1856
Cheatham	Tennessee	February 28, 1856
McLeod	Minnesota	March 1, 1856
Pine	Minnesota	March 1, 1856
Saint Louis	Minnesota	March 1, 1856
Calhoun	West Virginia	March 5, 1856
Towns	Georgia	March 6, 1856
Tucker	West Virginia	March 7, 1856
Roane	West Virginia	March 11, 1856

Rowan	Kentucky	March 15, 1856
Wood	Wisconsin	March 29, 1856
Burnett	Wisconsin	March 31, 1856
Tehama	California	April 9, 1856
Fresno	California	April 19, 1856
San Mateo	California	April 19, 1856
Brown	Texas	August 27, 1856
Jack	Texas	August 27, 1856
McCulloch	Texas	August 27, 1856
Palo Pinto	Texas	August 27, 1856
Eau Claire	Wisconsin	October 6, 1856
Juneau	Wisconsin	October 13, 1856
Hamilton	Iowa	December 22, 1856
Lafayette	Florida	December 23, 1856
Taylor	Florida	December 23, 1856
Kitsap	Washington	January 16, 1857
Sarpy	Nebraska	February 7, 1857
Knox	Nebraska	February 10, 1857
Cedar	Nebraska	February 12, 1857
Isanti	Minnesota	February 13, 1857
Iron	Missouri	February 17, 1857
Clay	Kansas	February 20, 1857
Dickinson	Kansas	February 20, 1857
Pottawatomie	Kansas	February 20, 1857
Washington	Kansas	February 20, 1857
Waseca	Minnesota	February 27, 1857
Del Norte	California	March 2, 1857
Howell	Missouri	March 2, 1857
Union	New Jersey	March 19, 1857
Bay	Michigan	April 20, 1857
Aitkin	Minnesota	May 23, 1857
Anoka	Minnesota	May 23, 1857
Carlton	Minnesota	May 23, 1857
Cottonwood	Minnesota	May 23, 1857
Crow Wing	Minnesota	May 23, 1857
Jackson	Minnesota	May 23, 1857
Martin	Minnesota	May 23, 1857
Mille Lacs	Minnesota	May 23, 1857
Murray	Minnesota	May 23, 1857
Nobles	Minnesota	May 23, 1857
Pipestone	Minnesota	May 23, 1857
Rock	Minnesota	May 23, 1857
Douglas	Missouri	October 29, 1857
Phelps	Missouri	November 13, 1857
Dawson	Georgia	December 3, 1857
Bee	Texas	December 8, 1857
Sequatchie	Tennessee	December 9, 1857
Pierce	Georgia	December 18, 1857
Glascock	Georgia	December 19, 1857
Mitchell	Georgia	December 21, 1857
Schley	Georgia	December 22, 1857
White	Georgia	December 22, 1857
Wilcox	Georgia	December 22, 1857
Clay	Texas	December 24, 1857

Montague	Texas	December 24, 1857
Throckmorton	Texas	January 13, 1858
Archer	Texas	January 22, 1858
Hamilton	Texas	January 22, 1858
Hardin	Texas	January 22, 1858
Kimble	Texas	January 22, 1858
Mason	Texas	January 22, 1858
Menard	Texas	January 22, 1858
Stephens	Texas	January 22, 1858
Zapata	Texas	January 22, 1858
Spokane	Washington	January 29, 1858
Baylor	Texas	February 1, 1858
Callahan	Texas	February 1, 1858
Coleman	Texas	February 1, 1858
Concho	Texas	February 1, 1858
Dimmitt	Texas	February 1, 1858
Duval	Texas	February 1, 1858
Eastland	Texas	February 1, 1858
Edwards	Texas	February 1, 1858
Frio	Texas	February 1, 1858
Hardeman	Texas	February 1, 1858
Haskell	Texas	February 1, 1858
Jones	Texas	February 1, 1858
Knox	Texas	February 1, 1858
La Salle	Texas	February 1, 1858
McMullen	Texas	February 1, 1858
Runnels	Texas	February 1, 1858
Shackelford	Texas	February 1, 1858
Taylor	Texas	February 1, 1858
Wichita	Texas	February 1, 1858
Wilbarger	Texas	February 1, 1858
Zavala	Texas	February 1, 1858
Jackson	Kentucky	February 2, 1858
Blanco	Texas	February 12, 1858
Chambers	Texas	February 12, 1858
Buchanan	Virginia	February 13, 1858
McDowell	West Virginia	February 20, 1858
Pepin	Wisconsin	February 25, 1858
Portsmouth (IC)	Virginia	March 1, 1858
Green Lake	Wisconsin	March 5, 1858
Douglas	Minnesota	March 8, 1858
Kanabec	Minnesota	March 13, 1858
Becker	Minnesota	March 18, 1858
Clay	Minnesota	March 18, 1858
Otter Tail	Minnesota	March 18, 1858
Wilkin	Minnesota	March 18, 1858
Kandiyohi	Minnesota	March 20, 1858
Clay	West Virginia	March 29, 1858
Wadena	Minnesota	June 11, 1858
Polk	Minnesota	July 20, 1858
Hall	Nebraska	November 4, 1858
Merrick	Nebraska	November 4, 1858
Clayton	Georgia	November 30, 1858
Quitman	Georgia	December 10, 1858

Banks	Georgia	December 11, 1858
Brooks	Georgia	December 11, 1858
Johnson	Georgia	December 11, 1858
Echols	Georgia	December 13, 1858
Bradford	Florida	December 21, 1858
Suwanee	Florida	December 21, 1858
Clay	Florida	December 31, 1858
Wyandotte	Kansas	January 29, 1859
Muskegon	Michigan	February 4, 1859
Douglas	Illinois	February 8, 1859
Chase	Kansas	February 11, 1859
Ford	Illinois	February 17, 1859
Craighead	Arkansas	February 19, 1859
Christian	Missouri	March 8, 1859
Carter	Missouri	March 10, 1859
Barron	Wisconsin	March 19, 1859
Klickitat	Washington	December 20, 1859
Alleghany	North Carolina	1859
Lincoln	Nebraska	January 7, 1860
Kearney	Nebraska	January 10, 1860
Webster	West Virginia	January 10, 1860
Dawson	Nebraska	January 11, 1860
Holt	Nebraska	January 13, 1860
Nuckolls	Nebraska	January 13, 1860
Metcalfe	Kentucky	February 1, 1860
Mora	New Mexico	February 1, 1860
Marion	Texas	February 8, 1860
Wilson	Texas	February 13, 1860
Saline	Kansas	February 15, 1860
Boyd	Kentucky	February 16, 1860
Magoffin	Kentucky	February 22, 1860
Watonwan	Minnesota	February 25, 1860
Cloud	Kansas	February 27, 1860
Ottawa	Kansas	February 27, 1860
Republic	Kansas	February 27, 1860
Webster	Kentucky	February 29, 1860
Wolfe	Kentucky	March 5, 1860
Knox	Maine	March 9, 1860
Ashland	Wisconsin	March 27, 1860
Cameron	Pennsylvania	March 29, 1860
Snohomish	Washington	January 14, 1861
Worth	Missouri	February 6, 1861
Baker	Florida	February 8, 1861
Polk	Florida	February 8, 1861
Transylvania	North Carolina	February 15, 1861
Mitchell	North Carolina	February 16, 1861
Clay	North Carolina	February 20, 1861
Keweenaw	Michigan	March 11, 1861
Menominee	Michigan	March 15, 1861
Bland	Virginia	March 30, 1861
Mono	California	April 24, 1861
Lake	California	May 20, 1861

Arapahoe	Colorado	November 1, 1861
Boulder	Colorado	November 1, 1861
Chaffee	Colorado	November 1, 1861
Clear Creek	Colorado	November 1, 1861
Conejos	Colorado	November 1, 1861
Costilla	Colorado	November 1, 1861
Douglas	Colorado	November 1, 1861
El Paso	Colorado	November 1, 1861
Fremont	Colorado	November 1, 1861
Gilpin	Colorado	November 1, 1861
Huerfano	Colorado	November 1, 1861
Jefferson	Colorado	November 1, 1861
Lake	Colorado	November 1, 1861
Larimer	Colorado	November 1, 1861
Park	Colorado	November 1, 1861
Pueblo	Colorado	November 1, 1861
Summit	Colorado	November 1, 1861
Weld	Colorado	November 1, 1861
Carson City (IC)	Nevada	November 25, 1861
Churchill	Nevada	November 25, 1861
Douglas	Nevada	November 25, 1861
Esmeralda	Nevada	November 25, 1861
Humboldt	Nevada	November 25, 1861
Lyon	Nevada	November 25, 1861
Storey	Nevada	November 25, 1861
Washoe	Nevada	November 25, 1861
Kendall	Texas	January 10, 1862
Morgan	Utah	January 17, 1862
Wasatch	Utah	January 17, 1862
Redwood	Minnesota	February 6, 1862
Big Stone	Minnesota	February 20, 1862
Chippewa	Minnesota	February 20, 1862
Pope	Minnesota	February 20, 1862
Stevens	Minnesota	February 20, 1862
Traverse	Minnesota	February 20, 1862
Bon Homme	South Dakota	April 5, 1862
Brookings	South Dakota	April 5, 1862
Deuel	South Dakota	April 5, 1862
Lincoln	South Dakota	April 5, 1862
Minnehaha	South Dakota	April 5, 1862
Clay	South Dakota	April 10, 1862
Union	South Dakota	April 10, 1862
Yankton	South Dakota	April 10, 1862
Charles Mix	South Dakota	May 8, 1862
Gregory	South Dakota	May 8, 1862
Hutchinson	South Dakota	May 8, 1862
Baker	Oregon	September 22, 1862
Umatilla	Oregon	September 27, 1862
Cross	Arkansas	November 15, 1862
Woodruff	Arkansas	November 26, 1862
Lander	Nevada	December 19, 1862
Stevens	Washington	January 20, 1863
Benzie	Michigan	February 27, 1863

Owyhee	Idaho	December 31, 1863
Buffalo	South Dakota	January 6, 1864
Kane	Utah	January 16, 1864
Rich	Utah	January 16, 1864
Oneida	Idaho	January 22, 1864
Boise	Idaho	February 4, 1864
Idaho	Idaho	February 4, 1864
Nez Perce	Idaho	February 4, 1864
Shoshone	Idaho	February 4, 1864
Nye	Nevada	February 16, 1864
Alpine	California	March 16, 1864
Lassen	California	April 1, 1864
Grant	Oregon	October 14, 1864
Union	Oregon	October 14, 1864
Pima	Arizona	December 15, 1864
Mohave	Arizona	December 21, 1864
Yavapai	Arizona	December 21, 1864
Yuma	Arizona	December 21, 1864
Ada	Idaho	December 22, 1864
Kootenai	Idaho	December 22, 1864
Latah	Idaho	December 22, 1864
Piute	Utah	January 16, 1865
Sevier	Utah	January 16, 1865
Yakima	Washington	January 21, 1865
Beaverhead	Montana	February 2, 1865
Chouteau	Montana	February 2, 1865
Custer	Montana	February 2, 1865
Deer Lodge	Montana	February 2, 1865
Gallatin	Montana	February 2, 1865
Jefferson	Montana	February 2, 1865
Lewis and Clark	Montana	February 2, 1865
Madison	Montana	February 2, 1865
Missoula	Montana	February 2, 1865
Mineral	West Virginia	February 1, 1866
Las Animas	Colorado	February 9, 1866
Grant	West Virginia	February 14, 1866
Elmore	Alabama	February 15, 1866
Lincoln	Nevada	February 26, 1866
Beltrami	Minnesota	February 28, 1866
Inyo	California	March 22, 1866
Kern	California	April 2, 1866
Lee	Mississippi	October 26, 1866
Hood	Texas	November 2, 1866
Crenshaw	Alabama	November 24, 1866
Bullock	Alabama	December 5, 1866
Lee	Alabama	December 5, 1866
Cleburne	Alabama	December 6, 1866
Clay	Alabama	December 7, 1866
Etowah	Alabama	December 7, 1866
Saguache	Colorado	December 29, 1866
Laramie	Wyoming	January 9, 1867

Pembina	North Dakota	January 9, 1867
Hale	Alabama	January 30, 1867
Lamar	Alabama	February 4, 1867
Colbert	Alabama	February 6, 1867
Labette	Kansas	February 7, 1867
Robertson	Kentucky	February 11, 1867
Crawford	Kansas	February 13, 1867
Adams	Nebraska	February 16, 1867
Clay	Nebraska	February 16, 1867
Franklin	Nebraska	February 16, 1867
Hamilton	Nebraska	February 16, 1867
Webster	Nebraska	February 16, 1867
Lincoln	West Virginia	February 23, 1867
Barber	Kansas	February 26, 1867
Barton	Kansas	February 26, 1867
Clark	Kansas	February 26, 1867
Comanche	Kansas	February 26, 1867
Cowley	Kansas	February 26, 1867
Ellis	Kansas	February 26, 1867
Ellsworth	Kansas	February 26, 1867
Graham	Kansas	February 26, 1867
Harper	Kansas	February 26, 1867
Hodgeman	Kansas	February 26, 1867
Jewell	Kansas	February 26, 1867
Kiowa	Kansas	February 26, 1867
Lincoln	Kansas	February 26, 1867
McPherson	Kansas	February 26, 1867
Mitchell	Kansas	February 26, 1867
Montgomery	Kansas	February 26, 1867
Ness	Kansas	February 26, 1867
Norton	Kansas	February 26, 1867
Osborne	Kansas	February 26, 1867
Pawnee	Kansas	February 26, 1867
Phillips	Kansas	February 26, 1867
Pratt	Kansas	February 26, 1867
Reno	Kansas	February 26, 1867
Rice	Kansas	February 26, 1867
Rooks	Kansas	February 26, 1867
Rush	Kansas	February 26, 1867
Russell	Kansas	February 26, 1867
Sedgwick	Kansas	February 26, 1867
Smith	Kansas	February 26, 1867
Stafford	Kansas	February 26, 1867
Sumner	Kansas	February 26, 1867
Trego	Kansas	February 26, 1867
Bell	Kentucky	February 28, 1867
Little River	Arkansas	March 5, 1867
Cheyenne	Nebraska	June 22, 1867
Wicomico	Maryland	August 17, 1867
Meagher	Montana	November 16, 1867
Sweetwater	Wyoming	December 27, 1867
Oconee	South Carolina	January 29, 1868
Grant	New Mexico	January 30, 1868
Gove	Kansas	March 2, 1868

Wallace	Kansas	March 2, 1868
Grant	Minnesota	March 6, 1868
Lyon	Minnesota	March 6, 1868
Sharp	Arkansas	July 18, 1868
Richland	Louisiana	September 29, 1868
Iberia	Louisiana	October 30, 1868
Escambia	Alabama	December 10, 1868
Albany	Wyoming	December 16, 1868
Carbon	Wyoming	December 16, 1868
Geneva	Alabama	December 26, 1868
Chilton	Alabama	December 30, 1868
Lemhi	Idaho	January 9, 1869
Dawson	Montana	January 15, 1869
Lincoln	New Mexico	January 16, 1869
Colfax	New Mexico	January 25, 1869
Elliott	Kentucky	January 26, 1869
Grant	Arkansas	February 4, 1869
Colfax	Nebraska	February 15, 1869
White Pine	Nevada	March 2, 1869
Grant	Louisiana	March 4, 1869
Elko	Nevada	March 5, 1869
Tangipahoa	Louisiana	March 6, 1869
Menifee	Kentucky	March 10, 1869
Boone	Arkansas	April 9, 1869
Uinta	Wyoming	December 1, 1869
Lee	Kentucky	January 29, 1870
Dare	North Carolina	February 2, 1870
Bent	Colorado	February 11, 1870
Swift	Minnesota	February 18, 1870
Martin	Kentucky	March 10, 1870
Cameron	Louisiana	March 15, 1870
Lincoln	Mississippi	April 7, 1870
Alcorn	Mississippi	April 15, 1870
Prentiss	Mississippi	April 15, 1870
Grenada	Mississippi	May 9, 1870
Loudon	Tennessee	June 2, 1870
Hamblen	Tennessee	June 8, 1870
Rains	Texas	June 9, 1870
Trousdale	Tennessee	June 21, 1870
Clay	Tennessee	June 24, 1870
Lake	Tennessee	June 24, 1870
Union	Mississippi	July 7, 1870
Benton	Mississippi	July 21, 1870
Delta	Texas	July 29, 1870
San Jacinto	Texas	August 13, 1870
Douglas	Georgia	October 17, 1870
McDuffie	Georgia	October 18, 1870
Rockdale	Georgia	October 18, 1870
Dodge	Georgia	October 26, 1870
Hanson	South Dakota	January 13, 1871
Turner	South Dakota	January 13, 1871
Houston	Tennessee	January 23, 1871

Maricopa	Arizona	February 14, 1871
Swain	North Carolina	February 24, 1871
Summers	West Virginia	February 27, 1871
Webster	Louisiana	February 27, 1871
Antelope	Nebraska	March 1, 1871
Boone	Nebraska	March 1, 1871
Greeley	Nebraska	March 1, 1871
Howard	Nebraska	March 1, 1871
Sherman	Nebraska	March 1, 1871
Valley	Nebraska	March 1, 1871
Wayne	Nebraska	March 4, 1871
Lac qui Parle	Minnesota	March 6, 1871
Yellow Medicine	Minnesota	March 6, 1871
Red River	Louisiana	March 7, 1871
Aiken	South Carolina	March 10, 1871
Leflore	Mississippi	March 15, 1871
Nevada	Arkansas	March 20, 1871
Logan	Arkansas	March 22, 1871
Lincoln	Arkansas	March 28, 1871
Vernon	Louisiana	March 30, 1871
Pecos	Texas	May 3, 1871
Clay	Mississippi	May 12, 1871
Montgomery	Mississippi	May 13, 1871
Harlan	Nebraska	June 3, 1871
Aransas	Texas	September 18, 1871
Whitman	Washington	November 29, 1871
Moore	Tennessee	December 14, 1871
Frontier	Nebraska	January 17, 1872
Graham	North Carolina	January 30, 1872
Pamlico	North Carolina	February 8, 1872
Harvey	Kansas	February 29, 1872
Kingman	Kansas	February 29, 1872
Ventura	California	March 22, 1872
Garrett	Maryland	April 1, 1872
Barnes	North Dakota	January 4, 1873
Bottineau	North Dakota	January 4, 1873
Burleigh	North Dakota	January 4, 1873
Cass	North Dakota	January 4, 1873
Cavalier	North Dakota	January 4, 1873
Foster	North Dakota	January 4, 1873
Grand Forks	North Dakota	January 4, 1873
Kidder	North Dakota	January 4, 1873
LaMoure	North Dakota	January 4, 1873
Logan	North Dakota	January 4, 1873
McHenry	North Dakota	January 4, 1873
Mountrail	North Dakota	January 4, 1873
Ramsey	North Dakota	January 4, 1873
Ransom	North Dakota	January 4, 1873
Renville	North Dakota	January 4, 1873
Richland	North Dakota	January 4, 1873
Rolette	North Dakota	January 4, 1873
Sheridan	North Dakota	January 4, 1873
Stutsman	North Dakota	January 4, 1873

Wells	North Dakota	January 4, 1873
Campbell	South Dakota	January 8, 1873
Clark	South Dakota	January 8, 1873
Davison	South Dakota	January 8, 1873
Dewey	South Dakota	January 8, 1873
Douglas	South Dakota	January 8, 1873
Edmunds	South Dakota	January 8, 1873
Faulk	South Dakota	January 8, 1873
Grant	South Dakota	January 8, 1873
Hamlin	South Dakota	January 8, 1873
Hand	South Dakota	January 8, 1873
Hughes	South Dakota	January 8, 1873
Hyde	South Dakota	January 8, 1873
Kingsbury	South Dakota	January 8, 1873
Lake	South Dakota	January 8, 1873
Lyman	South Dakota	January 8, 1873
McCook	South Dakota	January 8, 1873
McPherson	South Dakota	January 8, 1873
Miner	South Dakota	January 8, 1873
Moody	South Dakota	January 8, 1873
Morton	North Dakota	January 8, 1873
Potter	South Dakota	January 8, 1873
Spink	South Dakota	January 8, 1873
Stanley	South Dakota	January 8, 1873
Sully	South Dakota	January 8, 1873
Tripp	South Dakota	January 8, 1873
Walworth	South Dakota	January 8, 1873
Furnas	Nebraska	January 27, 1873
Phelps	Nebraska	February 11, 1873
Chase	Nebraska	February 27, 1873
Dundy	Nebraska	February 27, 1873
Hitchcock	Nebraska	February 27, 1873
Keith	Nebraska	February 27, 1873
Lincoln	Louisiana	February 27, 1873
Red Willow	Nebraska	February 27, 1873
Eureka	Nevada	March 1, 1873
Rockwall	Texas	March 1, 1873
Cheyenne	Kansas	March 6, 1873
Decatur	Kansas	March 6, 1873
Finney	Kansas	March 6, 1873
Ford	Kansas	March 6, 1873
Grant	Kansas	March 6, 1873
Greeley	Kansas	March 6, 1873
Hamilton	Kansas	March 6, 1873
Kearny	Kansas	March 6, 1873
Lane	Kansas	March 6, 1873
Meade	Kansas	March 6, 1873
Rawlins	Kansas	March 6, 1873
Scott	Kansas	March 6, 1873
Seward	Kansas	March 6, 1873
Sheridan	Kansas	March 6, 1873
Sherman	Kansas	March 6, 1873
Stanton	Kansas	March 6, 1873
Stevens	Kansas	March 6, 1873
Thomas	Kansas	March 6, 1873

Wichita	Kansas	March 6, 1873
Baxter	Arkansas	March 24, 1873
Clay	Arkansas	March 24, 1873
Garland	Arkansas	April 5, 1873
Faulkner	Arkansas	April 12, 1873
Gregg	Texas	April 12, 1873
Tate	Mississippi	April 15, 1873
Lonoke	Arkansas	April 16, 1873
Cleveland	Arkansas	April 17, 1873
Howard	Arkansas	April 17, 1873
Lee	Arkansas	April 17, 1873
Stone	Arkansas	April 21, 1873
Waller	Texas	April 28, 1873
San Juan	Washington	October 31, 1873
Lincoln	Minnesota	November 4, 1873
Gosper	Nebraska	November 26, 1873
Elbert	Colorado	February 2, 1874
Grand	Colorado	February 2, 1874
Hinsdale	Colorado	February 10, 1874
La Plata	Colorado	February 10, 1874
Rio Grande	Colorado	February 10, 1874
San Benito	California	February 12, 1874
Modoc	California	February 17, 1874
Lincoln	Wisconsin	March 4, 1874
Edwards	Kansas	March 7, 1874
Cook	Minnesota	March 9, 1874
Tom Green	Texas	March 13, 1874
Camp	Texas	April 6, 1874
Webster	Mississippi	April 6, 1874
Lee	Texas	April 14, 1874
Lake	Oregon	October 24, 1874
Miller	Arkansas	December 1874
Winchester (IC)	Virginia	1874
Bear Lake	Idaho	January 5, 1875
Custer	South Dakota	January 11, 1875
Lawrence	South Dakota	January 11, 1875
Pennington	South Dakota	January 11, 1875
Shannon	South Dakota	January 11, 1875
Traill	North Dakota	January 12, 1875
Brule	South Dakota	January 14, 1875
Mercer	North Dakota	January 14, 1875
Crockett	Texas	January 22, 1875
Pinal	Arizona	February 1, 1875
Pender	North Carolina	February 16, 1875
Baraga	Michigan	February 19, 1875
Oconee	Georgia	February 25, 1875
Chautauqua	Kansas	March 3, 1875
Elk	Kansas	March 3, 1875
Taylor	Wisconsin	March 4, 1875
Franklin	Texas	March 6, 1875
Morris	Texas	March 6, 1875
Somervell	Texas	March 13, 1875
Unicoi	Tennessee	March 23, 1875

Columbia	Washington	November 11, 1875
Crook	Wyoming	December 8, 1875
Johnson	Wyoming	December 8, 1875
San Juan	Colorado	January 31, 1876
Sharkey	Mississippi	March 29, 1876
Andrews	Texas	August 21, 1876
Armstrong	Texas	August 21, 1876
Bailey	Texas	August 21, 1876
Borden	Texas	August 21, 1876
Briscoe	Texas	August 21, 1876
Carson	Texas	August 21, 1876
Castro	Texas	August 21, 1876
Childress	Texas	August 21, 1876
Cochran	Texas	August 21, 1876
Collingsworth	Texas	August 21, 1876
Cottle	Texas	August 21, 1876
Crosby	Texas	August 21, 1876
Dallam	Texas	August 21, 1876
Dawson	Texas	August 21, 1876
Deaf Smith	Texas	August 21, 1876
Dickens	Texas	August 21, 1876
Donley	Texas	August 21, 1876
Fisher	Texas	August 21, 1876
Floyd	Texas	August 21, 1876
Gaines	Texas	August 21, 1876
Garza	Texas	August 21, 1876
Gray	Texas	August 21, 1876
Hale	Texas	August 21, 1876
Hall	Texas	August 21, 1876
Hansford	Texas	August 21, 1876
Hartley	Texas	August 21, 1876
Hemphill	Texas	August 21, 1876
Hockley	Texas	August 21, 1876
Howard	Texas	August 21, 1876
Hutchinson	Texas	August 21, 1876
Kent	Texas	August 21, 1876
King	Texas	August 21, 1876
Lamb	Texas	August 21, 1876
Lipscomb	Texas	August 21, 1876
Lubbock	Texas	August 21, 1876
Lynn	Texas	August 21, 1876
Martin	Texas	August 21, 1876
Mitchell	Texas	August 21, 1876
Moore	Texas	August 21, 1876
Motley	Texas	August 21, 1876
Nolan	Texas	August 21, 1876
Ochiltree	Texas	August 21, 1876
Oldham	Texas	August 21, 1876
Parmer	Texas	August 21, 1876
Potter	Texas	August 21, 1876
Randall	Texas	August 21, 1876
Roberts	Texas	August 21, 1876
Scurry	Texas	August 21, 1876
Sherman	Texas	August 21, 1876

Stonewall	Texas	August 21, 1876
Swisher	Texas	August 21, 1876
Terry	Texas	August 21, 1876
Wheeler	Texas	August 21, 1876
Yoakum	Texas	August 21, 1876
Ouray	Colorado	January 18, 1877
Cullman	Alabama	January 24, 1877
Routt	Colorado	January 29, 1877
Quitman	Mississippi	February 1, 1877
Codington	South Dakota	February 15, 1877
Custer	Nebraska	February 17, 1877
Wheeler	Nebraska	February 17, 1877
Hayes	Nebraska	February 19, 1877
Sioux	Nebraska	February 19, 1877
Saint Louis (IC)	Missouri	March 5, 1877
Custer	Colorado	March 9, 1877
Gunnison	Colorado	March 9, 1877
East Carroll	Louisiana	March 28, 1877
West Carroll	Louisiana	March 28, 1877
Hampton	South Carolina	February 18, 1878
Leslie	Kentucky	March 29, 1878
Lackawanna	Pennsylvania	August 21, 1878
Billings	North Dakota	February 10, 1879
Emmons	North Dakota	February 10, 1879
Stark	North Dakota	February 10, 1879
Nance	Nebraska	February 13, 1879
Apache	Arizona	February 14, 1879
Cassia	Idaho	February 20, 1879
Washington	Idaho	February 20, 1879
Aurora	South Dakota	February 22, 1879
Beadle	South Dakota	February 22, 1879
Brown	South Dakota	February 22, 1879
Marshall	Minnesota	February 25, 1879
Price	Wisconsin	February 26, 1879
Langlade	Wisconsin	February 27, 1879
Marinette	Wisconsin	February 27, 1879
Pickett	Tennessee	February 27, 1879
Chester	Tennessee	March 4, 1879
Day	South Dakota	October 1, 1879
Fredericksburg (IC)	Virginia	1879
Emery	Utah	February 12, 1880
San Juan	Utah	February 17, 1880
Uintah	Utah	February 18, 1880
Dickenson	Virginia	March 3, 1880
Custer	Idaho	January 8, 1881
Cochise	Arizona	February 1, 1881
Gila	Arizona	February 8, 1881
Silver Bow	Montana	February 16, 1881
Norman	Minnesota	February 17, 1881
Griggs	North Dakota	February 18, 1881

Walsh	North Dakota	February 18, 1881
Dolores	Colorado	February 19, 1881
Pitkin	Colorado	February 23, 1881
Durham	North Carolina	February 28, 1881
Logan	Kansas	March 4, 1881
Dickey	North Dakota	March 5, 1881
Harding	South Dakota	March 5, 1881
Vance	North Carolina	March 5, 1881
Graham	Arizona	March 10, 1881
Garfield	Washington	November 29, 1881
Berkeley	South Carolina	January 31, 1882
Garfield	Utah	March 9, 1882
Florence	Wisconsin	March 18, 1882
Klamath	Oregon	October 17, 1882
Crook	Oregon	October 24, 1882
Garfield	Colorado	February 10, 1883
Delta	Colorado	February 11, 1883
Eagle	Colorado	February 11, 1883
Montrose	Colorado	February 11, 1883
Mesa	Colorado	February 14, 1883
Brown	Nebraska	February 19, 1883
Cleburne	Arkansas	February 20, 1883
Cherry	Nebraska	February 23, 1883
Loup	Nebraska	February 23, 1883
Hubbard	Minnesota	February 26, 1883
Yellowstone	Montana	February 26, 1883
Butte	South Dakota	March 2, 1883
Nelson	North Dakota	March 2, 1883
Sargent	North Dakota	March 3, 1883
Bowman	North Dakota	March 8, 1883
Jackson	South Dakota	March 8, 1883
McLean	North Dakota	March 8, 1883
Roberts	South Dakota	March 8, 1883
Steele	North Dakota	March 8, 1883
Towner	North Dakota	March 8, 1883
Benson	North Dakota	March 9, 1883
Dunn	North Dakota	March 9, 1883
Hettinger	North Dakota	March 9, 1883
Jerauld	South Dakota	March 9, 1883
McIntosh	North Dakota	March 9, 1883
McKenzie	North Dakota	March 9, 1883
Sanborn	South Dakota	March 9, 1883
Sawyer	Wisconsin	March 10, 1883
Washburn	Wisconsin	March 27, 1883
Fall River	South Dakota	April 3, 1883
Reeves	Texas	April 14, 1883
Asotin	Washington	October 27, 1883
San Miguel	Colorado	November 1, 1883
Kittitas	Washington	November 24, 1883
Lincoln	Washington	November 24, 1883
Adams	Washington	November 28, 1883
Douglas	Washington	November 28, 1883
Franklin	Washington	November 28, 1883

Skagit	Washington	November 28, 1883
Fremont	Wyoming	March 5, 1884
Sierra	New Mexico	April 3, 1884
Knott	Kentucky	May 5, 1884
Keya Paha	Nebraska	November 4, 1884
Garfield	Nebraska	November 8, 1884
Roanoke (IC)	Virginia	1884
Williamsburg (IC)	Virginia	1884
Bingham	Idaho	January 13, 1885
Morrow	Oregon	February 16, 1885
Dawes	Nebraska	February 19, 1885
Val Verde	Texas	February 20, 1885
Logan	Nebraska	February 24, 1885
Gilliam	Oregon	February 25, 1885
Sheridan	Nebraska	February 25, 1885
Midland	Texas	March 4, 1885
Blaine	Nebraska	March 5, 1885
Marshall	South Dakota	March 10, 1885
Fergus	Montana	March 12, 1885
Oliver	North Dakota	March 12, 1885
Alger	Michigan	March 17, 1885
Eddy	North Dakota	March 31, 1885
Iron	Michigan	April 3, 1885
Forest	Wisconsin	April 11, 1885
Oneida	Wisconsin	April 11, 1885
Ward	North Dakota	April 14, 1885
Archuleta	Colorado	April 15, 1885
Morton	Kansas	February 18, 1886
Carlisle	Kentucky	April 3, 1886
Box Butte	Nebraska	November 2, 1886
Greer	Oklahoma	1886
Brewster	Texas	February 2, 1887
Gogebic	Michigan	February 7, 1887
Washington	Colorado	February 9, 1887
Wallowa	Oregon	February 11, 1887
Malheur	Oregon	February 17, 1887
Park	Montana	February 23, 1887
San Juan	New Mexico	February 24, 1887
Logan	Colorado	February 25, 1887
Crane	Texas	February 26, 1887
Ector	Texas	February 26, 1887
Loving	Texas	February 26, 1887
Upton	Texas	February 26, 1887
Ward	Texas	February 26, 1887
Winkler	Texas	February 26, 1887
Luce	Michigan	March 1, 1887
Gray	Kansas	March 5, 1887
Haskell	Kansas	March 5, 1887
Pierce	North Dakota	March 11, 1887
Jeff Davis	Texas	March 15, 1887
Mills	Texas	March 15, 1887

Arthur	Nebraska	March 31, 1887
Grant	Nebraska	March 31, 1887
McPherson	Nebraska	March 31, 1887
Thomas	Nebraska	March 31, 1887
Schleicher	Texas	April 1, 1887
Sutton	Texas	April 1, 1887
Glasscock	Texas	April 4, 1887
Osceola	Florida	May 12, 1887
Lee	Florida	May 13, 1887
DeSoto	Florida	May 19, 1887
Lake	Florida	May 27, 1887
Citrus	Florida	June 2, 1887
Pasco	Florida	June 2, 1887
Cascade	Montana	September 12, 1887
Perkins	Nebraska	November 1887
Okanogan	Washington	February 2, 1888
Converse	Wyoming	March 9, 1888
Natrona	Wyoming	March 9, 1888
Sheridan	Wyoming	March 9, 1888
Banner	Nebraska	November 6, 1888
Deuel	Nebraska	November 6, 1888
Kimball	Nebraska	November 6, 1888
Rock	Nebraska	November 6, 1888
Scotts Bluff	Nebraska	November 6, 1888
Florence	South Carolina	December 22, 1888
Charlottesville (IC)	Virginia	1888
Elmore	Idaho	February 7, 1889
Meade	South Dakota	February 7, 1889
Morgan	Colorado	February 19, 1889
Chaves	New Mexico	February 25, 1889
Eddy	New Mexico	February 25, 1889
Harney	Oregon	February 25, 1889
Sherman	Oregon	February 25, 1889
Irion	Texas	March 7, 1889
Orange	California	March 11, 1889
Coke	Texas	March 13, 1889
Yuma	Colorado	March 15, 1889
Cheyenne	Colorado	March 25, 1889
Otero	Colorado	March 25, 1889
Rio Blanco	Colorado	March 25, 1889
Phillips	Colorado	March 27, 1889
Hooker	Nebraska	March 29, 1889
Sedgwick	Colorado	April 9, 1889
Kiowa	Colorado	April 11, 1889
Kit Carson	Colorado	April 11, 1889
Lincoln	Colorado	April 11, 1889
Prowers	Colorado	April 11, 1889
Baca	Colorado	April 16, 1889
Montezuma	Colorado	April 16, 1889
Canadian	Oklahoma	1889
Bristol (IC)	Virginia	February 12, 1890
Pearl River	Mississippi	February 22, 1890
Big Horn	Wyoming	March 12, 1890

Weston	Wyoming	March 12, 1890
Grand	Utah	March 13, 1890
Beaver	Oklahoma	1890
Cleveland	Oklahoma	1890
Danville (IC)	Virginia	1890
Kingfisher	Oklahoma	1890
Logan	Oklahoma	1890
Oklahoma	Oklahoma	1890
Payne	Oklahoma	1890
Coconino	Arizona	February 19, 1891
Guadalupe	New Mexico	February 26, 1891
Foard	Texas	March 3, 1891
Sterling	Texas	March 4, 1891
Glenn	California	March 11, 1891
Boyd	Nebraska	March 20, 1891
Canyon	Idaho	May 7, 1891
Dickinson	Michigan	May 21, 1891
Lincoln	Oklahoma	1891
Pottawatomie	Oklahoma	1891
Wayne	Utah	March 10, 1892
Williams	North Dakota	November 30, 1892
Blaine	Oklahoma	1892
Buena Vista (IC)	Virginia	1892
Custer	Oklahoma	1892
Dewey	Oklahoma	1892
Radford (IC)	Virginia	1892
Roger Mills	Oklahoma	1892
Washita	Oklahoma	1892
Flathead	Montana	February 6, 1893
Valley	Montana	February 6, 1893
Teton	Montana	February 7, 1893
Ravalli	Montana	February 16, 1893
Lincoln	Oregon	February 20, 1893
Union	New Mexico	February 23, 1893
Iron	Wisconsin	March 1, 1893
Granite	Montana	March 2, 1893
Fremont	Idaho	March 4, 1893
Bannock	Idaho	March 6, 1893
Madera	California	March 11, 1893
Riverside	California	March 11, 1893
Kings	California	March 22, 1893
Mineral	Colorado	March 27, 1893
Vilas	Wisconsin	April 12, 1893
Garfield	Oklahoma	1893
Grant	Oklahoma	1893
Kay	Oklahoma	1893
Noble	Oklahoma	1893
Pawnee	Oklahoma	1893
Woods	Oklahoma	1893
Woodward	Oklahoma	1893
Roseau	Minnesota	February 28, 1894
Carbon	Utah	March 8, 1894

Mingo	West Virginia	January 30, 1895
Carbon	Montana	March 4, 1895
Blaine	Idaho	March 5, 1895
Sweet Grass	Montana	March 5, 1895
Lincoln	Idaho	March 18, 1895
Navajo	Arizona	March 21, 1895
Saluda	South Carolina	February 25, 1896
Red Lake	Minnesota	December 24, 1896
Broadwater	Montana	February 9, 1897
Bamberg	South Carolina	February 25, 1897
Cherokee	South Carolina	February 25, 1897
Dorchester	South Carolina	February 25, 1897
Greenwood	South Carolina	March 2, 1897
Nassau	New York	April 27, 1898
Otero	New Mexico	January 30, 1899
Wheeler	Oregon	February 17, 1899
Ferry	Washington	February 18, 1899
Scotland	North Carolina	February 20, 1899
McKinley	New Mexico	February 23, 1899
Chelan	Washington	March 13, 1899
Santa Cruz	Arizona	March 15, 1899
Teller	Colorado	March 23, 1899
Powell	Montana	January 31, 1901
Rosebud	Montana	February 11, 1901
Luna	New Mexico	March 16, 1901
Denver	Colorado	March 18, 1901
Adams	Colorado	April 15, 1901
Rusk	Wisconsin	May 15, 1901
Caddo	Oklahoma	1901
Comanche	Oklahoma	1901
Kiowa	Oklahoma	1901
Lee	South Carolina	February 25, 1902
Clearwater	Minnesota	December 20, 1902
Houston	Alabama	February 9, 1903
Quay	New Mexico	February 28, 1903
Roosevelt	New Mexico	February 28, 1903
Reagan	Texas	March 7, 1903
Sandoval	New Mexico	March 10, 1903
Torrance	New Mexico	March 16, 1903
Lamar	Mississippi	February 19, 1904
Sanders	Montana	February 7, 1905
Benton	Washington	March 8, 1905
Terrell	Texas	April 8, 1905
Saint Lucie	Florida	May 24, 1905
Hawaii	Hawaii	July 1905
Honolulu	Hawaii	July 1905

Kalawao	Hawaii	July 1905
Kauai	Hawaii	July 1905
Maui	Hawaii	July 1905
Crisp	Georgia	August 17, 1905
Grady	Georgia	August 17, 1905
Jenkins	Georgia	August 17, 1905
Tift	Georgia	August 17, 1905
Jeff Davis	Georgia	August 18, 1905
Stephens	Georgia	August 18, 1905
Toombs	Georgia	August 18, 1905
Turner	Georgia	August 18, 1905
Tulsa	Oklahoma	1905
Jefferson Davis	Mississippi	March 31, 1906
Forrest	Mississippi	April 19, 1906
Ben Hill	Georgia	July 31, 1906
Koochiching	Minnesota	December 19, 1906
Mahnomen	Minnesota	December 27, 1906
Clifton Forge (IC)	Virginia	1906
Bonner	Idaho	February 21, 1907
Twin Falls	Idaho	February 21, 1907
Lee	North Carolina	March 6, 1907
Adams	North Dakota	April 17, 1907
Adair	Oklahoma	July 16, 1907
Alfalfa	Oklahoma	July 16, 1907
Atoka	Oklahoma	July 16, 1907
Beckham	Oklahoma	July 16, 1907
Bryan	Oklahoma	July 16, 1907
Carter	Oklahoma	July 16, 1907
Cherokee	Oklahoma	July 16, 1907
Choctaw	Oklahoma	July 16, 1907
Cimarron	Oklahoma	July 16, 1907
Coal	Oklahoma	July 16, 1907
Craig	Oklahoma	July 16, 1907
Creek	Oklahoma	July 16, 1907
Delaware	Oklahoma	July 16, 1907
Ellis	Oklahoma	July 16, 1907
Garvin	Oklahoma	July 16, 1907
Grady	Oklahoma	July 16, 1907
Harper	Oklahoma	July 16, 1907
Haskell	Oklahoma	July 16, 1907
Hughes	Oklahoma	July 16, 1907
Jackson	Oklahoma	July 16, 1907
Jefferson	Oklahoma	July 16, 1907
Johnston	Oklahoma	July 16, 1907
Latimer	Oklahoma	July 16, 1907
Le Flore	Oklahoma	July 16, 1907
Love	Oklahoma	July 16, 1907
Major	Oklahoma	July 16, 1907
Marshall	Oklahoma	July 16, 1907
Mayes	Oklahoma	July 16, 1907
McClain	Oklahoma	July 16, 1907
McCurtain	Oklahoma	July 16, 1907
McIntosh	Oklahoma	July 16, 1907

Murray	Oklahoma	July 16, 1907
Muskogee	Oklahoma	July 16, 1907
Nowata	Oklahoma	July 16, 1907
Okfuskee	Oklahoma	July 16, 1907
Okmulgee	Oklahoma	July 16, 1907
Osage	Oklahoma	July 16, 1907
Ottawa	Oklahoma	July 16, 1907
Pittsburg	Oklahoma	July 16, 1907
Pontotoc	Oklahoma	July 16, 1907
Pushmataha	Oklahoma	July 16, 1907
Rogers	Oklahoma	July 16, 1907
Seminole	Oklahoma	July 16, 1907
Sequoyah	Oklahoma	July 16, 1907
Stephens	Oklahoma	July 16, 1907
Texas	Oklahoma	July 16, 1907
Tillman	Oklahoma	July 16, 1907
Wagoner	Oklahoma	July 16, 1907
Washington	Oklahoma	July 16, 1907
Imperial	California	August 6, 1907
Staunton (IC)	Virginia	January 16, 1908
Calhoun	South Carolina	February 14, 1908
Hood River	Oregon	June 23, 1908
La Salle	Louisiana	July 3, 1908
Perkins	South Dakota	November 3, 1908
Morrill	Nebraska	November 12, 1908
Clark	Nevada	February 9, 1909
Park	Wyoming	February 15, 1909
Grant	Washington	February 24, 1909
Curry	New Mexico	February 25, 1909
Corson	South Dakota	March 2, 1909
Bennett	South Dakota	March 9, 1909
Lincoln	Montana	March 9, 1909
Mellette	South Dakota	March 9, 1909
Todd	South Dakota	March 9, 1909
Greenlee	Arizona	March 10, 1909
Palm Beach	Florida	April 30, 1909
Jackson	Colorado	May 5, 1909
Harmon	Oklahoma	June 2, 1909
Garden	Nebraska	November 2, 1909
Burke	North Dakota	February 8, 1910
Dillon	South Carolina	February 15, 1910
George	Mississippi	March 16, 1910
Walthall	Mississippi	March 16, 1910
Evangeline	Louisiana	June 15, 1910
Suffolk	Virginia	October 10, 1910
Pennington	Minnesota	November 23, 1910
Divide	North Dakota	December 9, 1910
Ziebach	South Dakota	February 1, 1911
Bonneville	Idaho	February 7, 1911
Hoke	North Carolina	February 7, 1911
Goshen	Wyoming	February 9, 1911

Hot Springs	Wyoming	February 9, 1911
Platte	Wyoming	February 9, 1911
Washakie	Wyoming	February 9, 1911
Mineral	Nevada	February 10, 1911
Musselshell	Montana	February 11, 1911
Campbell	Wyoming	February 13, 1911
Niobrara	Wyoming	February 14, 1911
Lincoln	Wyoming	February 20, 1911
Avery	North Carolina	February 23, 1911
Clearwater	Idaho	February 27, 1911
Moffat	Colorado	February 27, 1911
Pend Oreille	Washington	March 1, 1911
Adams	Idaho	March 3, 1911
Lewis	Idaho	March 3, 1911
Culberson	Texas	March 10, 1911
Brooks	Texas	March 11, 1911
Willacy	Texas	March 11, 1911
Jim Wells	Texas	March 25, 1911
Pinellas	Florida	May 23, 1911
Crowley	Colorado	May 29, 1911
Jasper	South Carolina	January 30, 1912
Hill	Montana	February 28, 1912
Blaine	Montana	February 29, 1912
McCreary	Kentucky	March 12, 1912
Bronx	New York	April 19, 1912
Allen	Louisiana	June 12, 1912
Beauregard	Louisiana	June 12, 1912
Jefferson Davis	Louisiana	June 12, 1912
Bleckley	Georgia	July 30, 1912
Wheeler	Georgia	August 14, 1912
Cotton	Oklahoma	August 27, 1912
Golden Valley	North Dakota	November 19, 1912
Big Horn	Montana	January 13, 1913
Franklin	Idaho	January 20, 1913
Gooding	Idaho	January 28, 1913
Minidoka	Idaho	January 28, 1913
Power	Idaho	January 30, 1913
Jefferson	Idaho	February 18, 1913
Madison	Idaho	February 18, 1913
Kleberg	Texas	February 27, 1913
Duchesne	Utah	March 3, 1913
Alamosa	Colorado	March 8, 1913
Sheridan	Montana	March 24, 1913
Stillwater	Montana	March 24, 1913
Jim Hogg	Texas	March 31, 1913
Real	Texas	April 3, 1913
Bay	Florida	April 24, 1913
Seminole	Florida	April 25, 1913
Fallon	Montana	December 9, 1913
Toole	Montana	May 7, 1914
Richland	Montana	May 27, 1914
Barrow	Georgia	July 7, 1914

Candler	Georgia	July 17, 1914
Bacon	Georgia	July 27, 1914
Mineral	Montana	August 7, 1914
Evans	Georgia	August 11, 1914
Wibaux	Montana	August 17, 1914
Sioux	North Dakota	September 3, 1914
Slope	North Dakota	November 3, 1914
Haakon	South Dakota	November 1914
Jefferson	Oregon	December 12, 1914
Benewah	Idaho	January 23, 1915
Boundary	Idaho	January 23, 1915
Teton	Idaho	January 26, 1915
Phillips	Montana	February 5, 1915
Prairie	Montana	February 5, 1915
Gem	Idaho	March 19, 1915
Broward	Florida	April 30, 1915
Okaloosa	Florida	June 3, 1915
Jones	South Dakota	January 15, 1916
McCormick	South Carolina	February 19, 1916
Stone	Mississippi	April 3, 1916
Grant	North Dakota	November 25, 1916
Deschutes	Oregon	December 13, 1916
Harrisonburg (IC)	Virginia	1916
Hopewell (IC)	Virginia	1916
Butte	Idaho	February 6, 1917
Camas	Idaho	February 6, 1917
Hudspeth	Texas	February 16, 1917
Carter	Montana	February 22, 1917
Wheatland	Montana	February 22, 1917
Valley	Idaho	February 26, 1917
DeBaca	New Mexico	February 28, 1917
Payette	Idaho	February 28, 1917
Daggett	Utah	March 4, 1917
Lea	New Mexico	March 7, 1917
Flagler	Florida	April 28, 1917
Okeechobee	Florida	May 8, 1917
Atkinson	Georgia	August 15, 1917
Treutlen	Georgia	August 21, 1917
Humphreys	Mississippi	March 28, 1918
Cook	Georgia	July 30, 1918
Clark	Idaho	February 1, 1919
Allendale	South Carolina	February 6, 1919
Garfield	Montana	February 7, 1919
Treasure	Montana	February 7, 1919
Jerome	Idaho	February 8, 1919
Caribou	Idaho	February 11, 1919
Glacier	Montana	February 17, 1919
Pondera	Montana	February 17, 1919
Roosevelt	Montana	February 18, 1919
McCone	Montana	February 20, 1919

Hidalgo	New Mexico	February 25, 1919
Powder River	Montana	March 7, 1919
Pershing	Nevada	March 18, 1919
Lanier	Georgia	August 11, 1919
Liberty	Montana	February 11, 1920
Seminole	Georgia	July 8, 1920
Brantley	Georgia	August 14, 1920
Long	Georgia	August 14, 1920
Lamar	Georgia	August 17, 1920
Daniels	Montana	August 30, 1920
Golden Valley	Montana	October 4, 1920
Judith Basin	Montana	December 10, 1920
Sublette	Wyoming	February 15, 1921
Teton	Wyoming	February 15, 1921
Catron	New Mexico	February 25, 1921
Harding	New Mexico	March 4, 1921
Kenedy	Texas	April 2, 1921
Charlotte	Florida	April 23, 1921
Glades	Florida	April 23, 1921
Hardee	Florida	April 23, 1921
Highlands	Florida	April 23, 1921
Dixie	Florida	April 25, 1921
Sarasota	Florida	May 14, 1921
Union	Florida	May 20, 1921
Lake of the Woods	Minnesota	November 28, 1922
Collier	Florida	May 8, 1923
Hendry	Florida	May 11, 1923
Lake	Montana	May 11, 1923
Peach	Georgia	July 18, 1924
Petroleum	Montana	November 24, 1924
Indian River	Florida	May 30, 1925
Martin	Florida	May 30, 1925
Gulf	Florida	June 6, 1925
Gilchrist	Florida	December 4, 1925
Martinsville (IC)	Virginia	1928
Waynesboro (IC)	Virginia	February 1948
Falls Church (IC)	Virginia	1948
Los Alamos	New Mexico	March 16, 1949
Covington (IC)	Virginia	1952
Galax (IC)	Virginia	November 30, 1953
Norton (IC)	Virginia	1954
Menominee	Wisconsin	May 1, 1961

Fairfax (IC)	Virginia	June 30, 1961
Franklin (IC)	Virginia	December 21, 1961
Colonial Heights (IC)	Virginia	1961
Bristol Bay	Alaska	October 1962
Anchorage	Alaska	September 13, 1963
Kenai Peninsula	Alaska	September 13, 1963
Ketchikan Gateway	Alaska	September 13, 1963
Kodiak Island	Alaska	September 1963
Fairbanks North Star	Alaska	January 1, 1964
Matanuska-Susitna	Alaska	January 1964
Lexington (IC)	Virginia	December 31, 1965
Emporia (IC)	Virginia	July 31, 1967
Bedford (IC)	Virginia	August 30, 1968
Haines	Alaska	August 1968
Salem (IC)	Virginia	1968
Juneau	Alaska	December 1971
Sitka	Alaska	December 1971
North Slope	Alaska	July 1, 1972
Manassas (IC)	Virginia	May 1, 1975
Manassas Park (IC)	Virginia	June 1, 1975
Poquoson (IC)	Virginia	1976
Cibola	New Mexico	January 19, 1981
La Paz	Arizona	November 2, 1983
Northwest Arctic	Alaska	June 1986
Aleutians East	Alaska	October 23, 1987
Lake and Peninsula	Alaska	April 1989
Denali	Alaska	December 1990
Yakutat	Alaska	September 1992
Broomfield	Colorado	November 15, 2001

Appendix B:
Counties by State

This appendix lists counties alphabetically by state. The list includes the county seat and the date the county was created. Please see "Introduction to the 5th Edition" for a discussion of county seats and dates of creation. The information provided in this appendix at the beginning of each state's entry is meant to account for the political entity under which the counties were created. It is not meant to include the state's entire political history.

This appendix also includes the governmental action (statute) that created the county. This legislative information is included for the researcher who wants to pursue in detail the creation of a county. The enumeration of legislation varies widely between and within states. A lower number does not necessarily mean an earlier piece of legislation. The creation of a county may be by a general law, a private law, or a special law. Each category of laws may have its own numbering system within a state. The column heading is labeled "Statute" although the county was not always created by a law. Some original counties in a state were created by the state constitution; others were created by a petition and election.

Abbreviations used under "Statute" are Ch. = Chapter; Const. = Constitution; Conv. = Convention; H.B. = House Bill; P & E = Petition and Election; Proc. = Proclamation; Res. = Resolution; S.B. = Senate Bill; Unnumb. = Unnumbered.

ALABAMA (67 COUNTIES)

Mississippi Territory April 7, 1798
Alabama Territory March 3, 1817
Admitted as state December 14, 1819 (22nd)
Seceded January 11, 1861
Readmitted June 25, 1868

County	County Seat	Created	Statute
Autauga	Prattville	Nov. 21, 1818	Unnumb.
Baldwin	Bay Minette	Dec. 21, 1809	Unnumb.
Barbour	Clayton	Dec. 18, 1832	Act 11
Bibb[1]	Centreville	Feb. 7, 1818	Unnumb.
Blount	Oneonta	Feb. 6, 1818	Unnumb.
Bullock	Union Springs	Dec. 5, 1866	Act 84
Butler	Greenville	Dec. 13, 1819	Unnumb.
Calhoun[2]	Anniston	Dec. 18, 1832	Act 11
Chambers	Lafayette	Dec. 18, 1832	Act 11
Cherokee	Centre	Jan. 9, 1836	Act 179
Chilton[3]	Clanton	Dec. 30, 1868	Act 142
Choctaw	Butler	Dec. 29, 1847	Act 213
Clarke	Grove Hill	Dec. 10, 1812	Act 5
Clay	Ashland	Dec. 7, 1866	Act 110
Cleburne	Heflin	Dec. 6, 1866	Act 89
Coffee	New Brockton	Dec. 29, 1841	Act 190

Colbert	Tuscumbia	Feb. 6, 1867	Act 321
Conecuh	Evergreen	Feb. 13, 1818	Unnumb.
Coosa	Rockford	Dec. 18, 1832	Act 11
Covington[4]	Andalusia	Dec. 7, 1821	Unnumb.
Crenshaw	Luverne	Nov. 24, 1866	Act 39
Cullman	Cullman	Jan. 24, 1877	Act 56
Dale	Ozark	Dec. 22, 1824	Unnumb.
Dallas	Selma	Feb. 9. 1818	Unnumb.
DeKalb	Fort Payne	Jan. 9, 1836	Act 179
Elmore	Wetumpka	Feb. 15, 1866	Act 312
Escambia	Brewton	Dec. 10, 1868	Act 34
Etowah[5]	Gadsden	Dec. 7, 1866	Act 92
Fayette	Fayette	Dec. 20, 1824	Unnumb.
Franklin	Russellville	Feb. 6, 1818	Unnumb.
Geneva	Geneva	Dec. 26, 1868	Act 110
Greene	Eutaw	Dec. 13, 1819	Unnumb.
Hale	Greensboro	Jan. 30, 1867	Act 418
Henry	Abbeville	Dec. 13, 1819	Unnumb.
Houston	Dothan	Feb. 9, 1903	Act 27
Jackson	Scottsboro	Dec. 13, 1819	Unnumb.
Jefferson	Birmingham	Dec. 13, 1819	Unnumb.
Lamar[6]	Vernon	Feb. 4, 1867	Act 298
Lauderdale	Florence	Feb. 6, 1818	Unnumb.
Lawrence	Moulton	Feb. 6, 1818	Unnumb.
Lee	Opelika	Dec. 5, 1866	Act 61
Limestone	Athens	Feb. 6, 1818	Unnumb.
Lowndes	Hayneville	Jan. 20, 1830	Unnumb.
Macon	Tuskegee	Dec. 18, 1832	Act 11
Madison	Huntsville	Dec. 13, 1808	Proc.
Marengo	Linden	Feb. 6, 1818	Unnumb.
Marion	Hamilton	Feb. 13, 1818	Unnumb.
Marshall	Guntersville	Jan. 9, 1836	Act 47
Mobile	Mobile	Aug. 1, 1812	Proc.
Monroe	Monroeville	June 29, 1815	Proc.
Montgomery	Montgomery	Dec. 6, 1816	Act 8
Morgan[7]	Decatur	Feb. 6, 1818	Unnumb.
Perry	Marion	Dec. 13, 1819	Unnumb.
Pickens	Carrollton	Dec. 19, 1820	Act 26
Pike	Troy	Dec. 17, 1821	Act 32
Randolph	Wedowee	Dec. 18, 1832	Act 11
Russell	Phenix City	Dec. 18, 1832	Act 11
Saint Clair	Ashville	Nov. 20, 1818	Unnumb.
Shelby	Columbiana	Feb. 7, 1818	Unnumb.
Sumter	Livingston	Dec. 18, 1832	Act 11
Talladega	Talladega	Dec. 18, 1832	Act 11
Tallapoosa	Dadeville	Dec. 18, 1832	Act 11
Tuscaloosa	Tuscaloosa	Feb. 6, 1818	Unnumb.
Walker	Jasper	Dec. 26, 1823	Unnumb.
Washington	Chatom	June 4, 1800	Proc.
Wilcox	Camden	Dec. 13, 1819	Unnumb.
Winston[8]	Double Springs	Feb. 12, 1850	Act 58

Notes

1. Bibb created as Cahawba; name changed Dec. 20, 1820, Act 24
2. Calhoun created as Benton; name changed Jan. 29, 1856, Act 306

3. Chilton created as Baker; name changed Dec. 17, 1874, Act 72
4. Created as Covington; name changed to Jones, Aug. 6, 1868, unnumbered; renamed Covington, Oct. 10, 1868, Act 39
5. Etowah created as Baine; name changed Dec. 3, 1867, Act 20
6. Lamar created as Jones; name changed Feb. 8, 1877, Act 205
7. Morgan created as Cotaco; name changed June 14, 1821, unnumbered
8. Winston created as Hancock; name changed Jan. 22, 1858, Act 322

ALASKA (16 BOROUGHS; 11 CENSUS AREAS)

Alaska District May 17, 1884
Alaska Territory August 24, 1912
Admitted as state January 3, 1959 (49th)

Borough/Census Area[1]	Borough Center	Created
Aleutians East	Sand Point	Oct. 23, 1987
Aleutians West	—	—
Anchorage	Anchorage	Sep. 13, 1963
Bethel	—	—
Bristol Bay	Naknek	Oct. 1962
Denali	Healy	Dec. 1990
Dillingham	—	—
Fairbanks North Star	Fairbanks	Jan. 1, 1964
Haines	Haines	Aug. 1968
Juneau	Juneau	Dec. 1971
Kenai Peninsula	Soldotna	Sep. 13, 1963
Ketchikan Gateway	Ketchikan	Sep. 13, 1963
Kodiak Island	Kodiak	Sep. 1963
Lake and Peninsula	King Salmon	Apr. 1989
Matanuska-Susitna	Palmer	Jan. 1964
Nome	—	—
North Slope	Barrow	July 1, 1972
Northwest Arctic	Kotzebue	June 1986
Prince of Wales–Outer Ketchikan	—	—
Sitka	Sitka	Dec. 1971
Skagway-Hoonah-Angoon	—	—
Southeast Fairbanks	—	—
Valdez-Cordova	—	—
Wade Hampton	—	—
Wrangell-Petersburg	—	—
Yakutat	Yakutat	Sep. 1992
Yukon-Koyukuk	—	—

Note

1. If there is no borough center listed in the second column, the entity is a census area.

ARIZONA (15 COUNTIES)

Arizona Territory February 24, 1863
Admitted as state February 14, 1912 (48th)

County	County Seat	Created	Statute
Apache	Saint Johns	Feb. 14, 1879	Act 58
Cochise	Bisbee	Feb. 1, 1881	Act 7

Coconino	Flagstaff	Feb. 19, 1891	Act 14
Gila	Globe	Feb. 8, 1881	Act 17
Graham	Safford	Mar. 10, 1881	Act 87
Greenlee	Clifton	Mar. 10, 1909	Act 21
La Paz	Parker	Nov. 2, 1983	
Maricopa	Phoenix	Feb. 14, 1871	Unnumb.
Mohave	Kingman	Dec. 21, 1864	Unnumb.
Navajo	Holbrook	Mar. 21, 1895	Act 60
Pima	Tucson	Dec. 15, 1864	Unnumb.
Pinal	Florence	Feb. 1, 1875	Unnumb.
Santa Cruz	Nogales	Mar. 15, 1899	Act 44
Yavapai	Prescott	Dec. 21, 1864	Unnumb.
Yuma	Yuma	Dec. 21, 1864	Unnumb.

ARKANSAS (75 COUNTIES)

Missouri Territory June 14, 1812
Arkansas Territory March 2, 1819
Admitted as state June 15, 1836 (25th)
Seceded May 6, 1861
Readmitted June 22, 1868

County	County Seat	Created	Statute
Arkansas	De Witt	Dec. 31, 1813	Unnumb.
Ashley	Hamburg	Nov. 30, 1848	Unnumb.
Baxter	Mountain Home	Mar. 24, 1873	Act 26
Benton	Bentonville	Sep. 30, 1836	Unnumb.
Boone	Harrison	Apr. 9, 1869	Act 70
Bradley	Warren	Dec. 18, 1840	Unnumb.
Calhoun	Hampton	Dec. 6, 1850	Unnumb.
Carroll	Berryville	Nov. 1, 1833	Unnumb.
Chicot	Lake Village	Oct. 25, 1823	Unnumb.
Clark	Arkadelphia	Dec. 15, 1818	Unnumb.
Clay[1]	Piggott	Mar. 24, 1873	Act 27
Cleburne	Heber Springs	Feb. 20, 1883	Act 24
Cleveland[2]	Rison	Apr. 17, 1873	Act 58
Columbia	Magnolia	Dec. 17, 1852	Unnumb.
Conway	Morrilton	Oct. 20, 1825	Unnumb.
Craighead	Jonesboro	Feb. 19, 1859	Act 171
Crawford	Van Buren	Oct. 18, 1820	Unnumb.
Crittenden	Marion	Oct. 22, 1825	Unnumb.
Cross	Wynne	Nov. 15, 1862	Unnumb.
Dallas	Fordyce	Jan. 1, 1845	Unnumb.
Desha	Arkansas City	Dec. 12, 1838	Unnumb.
Drew	Monticello	Nov. 26, 1846	Unnumb.
Faulkner	Conway	Apr. 12, 1873	Act 44
Franklin	Ozark	Dec. 19, 1837	Unnumb.
Fulton	Salem	Dec. 21, 1842	Unnumb.
Garland	Hot Springs	Apr. 5, 1873	Act 34
Grant	Sheridan	Feb. 4, 1869	Act 15
Greene	Paragould	Nov. 5, 1833	Unnumb.
Hempstead	Hope	Dec. 15, 1818	Unnumb.
Hot Spring	Malvern	Nov. 2, 1829	Unnumb.
Howard	Nashville	Apr. 17, 1873	Act 57
Independence	Batesville	Oct. 23, 1820	Unnumb.

Izard	Melbourne	Oct. 27, 1825	Unnumb.
Jackson	Newport	Nov. 5, 1829	Unnumb.
Jefferson	Pine Bluff	Nov. 2, 1829	Unnumb.
Johnson	Clarksville	Nov. 16, 1833	Unnumb.
Lafayette	Lewisville	Oct. 15, 1827	Unnumb.
Lawrence	Walnut Ridge	Jan. 15, 1815	Unnumb.
Lee	Marianna	Apr. 17, 1873	Act 60
Lincoln	Star City	Mar. 28, 1871	Act 68
Little River	Ashdown	Mar. 5, 1867	Act 104
Logan[3]	Paris	Mar. 22, 1871	Act 25
Lonoke	Lonoke	Apr. 16, 1873	Act 47
Madison	Huntsville	Sep. 30, 1836	Unnumb.
Marion[4]	Yellville	Nov. 3, 1835	Unnumb.
Miller	Texarkana	Dec. 1874	Unnumb.
Mississippi	Blytheville	Nov. 1, 1833	Unnumb.
Monroe	Clarendon	Nov. 2, 1829	Unnumb.
Montgomery	Mount Ida	Dec. 9, 1842	Unnumb.
Nevada	Prescott	Mar. 20, 1871	Act 20
Newton	Jasper	Dec. 14, 1842	Unnumb.
Ouachita	Camden	Nov. 29, 1842	Unnumb.
Perry	Perryville	Dec. 18, 1840	Unnumb.
Phillips	Helena	May 1, 1820	Unnumb.
Pike	Murfreesboro	Nov. 1, 1833	Unnumb.
Poinsett	Harrisburg	Feb. 28, 1838	Unnumb.
Polk	Mena	Nov. 30, 1844	Unnumb.
Pope	Russellville	Nov. 2, 1829	Unnumb.
Prairie	Des Arc	Nov. 25, 1846	Unnumb.
Pulaski	Little Rock	Dec. 15, 1818	Unnumb.
Randolph	Pocahontas	Oct. 29, 1835	Unnumb.
Saint Francis	Forrest City	Oct. 13, 1827	Unnumb.
Saline	Benton	Nov. 2, 1835	Unnumb.
Scott	Waldron	Nov. 5, 1833	Unnumb.
Searcy	Marshall	Dec. 13, 1838	Unnumb.
Sebastian	Fort Smith	Jan. 6, 1851	Unnumb.
Sevier	De Queen	Oct. 17, 1828	Unnumb.
Sharp	Ash Flat	July 18, 1868	Act 42
Stone	Mountain View	Apr. 21, 1873	Act 74
Union	El Dorado	Nov. 2, 1829	Unnumb.
Van Buren	Clinton	Nov. 11, 1833	Unnumb.
Washington	Fayetteville	Oct. 17, 1828	Unnumb.
White	Searcy	Oct. 23, 1835	Unnumb.
Woodruff	Augusta	Nov. 26, 1862	Unnumb.
Yell	Danville	Dec. 5, 1840	Unnumb.

Notes

1. Clay created as Clayton; name changed Dec. 6, 1875, Act 42
2. Cleveland created as Dorsey; name changed Mar. 5, 1885, Act 38
3. Logan created as Sarber; name changed Dec. 14, 1875, Act 62
4. Marion created as Searcy; name changed Sep. 29, 1836, unnumbered

CALIFORNIA (58 COUNTIES)

Constitutional Convention 1849–50
Admitted as state September 9, 1850 (31st)

County	County Seat	Created	Statute
Alameda	Oakland	Mar. 25, 1853	Ch. 41
Alpine	Markleeville	Mar. 16, 1864	Ch. 180
Amador	Jackson	May 11, 1854	Ch. 42
Butte	Oroville	Feb. 18, 1850	Ch. 15
Calaveras	San Andreas	Feb. 18, 1850	Ch. 15
Colusa[1]	Colusa	Feb. 18, 1850	Ch. 15
Contra Costa	Martinez	Feb. 18, 1850	Ch. 15
Del Norte	Crescent City	Mar. 2, 1857	Ch. 52
El Dorado	Placerville	Feb. 18, 1850	Ch. 15
Fresno	Fresno	Apr. 19, 1856	Ch. 127
Glenn	Willows	Mar. 11, 1891	Ch. 94
Humboldt	Eureka	May 12, 1853	Ch. 114
Imperial	El Centro	Aug. 6, 1907	Unnumb.
Inyo	Independence	Mar. 22, 1866	Ch. 316
Kern	Bakersfield	Apr. 2, 1866	Ch. 569
Kings	Hanford	Mar. 22, 1893	Ch. 150
Lake	Lakeport	May 20, 1861	Ch. 498
Lassen	Susanville	Apr. 1, 1864	Ch. 261
Los Angeles	Los Angeles	Feb. 18, 1850	Ch. 15
Madera	Madera	Mar. 11, 1893	Ch. 143
Marin	San Rafael	Feb. 18, 1850	Ch. 15
Mariposa	Mariposa	Feb. 18, 1850	Ch. 15
Mendocino	Ukiah	Feb. 18, 1850	Ch. 15
Merced	Merced	Apr. 19, 1855	Ch. 104
Modoc	Alturas	Feb. 17, 1874	Ch. 107
Mono	Bridgeport	Apr. 24, 1861	Ch. 233
Monterey	Salinas	Feb. 18, 1850	Ch. 15
Napa	Napa	Feb. 18, 1850	Ch. 15
Nevada	Nevada City	Apr. 25, 1851	Ch. 14
Orange	Santa Ana	Mar. 11, 1889	Ch. 110
Placer	Auburn	Apr. 25, 1851	Ch. 14
Plumas	Quincy	Mar. 18, 1854	Ch. 1
Riverside	Riverside	Mar. 11, 1893	Ch. 142
Sacramento	Sacramento	Feb. 18, 1850	Ch. 15
San Benito	Hollister	Feb. 12, 1874	Ch. 87
San Bernardino	San Bernardino	Apr. 26, 1853	Ch. 78
San Diego	San Diego	Feb. 18, 1850	Ch. 15
San Francisco	San Francisco	Feb. 18, 1850	Ch. 15
San Joaquin	Stockton	Feb. 18, 1850	Ch. 15
San Luis Obispo	San Luis Obispo	Feb. 18, 1850	Ch. 15
San Mateo	Redwood City	Apr. 19, 1856	Ch. 125
Santa Barbara	Santa Barbara	Feb. 18, 1850	Ch. 15
Santa Clara	San Jose	Feb. 18, 1850	Ch. 15
Santa Cruz[2]	Santa Cruz	Feb. 18, 1850	Ch. 15
Shasta	Redding	Feb. 18, 1850	Ch. 15
Sierra	Downieville	Apr. 16, 1852	Ch. 145
Siskiyou	Yreka	Mar. 22, 1852	Ch. 146
Solano	Fairfield	Feb. 18, 1850	Ch. 15
Sonoma	Santa Rosa	Feb. 18, 1850	Ch. 15
Stanislaus	Modesto	Apr. 1, 1854	Ch. 81
Sutter	Yuba City	Feb. 18, 1850	Ch. 15
Tehama	Red Bluff	Apr. 9, 1856	Ch. 100
Trinity	Weaverville	Feb. 18, 1850	Ch. 15
Tulare	Visalia	Apr. 20, 1852	Ch. 153

Tuolumne	Sonora	Feb. 18, 1850	Ch. 15
Ventura	Ventura	Mar. 22, 1872	Ch. 151
Yolo	Woodland	Feb. 18, 1850	Ch. 15
Yuba	Marysville	Feb. 18, 1850	Ch. 15

Notes

1. Colusa created as Colusi; spelling changed 1854
2. Sanata Cruz created as Branciforte; name changed Apr. 5, 1850, Ch. 61

COLORADO (64 COUNTIES)

Colorado Territory February 28, 1861
Admitted as state August 1, 1876 (38th)

County	County Seat	Created	Statute
Adams	Brighton	Apr. 15, 1901	Ch. 57
Alamosa	Alamosa	Mar. 8, 1913	Ch. 6
Arapahoe	Littleton	Nov. 1, 1861	Unnumb.
Archuleta	Pagosa Springs	Apr. 15, 1885	S.B. 144
Baca	Springfield	Apr. 16, 1889	S.B. 37
Bent	Las Animas	Feb. 11, 1870	Unnumb.
Boulder	Boulder	Nov. 1, 1861	Unnumb.
Broomfield	Broomfield	Nov. 15, 2001	
Chaffee[1]	Salida	Nov. 1, 1861	Unnumb.
Cheyenne	Cheyenne Wells	March 25, 1889	S.B. 116
Clear Creek	Georgetown	Nov. 1, 1861	Unnumb.
Conejos[2]	Conejos	Nov. 1, 1861	Unnumb.
Costilla	San Luis	Nov. 1, 1861	Unnumb.
Crowley	Ordway	May 29, 1911	Ch. 111
Custer	Westcliffe	Mar. 9, 1877	Ch. 400
Delta	Delta	Feb. 11, 1883	Unnumb.
Denver	Denver	Mar. 18, 1901	Ch. 46
Dolores	Dove Creek	Feb. 19, 1881	Unnumb.
Douglas	Castle Rock	Nov. 1, 1861	Unnumb.
Eagle	Eagle	Feb. 11, 1883	Unnumb.
Elbert	Kiowa	Feb. 2, 1874	Unnumb.
El Paso	Colorado Springs	Nov. 1, 1861	Unnumb.
Fremont	Canon City	Nov. 1, 1861	Unnumb.
Garfield	Glenwood Springs	Feb. 10, 1883	Unnumb.
Gilpin	Central City	Nov. 1, 1861	Unnumb.
Grand	Hot Sulphur Springs	Feb. 2, 1874	Unnumb.
Gunnison	Gunnison	Mar. 9, 1977	Ch. 411
Hinsdale	Lake City	Feb. 10, 1874	Unnumb.
Huerfano	Walsenburg	Nov. 1, 1861	Unnumb.
Jackson	Walden	May 5, 1909	Ch. 179
Jefferson	Golden	Nov. 1, 1861	Unnumb.
Kiowa	Eads	Apr. 11, 1889	H.B. 337
Kit Carson	Burlington	Apr. 11, 1889	S.B. 48
Lake[3]	Leadville	Nov. 1, 1861	Unnumb.
La Plata	Durango	Feb. 10, 1874	Unnumb.
Larimer	Fort Collins	Nov. 1, 1861	Unnumb.
Las Animas	Trinidad	Feb. 9, 1866	Unnumb.
Lincoln	Hugo	Apr. 11, 1889	S.B. 106

Logan	Sterling	Feb. 25, 1887	S.B. 72
Mesa	Grand Junction	Feb. 14, 1883	Unnumb.
Mineral	Creede	Mar. 27, 1893	S.B. 57
Moffat	Craig	Feb. 27, 1911	Ch. 173
Montezuma	Cortez	Apr. 16, 1889	H.B. 230
Montrose	Montrose	Feb. 11, 1883	Unnumb.
Morgan	Fort Morgan	Feb. 19, 1889	S.B. 40
Otero	La Junta	Mar. 25, 1889	S.B. 34
Ouray[4]	Ouray	Jan. 18, 1877	Unnumb.
Park	Fairplay	Nov. 1, 1861	Unnumb.
Phillips	Holyoke	Mar. 27, 1889	H.B. 127
Pitkin	Aspen	Feb. 23, 1881	Unnumb.
Prowers	Lamar	Apr. 11, 1889	S.B. 35
Pueblo	Pueblo	Nov. 1, 1861	Unnumb.
Rio Blanco	Meeker	Mar. 25, 1889	H.B. 107
Rio Grande	Del Norte	Feb. 10, 1874	Unnumb.
Routt	Steamboat Springs	Jan. 29, 1877	Ch. 393
Saguache	Saguache	Dec. 29, 1866	Unnumb.
San Juan	Silverton	Jan. 31, 1876	Unnumb.
San Miguel	Telluride	Nov. 1, 1883	Unnumb.
Sedgwick	Julesburg	Apr. 9, 1889	H.B. 148
Summit	Breckenridge	Nov. 1, 1861	Unnumb.
Teller	Cripple Creek	Mar. 23, 1899	S.B. 52
Washington	Akron	Feb. 9, 1887	H.B. 51
Weld	Greeley	Nov. 1, 1861	Unnumb.
Yuma	Wray	Mar. 15, 1889	H.B. 90

Notes

1. Chaffee created as Lake; name changed Feb. 10, 1879, unnumbered
2. Conejos created as Guadalupe; name changed Nov. 7, 1861, unnumbered
3. Lake created as Carbonate; name changed Feb. 10, 1897, unnumbered
4. Ouray created as Uncompahgre; name changed Mar. 2, 1883, unnumbered

CONNECTICUT (8 COUNTIES)

Connecticut Colony established 1636
Connecticut and New Haven colonies consolidated 1662
Independence Resolution June 14, 1776
Ratified Constitution January 9, 1788 (admitted as 5th state)

County	County Seat	Created
Fairfield	Bridgeport	May 10, 1666 (Sess.)
Hartford	Hartford	May 10, 1666 (Sess.)
Litchfield	Litchfield	Oct. 14, 1751 (Sess.)
Middlesex	Middletown	May 2, 1785 (Sess.)
New Haven	New Haven	May 10, 1666 (Sess.)
New London	New London	May 10, 1666 (Sess.)
Tolland	Rockville	Oct. 13, 1785 (Sess.)
Windham	Putnam	May 12, 1726 (Sess.)

DELAWARE (3 COUNTIES)

Captured from Dutch by English 1664
Acquired by Pennsylvania 1682
Self-rule from Pennsylvania 1704

Declared independence July 4, 1776
Ratified Constitution December 7, 1787 (admitted as 1st state)

County	County Seat	Created
Kent[1]	Dover	1680
New Castle	Wilmington	Aug. 8, 1673
Sussex[2]	Georgetown	Aug. 8, 1673

Notes

1. Kent created as Saint Jones; name changed Dec. 31, 1683
2. Sussex created as Hoarkill; name changed to Deale 1681; name changed to Sussex Dec. 4, 1682

DISTRICT OF COLUMBIA (FEDERAL DISTRICT)

County	County Seat	Created
	Washington	July 16, 1790

FLORIDA (67 COUNTIES)

Military government 1819
Florida Territory March 30, 1822
Admitted as state March 3, 1845 (27th)
Seceded January 10, 1861
Readmitted June 25, 1868

County	County Seat	Created	Statute
Alachua	Gainesville	Dec. 29, 1824	Unnumb.
Baker	Macclenny	Feb. 8, 1861	Ch. 1,185
Bay	Panama City	Apr. 24, 1913	Ch. 6,505
Bradford[1]	Starke	Dec. 21, 1858	Ch. 895
Brevard[2]	Titusville	Mar. 14, 1844	Unnumb.
Broward	Fort Lauderdale	Apr. 30, 1915	Ch. 6,934
Calhoun	Blountstown	Jan. 26, 1838	Ch. 8
Charlotte	Port Charlotte	Apr. 23, 1921	Ch. 8,513
Citrus	Inverness	June 2, 1887	Ch. 3,772
Clay	Green Cove Springs	Dec. 31, 1858	Ch. 866
Collier	Naples	May 8, 1923	Ch. 9,362
Columbia	Lake City	Feb. 4, 1832	Ch. 25
DeSoto	Arcadia	May 19, 1887	Ch. 3,770
Dixie	Cross City	Apr. 25, 1921	Ch. 8,514
Duval	Jacksonville	Aug. 12, 1822	Unnumb.
Escambia	Pensacola	July 21, 1821	Unnumb.
Flagler	Bunnell	Apr. 28, 1917	Ch. 7,379
Franklin	Apalachicola	Feb. 8, 1832	Ch. 42
Gadsden	Quincy	June 24, 1823	Unnumb.
Gilchrist	Trenton	Dec. 4, 1925	Ch. 11,371
Glades	Moore Haven	Apr. 23, 1921	Ch. 8,513
Gulf	Port Saint Joe	June 6, 1925	Ch. 10,132
Hamilton	Jasper	Dec. 26, 1827	Unnumb.
Hardee	Wauchula	Apr. 23, 1921	Ch. 8,513
Hendry	La Belle	May 11, 1923	Ch. 9,360
Hernando[3]	Brooksville	Feb. 24, 1843	Ch. 51

Highlands	Sebring	Apr. 23, 1921	Ch. 8,513
Hillsborough	Tampa	Jan. 25, 1834	Ch. 764
Holmes	Bonifay	Jan. 8, 1848	Ch. 176
Indian River	Vero Beach	May 30, 1925	Ch. 10,148
Jackson	Marianna	Aug. 12, 1822	Unnumb.
Jefferson	Monticello	Jan. 6, 1827	Unnumb.
Lafayette	Mayo	Dec. 23, 1856	Ch. 806
Lake	Tavares	May 27, 1887	Ch. 3,771
Lee	Fort Myers	May 13, 1887	Ch. 3,769
Leon	Tallahassee	Dec. 29, 1824	Unnumb.
Levy	Bronson	Mar. 10, 1845	Ch. 30
Liberty	Bristol	Dec. 15, 1855	Ch. 771
Madison	Madison	Dec. 26, 1827	Unnumb.
Manatee	Bradenton	Jan. 9, 1855	Ch. 628
Marion	Ocala	Mar. 14, 1844	Unnumb.
Martin	Stuart	May 30, 1925	Ch. 10,180
Miami-Dade[4]	Miami	Feb. 4, 1836	Ch. 937
Monroe	Key West	July 3, 1823	Unnumb.
Nassau	Fernandina Beach	Dec. 29, 1824	Unnumb.
Okaloosa	Crestview	June 3, 1915	Ch. 6,937
Okeechobee	Okeechobee	May 8, 1917	Ch. 7,401
Orange[5]	Orlando	Dec. 29, 1824	Unnumb.
Osceola	Kissimmee	May 12, 1887	Ch. 3,768
Palm Beach	West Palm Beach	Apr. 30, 1909	Ch. 5,970
Pasco	Dade City	June 2, 1887	Ch. 3,772
Pinellas	Clearwater	May 23, 1911	Ch. 6,247
Polk	Bartow	Feb. 8, 1861	Ch. 1,201
Putnam	Palatka	Jan. 13, 1849	Ch. 280
Saint Johns	Saint Augustine	Aug. 12, 1822	Unnumb.
Saint Lucie	Fort Pierce	May 24, 1905	Ch. 5,567
Santa Rosa	Milton	Feb. 18, 1842	Unnumb.
Sarasota	Sarasota	May 14, 1921	Ch. 8,515
Seminole	Sanford	Apr. 25, 1913	Ch. 6,511
Sumter	Bushnell	Jan. 8, 1853	Ch. 548
Suwanee	Live Oak	Dec. 21, 1858	Ch. 895
Taylor	Perry	Dec. 23, 1856	Ch. 806
Union	Lake Butler	May 20, 1921	Ch. 8,516
Volusia	De Land	Dec. 29, 1854	Ch. 624
Wakulla	Crawfordville	Mar. 11, 1843	Ch. 25
Walton	De Funiak Springs	Dec. 29, 1824	Unnumb.
Washington	Chipley	Dec. 9, 1825	Unnumb.

Notes

1. Bradford created as New River; name changed Dec. 6, 1861, Ch. 1,300
2. Brevard created as Saint Lucie; name changed Jan 6. 1855, Ch. 651
3. Created as Hernando; name changed to Benton Mar. 6, 1844, unnumbered; renamed Hernando Dec. 24, 1850, Ch. 415
4. Miami-Dade created as Dade; name changed Dec. 2, 1997
5. Orange created as Mosquito; name changed Jan. 30, 1845, Ch. 31

GEORGIA (159 COUNTIES)

State Constitution Feb. 5, 1777
Ratified Constitution January 2, 1788 (admitted as 4th state)

Seceded January 19, 1861
Readmitted July 15, 1870

County	County Seat	Created	Statute
Appling	Baxley	Dec. 15, 1818	Unnumb.
Atkinson	Pearson	Aug. 15, 1917	Act 180
Bacon	Alma	July 27, 1914	Act 298
Baker	Newton	Dec. 12, 1825	Unnumb.
Baldwin	Milledgeville	May 11, 1803	Unnumb.
Banks	Homer	Dec. 11, 1858	Act 19
Barrow	Winder	July 7, 1914	Act 278
Bartow[1]	Cartersville	Dec. 3, 1832	Unnumb.
Ben Hill	Fitzgerald	July 31, 1906	Act 372
Berrien	Nashville	Feb. 25, 1856	Act 48
Bibb	Macon	Dec. 9, 1822	Unnumb.
Bleckley	Cochran	July 30, 1912	Act 355
Brantley	Nahunta	Aug. 14, 1920	Act 626
Brooks	Quitman	Dec. 11, 1858	Act 21
Bryan	Pembroke	Dec. 19, 1793	Unnumb.
Bulloch	Statesboro	Feb. 8, 1796	Unnumb.
Burke	Waynesboro	Feb. 5, 1777	Const.
Butts	Jackson	Dec. 24, 1825	Unnumb.
Calhoun	Morgan	Feb. 20, 1854	Act 217
Camden	Woodbine	Feb. 5, 1777	Const.
Candler	Metter	July 17, 1914	Act 282
Carroll	Carrollton	Dec. 11, 1826	Unnumb.
Catoosa	Ringgold	Dec. 5, 1853	Act 218
Charlton	Folkston	Feb. 18, 1854	Act 220
Chatham	Savannah	Feb. 5, 1777	Const.
Chattahoochee	Cusseta	Feb. 13, 1854	Act 219
Chattooga	Summerville	Dec. 28, 1838	Unnumb.
Cherokee	Canton	Dec. 26, 1831	Unumb.
Clarke	Athens	Dec. 5, 1801	Unnumb.
Clay	Fort Gaines	Feb. 16, 1854	Act 221
Clayton	Jonesboro	Nov. 30, 1858	Act 17
Clinch	Homerville	Feb. 14, 1850	Unnumb.
Cobb	Marietta	Dec. 3, 1832	Unnumb.
Coffee	Douglas	Feb. 9, 1854	Act 222
Colquitt	Moultrie	Feb. 25, 1856	Act 46
Columbia	Evans	Dec. 10, 1790	Unnumb.
Cook	Adel	July 30, 1918	Act 292
Coweta	Newman	Dec. 11, 1826	Unnumb.
Crawford	Roberta	Dec. 9, 1822	Unnumb.
Crisp	Cordele	Aug. 17, 1905	Act 19
Dade	Trenton	Dec. 25, 1837	Unnumb.
Dawson	Dawsonville	Dec. 3, 1857	Act 19
Decatur	Bainbridge	Dec. 8, 1823	Unnumb.
DeKalb	Decatur	Dec. 9, 1822	Unnumb.
Dodge	Eastman	Oct. 26, 1870	Act 7
Dooly	Vienna	May 15, 1821	Unnumb.
Dougherty	Albany	Dec. 15, 1853	Act 223
Douglas	Douglasville	Oct. 17, 1870	Act 5
Early	Blakely	Dec. 15, 1818	Unnumb.
Echols	Statenville	Dec. 13, 1858	Act 22
Effingham	Springfield	Feb. 5, 1777	Const.

Elbert	Elberton	Dec. 10, 1790	Unnumb.
Emanuel	Swainsboro	Dec. 10, 1812	Unnumb.
Evans	Claxton	Aug. 11, 1914	Act 371
Fannin	Blue Ridge	Jan. 21, 1854	Act 224
Fayette	Fayetteville	May 15, 1821	Unnumb.
Floyd	Rome	Dec. 3, 1832	Unnumb.
Forsyth	Cumming	Dec. 3, 1832	Unnumb.
Franklin	Carnesville	Feb. 25, 1784	Unnumb.
Fulton	Atlanta	Dec. 20, 1853	Act 225
Gilmer	Ellijay	Dec. 3, 1832	Unnumb.
Glascock	Gibson	Dec. 19, 1857	Act 20
Glynn	Brunswick	Feb. 5, 1777	Const.
Gordon	Calhoun	Feb. 13, 1850	Unnumb.
Grady	Cairo	Aug. 17, 1905	Act 31
Greene	Greensboro	Feb. 3, 1786	Unnumb.
Gwinnett	Lawrenceville	Dec. 15, 1818	Unnumb.
Habersham	Clarkesville	Dec. 15, 1818	Unnumb.
Hall	Gainesville	Dec. 15, 1818	Unnumb.
Hancock	Sparta	Dec. 17, 1793	Unnumb.
Haralson	Buchanan	Jan. 26, 1856	Act 47
Harris	Hamilton	Dec. 14, 1827	Unnumb.
Hart	Hartwell	Dec. 7, 1853	Act 226
Heard	Franklin	Dec. 22, 1830	Unnumb.
Henry	McDonough	May 15, 1821	Unnumb.
Houston	Perry	May 15, 1821	Unnumb.
Irwin	Ocilla	Dec. 15, 1818	Unnumb.
Jackson	Jefferson	Feb. 11, 1796	Unnumb.
Jasper[2]	Monticello	Dec. 10, 1807	Unnumb.
Jeff Davis	Hazlehurst	Aug. 18, 1905	Act 157
Jefferson	Louisville	Feb. 20, 1796	Unnumb.
Jenkins	Millen	Aug. 17, 1905	Act 142
Johnson	Wrightsville	Dec. 11, 1858	Act 20
Jones	Gray	Deo. 10, 1807	Unnumb.
Lamar	Barnesville	Aug. 17, 1920	Act 738
Lanier	Lakeland	Aug. 11, 1919	Act 78
Laurens	Dublin	Dec. 10, 1807	Unnumb.
Lee	Leesburg	Dec. 11, 1826	Unnumb.
Liberty	Hinesville	Feb. 5, 1777	Const.
Lincoln	Lincolnton	Feb. 20, 1796	Unnumb.
Long	Ludowici	Aug. 14, 1920	Act 814
Lowndes	Valdosta	Dec. 23, 1825	Unnumb.
Lumpkin	Dahlonega	Dec. 3, 1832	Unnumb.
Macon	Oglethorpe	Dec. 14, 1837	Unnumb.
Madison	Danielsville	Dec. 5, 1811	Unnumb.
Marion	Buena Vista	Dec. 24, 1827	Unnumb.
McDuffie	Thomson	Oct. 18, 1870	Act 8
McIntosh	Darien	Dec. 19, 1793	Unnumb.
Meriwether	Greenville	Dec. 24, 1827	Unnumb.
Miller	Colquitt	Feb. 26, 1856	Act 49
Mitchell	Camilla	Dec. 21, 1857	Act 22
Monroe	Forsyth	May 15, 1821	Unnumb.
Montgomery	Mount Vernon	Dec. 19, 1793	Unnumb.
Morgan	Madison	Dec. 10, 1807	Unnumb.
Murray	Chatsworth	Dec. 3, 1832	Unnumb.

Muscogee	Columbus	Dec. 11, 1826	Unnumb.
Newton	Covington	Dec. 24, 1821	Unnumb.
Oconee	Watkinsville	Feb. 25, 1875	Ch. 123
Oglethorpe	Lexington	Dec. 19, 1793	Unnumb.
Paulding	Dallas	Dec. 3, 1832	Unnumb.
Peach	Fort Valley	July 18, 1924	Act 274
Pickens	Jasper	Dec. 5, 1853	Act 228
Pierce	Blackshear	Dec. 18, 1857	Act 23
Pike	Zebulon	Dec. 9, 1822	Unnumb.
Polk	Cedartown	Dec. 20, 1851	Act 26
Pulaski	Hawkinsville	Dec. 13, 1808	Unnumb.
Putnam	Eatonton	Dec. 10, 1807	Unnumb.
Quitman	Georgetown	Dec. 10, 1858	Act 18
Rabun	Clayton	Dec. 21, 1819	Unnumb.
Randolph	Cuthbert	Dec. 20, 1828	Unnumb.
Richmond	Augusta	Feb. 5, 1777	Const.
Rockdale	Conyers	Oct. 18, 1870	Act 6
Schley	Ellaville	Dec. 22, 1857	Act 24
Screven	Sylvania	Dec. 14, 1793	Unnumb.
Seminole	Donalsonville	July 8, 1920	Act 319
Spalding	Griffin	Dec. 20, 1851	Act 28
Stephens	Toccoa	Aug. 18, 1905	Act 215
Stewart	Lumpkin	Dec. 23, 1830	Unnumb.
Sumter	Americus	Dec. 26, 1831	Unnumb.
Talbot	Talbotton	Dec. 14, 1827	Unnumb.
Taliaferro	Crawfordville	Dec. 24, 1825	Unnumb.
Tattnall	Reidsville	Dec. 5, 1801	Unnumb.
Taylor	Butler	Jan. 15, 1852	Act 29
Telfair	McRae	Dec. 10, 1807	Unnumb.
Terrell	Dawson	Feb. 16, 1856	Act 50
Thomas	Thomasville	Dec. 23, 1825	Unnumb.
Tift	Tifton	Aug. 17, 1905	Act 3
Toombs	Lyons	Aug. 18, 1905	Act 232
Towns	Hiawassee	Mar. 6, 1856	Act 51
Treutlen	Soperton	Aug. 21, 1917	Act 250
Troup	La Grange	Dec. 11, 1826	Unnumb.
Turner	Ashburn	Aug. 18, 1905	Act 75
Twiggs	Jeffersonville	Dec. 14, 1809	Unnumb.
Union	Blairsville	Dec. 3, 1832	Unnumb.
Upson	Thomaston	Dec. 15, 1824	Unnumb.
Walker	LaFayette	Dec. 18, 1833	Unnumb.
Walton	Monroe	Dec. 15, 1818	Unnumb.
Ware	Waycross	Dec. 15, 1824	Unnumb.
Warren	Warrenton	Dec. 19, 1793	Unnumb.
Washington	Sandersville	Feb. 25, 1784	Unnumb.
Wayne	Jesup	May 11, 1803	Unnumb.
Webster[3]	Preston	Dec. 16, 1853	Act 227
Wheeler	Alamo	Aug. 14, 1912	Act 449
White	Cleveland	Dec. 22, 1857	Act 25
Whitfield	Dalton	Dec. 30, 1851	Act 27
Wilcox	Abbeville	Dec. 22, 1857	Act 26
Wilkes	Washington	Feb. 5, 1777	Const.
Wilkinson	Irwinton	May 11, 1803	Unnumb.
Worth	Sylvester	Dec. 20, 1853	Act 229

Notes

1. Bartow created as Cass; name changed Dec. 6, 1861, Act 97
2. Jasper created as Randolph; name changed Dec. 10, 1812, unnumbered
3. Webster created as Kinchafoonee; name changed Feb. 21, 1856, Act 367

HAWAII (5 COUNTIES)

Territory of Hawaii April 30, 1900
Admitted as state August 21, 1959 (50th)

County	County Seat	Created
Hawaii	Hilo	July 1905
Honolulu	Honolulu	July 1905
Kalawao[1]		July 1905
Kauai	Lihue	July 1905
Maui	Wailuku	July 1905

Note

1. Kalawao County has no county-level government; it is administered by the State of Hawaii. It is usually statistically included in Maui County.

IDAHO (44 COUNTIES)

Idaho Territory March 3, 1863
Admitted as state July 3, 1890 (43rd)

County	County Seat	Created	Statute
Ada	Boise	Dec. 22, 1864	Ch. 29
Adams	Council	Mar. 3, 1911	Ch. 31
Bannock	Pocatello	Mar. 6, 1893	Unnumb.
Bear Lake	Paris	Jan. 5, 1875	Unnumb.
Benewah	Saint Maries	Jan. 23, 1915	Ch. 4
Bingham	Blackfoot	Jan. 13, 1885	Unnumb.
Blaine	Hailey	Mar. 5, 1895	S.B. 31
Boise	Idaho City	Feb. 4, 1864	Unnumb.
Bonner	Sandpoint	Feb. 21, 1907	H.B. 43
Bonneville	Idaho Falls	Feb. 7, 1911	Ch. 5
Boundary	Bonners Ferry	Jan. 23, 1915	Ch. 7
Butte	Arco	Feb. 6, 1917	Ch. 98
Camas	Fairfield	Feb. 6, 1917	Ch. 97
Canyon	Caldwell	May 7, 1891	Unumb.
Caribou	Soda Springs	Feb. 11, 1919	Ch. 5
Cassia	Burley	Feb. 20, 1879	Unnumb.
Clark	Dubois	Feb. 1, 1919	Ch. 3
Clearwater	Orofino	Feb. 27, 1911	Ch. 34
Custer	Challis	Jan. 8, 1881	Unnumb.
Elmore	Mountain Home	Feb. 7, 1889	Unnumb.
Franklin	Preston	Jan. 20, 1913	Ch. 5
Fremont	Saint Anthony	Mar. 4, 1893	Unnumb.
Gem	Emmett	Mar. 19, 1915	Ch. 165
Gooding	Gooding	Jan. 28, 1913	Ch. 4
Idaho	Grangeville	Feb. 4, 1864	Unnumb.

Jefferson	Rigby	Feb. 18, 1913	Ch. 25
Jerome	Jerome	Feb. 8, 1919	Ch. 4
Kootenai	Coeur d'Alene	Dec. 22, 1864	Ch. 30
Latah	Moscow	Dec. 22, 1864	Ch. 30
Lemhi	Salmon	Jan. 9, 1869	Ch. 19
Lewis	Nezperce	Mar. 3, 1911	Ch. 37
Lincoln	Shoshone	Mar. 18, 1895	S.B. 83
Madison	Rexburg	Feb. 18, 1913	Ch. 26
Minidoka	Rupert	Jan. 28, 1913	Ch. 3
Nez Perce	Lewiston	Feb. 4, 1864	Unnumb.
Oneida	Malad City	Jan. 22, 1864	Unnumb.
Owyhee	Murphy	Dec. 31, 1863	Unnumb.
Payette	Payette	Feb. 28, 1917	Ch. 11
Power	American Falls	Jan. 30, 1913	Ch. 6
Shoshone	Wallace	Feb. 4, 1864	Unnumb.
Teton	Driggs	Jan. 26, 1915	Ch. 8
Twin Falls	Twin Falls	Feb. 21, 1907	H.B. 48
Valley	Cascade	Feb. 26, 1917	Ch. 99
Washington	Weiser	Feb. 20, 1879	Unnumb.

ILLINOIS (102 COUNTIES)

Northwest Territory July 13, 1787
Indiana Territory May 7, 1800
Illinois Territory February 3, 1809
Admitted as state December 3, 1818 (21st)

County	County Seat	Created	Statute
Adams	Quincy	Jan. 13, 1825	Unnumb.
Alexander	Cairo	Mar. 4, 1819	Unnumb.
Bond	Greenville	Jan. 4, 1817	Unnumb.
Boone	Belvidere	Mar. 4, 1837	Unnumb.
Brown	Mount Sterling	Feb. 1, 1839	Unnumb.
Bureau	Princeton	Feb. 28, 1837	Unnumb.
Calhoun	Hardin	Jan. 10, 1825	Unnumb.
Carroll	Mount Carroll	Feb. 22, 1839	Unnumb.
Cass	Virginia	Mar. 3, 1837	Unnumb.
Champaign	Urbana	Feb. 20, 1833	Unnumb.
Christian[1]	Taylorville	Feb. 15, 1839	Unnumb.
Clark	Marshall	Mar. 22, 1819	Unnumb.
Clay	Louisville	Dec. 23, 1824	Unnumb.
Clinton	Carlyle	Dec. 27, 1824	Unnumb.
Coles	Charleston	Dec. 25, 1830	Unnumb.
Cook	Chicago	Jan. 15, 1831	Unnumb.
Crawford	Robinson	Dec. 31, 1816	Unnumb.
Cumberland	Toledo	Mar. 2, 1843	Unnumb.
DeKalb	Sycamore	Mar. 4, 1837	Unnumb.
De Witt	Clinton	Mar. 1, 1839	Unnumb.
Douglas	Tuscola	Feb. 8, 1859	Unnumb.
DuPage	Wheaton	Feb. 9, 1839	Unnumb.
Edgar	Paris	Jan. 3, 1823	Unnumb.
Edwards	Albion	Nov. 28, 1814	Unnumb.
Effingham	Effingham	Feb. 15, 1831	Unnumb.
Fayette	Vandalia	Feb. 14, 1821	Unnumb.

Ford	Paxton	Feb. 17, 1859	Unnumb.
Franklin	Benton	Jan. 2, 1818	Unnumb.
Fulton	Lewistown	Jan. 28, 1823	Unnumb.
Gallatin	Shawneetown	Sep. 14, 1812	Proc.
Greene	Carrollton	Jan. 20, 1821	Unnumb.
Grundy	Morris	Feb. 7, 1841	Unnumb.
Hamilton	McLeansboro	Feb. 8, 1821	Unnumb.
Hancock	Carthage	Jan. 13, 1825	Unnumb.
Hardin	Elizabethtown	Mar. 2, 1839	Unnumb.
Henderson	Oquawka	Jan. 20, 1841	Unnumb.
Henry	Cambridge	Jan. 13, 1825	Unnumb.
Iroquois	Watseka	Feb. 26, 1833	Unnumb.
Jackson	Murphysboro	Jan. 10, 1816	Unnumb.
Jasper	Newton	Feb. 15, 1831	Unnumb.
Jefferson	Mount Vernon	Mar. 26, 1819	Unnumb.
Jersey	Jerseyville	Feb. 28, 1839	Unnumb.
Jo Daviess	Galena	Feb. 17, 1827	Unnumb.
Johnson	Vienna	Sep. 14, 1812	Proc.
Kane	Geneva	Jan. 16, 1836	Unnumb.
Kankakee	Kankakee	Feb. 11, 1853	Unnumb.
Kendall	Yorkville	Feb. 19, 1841	Unnumb.
Knox	Galesburg	Jan. 13, 1825	Unnumb.
Lake	Waukegan	Mar. 1, 1839	Unnumb.
La Salle	Ottawa	Jan. 15, 1831	Unnumb.
Lawrence	Lawrenceville	Jan. 16, 1821	Unnumb.
Lee	Dixon	Feb. 27, 1839	Unnumb.
Livingston	Pontiac	Feb. 27, 1837	Unnumb.
Logan	Lincoln	Feb. 15, 1839	Unnumb.
Macon	Decatur	Jan. 19, 1829	Unnumb.
Macoupin	Carlinville	Jan. 17, 1829	Unnumb.
Madison	Edwardsville	Sep. 14, 1812	Proc.
Marion	Salem	Jan. 24, 1823	Unnumb.
Marshall	Lacon	Jan. 19, 1839	Unnumb.
Mason	Havana	Jan. 20, 1841	Unnumb.
Massac	Metropolis	Feb. 8, 1843	Unnumb.
McDonough	Macomb	Jan. 25, 1826	Unnumb.
McHenry	Woodstock	Jan. 16, 1836	Unnumb.
McLean	Bloomington	Dec. 25, 1830	Unnumb.
Menard	Petersburg	Feb. 15, 1839	Unnumb.
Mercer	Aledo	Jan. 13, 1825	Unnumb.
Monroe	Waterloo	Jan. 6, 1816	Unnumb.
Montgomery	Hillsboro	Feb. 12, 1821	Unnumb.
Morgan	Jacksonville	Jan. 31, 1823	Unnumb.
Moultrie	Sullivan	Feb. 16, 1843	Unnumb.
Ogle	Oregon	Jan. 16, 1836	Unnumb.
Peoria	Peoria	Jan. 13, 1825	Unnumb.
Perry	Pinckneyville	Jan. 29, 1827	Unnumb.
Piatt	Monticello	Jan. 27, 1841	Unnumb.
Pike	Pittsfield	Jan. 31, 1821	Unnumb.
Pope	Golconda	Jan. 10, 1816	Unnumb.
Pulaski	Mound City	Mar. 3, 1843	Unnumb.
Putnam	Hennepin	Jan. 13, 1825	Unnumb.
Randolph	Chester	Oct. 5, 1795	Proc.
Richland	Olney	Feb. 24, 1841	Unnumb.
Rock Island	Rock Island	Feb. 9, 1831	Unnumb.

Saint Clair	Belleville	Apr. 27, 1790	Proc.
Saline	Harrisburg	Feb. 25, 1847	Unnumb.
Sangamon	Springfield	Jan. 30, 1821	Unnumb.
Schuyler	Rushville	Jan. 13, 1825	Unnumb.
Scott	Winchester	Feb. 16, 1839	Unnumb.
Shelby	Shelbyville	Jan. 23, 1827	Unnumb.
Stark	Toulon	Mar. 2, 1839	Unnumb.
Stephenson	Freeport	Mar. 4, 1837	Unnumb.
Tazewell	Pekin	Jan. 31, 1827	Unnumb.
Union	Jonesboro	Jan. 2, 1818	Unnumb.
Vermilion	Danville	Jan. 18, 1826	Unnumb.
Wabash	Mount Carmel	Dec. 27, 1824	Unnumb.
Warren	Monmouth	Jan. 13, 1825	Unnumb.
Washington	Nashville	Jan. 2, 1818	Unnumb.
Wayne	Fairfield	Mar. 26, 1819	Unnumb.
White	Carmi	Dec. 9, 1815	Unnumb.
Whiteside	Morrison	Jan. 16, 1836	Unnumb.
Will	Joliet	Jan. 12, 1836	Unnumb.
Williamson	Marion	Feb. 28, 1839	Unnumb.
Winnebago	Rockford	Jan. 16, 1836	Unnumb.
Woodford	Eureka	Feb. 27, 1841	Unnumb.

Note

1. Christian created as Dane; name changed Feb. 1, 1840, unnumbered

INDIANA (92 COUNTIES)

Northwest Territory July 13, 1787
Indiana Territory May 7, 1800
Admitted as state December 11, 1816 (19th)

County	County Seat	Created	Statute
Adams	Decatur	Feb. 7, 1835	Ch. 25
Allen	Fort Wayne	Dec. 17, 1823	Ch. 18
Bartholomew	Columbus	Jan. 8, 1821	Ch. 31
Benton	Fowler	Feb. 18, 1840	Ch. 40
Blackford	Hartford City	Feb. 15, 1838	Ch. 97
Boone	Lebanon	Jan. 29, 1830	Ch. 24
Brown	Nashville	Feb. 4, 1836	Ch. 19
Carroll	Delphi	Jan. 7, 1828	Ch. 16
Cass	Logansport	Dec. 18, 1828	Ch. 19
Clark	Jeffersonville	Feb. 3, 1801	Proc.
Clay	Brazil	Feb. 12, 1825	Ch. 15
Clinton	Frankfort	Jan. 29, 1830	Ch. 25
Crawford	English	Jan. 29, 1818	Ch. 11
Daviess	Washington	Dec. 24, 1816	Ch. 63
Dearborn	Lawrenceburg	Mar. 7, 1803	Proc.
Decatur	Greensburg	Dec. 31, 1821	Ch. 33
DeKalb	Auburn	Feb. 7, 1835	Ch. 25
Delaware	Muncie	Jan. 26, 1827	Ch. 10
Dubois	Jasper	Dec. 20, 1817	Ch. 7
Elkhart	Goshen	Jan. 29, 1830	Ch. 23
Fayette	Connersville	Dec. 28, 1818	Ch. 28

Floyd	New Albany	Jan. 2, 1819	Ch. 27
Fountain	Covington	Dec. 20, 1825	Ch. 9
Franklin	Brookville	Nov. 27, 1810	Ch. 6
Fulton	Rochester	Feb. 7, 1835	Ch. 25
Gibson	Princeton	Mar. 9, 1813	Ch. 23
Grant	Marion	Feb. 10, 1831	Ch. 12
Greene	Bloomfield	Jan. 5, 1821	Ch. 49
Hamilton	Noblesville	Jan. 8, 1823	Ch. 52
Hancock	Greenfield	Jan. 26, 1827	Ch. 91
Harrison	Corydon	Oct. 11, 1808	Ch. 1
Hendricks	Danville	Dec. 20, 1823	Ch. 91
Henry	New Castle	Dec. 31, 1821	Ch. 60
Howard[1]	Kokomo	Jan. 15, 1844	Ch. 3
Huntington	Huntington	Feb. 2, 1832	Ch. 119
Jackson	Brownstown	Dec. 18, 1815	Ch. 1
Jasper	Rensselaer	Feb. 7, 1835	Ch. 25
Jay	Portland	Feb. 7, 1835	Ch. 25
Jefferson	Madison	Nov. 23, 1810	Ch. 2
Jennings	Vernon	Dec. 27, 1816	Ch. 45
Johnson	Franklin	Dec. 31, 1822	Ch. 15
Knox	Vincennes	June 20, 1790	Proc.
Kosciusko	Warsaw	Feb. 7, 1835	Ch. 25
LaGrange	Lagrange	Feb. 2, 1832	Ch. 117
Lake	Crown Point	Jan. 28, 1836	Ch. 18
LaPorte	La Porte	Jan. 9, 1832	Ch. 2
Lawrence	Bedford	Jan. 7, 1818	Ch. 5
Madison	Anderson	Jan. 4, 1823	Ch. 50
Marion	Indianapolis	Dec. 31, 1821	Ch. 60
Marshall	Plymouth	Feb. 7, 1835	Ch. 25
Martin	Shoals	Jan. 17, 1820	Ch. 31
Miami	Peru	Feb. 2, 1832	Ch. 119
Monroe	Bloomington	Jan. 14, 1818	Ch. 6
Montgomery	Crawfordsville	Dec. 21, 1822	Ch. 6
Morgan	Martinsville	Dec. 31, 1821	Ch. 24
Newton	Kentland	Feb. 7, 1835	Ch. 25
Noble	Albion	Feb. 7, 1835	Ch. 24
Ohio	Rising Sun	Jan. 4, 1844	Ch. 2
Orange	Paoli	Dec. 26, 1815	Ch. 12
Owen	Spencer	Dec. 21, 1818	Ch. 26
Parke	Rockville	Jan. 9, 1821	Ch. 24
Perry	Tell City	Sep. 7, 1814	Ch. 7
Pike	Petersburg	Dec. 21, 1816	Ch. 51
Porter	Valparaiso	Feb. 7, 1835	Ch. 25
Posey	Mount Vernon	Sep. 7, 1814	Ch. 7
Pulaski	Winamac	Feb. 7, 1835	Ch. 25
Putnam	Greencastle	Dec. 31, 1821	Ch. 36
Randolph	Winchester	Jan. 10, 1818	Ch. 8
Ripley	Versailles	Dec. 27, 1816	Ch. 45
Rush	Rushville	Dec. 31, 1821	Ch. 35
Saint Joseph	South Bend	Jan. 29, 1830	Ch. 23
Scott	Scottsburg	Jan. 12, 1820	Ch. 30
Shelby	Shelbyville	Dec. 31, 1821	Ch. 31
Spencer	Rockport	Jan. 10, 1818	Ch. 9
Starke	Knox	Feb. 7, 1835	Ch. 25
Steuben	Angola	Feb. 7, 1835	Ch. 25

Sullivan	Sullivan	Dec. 30, 1816	Ch. 49
Switzerland	Vevay	Sep. 7, 1814	Ch. 9
Tippecanoe	Lafayette	Jan. 20, 1826	Ch. 10
Tipton	Tipton	Jan. 15, 1844	Ch. 3
Union	Liberty	Jan. 5, 1821	Ch. 58
Vanderburgh	Evansville	Jan. 7, 1818	Ch. 10
Vermillion	Newport	Jan. 2, 1824	Ch. 20
Vigo	Terre Haute	Jan. 21, 1818	Ch. 14
Wabash	Wabash	Feb. 2, 1832	Ch. 119
Warren	Williamsport	Jan. 19, 1827	Ch. 11
Warrick	Boonville	Mar. 9, 1813	Ch. 23
Washington	Salem	Dec. 21, 1813	Ch. 10
Wayne	Richmond	Nov. 27, 1810	Ch. 6
Wells	Bluffton	Feb. 7, 1835	Ch. 25
White	Monticello	Feb. 1, 1834	Ch. 30
Whitley	Columbia City	Feb. 7, 1835	Ch. 25

Note

1. Howard created as Richardville; name changed Dec. 28, 1846, Ch. 168

IOWA (99 COUNTIES)

Included in Michigan Territory 1834
Included in Wisconsin Territory 1836
Iowa Territory June 12, 1838
Admitted as state December 28, 1846 (29th)

County	County Seat	Created	Statute
Adair	Greenfield	Jan. 15, 1851	Ch. 9
Adams	Corning	Jan. 15, 1851	Ch. 9
Allamakee	Waukon	Feb. 20, 1847	Ch. 66
Appanoose	Centerville	Feb. 17, 1843	Ch. 34
Audubon	Audubon	Jan. 15, 1851	Ch. 9
Benton	Vinton	Dec. 21, 1837	Ch. 6
Black Hawk	Waterloo	Feb. 17, 1843	Ch. 34
Boone	Boone	Jan. 13, 1846	Ch. 82
Bremer	Waverly	Jan. 15, 1851	Ch. 9
Buchanan	Independence	Dec. 21, 1837	Ch. 6
Buena Vista	Storm Lake	Jan. 15, 1851	Ch. 9
Butler	Allison	Jan. 15, 1851	Ch. 9
Calhoun[1]	Rockwell City	Jan. 15, 1851	Ch. 9
Carroll	Carroll	Jan. 15, 1851	Ch. 9
Cass	Atlantic	Jan. 15, 1851	Ch. 9
Cedar	Tipton	Dec. 21, 1837	Ch. 6
Cerro Gordo	Mason City	Jan. 15, 1851	Ch. 9
Cherokee	Cherokee	Jan. 15, 1851	Ch. 9
Chickasaw	New Hampton	Jan. 15, 1851	Ch. 9
Clarke	Osceola	Jan. 13, 1846	Ch. 82
Clay	Spencer	Jan. 15, 1851	Ch. 9
Clayton	Elkader	Dec. 21, 1837	Ch. 6
Clinton	Clinton	Dec. 21, 1837	Ch. 6
Crawford	Denison	Jan. 15, 1851	Ch. 9
Dallas	Adel	Jan. 13, 1846	Ch. 82

Davis	Bloomfield	Feb. 17, 1843	Ch. 34
Decatur	Leon	Jan. 13, 1846	Ch. 82
Delaware	Manchester	Dec. 21, 1837	Ch. 6
Des Moines	Burlington	Sep. 6, 1834	Unnumb.
Dickinson	Spirit Lake	Jan. 15, 1851	Ch. 9
Dubuque	Dubuque	Sep. 6, 1834	Unnumb.
Emmet	Estherville	Jan. 15, 1851	Ch. 9
Fayette	West Union	Dec. 21, 1837	Ch. 6
Floyd	Charles City	Jan. 15, 1851	Ch. 9
Franklin	Hampton	Jan. 15, 1851	Ch. 9
Fremont	Sidney	Feb. 24, 1847	Ch. 83
Greene	Jefferson	Jan. 15, 1851	Ch. 9
Grundy	Grundy Center	Jan. 15, 1851	Ch. 9
Guthrie	Guthrie Center	Jan. 15, 1851	Ch. 9
Hamilton	Webster City	Dec. 22, 1856	Ch. 15
Hancock	Garner	Jan. 15, 1851	Ch. 9
Hardin	Eldora	Jan. 15, 1851	Ch. 9
Harrison	Logan	Jan. 15, 1851	Ch. 9
Henry	Mount Pleasant	Dec. 7, 1836	Ch. 21
Howard	Cresco	Jan. 15, 1851	Ch. 9
Humboldt	Dakota City	Jan. 15, 1851	Ch. 9
Ida	Ida Grove	Jan. 15, 1851	Ch. 9
Iowa	Marengo	Feb. 17, 1843	Ch. 34
Jackson	Maquoketa	Dec. 21, 1837	Ch. 6
Jasper	Newton	Jan. 13, 1846	Ch. 82
Jefferson	Fairfield	Jan. 21, 1839	Unnumb.
Johnson	Iowa City	Dec. 21, 1837	Ch. 6
Jones	Anamosa	Dec. 21, 1837	Ch. 6
Keokuk	Sigourney	Dec. 21, 1837	Ch. 6
Kossuth	Algona	Jan. 15, 1851	Ch. 9
Lee	Fort Madison	Dec. 7, 1836	Ch. 21
Linn	Cedar Rapids	Dec. 21, 1837	Ch. 6
Louisa	Wapello	Dec. 7, 1836	Ch. 21
Lucas	Chariton	Jan. 13, 1846	Ch. 82
Lyon[2]	Rock Rapids	Jan. 15, 1851	Ch. 9
Madison	Winterset	Jan. 13, 1846	Ch. 82
Mahaska	Oskaloosa	Feb. 17, 1843	Ch. 34
Marion	Knoxville	June 10, 1845	Ch. 57
Marshall	Marshalltown	Jan. 13, 1846	Ch. 82
Mills	Glenwood	Jan. 15, 1851	Ch. 9
Mitchell	Osage	Jan. 15, 1851	Ch. 9
Monona	Onawa	Jan. 15, 1851	Ch. 9
Monroe[3]	Albia	Feb. 17, 1843	Ch. 34
Montgomery	Red Oak	Jan. 15, 1851	Ch. 9
Muscatine	Muscatine	Dec. 7, 1836	Ch. 21
O'Brien	Primghar	Jan. 15, 1851	Ch. 9
Osceola	Sibley	Jan. 15, 1851	Ch. 9
Page	Clarinda	Feb. 24, 1847	Ch. 83
Palo Alto	Emmetsburg	Jan. 15, 1851	Ch. 9
Plymouth	Le Mars	Jan. 15, 1851	Ch. 9
Pocahontas	Pocahontas	Jan. 15, 1851	Ch. 9
Polk	Des Moines	Jan. 13, 1846	Ch. 82
Pottawattanie	Council Bluffs	Jan. 15, 1851	Ch. 9
Poweshiek	Montezuma	Feb. 17, 1843	Ch. 34
Ringgold	Mount Ayr	Feb. 24, 1847	Ch. 83

Sac	Sac City	Jan. 15, 1851	Ch. 9
Scott	Davenport	Dec. 21, 1837	Ch. 6
Shelby	Harlan	Jan. 15, 1851	Ch. 9
Sioux	Orange City	Jan. 15, 1851	Ch. 9
Story	Nevada	Jan. 13, 1846	Ch. 82
Tama	Toledo	Feb. 17, 1843	Ch. 34
Taylor	Bedford	Feb. 24, 1847	Ch. 83
Union	Creston	Jan. 15, 1851	Ch. 9
Van Buren	Keosauqua	Dec. 7, 1836	Ch. 21
Wapello	Ottumwa	Feb. 17, 1843	Ch. 34
Warren	Indianola	Jan. 13, 1846	Ch. 82
Washington[4]	Washington	Jan. 16, 1837	Ch. 248
Wayne	Corydon	Jan. 13, 1846	Ch. 82
Webster[5]	Fort Dodge	Jan. 15, 1851	Ch. 9
Winnebago	Forest City	Feb. 20, 1847	Ch. 66
Winneshiek	Decorah	Feb. 20, 1847	Ch. 66
Woodbury[6]	Sioux City	Jan. 15, 1851	Ch. 9
Worth	Northwood	Jan. 15, 1851	Ch. 9
Wright	Clarion	Jan. 15, 1851	Ch. 9

Notes

1. Calhoun created as Fox; name changed Jan. 22, 1853, Ch. 12
2. Lyon created as Buncombe; name changed Sep. 11, 1862, Ch. 23
3. Monroe created as Kishkekosh; name changed Jan. 19, 1846, Ch. 21
4. Washington created as Slaughter; name changed Jan. 25, 1839, unnumbered
5. Webster created as Risley; name changed Jan. 12, 1853, Ch. 12
6. Woodbury created as Wahkaw; name changed Jan. 12, 1853, Ch. 12

KANSAS (105 COUNTIES)

Kansas Territory May 30, 1854
Admitted as state January 29, 1861 (34th)

County	County Seat	Created	Statute
Allen	Iola	Aug. 30, 1855	Ch. 30
Anderson	Garnett	Aug. 30, 1855	Ch. 30
Atchison	Atchison	Aug. 30, 1855	Ch. 30
Barber[1]	Medicine Lodge	Feb. 26, 1867	Ch. 33
Barton	Great Bend	Feb. 26, 1867	Ch. 33
Bourbon	Fort Scott	Aug. 30, 1855	Ch. 30
Brown	Hiawatha	Aug. 30, 1855	Ch. 30
Butler	El Dorado	Aug. 30, 1855	Ch. 30
Chase	Cottonwood Falls	Feb. 11, 1859	Ch. 46
Chautauqua	Sedan	Mar. 3, 1875	Ch. 106
Cherokee[2]	Columbus	Aug. 30, 1855	Ch. 30
Cheyenne	Saint Francis	Mar. 6, 1873	Ch. 72
Clark	Ashland	Feb. 26, 1867	Ch. 33
Clay	Clay Center	Feb. 20, 1857	Unnumb.
Cloud[3]	Concordia	Feb. 27, 1860	Ch. 43
Coffey	Burlington	Aug. 30, 1855	Ch. 30
Comanche	Coldwater	Feb. 26, 1867	Ch. 33
Cowley	Winfield	Feb. 26, 1867	Ch. 33
Crawford	Girard	Feb. 13, 1867	Ch. 32

Decatur	Oberlin	Mar. 6, 1873	Ch. 72
Dickinson	Abeline	Feb. 20, 1857	Unnumb.
Doniphan	Troy	Aug. 30, 1855	Ch. 30
Douglas	Lawrence	Aug. 30, 1855	Ch. 30
Edwards	Kinsley	Mar. 7, 1874	Ch. 59
Elk	Howard	Mar. 3, 1875	Ch. 106
Ellis	Hays	Feb. 26, 1867	Ch. 33
Ellsworth	Ellsworth	Feb. 26, 1867	Ch. 33
Finney[4]	Garden City	Mar. 6, 1873	Ch. 72
Ford	Dodge City	Mar. 6, 1873	Ch. 72
Franklin	Ottawa	Aug. 30, 1855	Ch. 30
Geary[5]	Junction City	Aug. 30, 1855	Ch. 30
Gove	Gove City	Mar. 2, 1868	Ch. 14
Graham	Hill City	Feb. 26, 1867	Ch. 33
Grant	Ulysses	Mar. 6, 1873	Ch. 72
Gray	Cimarron	Mar. 5, 1887	Ch. 81
Greeley	Tribune	Mar. 6, 1873	Ch. 72
Greenwood	Eureka	Aug. 30, 1855	Ch. 30
Hamilton	Syracuse	Mar. 6, 1873	Ch. 72
Harper	Anthony	Feb. 26, 1867	Ch. 33
Harvey	Newton	Feb. 29, 1872	Ch. 97
Haskell	Sublette	Mar. 5, 1887	Ch. 81
Hodgeman[6]	Jetmore	Feb. 26, 1867	Ch. 72
Jackson[7]	Holton	Aug. 30, 1855	Ch. 30
Jefferson	Oskaloosa	Aug. 30, 1855	Ch. 30
Jewell	Mankato	Feb. 26, 1867	Ch. 33
Johnson	Olathe	Aug. 30, 1855	Ch. 30
Kearny[8]	Lakin	Mar. 6, 1873	Ch. 72
Kingman	Kingman	Feb. 29, 1872	Ch. 97
Kiowa	Greensburg	Feb. 26, 1867	Ch. 33
Labette	Oswego	Feb. 7, 1867	Ch. 29
Lane	Dighton	Mar. 6, 1873	Ch. 72
Leavenworth	Leavenworth	Aug. 30, 1855	Ch. 30
Lincoln	Lincoln	Feb. 26, 1867	Ch. 33
Linn	Mound City	Aug. 30, 1855	Ch. 30
Logan[9]	Oakley	Mar. 4, 1881	Ch. 48
Lyon[10]	Emporia	Aug. 30, 1855	Ch. 30
Marion	Marion	Aug. 30, 1855	Ch. 30
Marshall	Marysville	Aug. 30, 1855	Ch. 30
McPherson	McPherson	Feb. 26, 1867	Ch. 33
Meade	Meade	Mar. 6, 1873	Ch. 72
Miami[11]	Paola	Aug. 30, 1855	Ch. 30
Mitchell	Beloit	Feb. 26, 1867	Ch. 33
Montgomery	Independence	Feb. 26, 1867	Ch. 33
Morris[12]	Council Grove	Aug. 30, 1855	Ch. 30
Morton	Elkhart	Feb. 18, 1886	Ch. 37
Nemaha	Seneca	Aug. 30, 1855	Ch. 30
Neosho[13]	Erie	Aug. 30, 1855	Ch. 30
Ness	Ness City	Feb. 26, 1867	Ch. 33
Norton[14]	Norton	Feb. 26, 1867	Ch. 33
Osage[15]	Lyndon	Aug. 30, 1855	Ch. 30
Osborne	Osborne	Feb. 26, 1867	Ch. 33
Ottawa	Minneapolis	Feb. 27, 1860	Ch. 43
Pawnee	Larned	Feb. 26, 1867	Ch. 33
Phillips	Phillipsburg	Feb. 26, 1867	Ch. 33

Pottawatomie	Westmoreland	Feb. 20, 1857	Unnumb.
Pratt	Pratt	Feb. 26, 1867	Ch. 33
Rawlins	Atwood	Mar. 6, 1873	Ch. 72
Reno	Hutchinson	Feb. 26, 1867	Ch. 33
Republic	Belleville	Feb. 27, 1860	Ch. 43
Rice	Lyons	Feb. 26, 1867	Ch. 33
Riley	Manhattan	Aug. 30, 1855	Ch. 30
Rooks	Stockton	Feb. 26, 1867	Ch. 33
Rush	La Crosse	Feb. 26, 1867	Ch. 33
Russell	Russell	Feb. 26, 1867	Ch. 33
Saline	Salina	Feb. 15, 1860	Ch. 44
Scott	Scott City	Mar. 6, 1873	Ch. 72
Sedgwick	Wichita	Feb. 26, 1867	Ch. 33
Seward	Liberal	Mar. 6, 1873	Ch. 72
Shawnee	Topeka	Aug. 30, 1855	Ch. 30
Sheridan	Hoxie	Mar. 6, 1873	Ch. 72
Sherman	Goodland	Mar. 6, 1873	Ch. 72
Smith	Smith Center	Feb. 26, 1867	Ch. 33
Stafford	Saint John	Feb. 26, 1867	Ch. 33
Stanton	Johnson	Mar. 6, 1873	Ch. 72
Stevens	Hugoton	Mar. 6, 1873	Ch. 72
Sumner	Wellington	Feb. 26, 1867	Ch. 33
Thomas	Colby	Mar. 6, 1873	Ch. 72
Trego	WaKeeney	Feb. 26, 1867	Ch. 33
Wabaunsee[16]	Alma	Aug. 30, 1855	Ch. 30
Wallace	Sharon Springs	Mar. 2, 1868	Ch. 14
Washington	Washington	Feb. 20, 1857	Unnumb.
Wichita	Leoti	Mar. 6, 1873	Ch. 72
Wilson	Fredonia	Aug. 30, 1855	Ch. 30
Woodson	Yates Center	Aug. 30, 1855	Ch. 30
Wyandotte	Kansas City	Jan. 29, 1859	Ch. 47

Notes

1. Barber created as Barbour; spelling corrected Mar. 1, 1883
2. Cherokee created as McGee; name changed Feb. 18, 1860, Ch. 30
3. Cloud created as Shirley; named changed Feb. 26, 1867, Ch. 40
4. Finney created as Sequoyah; name changed Feb. 21, 1883, Ch. 71
5. Geary created as Davis; name changed Feb. 28, 1889, Ch. 132
6. Hodgeman created as Hageman; name changed 1868
7. Jackson created as Calhoun; name changed Feb. 11, 1859, Ch. 99
8. Kearny created as Kearney; spelling corrected Mar. 5, 1887
9. Logan created as Saint John; name changed Feb. 24, 1887, Ch. 173
10. Lyon created as Breckenridge; name changed Feb. 5, 1862, Ch. 61
11. Miami created as Lykins; name changed June 3, 1861, Ch. 18
12. Morris created as Wise; name changed Feb. 11, 1859, Ch. 60
13. Neosho created as Dorn; name changed June 3, 1861, Ch. 18
14. Created as Norton; name changed to Billings Mar. 6, 1873, Ch. 72; renamed Norton Feb. 19, 1874, Ch. 55
15. Osage created as Weller; name changed Feb. 11, 1859, Ch. 100
16. Wabaunsee created as Richardson; name changed Feb. 11, 1859, Ch. 49

KENTUCKY (120 COUNTIES)

Part of Virginia 1780–92

Admitted as state June 1, 1792 (15th)

County	County Seat	Created	Statute
Adair	Columbia	Dec. 11, 1801	Ch. 43
Allen	Scottsville	Jan. 11, 1815	Ch. 188
Anderson	Lawrenceburg	Jan. 16, 1827	Ch. 35
Ballard	Wickliffe	Feb. 15, 1842	Ch. 188
Barren	Glasgow	Dec. 20, 1798	Ch. 43
Bath	Owingsville	Jan. 15, 1811	Ch. 221
Bell[1]	Pineville	Feb. 28, 1867	Ch. 1,553
Boone	Burlington	Dec. 13, 1798	Ch. 4
Bourbon	Paris	Oct. 17, 1785 (Sess.)	Ch. 37
Boyd	Catlettsburg	Feb. 16, 1860	Ch. 288
Boyle	Danville	Feb. 15, 1842	Ch. 189
Bracken	Brooksville	Dec. 14, 1796	Unnumb.
Breathitt	Jackson	Feb. 8, 1839	Ch. 1,192
Breckinridge	Hardinsburg	Dec. 9, 1799	Ch. 72
Bullitt	Sheperdsville	Dec. 13, 1796	Unnumb.
Butler	Morgantown	Jan. 18, 1810	Ch. 33
Caldwell	Princeton	Jan. 13, 1809	Ch. 33
Calloway	Murray	Dec. 19, 1821	Ch. 112
Campbell	Newport	Dec. 17, 1794	Ch. 19
Carlisle	Bardwell	Apr. 3, 1886	Ch. 495
Carroll	Carrollton	Feb. 9, 1838	Ch. 773
Carter	Grayson	Feb. 9, 1838	Ch. 760
Casey	Liberty	Nov. 14, 1806	Unnumb.
Christian	Hopkinsville	Dec. 13, 1796	Unnumb.
Clark	Winchester	Dec. 6, 1792	Ch. 16
Clay	Manchester	Dec. 2, 1806	Unnumb.
Clinton	Albany	Feb. 20, 1836	Ch. 245
Crittenden	Marion	Jan. 26, 1842	Ch. 97
Cumberland	Burkesville	Dec. 14, 1798	Ch. 54
Daviess	Owensboro	Jan. 14, 1815	Ch. 190
Edmonson	Brownsville	Jan. 12, 1825	Ch. 204
Elliott	Sandy Hook	Jan. 26, 1869	Ch. 1,297
Estill	Irvine	Jan. 27, 1808	Ch. 38
Fayette	Lexington	May 1, 1780 (Sess.)	Unnumb.
Fleming	Flemingsburg	Feb. 10, 1798	Ch. 32
Floyd	Prestonburg	Dec. 13, 1799	Ch. 73
Franklin	Frankfort	Dec. 7, 1794	Ch. 13
Fulton	Hickman	Jan. 15, 1845	Ch. 44
Gallatin	Warsaw	Dec. 14, 1798	Ch. 58
Garrard	Lancaster	Dec. 17, 1796	Unnumb.
Grant	Williamstown	Feb. 12, 1820	Ch. 561
Graves	Mayfield	Dec. 19, 1821	Ch. 112
Grayson	Leitchfield	Jan. 25, 1810	Ch. 133
Green	Greensburg	Dec. 20, 1792	Ch. 44
Greenup	Greenup	Dec. 12, 1803	Ch. 76
Hancock	Hawesville	Jan. 3, 1829	Ch. 32
Hardin	Elizabethtown	Dec. 15, 1792	Ch. 17
Harlan	Harlan	Jan. 28, 1819	Ch. 341
Harrison	Cynthiana	Dec. 21, 1793	Ch. 24
Hart	Munfordville	Jan. 28, 1819	Ch. 352
Henderson	Henderson	Dec. 21, 1798	Ch. 57
Henry	New Castle	Dec. 14, 1798	Ch. 49
Hickman	Clinton	Dec. 19, 1821	Ch. 112
Hopkins	Madisonville	Dec. 9, 1806	Unnumb.

Jackson	McKee	Feb 2, 1858	Ch. 167
Jefferson	Louisville	May 1, 1780 (Sess.)	Unnumb.
Jessamine	Nicholasville	Dec. 19, 1798	Ch. 62
Johnson	Paintsville	Feb. 24, 1843	Ch. 167
Kenton	Covington	Jan. 29, 1840	Ch. 175
Knott	Hindman	May 5, 1884	
Knox	Barbourville	Dec. 19, 1799	Ch. 74
Larue	Hodgenville	Mar. 4, 1843	Ch. 210
Laurel	London	Dec. 12, 1825	Ch. 29
Lawrence	Louisa	Dec. 14, 1821	Ch. 274
Lee	Beattyville	Jan. 29, 1870	Ch. 202
Leslie	Hyden	Mar. 29, 1878	Ch. 666
Letcher	Whitesburg	Mar. 3, 1842	Ch. 394
Lewis	Vanceburg	Dec. 2, 1806	Unnumb.
Lincoln	Stanford	May 1, 1780 (Sess.)	Unnumb.
Livingston	Smithland	Dec. 13, 1798	Ch. 61
Logan	Russellville	June 28, 1792	Ch. 12
Lyon	Eddyville	Jan. 14, 1854	Ch. 32
Madison	Richmond	Oct. 17, 1785 (Sess.)	Ch. 54
Magoffin	Salyersville	Feb. 22, 1860	Ch. 437
Marion	Lebanon	Jan. 25, 1834	Ch. 285
Marshall	Benton	Feb. 12, 1842	Ch. 180
Martin	Inez	Mar. 10, 1870	Ch. 554
Mason	Maysville	Nov. 5, 1788	Ch. 4
McCracken	Paducah	Dec. 17, 1824	Ch. 48
McCreary	Whitley City	Mar. 12, 1912	Ch. 46
McLean	Calhoun	Feb. 6, 1854	Ch. 125
Meade	Brandenburg	Dec. 17, 1823	Ch. 609
Menifee	Frenchburg	Mar. 10, 1869	Ch. 1,872
Mercer	Harrodsburg	Oct. 17, 1785 (Sess.)	Ch. 44
Metcalfe	Edmonton	Feb. 1, 1860	Ch. 104
Monroe	Tompkinsville	Jan. 19, 1820	Ch. 474
Montgomery	Mount Sterling	Dec. 14, 1796	Unnumb.
Morgan	West Liberty	Dec. 7, 1822	Ch. 460
Muhlenberg	Greenville	Dec. 14, 1798	Ch. 65
Nelson	Bardstown	Oct. 18, 1784 (Sess.)	Ch. 62
Nicholas	Carlisle	Dec. 18, 1799	Ch. 11
Ohio	Hartford	Dec. 17, 1798	Ch. 73
Oldham	La Grange	Dec. 15, 1823	Ch. 620
Owen	Owenton	Feb. 6, 1819	Ch. 387
Owsley	Booneville	Jan. 23, 1843	Ch. 43
Pendleton	Falmouth	Dec. 13, 1798	Ch. 47
Perry	Hazard	Nov. 2, 1820	Ch. 9
Pike	Pikeville	Dec. 19, 1821	Ch. 297
Powell	Stanton	Jan. 7, 1852	Ch. 325
Pulaski	Somerset	Dec. 10, 1798	Ch. 1
Robertson	Mount Olivet	Feb. 11, 1867	Ch. 1,317
Rockcastle	Mount Vernon	Jan. 8, 1810	Ch. 102
Rowan	Morehead	Mar. 15, 1856	
Russell	Jamestown	Dec. 14, 1825	Ch. 39
Scott	Georgetown	June 22, 1792	Ch. 3
Shelby	Shelbyville	June 23, 1792	Ch. 9
Simpson	Franklin	Jan. 28, 1819	Ch. 342
Spencer	Taylorsville	Jan. 7, 1824	Ch. 708
Taylor	Campbellsville	Jan. 13, 1848	Ch. 26

Todd	Elkton	Dec. 30, 1819	Ch. 460
Trigg	Cadiz	Jan. 27, 1820	Ch. 489
Trimble	Bedford	Feb. 9, 1837	Ch. 248
Union	Morganfield	Jan. 15, 1811	Ch. 220
Warren	Bowling Green	Dec. 14, 1796	Unnumb.
Washington	Springfield	June 22, 1792	Ch. 2
Wayne	Monticello	Dec. 18, 1800	Ch. 46
Webster	Dixon	Feb. 29, 1860	Ch. 822
Whitley	Williamsburg	Jan. 17, 1818	Ch. 183
Wolfe	Campton	Mar. 5, 1860	Ch. 1,326
Woodford	Versailles	Nov. 12, 1788	Ch. 10

Note

1. Bell created as Josh Bell; name changed 1873

LOUISIANA (64 PARISHES)

Louisiana Territory March 3, 1805
Admitted as state April 30, 1812 (18th)
Seceded January 26, 1861
Readmitted July 9, 1868

Parish	Parish Seat	Created	Statute
Acadia	Crowley	Apr. 10, 1805	Ch. 25
Allen	Oberlin	June 12, 1912	Act 6
Ascension	Donaldsonville	Mar. 31, 1807	Act 1
Assumption	Napoleonville	Mar. 31, 1807	Act 1
Avoyelles	Marksville	Mar. 31, 1807	Act 1
Beauregard	DeRidder	June 12, 1912	Act 8
Bienville	Arcadia	Mar. 14, 1848	Act 183
Bossier	Benton	Feb. 24, 1843	Act 33
Caddo	Shreveport	Jan. 18, 1838	Unnumb.
Calcasieu	Lake Charles	Mar. 24, 1840	Act 72
Caldwell	Columbia	Mar. 6, 1838	Act 48
Cameron	Cameron	Mar. 15, 1870	Act 102
Catahoula	Harrisonburg	Mar. 23, 1808	Act 9
Claiborne	Homer	Mar. 13, 1828	Act 42
Concordia	Vidalia	Apr. 10, 1805	Ch. 25
De Soto	Mansfield	Apr. 1, 1843	Act 88
East Baton Rouge	Baton Rouge	Dec. 22, 1810	
East Carroll	Lake Providence	Mar. 28, 1877	Act 24
East Feliciana	Clinton	Feb. 17, 1824	Unnumb.
Evangeline	Ville Platte	June 15, 1910	Act 15
Franklin	Winnsboro	Mar. 1, 1843	Act 41
Grant	Colfax	Mar. 4, 1869	Act 82
Iberia	New Iberia	Oct. 30, 1868	Act 208
Iberville	Plaquemine	Apr. 10, 1805	Ch. 25
Jackson	Jonesboro	Feb. 27, 1845	Act 38
Jefferson	Gretna	Feb. 11, 1825	Unnumb.
Jefferson Davis	Jennings	June 12, 1912	Act 7
Lafayette	Lafayette	Jan. 17, 1823	Unnumb.
Lafourche	Thibodaux	Apr. 10, 1805	Ch. 25
La Salle	Jena	July 3, 1908	Act 177

Lincoln	Ruston	Feb. 27, 1873	Act 32
Livingston	Livingston	Feb. 10, 1832	Unnumb.
Madison	Tallulah	Jan. 19, 1838	Unnumb.
Morehouse	Bastrop	Mar. 25, 1844	Act 118
Natchitoches	Natchitoches	Apr. 10, 1805	Ch. 25
Orleans	New Orleans	Apr. 10, 1805	Ch. 25
Ouachita	Monroe	Apr. 10, 1805	Ch. 25
Plaquemines	Pointe a la Hache	Mar. 31, 1807	Act 1
Pointe Coupee	New Roads	Apr. 10, 1805	Ch. 25
Rapides	Alexandria	Apr. 10, 1805	Ch. 25
Red River	Coushatta	Mar. 7, 1871	
Richland	Rayville	Sep. 29, 1868	
Sabine	Many	Mar. 7, 1843	Act 46
Saint Bernard	Chalmette	Mar. 31, 1807	Act 1
Saint Charles	Hahnville	Mar. 31, 1807	Act 1
Saint Helena	Greensburg	Oct. 27, 1810	
Saint James	Convent	Mar. 31, 1807	Act 1
Saint John the Baptist	Laplace	Mar. 31, 1807	Act 1
Saint Landry	Opelousas	Mar. 31, 1807	
Saint Martin	Saint Martinville	Mar. 31, 1807	
Saint Mary	Franklin	Apr. 17, 1811	Act 24
Saint Tammany	Covington	Oct. 27, 1810	
Tangipahoa	Amite	Mar. 6, 1869	Act 85
Tensas	Saint Joseph	Mar. 17, 1843	Act 61
Terrebonne	Houma	Mar. 22, 1822	Unnumb.
Union	Farmerville	Mar. 13, 1839	Act 22
Vermilion	Abbeville	Mar. 25, 1844	Act 81
Vernon	Leesville	Mar. 30, 1871	Act 71
Washington	Franklinton	Mar. 6, 1819	Unnumb.
Webster	Minden	Feb. 27, 1871	Act 26
West Baton Rouge[1]	Port Allen	Mar. 31, 1807	Act 1
West Carroll	Oak Grove	Mar. 28, 1877	Act 24
West Feliciana	Saint Francisville	Feb. 17, 1824	Unnumb.
Winn	Winnfield	Feb. 24, 1852	Act 85

Note

1. West Baton Rouge created as Baton Rouge; name changed 1812

MAINE (16 COUNTIES)

Part of Massachusetts 1652–1820
Admitted as state March 15, 1820 (23rd)

County	County Seat	Created	Statute
Androscoggin	Auburn	Mar. 18, 1854	Ch. 60
Aroostook	Caribou	Mar. 16, 1839	Ch. 395
Cumberland	Portland	May 28, 1760 (Sess.)	Ch. 2
Franklin	Farmington	Mar. 20, 1838	Ch. 328
Hancock	Ellsworth	June 25, 1789	Ch. 25
Kennebec	Augusta	Feb. 20, 1799	Ch. 23
Knox	Rockland	Mar. 9, 1860	Ch. 146
Lincoln	Wiscasset	May 28, 1760 (Sess.)	Ch. 2

Oxford	South Paris	Mar. 4, 1805	Ch. 24
Penobscot	Bangor	Feb. 15, 1816	Ch. 121
Piscataquis	Dover-Foxcroft	Mar. 23, 1838	Ch. 355
Sagadahoc	Bath	Apr. 4, 1854	Ch. 70
Somerset	Skowhegan	Mar. 1, 1809	Ch. 62
Waldo	Belfast	Feb. 7, 1827	Ch. 354
Washington	Machias	June 25, 1789	Ch. 25
York	Alfred	Nov. 20, 1652	Unnumb.

MARYLAND (23 COUNTIES; 1 INDEPENDENT CITY)

Colony granted to Lord Baltimore 1632
Independence declared July 4, 1776
Ratified Constitution April 28, 1788 (admitted as 7th state)

County/City	County Seat	Created	Statute
Allegany	Cumberland	Dec. 25. 1789	Ch. 29
Anne Arundel[1]	Annapolis	Apr. 9, 1650	Ch. 8
Baltimore	Towson	June 30, 1695	
Baltimore	(Independent City)	July 4, 1851	
Calvert[2]	Prince Frederick	July 3, 1654	
Caroline	Denton	Dec. 5, 1773	Ch. 10
Carroll	Westminster	Jan. 19, 1837	Ch. 19
Cecil	Elkton	Dec. 31, 1674	
Charles	La Plata	July 10, 1658	
Dorchester	Cambridge	Feb. 16, 1669	
Frederick	Frederick	June 10, 1748	Ch. 15
Garrett	Oakland	Apr. 1, 1872	Ch. 212
Harford	Bel Air	Mar. 2, 1774	
Howard	Ellicott City	July 4, 1851	
Kent	Chestertown	Aug. 2, 1642	
Montgomery	Rockville	Sep. 6, 1776	Conv.
Prince George's	Upper Marlboro	May 20, 1695	Ch. 13
Queen Anne's	Centreville	Apr. 18, 1706	Ch. 3
Saint Mary's[3]	Leonardtown	Feb. 9, 1637	
Somerset	Princess Anne	Aug. 22, 1666	Proc.
Talbot	Easton	Feb. 18, 1662	
Washington	Hagerstown	Sep. 6, 1776	Conv.
Wicomico	Salisbury	Aug. 17, 1867	Const.
Worcester	Snow Hill	Oct. 29, 1742	Ch. 19

Note

1. Created as Anne Arundel; name changed to Providence 1654; renamed Anne Arundel 1658
2. Created as Calvert; name changed to Patuxent Oct. 31, 1654; renamed Calvert Dec. 31, 1658
3. Created as Saint Mary's; name changed to Potomac 1654; renamed Saint Mary's 1658

MASSACHUSETTS (14 COUNTIES)

Massachusetts Bay Colony 1628
Declared independence July 4, 1776
Ratified Constitution February 6, 1788 (admitted as 6th state)

County	County Seat	Created	Statute
Barnstable	Barnstable	June 2, 1685	

Berkshire	Pittsfield	May 28, 1760 (Sess.)	Ch. 4
Bristol	Taunton	June 2, 1685	
Dukes	Edgartown	June 22, 1695	Ch. 7
Essex	Salem	May 10, 1643	
Franklin	Greenfield	June 24, 1811	Ch. 61
Hampden	Springfield	Feb. 25, 1812	Ch. 137
Hampshire	Northampton	May 7, 1662	
Middlesex	East Cambridge	May 10, 1643	
Nantucket	Nantucket	June 22, 1695	Ch. 7
Norfolk	Dedham	Mar. 26, 1793	Ch. 43
Plymouth	Plymouth	June 2, 1685	
Suffolk	Boston	May 10, 1643	
Worcester	Worcester	Apr. 5, 1731	Ch. 13

MICHIGAN (83 COUNTIES)

Michigan Territory January 11, 1805
Admitted as state January 26, 1837 (26th)

County	County Seat	Created	Statute
Alcona[1]	Harrisville	Apr. 1, 1840	Act 119
Alger	Munising	Mar. 17, 1885	Act 23
Allegan	Allegan	Mar. 2, 1831	Unnumb.
Alpena[2]	Alpena	Apr. 1, 1840	Act 119
Antrim[3]	Bellaire	Apr. 1, 1840	Act 119
Arenac	Standish	Mar. 2, 1831	Unnumb.
Baraga	L'Anse	Feb. 19, 1875	Act 14
Barry	Hastings	Oct. 29, 1829	Unnumb.
Bay	Bay City	Apr. 20, 1857	
Benzie	Beulah	Feb. 27, 1863	Act 48
Berrien	Saint Joseph	Oct. 29, 1829	Unnumb.
Branch	Coldwater	Oct. 29, 1829	Unnumb.
Calhoun	Marshall	Oct. 29, 1829	Unnumb.
Cass	Cassopolis	Oct. 29, 1829	Unnumb.
Charlevoix[4]	Charlevoix	Apr. 1, 1840	Act 119
Cheboygan	Cheboygan	Apr. 1, 1840	Act 119
Chippewa	Sault Sainte Marie	Dec. 22, 1826	Unnumb.
Clare[5]	Harrison	Apr. 1, 1840	Act 119
Clinton	Saint Johns	Mar. 2, 1831	Unnumb.
Crawford[6]	Grayling	Apr. 1, 1840	Act 119
Delta	Escanaba	Mar. 9, 1843	Act 89
Dickinson	Iron Mountain	May 21, 1891	Act 89
Eaton	Charlotte	Oct. 29, 1829	Unnumb.
Emmet[7]	Petoskey	Apr. 1, 1840	Act 119
Genesee	Flint	Mar. 28, 1835	Unnumb.
Gladwin	Gladwin	Mar. 2, 1831	Unnumb.
Gogebic	Bessemer	Feb. 7, 1887	Act 337
Grand Traverse	Traverse City	Apr. 7, 1851	
Gratiot	Ithaca	Mar. 2, 1831	Unnumb.
Hillsdale	Hillsdale	Oct. 29, 1829	Unnumb.
Houghton	Houghton	Mar. 19, 1845	Act 48
Huron	Bad Axe	Apr. 1, 1840	Act 119
Ingham	Mason	Oct. 29, 1829	Unnumb.
Ionia	Ionia	Mar. 2, 1831	Unnumb.

Iosco[8]	Tawas City	Apr. 1, 1840	Act 119
Iron	Crystal Falls	Apr. 3, 1885	Act 35
Isabella	Mount Pleasant	Mar. 2, 1831	Unnumb.
Jackson	Jackson	Oct. 29, 1829	Unnumb.
Kalamazoo	Kalamazoo	Oct. 29, 1829	Unnumb.
Kalkaska[9]	Kalkaska	Apr. 1, 1840	Unnumb.
Kent	Grand Rapids	Mar. 2, 1831	Unnumb.
Keweenaw	Eagle River	Mar. 11, 1861	Ch. 118
Lake[10]	Baldwin	Apr. 1, 1840	Act 119
Lapeer	Lapeer	Sep. 10, 1822	Unnumb.
Leelanau	Leland	Apr. 1, 1840	Act 119
Lenawee	Adrian	Sep. 10, 1822	Unnumb.
Livingston	Howell	Mar. 21, 1833	Unnumb.
Luce	Newberry	Mar. 1, 1887	Act 363
Mackinac[11]	Saint Ignance	Oct. 26, 1818	Proc.
Macomb	Mount Clemens	Jan. 15, 1818	Proc.
Manistee	Manistee	Apr. 1, 1840	Act 119
Marquette	Marquette	Mar. 9, 1843	Act 89
Mason[12]	Ludington	Apr. 1, 1840	Act 119
Mecosta	Big Rapids	Apr. 1, 1840	Act 119
Menominee[13]	Menominee	Mar. 15, 1861	Act 213
Midland	Midland	Mar. 2, 1831	Unnumb.
Missaukee	Lake City	Apr. 1, 1840	Act 119
Monroe	Monroe	July 14, 1817	Proc.
Montcalm	Stanton	Mar. 2, 1831	Unnumb.
Montmorency[14]	Atlanta	Apr. 1, 1840	Act 119
Muskegon	Muskegon	Feb. 4, 1859	Act 55
Newaygo	White Cloud	Apr. 1, 1840	Act 119
Oakland	Pontiac	Jan. 12, 1819	Proc.
Oceana	Hart	Mar. 2, 1831	Unnumb.
Ogemaw	West Branch	Apr. 1, 1840	Act 119
Ontonagon	Ontonagon	Mar. 9, 1843	Act 89
Osceola[15]	Reed City	Apr. 1, 1840	Act 119
Oscoda	Mio	Apr. 1, 1840	Act 119
Otsego[16]	Gaylord	Apr. 1, 1840	Act 119
Ottawa	Grand Haven	Mar. 2, 1831	Unnumb.
Presque Isle	Rogers City	Apr. 1, 1840	Act 119
Roscommon[17]	Roscommon	Apr. 1, 1840	Act 119
Saginaw	Saginaw	Sep. 10, 1822	Unnumb.
Saint Clair	Port Huron	Mar. 28, 1820	Proc.
Saint Joseph	Centreville	Oct. 29, 1829	Unnumb.
Sanilac	Sandusky	Sep. 10, 1822	Unnumb.
Schoolcraft	Manistique	Mar. 9, 1843	Ch. 89
Shiawassee	Corunna	Sep. 10, 1822	Unnumb.
Tuscola	Caro	Apr. 1, 1840	Act 119
Van Buren	Paw Paw	Oct. 29, 1829	Unnumb.
Washtenaw	Ann Arbor	Sep. 10, 1822	Unnumb.
Wayne	Detroit	Nov. 21, 1815	Proc.
Wexford[18]	Cadillac	Apr. 1, 1840	Act 119

Notes

1. Alcona created as Negwegon (or Newago); name changed Mar. 8, 1843, Act 67
2. Alpena created as Anamickee; name changed Mar. 8, 1843, Act 67
3. Antrim created as Meegisee; name changed Mar. 8, 1843, Act 67

4. Charlevoix created as Reshkauko (or Keskkauko); name changed Mar. 8, 1843, Act 67
5. Clare created as Kaykakee; name changed Mar. 8, 1843, Act 67
6. Crawford created as Shawano; name changed Mar. 8, 1843, Act 67
7. Emmett created as Tonedagana; name changed Mar. 8, 1843, Act 67
8. Iosco created as Kanotin; name changed Mar. 8, 1843, Act 67
9. Kalkaska created as Wabassee; name changed to Kalcasca Mar. 8, 1843, Act 67; spelling changed Jan. 27, 1871
10. Lake created as Aishcum; name changed Mar. 8, 1843, Act 67
11. Mackinac created as Michilimackinac; name changed Jan. 26, 1837, Act 89
12. Mason created as Notipekago; name changed Mar. 8, 1843, Act 67
13. Menominee created as Bleeker; name changed Mar. 19, 1863, Act 163
14. Montmorency created as Cheonoquet; name changed Mar. 8, 1843, Act 67
15. Osceola created as Unwattin; name changed Mar. 8, 1843, Act 67
16. Otsego created as Okkuddo; name changed Apr. 1, 1840, Act 119
17. Roscommon created as Mikenauk; name changed Mar. 8, 1843, Act 67
18. Wexford created as Kautawaubet; name changed Mar. 8, 1843, Act 67

MINNESOTA (87 COUNTIES)

Minnesota Territory May 3, 1849
Admitted as state May 11, 1858 (32nd)

County	County Seat	Created	Statute
Aitkin[1]	Aitkin	May 23, 1857	Ch. 5
Anoka	Anoka	May 23, 1857	Ch. 64
Becker	Detroit Lakes	Mar. 18, 1858	Ch. 34
Beltrami	Bemidji	Feb. 28, 1866	Ch. 46
Benton	Foley	Oct. 27, 1849	Ch. 5
Big Stone	Ortonville	Feb. 20, 1862	Ch. 22
Blue Earth	Mankato	Mar. 5, 1853	Ch. 11
Brown	New Ulm	Feb. 20, 1855	Ch. 6
Carlton	Carlton	May 23, 1857	Ch. 5
Carver	Chaska	Feb. 20, 1855	Ch. 6
Cass	Walker	Mar. 31, 1851	Unnumb.
Chippewa	Montevideo	Feb. 20, 1862	Ch. 22
Chisago	Center City	Mar. 31, 1851	Unnumb.
Clay[2]	Moorhead	Mar. 18, 1858	Ch. 34
Clearwater	Bagley	Dec. 20, 1902	Proc.
Cook	Grand Marais	Mar. 9, 1874	Ch. 100
Cottonwood	Windom	May 23, 1857	Ch. 14
Crow Wing	Brainerd	May 23, 1857	Ch. 5
Dakota	Hastings	Oct. 27, 1849	Ch. 5
Dodge	Mantorville	Feb. 20, 1855	Ch. 6
Douglas	Alexandria	Mar. 8, 1858	Ch. 74
Faribault	Blue Earth	Feb. 20, 1855	Ch. 6
Fillmore	Preston	Mar. 5, 1853	Ch. 11
Freeborn	Albert Lea	Feb. 20, 1855	Ch. 6
Goodhue	Red Wing	Mar. 5, 1853	Ch. 11
Grant	Elbow Lake	Mar. 6, 1868	Ch. 109
Hennepin	Minneapolis	Mar. 6, 1852	Ch. 32
Houston	Caledonia	Feb. 23, 1854	Ch. 29
Hubbard	Park Rapids	Feb. 26, 1883	Ch. 78
Isanti	Cambridge	Feb. 13, 1857	Ch. 70
Itasca	Grand Rapids	Oct. 27, 1849	Ch. 5
Jackson	Jackson	May 23, 1857	Ch. 14
Kanabec	Mora	Mar. 13, 1858	Ch. 56

Kandiyohi	Willmar	Mar. 20, 1858	Ch. 65
Kittson[3]	Hallock	Oct. 27, 1849	Ch. 5
Koochiching	International Falls	Dec. 19, 1906	Proc.
Lac qui Parle	Madison	Mar. 6, 1871	Ch. 100
Lake[4]	Two Harbors	Feb. 20, 1855	Ch. 6
Lake of the Woods	Baudette	Nov. 28, 1922	Proc.
Le Sueur	Le Center	Mar. 5, 1853	Ch. 11
Lincoln	Ivanhoe	Nov. 4, 1873	
Lyon	Marshall	Mar. 6, 1868	Ch. 112
Mahnomen	Mahnomen	Dec. 27, 1906	Proc.
Marshall	Warren	Feb. 25, 1879	Ch. 10
Martin	Fairmont	May 23, 1857	Ch. 14
McLeod	Glencoe	Mar. 1, 1856	Ch. 26
Meeker	Litchfield	Feb. 23, 1856	Ch. 68
Mille Lacs	Milaca	May 23, 1857	Ch. 5
Morrison	Little Falls	Feb. 25, 1856	Ch. 38
Mower	Austin	Feb. 20, 1855	Ch. 6
Murray	Slayton	May 23, 1857	Ch. 14
Nicollet	Saint Peter	Mar. 5, 1853	Ch. 11
Nobles	Worthington	May 23, 1857	Ch. 14
Norman	Ada	Feb. 17, 1881	Ch. 92
Olmsted	Rochester	Feb. 20, 1855	Ch. 6
Otter Tail	Fergus Falls	Mar. 18, 1858	Ch. 34
Pennington	Thief River Falls	Nov. 23, 1910	Proc.
Pine	Pine City	Mar. 1, 1856	Ch. 36
Pipestone[5]	Pipestone	May 23, 1857	Ch. 14
Polk	Crookston	July 20, 1858	Ch. 67
Pope	Glenwood	Feb. 20, 1862	Ch. 22
Ramsey	Saint Paul	Oct. 27, 1849	Ch. 5
Red Lake	Red Lake Falls	Dec. 24, 1896	Proc.
Redwood	Redwood Falls	Feb. 6, 1862	Ch. 21
Renville	Olivia	Feb. 20, 1855	Ch. 6
Rice	Faribault	Mar. 5, 1853	Ch. 11
Rock[6]	Luverne	May 23, 1857	Ch. 14
Roseau	Roseau	Feb. 28, 1894	Proc.
Saint Louis	Duluth	Mar. 1, 1856	Ch. 36
Scott	Shakopee	Mar. 5, 1853	Ch. 11
Sherburne	Elk River	Feb. 25, 1856	Ch. 38
Sibley	Gaylord	Mar. 5, 1853	Ch. 11
Stearns	Saint Cloud	Feb. 20, 1855	Ch. 6
Steele	Owatonna	Feb. 20, 1855	Ch. 6
Stevens	Morris	Feb. 20, 1862	Ch. 22
Swift	Benson	Feb. 18, 1870	Ch. 90
Todd	Long Prairie	Feb. 20, 1855	Ch. 6
Traverse	Wheaton	Feb. 20, 1862	Ch. 22
Wabasha	Wabasha	Oct. 27, 1849	Ch. 5
Wadena	Wadena	June 11, 1858	Ch. 179
Waseca	Waseca	Feb. 27, 1857	Ch. 57
Washington	Stillwater	Oct. 27, 1849	Ch. 5
Watonwan	Saint James	Feb. 25, 1860	Ch. 13
Wilkin[7]	Breckenridge	Mar. 18, 1858	Ch. 64
Winona	Winona	Feb. 23, 1854	Ch. 29
Wright	Buffalo	Feb. 20, 1855	Ch. 6
Yellow Medicine	Granite Falls	Mar. 6, 1871	Ch. 98

Notes

1. Aitkin created as Aiken; name changed 1872
2. Clay created as Breckinridge; name changed Mar. 6, 1862, Ch. 33
3. Kittson created as Pembina; name changed Mar. 9, 1878, Ch. 59
4. Lake created as Superior; name changed to St. Louis Mar. 3, 1855; name changed Mar. 1, 1856
5. Pipestone created as Rock; name changed Sep. 20, 1862
6. Rock created as Pipestone; name changed Feb. 20, 1862
7. Wilkin created as Toombs; name changed to Andy Johnson Mar. 18, 1862; name changed Mar. 6, 1868

MISSISSIPPI (82 COUNTIES)

Mississippi Territory April 7, 1798
Admitted as state December 10, 1817 (20th)
Seceded January 9, 1861
Readmitted February 23, 1870

County	County Seat	Created	Statute
Adams	Natchez	Apr. 2, 1799	Proc.
Alcorn	Corinth	Apr. 15, 1870	Ch. 51
Amite	Liberty	Feb. 24, 1809	Unnumb.
Attala	Kosciusko	Dec. 23, 1833	Unnumb.
Benton	Ashland	July 21, 1870	Ch. 50
Bolivar	Cleveland	Feb. 9, 1836	Unnumb.
Calhoun	Pittsboro	Mar. 8, 1852	Ch. 15
Carroll	Carrollton	Dec. 23, 1833	Unnumb.
Chickasaw	Houston	Feb. 9, 1836	Unnumb.
Choctaw	Ackerman	Dec. 23, 1833	Unnumb.
Claiborne	Port Gibson	Jan. 27, 1802	Unnumb.
Clarke	Quitman	Dec. 23, 1833	Unnumb.
Clay[1]	West Point	May 12, 1871	Ch. 430
Coahoma	Clarksdale	Feb. 9, 1836	Unnumb.
Copiah	Hazlehurst	Jan. 21, 1823	Ch. 49
Covington	Collins	Feb. 5, 1819	Unnumb.
DeSoto	Hernando	Feb. 9, 1836	Unnumb.
Forrest	Hattiesburg	Apr. 19, 1906	Ch. 165
Franklin	Meadville	Dec. 21, 1809	Unnumb.
George	Lucedale	Mar. 16, 1910	Ch. 248
Greene	Leaksville	Dec. 9, 1811	Unnumb.
Grenada	Grenada	May 9, 1870	Ch. 240
Hancock	Bay Saint Louis	Dec. 18, 1812	Unnumb.
Harrison	Gulfport	Feb. 5, 1841	Ch. 35
Hinds	Jackson	Feb. 12, 1821	Ch. 70
Holmes	Lexington	Feb. 19, 1833	Ch. 38
Humphreys	Belzoni	Mar. 28, 1918	Ch. 348
Issaquena	Mayersville	Jan. 23, 1844	Ch. 47
Itawamba	Fulton	Feb. 9, 1836	Unnumb.
Jackson	Pascagoula	Dec. 18, 1812	Unnumb.
Jasper	Bay Springs	Dec. 23, 1833	Unnumb.
Jefferson[2]	Fayette	Apr. 2, 1799	Proc.
Jefferson Davis	Prentiss	Mar. 31, 1906	Ch. 166
Jones[3]	Laurel	Jan. 24, 1826	Ch. 47
Kemper	De Kalb	Dec. 23, 1833	Unnumb.

Lafayette	Oxford	Feb. 9, 1836	Unnumb.
Lamar	Purvis	Feb. 19, 1904	Ch. 102
Lauderdale	Meridian	Dec. 23, 1833	Unnumb.
Lawrence	Monticello	Dec. 22, 1814	Unnumb.
Leake	Carthage	Dec. 23, 1833	Unnumb.
Lee	Tupelo	Oct. 26, 1866	Ch. 20
Leflore	Greenwood	Mar. 15, 1871	Ch. 238
Lincoln	Brookhaven	Apr. 7, 1870	Ch. 55
Lowndes	Columbus	Jan. 30, 1830	Ch. 14
Madison	Canton	Jan. 29, 1828	Ch. 14
Marion	Columbia	Dec. 9, 1811	Unnumb.
Marshall	Holly Springs	Feb. 9, 1836	Unnumb.
Monroe	Aberdeen	Feb. 9, 1821	Ch. 30
Montgomery	Winona	May 13, 1871	Ch. 241
Neshoba	Philadelphia	Dec. 23, 1833	Unnumb.
Newton	Decatur	Feb. 25, 1836	Unnumb.
Noxubee	Macon	Dec. 23, 1833	Unnumb.
Oktibbeha	Starkville	Dec. 23, 1833	Unnumb.
Panola	Batesville	Feb. 9, 1836	Unnumb.
Pearl River	Poplarville	Feb. 22, 1890	Ch. 76
Perry	New Augusta	Feb. 3, 1820	Ch. 18
Pike	Magnolia	Dec. 9, 1815	Unnumb.
Pontotoc	Pontotoc	Feb. 9, 1836	Unnumb.
Prentiss	Booneville	Apr. 15, 1870	Ch. 51
Quitman	Marks	Feb. 1, 1877	Ch. 35
Rankin	Brandon	Feb. 4, 1828	Ch. 93
Scott	Forest	Dec. 23, 1833	Unnumb.
Sharkey	Rolling Fork	Mar. 29, 1876	Ch. 63
Simpson	Mendenhall	Jan. 23, 1824	Unnumb.
Smith	Raleigh	Dec. 23, 1833	Ch. 5
Stone	Wiggins	Apr. 3, 1916	Ch. 527
Sunflower	Indianola	Feb. 15, 1844	Ch. 49
Tallahatchie	Charleston	Dec. 23, 1833	Unnumb.
Tate	Senatobia	Apr. 15, 1873	Ch. 1
Tippah	Ripley	Feb. 9, 1836	Unnumb.
Tishomingo	Iuka	Feb. 9, 1836	Unnumb.
Tunica	Tunica	Feb. 9, 1836	Unnumb.
Union	New Albany	July 7, 1870	Ch. 54
Walthall	Tylertown	Mar. 16, 1910	Ch. 321
Warren	Vicksburg	Dec. 22, 1809	Unnumb.
Washington	Greenville	Jan. 29, 1827	Ch. 80
Wayne	Waynesboro	Dec. 21, 1809	Unnumb.
Webster[4]	Walthall	Apr. 6, 1874	Ch. 112
Wilkinson	Woodville	Jan. 30, 1802	Unnumb.
Winston	Louisville	Dec. 23, 1833	Unnumb.
Yalobusha	Water Valley	Dec. 23, 1833	Unnumb.
Yazoo	Yazoo City	Jan. 21, 1823	Ch. 49

Notes

1. Clay created as Colfax; name changed Apr. 10, 1876, Ch. 103
2. Jefferson created as Pickering; name changed Jan. 11, 1802
3. Created as Jones; name changed to Davis 1865; renamed Jones 1869
4. Webster created as Sumner; name changed Jan. 20, 1882, Ch. 132

MISSOURI (114 COUNTIES; 1 INDEPENDENT CITY)

Missouri Territory March 3, 1805
Admitted as state August 10, 1821 (24th)

County/City	County Seat	Created	Statute
Adair	Kirksville	Jan. 29, 1841	Unnumb.
Andrew	Savannah	Jan. 29, 1841	Unnumb.
Atchison[1]	Rock Port	Feb. 23, 1843	Unnumb.
Audrain	Mexico	Jan. 12, 1831	Ch. 13
Barry	Cassville	Jan. 5, 1835	Unnumb.
Barton	Lamar	Dec. 12, 1855	Unnumb.
Bates	Butler	Jan. 29, 1841	Unnumb.
Benton	Warsaw	Jan. 3, 1835	Unnumb.
Bollinger	Marble Hill	Mar. 1, 1851	Unnumb.
Boone	Columbia	Nov. 16, 1820	Ch. 14
Buchanan	Saint Joseph	Dec. 31, 1838	Unnumb.
Butler	Poplar Bluff	Feb. 27, 1849	Unnumb.
Caldwell	Kingston	Dec. 29, 1836	Unnumb.
Callaway	Fulton	Nov. 25, 1820	Ch. 29
Camden[2]	Camdenton	Jan. 29, 1841	Unnumb.
Cape Girardeau	Jackson	Oct. 1, 1812	Proc.
Carroll	Carrollton	Jan. 2, 1833	Ch. 24
Carter	Van Buren	Mar. 10, 1859	Unnumb.
Cass[3]	Harrisonville	Mar. 3, 1835	Unnumb.
Cedar	Stockton	Feb. 14, 1845	Unnumb.
Chariton	Keytesville	Nov. 16, 1820	Ch. 14
Christian	Ozark	Mar. 8, 1859	Unnumb.
Clark	Kahoka	Dec. 16, 1836	Unnumb.
Clay	Liberty	Jan. 2, 1822	Ch. 39
Clinton	Plattsburg	Jan. 2, 1833	Ch. 25
Cole	Jefferson City	Nov. 16, 1820	Ch. 16
Cooper	Boonville	Dec. 17, 1818	Unnumb.
Crawford	Steelville	Jan. 23, 1829	Ch. 19
Dade	Greenfield	Jan. 29, 1841	Unnumb.
Dallas[4]	Buffalo	Jan. 29, 1841	Unnumb.
Daviess	Gallatin	Dec. 29, 1836	Unnumb.
DeKalb	Maysville	Feb. 25, 1845	Unnumb.
Dent	Salem	Feb. 10, 1851	Unnumb.
Douglas	Ava	Oct. 29, 1857	Unnumb.
Dunklin	Kennett	Feb. 14, 1845	Unnumb.
Franklin	Union	Dec. 11, 1818	Unnumb.
Gasconade	Hermann	Nov. 25, 1820	Ch. 28
Gentry	Albany	Feb. 12, 1841	Unnumb.
Greene	Springfield	Jan. 2, 1833	Ch. 26
Grundy	Trenton	Jan. 29, 1841	Unnumb.
Harrison	Bethany	Feb. 14, 1845	Unnumb.
Henry[5]	Clinton	Dec. 13, 1834	Unnumb.
Hickory	Hermitage	Feb. 14, 1845	Unnumb.
Holt[6]	Oregon	Jan. 29, 1841	Unnumb.
Howard	Fayette	Jan. 13, 1816	Unnumb.
Howell	West Plains	Mar. 2, 1857	Unnumb.
Iron	Ironton	Feb. 17, 1857	Unnumb.
Jackson	Kansas City	Dec. 15, 1826	Ch. 20

Jasper	Carthage	Jan. 29, 1841	Unnumb.
Jefferson	Hillsboro	Dec. 8, 1818	Unnumb.
Johnson	Warrensburg	Dec. 13, 1834	Unnumb.
Knox	Edina	Feb. 14, 1845	Unnumb.
Laclede	Lebanon	Feb. 24, 1849	Unnumb.
Lafayette[7]	Lexington	Nov. 16, 1820	Ch. 10
Lawrence	Mount Vernon	Feb. 14, 1845	Unnumb.
Lewis	Monticello	Jan. 2, 1833	Ch. 28
Lincoln	Troy	Dec. 14, 1818	Unnumb.
Linn	Linneus	Jan. 6, 1837	Unnumb.
Livingston	Chillicothe	Jan. 6, 1837	Unnumb.
Macon	Macon	Jan. 6, 1837	Unnumb.
Madison	Fredericktown	Dec. 14, 1818	Unnumb.
Maries	Vienna	Mar. 2, 1855	Unnumb.
Marion	Palmyra	Dec. 14, 1822	Ch. 38
McDonald	Pineville	Mar. 3, 1849	Unnumb.
Mercer	Princeton	Feb. 14, 1845	Unnumb.
Miller	Tuscumbia	Feb. 6, 1837	Unnumb.
Mississippi	Charleston	Feb. 14, 1845	Unnumb.
Moniteau	California	Feb. 14, 1845	Unnumb.
Monroe	Paris	Jan. 6, 1831	Ch. 15
Montgomery	Montgomery City	Dec. 14, 1818	Unnumb.
Morgan	Versailles	Jan. 5, 1833	Ch. 29
New Madrid	New Madrid	Oct. 1, 1812	Proc.
Newton	Neosho	Dec. 30, 1838	Unnumb.
Nodaway	Maryville	Jan. 2, 1843	
Oregon	Alton	Feb. 14, 1845	Unnumb.
Osage	Linn	Jan. 29, 1841	Unnumb.
Ozark[8]	Gainesville	Jan. 29, 1841	Unnumb.
Pemiscot	Caruthersville	Feb. 19, 1851	Unnumb.
Perry	Perryville	Nov. 16, 1820	Ch. 15
Pettis	Sedalia	Jan. 26, 1833	Ch. 30
Phelps	Rolla	Nov. 13, 1857	Unnumb.
Pike	Bowling Green	Dec. 14, 1818	Unnumb.
Platte	Platte City	Dec. 31, 1838	Unnumb.
Polk	Bolivar	Jan. 5, 1835	Unnumb.
Pulasaki	Waynesville	Jan. 19, 1833	Ch. 31
Putnam	Unionville	Feb. 22, 1843	Unnumb.
Ralls	New London	Nov. 16, 1820	Ch. 12
Randolph	Huntsville	Jan. 22, 1829	Ch. 29
Ray	Richmond	Nov. 16, 1820	Ch. 14
Reynolds	Centerville	Feb. 25, 1845	Unnumb.
Ripley	Doniphan	Jan. 5, 1833	Ch. 32
Saint Charles	Saint Charles	Oct. 1, 1812	Proc.
Saint Clair	Osceola	Jan. 16, 1833	Unnumb.
Sainte Genevieve	Sainte Genevieve	Oct. 1, 1812	Proc.
Saint Francois	Farmington	Dec. 19, 1821	Ch. 26
Saint Louis	Clayton	Oct. 1, 1812	Proc.
Saint Louis	(Independent City)	Mar. 5, 1877	
Saline	Marshall	Nov. 25, 1820	Ch. 27
Schuyler	Lancaster	Feb. 14, 1845	Unnumb.
Scotland	Memphis	Jan. 29, 1841	Unnumb.
Scott	Benton	Dec. 28, 1821	Ch. 28
Shannon	Eminence	Jan. 29, 1841	Unnumb.
Shelby	Shelbyville	Jan. 2, 1835	Unnumb.

Stoddard	Bloomfield	Jan. 2, 1835	Unnumb.
Stone	Galena	Feb. 10, 1851	Unnumb.
Sullivan[9]	Milan	Feb. 17, 1843	Unnumb.
Taney	Forsyth	Jan. 6, 1837	Unnumb.
Texas[10]	Houston	Feb. 17, 1843	Unnumb.
Vernon	Nevada	Feb. 17, 1851	Unnumb.
Warren	Warrenton	Jan. 5, 1833	Ch. 95
Washington	Potosi	Aug. 21, 1813	Unnumb.
Wayne	Greenville	Dec. 11, 1818	Unnumb.
Webster	Marshfield	Mar. 3, 1855	Unnumb.
Worth	Grant City	Feb. 6, 1861	Unnumb.
Wright	Hartville	Jan. 29, 1841	Unnumb.

Notes

1. Atchison created as Allen; name changed Feb. 14, 1845, unnumb.
2. Camden created as Kinderhook; name changed Feb. 23, 1843, unnumb.
3. Cass created as Van Buren; name changed Feb. 19, 1849, unnumb.
4. Dallas created as Niangaua; name changed Dec. 14, 1844, unnumb.
5. Henry created as Rives; name changed Feb. 15, 1841, unnumb.
6. Holt created as Nodaway; name changed Feb. 15, 1841, unnumb.
7. Lafayette created as Lillard; name changed Feb. 16, 1825, Ch. 1
8. Created as Ozark; name changed to Decatur Feb. 22, 1843, unnumb.; renamed Ozark Mar. 24, 1845, unnumb.
9. Sullivan created as Highland; name changed Feb. 14, 1845, unnumb.
10. Texas created as Ashley; name changed Feb. 14, 1845, unnumb.

MONTANA (56 COUNTIES)

Montana Territory May 26, 1864
Admitted as state November 8, 1889 (41st)

County	County Seat	Created	Statute
Beaverhead	Dillon	Feb. 2, 1865	Unnumb.
Big Horn	Hardin	Jan. 13, 1913	P & E
Blaine	Chinook	Feb. 29, 1912	P & E
Broadwater	Townsend	Feb. 9, 1897	H.B. 24
Carbon	Red Lodge	Mar. 4, 1895	H.B. 9
Carter	Ekalaka	Feb. 22, 1917	Ch. 56
Cascade	Great Falls	Sep. 12, 1887	Unnumb.
Chouteau	Fort Benton	Feb. 2, 1865	Unnumb.
Custer[1]	Miles City	Feb. 2, 1865	Unnumb.
Daniels	Scobey	Aug. 30, 1920	P & E
Dawson	Glendive	Jan. 15, 1869	Unnumb.
Deer Lodge	Anaconda	Feb. 2, 1865	Unnumb.
Fallon	Baker	Dec. 9, 1913	P & E
Fergus	Lewistown	Mar. 12, 1885	Unnumb.
Flathead	Kalispell	Feb. 6, 1893	Unnumb.
Gallatin	Bozeman	Feb. 2, 1865	Unnumb.
Garfield	Jordan	Feb. 7, 1919	Ch. 4
Glacier	Cut Bank	Feb. 17, 1919	Ch. 21
Golden Valley	Ryegate	Oct. 4, 1920	P & E
Granite	Philipsburg	Mar. 2, 1893	Unnumb.
Hill	Havre	Feb. 28, 1912	P & E
Jefferson	Boulder	Feb. 2, 1865	Unnumb.
Judith Basin	Stanford	Dec. 10, 1920	P & E

Lake	Polson	May 11, 1923	Proc.
Lewis and Clark[2]	Helena	Feb. 2, 1865	Unnumb.
Liberty	Chester	Feb. 11, 1920	P & E
Lincoln	Libby	Mar. 9, 1909	Ch. 133
Madison	Virginia City	Feb. 2, 1865	Unnumb.
McCone	Circle	Feb. 20, 1919	Ch. 33
Meagher	White Sulphur Springs	Nov. 16, 1867	Unnumb.
Mineral	Superior	Aug. 7, 1914	P & E
Missoula	Missoula	Feb. 2, 1865	Unnumb.
Musselshell	Roundup	Feb. 11, 1911	Ch. 25
Park	Livingston	Feb. 23, 1887	Unnumb.
Petroleum	Winnett	Nov. 24, 1924	Proc.
Phillips	Malta	Feb. 5, 1915	P & E
Pondera	Conrad	Feb. 17, 1919	Ch. 22
Powder River	Broadus	Mar. 7, 1919	Ch. 141
Powell	Deer Lodge	Jan. 31, 1901	S.B. 3
Prairie	Terry	Feb. 5, 1915	P & E
Ravalli	Hamilton	Feb. 16, 1893	Unnumb.
Richland	Sidney	May 27, 1914	P & E
Roosevelt	Wolf Point	Feb. 18, 1919	Ch. 23
Rosebud	Forsyth	Feb. 11, 1901	S.B. 21
Sanders	Thompson Falls	Feb. 7, 1905	Ch. 9
Sheridan	Plentywood	Mar. 24, 1913	P & E
Silver Bow	Butte	Feb. 16, 1881	Unnumb.
Stillwater	Columbus	Mar. 24, 1913	P & E
Sweet Grass	Big Timber	Mar. 5, 1895	H.B. 17
Teton	Choteau	Feb. 7, 1893	Unnumb.
Toole	Shelby	May 7, 1914	P & E
Treasure	Hysham	Feb. 7, 1919	Ch. 5
Valley	Glasgow	Feb. 6, 1893	Unnumb.
Wheatland	Harlowton	Feb. 22, 1917	Ch. 55
Wibaux	Wibaux	Aug. 17, 1914	P & E
Yellowstone	Billings	Feb. 26, 1883	Unnumb.

Notes

1. Custer created as Big Horn; name changed Apr. 1, 1882, unnumb.
2. Lewis and Clark created as Edgerton; name changed Dec. 20, 1867, unnumb.

NEBRASKA (93 COUNTIES)

Nebraska Territory May 30, 1854
Admitted as state March 1, 1867 (37th)

County	County Seat	Created	Statute
Adams	Hastings	Feb. 16, 1867	Unnumb.
Antelope	Neligh	Mar. 1, 1871	Unnumb.
Arthur	Arthur	Mar. 31, 1887	Ch. 21
Banner	Harrisburg	Nov. 6, 1888	Proc.
Blaine	Brewster	Mar. 5, 1885	Ch. 31
Boone	Albion	Mar. 1, 1871	Unnumb.
Box Butte	Alliance	Nov. 2, 1886	Proc.
Boyd	Butte	Mar. 20, 1891	Ch. 20

Brown	Ainsworth	Feb. 19, 1883	Ch. 31
Buffalo	Kearney	Mar. 14, 1855	Unnumb.
Burt	Tekamah	Nov. 23, 1854	Proc.
Butler	David City	Jan. 26, 1856	Unnumb.
Cass	Plattsmouth	Nov. 3, 1854	Proc.
Cedar	Hartington	Feb. 12, 1857	Unnumb.
Chase	Imperial	Feb. 27, 1873	Unnumb.
Cherry	Valentine	Feb. 23, 1883	Ch. 32
Cheyenne	Sidney	June 22, 1867	Unnumb.
Clay	Clay Center	Feb. 16, 1867	Unnumb.
Colfax	Schuyler	Feb. 15, 1869	Unnumb.
Cuming	West Point	Mar. 16, 1855	Unnumb.
Custer	Broken Bow	Feb. 17, 1877	Unnumb.
Dakota	Dakota City	Mar. 7, 1855	Unnumb.
Dawes	Chadron	Feb. 19, 1885	Ch. 32
Dawson	Lexington	Jan. 11, 1860	Unnumb.
Deuel	Chappell	Nov. 6, 1888	Unnumb.
Dixon	Ponca	Jan. 26, 1856	Unnumb.
Dodge	Fremont	Nov. 23, 1854	Proc.
Douglas	Omaha	Nov. 23, 1854	Proc.
Dundy	Benkelman	Feb. 27, 1873	Unnumb.
Fillmore	Geneva	Jan. 26, 1856	Unnumb.
Franklin	Franklin	Feb. 16, 1867	Unnumb.
Frontier	Stockville	Jan. 17, 1872	Unnumb.
Furnas	Beaver City	Feb. 27, 1873	Unnumb.
Gage	Beatrice	Mar. 16, 1855	Unnumb.
Garden	Oshkosh	Nov. 2, 1909	Election
Garfield	Burwell	Nov. 8, 1884	Proc.
Gosper	Elwood	Nov. 26, 1873	Unnumb.
Grant	Hyannis	Mar. 31, 1887	Ch. 22
Greeley	Greeley	Mar. 1, 1871	Unnumb.
Hall	Grand Island	Nov. 4, 1858	Unnumb.
Hamilton	Aurora	Feb. 16, 1867	Unnumb.
Harlan	Alma	June 3, 1871	Unnumb.
Hayes	Hayes Center	Feb. 19, 1877	Unnumb.
Hitchcock	Trenton	Feb. 27, 1873	Unnumb.
Holt[1]	O'Neill	Jan. 13, 1860	Unnumb.
Hooker	Mullen	Mar. 29, 1889	Ch. 1
Howard	Saint Paul	Mar. 1, 1871	Unnumb.
Jefferson[2]	Fairbury	Jan. 26, 1856	Unnumb.
Johnson	Tecumseh	Mar. 2, 1855	Unnumb.
Kearney	Minden	Jan. 10, 1860	Unnumb.
Keith	Ogallala	Feb. 27, 1873	Unnumb.
Keya Paha	Springview	Nov. 4, 1884	Proc.
Kimball	Kimball	Nov. 6, 1888	Proc.
Knox[3]	Center	Feb. 10, 1857	Unnumb.
Lancaster	Lincoln	Mar. 6, 1855	Unnumb.
Lincoln[4]	North Platte	Jan. 7, 1860	Unnumb.
Logan	Stapleton	Feb. 24, 1885	Ch. 33
Loup	Taylor	Feb. 23, 1883	
Madison	Madison	Jan. 26, 1856	Unnumb.
McPherson	Tryon	Mar. 31, 1887	Ch. 23
Merrick	Central City	Nov. 4, 1858	Unnumb.
Morrill	Bridgeport	Nov. 12, 1908	
Nance	Fullerton	Feb. 13, 1879	Unnumb.

Nemaha[5]	Auburn	Nov. 23, 1854	Proc.
Nuckolls	Nelson	Jan. 13, 1860	Unnumb.
Otoe[6]	Nebraska City	Nov. 23, 1854	Proc.
Pawnee	Pawnee City	Mar. 6, 1855	Unnumb.
Perkins	Grant	Nov. 1887	Proc.
Phelps	Holdrege	Feb. 11, 1873	Unnumb.
Pierce[7]	Pierce	Jan. 26, 1856	Proc.
Platte	Columbus	Jan. 26, 1856	Unnumb.
Polk	Osceola	Jan. 26, 1856	Unnumb.
Red Willow	McCook	Feb. 27, 1873	Unnumb.
Richardson	Falls City	Nov. 23, 1854	Proc.
Rock	Bassett	Nov. 6, 1888	
Saline	Wilber	Mar. 6, 1855	Unnumb.
Sarpy	Papillion	Feb. 7, 1857	Unnumb.
Saunders[8]	Wahoo	Jan. 26, 1856	Unnumb.
Scotts Bluff	Gering	Nov. 6, 1888	
Seward[9]	Seward	Mar. 6, 1855	Unnumb.
Sheridan	Rushville	Feb. 25, 1885	Ch. 34
Sherman	Loup City	Mar. 1, 1871	Unnumb.
Sioux	Harrison	Feb. 19, 1877	Unnumb.
Stanton[10]	Stanton	Mar. 6, 1855	Unnumb.
Thayer[11]	Hebron	Jan. 26, 1856	Unnumb.
Thomas	Thedford	Mar. 31, 1887	Ch. 24
Thurston[12]	Pender	Mar. 7, 1855	
Valley	Ord	Mar. 1, 1871	Unnumb.
Washington	Blair	Nov. 23, 1854	Proc.
Wayne	Wayne	Mar. 4, 1871	Unnumb.
Webster	Red Cloud	Feb. 16, 1867	Unnumb.
Wheeler	Bartlett	Feb. 17, 1877	Unnumb.
York	York	Mar. 13, 1855	Unnumb.

Notes

1. Holt created as West; name changed Jan. 9, 1862, unnumb.
2. Jefferson created as Jones; name changed 1867
3. Knox created as L'eau qui Court; name changed to Emmett Feb. 18, 1867; name changed Feb. 21, 1873
4. Lincoln created as Shorter; name changed Dec. 11, 1861, unnumb.
5. Nemaha created as Forney; name changed Mar. 17, 1855
6. Otoe created as Pierce; name changed 1855
7. Pierce created as Otoe; name changed 1856
8. Saunders created as Calhoun; name changed Jan. 8, 1862, unnumb.
9. Seward created as Greene; name changed Jan. 3, 1862
10. Stanton created as Izard; name changed Jan. 10, 1862
11. Thayer created as Jefferson; name changed Jan. 26, 1871
12. Thurston created as Blackbird; name changed Mar. 28, 1889

NEVADA (16 COUNTIES; 1 INDEPENDENT CITY)

Nevada Territory March 2, 1861
Admitted as state October 31, 1864 (36th)

County/City	County Seat	Created	Statute
Carson City[1]	(Independent City)	Nov. 25, 1861	Ch. 24
Churchill	Fallon	Nov. 25, 1861	Ch. 24
Clark	Las Vegas	Feb. 9, 1909	Ch. 11

Douglas	Minden	Nov. 25, 1861	Ch. 24
Elko	Elko	Mar. 5, 1869	Ch. 94
Esmeralda	Goldfield	Nov. 25, 1861	Ch. 24
Eureka	Eureka	Mar. 1, 1873	Ch. 46
Humboldt	Winnemucca	Nov. 25, 1861	Ch. 24
Lander	Battle Mountain	Dec. 19, 1862	Ch. 58
Lincoln	Pioche	Feb. 26, 1866	Ch. 48
Lyon	Yerington	Nov. 25, 1861	Ch. 24
Mineral	Hawthorne	Feb. 10, 1911	Ch. 13
Nye	Tonopah	Feb. 16, 1864	Ch. 102
Pershing	Lovelock	Mar. 18, 1919	Ch. 62
Storey	Virginia City	Nov. 25, 1861	Ch. 24
Washoe	Reno	Nov. 25, 1861	Ch. 24
White Pine	Ely	Mar. 2, 1869	Ch. 60

Note

1. Carson City created as Ormsby County; consolidated into Carson City 1969

NEW HAMPSHIRE (10 COUNTIES)

Separated from Massachusetts Colony 1680
Declared independence July 4, 1776
Ratified Constitution June 21, 1788 (admitted as 9th state)

County	County Seat	Created	Statute
Belknap	Laconia	Dec. 22, 1840	Ch. 539
Carroll	Ossipee	Dec. 22, 1840	Ch. 539
Cheshire	Keene	Apr. 29, 1769	
Coos	Lancaster	Dec. 24, 1803	Unnumb.
Grafton	North Haverhill	Apr. 29, 1769	
Hillsborough	Nashua	Apr. 29, 1769	
Merrimack	Concord	July 1, 1823	Ch. 40
Rockingham	Brentwood	Apr. 29, 1769	
Strafford	Dover	Apr. 29, 1769	
Sullivan	Newport	July 5, 1827	Ch. 48

NEW JERSEY (21 COUNTIES)

Provinces of East Jersey and West Jersey 1675–1702
East and West Jersey merged into New Jersey 1702
Declared independence July 4, 1776
Ratified Constitution December 18, 1787 (admitted as 3rd state)

County	County Seat	Created	Statute
Atlantic	Mays Landing	Feb. 7, 1837	Unnumb.
Bergen[1]	Hackensack	Mar. 1, 1683	Unnumb.
Burlington[2]	Mount Holly	May 17, 1694	Unnumb.
Camden	Camden	Mar. 13, 1844	Unnumb.
Cape May[2]	Cape May Court House	Nov. 12, 1692	Unnumb.
Cumberland	Bridgeton	Jan. 19, 1748	Ch. 92
Essex[1]	Newark	Mar. 1, 1683	Unnumb.

Gloucester[2]	Woodbury	May 28, 1686	Unnumb.
Hudson	Jersey City	Feb. 22, 1840	Unnumb.
Hunterdon	Flemington	Mar. 13, 1714	Unnumb.
Mercer	Trenton	Feb. 22, 1838	Unnumb.
Middlesex[1]	New Brunswick	Mar. 1, 1683	Unnumb.
Monmouth[1]	Freehold	Mar. 1, 1683	Unnumb.
Morris	Morristown	Mar. 15, 1739	Ch. 63
Ocean	Toms River	Feb. 15, 1850	Unnumb.
Passaic	Paterson	Feb. 7, 1837	Unnumb.
Salem[2]	Salem	May 17, 1694	Unnumb.
Somerset[1]	Somerville	May 1688	Unnumb.
Sussex	Newton	May 16, 1753 (Sess.)	Unnumb.
Union	Elizabeth	Mar. 19, 1857	Ch. 82
Warren	Belvidere	Nov. 20, 1824	Unnumb.

Notes

1. East Jersey
2. West Jersey

NEW MEXICO (33 COUNTIES)

New Mexico Territory September 9, 1850
Admitted as state January 6, 1912 (47th)

County	County Seat	Created	Statute
Bernalillo	Albuquerque	Jan. 9, 1852	Unnumb.
Catron	Reserve	Feb. 25, 1921	Ch. 28
Chaves	Roswell	Feb. 25, 1889	Ch. 87
Cibola	Grants	Jan. 19, 1981	
Colfax	Raton	Jan. 25, 1869	Ch. 24
Curry	Clovis	Feb. 25, 1909	Ch. 6
DeBaca	Fort Sumner	Feb. 28, 1917	Ch. 11
Dona Ana	Las Cruces	Jan. 9, 1852	Unnumb.
Eddy	Carlsbad	Feb. 25, 1889	Ch. 87
Grant	Silver City	Jan. 30, 1868	Ch. 20
Guadalupe	Santa Rosa	Feb. 26, 1891	Ch. 88
Harding	Mosquero	Mar. 4, 1921	Ch. 48
Hidalgo	Lordsburg	Feb. 25, 1919	Ch. 11
Lea	Lovington	Mar. 7, 1917	Ch. 23
Lincoln	Carrizozo	Jan. 16, 1869	Ch. 8
Los Alamos	Los Alamos	Mar. 16, 1949	Ch. 134
Luna	Deming	Mar. 16, 1901	Ch. 38
McKinley	Gallup	Feb. 23, 1899	Ch. 19
Mora	Mora	Feb. 1, 1860	Unnumb.
Otero	Alamogordo	Jan. 30, 1899	Ch. 3
Quay	Tucumcari	Feb. 28, 1903	Ch. 8
Rio Arriba	Tierra Amarilla	Jan. 9, 1852	Unnumb.
Roosevelt	Portales	Feb. 28, 1903	Ch. 7
Sandoval	Bernalillo	Mar. 10, 1903	Ch. 27
San Juan	Aztec	Feb. 24, 1887	Ch. 13
San Miguel	Las Vegas	Jan. 9, 1852	Unnumb.
Santa Fe	Santa Fe	Jan. 9, 1852	Unnumb.

Sierra	Truth or Consequences	Apr. 3, 1884	Ch. 59
Socorro	Socorro	Jan. 9, 1852	Unnumb.
Taos	Taos	Jan. 9, 1852	Unnumb.
Torrance	Estancia	Mar. 16, 1903	Ch. 70
Union	Clayton	Feb. 23, 1893	Ch. 49
Valencia	Los Lunas	Jan. 9, 1852	Unnumb.

NEW YORK (62 COUNTIES)

Surrendered to England by Dutch 1664
Declared independence July 4, 1776
Ratified Constitution July 26, 1788 (admitted as 11th state)

County	County Seat	Created	Statute
Albany	Albany	Nov. 1, 1683	Ch. 4
Allegany	Belmont	Apr. 7, 1806	Ch. 162
Bronx	Bronx	Apr. 19, 1912	Ch. 548
Broome	Binghamton	Mar. 28, 1806	Ch. 89
Cattaraugus	Little Valley	Mar. 11, 1808	Ch. 60
Cayuga	Auburn	Mar. 8, 1799	Ch. 26
Chautauqua	Mayville	Mar. 11, 1808	Ch. 60
Chemung	Elmira	Mar. 29, 1836	Ch. 77
Chenango	Norwich	Mar. 15, 1798	Ch. 31
Clinton	Plattsburgh	Mar. 17, 1788	Ch. 63
Columbia	Hudson	Apr. 4, 1786	Ch. 28
Cortland	Cortland	Apr. 8, 1808	Ch. 194
Delaware	Delhi	Mar. 10, 1797	Ch. 33
Dutchess	Poughkeepsie	Nov. 1, 1683	Ch. 4
Erie	Buffalo	Apr. 2, 1821	Ch. 228
Essex	Elizabethtown	Mar. 1, 1799	Ch. 24
Franklin	Malone	Mar. 11, 1808	Ch. 43
Fulton	Johnstown	Apr. 18, 1838	Ch. 332
Genesee	Batavia	Mar. 30, 1802	Ch. 64
Greene	Catskill	Mar. 25, 1800	Ch. 59
Hamilton	Lake Pleasant	Apr. 12, 1816	Ch. 120
Herkimer	Herkimer	Feb. 16, 1791	Ch. 10
Jefferson	Watertown	Mar. 28, 1805	Ch. 51
Kings	Brooklyn	Nov. 1, 1683	Ch. 4
Lewis	Lowville	Mar. 28, 1805	Ch. 51
Livingston	Geneseo	Feb. 23, 1821	Ch. 58
Madison	Wampsville	Mar. 21, 1806	Ch. 70
Monroe	Rochester	Feb. 23, 1821	Ch. 57
Montgomery[1]	Fonda	Mar. 12, 1772	Ch. 613
Nassau	Mineola	Apr. 27, 1898	Ch. 558
New York	New York	Nov. 1, 1683	Ch. 4
Niagara	Lockport	Mar. 11, 1808	Ch. 60
Oneida	Utica	Mar. 15, 1798	Ch. 31
Onondaga	Syracuse	Mar. 5, 1794	Ch. 18
Ontario	Canandaigua	Jan. 27, 1789	Ch. 11
Orange	Goshen	Nov. 1, 1683	Ch. 4
Orleans	Albion	Nov. 12, 1824	Ch. 266
Oswego	Oswego	Mar. 1, 1816	Ch. 22

Otsego	Cooperstown	Feb. 16, 1791	Ch. 10
Putnam	Carmel	June 12, 1812	Ch. 143
Queens	Jamaica	Nov. 1, 1683	Ch. 4
Rensselaer	Troy	Feb. 7, 1791	Ch. 4
Richmond	Saint George	Nov. 1, 1683	Ch. 4
Rockland	New City	Feb. 23, 1798	Ch. 16
Saint Lawrence	Canton	Mar. 3, 1802	Ch. 16
Saratoga	Ballston Spa	Feb. 7, 1791	Ch. 4
Schenectady	Schenectady	Mar. 7, 1809	Ch. 65
Schoharie	Schoharie	Apr. 6, 1795	Ch. 42
Schuyler	Watkins Glen	Apr. 17, 1854	Ch. 386
Seneca	Waterloo	Mar. 24, 1804	Ch. 331
Steuben	Bath	Mar. 18, 1796	Ch. 29
Suffolk	Riverhead	Nov. 1, 1683	Ch. 4
Sullivan	Monticello	Mar. 27, 1809	Ch. 126
Tioga	Owego	Feb. 16, 1791	Ch. 10
Tompkins	Ithaca	Apr. 7, 1817	Ch. 189
Ulster	Kingston	Nov. 1, 1683	Ch. 4
Warren	Lake George	Mar. 12, 1813	Ch. 50
Washington[2]	Fort Edward	Mar. 12, 1772	Ch. 613
Wayne	Lyons	Apr. 11, 1823	Ch. 138
Westchester	White Plains	Nov. 1, 1683	Ch. 4
Wyoming	Warsaw	May 19, 1841	Ch. 196
Yates	Penn Yan	Feb. 5, 1823	Ch. 30

Notes

1. Montgomery created as Tryon; name changed Apr. 2, 1784, Ch. 17
2. Washington created as Charlotte; name changed Apr. 2, 1784, Ch. 17

NORTH CAROLINA (100 COUNTIES)

Carolina proprietary colony 1663
North and South Carolina made separate provinces 1710
Declared independence July 4, 1776
Ratified Constitution November 21, 1789 (admitted as 12th state)
Seceded May 20, 1861
Readmitted July 4, 1868

County	County Seat	Created	Statute
Alamance	Graham	Jan. 29, 1849	Ch. 14
Alexander	Taylorsville	Jan. 15, 1847	Ch. 22
Alleghany	Sparta	1859	Ch. 3
Anson	Wadesboro	Mar. 17, 1749 (Sess.)	Ch. 2
Ashe	Jefferson	Nov. 18, 1799 (Sess.)	Ch. 36
Avery	Newland	Feb. 23, 1911	Ch. 33
Beaufort[1]	Washington	Dec. 3, 1705	
Bertie	Windsor	Oct. 2, 1722 (Sess.)	Ch. 5
Bladen	Elizabethtown	1734 (Sess.)	Ch. 8
Brunswick	Bolivia	Jan. 30, 1764 (Sess.)	Ch. 14
Buncombe	Asheville	Dec. 5, 1791 (Sess.)	Ch. 52
Burke	Morganton	Apr. 8, 1777	Ch. 19
Cabarrus	Concord	Nov. 15, 1792 (Sess.)	Ch. 21
Caldwell	Lenoir	Jan. 11, 1841	Ch. 11

Camden	Camden	Apr. 8, 1777	Ch. 18
Carteret	Beaufort	1722	
Caswell	Yanceyville	Apr. 8, 1777	Ch. 17
Catawba	Newton	Dec. 12, 1842	Ch. 8
Chatham	Pittsboro	Dec. 5, 1770 (Sess.)	Ch. 27
Cherokee	Murphy	Jan. 4, 1839	Ch. 10
Chowan	Edenton	1670	
Clay	Hayesville	Feb. 20, 1861	Ch. 6
Cleveland[2]	Shelby	Jan. 11, 1841	Ch. 9
Columbus	Whiteville	Dec. 15, 1808	Ch 1
Craven[3]	New Bern	Dec. 3, 1705	
Cumberland	Fayetteville	Feb. 19, 1754 (Sess.)	Ch. 8
Currituck	Currituck	1670	
Dare	Manteo	Feb. 2, 1870	Ch. 36
Davidson	Lexington	Dec. 9, 1822	Ch. 47
Davie	Mocksville	Dec. 20, 1836	Ch. 4
Duplin	Kenansville	Mar. 17, 1749 (Sess.)	Ch. 1
Durham	Durham	Feb. 28, 1881	Ch. 138
Edgecombe	Tarboro	Apr. 4, 1741	Ch. 7
Forsyth	Winston-Salem	Jan. 16, 1849	Ch. 23
Franklin	Louisburg	Apr. 14, 1778 (Sess.)	Ch. 19
Gaston	Gastonia	Dec. 21, 1846	Ch. 24
Gates	Gatesville	Apr. 14, 1778 (Sess.)	Ch. 20
Graham	Robbinsville	Jan. 30, 1872	Ch. 77
Granville	Oxford	June 28, 1746 (Sess.)	Ch. 3
Greene	Snow Hill	Nov. 18, 1799 (Sess.)	Ch. 39
Guilford	Greensboro	Dec. 5, 1770 (Sess.)	Ch. 24
Halifax	Halifax	Dec. 12, 1754 (Sess.)	Ch. 13
Harnett	Lillington	Feb. 7, 1855	Ch. 8
Haywood	Waynesville	Dec. 15, 1808	Ch. 1
Henderson	Hendersonville	Dec. 15, 1838	Ch. 12
Hertford	Winton	Dec. 12, 1754 (Sess.)	Ch. 4
Hoke	Raeford	Feb. 7, 1911	Ch. 24
Hyde[4]	Swanquarter	Dec. 3, 1705	
Iredell	Statesville	Nov. 3, 1788 (Sess.)	Ch. 36
Jackson	Sylva	Jan. 29, 1851	Ch. 38
Johnston	Smithfield	June 28, 1746 (Sess.)	Ch. 2
Jones	Trenton	Apr. 14, 1778 (Sess.)	Ch. 18
Lee	Sanford	Mar. 6, 1907	Ch 624
Lenoir	Kinston	Dec. 5, 1791 (Sess.)	Ch. 47
Lincoln	Lincolnton	Apr. 14, 1778 (Sess.)	Ch. 23
Macon	Franklin	1828	Ch. 50
Madison	Marshall	Jan. 27, 1851	Ch. 36
Martin	Williamston	Mar. 2, 1774	Ch. 32
McDowell	Marion	Dec. 19, 1842	Ch .10
Mecklenburg	Charlotte	Nov. 3, 1762 (Sess.)	Ch. 12
Mitchell	Bakersville	Feb. 16, 1861	Ch. 8
Montgomery	Troy	Apr. 14, 1778 (Sess.)	Ch. 21
Moore	Carthage	Apr. 18, 1784 (Sess.)	Ch. 76
Nash	Nashville	Nov. 15, 1777 (Sess.)	Ch. 30
New Hanover	Wilmington	Nov. 27, 1729 (Sess.)	Ch. 10
Northampton	Jackson	1741 (Sess.)	Ch. 1
Onslow	Jacksonville	1734 (Sess.)	Ch. 8
Orange	Hillsborough	Mar. 31, 1752 (Sess.)	Ch. 6
Pamlico	Bayboro	Feb. 8, 1872	Ch. 132

Pasquotank	Elizabeth City	1670	
Pender	Burgaw	Feb. 16, 1875	Ch. 91
Perquimans[5]	Hertford	1670	
Person	Roxboro	Dec. 5, 1791 (Sess.)	Ch. 53
Pitt	Greenville	Apr. 24, 1760 (Sess.)	Ch. 3
Polk	Columbus	Jan. 18, 1847	Ch. 26
Randolph	Asheboro	Apr. 14, 1778 (Sess.)	Ch. 22
Richmond	Rockingham	Oct. 18, 1779 (Sess.)	Ch. 16
Robeson	Lumberton	Nov. 18, 1786 (Sess.)	Ch. 40
Rockingham	Wentworth	Nov. 19, 1785 (Sess.)	Ch. 23
Rowan	Salisbury	Mar. 25, 1753 (Sess.)	Ch. 7
Rutherford	Rutherfordton	Apr. 14, 1779 (Sess.)	Ch. 23
Sampson	Clinton	Apr. 18, 1784 (Sess.)	Ch. 75
Scotland	Laurinburg	Feb. 20, 1899	Ch. 127
Stanly	Albemarle	Jan. 11, 1841	Ch. 13
Stokes	Danbury	Nov. 2, 1789 (Sess.)	Ch. 14
Surry	Dobson	Dec. 5, 1770 (Sess.)	Ch. 42
Swain	Bryson City	Feb. 24, 1871	Ch. 94
Transylvania	Brevard	Feb. 15, 1861	Ch. 10
Tyrrell	Columbia	Nov. 27, 1729 (Sess.)	Ch. 4
Union	Monroe	Dec. 19, 1842	Ch. 12
Vance	Henderson	Mar. 5, 1881	Ch. 113
Wake	Raleigh	Dec. 5, 1770 (Sess.)	Ch. 22
Warren	Warrenton	Apr. 19, 1779 (Sess.)	Ch. 19
Washington	Plymouth	Nov. 15, 1799 (Sess.)	Ch. 36
Watauga	Boone	Jan. 27, 1849	Ch. 25
Wayne	Goldsboro	Oct. 18, 1779 (Sess.)	Ch. 17
Wilkes	Wilkesboro	Nov. 15, 1777 (Sess.)	Ch. 32
Wilson	Wilson	Feb. 13, 1855	Ch. 12
Yadkin	Yadkinville	Dec. 28, 1850	Ch. 40
Yancey	Burnsville	1833	Ch. 83

Notes

1. Beaufort created as Pamptecough; name changed 1712
2. Cleveland created as Cleaveland; spelling changed 1885
3. Craven created as Archdale; name changed 1712
4. Hyde created as Wickham; name changed 1712
5. Perquimans created as Berkeley; name changed 1681

NORTH DAKOTA (53 COUNTIES)

Dakota Territory March 2, 1861
Admitted as state November 2, 1889 (39th)

County	County Seat	Created	Statute
Adams	Hettinger	Apr. 17, 1907	Proc.
Barnes[1]	Valley City	Jan. 4, 1873	Ch. 30
Benson	Minnewaukan	Mar. 9, 1883	Ch. 12
Billings	Medora	Feb. 10, 1879	Ch. 11
Bottineau	Bottineau	Jan. 4, 1873	Ch. 18
Bowman	Bowman	Mar. 8, 1883	Ch. 38
Burke	Bowbells	Feb. 8, 1910	
Burleigh	Bismarck	Jan. 4, 1873	Ch. 18
Cass	Fargo	Jan. 4, 1873	Ch. 20

Cavalier	Langdon	Jan. 4, 1873	Ch. 18
Dickey	Ellendale	Mar. 5, 1881	Ch. 40
Divide	Crosby	Dec. 9, 1910	
Dunn	Manning	Mar. 9, 1883	Ch. 39
Eddy	New Rockford	Mar. 31, 1885	Ch. 15
Emmons	Linton	Feb. 10, 1879	Ch. 11
Foster	Carrington	Jan. 4, 1873	Ch. 18
Golden Valley	Beach	Nov. 19, 1912	
Grand Forks	Grand Forks	Jan. 4, 1873	Ch. 20
Grant	Carson	Nov. 25, 1916	Unnumb.
Griggs	Cooperstown	Feb. 18, 1881	Ch. 41
Hettinger	Mott	Mar. 9, 1883	Ch. 39
Kidder	Steele	Jan. 4, 1873	Ch. 18
LaMoure	LaMoure	Jan. 4, 1873	Ch. 20
Logan	Napoleon	Jan. 4, 1873	Ch. 18
McHenry	Towner	Jan. 4, 1873	Ch. 18
McIntosh	Ashley	Mar. 9, 1883	Ch. 26
McKenzie	Watford City	Mar. 9, 1883	Ch. 39
McLean	Washburn	Mar. 8, 1883	Ch. 25
Mercer	Stanton	Jan. 14, 1875	Ch. 30
Morton	Mandan	Jan. 8, 1873	Ch. 19
Mountrail	Stanley	Jan. 4, 1873	Ch. 18
Nelson	Lakota	Mar. 2, 1883	Ch. 27
Oliver	Center	Mar. 12, 1885	Ch. 31
Pembina	Cavalier	Jan. 9, 1867	Ch. 15
Pierce	Rugby	Mar. 11, 1887	Ch. 180
Ramsey	Devils Lake	Jan. 4, 1873	Ch. 18
Ransom	Lisbon	Jan. 4, 1873	Ch. 18
Renville	Mohall	Jan. 4, 1873	Ch. 18
Richland	Wahpeton	Jan. 4, 1873	Ch. 20
Rolette	Rolla	Jan. 4, 1873	Ch. 18
Sargent	Forman	Mar. 3, 1883	Ch. 32
Sheridan	McClusky	Jan. 4, 1873	Ch. 18
Sioux	Fort Yates	Sep. 3, 1914	
Slope	Amidon	Nov. 3, 1914	
Stark	Dickinson	Feb. 10, 1879	Ch. 11
Steele	Finley	Mar. 8, 1883	Ch. 36
Stutsman	Jamestown	Jan. 4, 1873	Ch. 20
Towner	Cando	Mar. 8, 1883	Ch. 37
Traill	Hillsboro	Jan. 12, 1875	Ch. 32
Walsh	Grafton	Feb. 18, 1881	Ch. 51
Ward	Minot	Apr. 14, 1885	Ch. 42
Wells[2]	Fessenden	Jan. 4, 1873	Ch. 18
Williams	Williston	Nov. 30, 1892	

Notes

1. Barnes created as Burbank; name changed Jan. 14, 1875
2. Wells created as Gingras; name changed Feb. 26, 1881, Ch. 53

OHIO (88 COUNTIES)

Northwest Territory July 13, 1787
Admitted as state February 19, 1803 (17th)

County	County Seat	Created	Statute
Adams	West Union	July 10, 1797	Proc.
Allen	Lima	Feb. 12, 1820	Ch. 37
Ashland	Ashland	Feb. 24, 1846	Unnumb.
Ashtabula	Jefferson	Feb. 10, 1807	Ch. 1
Athens	Athens	Feb. 20, 1805	Ch. 68
Auglaize	Wapakoneta	Feb. 14, 1848	Unnumb.
Belmont	Saint Clairsville	Sep. 7, 1801	Proc.
Brown	Georgetown	Dec. 27, 1817	Ch. 12
Butler	Hamilton	Mar. 24, 1803	Ch. 4
Carroll	Carrollton	Dec. 25, 1832	Unnumb.
Champaign	Urbana	Feb. 20, 1805	Ch. 69
Clark	Springfield	Dec. 26, 1817	Ch. 14
Clermont	Batavia	Dec. 6, 1800	Proc.
Clinton	Wilmington	Feb. 19, 1810	Ch. 63
Columbiana	Lisbon	Mar. 25, 1803	Ch. 6
Coshocton	Coshocton	Jan. 31, 1810	Ch. 26
Crawford	Bucyrus	Feb. 12, 1820	Ch. 37
Cuyahoga	Cleveland	Feb. 10, 1807	Ch. 1
Darke	Greenville	Jan. 3, 1809	Ch. 6
Defiance	Defiance	Mar. 4, 1845	Unnumb.
Delaware	Delaware	Feb. 10, 1808	Ch. 10
Erie	Sandusky	Mar. 15, 1838	Unnumb.
Fairfield	Lancaster	Dec. 9, 1800	Proc.
Fayette	Washington Court House	Feb. 19, 1810	Ch. 39
Franklin	Columbus	Mar. 30, 1803	Ch. 11
Fulton	Wauseon	Feb. 28, 1850	Unnumb.
Gallia	Gallipolis	Mar. 25, 1803	Ch. 8
Geauga	Chardon	Dec. 31, 1805	Unnumb.
Greene	Xenia	Mar. 24, 1803	Ch. 4
Guernsey	Cambridge	Jan. 31, 1810	Ch. 20
Hamilton	Cincinnati	Jan. 2, 1790	Proc.
Hancock	Findlay	Feb. 12, 1820	Ch. 37
Hardin	Kenton	Feb. 12, 1820	Ch. 37
Harrison	Cadiz	Jan. 12, 1813	Ch. 5
Henry	Napoleon	Feb. 12 1820	Ch. 37
Highland	Hillsboro	Feb. 18, 1805	Ch. 60
Hocking	Logan	Jan. 3, 1818	Ch. 24
Holmes	Millersburg	Jan. 20, 1824	Ch. 36
Huron	Norwalk	Feb. 7, 1809	Ch. 48
Jackson	Jackson	Jan. 12, 1816	Ch. 25
Jefferson	Steubenville	July 27, 1797	Proc.
Knox	Mount Vernon	Jan. 30, 1808	Ch. 8
Lake	Painesville	Mar. 6, 1840	Unnumb.
Lawrence	Ironton	Dec. 21, 1815	Ch. 8
Licking	Newark	Jan. 30, 1808	Ch. 8
Logan	Bellefontaine	Dec. 30, 1817	Ch. 20
Lorain	Elyria	Dec. 26, 1822	Ch. 5
Lucas	Toledo	June 20, 1835	Unnumb.
Madison	London	Feb. 16, 1810	Ch. 67
Mahoning	Youngstown	Feb. 16, 1846	Unnumb.
Marion	Marion	Feb. 12, 1820	Ch. 37
Medina	Medina	Feb. 18, 1812	Ch. 46
Meigs	Pomeroy	Jan. 21, 1819	Ch. 25

Mercer	Celina	Feb. 12, 1820	Ch. 37
Miami	Troy	Jan. 16, 1807	Ch. 32
Monroe	Woodsfield	Jan. 29, 1813	Ch. 25
Montgomery	Dayton	Mar. 24, 1803	Ch. 4
Morgan	McConnelsville	Dec. 29, 1817	Ch. 18
Morrow	Mount Gilead	Feb. 24, 1848	Unnumb.
Muskingum	Zanesville	Jan. 7, 1804	Ch. 22
Noble	Caldwell	Mar. 11, 1851	Unnumb.
Ottawa	Port Clinton	Mar. 6, 1840	Unnumb.
Paulding	Paulding	Feb. 12, 1820	Ch. 37
Perry	New Lexington	Dec. 26, 1817	Ch. 11
Pickaway	Circleville	Jan. 12, 1810	Ch. 13
Pike	Waverly	Jan. 4, 1815	Ch. 16
Portage	Ravenna	Feb. 10, 1807	Ch. 1
Preble	Eaton	Feb. 15, 1808	Ch. 51
Putnam	Ottawa	Feb. 12, 1820	Ch. 37
Richland	Mansfield	Jan. 30, 1808	Ch. 8
Ross	Chillicothe	Aug. 20, 1798	Proc.
Sandusky	Fremont	Feb. 12, 1820	Ch. 37
Scioto	Portsmouth	Mar. 24, 1803	Ch. 3
Seneca	Tiffin	Feb. 12, 1820	Ch. 37
Shelby	Sidney	Jan. 7, 1819	Ch. 12
Stark	Canton	Feb. 13, 1808	Ch. 46
Summit	Akron	Mar. 3, 1840	Unnumb.
Trumbull	Warren	July 10, 1800	Proc.
Tuscarawas	New Philadelphia	Feb. 13, 1808	Ch. 50
Union	Marysville	Jan. 10, 1820	Ch. 16
Van Wert	Van Wert	Feb. 12, 1820	Ch. 37
Vinton	McArthur	Mar. 23, 1850	Unnumb.
Warren	Lebanon	Mar. 24, 1803	Ch. 4
Washington	Marietta	July 27, 1788	Proc.
Wayne	Wooster	Feb. 13, 1808	Ch. 46
Williams	Bryan	Feb. 12, 1820	Ch. 37
Wood	Bowling Green	Feb. 12, 1820	Ch. 37
Wyandot	Upper Sandusky	Feb. 3, 1845	Unnumb.

OKLAHOMA (77 COUNTIES)

Indian Lands 1819–1890
Oklahoma Territory May 2, 1890
Admitted as state November 16, 1907 (46th)

County	County Seat	Created	Statute
Adair	Stilwell	July 16, 1907	Const.
Alfalfa	Cherokee	July 16, 1907	Const.
Atoka	Atoka	July 16, 1907	Const.
Beaver[1]	Beaver	1890	
Beckham	Sayre	July 16, 1907	Const.
Blaine[2]	Watonga	1892	
Bryan	Durant	July 16, 1907	Const.
Caddo[3]	Anadarko	1901	
Canadian	El Reno	1889	
Carter	Ardmore	July 16, 1907	Const.
Cherokee	Tahlequah	July 16, 1907	Const.

Choctaw	Hugo	July 16, 1907	Const.
Cimarron	Boise City	July 16, 1907	Const.
Cleveland	Norman	1890	
Coal	Coalgate	July 16, 1907	Const.
Comanche	Lawton	1901	
Cotton	Walters	Aug. 27, 1912	Proc.
Craig	Vinita	July 16, 1907	Const.
Creek	Sapulpa	July 16, 1907	Const.
Custer[4]	Arapaho	1892	
Delaware	Jay	July 16, 1907	Const.
Dewey[5]	Taloga	1892	
Ellis	Arnett	July 16, 1907	Const.
Garfield[6]	Enid	1893	
Garvin	Pauls Valley	July 16, 1907	Const.
Grady	Chickasha	July 16, 1907	Const.
Grant[7]	Medford	1893	
Greer	Mangum	1886	
Harmon	Hollis	June 2, 1909	Proc.
Harper	Buffalo	July 16, 1907	Const.
Haskell	Stigler	July 16, 1907	Const.
Hughes	Holdenville	July 16, 1907	Const.
Jackson	Altus	July 16, 1907	Const.
Jefferson	Waurika	July 16, 1907	Const.
Johnston	Tishomingo	July 16, 1907	Const.
Kay[8]	Newkirk	1893	
Kingfisher	Kingfisher	1890	
Kiowa	Hobart	1901	
Latimer	Wilburton	July 16, 1907	Const.
Le Flore	Poteau	July 16, 1907	Const.
Lincoln	Chandler	1891	
Logan	Guthrie	1890	
Love	Marietta	July 16, 1907	Const.
Major	Fairview	July 16, 1907	Const.
Marshall	Madill	July 16, 1907	Const.
Mayes	Pryor	July 16, 1907	Const.
McClain	Purcell	July 16, 1907	Const.
McCurtain	Idabel	July 16, 1907	Const.
McIntosh	Eufala	July 16, 1907	Const.
Murray	Sulphur	July 16, 1907	Const.
Muskogee	Muskogee	July 16, 1907	Const.
Noble[9]	Perry	1893	
Nowata	Nowata	July 16, 1907	Const.
Okfuskee	Okemah	July 16, 1907	Const.
Oklahoma	Oklahoma City	1890	
Okmulgee	Okmulgee	July 16, 1907	Const.
Osage	Pawhuska	July 16, 1907	Const.
Ottawa	Miami	July 16, 1907	Const.
Pawnee[10]	Pawnee	1893	
Payne	Stillwater	1890	
Pittsburg	McAlester	July 16, 1907	Const.
Pontotoc	Ada	July 16, 1907	Const.
Pottawatomie	Shawnee	1891	
Pushmataha	Antlers	July 16, 1907	Const.
Roger Mills[11]	Cheyenne	1892	
Rogers	Claremore	July 16, 1907	Const.

Seminole	Wewoka	July 16, 1907	Const.
Sequoyah	Sallisaw	July 16, 1907	Const.
Stephens	Duncan	July 16, 1907	Const.
Texas	Guymon	July 16, 1907	Const.
Tillman	Frederick	July 16, 1907	Const.
Tulsa	Tulsa	1905	
Wagoner	Wagoner	July 16, 1907	Const.
Washington	Bartlesville	July 16, 1907	Const.
Washita[12]	Cordell	1892	
Woods[13]	Alva	1893	
Woodward[14]	Woodward	1893	

Notes

1. Beaver created as County 7; name changed July 16, 1907
2. Blaine created as County C; name changed July 16, 1907
3. Caddo created as County I; name changed Nov. 8, 1902
4. Custer created as County G; name changed Nov. 8, 1892
5. Dewey created as County D; name changed Nov. 8, 1898
6. Garfield created as County O; name changed Nov. 6, 1894
7. Grant created as County L; name changed Nov. 6, 1894
8. Kay created as County K; name changed 1895
9. Noble created as County P; name changed Nov. 6, 1894
10. Pawnee created as County Q; name changed 1895
11. Roger Mills created as County F; name changed Nov. 8, 1892
12. Washita created as County H; name changed 1900
13. Woods created as County M; name changed Nov. 6, 1894
14. Woodward created as County N; name changed Nov. 6, 1894

OREGON (36 COUNTIES)

Provisional government 1843
Oregon Territory August 14, 1848
Admitted as state February 14, 1859 (33rd)

County	County Seat	Created	Statute
Baker	Baker City	Sep. 22, 1862	Unnumb.
Benton	Corvallis	Dec. 23, 1847	Unnumb.
Clackamas	Oregon City	July 5, 1843	Unnumb.
Clatsop	Astoria	June 22, 1844	Unnumb.
Columbia	Saint Helens	Jan. 16, 1854	Unnumb.
Coos	Coquille	Dec. 22, 1853	Unnumb.
Crook	Prineville	Oct. 24, 1882	Unnumb.
Curry	Gold Beach	Dec. 18, 1855	Unnumb.
Deschutes	Bend	Dec. 13, 1916	Proc.
Douglas	Roseburg	Jan. 7, 1852	Unnumb.
Gilliam	Condon	Feb. 25, 1885	Unnumb.
Grant	Canyon City	Oct. 14, 1864	Unnumb.
Harney	Burns	Feb. 25, 1889	Unnumb.
Hood River	Hood River	June 23, 1908	Proc.
Jackson	Medford	Jan. 12, 1852	Unnumb.
Jefferson	Madras	Dec. 12, 1914	Proc.
Josephine	Grants Pass	Jan. 22, 1856	Unnumb.
Klamath	Klamath Falls	Oct. 17, 1882	Unnumb.
Lake	Lakeview	Oct. 24, 1874	Unnumb.

Lane	Eugene	Jan. 28, 1851	Unnumb.
Lincoln	Newport	Feb. 20, 1893	S.B. 119
Linn	Albany	Dec. 28, 1847	Unnumb.
Malheur	Vale	Feb. 17, 1887	Unnumb.
Marion[1]	Salem	July 5, 1843	Unnumb.
Morrow	Heppner	Feb. 16, 1885	Unnumb.
Multnomah	Portland	Dec. 22, 1854	Unnumb.
Polk	Dallas	Dec. 22, 1845	Unnumb.
Sherman	Moro	Feb. 25, 1889	Unnumb.
Tillamook	Tillamook	Dec. 15, 1853	Unnumb.
Umatilla	Pendleton	Sep. 27, 1862	Unnumb.
Union	La Grande	Oct. 14, 1864	Unnumb.
Wallowa	Enterprise	Feb. 11, 1887	Unnumb.
Wasco	The Dalles	Jan. 11, 1854	Unnumb.
Washington[2]	Hillsboro	July 5, 1843	Unnumb.
Wheeler	Fossil	Feb. 17, 1899	H.B. 153
Yamhill	McMinnville	July 5, 1843	Unnumb.

Notes

1. Marion created as Champoeg; name changed Sep. 3, 1849, unnumb.
2. Washington created as Twality; name changed Sep. 3, 1849, unnumb.

PENNSYLVANIA (67 COUNTIES)

William Penn's colony established 1682
Declared independence July 4, 1776
Ratified Constitution December 12, 1787 (admitted as 2nd state)

County	County Seat	Created	Statute
Adams	Gettysburg	Jan. 22, 1800	Ch. 231
Allegheny	Pittsburgh	Sep. 24, 1788	Ch. 408
Armstrong	Kittanning	Mar. 12, 1800	Ch. 264
Beaver	Beaver	Mar. 12, 1800	Ch. 264
Bedford	Bedford	Mar. 9, 1771	Unnumb.
Berks	Reading	Oct. 14, 1751 (Sess.)	Unnumb.
Blair	Hollidaysburg	Feb. 26, 1846	Act 55
Bradford[1]	Towanda	Feb. 21, 1810	Ch. 30
Bucks	Doylestown	Mar. 10, 1682	Unnumb.
Butler	Butler	Mar. 12, 1800	Ch. 264
Cambria	Ebensburg	Mar. 26, 1804	Act 78
Cameron	Emporium	Mar. 29, 1860	Act 598
Carbon	Jim Thorpe	Mar. 13, 1843	Act 141
Centre	Bellefonte	Feb. 13, 1800	Ch. 237
Chester	West Chester	Mar. 10, 1682	Unnumb.
Clarion	Clarion	Mar. 11, 1839	Act 27
Clearfield	Clearfield	Mar. 26, 1804	Act 78
Clinton	Lock Haven	June 21, 1839	Act 145
Columbia	Bloomsburg	Mar. 22, 1813	Act 109
Crawford	Meadville	Mar. 12, 1800	Ch. 264
Cumberland	Carlisle	Jan. 27, 1750	Ch. 1
Dauphin	Harrisburg	Mar. 4, 1785	Ch. 182
Delaware	Media	Sep. 26, 1789	Ch. 492
Elk	Ridgway	Apr. 18, 1843	Act 150

Erie	Erie	Mar. 12, 1800	Ch. 264
Fayette	Uniontown	Sep. 26, 1783	Ch. 155
Forest	Tionesta	Apr. 11, 1848	Res. 9
Franklin	Chambersburg	Sep. 9, 1784	Ch. 153
Fulton	McConnellsburg	Apr. 19, 1850	Act 495
Greene	Waynesburg	Feb. 9, 1796	Ch. 4
Huntingdon	Huntingdon	Sep. 20, 1787	Ch. 359
Indiana	Indiana	Mar. 30, 1803	Act 161
Jefferson	Brookville	Mar. 26, 1804	Act 78
Juniata	Mifflintown	Mar. 2, 1831	Act 67
Lackawanna	Scranton	Aug. 21, 1878	Proc.
Lancaster	Lancaster	Oct. 14, 1728 (Sess.)	Ch. 299
Lawrence	New Castle	Mar. 20, 1849	Act 366
Lebanon	Lebanon	Feb. 16, 1813	Act 52
Lehigh	Allentown	Mar. 6, 1812	Act 49
Luzerne	Wilkes-Barre	Sep. 25, 1786	Ch. 291
Lycoming	Williamsport	Apr. 13, 1795	Ch. 314
McKean	Smethport	Mar. 26, 1804	Ch. 78
Mercer	Mercer	Mar. 12, 1800	Ch. 264
Mifflin	Lewistown	Sep. 19, 1789	Ch. 485
Monroe	Stroudsburg	Apr. 1, 1836	Act 144
Montgomery	Norristown	Sep. 10, 1784	Ch. 154
Montour	Danville	May 3, 1850	Act 387
Northampton	Easton	Oct. 14, 1751 (Sess.)	Unnumb.
Northumberland	Sunbury	Mar. 21, 1772	Unnumb.
Perry	New Bloomfield	Mar. 22, 1820	Act 68
Philadelphia	Philadelphia	Mar. 10, 1682	Unnumb.
Pike	Milford	Mar. 26, 1814	Act 109
Potter	Coudersport	Mar. 26, 1804	Act 78
Schuylkill	Pottsville	Mar. 1, 1811	Act 54
Snyder	Middleburg	Mar. 2, 1855	Act 555
Somerset	Somerset	Apr. 17, 1795	Ch. 331
Sullivan	Laporte	Mar. 15, 1847	Act 365
Susquehanna	Montrose	Feb. 21, 1810	Ch. 30
Tioga	Wellsboro	Mar. 26, 1804	Act 78
Union	Lewisburg	Mar. 22, 1813	Act 110
Venango	Franklin	Mar. 12, 1800	Ch. 264
Warren	Warren	Mar. 12, 1800	Ch. 264
Washington	Washington	Mar. 28, 1781	Ch. 189
Wayne	Honesdale	Mar. 21, 1798	Ch. 120
Westmoreland	Greensburg	Feb. 26, 1773	Ch. 8
Wyoming	Tunkhannock	Apr. 4, 1842	Act 79
York	York	Oct. 14, 1748 (Sess.)	Unnumb.

Note

1. Bradford created as Ontario; name changed Mar. 24, 1812, Ch. 109

RHODE ISLAND (5 COUNTIES)

Chartered 1663
Renounced allegiance to England May 14, 1776
Ratified Constitution May 29, 1790 (admitted as 13th state)

County	County Seat	Created
Bristol	Bristol	Feb 17, 1747
Kent	West Warwick	June 11, 1750
Newport[1]	Newport	June 22, 1703
Providence[2]	Providence	June 22, 1703
Washington[3]	West Kingston	June 3, 1729

Notes

1. Kent created as Rhode Island; name changed June 16, 1729
2. Providence created as Providence Plantations; name changed June 16, 1729
3. Washington created as King's; name changed Oct. 29, 1781

SOUTH CAROLINA (46 COUNTIES)

Carolina proprietary colony 1663
North and South Carolina made separate provinces 1710
Declared independence July 4, 1776
Ratified Constitution May 23, 1788 (admitted as 8th state)
Seceded December 20, 1860
Readmitted July 9, 1868

Prior to 1868, South Carolina political subdivisions were changed from counties (1682) to parishes (1706), to townships (1731), to judicial districts (1769), and back to counties (1785 and 1868). These subdivisions overlapped each other in both time and area. The date of creation in this table is as close as possible to the subdivision that evolved into today's county.

County	County Seat	Created	Statute
Abbeville	Abbeville	Mar. 12, 1785	Unnumb.
Aiken	Aiken	Mar. 10, 1871	Act 420
Allendale	Allendale	Feb. 6, 1919	Act 6
Anderson	Anderson	Dec. 20, 1826	Act 9
Bamberg	Bamberg	Feb. 25, 1897	Act 344
Barnwell	Barnwell	1798	
Beaufort	Beaufort	Mar. 12, 1785	Unnumb.
Berkeley	Moncks Corner	Jan. 31, 1882	Act 527
Calhoun	Saint Matthews	Feb. 14, 1908	Act 567
Charleston	Charleston	1769	
Cherokee	Gaffney	Feb. 25, 1897	Act 345
Chester	Chester	Mar. 12, 1785	Unnumb.
Chesterfield	Chesterfield	Mar. 12, 1785	Unnumb.
Clarendon	Manning	Mar. 12, 1785	Unnumb.
Colleton	Walterboro	1682	
Darlington	Darlington	Mar. 12, 1785	Unnumb.
Dillon	Dillon	Feb. 15, 1910	Act 436
Dorchester	Saint George	Feb. 25, 1897	Act 346
Edgefield	Edgefield	Mar. 12, 1785	Unnumb.
Fairfield	Winnsboro	Mar. 12, 1785	Unnumb.
Florence	Florence	Dec. 22, 1888	Act 99
Georgetown	Georgetown	1769	
Greenville	Greenville	Mar. 22, 1786	Unnumb.
Greenwood	Greenwood	Mar. 2, 1897	Act 347
Hampton	Hampton	Feb. 18, 1878	Act 353
Horry	Conway	Dec. 19, 1801	Unnumb.
Jasper	Ridgeland	Jan. 30, 1912	Act 459

Kershaw	Camden	Feb. 19, 1791	
Lancaster	Lancaster	Mar. 12, 1785	Unnumb.
Laurens	Laurens	Mar. 12, 1785	Unnumb.
Lee	Bishopville	Feb. 25, 1902	Act 651
Lexington	Lexington	Mar. 12, 1785	Unnumb.
Marion	Marion	1798	
Marlboro	Bennettsville	Mar. 12, 1785	Unnumb.
McCormick	McCormick	Feb. 19, 1916	Act 398
Newberry	Newberry	Mar. 12, 1785	Unnumb.
Oconee	Walhalla	Jan. 29, 1868	
Orangeburg	Orangeburg	1769	
Pickens	Pickens	Dec. 20, 1826	Act 9
Richland	Columbia	Mar. 12, 1785	Unnumb.
Saluda	Saluda	Feb. 25, 1896	Act. 118
Spartanburg	Spartanburg	Mar. 12, 1785	Unnumb.
Sumter	Sumter	1798	
Union	Union	Mar. 12, 1785	Unnumb.
Williamsburg	Kingstree	Mar. 12, 1785	Unnumb.
York	York	Mar. 12, 1785	Unnumb.

SOUTH DAKOTA (66 COUNTIES)

Dakota Territory March 2, 1861
Admitted as state November 2, 1889 (40th)

County	County Seat	Created	Statute
Aurora	Plankinton	Feb. 22, 1879	Ch. 12
Beadle	Huron	Feb. 22, 1879	Ch. 12
Bennett	Martin	Mar. 9, 1909	Ch. 280
Bon Homme	Tyndall	Apr. 5, 1862	Ch. 12
Brookings	Brookings	Apr. 5, 1862	Ch. 16
Brown	Aberdeen	Feb. 22, 1879	Ch. 12
Brule	Chamberlain	Jan. 14, 1875	Ch. 31
Buffalo	Gann Valley	Jan. 6, 1864	
Butte	Belle Fourche	Mar. 2, 1883	Ch. 15
Campbell	Mound City	Jan. 8, 1873	Ch. 16
Charles Mix	Lake Andes	May 8, 1862	Ch. 18
Clark	Clark	Jan. 8, 1873	Ch. 16
Clay	Vermillion	Apr. 10, 1862	Ch. 13
Codington	Watertown	Feb. 15, 1877	
Corson	McIntosh	Mar. 2, 1909	Ch. 133
Custer	Custer	Jan. 11, 1875	Ch. 29
Davison	Mitchell	Jan. 8, 1873	Ch. 16
Day	Webster	Oct. 1, 1879	
Deuel	Clear Lake	Apr. 5, 1862	Ch. 16
Dewey[1]	Timber Lake	Jan. 8, 1873	Ch. 19
Douglas	Armour	Jan. 8, 1873	Ch. 16
Edmunds	Ipswich	Jan. 8, 1873	Ch. 16
Fall River	Hot Springs	Apr. 3, 1883	
Faulk	Faulkton	Jan. 8, 1873	Ch. 16
Grant	Milbank	Jan. 8, 1873	Ch. 16
Gregory	Burke	May 8, 1862	Ch. 18
Haakon	Phillip	Nov. 1914	
Hamlin	Hayti	Jan. 8, 1873	Ch. 16

Hand	Miller	Jan. 8, 1873	Ch. 16
Hanson	Alexandria	Jan. 13, 1871	Ch. 10
Harding	Buffalo	Mar. 5, 1881	
Hughes	Pierre	Jan. 8, 1873	Ch. 16
Hutchinson	Olivet	May 8, 1862	Ch. 15
Hyde	Highmore	Jan. 8, 1873	Ch. 16
Jackson	Kadoka	Mar. 8, 1883	
Jerauld	Wessington Springs	Mar. 9, 1883	Ch. 23
Jones	Murdo	Jan. 15, 1916	
Kingsbury	De Smet	Jan. 8, 1873	Ch. 16
Lake	Madison	Jan. 8, 1873	Ch. 16
Lawrence	Deadwood	Jan. 11, 1875	Ch. 29
Lincoln	Canton	Apr. 5, 1862	Ch. 16
Lyman	Kennebec	Jan. 8, 1873	Ch. 19
Marshall	Britton	Mar. 10, 1885	Ch. 12
McCook	Salem	Jan. 8, 1873	Ch. 16
McPherson	Leola	Jan. 8, 1873	Ch. 16
Meade	Sturgis	Feb. 7, 1889	Ch. 57
Mellette	White River	Mar. 9, 1909	Ch. 280
Miner	Howard	Jan. 8, 1873	Ch. 16
Minnehaha	Sioux Falls	Apr. 5, 1862	Ch. 16
Moody	Flandreau	Jan. 8, 1873	Ch. 16
Pennington	Rapid City	Jan. 11, 1875	Ch. 29
Perkins	Bison	Nov. 3, 1908	
Potter[2]	Gettysburg	Jan. 8, 1873	
Roberts	Sisseton	Mar. 8, 1883	Ch. 30
Sanborn	Woonsocket	Mar. 9, 1883	Ch. 31
Shannon	(Unorganized)[3]	Jan. 11, 1875	Ch. 29
Spink	Redfield	Jan. 8, 1873	Ch. 16
Stanley	Fort Pierre	Jan. 8, 1873	Ch. 19
Sully	Onida	Jan. 8, 1873	Ch. 16
Todd	(Unorganized)[4]	Mar. 9, 1909	Ch. 280
Tripp	Winner	Jan. 8, 1873	Ch. 19
Turner	Parker	Jan. 13, 1871	Ch. 10
Union[5]	Elk Point	Apr. 10, 1862	Ch. 14
Walworth	Selby	Jan. 8, 1873	Ch. 16
Yankton	Yankton	Apr. 10, 1862	Ch. 19
Ziebach	Dupree	Feb. 1, 1911	Ch. 107

Notes

1. Dewey created as Rusk; name changed Mar. 9, 1883, Ch. 17
2. Potter created as Ashmore; name changed Jan. 14, 1875
3. Shannon attached to Fall River County
4. Todd attached to Tripp County
5. Union created as Cole; name changed Jan. 7, 1864, Ch. 14

TENNESSEE (95 COUNTIES)

Part of North Carolina
Provisional State of Franklin 1784–1788
Ceded to federal government by North Carolina 1789
Territory South of the Ohio River May 26, 1790
Admitted as state June 1, 1796 (16th)

Seceded June 8, 1861
Readmitted July 24, 1866

County	County Seat	Created	Statute
Anderson	Clinton	Nov. 6, 1801	Ch. 45
Bedford	Shelbyville	Dec. 3, 1807	Ch. 37
Benton	Camden	Dec. 19, 1835	Ch. 30
Bledsoe	Pikeville	Nov. 30, 1807	Ch. 9
Blount	Maryville	July 11, 1795	Ch. 6
Bradley	Cleveland	Feb. 10, 1836	Ch. 32
Campbell	Jacksboro	Sep. 11, 1806	Ch. 21
Cannon	Woodbury	Jan. 31, 1836	Ch. 33
Carroll	Huntingdon	Nov. 7, 1821	Ch. 32
Carter	Elizabethton	Apr. 9, 1796	Ch. 31
Cheatham	Ashland City	Feb. 28, 1856	Ch. 122
Chester	Henderson	Mar. 4, 1879	Ch. 42
Claiborne	Tazewell	Oct. 29, 1801	Ch. 46
Clay	Celina	June 24, 1870	Ch. 29
Cocke[1]	Newport	Oct. 9, 1797	Ch. 8
Coffee	Manchester	Jan. 8, 1836	Ch. 36
Crockett	Alamo	Dec. 20, 1845	Ch. 25
Cumberland	Crossville	Nov. 16, 1855	Ch. 9
Davidson	Nashville	Apr. 18, 1783 (Sess.)	Ch. 52
Decatur	Decaturville	Nov. 1845	Ch. 7
DeKalb	Smithville	Dec. 11, 1837	
Dickson	Charlotte	Oct. 25, 1803	Ch. 66
Dyer	Dyersburg	Oct. 16, 1823	Ch. 108
Fayette	Somerville	Sep. 29, 1824	Ch. 36
Fentress	Jamestown	Nov. 28, 1823	Ch. 302
Franklin	Winchester	Dec. 3, 1807	Ch. 72
Gibson	Trenton	Oct. 21, 1823	Ch. 111
Giles	Pulaski	Nov. 14, 1809	Ch. 55
Grainger	Rutledge	Apr. 22, 1796	Ch. 28
Greene	Greenville	Apr. 18, 1783 (Sess.)	Ch. 51
Grundy	Altamont	Jan. 29, 1844	Ch. 204
Hamblen	Morristown	June 8, 1870	Ch. 6
Hamilton	Chattanooga	Oct. 25, 1819	Ch. 113
Hancock	Sneedville	Jan. 7, 1844	Ch. 71
Hardeman	Bolivar	Oct. 16, 1823	Ch. 108
Hardin	Savannah	Nov. 13, 1819	Ch. 6
Hawkins	Rogersville	Nov. 18, 1786 (Sess.)	Ch. 34
Haywood	Brownsville	Nov. 3, 1823	Ch. 145
Henderson	Lexington	Nov. 7, 1821	Ch. 32
Henry	Paris	Nov. 7, 1821	Ch. 32
Hickman	Centerville	Dec. 3, 1807	Ch. 44
Houston	Erin	Jan. 23, 1871	Ch. 46
Humphreys	Waverly	Oct. 19, 1809	Ch. 31
Jackson	Gainesboro	Nov. 6, 1801	Ch. 48
Jefferson	Dandridge	June 11, 1792	Unnumb.
Johnson	Mountain City	Jan. 2, 1836	Ch. 31
Knox	Knoxville	June 11, 1792	Unnumb.
Lake	Tiptonville	June 24, 1870	Ch. 30
Lauderdale	Ripley	Nov. 24, 1835	Ch. 28
Lawrence	Lawrenceburg	Oct. 21, 1817	Ch. 42
Lewis	Hohenwald	Dec. 21, 1843	Ch. 38

Lincoln	Fayetteville	Nov. 14, 1809	Ch. 48
Loudon[2]	Loudon	June 2, 1870	Ch. 2
Macon	Lafayette	Jan. 18, 1842	Ch. 45
Madison	Jackson	Nov. 7, 1821	Ch. 32
Marion	Jasper	Nov. 20, 1817	Ch. 109
Marshall	Lewisburg	Feb. 20, 1836	Ch. 35
Maury	Columbia	Nov. 16, 1807	Ch. 94
McMinn	Athens	Nov. 13, 1819	Ch. 7
McNairy	Selmer	Oct. 8, 1823	Ch. 96
Meigs	Decatur	Jan. 20, 1836	Ch. 34
Monroe	Madisonville	Nov. 13, 1819	Ch. 7
Montgomery	Clarksville	Apr. 9, 1796	Ch. 30
Moore	Lynchburg	Dec. 14, 1871	Ch. 96
Morgan	Wartburg	Oct. 15, 1817	Ch. 38
Obion	Union City	Oct. 24, 1823	Ch. 114
Overton	Livingston	Sep. 11, 1806	Ch. 27
Perry	Linden	Nov. 14, 1818	
Pickett	Byrdstown	Feb. 27, 1879	Ch. 34
Polk	Benton	Nov. 28, 1839	Ch. 10
Putnam	Cookeville	Feb. 2, 1842	Ch. 169
Rhea	Dayton	Nov. 30, 1807	Ch. 9
Roane	Kingston	Nov. 6, 1801	Ch. 45
Robertson	Springfield	Apr. 9, 1796	Ch. 30
Rutherford	Murfreesboro	Oct. 25, 1803	Ch. 70
Scott	Huntsville	Dec. 17, 1849	Ch. 45
Sequatchie	Dunlap	Dec. 9, 1857	Ch. 11
Sevier	Sevierville	Sep. 27, 1794	Ch. 11
Shelby	Memphis	Nov. 24, 1819	Ch. 218
Smith	Carthage	Oct. 26, 1799	Ch. 2
Stewart	Dover	Nov. 1, 1803	Ch. 68
Sullivan	Blountsville	Oct. 18, 1779 (Sess.)	Ch. 29
Sumner	Gallatin	Nov. 18, 1786 (Sess.)	Ch. 32
Tipton	Covington	Oct. 29, 1823	Ch. 126
Trousdale	Hartsville	June 21, 1870	Ch. 27
Unicoi	Erwin	Mar. 23, 1875	Ch. 68
Union	Maynardville	Jan. 3, 1850	
Van Buren	Spencer	Jan. 3, 1840	Ch. 59
Warren	McMinnville	Nov. 26, 1807	Ch. 28
Washington	Jonesborough	Nov. 15, 1777 (Sess.)	Ch. 31
Wayne	Waynesboro	Nov. 24, 1817	Ch. 175
Weakley	Dresden	Oct. 21, 1823	Ch. 112
White	Sparta	Sep. 11, 1806	Ch. 36
Williamson	Franklin	Oct. 26, 1799	Ch. 2
Wilson	Lebanon	Oct. 26, 1799	Ch. 2

Notes

1. Created as Cocke; name changed to Union Jan. 28, 1846; renamed Cocke Jan. 3, 1850

2. Loudon created as Christiana; name changed July 7, 1870, Ch. 77

TEXAS (254 COUNTIES)

Republic of Texas March 2, 1836
Admitted as state December 29, 1845 (28th)

Seceded March 2, 1861
Readmitted March 30, 1870

County	County Seat	Created	Statute
Anderson	Palestine	Mar. 24, 1846	Unnumb.
Andrews	Andrews	Aug. 21, 1876	Ch. 144
Angelina	Lufkin	Apr. 22, 1846	Unnumb.
Aransas	Rockport	Sep. 18, 1871	Ch. 1
Archer	Archer City	Jan. 22, 1858	Ch. 55
Armstrong	Claude	Aug. 21, 1876	Ch. 144
Atascosa	Jourdanton	Jan. 25, 1856	Ch. 33
Austin	Bellville	Mar. 17, 1836	Const.
Bailey	Muleshoe	Aug. 21, 1876	Ch. 144
Bandera	Bandera	Jan. 26, 1856	Ch. 42
Bastrop[1]	Bastrop	Mar. 17, 1836	Const.
Baylor	Seymour	Feb. 1, 1858	Ch. 75
Bee	Beeville	Dec. 8, 1857	Ch. 14
Bell	Belton	Jan. 22, 1850	Ch. 55
Bexar	San Antonio	Mar. 17, 1836	Const.
Blanco	Johnson City	Feb. 12, 1858	Ch. 130
Borden	Gail	Aug. 21, 1876	Ch. 144
Bosque	Meridian	Feb. 4, 1854	Ch. 38
Bowie	New Boston	Dec. 17, 1840	Unnumb.
Brazoria	Angleton	Mar. 17, 1836	Const.
Brazos[2]	Bryan	Jan. 30, 1841	Unnumb.
Brewster	Alpine	Feb. 2, 1887	Ch. 4
Briscoe	Silverton	Aug. 21, 1876	Ch. 144
Brooks	Falfurrias	Mar. 11, 1911	Ch. 39
Brown	Brownwood	Aug. 27, 1856	Ch. 139
Burleson	Caldwell	Mar. 24, 1846	Unnumb.
Burnet	Burnet	Feb. 5, 1852	Ch. 60
Caldwell	Lockhart	Mar. 6, 1848	Ch. 65
Calhoun	Port Lavaca	Apr. 4, 1846	Unnumb.
Callahan	Baird	Feb. 1, 1858	Ch. 75
Cameron	Brownsville	Feb. 12, 1848	Ch. 35
Camp	Pittsburg	Apr. 6, 1874	Ch. 55
Carson	Panhandle	Aug. 21, 1876	Ch. 144
Cass[3]	Linden	Apr. 25, 1846	Unnumb.
Castro	Dimmitt	Aug. 21, 1876	Ch. 144
Chambers	Anahuac	Feb. 12, 1858	Ch. 125
Cherokee	Rusk	Apr. 11, 1846	Unnumb.
Childress	Childress	Aug. 21, 1876	Ch. 144
Clay	Henrietta	Dec. 24, 1857	Ch. 34
Cochran	Morton	Aug. 21, 1876	Ch. 144
Coke	Robert Lee	Mar. 13, 1889	Ch. 77
Coleman	Coleman	Feb. 1, 1858	Ch. 75
Collin	McKinney	Apr. 3, 1846	Unnumb.
Collingsworth	Wellington	Aug. 21, 1876	Ch. 144
Colorado	Columbus	Mar. 17, 1836	Const.
Comal	New Braunfels	Mar. 24, 1846	Unnumb.
Comanche	Comanche	Jan. 25, 1856	Ch. 35
Concho	Paint Rock	Feb. 1, 1858	Ch. 75
Cooke	Gainesville	Mar. 20, 1848	Ch. 130
Coryell	Gatesville	Feb. 4, 1854	Ch. 36
Cottle	Paducah	Aug. 21, 1876	Ch. 144

Crane	Crane	Feb. 26, 1887	Ch. 12
Crockett	Ozona	Jan. 22, 1875	Ch. 2
Crosby	Crosbyton	Aug. 21, 1876	Ch. 144
Culberson	Van Horn	Mar. 10, 1911	Ch. 38
Dallam	Dalhart	Aug. 21, 1876	Ch. 144
Dallas	Dallas	Mar. 30, 1846	Unnumb.
Dawson	Lamesa	Aug. 21, 1876	Ch. 144
Deaf Smith	Hereford	Aug. 21, 1876	Ch. 144
Delta	Cooper	July 29, 1870	Ch. 30
Denton	Denton	Apr. 11, 1846	Unnumb.
DeWitt	Cuero	Mar. 24, 1846	Unnumb.
Dickens	Dickens	Aug. 21, 1876	Ch. 144
Dimmitt	Carrizo Springs	Feb. 1, 1858	Ch. 75
Donley	Clarendon	Aug. 21, 1876	Ch. 144
Duval	San Diego	Feb. 1, 1858	Ch. 75
Eastland	Eastland	Feb. 1, 1858	Ch. 75
Ector	Odessa	Feb. 26, 1887	Ch. 12
Edwards	Rocksprings	Feb. 1, 1858	Ch. 75
Ellis	Waxahachie	Dec. 20, 1849	Ch. 18
El Paso	El Paso	Jan. 3, 1850	Ch. 29
Erath	Stephenville	Jan. 25, 1856	Ch. 34
Falls	Marlin	Jan. 28, 1850	Ch. 80
Fannin	Bonham	Dec. 14, 1837	Unnumb.
Fayette	La Grange	Dec. 14, 1837	Unnumb.
Fisher	Roby	Aug. 21, 1876	Ch. 144
Floyd	Floydada	Aug. 21, 1876	Ch. 144
Foard	Crowell	Mar. 3, 1891	Ch. 15
Fort Bend	Richmond	Dec. 29, 1837	Unnumb.
Franklin	Mount Vernon	Mar. 6, 1875	Ch. 81
Freestone	Fairfield	Sep. 6, 1850	Ch. 39
Frio	Pearsall	Feb. 1, 1858	Ch. 75
Gaines	Seminole	Aug. 21, 1876	Ch. 144
Galveston	Galveston	May 15, 1838	Unnumb.
Garza	Post	Aug. 21, 1876	Ch. 144
Gillespie	Fredericksburg	Feb. 23, 1848	Ch. 47
Glasscock	Garden City	Apr. 4, 1887	Ch. 143
Goliad	Goliad	Mar. 17, 1836	Const.
Gonzales	Gonzales	Mar. 17, 1836	Const.
Gray	Pampa	Aug. 21, 1876	Ch. 144
Grayson	Sherman	Mar. 17, 1846	Unnumb.
Gregg	Longview	Apr. 12, 1873	Ch. 27
Grimes	Anderson	Apr. 6, 1846	Unnumb.
Guadalupe	Seguin	Mar. 30, 1846	Unnumb.
Hale	Plainview	Aug. 21, 1876	Ch. 144
Hall	Memphis	Aug. 21, 1876	Ch. 144
Hamilton	Hamilton	Jan. 22, 1858	Unnumb.
Hansford	Spearman	Aug. 21, 1876	Ch. 144
Hardeman	Quanah	Feb. 1, 1858	Ch. 75
Hardin	Kountze	Jan. 22, 1858	Ch. 55
Harris[4]	Houston	Mar. 17, 1836	Const.
Harrison	Marshall	Jan. 28, 1839	Unnumb.
Hartley	Channing	Aug. 21, 1876	Ch. 144
Haskell	Haskell	Feb. 1, 1858	Ch. 75
Hays	San Marcos	Mar. 1, 1848	Ch. 57
Hemphill	Canadian	Aug. 21, 1876	Ch. 144

Henderson	Athens	Apr. 27, 1846	Unnumb.
Hidalgo	Edinburg	Jan. 24, 1852	Ch. 42
Hill	Hillsboro	Feb. 7, 1853	Ch. 26
Hockley	Levelland	Aug. 21, 1876	Ch. 144
Hood	Granbury	Nov. 2, 1866	Ch. 85
Hopkins	Sulphur Springs	Mar. 25, 1846	Unnumb.
Houston	Crockett	June 12, 1837	Unnumb.
Howard	Big Spring	Aug. 21, 1876	Ch. 144
Hudspeth	Sierra Blanca	Feb. 16, 1917	Ch. 25
Hunt	Greenville	Apr. 11, 1846	Unnumb.
Hutchinson	Stinnett	Aug. 21, 1876	Ch. 144
Irion	Mertzon	Mar. 7, 1889	Ch. 87
Jack	Jacksboro	Aug. 27, 1856	Ch. 135
Jackson	Edna	Mar. 17, 1836	Const.
Jasper	Jasper	Mar. 17, 1836	Const.
Jeff Davis	Fort Davis	Mar. 15, 1887	Ch. 38
Jefferson	Beaumont	Mar. 17, 1836	Const.
Jim Hogg	Hebbronville	Mar. 31, 1913	Ch. 73
Jim Wells	Alice	Mar. 25, 1911	Ch. 140
Johnson	Cleburne	Feb. 13, 1854	Ch. 76
Jones	Anson	Feb. 1, 1858	Ch. 75
Karnes	Karnes City	Feb. 4, 1854	Ch. 35
Kaufman	Kaufman	Feb. 26, 1848	Ch. 52
Kendall	Boerne	Jan. 10, 1862	Ch. 38
Kenedy	Sarita	Apr. 2, 1921	Ch. 104
Kent	Jayton	Aug. 21, 1876	Ch. 144
Kerr	Kerrville	Jan. 26, 1856	Ch. 40
Kimble	Junction	Jan. 22, 1858	Ch. 55
King	Guthrie	Aug. 21, 1876	Ch. 144
Kinney	Brackettville	Jan. 28, 1850	Ch. 81
Kleberg	Kingsville	Feb. 27, 1913	Ch. 10
Knox	Benjamin	Feb. 1, 1858	Ch. 75
Lamar	Paris	Dec. 17, 1840	Unnumb.
Lamb	Littlefield	Aug. 21, 1876	Ch. 144
Lampasas	Lampasas	Feb. 1, 1856	Ch. 44
La Salle	Cotulla	Feb. 1, 1858	Ch. 75
Lavaca	Hallettsville	Apr. 6, 1846	Unnumb.
Lee	Giddings	Apr. 14, 1874	Ch. 75
Leon	Centerville	Mar. 17, 1846	Unnumb.
Liberty	Liberty	Mar. 17, 1836	Const.
Limestone	Groesbeck	Apr. 11, 1846	Unnumb.
Lipscomb	Lipscomb	Aug. 21, 1876	Ch. 144
Live Oak	George West	Feb. 2, 1856	Ch. 59
Llano	Llano	Feb. 1, 1856	Ch. 48
Loving	Mentone	Feb. 26, 1887	Ch. 12
Lubbock	Lubbock	Aug. 21, 1876	Ch. 144
Lynn	Tahoka	Aug. 21, 1876	Ch. 144
Madison	Madisonville	Jan. 27, 1853	
Marion	Jefferson	Feb. 8, 1860	Ch. 48
Martin	Stanton	Aug. 21, 1876	Ch. 144
Mason	Mason	Jan. 22, 1858	Ch. 55
Matagorda	Bay City	Mar. 17, 1836	Const.
Maverick	Eagle Pass	Feb. 2, 1856	Ch. 69
McCulloch	Brady	Aug. 27, 1856	Ch. 141
McLennan	Waco	Jan. 22, 1850	Ch. 54

McMullen	Tilden	Feb. 1, 1858	Ch. 75
Medina	Hondo	Feb. 12, 1848	Ch. 36
Menard	Menard	Jan. 22, 1858	Ch. 55
Midland	Midland	Mar. 4, 1885	Ch. 23
Milam	Cameron	Mar. 17, 1836	Const.
Mills	Goldthwaite	Mar. 15, 1887	Ch. 37
Mitchell	Colorado City	Aug. 21, 1876	Ch. 144
Montague	Montague	Dec. 24, 1857	Ch. 33
Montgomery	Conroe	Dec. 14, 1837	Unnumb.
Moore	Dumas	Aug. 21, 1876	Ch. 144
Morris	Daingerfield	Mar. 6, 1875	Ch. 82
Motley	Matador	Aug. 21, 1876	Ch. 144
Nacogdoches	Nacogdoches	Mar. 17, 1836	Const.
Navarro	Corsicana	Apr. 25, 1846	Unnumb.
Newton	Newton	Apr. 22, 1846	Unnumb.
Nolan	Sweetwater	Aug. 21, 1876	Ch. 144
Nueces	Corpus Christi	Apr. 18, 1846	Unnumb.
Ochiltree	Perryton	Aug. 21, 1876	Ch. 144
Oldham	Vega	Aug. 21, 1876	Ch. 144
Orange	Orange	Feb. 5, 1852	Ch. 59
Palo Pinto	Palo Pinto	Aug. 27, 1856	Ch. 138
Panola	Carthage	Mar. 30, 1846	Unnumb.
Parker	Weatherford	Dec. 12, 1855	Ch. 1
Parmer	Farwell	Aug. 21, 1876	Ch. 144
Pecos	Fort Stockton	May 3, 1871	Ch. 70
Polk	Livingston	Mar. 30, 1846	Unnumb.
Potter	Amarillo	Aug. 21, 1876	Ch. 144
Presidio	Marfa	Jan. 3, 1850	Ch. 29
Rains	Emory	June 9, 1870	Ch. 3
Randall	Canyon	Aug. 21, 1876	Ch. 144
Reagan	Big Lake	Mar. 7, 1903	Ch. 32
Real	Leakey	Apr. 3, 1913	Ch. 133
Red River	Clarksville	Mar. 17, 1836	Const.
Reeves	Pecos	Apr. 14, 1883	Ch. 103
Refugio	Refugio	Mar. 17, 1836	Const.
Roberts	Miami	Aug. 21, 1876	Ch. 144
Robertson	Franklin	Dec. 14, 1837	Unnumb.
Rockwall	Rockwall	Mar. 1, 1873	Ch. 7
Runnels	Ballinger	Feb. 1, 1858	Ch. 75
Rusk	Henderson	Jan. 16, 1843	Unnumb.
Sabine	Hemphill	Mar. 17, 1836	Const.
San Augustine	San Augustine	Mar. 17, 1836	Const.
San Jacinto	Coldspring	Aug. 13, 1870	Ch. 59
San Patricio	Sinton	Mar. 17, 1836	Const.
San Saba	San Saba	Feb. 1, 1856	Ch. 49
Schleicher	Eldorado	Apr. 1, 1887	Ch. 103
Scurry	Snyder	Aug. 21, 1876	Ch. 144
Shackelford	Albany	Feb. 1, 1858	Ch. 75
Shelby	Center	Mar. 17, 1836	Const.
Sherman	Stratford	Aug. 21, 1876	Ch. 144
Smith	Tyler	Apr. 11, 1846	Unnumb.
Somervell	Glen Rose	Mar. 13, 1875	Ch. 83
Starr	Rio Grande City	Feb. 10, 1848	Ch. 31
Stephens[5]	Breckenridge	Jan. 22, 1858	Ch. 55
Sterling	Sterling City	Mar. 4, 1891	Ch. 16

Stonewall	Aspermont	Aug. 21, 1876	Ch. 144
Sutton	Sonora	Apr. 1, 1887	Ch. 103
Swisher	Tulia	Aug. 21, 1876	Ch. 144
Tarrant	Fort Worth	Dec. 20, 1849	Ch. 17
Taylor	Abeline	Feb. 1, 1858	Ch. 75
Terrell	Sanderson	Apr. 8, 1905	Ch. 70
Terry	Brownfield	Aug. 21, 1876	Ch. 144
Throckmorton	Throckmorton	Jan. 13, 1858	Ch. 30
Titus	Mount Pleasant	May 11, 1846	Unnumb.
Tom Green	San Angelo	Mar. 13, 1874	Ch. 26
Travis	Austin	Jan. 25, 1840	Unnumb.
Trinity	Groveton	Feb. 11, 1850	Ch. 160
Tyler	Woodville	Apr. 3, 1846	Unnumb.
Upshur	Gilmer	Apr. 27, 1846	Unnumb.
Upton	Rankin	Feb. 26, 1887	Ch. 12
Uvalde	Uvalde	Feb. 8, 1850	Ch. 112
Val Verde	Del Rio	Feb. 20, 1885	Ch. 50
Van Zandt	Canton	Mar. 20, 1848	Ch. 119
Victoria	Victoria	Mar. 17, 1836	Const.
Walker	Huntsville	Apr. 6, 1846	Unnumb.
Waller	Hempstead	Apr. 28, 1873	Ch. 38
Ward	Monahans	Feb. 26, 1887	Ch. 12
Washington	Brenham	Mar. 17, 1836	Const.
Webb	Laredo	Jan. 28, 1848	Ch. 32
Wharton	Wharton	Apr. 3, 1846	Unnumb.
Wheeler	Wheeler	Aug. 21, 1876	Ch. 144
Wichita	Wichita Falls	Feb. 1, 1858	Ch. 75
Wilbarger	Vernon	Feb. 1, 1858	Ch. 75
Willacy	Raymondville	Mar. 11, 1911	Ch. 48
Williamson	Georgetown	Mar. 13, 1848	Ch. 78
Wilson	Floresville	Feb. 13, 1860	Ch. 76
Winkler	Kermit	Feb. 26, 1887	Ch. 12
Wise	Decatur	Jan. 23, 1856	Ch. 31
Wood	Quitman	Feb. 5, 1850	Ch. 98
Yoakum	Plains	Aug. 21, 1876	Ch. 144
Young	Graham	Feb. 2, 1856	Ch. 71
Zapata	Zapata	Jan. 22, 1858	Ch. 55
Zavala	Crystal City	Feb. 1, 1858	Ch. 75

Notes

1. Bastrop created as Mina; name changed Dec. 18, 1837
2. Brazos created as Navasota; name changed Jan. 30, 1841, unnumb.
3. Created as Cass; name changed to Davis Dec. 17, 1861, Ch. 14; renamed Cass May 16, 1871, Ch. 95
4. Harris created as Harrisburg; name changed Dec. 28, 1839, res.
5. Stephens created as Buchanan; name changed Dec. 17, 1861, Ch. 14

UTAH (29 COUNTIES)

Utah Territory September 9, 1850
Admitted as state January 4, 1896 (45th)

County	County Seat	Created	Statute
Beaver	Beaver	Jan. 5, 1856	Unnumb.
Box Elder	Brigham City	Jan. 5, 1856	Unnumb.

Cache	Logan	Jan. 5, 1856	Unnumb.
Carbon	Price	Mar. 8, 1894	Ch. 58
Daggett	Manila	Mar. 4, 1917	
Davis	Farmington	Mar. 3, 1852	Unnumb.
Duchesne	Duchesne	Mar. 3, 1913	Ch. 28
Emery	Castle Dale	Feb. 12, 1880	Ch. 4
Garfield	Panguitch	Mar. 9, 1882	Ch. 52
Grand	Moab	Mar. 13, 1890	Ch. 60
Iron[1]	Parowan	Jan. 31, 1850	Unnumb.
Juab	Nephi	Mar. 3, 1852	Unnumb.
Kane	Kanab	Jan. 16, 1864	Unnumb.
Millard	Fillmore	Oct. 4, 1851	Ch. 38
Morgan	Morgan	Jan. 17, 1862	Unnumb.
Piute	Junction	Jan. 16, 1865	Unnumb.
Rich[2]	Randolph	Jan. 16, 1864	Unnumb.
Salt Lake[3]	Salt Lake City	Mar. 3, 1852	Unnumb.
San Juan	Monticello	Feb. 17, 1880	Unnumb.
Sanpete	Manti	Mar. 3, 1852	Unnumb.
Sevier	Richfield	Jan. 16, 1865	Unnumb.
Summit	Coalville	Jan. 13, 1854	Ch. 63
Tooele	Tooele	Mar. 3, 1852	Unnumb.
Uintah	Vernal	Feb. 18, 1880	Ch. 10
Utah	Provo	Mar. 3, 1852	Unnumb.
Wasatch	Heber City	Jan. 17, 1862	Unnumb.
Washington	Saint George	Mar. 3, 1852	Unnumb.
Wayne	Loa	Mar. 10, 1892	Ch. 71
Weber	Ogden	Mar. 3, 1852	Unnumb.

Notes

1. Iron created as Little Salt Lake; name changed Dec. 3, 1850
2. Rich created as Richland; name changed Jan. 29, 1868, Ch. 2
3. Salt Lake created as Great Salt Lake; name changed Jan. 29, 1868, Ch. 3

VERMONT (14 COUNTIES)

Declared independence from New York 1777
Admitted as state March 4, 1791 (14th)

County	County Seat	Created	Statute
Addison	Middlebury	Oct. 18, 1785	Unnumb.
Bennington	Bennington	Feb. 11, 1779 (Sess.)	Unnumb.
Caledonia	Saint Johnsbury	Nov. 5, 1792	Unnumb.
Chittenden	Burlington	Oct. 22, 1787	Unnumb.
Essex	Guildhall	Nov. 5, 1792	Unnumb.
Franklin	Saint Albans	Nov. 5, 1792	Unnumb.
Grand Isle	North Hero	Nov. 9, 1802	Ch. 84
Lamoille	Hyde Park	Oct. 26, 1835	Act 41
Orange	Chelsea	Feb. 22, 1781	Unnumb.
Orleans	Newport	Nov. 5, 1792	Unnumb.
Rutland	Rutland	Feb. 22, 1781	Unnumb.
Washington[1]	Montpelier	Nov. 1, 1810	Ch. 74
Windham	Newfane	Feb. 22, 1781	Unnumb.
Windsor	Woodstock	Feb. 22, 1781	Unnumb.

Note

1. Washington created as Jefferson; name changed Nov. 4, 1814, Ch. 79

VIRGINIA (95 COUNTIES, 40 INDEPENDENT CITIES)

Royal colony 1624
Declared independence 1776
Ratified Constitution June 25, 1788 (admitted as 10th state)
Seceded April 17, 1861
Readmitted January 26, 1870

County/City	County Seat	Created	Statute
Accomack	Accomac	1661	
Albemarle	Charlottesville	May 6, 1744 (Sess.)	Ch. 31
Alexandria	(Independent City)	Mar. 13, 1852	
Alleghany	Covington	Jan. 5, 1822	Ch. 28
Amelia	Amelia Court House	Feb. 1, 1734 (Sess.)	Ch. 31
Amherst	Amherst	Sep. 14, 1758 (Sess.)	Ch. 20
Appomattox	Appomattox	Feb. 8, 1845	Ch. 41
Arlington[1]	Arlington	Mar. 13, 1847	Ch. 53
Augusta	Staunton	Aug. 1, 1738 (Sess.)	Ch. 21
Bath	Warm Springs	Dec. 14, 1790	Ch. 43
Bedford	Bedford	Feb. 27, 1752 (Sess.)	Ch. 16
Bedford	(Independent City)	August 30, 1968	
Bland	Bland	Mar. 30, 1861	Ch. 23
Botetourt	Fincastle	Nov. 7, 1769 (Sess.)	Ch. 40
Bristol	(Independent City)	Feb. 12, 1890	
Brunswick	Lawrenceville	Nov. 2, 1720 (Sess.)	Act 1
Buchanan	Grundy	Feb. 13, 1858	Ch. 156
Buckingham	Buckingham	Sep. 14, 1758 (Sess.)	Ch. 20
Buena Vista	(Independent City)	1892	
Campbell	Rustburg	Nov. 5, 1781 (Sess.)	Ch. 7
Caroline	Bowling Green	Feb. 1, 1727 (Sess.)	Ch. 17
Carroll	Hillsville	Jan. 17, 1842	Ch. 58
Charles City	Charles City	1634	
Charlotte	Charlotte Court House	May 26, 1764 (Sess.)	Ch. 4
Charlottesville	(Independent City)	1888	
Chesapeake[2]	(Independent City)	1691	
Chesterfield	Chesterfield	May 1, 1749	
Clarke	Berryville	Mar. 8, 1836	Ch. 19
Clifton Forge	(Independent City)	1906	
Colonial Heights	(Independent City)	1961	
Covington	(Independent City)	1952	
Craig	New Castle	Mar. 21, 1851	Ch. 25
Culpeper	Culpeper	Mar. 23, 1748	
Cumberland	Cumberland	March 23, 1749	
Danville	(Independent City)	1890	
Dickenson	Clintwood	Mar. 3, 1880	Ch. 140
Dinwiddie	Dinwiddie	Feb. 27, 1752 (Sess.)	Ch. 19
Emporia	(Independent City)	July 31, 1967	
Essex	Tappahannock	Apr. 16, 1692 (Sess.)	Act 5
Fairfax	Fairfax	May 6, 1742 (Sess.)	Ch. 27

Fairfax	(Independent City)	June 30, 1961	
Falls Church	(Independent City)	1948	
Fauquier	Warrenton	Sep. 14, 1758 (Sess.)	Ch. 27
Floyd	Floyd	Jan. 15, 1831	Ch. 72
Fluvanna	Palmyra	May 5, 1777 (Sess.)	Ch. 25
Franklin	Rocky Mount	Oct. 17, 1785 (Sess.)	Ch. 25
Franklin	(Independent City)	Dec. 21, 1961	
Frederick	Winchester	Aug. 1, 1738 (Sess.)	Ch. 21
Fredericksburg	(Independent City)	1879	
Galax	(Independent City)	Nov. 30, 1953	
Giles	Pearisburg	Jan. 6, 1806	Ch. 53
Gloucester	Gloucester	1651	
Goochland	Goochland	Feb. 1, 1727 (Sess.)	Ch. 18
Grayson	Independence	Nov. 7, 1792	Ch. 51
Greene	Stanardsville	Jan. 24, 1838	Ch. 59
Greensville	Emporia	Oct. 16, 1780 (Sess.)	Ch. 17
Halifax	Halifax	Feb. 27, 1752 (Sess.)	Ch. 18
Hampton[3]	(Independent City)	March 19, 1849	
Hanover	Hanover	Nov. 2, 1720 (Sess.)	Ch. 15
Harrisonburg	(Independent City)	1634	
Henrico	Richmond	1634	
Henry	Martinsville	Oct. 7, 1776 (Sess.)	Ch. 38
Highland	Monterey	Mar. 19, 1847	Ch. 56
Hopewell	(Independent City)	1916	
Isle of Wight[4]	Isle of Wight	1634	
James City	Williamsburg	1634	
King and Queen	King and Queen Court House	Apr. 16, 1691 (Sess.)	Act 19
King George	King George	Nov. 2, 1720 (Sess.)	Ch. 14
King William	King William	Dec. 5, 1700 (Sess.)	Act 4
Lancaster	Lancaster	1652	
Lee	Jonesville	Oct. 25, 1792 (Sess.)	Ch. 49
Lexington	(Independent City)	Dec. 31, 1965	
Loudoun	Leesburg	Mar. 25, 1757 (Sess.)	Ch. 22
Louisa	Louisa	May 6, 1742 (Sess.)	Ch. 28
Lunenburg	Lunenburg	May 6, 1745 (Sess.)	Ch. 22
Lynchburg	(Independent City)	Aug. 27, 1852	
Madison	Madison	Dec. 4, 1792 (Sess.)	Ch. 50
Manassas	(Independent City)	May 1, 1975	
Manassas Park	(Independent City)	June 1, 1975	
Martinsville	(Independent City)	1928	
Mathews	Mathews	Dec.16, 1790	Ch. 41
Mecklenburg	Boydton	May 26, 1764 (Sess.)	Ch. 4
Middlesex	Saluda	Sep. 21, 1674 (Sess.)	Act 1
Montgomery	Christiansburg	Oct. 7, 1776 (Sess.)	Ch. 44
Nelson	Lovingston	Dec. 25, 1807	Ch. 26
New Kent	New Kent	Nov. 20, 1654 (Sess.)	
Newport News[5]	(Independent City)	July 1, 1958	
Norfolk	(Independent City)	Feb. 11, 1845	
Northampton[6]	Eastville	1634	
Northumberland	Heathsville	Oct. 12, 1648 (Sess.)	Act 1
Norton	(Independent City)	1954	
Nottoway	Nottoway	Dec. 22, 1788	Ch. 64
Orange	Orange	Feb. 1, 1734 (Sess.)	Ch. 24

Page	Luray	Mar. 30, 1831	Ch. 74
Patrick	Stuart	Nov. 26, 1790	Ch. 40
Petersburg	(Independent City)	Mar. 16, 1850	
Pittsylvania	Chatham	Nov. 6, 1766 (Sess.)	Ch. 16
Poquoson	(Independent City)	1976	
Portsmouth	(Independent City)	Mar. 1, 1858	
Powhatan	Powhatan	May 5, 1777 (Sess.)	Ch. 24
Prince Edward	Farmville	Feb. 27, 1752 (Sess.)	Ch. 15
Prince George	Prince George	Dec. 5, 1700 (Sess.)	Ch. 2
Prince William	Manassas	Feb. 1, 1727 (Sess.)	Ch. 17
Pulaski	Pulaski	Mar. 30, 1839	Ch. 50
Radford	(Independent City)	1892	
Rappahannock	Washington	Feb. 8, 1833	Ch. 73
Richmond	Warsaw	Apr. 16, 1692 (Sess.)	Act 5
Richmond	(Independent City)	1782	
Roanoke	Salem	Mar. 30, 1838	Ch. 60
Roanoke	(Independent City)	1884	
Rockbridge	Lexington	Oct. 20, 1777 (Sess.)	Ch. 18
Rockingham	Harrisonburg	Oct. 20, 1777 (Sess.)	Ch. 18
Russell	Lebanon	Oct. 17, 1785 (Sess.)	Ch. 46
Salem	(Independent City)	1968	
Scott	Gate City	Nov. 24, 1814	Ch. 38
Shenandoah[7]	Woodstock	Mar. 24, 1772	Ch. 43
Smyth	Marion	Feb. 23, 1832	Ch. 67
Southampton	Courtland	Apr. 30, 1749	
Spotsylvania	Spotsylvania	Nov. 2, 1720 (Sess.)	Ch. 1
Stafford	Stafford	June 5, 1666 (Sess)	
Staunton	(Independent City)	Jan. 16, 1908	
Suffolk[8]	(Independent City)	1637	
Surry	Surry	1652	
Sussex	Sussex	Feb. 27, 1752 (Sess.)	Ch. 17
Tazewell	Tazewell	Dec. 7, 1799 (Sess.)	Ch. 27
Virginia Beach[9]	(Independent City)	1691	
Warren	Front Royal	Mar. 9, 1836	Ch. 20
Washington	Abingdon	Oct. 7, 1776 (Sess.)	Ch. 44
Waynesboro	(Independent City)	Feb. 1948	
Westmoreland	Montross	July 5, 1653 (Sess.)	Unnumb.
Williamsburg	(Independent City)	1884	
Winchester	(Independent City)	1874	
Wise	Wise	Feb. 16, 1856	Ch. 107
Wythe	Wytheville	Dec. 1, 1789	Ch. 56
York[10]	Yorktown	1634	

Notes

1. Arlington created as Alexandria; name changed Mar. 16, 1920
2. Chesapeake created as Norfolk County 1691; consolidated with City of South Norfolk January 1, 1963
3. Hampton created as Elizabeth City County 1634; merged with City of Hampton July 1, 1952
4. Isle of Wight created as Warrosquyoake; name changed 1637
5. Newport News created as Warwick River 1634; name changed to Warwick 1643; merged with City of Newport News July 1, 1958
6. Northampton created as Accawmack; name changed 1643
7. Shenandoah created as Dunmore; name changed Feb. 1, 1778
8. Suffolk created as Upper Norfolk March 1645 (session); name changed to Nansemond 1642; merged with City of Sufolk 1974
9. Virginia Beach created as Princess Anne April 16, 1691 (session); merged with City of Virginia Beach January 1, 1963
10. York created as Charles River; name changed 1642

WASHINGTON (39 COUNTIES)

Champeog provisional government May 2, 1843
Oregon Territory August 14, 1848
Washington Territory March 2, 1853
Admitted as state November 11, 1889 (42nd)

County	County Seat	Created	Statute
Adams	Ritzville	Nov. 28, 1883	Unnumb.
Asotin	Asotin	Oct. 27, 1883	Unnumb.
Benton	Prosser	Mar. 8, 1905	Ch. 89
Chelan	Wenatchee	Mar. 13, 1899	Ch. 95
Clallam	Port Angeles	Apr. 26, 1854	Unnumb.
Clark[1]	Vancouver	June 27, 1844	Unnumb.
Columbia	Dayton	Nov. 11, 1875	Unnumb.
Cowlitz	Kelso	Apr. 21, 1854	Unnumb.
Douglas	Waterville	Nov. 28, 1883	Unnumb.
Ferry	Republic	Feb. 18, 1899	Ch. 18
Franklin	Pasco	Nov. 28, 1883	Unnumb.
Garfield	Pomeroy	Nov. 29, 1881	Unnumb.
Grant	Ephrata	Feb. 24, 1909	Ch. 17
Grays Harbor[2]	Montesano	Apr. 14, 1854	Unnumb.
Island	Coupeville	Jan. 6, 1853	Unnumb.
Jefferson	Port Townsend	Dec. 22, 1852	Unnumb.
King	Seattle	Dec. 22, 1852	Unnumb.
Kitsap[3]	Port Orchard	Jan. 16, 1857	Unnumb.
Kittitas	Ellensburg	Nov. 24, 1883	Unnumb.
Klickitat	Goldendale	Dec. 20, 1859	Unnumb.
Lewis	Chehalis	Dec. 21, 1845	Unnumb.
Lincoln	Davenport	Nov. 24, 1883	Unnumb.
Mason[4]	Shelton	Mar. 13, 1854	Unnumb.
Okanogan	Okanogan	Feb. 2, 1888	Ch. 35
Pacific	South Bend	Feb. 4, 1851	Unnumb.
Pend Oreille	Newport	Mar. 1, 1911	Ch. 28
Pierce	Tacoma	Dec. 22, 1852	Unnumb.
San Juan	Friday Harbor	Oct. 31, 1873	Unnumb.
Skagit	Mount Vernon	Nov. 28, 1883	Unnumb.
Skamania	Stevenson	Mar. 9, 1854	Unnumb.
Snohomish	Everett	Jan. 14, 1861	Unnumb.
Spokane[5]	Spokane	Jan. 29, 1858	Unnumb.
Stevens	Colville	Jan. 20, 1863	Unnumb.
Thurston	Olympia	Jan. 12, 1852	Unnumb.
Wahkiakum	Cathlamet	Apr. 24, 1854	Unnumb.
Walla Walla	Walla Walla	Apr. 25, 1854	Unnumb.
Whatcom	Bellingham	Mar. 9, 1854	Unnumb.
Whitman	Colfax	Nov. 29, 1871	Unnumb.
Yakima	Yakima	Jan. 21, 1865	Unnumb.

Notes

1. Clark created as Vancouver; name changed Sep. 3, 1849, unnumb.
2. Grays Harbor created as Chehalis; name changed Mar. 15, 1915, Ch. 77
3. Kitsap created as Slaughter; name changed July 13, 1857
4. Mason created as Sawamish; name changed Jan. 8, 1864, unnumb.
5. Spokane created as Shoshone; name changed 1860

WEST VIRGINIA (55 COUNTIES)

Part of Virginia
Repudiated Virginia's secession June 11, 1861
Admitted as state June 20, 1863 (35th)

County	County Seat	Created	Statute
Barbour	Philippi	Mar. 3, 1843	Ch. 53
Berkeley	Martinsburg	Feb. 10, 1772 (Sess.)	Ch. 43
Boone	Madison	Mar. 11, 1847	Ch. 55
Braxton	Sutton	Jan. 15, 1836	Ch. 18
Brooke	Wellsburg	Nov. 30, 1796	Ch. 58
Cabell	Huntington	Jan. 2, 1809	Ch. 45
Calhoun	Grantsville	Mar. 5, 1856	Ch. 108
Clay	Clay	Mar. 29, 1858	Ch. 158
Doddridge	West Union	Feb. 4, 1845	Ch. 42
Fayette	Fayetteville	Feb. 28, 1831	Ch. 70
Gilmer	Glenville	Feb. 3, 1845	Ch. 43
Grant	Petersburg	Feb. 14, 1866	Ch. 29
Greenbrier	Lewisburg	Oct. 20, 1777 (Sess.)	Ch. 18
Hampshire	Romney	Feb. 27, 1752 (Sess.)	Ch. 14
Hancock	New Cumberland	Jan. 15, 1848	Ch. 58
Hardy	Moorefield	Oct. 17, 1785 (Sess.)	Ch. 35
Harrison	Clarksburg	May 3, 1784 (Sess.)	Ch. 6
Jackson	Ripley	Mar. 1, 1831	Ch. 73
Jefferson	Charles Town	Jan. 8, 1801	Ch. 31
Kanawha	Charleston	Nov. 14, 1788	Ch. 14
Lewis	Weston	Dec. 18, 1816	Ch. 85
Lincoln	Hamlin	Feb. 23, 1867	Ch. 61
Logan	Logan	Jan. 12, 1824	Unnumb.
Marion	Fairmont	Jan. 14, 1842	Ch. 59
Marshall	Moundsville	Mar. 12, 1835	Ch. 57
Mason	Point Pleasant	Jan. 2, 1804	Ch. 102
McDowell	Welch	Feb. 20, 1858	Ch. 155
Mercer	Princeton	Mar. 17, 1837	Ch. 53
Mineral	Keyser	Feb. 1, 1866	Ch. 7
Mingo	Williamson	Jan. 30, 1895	Ch. 68
Monongalia	Morgantown	Oct. 7, 1776 (Sess.)	Unnumb.
Monroe	Union	Jan. 14, 1799	Ch. 41
Morgan	Berkeley Springs	Feb. 9, 1820	Ch. 34
Nicholas	Summersville	Jan. 30, 1818	Ch. 33
Ohio	Wheeling	Oct. 7, 1776	Unnumb.
Pendleton	Franklin	Dec. 4, 1787	Ch. 94
Pleasants	Saint Marys	Mar. 29, 1851	Ch. 27
Pocahontas	Marlinton	Dec. 21, 1821	Ch. 27
Preston	Kingwood	Jan. 19, 1818	Ch. 32
Putnam	Winfield	Mar. 11, 1848	Ch. 59
Raleigh	Beckley	Jan. 23, 1850	Ch. 24
Randolph	Elkins	Oct. 16, 1786 (Sess.)	Ch. 101
Ritchie	Harrisville	Feb. 18, 1843	Ch. 52
Roane	Spencer	Mar. 11, 1856	Ch. 109
Summers	Hinton	Feb. 27, 1871	Ch. 134
Taylor	Grafton	Jan. 19, 1844	Ch. 44
Tucker	Parsons	Mar. 7, 1856	Ch. 110
Tyler	Middlebourne	Dec. 6, 1814	Ch. 40

Upshur	Buckhannon	Mar. 26, 1851	Ch. 26
Wayne	Wayne	Jan. 18, 1842	Ch. 60
Webster	Webster Springs	Jan. 10, 1860	Ch. 47
Wetzel	New Martinsville	Jan. 10, 1846	Ch. 65
Wirt	Elizabeth	Jan. 19, 1848	Ch. 60
Wood	Parkersburg	Dec. 21, 1798	Ch. 43
Wyoming	Pineville	Jan. 26, 1850	Ch. 25

WISCONSIN (72 COUNTIES)

Michigan Territory January 11, 1805
Wisconsin Territory April 20, 1836
Admitted as state May 29, 1848 (30th)

County	County Seat	Created	Statute
Adams	Friendship	Mar. 11, 1848	Unnumb.
Ashland	Ashland	Mar. 27, 1860	Ch. 211
Barron[1]	Barron	Mar. 19, 1859	Ch. 191
Bayfield[2]	Washburn	Feb. 19, 1845	
Brown	Green Bay	Oct. 26, 1818	Proc.
Buffalo	Alma	July 6, 1853	Ch. 100
Burnett	Siren	Mar. 31, 1856	Ch. 94
Calumet	Chilton	Dec. 7, 1836	Ch. 28
Chippewa	Chippewa Falls	Feb. 3, 1845	Unnumb.
Clark	Neillsville	July 6, 1853	Ch. 100
Columbia	Portage	Feb. 3, 1846	Unnumb.
Crawford	Prairie du Chien	Oct. 26, 1818	Proc.
Dane	Madison	Dec. 7, 1836	Ch. 28
Dodge	Juneau	Dec. 7, 1836	Ch. 28
Door	Sturgeon Bay	Feb. 11, 1851	Ch. 56
Douglas	Superior	Feb. 9, 1854	Ch. 10
Dunn	Menomonie	Feb. 3, 1854	Ch. 7
Eau Claire	Eau Claire	Oct. 6, 1856	Ch. 114
Florence	Florence	Mar. 18, 1882	Ch. 165
Fond du Lac	Fond du Lac	Dec. 7, 1836	Ch. 28
Forest	Crandon	Apr. 11, 1885	Ch. 436
Grant	Lancaster	Dec. 8, 1836	Ch. 31
Green	Monroe	Dec. 8, 1836	Ch. 31
Green Lake	Green Lake	Mar. 5, 1858	Ch. 17
Iowa	Dodgeville	Oct. 9, 1829	Unnumb.
Iron	Hurley	Mar. 1, 1893	Ch. 8
Jackson	Black River Falls	Feb. 11, 1853	Ch. 8
Jefferson	Jefferson	Dec. 7, 1836	Ch. 28
Juneau	Mauston	Oct. 13, 1856	Ch. 130
Kenosha	Kenosha	Jan. 30, 1850	Ch. 39
Kewaunee	Kewaunee	Apr. 16, 1852	Ch. 363
La Crosse	La Crosse	Mar. 1, 1851	Ch. 131
Lafayette	Darlington	Jan. 31, 1846	Unnumb.
Langlade[3]	Antigo	Feb. 27, 1879	Ch. 114
Lincoln	Merrill	Mar. 4, 1874	Ch. 128
Manitowoc	Manitowoc	Dec. 7, 1836	Ch. 28
Marathon	Wausau	Feb. 9, 1850	Ch. 226
Marinette	Marinette	Feb. 27, 1879	Ch. 114
Marquette	Montello	Dec. 7, 1836	Ch. 28

Menominee	Keshena	May 1, 1961	
Milwaukee	Milwaukee	Sep. 6, 1834	Unnumb.
Monroe	Sparta	Mar. 21, 1854	Ch. 35
Oconto	Oconto	Feb. 6, 1851	Ch. 44
Oneida	Rhinelander	Apr. 11, 1885	Ch. 411
Outagamie	Appleton	Feb. 17, 1851	Ch. 83
Ozaukee	Port Washington	Mar. 7, 1853	Ch. 21
Pepin	Durand	Feb. 25, 1858	Ch. 15
Pierce	Ellsworth	Mar. 14, 1853	Ch. 31
Polk	Balsam Lake	Mar. 14, 1853	Ch. 31
Portage	Stevens Point	Dec. 7, 1836	Ch. 28
Price	Phillips	Feb. 26, 1879	Ch. 103
Racine	Racine	Dec. 7, 1836	Ch. 28
Richland	Richland Center	Feb. 18, 1842	Unnumb.
Rock	Janesville	Dec. 7, 1836	Ch. 28
Rusk[4]	Ladysmith	May 15, 1901	Ch. 469
Saint Croix	Hudson	Jan. 9, 1840	Ch. 20
Sauk	Baraboo	Jan. 11, 1840	Ch. 20
Sawyer	Hayward	Mar. 10, 1883	Ch. 47
Shawano[5]	Shawano	Feb. 16, 1853	Ch. 9
Sheboygan	Sheboygan	Dec. 7, 1836	Ch. 28
Taylor	Medford	Mar. 4, 1875	Ch. 178
Trempealeau	Whitehall	Jan. 27, 1854	Ch. 2
Vernon[6]	Viroqua	Mar. 1, 1851	Ch. 131
Vilas	Eagle River	Apr. 12, 1893	Ch. 150
Walworth	Elkhorn	Dec. 7, 1836	Ch. 28
Washburn	Shell Lake	Mar. 27, 1883	Ch. 172
Washington	West Bend	Dec. 7, 1836	Ch. 28
Waukesha	Waukesha	Jan. 31, 1846	Unnumb.
Waupaca	Waupaca	Feb. 17, 1851	Ch. 78
Waushara	Wautoma	Feb. 15, 1851	Ch. 77
Winnebago	Oshkosh	Jan. 6, 1840	Ch. 12
Wood	Wisconsin Rapids	Mar. 29, 1856	Ch. 54

Notes

1. Barron created as Dallas; name changed Mar. 4, 1869, Ch. 75
2. Bayfield created as La Pointe; name changed Apr. 12, 1866, Ch. 146
3. Langlade created as New; name changed Feb. 19, 1880, Ch. 19
4. Rusk created as Gates; name changed June 19, 1905, Ch. 463
5. Shawano created as Shawanaw; spelling changed 1864
6. Vernon created as Bad Ax; name changed Mar. 22, 1862, Ch. 137

WYOMING (23 COUNTIES)

Dakota Territory March 2, 1861
Wyoming Territory July 25, 1868
Admitted as state July 10, 1890 (44th)

County	County Seat	Created	Statute
Albany	Laramie	Dec. 16, 1868	Ch. 28
Big Horn	Basin	Mar. 12, 1890	Ch. 48
Campbell	Gillette	Feb. 13, 1911	Ch. 14
Carbon	Rawlins	Dec. 16, 1868	Ch. 35
Converse	Douglas	Mar. 9, 1888	Ch. 90

Crook	Sundance	Dec. 8, 1875	Unnumb.
Fremont	Lander	Mar. 5, 1884	Ch. 46
Goshen	Torrington	Feb. 9, 1911	Ch. 10
Hot Springs	Thermopolis	Feb. 9, 1911	Ch. 9
Johnson[1]	Buffalo	Dec. 8, 1875	Unnumb.
Laramie	Cheyenne	Jan. 9, 1867	Ch. 14
Lincoln	Kemmerer	Feb. 20, 1911	Ch. 67
Natrona	Casper	Mar. 9, 1888	Ch. 90
Niobrara	Lusk	Feb. 14, 1911	Ch. 20
Park	Cody	Feb. 15, 1909	Ch. 19
Platte	Wheatland	Feb. 9, 1911	Ch. 7
Sheridan	Sheridan	Mar. 9, 1888	Ch. 90
Sublette	Pinedale	Feb. 15, 1921	Ch. 52
Sweetwater[2]	Green River	Dec. 27, 1867	Ch. 7
Teton	Jackson	Feb. 15, 1921	Ch. 53
Uinta	Evanston	Dec. 1, 1869	Ch. 34
Washakie	Worland	Feb. 9, 1911	Ch. 8
Weston	Newcastle	Mar. 12, 1890	Ch. 47

Notes

1. Johnson created as Pease; name changed Dec. 13, 1879, Ch. 31
2. Sweetwater created as Carter; name changed Dec. 13, 1869, Ch. 35

Appendix C: County Seats

Note: The counties Kalawao, Hawaii, and Shannon and Todd, South Dakota, do not have county seats. The census area of Alaska, Connecticut, and Rhode Island do not have county governments; the cities listed as county seats in these states and for the District of Columbia are governmental centers as listed by the National Association of Counties.

County Seat	County	State
Abbeville	Abbeville	South Carolina
Abbeville	Henry	Alabama
Abbeville	Vermilion	Louisiana
Abbeville	Wilcox	Georgia
Abeline	Dickinson	Kansas
Abeline	Taylor	Texas
Aberdeen	Brown	South Dakota
Aberdeen	Monroe	Mississippi
Abingdon	Washington	Virginia
Accomac	Accomack	Virginia
Ackerman	Choctaw	Mississippi
Ada	Norman	Minnesota
Ada	Pontotoc	Oklahoma
Adel	Cook	Georgia
Adel	Dallas	Iowa
Adrian	Lenawee	Michigan
Aiken	Aiken	South Carolina
Ainsworth	Brown	Nebraska
Aitkin	Aitkin	Minnesota
Akron	Summit	Ohio
Akron	Washington	Colorado
Alamo	Crockett	Tennessee
Alamo	Wheeler	Georgia
Alamogordo	Otero	New Mexico
Alamosa	Alamosa	Colorado
Albany	Albany	New York
Albany	Clinton	Kentucky
Albany	Dougherty	Georgia
Albany	Gentry	Missouri
Albany	Linn	Oregon
Albany	Shackelford	Texas
Albemarle	Stanly	North Carolina

Albert Lea	Freeborn	Minnesota
Albia	Monroe	Iowa
Albion	Boone	Nebraska
Albion	Edwards	Illinois
Albion	Noble	Indiana
Albion	Orleans	New York
Albuquerque	Bernalillo	New Mexico
Aledo	Mercer	Illinois
Alexandria	Douglas	Minnesota
Alexandria	Hanson	South Dakota
Alexandria	Rapides	Louisiana
Alfred	York	Maine
Algona	Kossuth	Iowa
Alice	Jim Wells	Texas
Allegan	Allegan	Michigan
Allendale	Allendale	South Carolina
Allentown	Lehigh	Pennsylvania
Alliance	Box Buttc	Ncbraska
Allison	Butler	Iowa
Alma	Bacon	Georgia
Alma	Buffalo	Wisconsin
Alma	Harlan	Nebraska
Alma	Wabaunsee	Kansas
Alpena	Alpena	Michigan
Alpine	Brewster	Texas
Altamont	Grundy	Tennessee
Alton	Oregon	Missouri
Alturas	Modoc	California
Altus	Jackson	Oklahoma
Alva	Woods	Oklahoma
Amarillo	Potter	Texas
Amelia Court House	Amelia	Virginia
American Falls	Power	Idaho
Americus	Sumter	Georgia
Amherst	Amherst	Virginia
Amidon	Slope	North Dakota
Amite	Tangipahoa	Louisiana
Anaconda	Deer Lodge	Montana
Anadarko	Caddo	Oklahoma
Anahuac	Chambers	Texas
Anamosa	Jones	Iowa
Anchorage	Anchorage	Alaska
Andalusia	Covington	Alabama
Anderson	Anderson	South Carolina
Anderson	Grimes	Texas
Anderson	Madison	Indiana
Andrews	Andrews	Texas
Angleton	Brazoria	Texas
Angola	Steuben	Indiana
Annapolis	Anne Arundel	Maryland
Ann Arbor	Washtenaw	Michigan
Anniston	Calhoun	Alabama
Anoka	Anoka	Minnesota
Anson	Jones	Texas
Anthony	Harper	Kansas

Antigo	Langlade	Wisconsin
Antlers	Pushmataha	Oklahoma
Apalachicola	Franklin	Florida
Appleton	Outagamie	Wisconsin
Appomattox	Appomattox	Virginia
Arapahoe	Custer	Oklahoma
Arcadia	Bienville	Louisiana
Arcadia	DeSoto	Florida
Archer City	Archer	Texas
Arco	Butte	Idaho
Ardmore	Carter	Oklahoma
Arkadelphia	Clark	Arkansas
Arkansas City	Desha	Arkansas
Arlington	Arlington	Virginia
Armour	Douglas	South Dakota
Arnett	Ellis	Oklahoma
Arthur	Arthur	Nebraska
Ashburn	Turner	Georgia
Ashdown	Little River	Arkansas
Asheboro	Randolph	North Carolina
Asheville	Buncombe	North Carolina
Ash Flat	Sharp	Arkansas
Ashland	Ashland	Ohio
Ashland	Ashland	Wisconsin
Ashland	Benton	Mississippi
Ashland	Clark	Kansas
Ashland	Clay	Alabama
Ashland City	Cheatham	Tennessee
Ashley	McIntosh	North Dakota
Ashville	Saint Clair	Alabama
Asotin	Asotin	Washington
Aspen	Pitkin	Colorado
Aspermont	Stonewall	Texas
Astoria	Clatsop	Oregon
Atchison	Atchison	Kansas
Athens	Athens	Ohio
Athens	Clarke	Georgia
Athens	Henderson	Texas
Athens	Limestone	Alabama
Athens	McMinn	Tennessee
Atlanta	Fulton	Georgia
Atlanta	Montmorency	Michigan
Atlantic	Cass	Iowa
Atoka	Atoka	Oklahoma
Atwood	Rawlins	Kansas
Auburn	Androscoggin	Maine
Auburn	Cayuga	New York
Auburn	DeKalb	Indiana
Auburn	Nemaha	Nebraska
Auburn	Placer	California
Audubon	Audubon	Iowa
Augusta	Kennebec	Maine
Augusta	Richmond	Georgia
Augusta	Woodruff	Arkansas
Aurora	Hamilton	Nebraska

Austin	Mower	Minnesota
Austin	Travis	Texas
Ava	Douglas	Missouri
Aztec	San Juan	New Mexico
Bad Axe	Huron	Michigan
Bagley	Clearwater	Minnesota
Bainbridge	Decatur	Georgia
Baird	Callahan	Texas
Baker	Fallon	Montana
Baker City	Baker	Oregon
Bakersfield	Kern	California
Bakersville	Mitchell	North Carolina
Baldwin	Lake	Michigan
Ballinger	Runnels	Texas
Ballston Spa	Saratoga	New York
Balsam Lake	Polk	Wisconsin
Bamberg	Bamberg	South Carolina
Bandera	Bandera	Texas
Bangor	Penobscot	Maine
Baraboo	Sauk	Wisconsin
Barbourville	Knox	Kentucky
Bardstown	Nelson	Kentucky
Bardwell	Carlisle	Kentucky
Barnesville	Lamar	Georgia
Barnstable	Barnstable	Massachusetts
Barnwell	Barnwell	South Carolina
Barron	Barron	Wisconsin
Barrow	North Slope	Alaska
Bartlesville	Washington	Oklahoma
Bartlett	Wheeler	Nebraska
Bartow	Polk	Florida
Basin	Big Horn	Wyoming
Bassett	Rock	Nebraska
Bastrop	Bastrop	Texas
Bastrop	Morehouse	Louisiana
Batavia	Clermont	Ohio
Batavia	Genesee	New York
Batesville	Independence	Arkansas
Batesville	Panola	Mississippi
Bath	Sagadahoc	Maine
Bath	Steuben	New York
Baton Rouge	East Baton Rouge	Louisiana
Battle Mountain	Lander	Nevada
Baudette	Lake of the Woods	Minnesota
Baxley	Appling	Georgia
Bayboro	Pamlico	North Carolina
Bay City	Bay	Michigan
Bay City	Matagorda	Texas
Bay Minette	Baldwin	Alabama
Bay Saint Louis	Hancock	Mississippi
Bay Springs	Jasper	Mississippi
Beach	Golden Valley	North Dakota
Beatrice	Gage	Nebraska
Beattyville	Lee	Kentucky

Beaufort	Beaufort	South Carolina
Beaufort	Carteret	North Carolina
Beaumont	Jefferson	Texas
Beaver	Beaver	Oklahoma
Beaver	Beaver	Pennsylvania
Beaver	Beaver	Utah
Beaver City	Furnas	Nebraska
Beckley	Raleigh	West Virginia
Bedford	Bedford	Pennsylvania
Bedford	Bedford	Virginia
Bedford	Lawrence	Indiana
Bedford	Taylor	Iowa
Bedford	Trimble	Kentucky
Beeville	Bee	Texas
Bel Air	Harford	Maryland
Belfast	Waldo	Maine
Bellaire	Antrim	Michigan
Bellefontaine	Logan	Ohio
Bellefonte	Centre	Pennsylvania
Belle Fourche	Butte	South Dakota
Belleville	Republic	Kansas
Belleville	Saint Clair	Illinois
Bellingham	Whatcom	Washington
Bellville	Austin	Texas
Belmont	Allegany	New York
Beloit	Mitchell	Kansas
Belton	Bell	Texas
Belvidere	Boone	Illinois
Belvidere	Warren	New Jersey
Belzoni	Humphreys	Mississippi
Bemidji	Beltrami	Minnesota
Bend	Deschutes	Oregon
Benjamin	Knox	Texas
Benkelman	Dundy	Nebraska
Bennettsville	Marlboro	South Carolina
Bennington	Bennington	Vermont
Benson	Swift	Minnesota
Benton	Bossier	Louisiana
Benton	Franklin	Illinois
Benton	Marshall	Kentucky
Benton	Polk	Tennessee
Benton	Saline	Arkansas
Benton	Scott	Missouri
Bentonville	Benton	Arkansas
Berkeley Springs	Morgan	West Virginia
Bernalillo	Sandoval	New Mexico
Berryville	Carroll	Arkansas
Berryville	Clarke	Virginia
Bessemer	Gogebic	Michigan
Bethany	Harrison	Missouri
Beulah	Benzie	Michigan
Big Lake	Reagan	Texas
Big Rapids	Mecosta	Michigan
Big Spring	Howard	Texas
Big Timber	Sweet Grass	Montana

Billings	Yellowstone	Montana
Binghamton	Broome	New York
Birmingham	Jefferson	Alabama
Bisbee	Cochise	Arizona
Bishopville	Lee	South Carolina
Bismarck	Burleigh	North Dakota
Bison	Perkins	South Dakota
Blackfoot	Bingham	Idaho
Black River Falls	Jackson	Wisconsin
Blackshear	Pierce	Georgia
Blair	Washington	Nebraska
Blairsville	Union	Georgia
Blakely	Early	Georgia
Bland	Bland	Virginia
Bloomfield	Davis	Iowa
Bloomfield	Greene	Indiana
Bloomfield	Stoddard	Missouri
Bloomington	McLean	Illinois
Bloomington	Monroe	Indiana
Bloomsburg	Columbia	Pennsylvania
Blountstown	Calhoun	Florida
Blountsville	Sullivan	Tennessee
Blue Earth	Faribault	Minnesota
Blue Ridge	Fannin	Georgia
Bluffton	Wells	Indiana
Blytheville	Mississippi	Arkansas
Boerne	Kendall	Texas
Boise	Ada	Idaho
Boise City	Cimarron	Oklahoma
Bolivar	Hardeman	Tennessee
Bolivar	Polk	Missouri
Bolivia	Brunswick	North Carolina
Bonham	Fannin	Texas
Bonifay	Holmes	Florida
Bonners Ferry	Boundary	Idaho
Boone	Boone	Iowa
Boone	Watauga	North Carolina
Booneville	Owsley	Kentucky
Booneville	Prentiss	Mississippi
Boonville	Cooper	Missouri
Boonville	Warrick	Indiana
Boston	Suffolk	Massachusetts
Bottineau	Bottineau	North Dakota
Boulder	Boulder	Colorado
Boulder	Jefferson	Montana
Bowbells	Burke	North Dakota
Bowling Green	Caroline	Virginia
Bowling Green	Pike	Missouri
Bowling Green	Warren	Kentucky
Bowling Green	Wood	Ohio
Bowman	Bowman	North Dakota
Boydton	Mecklenburg	Virginia
Bozeman	Gallatin	Montana
Brackettville	Kinney	Texas
Bradenton	Manatee	Florida

Brady	McCulloch	Texas
Brainerd	Crow Wing	Minnesota
Brandenburg	Meade	Kentucky
Brandon	Rankin	Mississippi
Brazil	Clay	Indiana
Breckenridge	Stephens	Texas
Breckenridge	Summit	Colorado
Breckenridge	Wilkin	Minnesota
Brenham	Washington	Texas
Brentwood	Rockingham	New Hampshire
Brevard	Transylvania	North Carolina
Brewster	Blaine	Nebraska
Brewton	Escambia	Alabama
Bridgeport	Fairfield	Connecticut
Bridgeport	Mono	California
Bridgeport	Morrill	Nebraska
Bridgeton	Cumberland	New Jersey
Brigham City	Box Elder	Utah
Brighton	Adams	Colorado
Bristol	Bristol	Rhode Island
Bristol	Liberty	Florida
Britton	Marshall	South Dakota
Broadus	Powder River	Montana
Broken Bow	Custer	Nebraska
Bronson	Levy	Florida
Bronx	Bronx	New York
Brookhaven	Lincoln	Mississippi
Brookings	Brookings	South Dakota
Brooklyn	Kings	New York
Brooksville	Bracken	Kentucky
Brooksville	Hernando	Florida
Brookville	Franklin	Indiana
Brookville	Jefferson	Pennsylvania
Broomfield	Broomfield	Colorado
Brownfield	Terry	Texas
Brownstown	Jackson	Indiana
Brownsville	Cameron	Texas
Brownsville	Edmonson	Kentucky
Brownsville	Haywood	Tennessee
Brownwood	Brown	Texas
Brunswick	Glynn	Georgia
Bryan	Brazos	Texas
Bryan	Williams	Ohio
Bryson City	Swain	North Carolina
Buchanan	Haralson	Georgia
Buckhannon	Upshur	West Virginia
Buckingham	Buckingham	Virginia
Bucyrus	Crawford	Ohio
Buena Vista	Marion	Georgia
Buffalo	Dallas	Missouri
Buffalo	Erie	New York
Buffalo	Harding	South Dakota
Buffalo	Harper	Oklahoma
Buffalo	Johnson	Wyoming
Buffalo	Wright	Minnesota

Bunnell	Flagler	Florida
Burgaw	Pender	North Carolina
Burke	Gregory	South Dakota
Burkesville	Cumberland	Kentucky
Burley	Cassia	Idaho
Burlington	Boone	Kentucky
Burlington	Chittenden	Vermont
Burlington	Coffey	Kansas
Burlington	Des Moines	Iowa
Burlington	Kit Carson	Colorado
Burnet	Burnet	Texas
Burns	Harney	Oregon
Burnsville	Yancey	North Carolina
Burwell	Garfield	Nebraska
Bushnell	Sumter	Florida
Butler	Bates	Missouri
Butler	Butler	Pennsylvania
Butler	Choctaw	Alabama
Butler	Taylor	Georgia
Butte	Boyd	Nebraska
Butte	Silver Bow	Montana
Byrdstown	Pickett	Tennessee
Cadillac	Wexford	Michigan
Cadiz	Harrison	Ohio
Cadiz	Trigg	Kentucky
Cairo	Alexander	Illinois
Cairo	Grady	Georgia
Caldwell	Burleson	Texas
Caldwell	Canyon	Idaho
Caldwell	Noble	Ohio
Caledonia	Houston	Minnesota
Calhoun	Gordon	Georgia
Calhoun	McLean	Kentucky
California	Moniteau	Missouri
Cambridge	Dorchester	Maryland
Cambridge	Guernsey	Ohio
Cambridge	Henry	Illinois
Cambridge	Isanti	Minnesota
Camden	Benton	Tennessee
Camden	Camden	New Jersey
Camden	Camden	North Carolina
Camden	Kershaw	South Carolina
Camden	Ouachita	Arkansas
Camden	Wilcox	Alabama
Camdenton	Camden	Missouri
Cameron	Cameron	Louisiana
Cameron	Milam	Texas
Camilla	Mitchell	Georgia
Campbellsville	Taylor	Kentucky
Campton	Wolfe	Kentucky
Canadian	Hemphill	Texas
Canandaigua	Ontario	New York
Cando	Towner	North Dakota
Canon City	Fremont	Colorado

Canton	Cherokee	Georgia
Canton	Lincoln	South Dakota
Canton	Madison	Mississippi
Canton	Saint Lawrence	New York
Canton	Stark	Ohio
Canton	Van Zandt	Texas
Canyon	Randall	Texas
Canyon City	Grant	Oregon
Cape May Court House	Cape May	New Jersey
Caribou	Aroostook	Maine
Carlinville	Macoupin	Illinois
Carlisle	Cumberland	Pennsylvania
Carlisle	Nicholas	Kentucky
Carlsbad	Eddy	New Mexico
Carlton	Carlton	Minnesota
Carlyle	Clinton	Illinois
Carmel	Putnam	New York
Carmi	White	Illinois
Carnesville	Franklin	Georgia
Caro	Tuscola	Michigan
Carrington	Foster	North Dakota
Carrizo Springs	Dimmitt	Texas
Carrizozo	Lincoln	New Mexico
Carroll	Carroll	Iowa
Carrollton	Carroll	Georgia
Carrollton	Carroll	Kentucky
Carrollton	Carroll	Mississippi
Carrollton	Carroll	Missouri
Carrollton	Carroll	Ohio
Carrollton	Greene	Illinois
Carrollton	Pickens	Alabama
Carson	Grant	North Dakota
Cartersville	Bartow	Georgia
Carthage	Hancock	Illinois
Carthage	Jasper	Missouri
Carthage	Leake	Mississippi
Carthage	Moore	North Carolina
Carthage	Panola	Texas
Carthage	Smith	Tennessee
Caruthersville	Pemiscot	Missouri
Cascade	Valley	Idaho
Casper	Natrona	Wyoming
Cassopolis	Cass	Michigan
Cassville	Barry	Missouri
Castle Dale	Emery	Utah
Castle Rock	Douglas	Colorado
Cathlamet	Wahkiakum	Washington
Catlettsburg	Boyd	Kentucky
Catskill	Greene	New York
Cavalier	Pembina	North Dakota
Cedar Rapids	Linn	Iowa
Cedartown	Polk	Georgia
Celina	Clay	Tennessee
Celina	Mercer	Ohio
Center	Knox	Nebraska

Center	Oliver	North Dakota
Center	Shelby	Texas
Center City	Chisago	Minnesota
Centerville	Appanoose	Iowa
Centerville	Hickman	Tennessee
Centerville	Leon	Texas
Centerville	Reynolds	Missouri
Centerville	Saint Joseph	Michigan
Central City	Gilpin	Colorado
Central City	Merrick	Nebraska
Centre	Cherokee	Alabama
Centreville	Bibb	Alabama
Centreville	Queen Anne's	Maryland
Chadron	Dawes	Nebraska
Challis	Custer	Idaho
Chalmette	Saint Bernard	Louisiana
Chamberlain	Brule	South Dakota
Chambersburg	Franklin	Pennsylvania
Chandler	Lincoln	Oklahoma
Channing	Hartley	Texas
Chappell	Deuel	Nebraska
Chardon	Geauga	Ohio
Chariton	Lucas	Iowa
Charles City	Charles City	Virginia
Charles City	Floyd	Iowa
Charleston	Charleston	South Carolina
Charleston	Coles	Illinois
Charleston	Kanawha	West Virginia
Charleston	Mississippi	Missouri
Charleston	Tallahatchie	Mississippi
Charles Town	Jefferson	West Virginia
Charlevoix	Charlevoix	Michigan
Charlotte	Dickson	Tennessee
Charlotte	Eaton	Michigan
Charlotte	Mecklenburg	North Carolina
Charlotte Court House	Charlotte	Virginia
Charlottesville	Albemarle	Virginia
Chaska	Carver	Minnesota
Chatham	Pittsylvania	Virginia
Chatom	Washington	Alabama
Chatsworth	Murray	Georgia
Chattanooga	Hamilton	Tennessee
Cheboygan	Cheboygan	Michigan
Chehalis	Lewis	Washington
Chelsea	Orange	Vermont
Cherokee	Alfalfa	Oklahoma
Cherokee	Cherokee	Iowa
Chester	Chester	South Carolina
Chester	Liberty	Montana
Chester	Randolph	Illinois
Chesterfield	Chesterfield	South Carolina
Chesterfield	Chesterfield	Virginia
Chestertown	Kent	Maryland
Cheyenne	Laramie	Wyoming
Cheyenne	Roger Mills	Oklahoma

Cheyenne Wells	Cheyenne	Colorado
Chicago	Cook	Illinois
Chickasha	Grady	Oklahoma
Childress	Childress	Texas
Chillicothe	Livingston	Missouri
Chillicothe	Ross	Ohio
Chilton	Calumet	Wisconsin
Chinook	Blaine	Montana
Chipley	Washington	Florida
Chippewa Falls	Chippewa	Wisconsin
Choteau	Teton	Montana
Christiansburg	Montgomery	Virginia
Cimarron	Gray	Kansas
Cincinnati	Hamilton	Ohio
Circle	McCone	Montana
Circleville	Pickaway	Ohio
Clanton	Chilton	Alabama
Claremore	Rogers	Oklahoma
Clarendon	Donley	Texas
Clarendon	Monroe	Arkansas
Clarinda	Page	Iowa
Clarion	Clarion	Pennsylvania
Clarion	Wright	Iowa
Clark	Clark	South Dakota
Clarkesville	Habersham	Georgia
Clarksburg	Harrison	West Virginia
Clarksdale	Coahoma	Mississippi
Clarksville	Johnson	Arkansas
Clarksville	Montgomery	Tennessee
Clarksville	Red River	Texas
Claude	Armstrong	Texas
Claxton	Evans	Georgia
Clay	Clay	West Virginia
Clay Center	Clay	Kansas
Clay Center	Clay	Nebraska
Clayton	Barbour	Alabama
Clayton	Rabun	Georgia
Clayton	Saint Louis	Missouri
Clayton	Union	New Mexico
Clearfield	Clearfield	Pennsylvania
Clear Lake	Deuel	South Dakota
Clearwater	Pinellas	Florida
Cleburne	Johnson	Texas
Cleveland	Bolivar	Mississippi
Cleveland	Bradley	Tennessee
Cleveland	Cuyahoga	Ohio
Cleveland	White	Georgia
Clifton	Greenlee	Arizona
Clinton	Anderson	Tennessee
Clinton	Clinton	Iowa
Clinton	De Witt	Illinois
Clinton	East Feliciana	Louisiana
Clinton	Henry	Missouri
Clinton	Hickman	Kentucky
Clinton	Sampson	North Carolina

Clinton	Van Buren	Arkansas
Clintwood	Dickenson	Virginia
Clovis	Curry	New Mexico
Coalgate	Coal	Oklahoma
Coalville	Summit	Utah
Cochran	Bleckley	Georgia
Cody	Park	Wyoming
Coeur d'Alene	Kootenai	Idaho
Colby	Thomas	Kansas
Coldspring	San Jacinto	Texas
Coldwater	Branch	Michigan
Coldwater	Comanche	Kansas
Coleman	Coleman	Texas
Colfax	Grant	Louisiana
Colfax	Whitman	Washington
Collins	Covington	Mississippi
Colorado City	Mitchell	Texas
Colorado Springs	El Paso	Colorado
Colquitt	Miller	Georgia
Columbia	Adair	Kentucky
Columbia	Boone	Missouri
Columbia	Caldwell	Louisiana
Columbia	Marion	Mississippi
Columbia	Maury	Tennessee
Columbia	Richland	South Carolina
Columbia	Tyrrell	North Carolina
Columbia City	Whitley	Indiana
Columbiana	Shelby	Alabama
Columbus	Bartholomew	Indiana
Columbus	Cherokee	Kansas
Columbus	Colorado	Texas
Columbus	Franklin	Ohio
Columbus	Lowndes	Mississippi
Columbus	Muscogee	Georgia
Columbus	Platte	Nebraska
Columbus	Polk	North Carolina
Columbus	Stillwater	Montana
Colusa	Colusa	California
Colville	Stevens	Washington
Comanche	Comanche	Texas
Concord	Cabarrus	North Carolina
Concord	Merrimack	New Hampshire
Concordia	Cloud	Kansas
Condon	Gilliam	Oregon
Conejos	Conejos	Colorado
Connersville	Fayette	Indiana
Conrad	Pondera	Montana
Conroe	Montgomery	Texas
Convent	Saint James	Louisiana
Conway	Faulkner	Arkansas
Conway	Horry	South Carolina
Conyers	Rockdale	Georgia
Cookeville	Putnam	Tennessee
Cooper	Delta	Texas
Cooperstown	Griggs	North Dakota

Cooperstown	Otsego	New York
Coquille	Coos	Oregon
Cordele	Crisp	Georgia
Cordell	Washita	Oklahoma
Corinth	Alcorn	Mississippi
Corning	Adams	Iowa
Corpus Christi	Nueces	Texas
Corsicana	Navarro	Texas
Cortez	Montezuma	Colorado
Cortland	Cortland	New York
Corunna	Shiawassee	Michigan
Corvallis	Benton	Oregon
Corydon	Harrison	Indiana
Corydon	Wayne	Iowa
Coshocton	Coshocton	Ohio
Cottonwood Falls	Chase	Kansas
Cotulla	La Salle	Texas
Coudersport	Potter	Pennsylvania
Council	Adams	Idaho
Council Bluffs	Pottawattamie	Iowa
Council Grove	Morris	Kansas
Coupeville	Island	Washington
Courtland	Southampton	Virginia
Coushatta	Red River	Louisiana
Covington	Alleghany	Virginia
Covington	Fountain	Indiana
Covington	Kenton	Kentucky
Covington	Newton	Georgia
Covington	Saint Tammany	Louisiana
Covington	Tipton	Tennessee
Craig	Moffat	Colorado
Crandon	Forest	Wisconsin
Crane	Crane	Texas
Crawfordsville	Montgomery	Indiana
Crawfordville	Taliaferro	Georgia
Crawfordville	Wakulla	Florida
Creede	Mineral	Colorado
Crescent City	Del Norte	California
Cresco	Howard	Iowa
Creston	Union	Iowa
Crestview	Okaloosa	Florida
Cripple Creek	Teller	Colorado
Crockett	Houston	Texas
Crookston	Polk	Minnesota
Crosby	Divide	North Dakota
Crosbyton	Crosby	Texas
Cross City	Dixie	Florida
Crossville	Cumberland	Tennessee
Crowell	Foard	Texas
Crowley	Acadia	Louisiana
Crown Point	Lake	Indiana
Crystal City	Zavala	Texas
Crystal Falls	Iron	Michigan
Cuero	DeWitt	Texas
Cullman	Cullman	Alabama

Culpeper	Culpeper	Virginia
Cumberland	Allegany	Maryland
Cumberland	Cumberland	Virginia
Cumming	Forsyth	Georgia
Currituck	Currituck	North Carolina
Cusseta	Chattahoochee	Georgia
Custer	Custer	South Dakota
Cut Bank	Glacier	Montana
Cuthbert	Randolph	Georgia
Cynthiana	Harrison	Kentucky
Dade City	Pasco	Florida
Dadeville	Tallapoosa	Alabama
Dahlonega	Lumpkin	Georgia
Daingerfield	Morris	Texas
Dakota City	Dakota	Nebraska
Dakota City	Humboldt	Iowa
Dalhart	Dallam	Texas
Dallas	Dallas	Texas
Dallas	Paulding	Georgia
Dallas	Polk	Oregon
Dalton	Whitfield	Georgia
Danbury	Stokes	North Carolina
Dandridge	Jefferson	Tennessee
Danielsville	Madison	Georgia
Danville	Boyle	Kentucky
Danville	Hendricks	Indiana
Danville	Montour	Pennsylvania
Danville	Vermilion	Illinois
Danville	Yell	Arkansas
Darien	McIntosh	Georgia
Darlington	Darlington	South Carolina
Darlington	Lafayette	Wisconsin
Davenport	Lincoln	Washington
Davenport	Scott	Iowa
David City	Butler	Nebraska
Dawson	Terrell	Georgia
Dawsonville	Dawson	Georgia
Dayton	Columbia	Washington
Dayton	Montgomery	Ohio
Dayton	Rhea	Tennessee
Deadwood	Lawrence	South Dakota
Decatur	Adams	Indiana
Decatur	DeKalb	Georgia
Decatur	Macon	Illinois
Decatur	Meigs	Tennessee
Decatur	Morgan	Alabama
Decatur	Newton	Mississippi
Decatur	Wise	Texas
Decaturville	Decatur	Tennessee
Decorah	Winneshiek	Iowa
Dedham	Norfolk	Massachusetts
Deer Lodge	Powell	Montana
Defiance	Defiance	Ohio
De Funiak Springs	Walton	Florida

De Kalb	Kemper	Mississippi
De Land	Volusia	Florida
Delaware	Delaware	Ohio
Delhi	Delaware	New York
Del Norte	Rio Grande	Colorado
Delphi	Carroll	Indiana
Del Rio	Val Verde	Texas
Delta	Delta	Colorado
Deming	Luna	New Mexico
Denison	Crawford	Iowa
Denton	Caroline	Maryland
Denton	Denton	Texas
Denver	Denver	Colorado
De Queen	Sevier	Arkansas
DeRidder	Beauregard	Louisiana
Des Arc	Prairie	Arkansas
De Smet	Kingsbury	South Dakota
Des Moines	Polk	Iowa
Detroit	Wayne	Michigan
Detroit Lakes	Becker	Minnesota
Devils Lake	Ramsey	North Dakota
De Witt	Arkansas	Arkansas
Dickens	Dickens	Texas
Dickinson	Stark	North Dakota
Dighton	Lane	Kansas
Dillon	Beaverhead	Montana
Dillon	Dillon	South Carolina
Dimmitt	Castro	Texas
Dinwiddie	Dinwiddie	Virginia
Dixon	Lee	Illinois
Dixon	Webster	Kentucky
Dobson	Surry	North Carolina
Dodge City	Ford	Kansas
Dodgeville	Iowa	Wisconsin
Donaldsonville	Ascension	Louisiana
Donalsonville	Seminole	Georgia
Doniphan	Ripley	Missouri
Dothan	Houston	Alabama
Double Springs	Winston	Alabama
Douglas	Coffee	Georgia
Douglas	Converse	Wyoming
Douglasville	Douglas	Georgia
Dove Creek	Dolores	Colorado
Dover	Kent	Delaware
Dover	Stewart	Tennessee
Dover	Strafford	New Hampshire
Dover-Foxcroft	Piscataquis	Maine
Downieville	Sierra	California
Doylestown	Bucks	Pennsylvania
Dresden	Weakley	Tennessee
Driggs	Teton	Idaho
Dublin	Laurens	Georgia
Dubois	Clark	Idaho
Dubuque	Dubuque	Iowa
Duchesne	Duchesne	Utah

Duluth	Saint Louis	Minnesota
Dumas	Moore	Texas
Duncan	Stephens	Oklahoma
Dunlap	Sequatchie	Tennessee
Dupree	Ziebach	South Dakota
Durand	Pepin	Wisconsin
Durango	La Plata	Colorado
Durant	Bryan	Oklahoma
Durham	Durham	North Carolina
Dyersburg	Dyer	Tennessee
Eads	Kiowa	Colorado
Eagle	Eagle	Colorado
Eagle Pass	Maverick	Texas
Eagle River	Keweenaw	Michigan
Eagle River	Vilas	Wisconsin
East Cambridge	Middlesex	Massachusetts
Eastland	Eastland	Texas
Eastman	Dodge	Georgia
Easton	Northampton	Pennsylvania
Easton	Talbot	Maryland
Eastville	Northampton	Virginia
Eaton	Preble	Ohio
Eatonton	Putnam	Georgia
Eau Claire	Eau Claire	Wisconsin
Ebensburg	Cambria	Pennsylvania
Eddyville	Lyon	Kentucky
Edenton	Chowan	North Carolina
Edgartown	Dukes	Massachusetts
Edgefield	Edgefield	South Carolina
Edina	Knox	Missouri
Edinburg	Hidalgo	Texas
Edmonton	Metcalfe	Kentucky
Edna	Jackson	Texas
Edwardsville	Madison	Illinois
Effingham	Effingham	Illinois
Ekalaka	Carter	Montana
Elberton	Elbert	Georgia
Elbow Lake	Grant	Minnesota
El Centro	Imperial	California
Eldora	Hardin	Iowa
El Dorado	Butler	Kansas
Eldorado	Schleicher	Texas
El Dorado	Union	Arkansas
Elizabeth	Union	New Jersey
Elizabeth	Wirt	West Virginia
Elizabeth City	Pasquotank	North Carolina
Elizabethton	Carter	Tennessee
Elizabethtown	Bladen	North Carolina
Elizabethtown	Essex	New York
Elizabethtown	Hardin	Illinois
Elizabethtown	Hardin	Kentucky
Elkader	Clayton	Iowa
Elkhart	Morton	Kansas
Elkhorn	Walworth	Wisconsin

Elkins	Randolph	West Virginia
Elko	Elko	Nevada
Elk Point	Union	South Dakota
Elk River	Sherburne	Minnesota
Elkton	Cecil	Maryland
Elkton	Todd	Kentucky
Ellaville	Schley	Georgia
Ellendale	Dickey	North Dakota
Ellensburg	Kittitas	Washington
Ellicott City	Howard	Maryland
Ellijay	Gilmer	Georgia
Ellsworth	Ellsworth	Kansas
Ellsworth	Hancock	Maine
Ellsworth	Pierce	Wisconsin
Elmira	Chemung	New York
El Paso	El Paso	Texas
El Reno	Canadian	Oklahoma
Elwood	Gosper	Nebraska
Ely	White Pine	Nevada
Elyria	Lorain	Ohio
Eminence	Shannon	Missouri
Emmetsburg	Palo Alto	Iowa
Emmett	Gem	Idaho
Emory	Rains	Texas
Emporia	Greensville	Virginia
Emporia	Lyon	Kansas
Emporium	Cameron	Pennsylvania
English	Crawford	Indiana
Enid	Garfield	Oklahoma
Enterprise	Wallowa	Oregon
Ephrata	Grant	Washington
Erie	Erie	Pennsylvania
Erie	Neosho	Kansas
Erin	Houston	Tennessee
Erwin	Unicoi	Tennessee
Escanaba	Delta	Michigan
Estancia	Torrance	New Mexico
Estherville	Emmet	Iowa
Eufala	McIntosh	Oklahoma
Eugene	Lane	Oregon
Eureka	Eureka	Nevada
Eureka	Greenwood	Kansas
Eureka	Humboldt	California
Eureka	Woodford	Illinois
Eutaw	Greene	Alabama
Evans	Columbia	Georgia
Evanston	Uinta	Wyoming
Evansville	Vanderburgh	Indiana
Everett	Snohomish	Washington
Evergreen	Conecuh	Alabama
Fairbanks	Fairbanks North Star	Alaska
Fairbury	Jefferson	Nebraska
Fairfax	Fairfax	Virginia
Fairfield	Camas	Idaho

Fairfield	Freestone	Texas
Fairfield	Jefferson	Iowa
Fairfield	Solano	California
Fairfield	Wayne	Illinois
Fairmont	Marion	West Virginia
Fairmont	Martin	Minnesota
Fairplay	Park	Colorado
Fairview	Major	Oklahoma
Falfurrias	Brooks	Texas
Fallon	Churchill	Nevada
Falls City	Richardson	Nebraska
Falmouth	Pendleton	Kentucky
Fargo	Cass	North Dakota
Faribault	Rice	Minnesota
Farmersville	Union	Louisiana
Farmington	Davis	Utah
Farmington	Franklin	Maine
Farmington	Saint Francois	Missouri
Farmville	Prince Edward	Virginia
Farwell	Parmer	Texas
Faulkton	Faulk	South Dakota
Fayette	Fayette	Alabama
Fayette	Howard	Missouri
Fayette	Jefferson	Mississippi
Fayetteville	Cumberland	North Carolina
Fayetteville	Fayette	Georgia
Fayetteville	Fayette	West Virginia
Fayetteville	Lincoln	Tennessee
Fayetteville	Washington	Arkansas
Fergus Falls	Otter Tail	Minnesota
Fernandina Beach	Nassau	Florida
Fessenden	Wells	North Dakota
Fillmore	Millard	Utah
Fincastle	Botetourt	Virginia
Findlay	Hancock	Ohio
Finley	Steele	North Dakota
Fitzgerald	Ben Hill	Georgia
Flagstaff	Coconino	Arizona
Flandreau	Moody	South Dakota
Flemingsburg	Fleming	Kentucky
Flemington	Hunterdon	New Jersey
Flint	Genesee	Michigan
Florence	Florence	South Carolina
Florence	Florence	Wisconsin
Florence	Lauderdale	Alabama
Florence	Pinal	Arizona
Floresville	Wilson	Texas
Floyd	Floyd	Virginia
Floydada	Floyd	Texas
Foley	Benton	Minnesota
Folkston	Charlton	Georgia
Fonda	Montgomery	New York
Fond du Lac	Fond du Lac	Wisconsin
Fordyce	Dallas	Arkansas
Forest	Scott	Mississippi

Forest City	Winnebago	Iowa
Forman	Sargent	North Dakota
Forrest City	Saint Francis	Arkansas
Forsyth	Monroe	Georgia
Forsyth	Rosebud	Montana
Forsyth	Taney	Missouri
Fort Benton	Chouteau	Montana
Fort Collins	Larimer	Colorado
Fort Davis	Jeff Davis	Texas
Fort Dodge	Webster	Iowa
Fort Edward	Washington	New York
Fort Gaines	Clay	Georgia
Fort Lauderdale	Broward	Florida
Fort Madison	Lee	Iowa
Fort Morgan	Morgan	Colorado
Fort Myers	Lee	Florida
Fort Payne	DeKalb	Alabama
Fort Pierce	Saint Lucie	Florida
Fort Pierre	Stanley	South Dakota
Fort Scott	Bourbon	Kansas
Fort Smith	Sebastian	Arkansas
Fort Stockton	Pecos	Texas
Fort Sumner	DeBaca	New Mexico
Fort Valley	Peach	Georgia
Fort Wayne	Allen	Indiana
Fort Worth	Tarrant	Texas
Fort Yates	Sioux	North Dakota
Fossil	Wheeler	Oregon
Fowler	Benton	Indiana
Frankfort	Clinton	Indiana
Frankfort	Franklin	Kentucky
Franklin	Franklin	Nebraska
Franklin	Heard	Georgia
Franklin	Johnson	Indiana
Franklin	Macon	North Carolina
Franklin	Pendleton	West Virginia
Franklin	Robertson	Texas
Franklin	Saint Mary	Louisiana
Franklin	Simpson	Kentucky
Franklin	Venango	Pennsylvania
Franklin	Williamson	Tennessee
Franklinton	Washington	Louisiana
Frederick	Frederick	Maryland
Frederick	Tillman	Oklahoma
Fredericksburg	Gillespie	Texas
Fredericktown	Madison	Missouri
Fredonia	Wilson	Kansas
Freehold	Monmouth	New Jersey
Freeport	Stephenson	Illinois
Fremont	Dodge	Nebraska
Fremont	Sandusky	Ohio
Frenchburg	Menifee	Kentucky
Fresno	Fresno	California
Friday Harbor	San Juan	Washington
Friendship	Adams	Wisconsin

Front Royal	Warren	Virginia
Fullerton	Nance	Nebraska
Fulton	Callaway	Missouri
Fulton	Itawamba	Mississippi
Gadsden	Etowah	Alabama
Gaffney	Cherokee	South Carolina
Gail	Borden	Texas
Gainesboro	Jackson	Tennessee
Gainesville	Alachua	Florida
Gainesville	Cooke	Texas
Gainesville	Hall	Georgia
Gainesville	Ozark	Missouri
Galena	Jo Daviess	Illinois
Galena	Stone	Missouri
Galesburg	Knox	Illinois
Gallatin	Daviess	Missouri
Gallatin	Sumner	Tennessee
Gallipolis	Gallia	Ohio
Gallup	McKinley	New Mexico
Galveston	Galveston	Texas
Gann Valley	Buffalo	South Dakota
Garden City	Finney	Kansas
Garden City	Glasscock	Texas
Garner	Hancock	Iowa
Garnett	Anderson	Kansas
Gastonia	Gaston	North Carolina
Gate City	Scott	Virginia
Gatesville	Coryell	Texas
Gatesville	Gates	North Carolina
Gaylord	Otsego	Michigan
Gaylord	Sibley	Minnesota
Geneseo	Livingston	New York
Geneva	Fillmore	Nebraska
Geneva	Geneva	Alabama
Geneva	Kane	Illinois
Georgetown	Brown	Ohio
Georgetown	Clear Creek	Colorado
Georgetown	Georgetown	South Carolina
Georgetown	Quitman	Georgia
Georgetown	Scott	Kentucky
Georgetown	Sussex	Delaware
Georgetown	Williamson	Texas
George West	Live Oak	Texas
Gering	Scotts Bluff	Nebraska
Gettysburg	Adams	Pennsylvania
Gettysburg	Potter	South Dakota
Gibson	Glascock	Georgia
Giddings	Lee	Texas
Gillette	Campbell	Wyoming
Gilmer	Upshur	Texas
Girard	Crawford	Kansas
Gladwin	Gladwin	Michigan
Glasgow	Barren	Kentucky
Glasgow	Valley	Montana

Glencoe	McLeod	Minnesota
Glendive	Dawson	Montana
Glen Rose	Somervell	Texas
Glensville	Gilmer	West Virginia
Glenwood	Mills	Iowa
Glenwood	Pope	Minnesota
Glenwood Springs	Garfield	Colorado
Globe	Gila	Arizona
Gloucester	Gloucester	Virginia
Golconda	Pope	Illinois
Gold Beach	Curry	Oregon
Golden	Jefferson	Colorado
Goldendale	Klickitat	Washington
Goldfield	Esmeralda	Nevada
Goldsboro	Wayne	North Carolina
Goldthwaite	Mills	Texas
Goliad	Goliad	Texas
Gonzales	Gonzales	Texas
Goochland	Goochland	Virginia
Gooding	Gooding	Idaho
Goodland	Sherman	Kansas
Goshen	Elkhart	Indiana
Goshen	Orange	New York
Gove City	Gove	Kansas
Grafton	Taylor	West Virginia
Grafton	Walsh	North Dakota
Graham	Alamance	North Carolina
Graham	Young	Texas
Granbury	Hood	Texas
Grand Forks	Grand Forks	North Dakota
Grand Haven	Ottawa	Michigan
Grand Island	Hall	Nebraska
Grand Junction	Mesa	Colorado
Grand Marais	Cook	Minnesota
Grand Rapids	Itasca	Minnesota
Grand Rapids	Kent	Michigan
Grangeville	Idaho	Idaho
Granite Falls	Yellow Medicine	Minnesota
Grant	Perkins	Nebraska
Grant City	Worth	Missouri
Grants	Cibola	New Mexico
Grants Pass	Josephine	Oregon
Grantsville	Calhoun	West Virginia
Gray	Jones	Georgia
Grayling	Crawford	Michigan
Grayson	Carter	Kentucky
Great Bend	Barton	Kansas
Great Falls	Cascade	Montana
Greeley	Greeley	Nebraska
Greeley	Weld	Colorado
Green Bay	Brown	Wisconsin
Greencastle	Putnam	Indiana
Green Cove Springs	Clay	Florida
Greenfield	Adair	Iowa
Greenfield	Dade	Missouri

Greenfield	Franklin	Massachusetts
Greenfield	Hancock	Indiana
Green Lake	Green Lake	Wisconsin
Green River	Sweetwater	Wyoming
Greensboro	Greene	Georgia
Greensboro	Guilford	North Carolina
Greensboro	Hale	Alabama
Greensburg	Decatur	Indiana
Greensburg	Green	Kentucky
Greensburg	Kiowa	Kansas
Greensburg	Saint Helena	Louisiana
Greensburg	Westmoreland	Pennsylvania
Greenup	Greenup	Kentucky
Greenville	Bond	Illinois
Greenville	Butler	Alabama
Greenville	Darke	Ohio
Greenville	Greene	Tennessee
Greenville	Greenville	South Carolina
Greenville	Hunt	Texas
Greenville	Meriwether	Georgia
Greenville	Muhlenberg	Kentucky
Greenville	Pitt	North Carolina
Greenville	Washington	Mississippi
Greenville	Wayne	Missouri
Greenwood	Greenwood	South Carolina
Greenwood	Leflore	Mississippi
Grenada	Grenada	Mississippi
Gretna	Jefferson	Louisiana
Griffin	Spalding	Georgia
Groesbeck	Limestone	Texas
Grove Hill	Clarke	Alabama
Groveton	Trinity	Texas
Grundy	Buchanan	Virginia
Grundy Center	Grundy	Iowa
Guildhall	Essex	Vermont
Gulfport	Harrison	Mississippi
Gunnison	Gunnison	Colorado
Guntersville	Marshall	Alabama
Guthrie	King	Texas
Guthrie	Logan	Oklahoma
Guthrie Center	Guthrie	Iowa
Guymon	Texas	Oklahoma
Hackensack	Bergen	New Jersey
Hagerstown	Washington	Maryland
Hahnville	Saint Charles	Louisiana
Hailey	Blaine	Idaho
Haines	Haines	Alaska
Halifax	Halifax	North Carolina
Halifax	Halifax	Virginia
Hallettsville	Lavaca	Texas
Hallock	Kittson	Minnesota
Hamburg	Ashley	Arkansas
Hamilton	Butler	Ohio
Hamilton	Hamilton	Texas

Hamilton	Harris	Georgia
Hamilton	Marion	Alabama
Hamilton	Ravalli	Montana
Hamlin	Lincoln	West Virginia
Hampton	Calhoun	Arkansas
Hampton	Franklin	Iowa
Hampton	Hampton	South Carolina
Hanford	Kings	California
Hanover	Hanover	Virginia
Hardin	Big Horn	Montana
Hardin	Calhoun	Illinois
Hardinsburg	Breckinridge	Kentucky
Harlan	Harlan	Kentucky
Harlan	Shelby	Iowa
Harlowton	Wheatland	Montana
Harrisburg	Banner	Nebraska
Harrisburg	Dauphin	Pennsylvania
Harrisburg	Poinsett	Arkansas
Harrisburg	Saline	Illinois
Harrison	Boone	Arkansas
Harrison	Clare	Michigan
Harrison	Sioux	Nebraska
Harrisonburg	Catahoula	Louisiana
Harrisonburg	Rockingham	Virginia
Harrisonville	Cass	Missouri
Harrisville	Alcona	Michigan
Harrisville	Ritchie	West Virginia
Harrodsburg	Mercer	Kentucky
Hart	Oceana	Michigan
Hartford	Hartford	Connecticut
Hartford	Ohio	Kentucky
Hartford City	Blackford	Indiana
Hartington	Cedar	Nebraska
Hartsville	Trousdale	Tennessee
Hartville	Wright	Missouri
Hartwell	Hart	Georgia
Haskell	Haskell	Texas
Hastings	Adams	Nebraska
Hastings	Barry	Michigan
Hastings	Dakota	Minnesota
Hattiesburg	Forrest	Mississippi
Havana	Mason	Illinois
Havre	Hill	Montana
Hawesville	Hancock	Kentucky
Hawkinsville	Pulaski	Georgia
Hawthorne	Mineral	Nevada
Hayes Center	Hayes	Nebraska
Hayesville	Clay	North Carolina
Hayneville	Lowndes	Alabama
Hays	Ellis	Kansas
Hayti	Hamlin	South Dakota
Hayward	Sawyer	Wisconsin
Hazard	Perry	Kentucky
Hazlehurst	Copiah	Mississippi
Hazlehurst	Jeff Davis	Georgia

Healy	Denali	Alaska
Heathsville	Northumberland	Virginia
Hebbronville	Jim Hogg	Texas
Heber City	Wasatch	Utah
Heber Springs	Cleburne	Arkansas
Hebron	Thayer	Nebraska
Heflin	Cleburne	Alabama
Helena	Lewis and Clark	Montana
Helena	Phillips	Arkansas
Hemphill	Sabine	Texas
Hempstead	Waller	Texas
Henderson	Chester	Tennessee
Henderson	Henderson	Kentucky
Henderson	Rusk	Texas
Henderson	Vance	North Carolina
Hendersonville	Henderson	North Carolina
Hennepin	Putnam	Illinois
Henrietta	Clay	Texas
Heppner	Morrow	Oregon
Hereford	Deaf Smith	Texas
Herkimer	Herkimer	New York
Hermann	Gasconade	Missouri
Hermitage	Hickory	Missouri
Hernando	DeSoto	Mississippi
Hertford	Perquimans	North Carolina
Hettinger	Adams	North Dakota
Hiawassee	Towns	Georgia
Hiawatha	Brown	Kansas
Hickman	Fulton	Kentucky
Highmore	Hyde	South Dakota
Hill City	Graham	Kansas
Hillsboro	Highland	Ohio
Hillsboro	Hill	Texas
Hillsboro	Jefferson	Missouri
Hillsboro	Montgomery	Illinois
Hillsboro	Traill	North Dakota
Hillsboro	Washington	Oregon
Hillsborough	Orange	North Carolina
Hillsdale	Hillsdale	Michigan
Hillsville	Carroll	Virginia
Hilo	Hawaii	Hawaii
Hindman	Knott	Kentucky
Hinesville	Liberty	Georgia
Hinton	Summers	West Virginia
Hobart	Kiowa	Oklahoma
Hodgenville	Larue	Kentucky
Hohenwald	Lewis	Tennessee
Holbrook	Navajo	Arizona
Holdenville	Hughes	Oklahoma
Holdrege	Phelps	Nebraska
Hollidaysburg	Blair	Pennsylvania
Hollis	Harmon	Oklahoma
Hollister	San Benito	California
Holly Springs	Marshall	Mississippi
Holton	Jackson	Kansas

Holyoke	Phillips	Colorado
Homer	Banks	Georgia
Homer	Claiborne	Louisiana
Homerville	Clinch	Georgia
Hondo	Medina	Texas
Honesdale	Wayne	Pennsylvania
Honolulu	Honolulu	Hawaii
Hood River	Hood River	Oregon
Hope	Hempstead	Arkansas
Hopkinsville	Christian	Kentucky
Hot Springs	Fall River	South Dakota
Hot Springs	Garland	Arkansas
Hot Sulphur Springs	Grand	Colorado
Houghton	Houghton	Michigan
Houma	Terrebonne	Louisiana
Houston	Chickasaw	Mississippi
Houston	Harris	Texas
Houston	Texas	Missouri
Howard	Elk	Kansas
Howard	Miner	South Dakota
Howell	Livingston	Michigan
Hoxie	Sheridan	Kansas
Hudson	Columbia	New York
Hudson	Saint Croix	Wisconsin
Hugo	Choctaw	Oklahoma
Hugo	Lincoln	Colorado
Hugoton	Stevens	Kansas
Huntingdon	Carroll	Tennessee
Huntingdon	Huntingdon	Pennsylvania
Huntington	Cabell	West Virginia
Huntington	Huntington	Indiana
Huntsville	Madison	Alabama
Huntsville	Madison	Arkansas
Huntsville	Randolph	Missouri
Huntsville	Scott	Tennessee
Huntsville	Walker	Texas
Hurley	Iron	Wisconsin
Huron	Beadle	South Dakota
Hutchinson	Reno	Kansas
Hyannis	Grant	Nebraska
Hyden	Leslie	Kentucky
Hyde Park	Lamoille	Vermont
Hysham	Treasure	Montana
Idabel	McCurtain	Oklahoma
Ida Grove	Ida	Iowa
Idaho City	Boise	Idaho
Idaho Falls	Bonneville	Idaho
Imperial	Chase	Nebraska
Independence	Buchanan	Iowa
Independence	Grayson	Virginia
Independence	Inyo	California
Independence	Montgomery	Kansas
Indiana	Indiana	Pennsylvania
Indianapolis	Marion	Indiana

Indianola	Sunflower	Mississippi
Indianola	Warren	Iowa
Inez	Martin	Kentucky
International Falls	Koochiching	Minnesota
Inverness	Citrus	Florida
Iola	Allen	Kansas
Ionia	Ionia	Michigan
Iowa City	Johnson	Iowa
Ipswich	Edmunds	South Dakota
Iron Mountain	Dickinson	Michigan
Ironton	Iron	Missouri
Ironton	Lawrence	Ohio
Irvine	Estill	Kentucky
Irwinton	Wilkinson	Georgia
Isle of Wight	Isle of Wight	Virginia
Ithaca	Gratiot	Michigan
Ithaca	Tompkins	New York
Iuka	Tishomingo	Mississippi
Ivanhoe	Lincoln	Minnesota
Jacksboro	Campbell	Tennessee
Jacksboro	Jack	Texas
Jackson	Amador	California
Jackson	Breathitt	Kentucky
Jackson	Butts	Georgia
Jackson	Cape Girardeau	Missouri
Jackson	Hinds	Mississippi
Jackson	Jackson	Michigan
Jackson	Jackson	Minnesota
Jackson	Jackson	Ohio
Jackson	Madison	Tennessee
Jackson	Northampton	North Carolina
Jackson	Teton	Wyoming
Jacksonville	Duval	Florida
Jacksonville	Morgan	Illinois
Jacksonville	Onslow	North Carolina
Jamaica	Queens	New York
Jamestown	Fentress	Tennessee
Jamestown	Russell	Kentucky
Jamestown	Stutsman	North Dakota
Janesville	Rock	Wisconsin
Jasper	Dubois	Indiana
Jasper	Hamilton	Florida
Jasper	Jasper	Texas
Jasper	Marion	Tennessee
Jasper	Newton	Arkansas
Jasper	Pickens	Georgia
Jasper	Walker	Alabama
Jay	Delaware	Oklahoma
Jayton	Kent	Texas
Jefferson	Ashe	North Carolina
Jefferson	Ashtabula	Ohio
Jefferson	Greene	Iowa
Jefferson	Jackson	Georgia
Jefferson	Jefferson	Wisconsin

Jefferson	Marion	Texas
Jefferson City	Cole	Missouri
Jeffersonville	Clark	Indiana
Jeffersonville	Twiggs	Georgia
Jena	La Salle	Louisiana
Jennings	Jefferson Davis	Louisiana
Jerome	Jerome	Idaho
Jersey City	Hudson	New Jersey
Jerseyville	Jersey	Illinois
Jessup	Wayne	Georgia
Jetmore	Hodgeman	Kansas
Jim Thorpe	Carbon	Pennsylvania
Johnson	Stanton	Kansas
Johnson City	Blanco	Texas
Johnstown	Fulton	New York
Joliet	Will	Illinois
Jonesboro	Clayton	Georgia
Jonesboro	Craighead	Arkansas
Jonesboro	Jackson	Louisiana
Jonesboro	Union	Illinois
Jonesborough	Washington	Tennessee
Jonesville	Lee	Virginia
Jordan	Garfield	Montana
Jourdanton	Atascosa	Texas
Julesburg	Sedgwick	Colorado
Junction	Kimble	Texas
Junction	Piute	Utah
Junction City	Geary	Kansas
Juneau	Dodge	Wisconsin
Juneau	Juneau	Alaska
Kadoka	Jackson	South Dakota
Kahoka	Clark	Missouri
Kalamazoo	Kalamazoo	Michigan
Kalispell	Flathead	Montana
Kalkaska	Kalkaska	Michigan
Kanab	Kane	Utah
Kankakee	Kankakee	Illinois
Kansas City	Jackson	Missouri
Kansas City	Wyandotte	Kansas
Karnes City	Karnes	Texas
Kaufman	Kaufman	Texas
Kearney	Buffalo	Nebraska
Keene	Cheshire	New Hampshire
Kelso	Cowlitz	Washington
Kemmerer	Lincoln	Wyoming
Kenansville	Duplin	North Carolina
Kennebec	Lyman	South Dakota
Kennett	Dunklin	Missouri
Kenosha	Kenosha	Wisconsin
Kentland	Newton	Indiana
Kenton	Hardin	Ohio
Keosauqua	Van Buren	Iowa
Kermit	Winkler	Texas
Kerrville	Kerr	Texas

Keshena	Menominee	Wisconsin
Ketchikan	Ketchikan Gateway	Alaska
Kewaunee	Kewaunee	Wisconsin
Keyser	Mineral	West Virginia
Keytesville	Chariton	Missouri
Key West	Monroe	Florida
Kimball	Kimball	Nebraska
King and Queen Court House	King and Queen	Virginia
Kingfisher	Kingfisher	Oklahoma
King George	King George	Virginia
Kingman	Kingman	Kansas
Kingman	Mohave	Arizona
King Salmon	Lake and Peninsula	Alaska
Kingston	Caldwell	Missouri
Kingston	Roane	Tennessee
Kingston	Ulster	New York
Kingstree	Williamsburg	South Carolina
Kingsville	Kleberg	Texas
King William	King William	Virginia
Kingwood	Preston	West Virginia
Kinsley	Edwards	Kansas
Kinston	Lenoir	North Carolina
Kiowa	Elbert	Colorado
Kirksville	Adair	Missouri
Kissimmee	Osceola	Florida
Kittanning	Armstrong	Pennsylvania
Klamath Falls	Klamath	Oregon
Knox	Starke	Indiana
Knoxville	Knox	Tennessee
Knoxville	Marion	Iowa
Kodiak	Kodiak Island	Alaska
Kokomo	Howard	Indiana
Kosciusko	Attala	Mississippi
Kotzebue	Northwest Arctic	Alaska
Kountze	Hardin	Texas
La Belle	Hendry	Florida
Lacon	Marshall	Illinois
Laconia	Belknap	New Hampshire
La Crosse	La Crosse	Wisconsin
La Crosse	Rush	Kansas
Ladysmith	Rusk	Wisconsin
Lafayette	Chambers	Alabama
Lafayette	Lafayette	Louisiana
Lafayette	Macon	Tennessee
Lafayette	Tippecanoe	Indiana
LaFayette	Walker	Georgia
La Grande	Union	Oregon
La Grange	Fayette	Texas
Lagrange	LaGrange	Indiana
La Grange	Oldham	Kentucky
La Grange	Troup	Georgia
La Junta	Otero	Colorado
Lake Andes	Charles Mix	South Dakota
Lake Butler	Union	Florida

Lake Charles	Calcasieu	Louisiana
Lake City	Columbia	Florida
Lake City	Hinsdale	Colorado
Lake City	Missaukee	Michigan
Lake George	Warren	New York
Lakeland	Lanier	Georgia
Lake Pleasant	Hamilton	New York
Lakeport	Lake	California
Lake Providence	East Carroll	Louisiana
Lakeview	Lake	Oregon
Lake Village	Chicot	Arkansas
Lakin	Kearny	Kansas
Lakota	Nelson	North Dakota
Lamar	Barton	Missouri
Lamar	Prowers	Colorado
Lamesa	Dawson	Texas
LaMoure	LaMoure	North Dakota
Lampasas	Lampasas	Texas
Lancaster	Coos	New Hampshire
Lancaster	Fairfield	Ohio
Lancaster	Garrard	Kentucky
Lancaster	Grant	Wisconsin
Lancaster	Lancaster	Pennsylvania
Lancaster	Lancaster	South Carolina
Lancaster	Lancaster	Virginia
Lancaster	Schuyler	Missouri
Lander	Fremont	Wyoming
Langdon	Cavalier	North Dakota
L'Anse	Baraga	Michigan
Lapeer	Lapeer	Michigan
Laplace	Saint John the Baptist	Louisiana
La Plata	Charles	Maryland
La Porte	LaPorte	Indiana
Laporte	Sullivan	Pennsylvania
Laramie	Albany	Wyoming
Laredo	Webb	Texas
Larned	Pawnee	Kansas
Las Animas	Bent	Colorado
Las Cruces	Dona Ana	New Mexico
Las Vegas	Clark	Nevada
Las Vegas	San Miguel	New Mexico
Laurel	Jones	Mississippi
Laurens	Laurens	South Carolina
Laurinburg	Scotland	North Carolina
Lawrence	Douglas	Kansas
Lawrenceburg	Anderson	Kentucky
Lawrenceburg	Dearborn	Indiana
Lawrenceburg	Lawrence	Tennessee
Lawrenceville	Brunswick	Virginia
Lawrenceville	Gwinnett	Georgia
Lawrenceville	Lawrence	Illinois
Lawton	Comanche	Oklahoma
Leadville	Lake	Colorado
Leakey	Real	Texas
Leaksville	Greene	Mississippi

Leavenworth	Leavenworth	Kansas
Lebanon	Boone	Indiana
Lebanon	Laclede	Missouri
Lebanon	Lebanon	Pennsylvania
Lebanon	Marion	Kentucky
Lebanon	Russell	Virginia
Lebanon	Warren	Ohio
Lebanon	Wilson	Tennessee
Le Center	Le Seuer	Minnesota
Leesburg	Lee	Georgia
Leesburg	Loudoun	Virginia
Leesville	Vernon	Louisiana
Leitchfield	Grayson	Kentucky
Leland	Leelanau	Michigan
Le Mars	Plymouth	Iowa
Lenoir	Caldwell	North Carolina
Leola	McPherson	South Dakota
Leon	Decatur	Iowa
Leonardtown	Saint Mary's	Maryland
Leoti	Wichita	Kansas
Levelland	Hockley	Texas
Lewisburg	Greenbrier	West Virginia
Lewisburg	Marshall	Tennessee
Lewisburg	Union	Pennsylvania
Lewiston	Nez Perce	Idaho
Lewistown	Fergus	Montana
Lewistown	Fulton	Illinois
Lewistown	Mifflin	Pennsylvania
Lewisville	Lafayette	Arkansas
Lexington	Davidson	North Carolina
Lexington	Dawson	Nebraska
Lexington	Fayette	Kentucky
Lexington	Henderson	Tennessee
Lexington	Holmes	Mississippi
Lexington	Lafeyette	Missouri
Lexington	Lexington	South Carolina
Lexington	Oglethorpe	Georgia
Lexington	Rockbridge	Virginia
Libby	Lincoln	Montana
Liberal	Seward	Kansas
Liberty	Amite	Mississippi
Liberty	Casey	Kentucky
Liberty	Clay	Missouri
Liberty	Liberty	Texas
Liberty	Union	Indiana
Lihue	Kauai	Hawaii
Lillington	Harnett	North Carolina
Lima	Allen	Ohio
Lincoln	Lancaster	Nebraska
Lincoln	Lincoln	Kansas
Lincoln	Logan	Illinois
Lincolnton	Lincoln	Georgia
Lincolnton	Lincoln	North Carolina
Linden	Cass	Texas
Linden	Marengo	Alabama

Linden	Perry	Tennessee
Linn	Osage	Missouri
Linneus	Linn	Missouri
Linton	Emmons	North Dakota
Lipscomb	Lipscomb	Texas
Lisbon	Columbiana	Ohio
Lisbon	Ransom	North Dakota
Litchfield	Litchfield	Connecticut
Litchfield	Meeker	Minnesota
Little Falls	Morrison	Minnesota
Littlefield	Lamb	Texas
Little Rock	Pulaski	Arkansas
Littleton	Arapahoe	Colorado
Little Valley	Cattaraugus	New York
Live Oak	Suwanee	Florida
Livingston	Livingston	Louisiana
Livingston	Overton	Tennessee
Livingston	Park	Montana
Livingston	Polk	Texas
Livingston	Sumter	Alabama
Llano	Llano	Texas
Loa	Wayne	Utah
Lockhart	Caldwell	Texas
Lock Haven	Clinton	Pennsylvania
Lockport	Niagara	New York
Logan	Cache	Utah
Logan	Harrison	Iowa
Logan	Hocking	Ohio
Logan	Logan	West Virginia
Logansport	Cass	Indiana
London	Laurel	Kentucky
London	Madison	Ohio
Long Prairie	Todd	Minnesota
Longview	Gregg	Texas
Lonoke	Lonoke	Arkansas
Lordsburg	Hidalgo	New Mexico
Los Alamos	Los Alamos	New Mexico
Los Angeles	Los Angeles	California
Los Lunas	Valencia	New Mexico
Loudon	Loudon	Tennessee
Louisa	Lawrence	Kentucky
Louisa	Louisa	Virginia
Louisburg	Franklin	North Carolina
Louisville	Clay	Illinois
Louisville	Jefferson	Georgia
Louisville	Jefferson	Kentucky
Louisville	Winston	Mississippi
Loup City	Sherman	Nebraska
Lovelock	Pershing	Nevada
Lovingston	Nelson	Virginia
Lovington	Lea	New Mexico
Lowville	Lewis	New York
Lubbock	Lubbock	Texas
Lucedale	George	Mississippi
Ludington	Mason	Michigan

Ludowici	Long	Georgia
Lufkin	Angelina	Texas
Lumberton	Robeson	North Carolina
Lumpkin	Stewart	Georgia
Lunenburg	Lunenburg	Virginia
Luray	Page	Virginia
Lusk	Niobrara	Wyoming
Luverne	Crenshaw	Alabama
Luverne	Rock	Minnesota
Lynchburg	Moore	Tennessee
Lyndon	Osage	Kansas
Lyons	Rice	Kansas
Lyons	Toombs	Georgia
Lyons	Wayne	New York
Macclenny	Baker	Florida
Machias	Washington	Maine
Macomb	McDonough	Illinois
Macon	Bibb	Georgia
Macon	Macon	Missouri
Macon	Noxubee	Mississippi
Madera	Madera	California
Madill	Marshall	Oklahoma
Madison	Boone	West Virginia
Madison	Dane	Wisconsin
Madison	Jefferson	Indiana
Madison	Lac qui Parle	Minnesota
Madison	Lake	South Dakota
Madison	Madison	Florida
Madison	Madison	Nebraska
Madison	Madison	Virginia
Madison	Morgan	Georgia
Madisonville	Hopkins	Kentucky
Madisonville	Madison	Texas
Madisonville	Monroe	Tennessee
Madras	Jefferson	Oregon
Magnolia	Columbia	Arkansas
Magnolia	Pike	Mississippi
Mahnomen	Mahnomen	Minnesota
Malad City	Oneida	Idaho
Malone	Franklin	New York
Malta	Phillips	Montana
Malvern	Hot Spring	Arkansas
Manassas	Prince William	Virginia
Manchester	Clay	Kentucky
Manchester	Coffee	Tennessee
Manchester	Delaware	Iowa
Mandan	Morton	North Dakota
Mangum	Greer	Oklahoma
Manhattan	Riley	Kansas
Manila	Daggett	Utah
Manistee	Manistee	Michigan
Manistique	Schoolcraft	Michigan
Manitowoc	Manitowoc	Wisconsin
Mankato	Blue Earth	Minnesota

Mankato	Jewell	Kansas
Manning	Clarendon	South Carolina
Manning	Dunn	North Dakota
Mansfield	De Soto	Louisiana
Mansfield	Richland	Ohio
Manteo	Dare	North Carolina
Manti	Sanpete	Utah
Mantorville	Dodge	Minnesota
Many	Sabine	Louisiana
Maquoketa	Jackson	Iowa
Marble Hill	Bollinger	Missouri
Marengo	Iowa	Iowa
Marfa	Presidio	Texas
Marianna	Jackson	Florida
Marianna	Lee	Arkansas
Marietta	Cobb	Georgia
Marietta	Love	Oklahoma
Marietta	Washington	Ohio
Marinette	Marinette	Wisconsin
Marion	Crittenden	Arkansas
Marion	Crittenden	Kentucky
Marion	Grant	Indiana
Marion	Marion	Kansas
Marion	Marion	Ohio
Marion	Marion	South Carolina
Marion	McDowell	North Carolina
Marion	Perry	Alabama
Marion	Smyth	Virginia
Marion	Williamson	Illinois
Mariposa	Mariposa	California
Markleeville	Alpine	California
Marks	Quitman	Mississippi
Marksville	Avoyelles	Louisiana
Marlin	Falls	Texas
Marlinton	Pocahontas	West Virginia
Marquette	Marquette	Michigan
Marshall	Calhoun	Michigan
Marshall	Clark	Illinois
Marshall	Harrison	Texas
Marshall	Lyon	Minnesota
Marshall	Madison	North Carolina
Marshall	Saline	Missouri
Marshall	Searcy	Arkansas
Marshalltown	Marshall	Iowa
Marshfield	Webster	Missouri
Martin	Bennett	South Dakota
Martinez	Contra Costa	California
Martinsburg	Berkeley	West Virginia
Martinsville	Henry	Virginia
Martinsville	Morgan	Indiana
Marysville	Marshall	Kansas
Marysville	Union	Ohio
Marysville	Yuba	California
Maryville	Blount	Tennessee
Maryville	Nodaway	Missouri

Mason	Ingham	Michigan
Mason	Mason	Texas
Mason City	Cerro Gordo	Iowa
Matador	Motley	Texas
Mathews	Mathews	Virginia
Mauston	Juneau	Wisconsin
Mayersville	Issaquena	Mississippi
Mayfield	Graves	Kentucky
Maynardville	Union	Tennessee
Mayo	Lafayette	Florida
Mays Landing	Atlantic	New Jersey
Maysville	DeKalb	Missouri
Maysville	Mason	Kentucky
Mayville	Chautauqua	New York
McAlester	Pittsburg	Oklahoma
McArthur	Vinton	Ohio
McClusky	Sheridan	North Dakota
McConnellsburg	Fulton	Pennsylvania
McConnelsville	Morgan	Ohio
McCook	Red Willow	Nebraska
McCormick	McCormick	South Carolina
McDonough	Henry	Georgia
McIntosh	Corson	South Dakota
McKee	Jackson	Kentucky
McKinney	Collin	Texas
McLeansboro	Hamilton	Illinois
McMinnville	Warren	Tennessee
McMinnville	Yamhill	Oregon
McPherson	McPherson	Kansas
McRae	Telfair	Georgia
Meade	Meade	Kansas
Meadville	Crawford	Pennsylvania
Meadville	Franklin	Mississippi
Medford	Grant	Oklahoma
Medford	Jackson	Oregon
Medford	Taylor	Wisconsin
Media	Delaware	Pennsylvania
Medicine Lodge	Barber	Kansas
Medina	Medina	Ohio
Medora	Billings	North Dakota
Meeker	Rio Blanco	Colorado
Melbourne	Izard	Arkansas
Memphis	Hall	Texas
Memphis	Scotland	Missouri
Memphis	Shelby	Tennessee
Mena	Polk	Arkansas
Menard	Menard	Texas
Mendenhall	Simpson	Mississippi
Menominee	Dunn	Wisconsin
Menominee	Menominee	Michigan
Mentone	Loving	Texas
Merced	Merced	California
Mercer	Mercer	Pennsylvania
Meridian	Bosque	Texas
Meridian	Lauderdale	Mississippi

Merrill	Lincoln	Wisconsin
Mertzon	Irion	Texas
Metropolis	Massac	Illinois
Metter	Candler	Georgia
Mexico	Audrain	Missouri
Miami	Miami-Dade	Florida
Miami	Ottawa	Oklahoma
Miami	Roberts	Texas
Middlebourne	Tyler	West Virginia
Middleburg	Snyder	Pennsylvania
Middlebury	Addison	Vermont
Middletown	Middlesex	Connecticut
Midland	Midland	Michigan
Midland	Midland	Texas
Mifflintown	Juniata	Pennsylvania
Milaca	Mille Lacs	Minnesota
Milan	Sullivan	Missouri
Milbank	Grant	South Dakota
Miles City	Custer	Montana
Milford	Pike	Pennsylvania
Milledgeville	Baldwin	Georgia
Millen	Jenkins	Georgia
Miller	Hand	South Dakota
Millersburg	Holmes	Ohio
Milton	Santa Rosa	Florida
Milwaukee	Milwaukee	Wisconsin
Minden	Douglas	Nevada
Minden	Kearney	Nebraska
Minden	Webster	Louisiana
Mineola	Nassau	New York
Minneapolis	Hennepin	Minnesota
Minneapolis	Ottawa	Kansas
Minnewaukan	Benson	North Dakota
Minot	Ward	North Dakota
Mio	Oscoda	Michigan
Missoula	Missoula	Montana
Mitchell	Davison	South Dakota
Moab	Grand	Utah
Mobile	Mobile	Alabama
Mocksville	Davie	North Carolina
Modesto	Stanislaus	California
Mohall	Renville	North Dakota
Monahans	Ward	Texas
Moncks Corner	Berkeley	South Carolina
Monmouth	Warren	Illinois
Monroe	Green	Wisconsin
Monroe	Monroe	Michigan
Monroe	Ouachita	Louisiana
Monroe	Union	North Carolina
Monroe	Walton	Georgia
Monroeville	Monroe	Alabama
Montague	Montague	Texas
Montello	Marquette	Wisconsin
Monterey	Highland	Virginia
Montesano	Grays Harbor	Washington

Montevideo	Chippewa	Minnesota
Montezuma	Poweshiek	Iowa
Montgomery	Montgomery	Alabama
Montgomery City	Montgomery	Missouri
Monticello	Drew	Arkansas
Monticello	Jasper	Georgia
Monticello	Jefferson	Florida
Monticello	Lawrence	Mississippi
Monticello	Lewis	Missouri
Monticello	Piatt	Illinois
Monticello	San Juan	Utah
Monticello	Sullivan	New York
Monticello	Wayne	Kentucky
Monticello	White	Indiana
Montpelier	Washington	Vermont
Montrose	Montrose	Colorado
Montrose	Susquehanna	Pennsylvania
Montross	Westmoreland	Virginia
Moorefield	Hardy	West Virginia
Moore Haven	Glades	Florida
Moorhead	Clay	Minnesota
Mora	Kanabec	Minnesota
Mora	Mora	New Mexico
Morehead	Rowan	Kentucky
Morgan	Calhoun	Georgia
Morgan	Morgan	Utah
Morganfield	Union	Kentucky
Morganton	Burke	North Carolina
Morgantown	Butler	Kentucky
Morgantown	Monongalia	West Virginia
Moro	Sherman	Oregon
Morrilton	Conway	Arkansas
Morris	Grundy	Illinois
Morris	Stevens	Minnesota
Morrison	Whiteside	Illinois
Morristown	Hamblen	Tennessee
Morristown	Morris	New Jersey
Morton	Cochran	Texas
Moscow	Latah	Idaho
Mosquero	Harding	New Mexico
Mott	Hettinger	North Dakota
Moulton	Lawrence	Alabama
Moultrie	Colquitt	Georgia
Mound City	Campbell	South Dakota
Mound City	Linn	Kansas
Mound City	Pulaski	Illinois
Moundsville	Marshall	West Virginia
Mountain City	Johnson	Tennessee
Mountain Home	Baxter	Arkansas
Mountain Home	Elmore	Idaho
Mountain View	Stone	Arkansas
Mount Ayr	Ringgold	Iowa
Mount Carmel	Wabash	Illinois
Mount Carroll	Carroll	Illinois
Mount Clemens	Macomb	Michigan

Mount Gilead	Morrow	Ohio
Mount Holly	Burlington	New Jersey
Mount Ida	Montgomery	Arkansas
Mount Olivet	Robertson	Kentucky
Mount Pleasant	Henry	Iowa
Mount Pleasant	Isabella	Michigan
Mount Pleasant	Titus	Texas
Mount Sterling	Brown	Illinois
Mount Sterling	Montgomery	Kentucky
Mount Vernon	Franklin	Texas
Mount Vernon	Jefferson	Illinois
Mount Vernon	Knox	Ohio
Mount Vernon	Lawrence	Missouri
Mount Vernon	Montgomery	Georgia
Mount Vernon	Posey	Indiana
Mount Vernon	Rockcastle	Kentucky
Mount Vernon	Skagit	Washington
Muleshoe	Bailey	Texas
Mullen	Hooker	Nebraska
Muncie	Delaware	Indiana
Munfordville	Hart	Kentucky
Munising	Alger	Michigan
Murdo	Jones	South Dakota
Murfreesboro	Pike	Arkansas
Murfreesboro	Rutherford	Tennessee
Murphy	Cherokee	North Carolina
Murphy	Owyhee	Idaho
Murphysboro	Jackson	Illinois
Murray	Calloway	Kentucky
Muscatine	Muscatine	Iowa
Muskegon	Muskegon	Michigan
Muskogee	Muskogee	Oklahoma
Nacogdoshes	Nacogdoches	Texas
Nahunta	Brantley	Georgia
Naknek	Bristol Bay	Alaska
Nantucket	Nantucket	Massachusetts
Napa	Napa	California
Naples	Collier	Florida
Napoleon	Henry	Ohio
Napoleon	Logan	North Dakota
Napoleonville	Assumption	Louisiana
Nashua	Hillsborough	New Hampshire
Nashville	Berrien	Georgia
Nashville	Brown	Indiana
Nashville	Davidson	Tennessee
Nashville	Howard	Arkansas
Nashville	Nash	North Carolina
Nashville	Washington	Illinois
Natchez	Adams	Mississippi
Natchitoches	Natchitoches	Louisiana
Nebraska City	Otoe	Nebraska
Neillsville	Clark	Wisconsin
Neligh	Antelope	Nebraska
Nelson	Nuckolls	Nebraska

Neosho	Newton	Missouri
Nephi	Juab	Utah
Ness City	Ness	Kansas
Nevada	Story	Iowa
Nevada	Vernon	Missouri
Nevada City	Nevada	California
New Albany	Floyd	Indiana
New Albany	Union	Mississippi
Newark	Essex	New Jersey
Newark	Licking	Ohio
New Augusta	Perry	Mississippi
New Bern	Craven	North Carolina
Newberry	Luce	Michigan
Newberry	Newberry	South Carolina
New Bloomfield	Perry	Pennsylvania
New Boston	Bowie	Texas
New Braunfels	Comal	Texas
New Brockton	Coffee	Alabama
New Brunswick	Middlesex	New Jersey
New Castle	Craig	Virginia
New Castle	Henry	Indiana
New Castle	Henry	Kentucky
New Castle	Lawrence	Pennsylvania
Newcastle	Weston	Wyoming
New City	Rockland	New York
New Cumberland	Hancock	West Virginia
Newfane	Windham	Vermont
New Hampton	Chickasaw	Iowa
New Haven	New Haven	Connecticut
New Iberia	Iberia	Louisiana
New Kent	New Kent	Virginia
Newkirk	Kay	Oklahoma
Newland	Avery	North Carolina
New Lexington	Perry	Ohio
New London	New London	Connecticut
New London	Ralls	Missouri
New Madrid	New Madrid	Missouri
Newman	Coweta	Georgia
New Martinsville	Wetzel	West Virginia
New Orleans	Orleans	Louisiana
New Philadelphia	Tuscarawas	Ohio
Newport	Campbell	Kentucky
Newport	Cocke	Tennessee
Newport	Jackson	Arkansas
Newport	Lincoln	Oregon
Newport	Newport	Rhode Island
Newport	Orleans	Vermont
Newport	Pend Oreille	Washington
Newport	Sullivan	New Hampshire
Newport	Vermillion	Indiana
New Roads	Pointe Coupee	Louisiana
New Rockford	Eddy	North Dakota
Newton	Baker	Georgia
Newton	Catawba	North Carolina
Newton	Harvey	Kansas

Newton	Jasper	Illinois
Newton	Jasper	Iowa
Newton	Newton	Texas
Newton	Sussex	New Jersey
New Ulm	Brown	Minnesota
New York	New York	New York
Nezperce	Lewis	Idaho
Nicholasville	Jessamine	Kentucky
Noblesville	Hamilton	Indiana
Nogales	Santa Cruz	Arizona
Norman	Cleveland	Oklahoma
Norristown	Montgomery	Pennsylvania
Northampton	Hampshire	Massachusetts
North Haverhill	Grafton	New Hampshire
North Hero	Grand Isle	Vermont
North Platte	Lincoln	Nebraska
Northwood	Worth	Iowa
Norton	Norton	Kansas
Norwalk	Huron	Ohio
Norwich	Chenango	New York
Nottoway	Nottoway	Virginia
Nowata	Nowata	Oklahoma
Oak Grove	West Carroll	Louisiana
Oakland	Alameda	California
Oakland	Garrett	Maryland
Oakley	Logan	Kansas
Oberlin	Allen	Louisiana
Oberlin	Decatur	Kansas
Ocala	Marion	Florida
Ocilla	Irwin	Georgia
Oconto	Oconto	Wisconsin
Odessa	Ector	Texas
Ogallala	Keith	Nebraska
Ogden	Weber	Utah
Oglethorpe	Macon	Georgia
Okanogan	Okanogan	Washington
Okeechobee	Okeechobee	Florida
Okemah	Okfuskee	Oklahoma
Oklahoma City	Oklahoma	Oklahoma
Okmulgee	Okmulgee	Oklahoma
Olathe	Johnson	Kansas
Olivet	Hutchinson	South Dakota
Olivia	Renville	Minnesota
Olney	Richland	Illinois
Olympia	Thurston	Washington
Omaha	Douglas	Nebraska
Onawa	Monona	Iowa
O'Neill	Holt	Nebraska
Oneonta	Blount	Alabama
Onida	Sully	South Dakota
Ontonagon	Ontonagon	Michigan
Opelika	Lee	Alabama
Opelousas	Saint Landry	Louisiana
Oquawka	Henderson	Illinois

Orange	Orange	Texas
Orange	Orange	Virginia
Orangeburg	Orangeburg	South Carolina
Orange City	Sioux	Iowa
Ord	Valley	Nebraska
Ordway	Crowley	Colorado
Oregon	Holt	Missouri
Oregon	Ogle	Illinois
Oregon City	Clackamas	Oregon
Orlando	Orange	Florida
Orofino	Clearwater	Idaho
Oroville	Butte	California
Ortonville	Big Stone	Minnesota
Osage	Mitchell	Iowa
Osborne	Osborne	Kansas
Osceola	Clarke	Iowa
Osceola	Polk	Nebraska
Osceola	Saint Clair	Missouri
Oshkosh	Garden	Nebraska
Oshkosh	Winnebago	Wisconsin
Oskaloosa	Jefferson	Kansas
Oskaloosa	Mahaska	Iowa
Ossipee	Carroll	New Hampshire
Oswego	Labette	Kansas
Oswego	Oswego	New York
Ottawa	Franklin	Kansas
Ottawa	La Salle	Illinois
Ottawa	Putnam	Ohio
Ottumwa	Wapello	Iowa
Ouray	Ouray	Colorado
Owatonna	Steele	Minnesota
Owego	Tioga	New York
Owensboro	Daviess	Kentucky
Owenton	Owen	Kentucky
Owingsville	Bath	Kentucky
Oxford	Granville	North Carolina
Oxford	Lafayette	Mississippi
Ozark	Christian	Missouri
Ozark	Dale	Alabama
Ozark	Franklin	Arkansas
Ozona	Crockett	Texas
Paducah	Cottle	Texas
Paducah	McCracken	Kentucky
Pagosa Springs	Archuleta	Colorado
Painesville	Lake	Ohio
Paint Rock	Concho	Texas
Paintsville	Johnson	Kentucky
Palatka	Putnam	Florida
Palestine	Anderson	Texas
Palmer	Matanuska-Susitna	Alaska
Palmyra	Fluvanna	Virginia
Palmyra	Marion	Missouri
Palo Pinto	Palo Pinto	Texas
Pampa	Gray	Texas

Panama City	Bay	Florida
Panguitch	Garfield	Utah
Panhandle	Carson	Texas
Paola	Miami	Kansas
Paoli	Orange	Indiana
Papillion	Sarpy	Nebraska
Paragould	Greene	Arkansas
Paris	Bear Lake	Idaho
Paris	Bourbon	Kentucky
Paris	Edgar	Illinois
Paris	Henry	Tennessee
Paris	Lamar	Texas
Paris	Logan	Arkansas
Paris	Monroe	Missouri
Parker	La Paz	Arizona
Parker	Turner	South Dakota
Parkersburg	Wood	West Virginia
Park Rapids	Hubbard	Minnesota
Parowan	Iron	Utah
Parsons	Tucker	West Virginia
Pascagoula	Jackson	Mississippi
Pasco	Franklin	Washington
Paterson	Passaic	New Jersey
Paulding	Paulding	Ohio
Pauls Valley	Garvin	Oklahoma
Pawhuska	Osage	Oklahoma
Pawnee	Pawnee	Oklahoma
Pawnee City	Pawnee	Nebraska
Paw Paw	Van Buren	Michigan
Paxton	Ford	Illinois
Payette	Payette	Idaho
Pearisburg	Giles	Virginia
Pearsall	Frio	Texas
Pearson	Atkinson	Georgia
Pecos	Reeves	Texas
Pekin	Tazewell	Illinois
Pembroke	Bryan	Georgia
Pender	Thurston	Nebraska
Pendleton	Umatilla	Oregon
Penn Yan	Yates	New York
Pensacola	Escambia	Florida
Peoria	Peoria	Illinois
Perry	Houston	Georgia
Perry	Noble	Oklahoma
Perry	Taylor	Florida
Perryton	Ochiltree	Texas
Perryville	Perry	Arkansas
Perryville	Perry	Missouri
Peru	Miami	Indiana
Petersburg	Grant	West Virginia
Petersburg	Menard	Illinois
Petersburg	Pike	Indiana
Petoskey	Emmet	Michigan
Phenix City	Russell	Alabama
Philadelphia	Neshoba	Mississippi

Philadelphia	Philadelphia	Pennsylvania
Philippi	Barbour	West Virginia
Phillip	Haakon	South Dakota
Phillips	Price	Wisconsin
Phillipsburg	Granite	Montana
Phillipsburg	Phillips	Kansas
Phoenix	Maricopa	Arizona
Pickens	Pickens	South Carolina
Pierce	Pierce	Nebraska
Pierre	Hughes	South Dakota
Piggott	Clay	Arkansas
Pikeville	Bledsoe	Tennessee
Pikeville	Pike	Kentucky
Pinckneyville	Perry	Illinois
Pine Bluff	Jefferson	Arkansas
Pine City	Pine	Minnesota
Pinedale	Sublette	Wyoming
Pineville	Bell	Kentucky
Pineville	McDonald	Missouri
Pineville	Wyoming	West Virginia
Pioche	Lincoln	Nevada
Pipestone	Pipestone	Minnesota
Pittsboro	Calhoun	Mississippi
Pittsboro	Chatham	North Carolina
Pittsburg	Camp	Texas
Pittsburgh	Allegheny	Pennsylvania
Pittsfield	Berkshire	Massachusetts
Pittsfield	Pike	Illinois
Placerville	El Dorado	California
Plaine	Yoakum	Texas
Plainview	Hale	Texas
Plankinton	Aurora	South Dakota
Plaquemine	Iberville	Louisiana
Platte City	Platte	Missouri
Plattsburg	Clinton	Missouri
Plattsburgh	Clinton	New York
Plattsmouth	Cass	Nebraska
Plentywood	Sheridan	Montana
Plymouth	Marshall	Indiana
Plymouth	Plymouth	Massachusetts
Plymouth	Washington	North Carolina
Pocahontas	Pocahontas	Iowa
Pocahontas	Randolph	Arkansas
Pocatello	Bannock	Idaho
Pointe a la Hache	Plaquemines	Louisiana
Point Pleasant	Mason	West Virginia
Polson	Lake	Montana
Pomeroy	Garfield	Washington
Pomeroy	Meigs	Ohio
Ponca	Dixon	Nebraska
Pontiac	Livingston	Illinois
Pontiac	Oakland	Michigan
Pontotoc	Pontotoc	Mississippi
Poplar Bluff	Butler	Missouri

Poplarville	Pearl River	Mississippi
Portage	Columbia	Wisconsin
Portales	Roosevelt	New Mexico
Port Allen	West Baton Rouge	Louisiana
Port Angeles	Clallam	Washington
Port Charlotte	Charlotte	Florida
Port Clinton	Ottawa	Ohio
Port Gibson	Claiborne	Mississippi
Port Huron	Saint Clair	Michigan
Portland	Cumberland	Maine
Portland	Jay	Indiana
Portland	Multnomah	Oregon
Port Lavaca	Calhoun	Texas
Port Orchard	Kitsap	Washington
Port Saint Joe	Gulf	Florida
Portsmouth	Scioto	Ohio
Port Townsend	Jefferson	Washington
Port Washington	Ozaukee	Wisconsin
Post	Garza	Texas
Poteau	Le Flore	Oklahoma
Potosi	Washington	Missouri
Pottsville	Schuylkill	Pennsylvania
Poughkeepsie	Dutchess	New York
Powhatan	Powhatan	Virginia
Prairie du Chien	Crawford	Wisconsin
Pratt	Pratt	Kansas
Prattville	Autauga	Alabama
Prentiss	Jefferson Davis	Mississippi
Prescott	Nevada	Arkansas
Prescott	Yavapai	Arizona
Preston	Fillmore	Minnesota
Preston	Franklin	Idaho
Preston	Webster	Georgia
Prestonburg	Floyd	Kentucky
Price	Carbon	Utah
Primghar	O'Brien	Iowa
Prince Frederick	Calvert	Maryland
Prince George	Prince George	Virginia
Princess Anne	Somerset	Maryland
Princeton	Bureau	Illinois
Princeton	Caldwell	Kentucky
Princeton	Gibson	Indiana
Princeton	Mercer	Missouri
Princeton	Mercer	West Virginia
Prineville	Crook	Oregon
Prosser	Benton	Washington
Providence	Providence	Rhode Island
Provo	Utah	Utah
Pryor	Mayes	Oklahoma
Pueblo	Pueblo	Colorado
Pulaski	Giles	Tennessee
Pulaski	Pulaski	Virginia
Purcell	McClain	Oklahoma
Purvis	Lamar	Mississippi

Quanah	Hardeman	Texas
Quincy	Adams	Illinois
Quincy	Gadsden	Florida
Quincy	Plumas	California
Quitman	Brooks	Georgia
Quitman	Clarke	Mississippi
Quitman	Wood	Texas
Racine	Racine	Wisconsin
Raeford	Hoke	North Carolina
Raleigh	Smith	Mississippi
Raleigh	Wake	North Carolina
Randolph	Rich	Utah
Rankin	Upton	Texas
Rapid City	Pennington	South Dakota
Raton	Colfax	New Mexico
Ravenna	Portage	Ohio
Rawlins	Carbon	Wyoming
Raymondville	Willacy	Texas
Rayville	Richland	Louisiana
Reading	Berks	Pennsylvania
Red Bluff	Tehama	California
Red Cloud	Webster	Nebraska
Redding	Shasta	California
Redfield	Spink	South Dakota
Red Lake Falls	Red Lake	Minnesota
Red Lodge	Carbon	Montana
Red Oak	Montgomery	Iowa
Red Wing	Goodhue	Minnesota
Redwood City	San Mateo	California
Redwood Falls	Redwood	Minnesota
Reed City	Osceola	Michigan
Refugio	Refugio	Texas
Reidsville	Tattnall	Georgia
Reno	Washoe	Nevada
Rensselaer	Jasper	Indiana
Republic	Ferry	Washington
Reserve	Catron	New Mexico
Rexburg	Madison	Idaho
Rhinelander	Oneida	Wisconsin
Richfield	Sevier	Utah
Richland Center	Richland	Wisconsin
Richmond	Fort Bend	Texas
Richmond	Henrico	Virginia
Richmond	Madison	Kentucky
Richmond	Ray	Missouri
Richmond	Wayne	Indiana
Ridgeland	Jasper	South Carolina
Ridgway	Elk	Pennsylvania
Rigby	Jefferson	Idaho
Ringgold	Catoosa	Georgia
Rio Grande City	Starr	Texas
Ripley	Jackson	West Virginia
Ripley	Lauderdale	Tennessee
Ripley	Tippah	Mississippi

Rising Sun	Ohio	Indiana
Rison	Cleveland	Arkansas
Ritzville	Adams	Washington
Riverhead	Suffolk	New York
Riverside	Riverside	California
Robbinsville	Graham	North Carolina
Roberta	Crawford	Georgia
Robert Lee	Coke	Texas
Robinson	Crawford	Illinois
Roby	Fisher	Texas
Rochester	Fulton	Indiana
Rochester	Monroe	New York
Rochester	Olmsted	Minnesota
Rockford	Coosa	Alabama
Rockford	Winnebago	Illinois
Rockingham	Richmond	North Carolina
Rock Island	Rock Island	Illinois
Rockland	Knox	Maine
Rockport	Aransas	Texas
Rock Port	Atchison	Missouri
Rockport	Spencer	Indiana
Rock Rapids	Lyon	Iowa
Rocksprings	Edwards	Texas
Rockville	Montgomery	Maryland
Rockville	Parke	Indiana
Rockville	Tolland	Connecticut
Rockwall	Rockwall	Texas
Rockwell City	Calhoun	Iowa
Rocky Mount	Franklin	Virginia
Rogers City	Presque Isle	Michigan
Rogersville	Hawkins	Tennessee
Rolla	Phelps	Missouri
Rolla	Rolette	North Dakota
Rolling Fork	Sharkey	Mississippi
Rome	Floyd	Georgia
Romney	Hampshire	West Virginia
Roscommon	Roscommon	Michigan
Roseau	Roseau	Minnesota
Roseburg	Douglas	Oregon
Roswell	Chaves	New Mexico
Roundup	Musselshell	Montana
Roxboro	Person	North Carolina
Rugby	Pierce	North Dakota
Rupert	Minidoka	Idaho
Rushville	Rush	Indiana
Rushville	Schuyler	Illinois
Rushville	Sheridan	Nebraska
Rusk	Cherokee	Texas
Russell	Russell	Kansas
Russellville	Franklin	Alabama
Russellville	Logan	Kentucky
Russellville	Pope	Arkansas
Rustburg	Campbell	Virginia
Ruston	Lincoln	Louisiana
Rutherfordton	Rutherford	North Carolina

Rutland	Rutland	Vermont
Rutledge	Grainger	Tennessee
Ryegate	Golden Valley	Montana
Sac City	Sac	Iowa
Sacramento	Sacramento	California
Safford	Graham	Arizona
Saginaw	Saginaw	Michigan
Saguache	Saguache	Colorado
Saint Albans	Franklin	Vermont
Saint Anthony	Fremont	Idaho
Saint Augustine	Saint Johns	Florida
Saint Charles	Saint Charles	Missouri
Saint Clairsville	Belmont	Ohio
Saint Cloud	Stearns	Minnesota
Sainte Genevieve	Sainte Genevieve	Missouri
Saint Francis	Cheyenne	Kansas
Saint Francisville	West Feliciana	Louisiana
Saint George	Dorchester	South Carolina
Saint George	Richmond	New York
Saint George	Washington	Utah
Saint Helens	Columbia	Oregon
Saint Ignance	Mackinac	Michigan
Saint James	Watonwan	Minnesota
Saint John	Stafford	Kansas
Saint Johns	Apache	Arizona
Saint Johns	Clinton	Michigan
Saint Johnsbury	Caledonia	Vermont
Saint Joseph	Berrien	Michigan
Saint Joseph	Buchanan	Missouri
Saint Joseph	Tensas	Louisiana
Saint Maries	Benewah	Idaho
Saint Martinville	Saint Martin	Louisiana
Saint Marys	Pleasants	West Virginia
Saint Matthews	Calhoun	South Carolina
Saint Paul	Howard	Nebraska
Saint Paul	Ramsey	Minnesota
Saint Peter	Nicollet	Minnesota
Salem	Dent	Missouri
Salem	Essex	Massachusetts
Salem	Fulton	Arkansas
Salem	Marion	Illinois
Salem	Marion	Oregon
Salem	McCook	South Dakota
Salem	Roanoke	Virginia
Salem	Salem	New Jersey
Salem	Washington	Indiana
Salida	Chaffee	Colorado
Salina	Saline	Kansas
Salinas	Monterey	California
Salisbury	Rowan	North Carolina
Salisbury	Wicomico	Maryland
Sallisaw	Sequoyah	Oklahoma
Salmon	Lemhi	Idaho
Salt Lake City	Salt Lake	Utah

Saluda	Middlesex	Virginia
Saluda	Saluda	South Carolina
Salyersville	Magoffin	Kentucky
San Andreas	Calaveras	California
San Angelo	Tom Green	Texas
San Antonio	Bexar	Texas
San Augustine	San Augustine	Texas
San Bernardino	San Bernardino	California
Sanderson	Terrell	Texas
Sandersville	Washington	Georgia
San Diego	Duval	Texas
San Diego	San Diego	California
Sand Point	Aleutians East	Alaska
Sandpoint	Bonner	Idaho
Sandusky	Erie	Ohio
Sandusky	Sanilac	Michigan
Sandy Hook	Elliott	Kentucky
Sanford	Lee	North Carolina
Sanford	Seminole	Florida
San Francisco	San Francisco	California
San Jose	Santa Clara	California
San Luis	Costilla	Colorado
San Luis Obispo	San Luis Obispo	California
San Marcos	Hays	Texas
San Rafael	Marin	California
San Saba	San Saba	Texas
Santa Ana	Orange	California
Santa Barbara	Santa Barbara	California
Santa Cruz	Santa Cruz	California
Santa Fe	Santa Fe	New Mexico
Santa Rosa	Guadalupe	New Mexico
Santa Rosa	Sonoma	California
Sapulpa	Creek	Oklahoma
Sarasota	Sarasota	Florida
Sarita	Kenedy	Texas
Sault Sainte Marie	Chippewa	Michigan
Savannah	Andrew	Missouri
Savannah	Chatham	Georgia
Savannah	Hardin	Tennessee
Sayre	Beckham	Oklahoma
Schenectady	Schenectady	New York
Schoharie	Schoharie	New York
Schuyler	Colfax	Nebraska
Scobey	Daniels	Montana
Scott City	Scott	Kansas
Scottsboro	Jackson	Alabama
Scottsburg	Scott	Indiana
Scottsville	Allen	Kentucky
Scranton	Lackawanna	Pennsylvania
Searcy	White	Arkansas
Seattle	King	Washington
Sebring	Highlands	Florida
Sedalia	Pettis	Missouri
Sedan	Chautauqua	Kansas
Seguin	Guadalupe	Texas

Selby	Walworth	South Dakota
Selma	Dallas	Alabama
Selmer	McNairy	Tennessee
Seminole	Gaines	Texas
Senatobia	Tate	Mississippi
Seneca	Nemaha	Kansas
Sevierville	Sevier	Tennessee
Seward	Seward	Nebraska
Seymour	Baylor	Texas
Shakope	Scott	Minnesota
Sharon Springs	Wallace	Kansas
Shawano	Shawano	Wisconsin
Shawnee	Pottawatomie	Oklahoma
Shawneetown	Gallatin	Illinois
Sheboygan	Sheboygan	Wisconsin
Shelby	Cleveland	North Carolina
Shelby	Toole	Montana
Shelbyville	Bedford	Tennessee
Shelbyville	Shelby	Illinois
Shelbyville	Shelby	Indiana
Shelbyville	Shelby	Kentucky
Shelbyville	Shelby	Missouri
Shell Lake	Washburn	Wisconsin
Shelton	Mason	Washington
Sheperdsville	Bullitt	Kentucky
Sheridan	Grant	Arkansas
Sheridan	Sheridan	Wyoming
Sherman	Grayson	Texas
Shoals	Martin	Indiana
Shoshone	Lincoln	Idaho
Shreveport	Caddo	Louisiana
Sibley	Osceola	Iowa
Sidney	Cheyenne	Nebraska
Sidney	Fremont	Iowa
Sidney	Richland	Montana
Sidney	Shelby	Ohio
Sierra Blanca	Hudspeth	Texas
Sigourney	Keokuk	Iowa
Silver City	Grant	New Mexico
Silverton	Briscoe	Texas
Silverton	San Juan	Colorado
Sinton	San Patricio	Texas
Sioux City	Woodbury	Iowa
Sioux Falls	Minnehaha	South Dakota
Siren	Burnett	Wisconsin
Sisseton	Roberts	South Dakota
Sitka	Sitka	Alaska
Skowhegan	Somerset	Maine
Slayton	Murray	Minnesota
Smethport	McKean	Pennsylvania
Smith Center	Smith	Kansas
Smithfield	Johnston	North Carolina
Smithland	Livingston	Kentucky
Smithville	DeKalb	Tennessee
Sneedville	Hancock	Tennessee

Snow Hill	Greene	North Carolina
Snow Hill	Worcester	Maryland
Snyder	Scurry	Texas
Socorro	Socorro	New Mexico
Soda Springs	Caribou	Idaho
Soldotna	Kenai Peninsula	Alaska
Somerset	Pulaski	Kentucky
Somerset	Somerset	Pennsylvania
Somerville	Fayette	Tennessee
Somerville	Somerset	New Jersey
Sonora	Sutton	Texas
Sonora	Tuolumne	California
Soperton	Treutlen	Georgia
South Bend	Pacific	Washington
South Bend	Saint Joseph	Indiana
South Paris	Oxford	Maine
Sparta	Alleghany	North Carolina
Sparta	Hancock	Georgia
Sparta	Monroe	Wisconsin
Sparta	White	Tennessee
Spartanburg	Spartanburg	South Carolina
Spearman	Hansford	Texas
Spencer	Clay	Iowa
Spencer	Owen	Indiana
Spencer	Roane	West Virginia
Spencer	Van Buren	Tennessee
Spirit Lake	Dickinson	Iowa
Spokane	Spokane	Washington
Spotsylvania	Spotsylvania	Virginia
Springfield	Baca	Colorado
Springfield	Clark	Ohio
Springfield	Effingham	Georgia
Springfield	Greene	Missouri
Springfield	Hampden	Massachusetts
Springfield	Robertson	Tennessee
Springfield	Sangamon	Illinois
Springfield	Washington	Kentucky
Springview	Keya Paha	Nebraska
Stafford	Stafford	Virginia
Stanardsville	Greene	Virginia
Standish	Arenac	Michigan
Stanford	Judith Basin	Montana
Stanford	Lincoln	Kentucky
Stanley	Mountrail	North Dakota
Stanton	Martin	Texas
Stanton	Mercer	North Dakota
Stanton	Montcalm	Michigan
Stanton	Powell	Kentucky
Stanton	Stanton	Nebraska
Stapleton	Logan	Nebraska
Star City	Lincoln	Arkansas
Starke	Bradford	Florida
Starkville	Oktibbeha	Mississippi
Statenville	Echols	Georgia
Statesboro	Bulloch	Georgia

Statesville	Iredell	North Carolina
Staunton	Augusta	Virginia
Steamboat Springs	Routt	Colorado
Steele	Kidder	North Dakota
Steelville	Crawford	Missouri
Stephenville	Erath	Texas
Sterling	Logan	Colorado
Sterling City	Sterling	Texas
Steubenville	Jefferson	Ohio
Stevenson	Skamania	Washington
Stevens Point	Portage	Wisconsin
Stigler	Haskell	Oklahoma
Stillwater	Payne	Oklahoma
Stillwater	Washington	Minnesota
Stilwell	Adair	Oklahoma
Stinnett	Hutchinson	Texas
Stockton	Cedar	Missouri
Stockton	Rooks	Kansas
Stockton	San Joaquin	California
Stockville	Frontier	Nebraska
Storm Lake	Buena Vista	Iowa
Stratford	Sherman	Texas
Stroudsburg	Monroe	Pennsylvania
Stuart	Martin	Florida
Stuart	Patrick	Virginia
Sturgeon Bay	Door	Wisconsin
Sturgis	Meade	South Dakota
Sublette	Haskell	Kansas
Sullivan	Moultrie	Illinois
Sullivan	Sullivan	Indiana
Sulphur	Murray	Oklahoma
Sulphur Springs	Hopkins	Texas
Summersville	Nicholas	West Virginia
Summerville	Chattooga	Georgia
Sumter	Sumter	South Carolina
Sunbury	Northumberland	Pennsylvania
Sundance	Crook	Wyoming
Superior	Douglas	Wisconsin
Superior	Mineral	Montana
Surry	Surry	Virginia
Susanville	Lassen	California
Sussex	Sussex	Virginia
Sutton	Braxton	West Virginia
Swainsboro	Emanuel	Georgia
Swanquarter	Hyde	North Carolina
Sweetwater	Nolan	Texas
Sycamore	DeKalb	Illinois
Sylva	Jackson	North Carolina
Sylvania	Screven	Georgia
Sylvester	Worth	Georgia
Syracuse	Hamilton	Kansas
Syracuse	Onondaga	New York
Tacoma	Pierce	Washington
Tahlequah	Cherokee	Oklahoma

Tahoka	Lynn	Texas
Talbotton	Talbot	Georgia
Talladega	Talladega	Alabama
Tallahassee	Leon	Florida
Tallulah	Madison	Louisiana
Taloga	Dewey	Oklahoma
Tampa	Hillsborough	Florida
Taos	Taos	New Mexico
Tappahannock	Essex	Virginia
Tarboro	Edgecombe	North Carolina
Taunton	Bristol	Massachusetts
Tavares	Lake	Florida
Tawas City	Iosco	Michigan
Taylor	Loup	Nebraska
Taylorsville	Alexander	North Carolina
Taylorsville	Spencer	Kentucky
Taylorville	Christian	Illinois
Tazewell	Claiborne	Tennessee
Tazewell	Tazewell	Virginia
Tecumseh	Johnson	Nebraska
Tekamah	Burt	Nebraska
Tell City	Perry	Indiana
Telluride	San Miguel	Colorado
Terre Haute	Vigo	Indiana
Terry	Prairie	Montana
Texarkana	Miller	Arkansas
The Dalles	Wasco	Oregon
Thedford	Thomas	Nebraska
Thermopolis	Hot Springs	Wyoming
Thibodaux	Lafourche	Louisiana
Thief River Falls	Pennington	Minnesota
Thomaston	Upson	Georgia
Thomasville	Thomas	Georgia
Thompson Falls	Sanders	Montana
Thomson	McDuffie	Georgia
Throckmorton	Throckmorton	Texas
Tierra Amarilla	Rio Arriba	New Mexico
Tiffin	Seneca	Ohio
Tifton	Tift	Georgia
Tilden	McMullen	Texas
Tillamook	Tillamook	Oregon
Timber Lake	Dewey	South Dakota
Tionesta	Forest	Pennsylvania
Tipton	Cedar	Iowa
Tipton	Tipton	Indiana
Tiptonville	Lake	Tennessee
Tishomingo	Johnston	Oklahoma
Titusville	Brevard	Florida
Toccoa	Stephens	Georgia
Toledo	Cumberland	Illinois
Toledo	Lucas	Ohio
Toledo	Tama	Iowa
Tompkinsville	Monroe	Kentucky
Toms River	Ocean	New Jersey
Tonopah	Nye	Nevada

Tooele	Tooele	Utah
Topeka	Shawnee	Kansas
Torrington	Goshen	Wyoming
Toulon	Stark	Illinois
Towanda	Bradford	Pennsylvania
Towner	McHenry	North Dakota
Townsend	Broadwater	Montana
Towson	Baltimore	Maryland
Traverse City	Grand Traverse	Michigan
Trenton	Dade	Georgia
Trenton	Gibson	Tennessee
Trenton	Gilchrist	Florida
Trenton	Grundy	Missouri
Trenton	Hitchcock	Nebraska
Trenton	Jones	North Carolina
Trenton	Mercer	New Jersey
Tribune	Greeley	Kansas
Trinidad	Las Animas	Colorado
Troy	Doniphan	Kansas
Troy	Lincoln	Missouri
Troy	Miami	Ohio
Troy	Montgomery	North Carolina
Troy	Pike	Alabama
Troy	Rensselaer	New York
Truth or Consequences	Sierra	New Mexico
Tryon	McPherson	Nebraska
Tucson	Pima	Arizona
Tucumcari	Quay	New Mexico
Tulia	Swisher	Texas
Tulsa	Tulsa	Oklahoma
Tunica	Tunica	Mississippi
Tunkhannock	Wyoming	Pennsylvania
Tupelo	Lee	Mississippi
Tuscaloosa	Tuscaloosa	Alabama
Tuscola	Douglas	Illinois
Tuscumbia	Colbert	Alabama
Tuscumbia	Miller	Missouri
Tuskegee	Macon	Alabama
Twin Falls	Twin Falls	Idaho
Two Harbors	Lake	Minnesota
Tyler	Smith	Texas
Tylertown	Walthall	Mississippi
Tyndall	Bon Homme	South Dakota
Ukiah	Mendocino	California
Ulysses	Grant	Kansas
Union	Franklin	Missouri
Union	Monroe	West Virginia
Union	Union	South Carolina
Union City	Obion	Tennessee
Union Springs	Bullock	Alabama
Uniontown	Fayette	Pennsylvania
Unionville	Putnam	Missouri
Upper Marlboro	Prince George's	Maryland
Upper Sandusky	Wyandot	Ohio

Urbana	Champaign	Illinois
Urbana	Champaign	Ohio
Utica	Oneida	New York
Uvalde	Uvalde	Texas
Valdosta	Lowndes	Georgia
Vale	Malheur	Oregon
Valentine	Cherry	Nebraska
Valley City	Barnes	North Dakota
Valparaiso	Porter	Indiana
Van Buren	Carter	Missouri
Van Buren	Crawford	Arkansas
Vanceburg	Lewis	Kentucky
Vancouver	Clark	Washington
Vandalia	Fayette	Illinois
Van Horn	Culberson	Texas
Van Wert	Van Wert	Ohio
Vega	Oldham	Texas
Ventura	Ventura	California
Vermilion	Clay	South Dakota
Vernal	Uintah	Utah
Vernon	Jennings	Indiana
Vernon	Lamar	Alabama
Vernon	Wilbarger	Texas
Vero Beach	Indian River	Florida
Versailles	Morgan	Missouri
Versailles	Ripley	Indiana
Versailles	Woodford	Kentucky
Vevay	Switzerland	Indiana
Vicksburg	Warren	Mississippi
Victoria	Victoria	Texas
Vidalia	Concordia	Louisiana
Vienna	Dooly	Georgia
Vienna	Johnson	Illinois
Vienna	Maries	Missouri
Ville Platte	Evangeline	Louisiana
Vincennes	Knox	Indiana
Vinita	Craig	Oklahoma
Vinton	Benton	Iowa
Virginia	Cass	Illinois
Virginia City	Madison	Montana
Virginia City	Storey	Nevada
Viroqua	Vernon	Wisconsin
Visalia	Tulare	California
Wabash	Wabash	Indiana
Wabasha	Wabasha	Minnesota
Waco	McLennan	Texas
Wadena	Wadena	Minnesota
Wadesboro	Anson	North Carolina
Wagoner	Wagoner	Oklahoma
Wahoo	Saunders	Nebraska
Wahpeton	Richland	North Dakota
Wailuku	Maui	Hawaii
WaKeeney	Trego	Kansas

Wakefield	Washington	Rhode Island
Walden	Jackson	Colorado
Waldron	Scott	Arkansas
Walhalla	Oconee	South Carolina
Walker	Cass	Minnesota
Wallace	Shoshone	Idaho
Walla Walla	Walla Walla	Washington
Walnut Ridge	Lawrence	Arkansas
Walsenburg	Huerfano	Colorado
Walterboro	Colleton	South Carolina
Walters	Cotton	Oklahoma
Walthall	Webster	Mississippi
Wampsville	Madison	New York
Wapakoneta	Auglaize	Ohio
Wapello	Louisa	Iowa
Warm Springs	Bath	Virginia
Warren	Bradley	Arkansas
Warren	Marshall	Minnesota
Warren	Trumbull	Ohio
Warren	Warren	Pennsylvania
Warrensburg	Johnson	Missouri
Warrenton	Fauquier	Virginia
Warrenton	Warren	Georgia
Warrenton	Warren	Missouri
Warrenton	Warren	North Carolina
Warsaw	Benton	Missouri
Warsaw	Gallatin	Kentucky
Warsaw	Kosciusko	Indiana
Warsaw	Richmond	Virginia
Warsaw	Wyoming	New York
Wartburg	Morgan	Tennessee
Waseca	Waseca	Minnesota
Washburn	Bayfield	Wisconsin
Washburn	McLean	North Dakota
Washington	Beaufort	North Carolina
Washington	Daviess	Indiana
Washington	District of Columbia	
Washington	Rappahannock	Virginia
Washington	Washington	Iowa
Washington	Washington	Kansas
Washington	Washington	Pennsylvania
Washington	Wilkes	Georgia
Washington Court House	Fayette	Ohio
Waterloo	Black Hawk	Iowa
Waterloo	Monroe	Illinois
Waterloo	Seneca	New York
Watertown	Codington	South Dakota
Watertown	Jefferson	New York
Water Valley	Yalobusha	Mississippi
Waterville	Douglas	Washington
Watford City	McKenzie	North Dakota
Watkins Glen	Schuyler	New York
Watkinsville	Oconee	Georgia
Watonga	Blaine	Oklahoma
Watseka	Iroquois	Illinois

Wauchula	Hardee	Florida
Waukegan	Lake	Illinois
Waukesha	Waukesha	Wisconsin
Waukon	Allamakee	Iowa
Waupaca	Waupaca	Wisconsin
Waurika	Jefferson	Oklahoma
Wausau	Marathon	Wisconsin
Wauseon	Fulton	Ohio
Wautoma	Waushara	Wisconsin
Waverly	Bremer	Iowa
Waverly	Humphreys	Tennessee
Waverly	Pike	Ohio
Waxahachie	Ellis	Texas
Waycross	Ware	Georgia
Wayne	Wayne	Nebraska
Wayne	Wayne	West Virginia
Waynesboro	Burke	Georgia
Waynesboro	Wayne	Mississippi
Waynesboro	Wayne	Tennessee
Waynesburg	Greene	Pennsylvania
Waynesville	Haywood	North Carolina
Waynesville	Pulaski	Missouri
Weatherford	Parker	Texas
Weaverville	Trinity	California
Webster	Day	South Dakota
Webster City	Hamilton	Iowa
Webster Springs	Webster	West Virginia
Wedowee	Randolph	Alabama
Weiser	Washington	Idaho
Welch	McDowell	West Virginia
Wellington	Collingsworth	Texas
Wellington	Sumner	Kansas
Wellsboro	Tioga	Pennsylvania
Wellsburg	Brooke	West Virginia
Wenatchee	Chelan	Washington
Wentworth	Rockingham	North Carolina
Wessington Springs	Jerauld	South Dakota
West Bend	Washington	Wisconsin
West Branch	Ogemaw	Michigan
West Chester	Chester	Pennsylvania
Westcliffe	Custer	Colorado
West Liberty	Morgan	Kentucky
Westminster	Carroll	Maryland
Westmoreland	Pottawatomie	Kansas
Weston	Lewis	West Virginia
West Palm Beach	Palm Beach	Florida
West Plaines	Howell	Missouri
West Point	Clay	Mississippi
West Point	Cuming	Nebraska
West Union	Adams	Ohio
West Union	Doddrodge	West Virginia
West Union	Fayette	Iowa
West Warrick	Kent	Rhode Island
Wetumpka	Elmore	Alabama
Wewoka	Seminole	Oklahoma

Wharton	Wharton	Texas
Wheatland	Platte	Wyoming
Wheaton	DuPage	Illinois
Wheaton	Traverse	Minnesota
Wheeler	Wheeler	Texas
Wheeling	Ohio	West Virginia
White Cloud	Newaygo	Michigan
Whitehall	Trempealeau	Wisconsin
White Plains	Westchester	New York
White River	Mellette	South Dakota
Whitesburg	Letcher	Kentucky
White Sulphur Springs	Meagher	Montana
Whiteville	Columbus	North Carolina
Whitley City	McCreary	Kentucky
Wibaux	Wibaux	Montana
Wichita	Sedgwick	Kansas
Wichita Falls	Wichita	Texas
Wickliffe	Ballard	Kentucky
Wiggins	Stone	Mississippi
Wilber	Saline	Nebraska
Wilburton	Latimer	Oklahoma
Wilkes-Barre	Luzerne	Pennsylvania
Wilkesboro	Wilkes	North Carolina
Willamantic	Windham	Connecticut
Williamsburg	James City	Virginia
Williamsburg	Whitley	Kentucky
Williamson	Mingo	West Virginia
Williamsport	Lycoming	Pennsylvania
Williamsport	Warren	Indiana
Williamston	Martin	North Carolina
Williamstown	Grant	Kentucky
Williston	Williams	North Dakota
Willmar	Kandiyohi	Minnesota
Willows	Glenn	California
Wilmington	Clinton	Ohio
Wilmington	New Castle	Delaware
Wilmington	New Hanover	North Carolina
Wilson	Wilson	North Carolina
Winamac	Pulaski	Indiana
Winchester	Clark	Kentucky
Winchester	Franklin	Tennessee
Winchester	Frederick	Virginia
Winchester	Randolph	Indiana
Winchester	Scott	Illinois
Winder	Barrow	Georgia
Windom	Cottonwood	Minnesota
Windsor	Bertie	North Carolina
Winfield	Cowley	Kansas
Winfield	Putnam	West Virginia
Winnemucca	Humboldt	Nevada
Winner	Tripp	South Dakota
Winnett	Petroleum	Montana
Winnfield	Winn	Louisiana
Winnsboro	Fairfield	South Carolina
Winnsboro	Franklin	Louisiana

Winona	Montgomery	Mississippi
Winona	Winona	Minnesota
Winston-Salem	Forsyth	North Carolina
Winterset	Madison	Iowa
Winton	Hertford	North Carolina
Wiscasset	Lincoln	Maine
Wisconsin Rapids	Wood	Wisconsin
Wise	Wise	Virginia
Wolf Point	Roosevelt	Montana
Woodbine	Camden	Georgia
Woodbury	Cannon	Tennessee
Woodbury	Gloucester	New Jersey
Woodland	Yolo	California
Woodsfield	Monoe	Ohio
Woodstock	McHenry	Illinois
Woodstock	Shenandoah	Virginia
Woodstock	Windsor	Vermont
Woodville	Tyler	Texas
Woodville	Wilkinson	Mississippi
Woodward	Woodward	Oklahoma
Woonsocket	Sanborn	South Dakota
Wooster	Wayne	Ohio
Worcester	Worcester	Massachusetts
Worland	Washakie	Wyoming
Worthington	Nobles	Minnesota
Wray	Yuma	Colorado
Wrightsville	Johnson	Georgia
Wynne	Cross	Arkansas
Wytheville	Wythe	Virginia
Xenia	Greene	Ohio
Yadkinville	Yadkin	North Carolina
Yakima	Yakima	Washington
Yakutat	Yakutat	Alaska
Yanceyville	Caswell	North Carolina
Yankton	Yankton	South Dakota
Yates Center	Woodson	Kansas
Yazoo City	Yazoo	Mississippi
Yellville	Marion	Arkansas
Yerington	Lyon	Nevada
York	York	Nebraska
York	York	Pennsylvania
York	York	South Carolina
Yorktown	York	Virginia
Yorkville	Kendall	Illinois
Youngstown	Mahoning	Ohio
Yreka	Siskiyou	California
Yuba City	Sutter	California
Yuma	Yuma	Arizona
Zanesville	Muskingum	Ohio
Zapata	Zapata	Texas
Zebulon	Pike	Georgia

Bibliography

The primary sources used in the compilation of this book were, of course, previous editions of Kane's *The American Counties*. A close second was Michael Beatty's *County Name Origins of the United States* (Jefferson, N.C.: McFarland & Co., Inc., 2001). This is a huge book listing the name origin of every county and parish in the United States. It does not, however, address independent cities and Alaska. The book is divided into sections by states. At the end of each state's section is a bibliography for counties in that state. The bibliographies are extensive but rather difficult to use because they are arranged alphabetically, in proper bibliographic form, by author or title rather than by county. Nonetheless, this is an excellent resource devoted to the how and why of county name origins.

The main sources consulted for Alaska's "counties" were (1) Orth, Donald J., *Dictionary of Alaska Place Names, Geological Professional Paper 567*, Washington, D.C.: U.S. Government Printing Office, 1967; and (2) Phillips, James W., *Alaska-Yukon Place Names*, Seattle: University of Washington Press, 1973. Name origins for Virginia's independent cities were found in Hanson, Raus McDill, *Virginia Place Names*, Verona, Va.: McClure Printing Company, Inc., 1969.

Population figures given in Kane's previous editions were checked against data compiled and edited by Richard L. Forstall, *Population of States and Counties of the United State: 1790 to 1990*, Washington, D.C.: U.S. Bureau of the Census, 1996. This same information is available on the Bureau of the Census's website at http://www.census.gov/population/cencounts. The website does not provide the explanatory notes included in Forstall. The Census Bureau's website was also the source for the 2000 Census population figures and county areas. Access the American Factfinder at http://www.census.gov.

An overwhelming amount of information is available on the Internet. The problem is deciding when to end the search. I used Google to initiate most searches for individuals for whom counties were named. Google led me into county histories or genealogical sites where I had varying degrees of success in finding the sought-after information, usually dates of birth or death.

The Department of Commerce's definition of "first-order subdivision" used to define counties and other entities listed in this book is from the National Institute of Standards and Technology's website at: http://www.itl.nist.gov/fipspubs/fip6-4.htm. Disputed spellings of counties and county seats were resolved by two websites: (1) the U.S. Geological Survey's Geographic Names Information System at http://geonames.usgs.gov; and (2) the National Association of Counties (NACO) at http://www.naco.org. NACO's website provided the names and addresses of county officials whom I could contact to determine preferred spellings.

Information on eponymous persons to supplement that given by Kane and by Beatty's *County Name Origins* was found at various Internet locations. Information on anybody who has served in Congress is available at "The Biographical Directory of the United States Congress; 1774–Present" at http://bioguide.congress.gov/biosearch/biosearch.asp. An interesting website that includes most all politicians who have served at national, state, and local levels is the "Political Graveyard" at http://politicalgraveyard.com/index.html. The biographies of saints for whom counties have been named were found at the Catholic Forum's patron saint index at http://www.catholic-forum.com/saints/patron02.htm. Brief descriptions of American Indian names are given at http://www.americanindian.net/names.html. Most states have websites providing various data, but the most helpful I found was the "The Handbook of Texas Online" at http://www.tsha.utexas.edu/handbook/online/index.html.

Information on the dates of county creation was found in "AniMap Plus," a compact disc available from The Gold Bug, Alamo, California. This is a fascinating collection of maps for each state showing the boundary changes for all counties from 1634. Another source for county creation dates, as well as spellings and county seats, is *The Handybook for Genealogists*:

United States of America, 10th edition, Draper, Utah: Everton Publishers, 2002. Because of their reliance on county records, genealogical books and websites are excellent sources of information on counties.

By now, almost every county in the United States has its own website. Some sites are better than others but they all provide a point of departure for exploring counties. Some provide county histories and other categories of information. Listing all the county sites I checked in compiling this book would essentially be a list of all counties in the United States. I will leave it up to the readers to track down the ones of interest to them. Happy hunting.

About the Authors

The late **Joseph Nathan Kane** is the author of the previous editions of *The American Counties* and laid the groundwork for this revision.

Charles Curry Aiken is an occupational safety and health consultant. Previously employed with the Navy Safety School, he traveled across the United States and fostered an interest in U.S. geography, especially counties.